TADATOSHI FUJIMAKI

There's a scene in this volume that involves meatballs. When drawing that scene, I passed the first draft over to my assistant, H-san.

> Me: Make it clear that these are handmade meatballs and not frozen ones.

> H: Showing that difference just through the drawings... is too hard.

Yes, it is. I agree.

—2012

Tadatoshi Fujimaki was born on June 9, 1982, in Tokyo. He made his debut in 2007 in *Akamaru Jump* with *Kuroko's Basketball*, which was later serialized in *Weekly Shonen Jump*. *Kuroko's Basketball* quickly gained popularity and became an anime in Japan in 2012.

Kuroko's BASKETBALL

19 & 20

SHONEN JUMP Manga Edition
BY TADATOSHI FUJIMAKI

Translation/Caleb Cook
Touch-Up Art & Lettering/Mark McMurray
Design/Julian [JR] Robinson
Editor/John Bae

KUROKO NO BASUKE © 2008 by Tadatoshi Fujimaki
All rights reserved.
First published in Japan in 2008 by SHUEISHA Inc., Tokyo.
English translation rights arranged by SHUEISHA Inc.

Printed in the U.S.A.

Published by VIZ Media, LLC
P.O. Box 77010
San Francisco, CA 94107

10 9 8 7 6 5 4 3 2 1
First printing, February 2018

THE WORLD'S
MOST POPULAR MANGA
SHONEN JUMP
www.shonenjump.com

www.viz.com

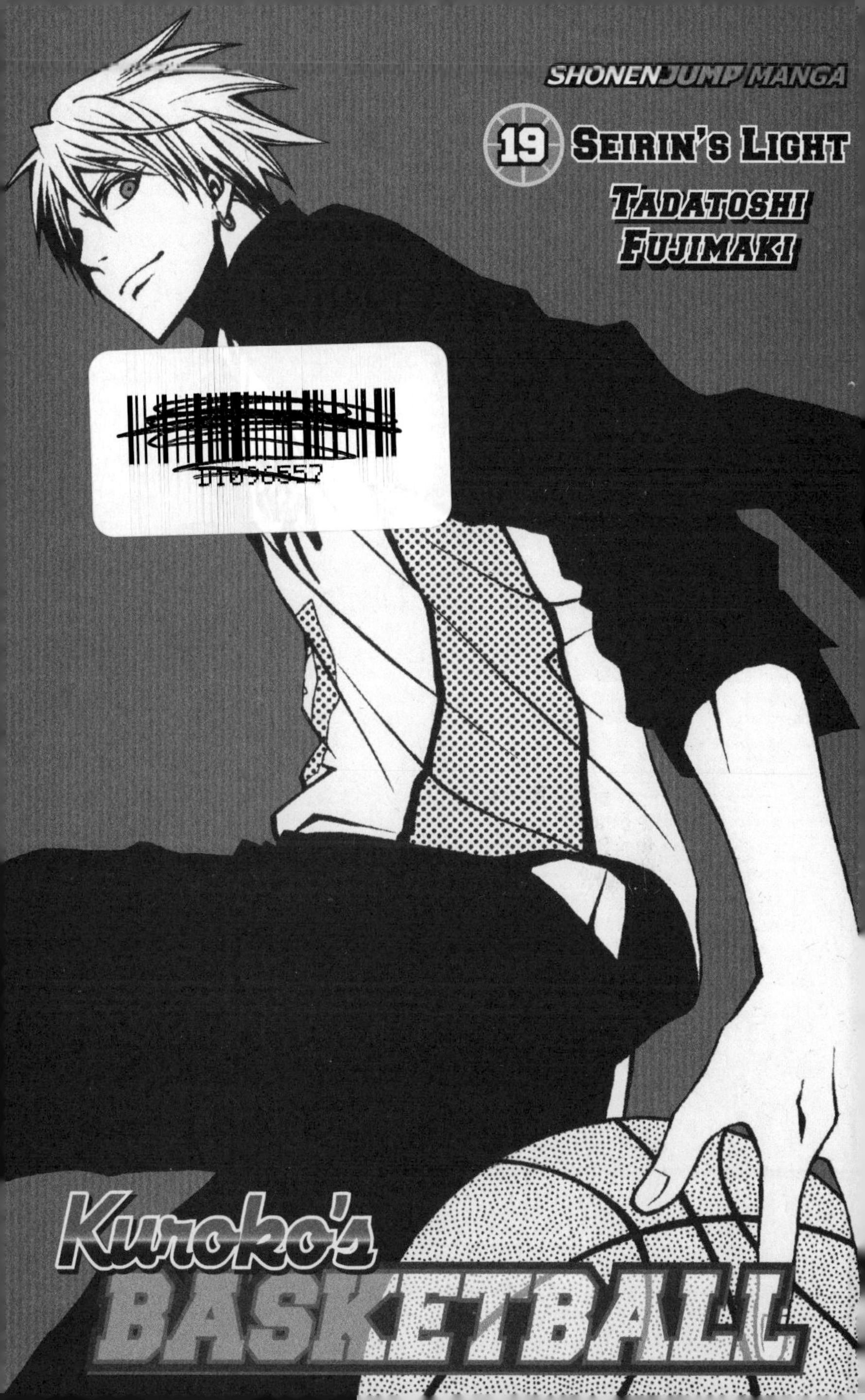
SHONEN JUMP MANGA
19 Seirin's Light
Tadatoshi Fujimaki
Kuroko's
BASKETBALL

CHARACTERS

TAIGA KAGAMI

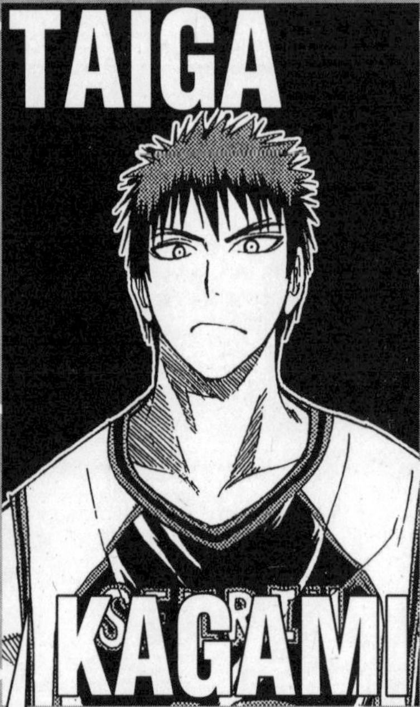

A first-year on Seirin High's basketball team. Though he's rough around the edges, he's a gifted player with a lot of potential. His goal is to beat the Miracle Generation.

TETSUYA KUROKO

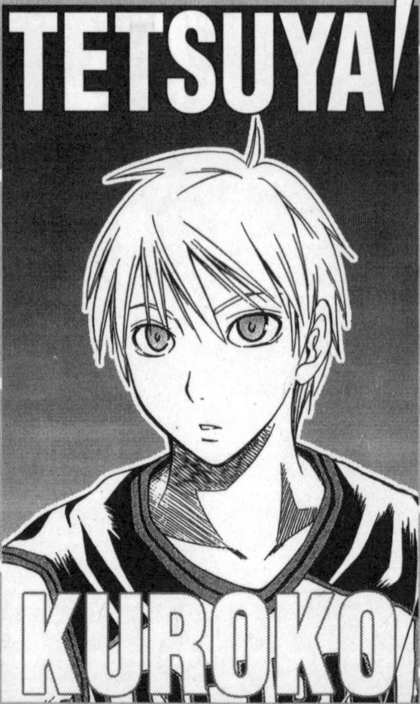

A first-year on Seirin High's basketball team. Gifted with a natural lack of presence, he utilizes misdirection on the court to make nearly invisible passes.

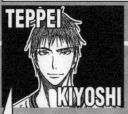

TEPPEI KIYOSHI

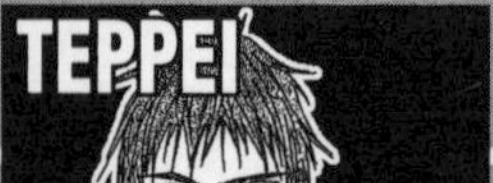

A second-year on Seirin High's basketball team and the club's founder. He was hospitalized but returned shortly after Inter-High.

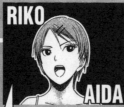

RIKO AIDA

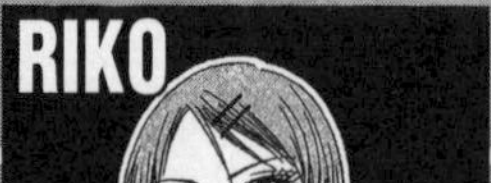

A second-year and coach of the Seirin High basketball team.

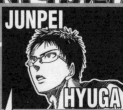

JUNPEI HYUGA

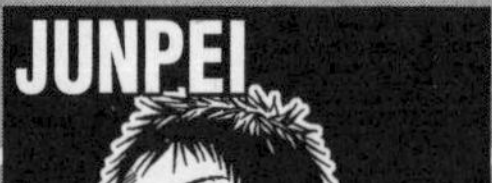

A second-year on Seirin High's basketball team. As captain, he led his team to the Finals League last year despite only playing first-year players.

KUROKO'S BASKETBALL

RYOTA
KISE

One of the Miracle Generation. Any basketball move he sees, he can mimic in an instant.

SHINTARO
MIDORIMA

A first-year at Shutoku High, he's the top shooter of the Miracle Generation.

DAIKI
AOMINE

The ace of the Miracle Generation and Kuroko's former friend, he's now a first-year at To-oh Academy.

SATSUKI
MOMOI

A first-year member of To-oh Academy's basketball team, she was the team manager for the Miracle Generation. She likes Kuroko.

TATSUYA
HIMURO

A second-year on Yosen High's basketball team, he's a cool shooting guard who was also an older-brother figure to Kagami in the U.S.

ATSUSHI
MURASAKIBARA

One of the Miracle Generation. A first-year on Yosen High's basketball team. He plays center, but he doesn't actually enjoy basketball all that much.

Teiko Middle School is an elite championship school whose basketball team once fielded five prodigies collectively known as "the Miracle Generation." But supporting those five was a phantom sixth man—Tetsuya Kuroko. Now Kuroko's a first-year high school student with zero presence who joins Seirin High's basketball club. Though his physical abilities and stats are well below average, Kuroko thrives on the court by making passes his opponents can't detect!

Aiming for the Winter Cup title, Seirin barely defeats To-oh and Aomine in its first game of the tournament. Games two and three also prove to be difficult, but the team pushes through, setting up an epic game against Yosen. Yosen's "Aegis Shield" defense is anchored by Murasakibara and seems to overwhelm Seirin, but Kuroko's Phantom Shot and Kiyoshi's skills as a point guard close the gap. That is, until Murasakibara goes on the offensive and starts giving them a real run for their money...

STORY THUS FAR

TABLE OF CONTENTS

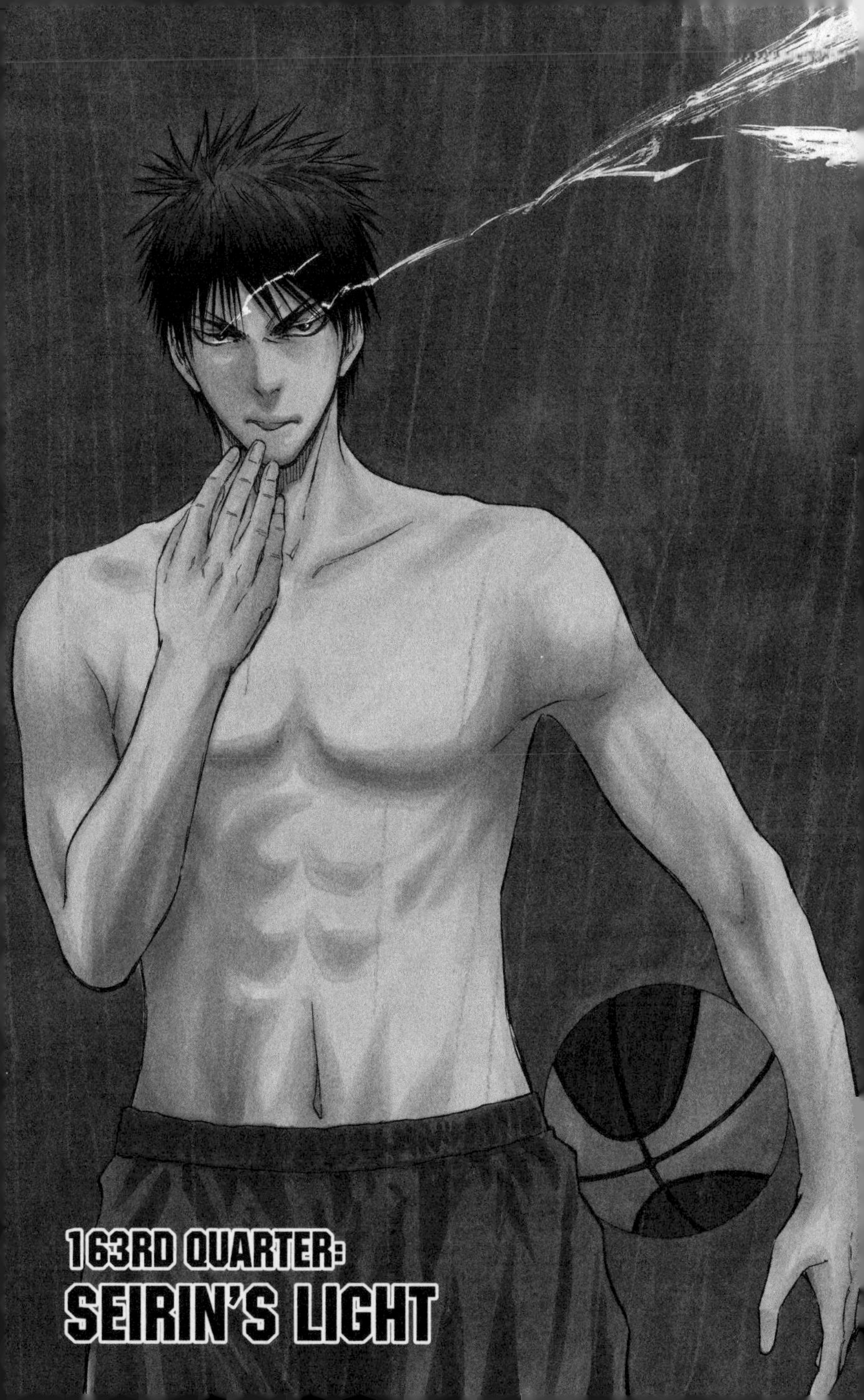
163RD QUARTER:
SEIRIN'S LIGHT

Kuroko's
BASKETBALL

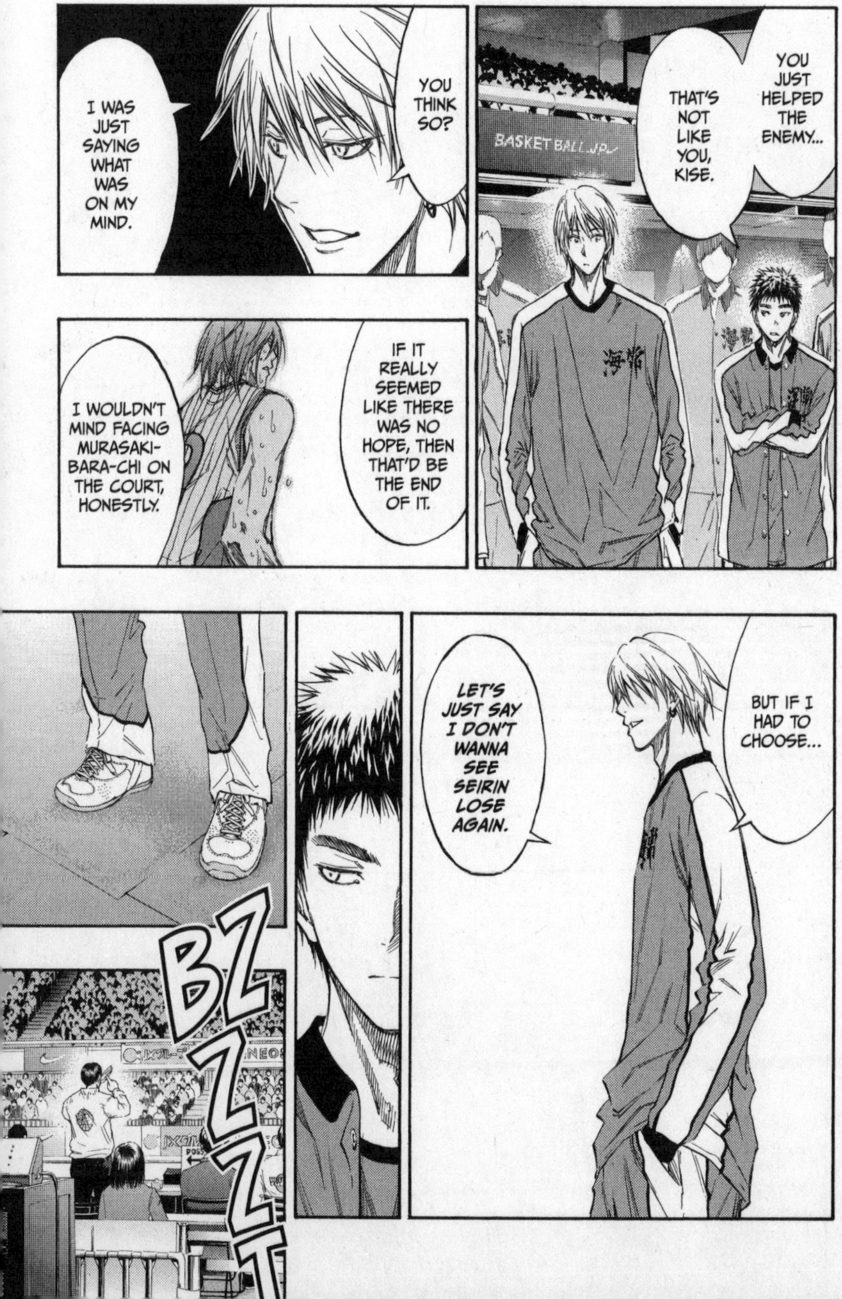
YOU JUST HELPED THE ENEMY...
THAT'S NOT LIKE YOU, KISE.
YOU THINK SO?
I WAS JUST SAYING WHAT WAS ON MY MIND.
IF IT REALLY SEEMED LIKE THERE WAS NO HOPE, THEN THAT'D BE THE END OF IT.
I WOULDN'T MIND FACING MURASAKIBARA-CHI ON THE COURT, HONESTLY.
BUT IF I HAD TO CHOOSE...
LET'S JUST SAY I DON'T WANNA SEE SEIRIN LOSE AGAIN.
BZZZT

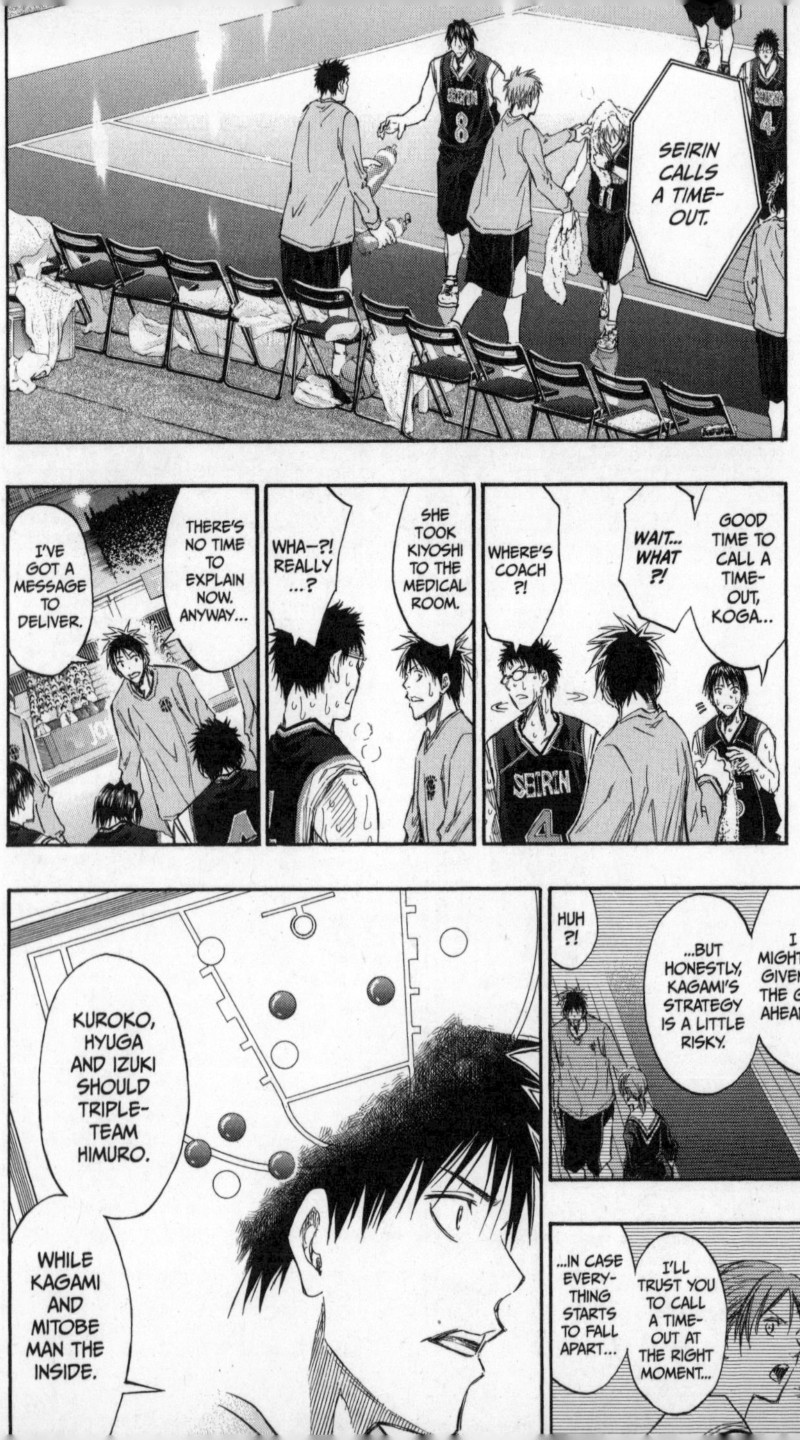
SEIRIN CALLS A TIME-OUT.
GOOD TIME TO CALL A TIME-OUT, KOGA...
WAIT... WHAT?!
WHERE'S COACH?!
SHE TOOK KIYOSHI TO THE MEDICAL ROOM.
WHA—?! REALLY...?
THERE'S NO TIME TO EXPLAIN NOW. ANYWAY...
I'VE GOT A MESSAGE TO DELIVER.
I MIGHT'VE GIVEN IT THE GO-AHEAD...
...BUT HONESTLY, KAGAMI'S STRATEGY IS A LITTLE RISKY.
HUH?!
I'LL TRUST YOU TO CALL A TIME-OUT AT THE RIGHT MOMENT...
...IN CASE EVERYTHING STARTS TO FALL APART...
KUROKO, HYUGA AND IZUKI SHOULD TRIPLE-TEAM HIMURO.
WHILE KAGAMI AND MITOBE MAN THE INSIDE.

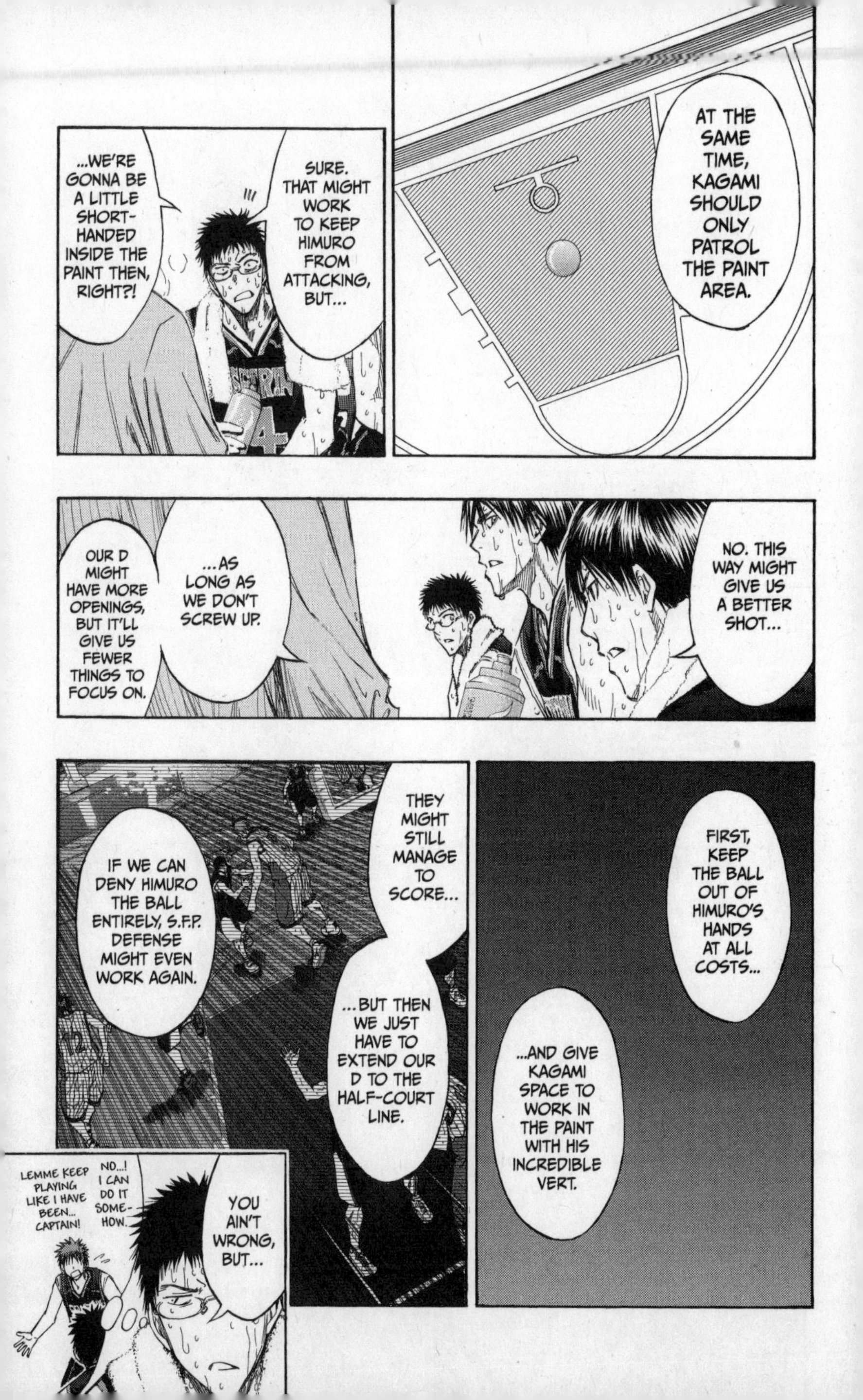
AT THE SAME TIME, KAGAMI SHOULD ONLY PATROL THE PAINT AREA.
SURE. THAT MIGHT WORK TO KEEP HIMURO FROM ATTACKING, BUT...
...WE'RE GONNA BE A LITTLE SHORT-HANDED INSIDE THE PAINT THEN, RIGHT?!
NO. THIS WAY MIGHT GIVE US A BETTER SHOT...
OUR D MIGHT HAVE MORE OPENINGS, BUT IT'LL GIVE US FEWER THINGS TO FOCUS ON.
...AS LONG AS WE DON'T SCREW UP.
FIRST, KEEP THE BALL OUT OF HIMURO'S HANDS AT ALL COSTS...
...AND GIVE KAGAMI SPACE TO WORK IN THE PAINT WITH HIS INCREDIBLE VERT.
THEY MIGHT STILL MANAGE TO SCORE...
...BUT THEN WE JUST HAVE TO EXTEND OUR D TO THE HALF-COURT LINE.
IF WE CAN DENY HIMURO THE BALL ENTIRELY, S.F.P. DEFENSE MIGHT EVEN WORK AGAIN.
YOU AIN'T WRONG, BUT...
NO...! I CAN DO IT SOME-HOW.
LEMME KEEP PLAYING LIKE I HAVE BEEN... CAPTAIN!

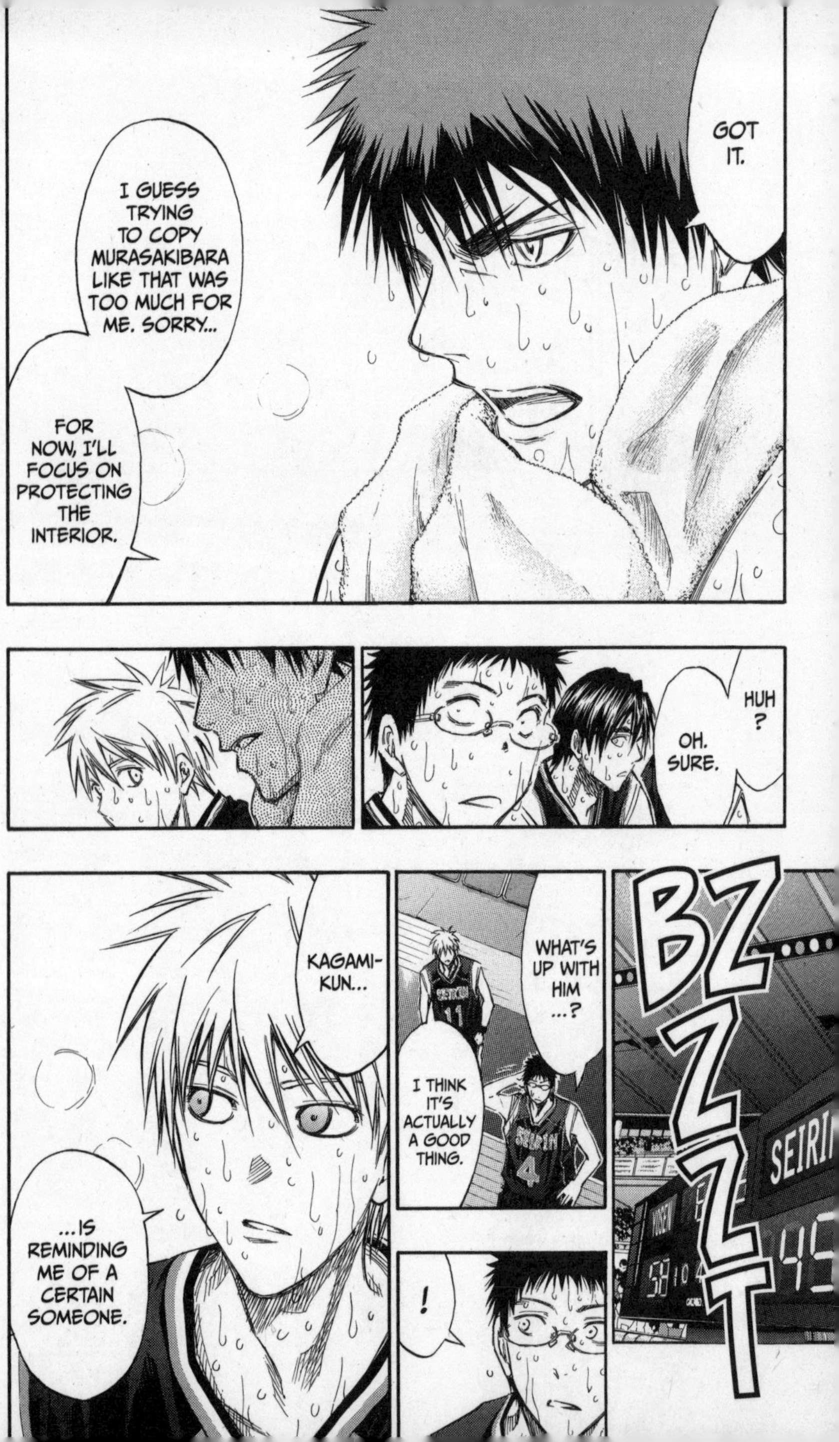
GOT IT.
I GUESS TRYING TO COPY MURASAKIBARA LIKE THAT WAS TOO MUCH FOR ME. SORRY...
FOR NOW, I'LL FOCUS ON PROTECTING THE INTERIOR.
HUH?
OH. SURE.
BZZZT
WHAT'S UP WITH HIM ...?
I THINK IT'S ACTUALLY A GOOD THING.
!
KAGAMI-KUN...
...IS REMINDING ME OF A CERTAIN SOMEONE.

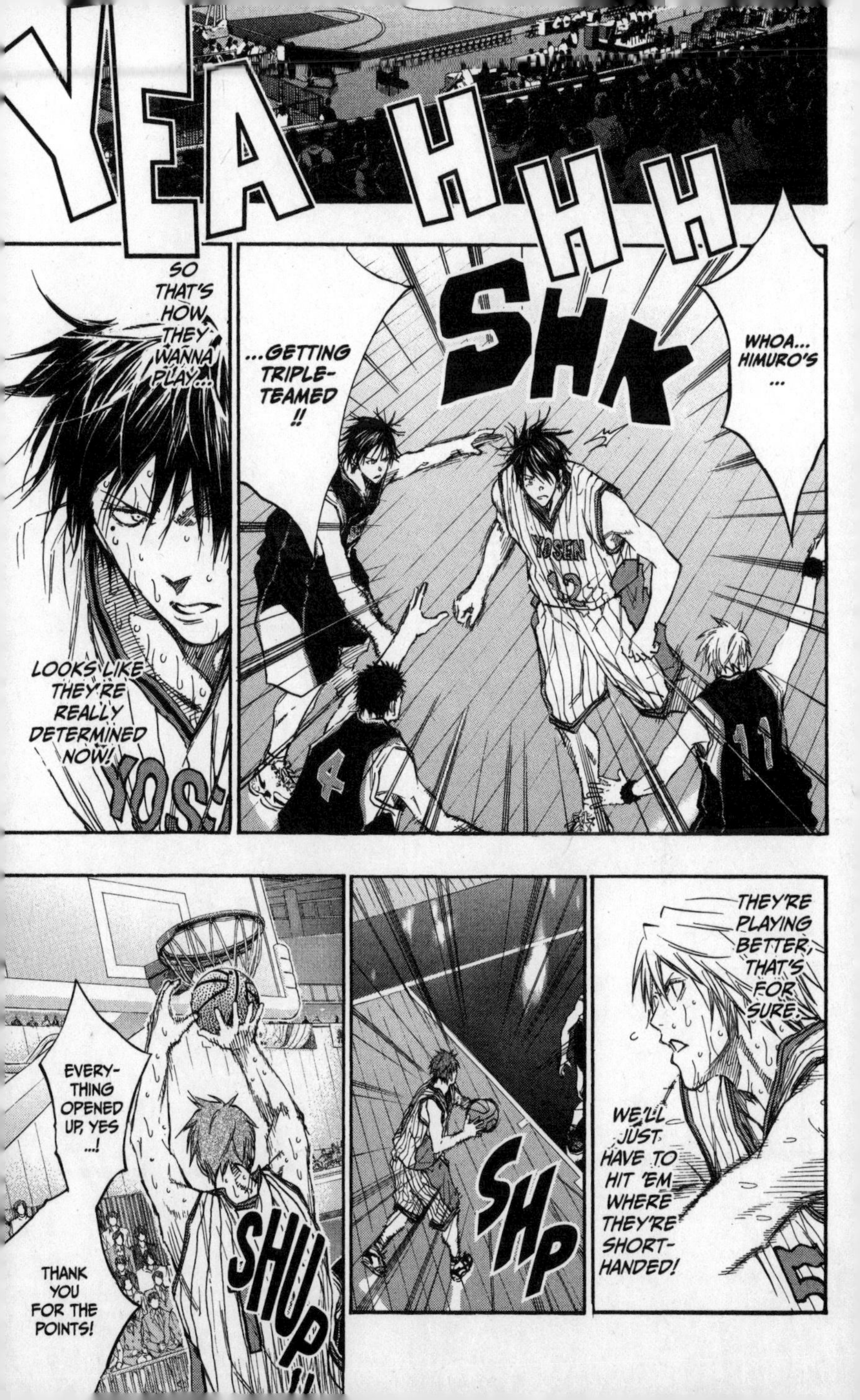
YEAHHHH
WHOA... HIMURO'S ...
SHK
...GETTING TRIPLE-TEAMED!!
SO THAT'S HOW THEY WANNA PLAY...
LOOKS LIKE THEY'RE REALLY DETERMINED NOW!
YOS
THEY'RE PLAYING BETTER, THAT'S FOR SURE.
WE'LL JUST HAVE TO HIT 'EM WHERE THEY'RE SHORT-HANDED!
SHP
EVERY-THING OPENED UP, YES ...!
SHUP
THANK YOU FOR THE POINTS!

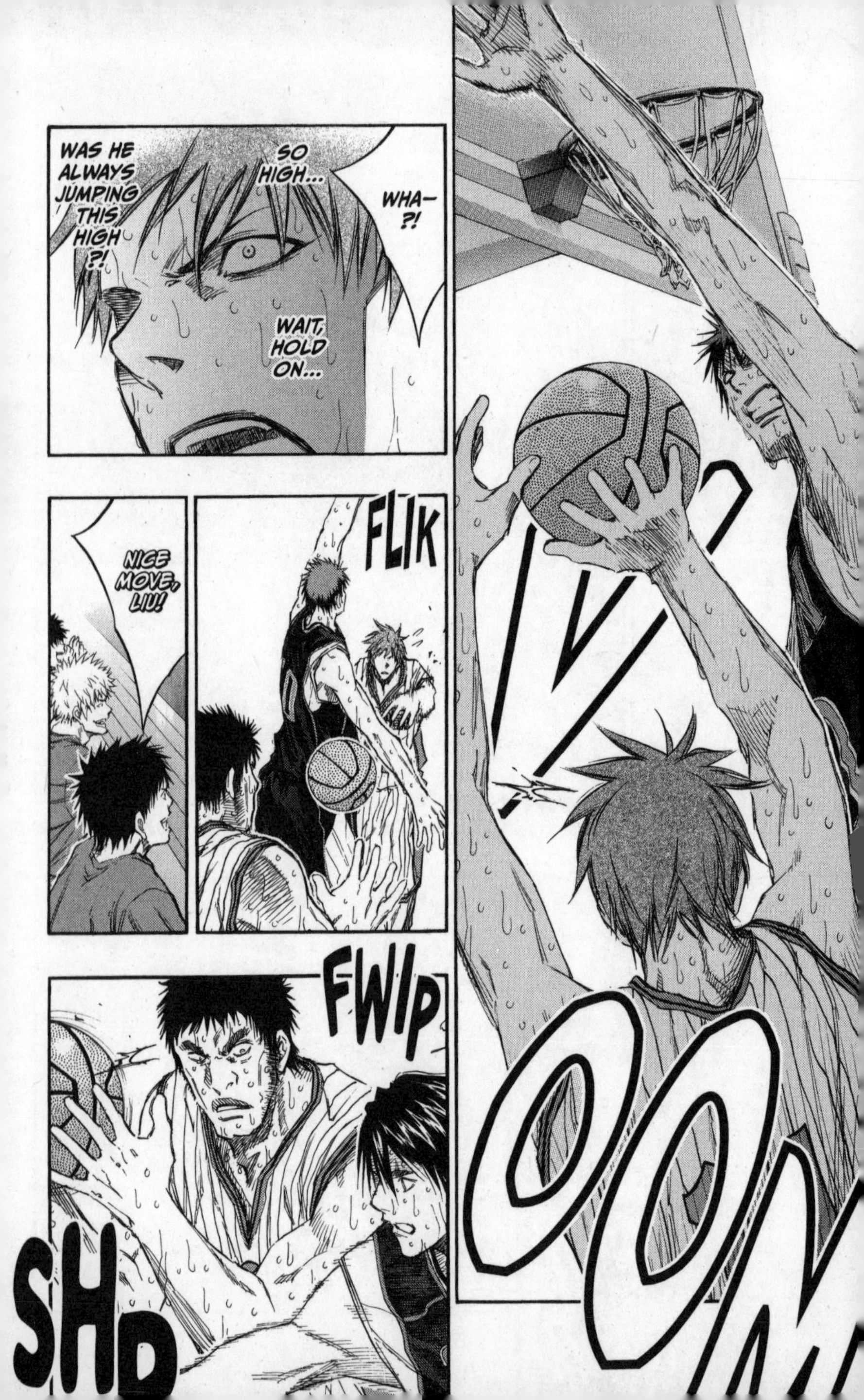

WHA—?!
SO HIGH...
WAS HE ALWAYS JUMPING THIS HIGH?!
WAIT, HOLD ON...
FLIK
NICE MOVE, LIU!
FWIP
SHD

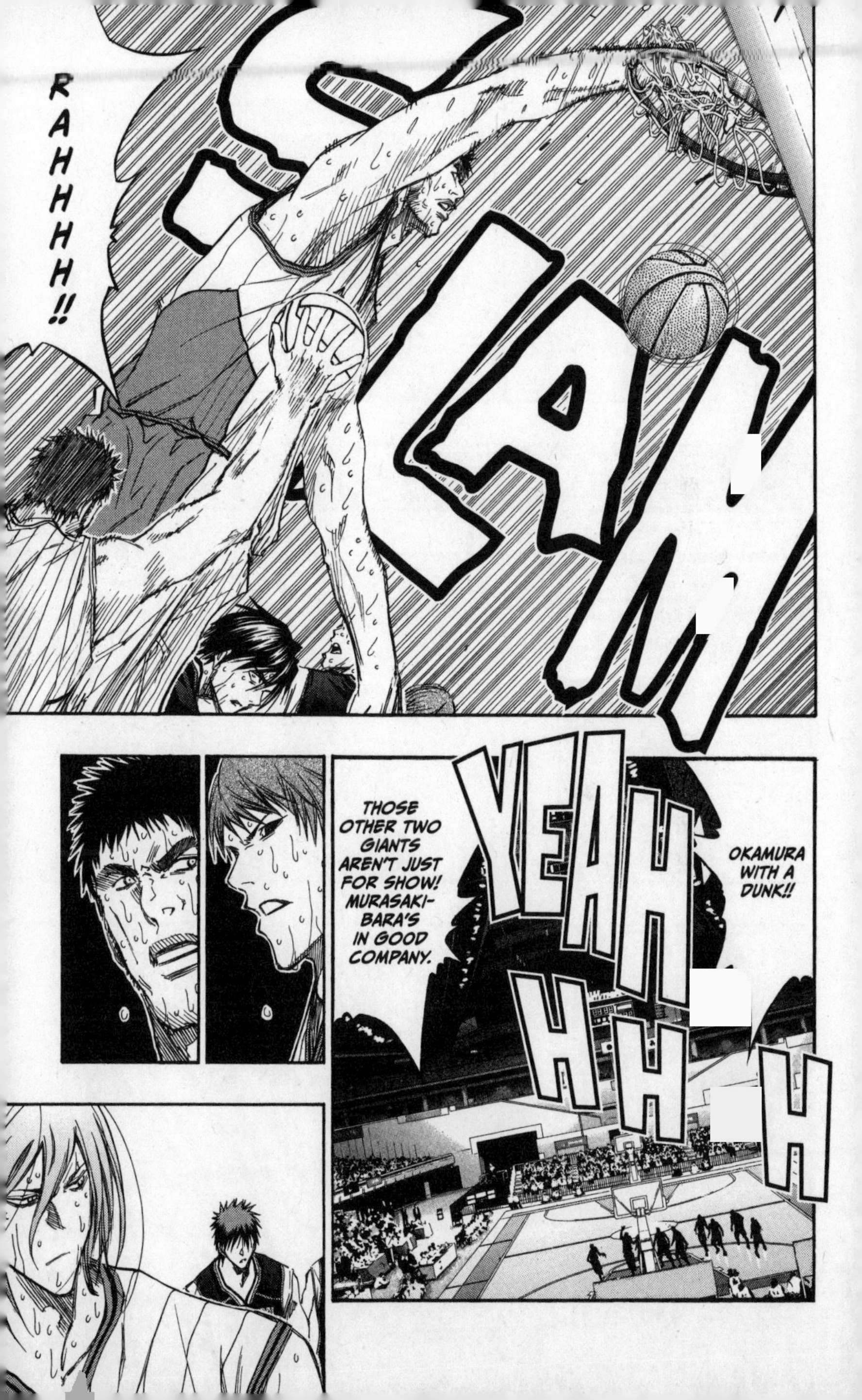
RAHHHHHH!!
OKAMURA WITH A DUNK!!
YEAHHHH
THOSE OTHER TWO GIANTS AREN'T JUST FOR SHOW! MURASAKIBARA'S IN GOOD COMPANY.

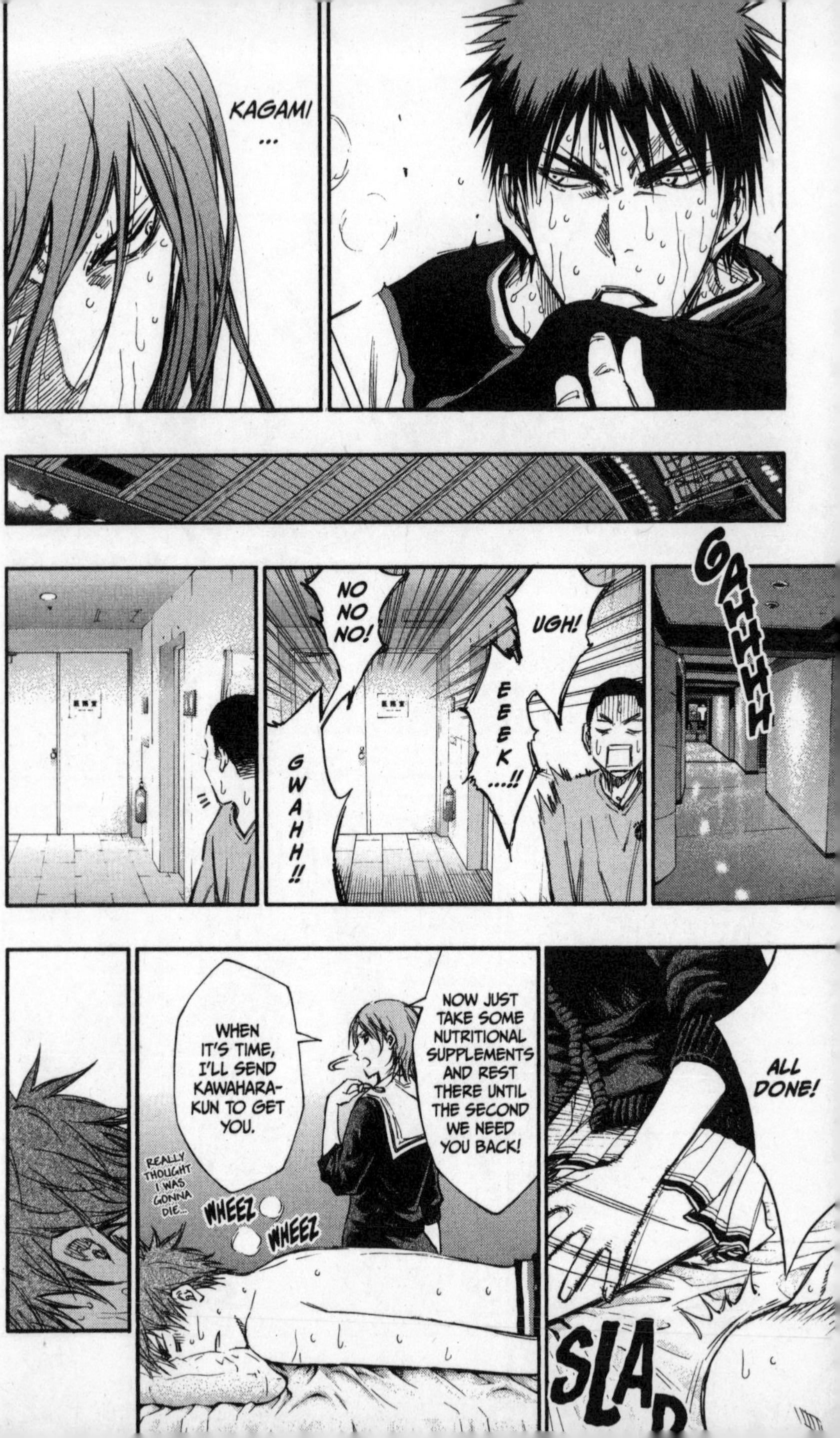
KAGAMI ...
GAHHHHH
UGH!
EEEK...!!
NO NO NO!
GWAHH!!
ALL DONE!
SLAP
NOW JUST TAKE SOME NUTRITIONAL SUPPLEMENTS AND REST THERE UNTIL THE SECOND WE NEED YOU BACK!
WHEN IT'S TIME, I'LL SEND KAWAHARA-KUN TO GET YOU.
WHEEZ
WHEEZ
REALLY THOUGHT I WAS GONNA DIE...

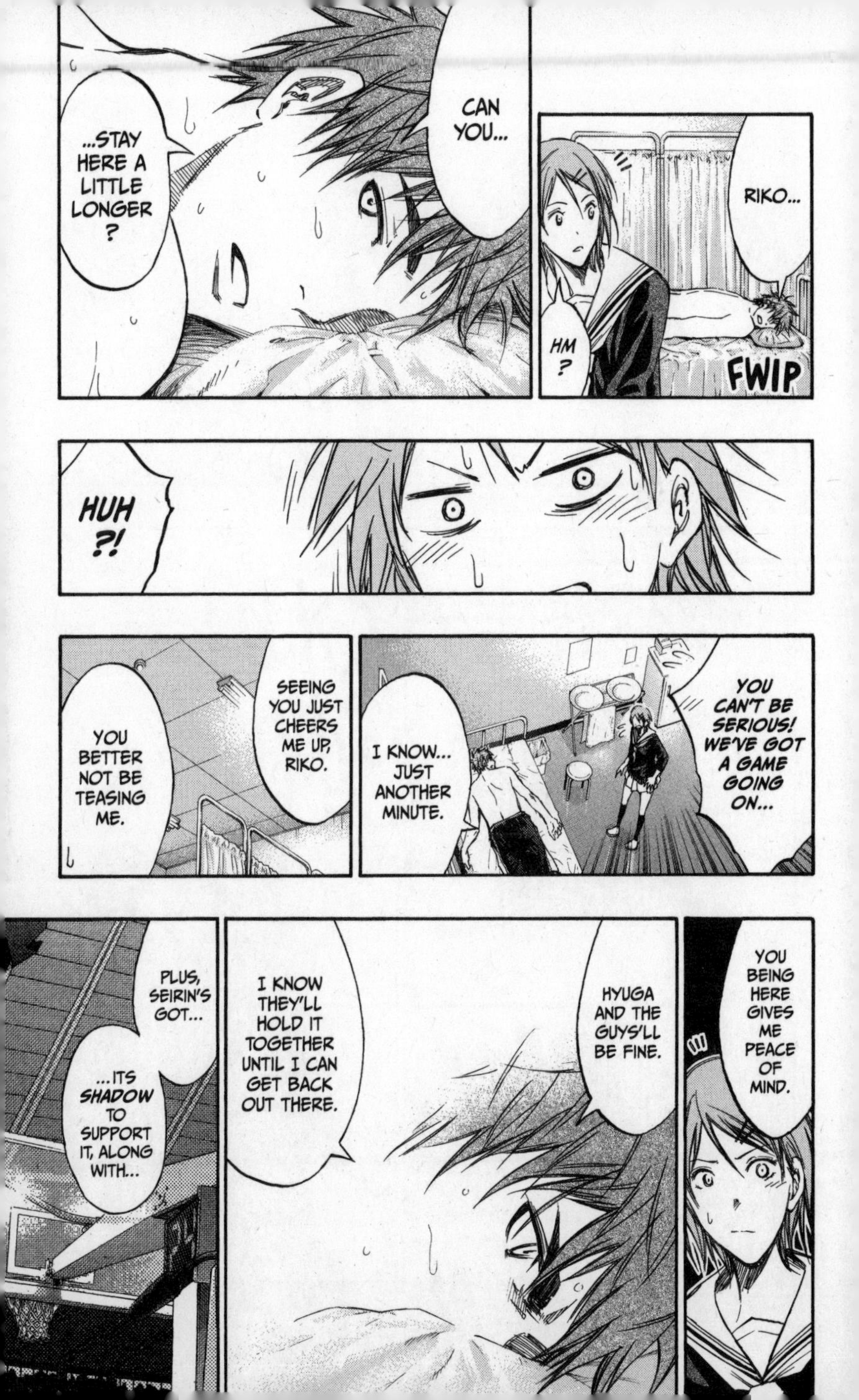
RIKO...
HM ?
FWIP
CAN YOU...
...STAY HERE A LITTLE LONGER ?
HUH ?!
YOU CAN'T BE SERIOUS! WE'VE GOT A GAME GOING ON...
I KNOW... JUST ANOTHER MINUTE.
SEEING YOU JUST CHEERS ME UP, RIKO.
YOU BETTER NOT BE TEASING ME.
YOU BEING HERE GIVES ME PEACE OF MIND.
HYUGA AND THE GUYS'LL BE FINE.
I KNOW THEY'LL HOLD IT TOGETHER UNTIL I CAN GET BACK OUT THERE.
PLUS, SEIRIN'S GOT...
...ITS SHADOW TO SUPPORT IT, ALONG WITH...

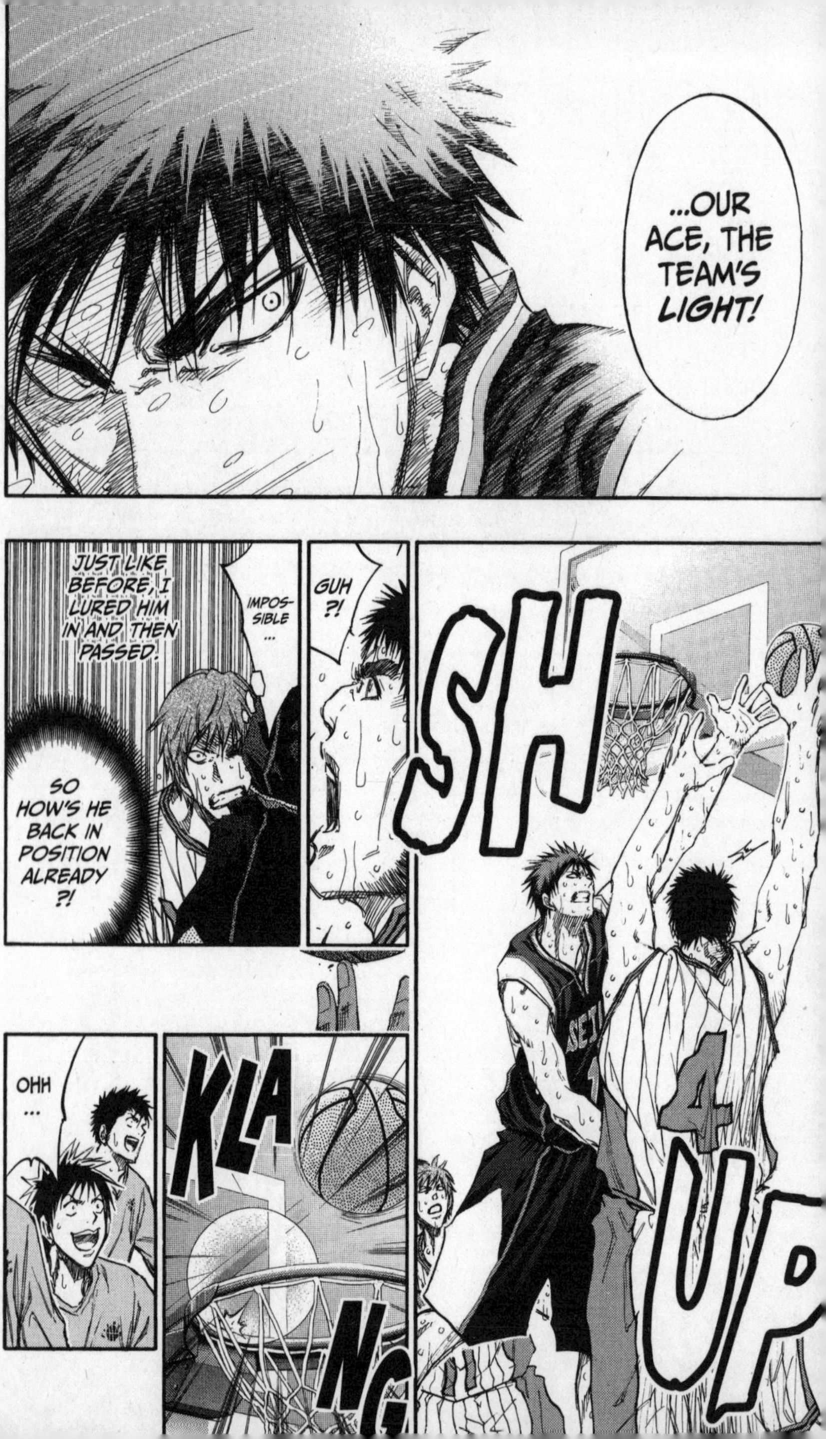
...OUR ACE, THE TEAM'S LIGHT!
SHUP
GUH ?!
IMPOS-SIBLE ...
JUST LIKE BEFORE, I LURED HIM IN AND THEN PASSED.
SO HOW'S HE BACK IN POSITION ALREADY ?!
KLANG
OHH ...

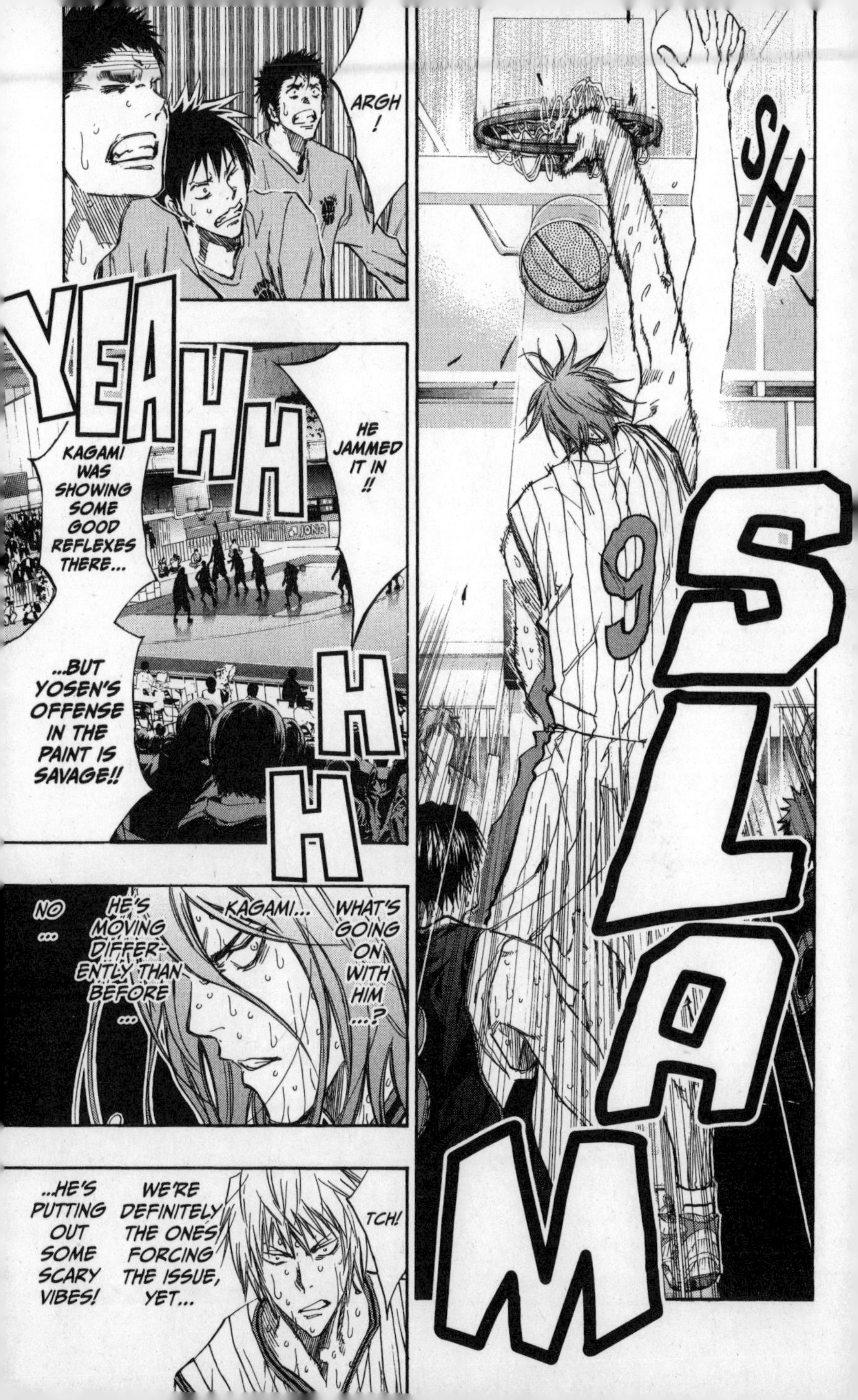
SHP
SLAM
ARGH!
YEAHHHHHH
HE JAMMED IT IN!!
KAGAMI WAS SHOWING SOME GOOD REFLEXES THERE...
...BUT YOSEN'S OFFENSE IN THE PAINT IS SAVAGE!!
WHAT'S GOING ON WITH HIM...?
KAGAMI...
HE'S MOVING DIFFERENTLY THAN BEFORE...
NO...
TCH!
WE'RE DEFINITELY THE ONES FORCING THE ISSUE, YET...
...HE'S PUTTING OUT SOME SCARY VIBES!

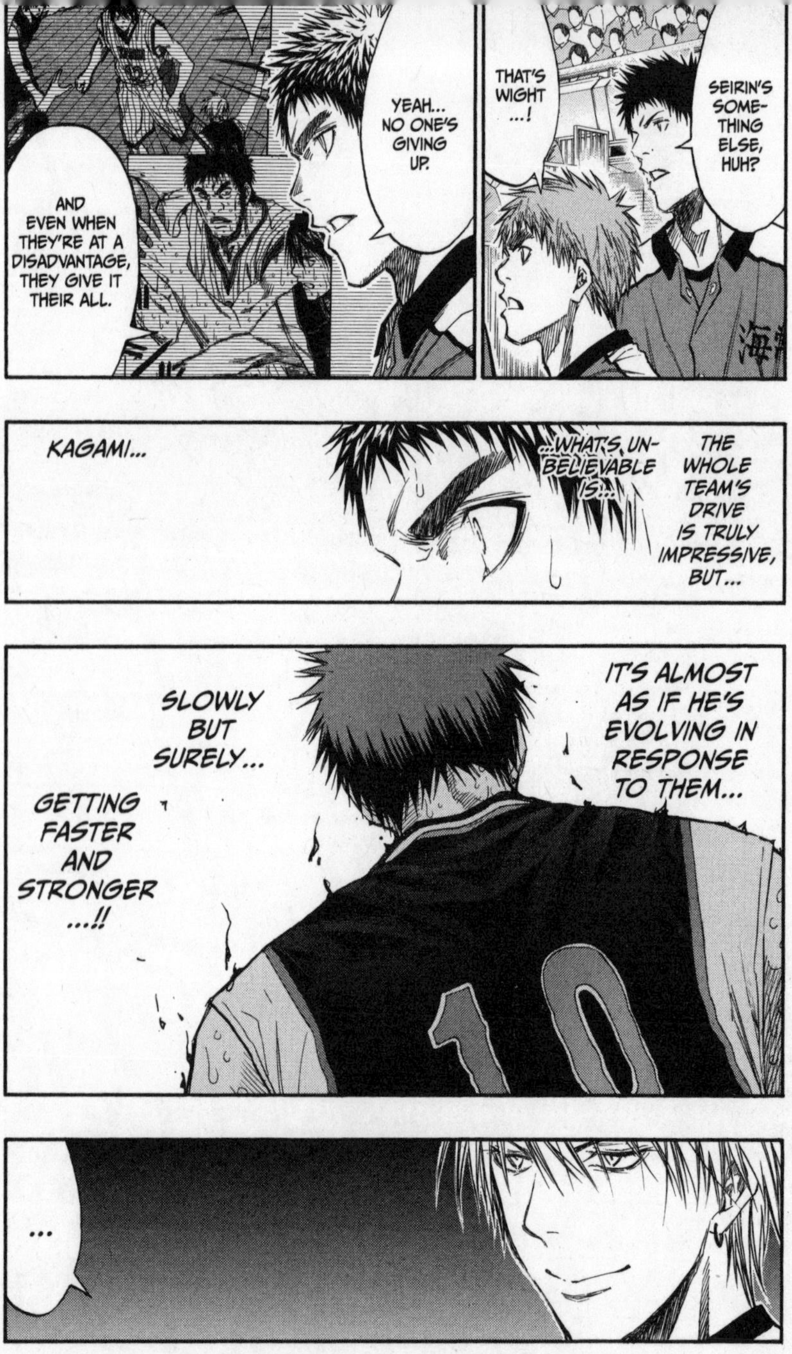
SEIRIN'S SOME-THING ELSE, HUH?
THAT'S WIGHT ...!
YEAH... NO ONE'S GIVING UP.
AND EVEN WHEN THEY'RE AT A DISADVANTAGE, THEY GIVE IT THEIR ALL.
THE WHOLE TEAM'S DRIVE IS TRULY IMPRESSIVE, BUT...
...WHAT'S UN-BELIEVABLE IS...
KAGAMI...
IT'S ALMOST AS IF HE'S EVOLVING IN RESPONSE TO THEM...
SLOWLY BUT SURELY...
GETTING FASTER AND STRONGER ...!!
...

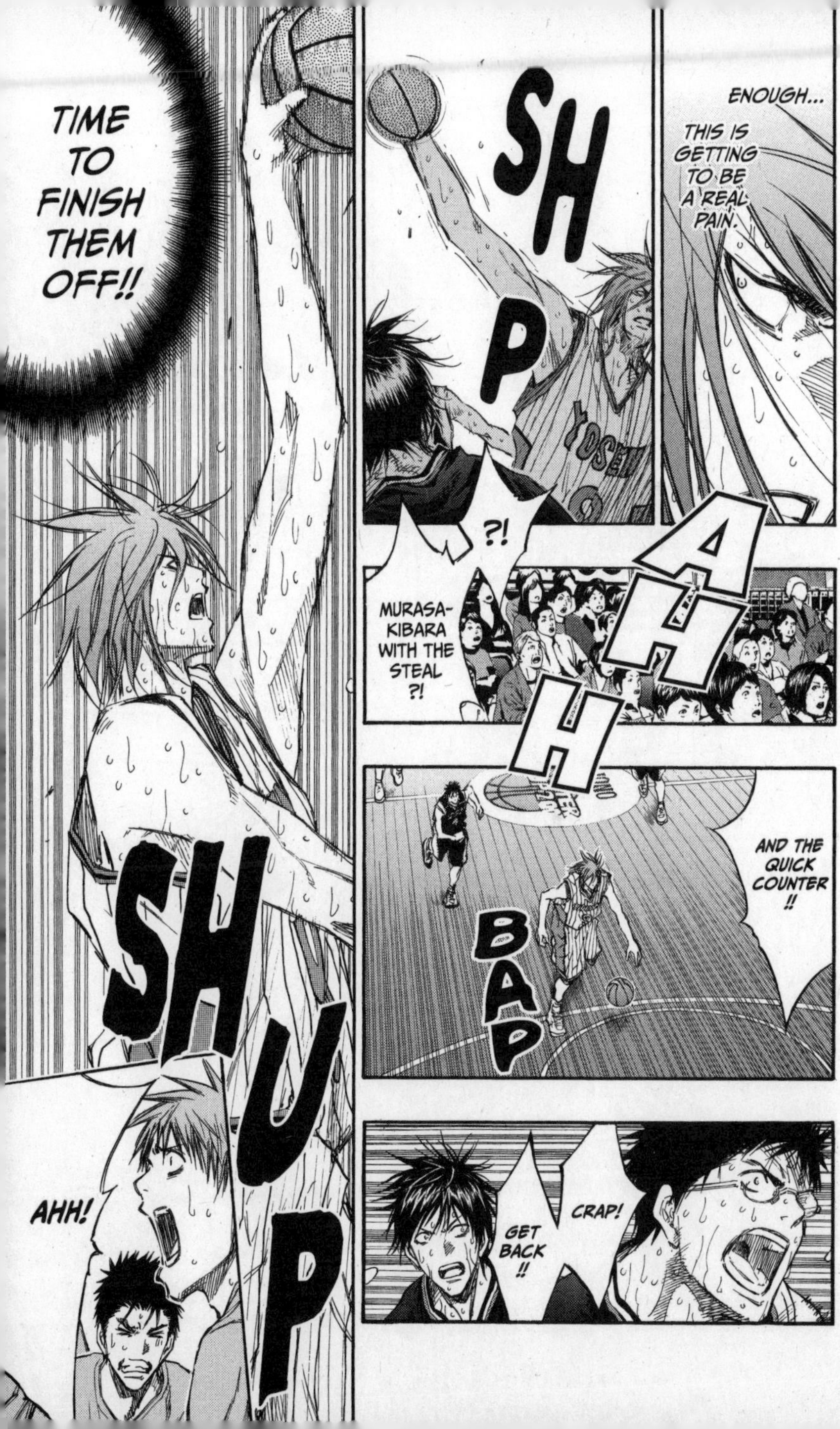
ENOUGH...
THIS IS GETTING TO BE A REAL PAIN.
SHP
?!
AHH
MURASA-KIBARA WITH THE STEAL ?!
BAP
AND THE QUICK COUNTER !!
CRAP!
GET BACK !!
TIME TO FINISH THEM OFF!!
SHUP
AHH!

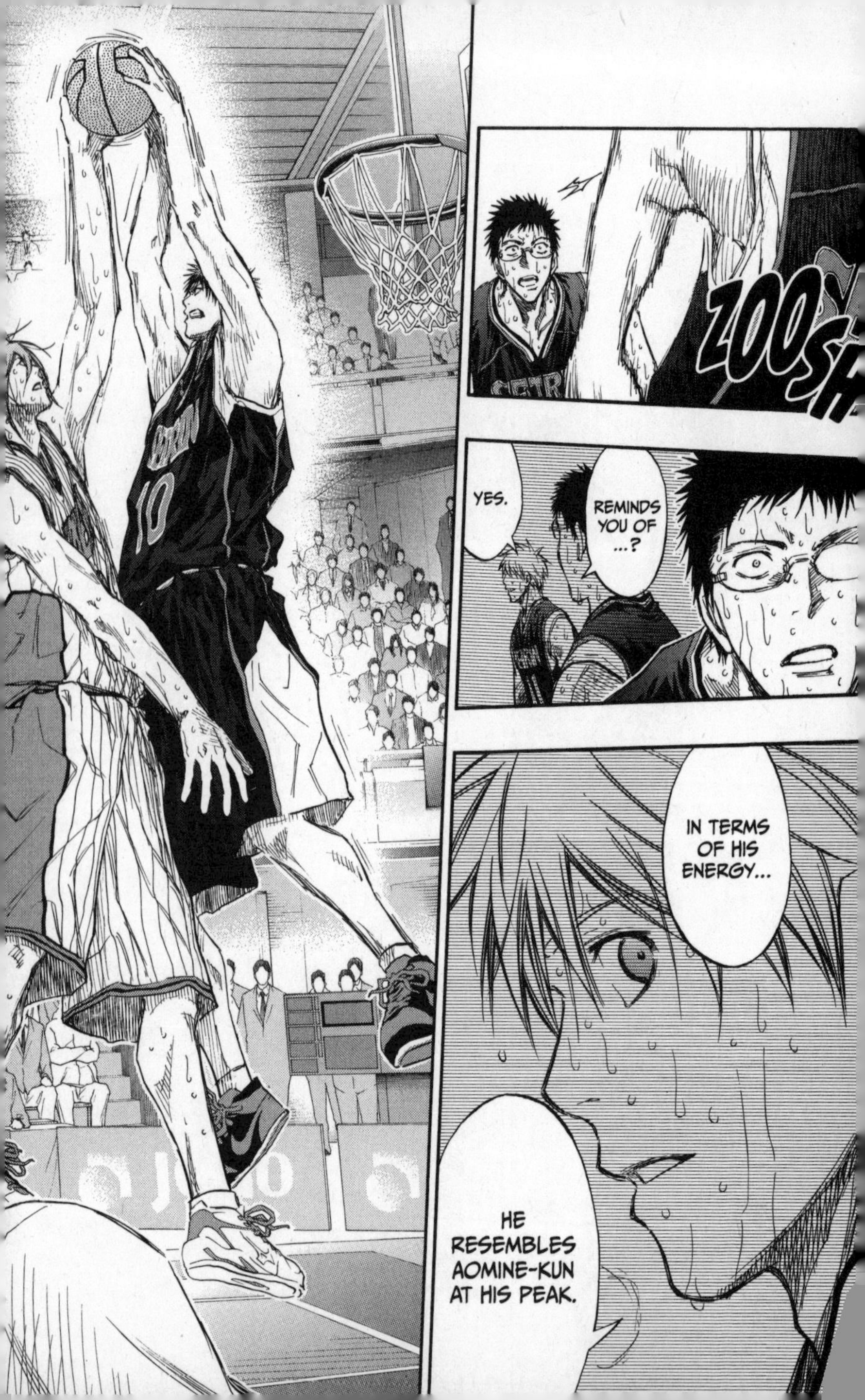
ZOOSH
REMINDS YOU OF ...?
YES.
IN TERMS OF HIS ENERGY...
HE RESEMBLES AOMINE-KUN AT HIS PEAK.

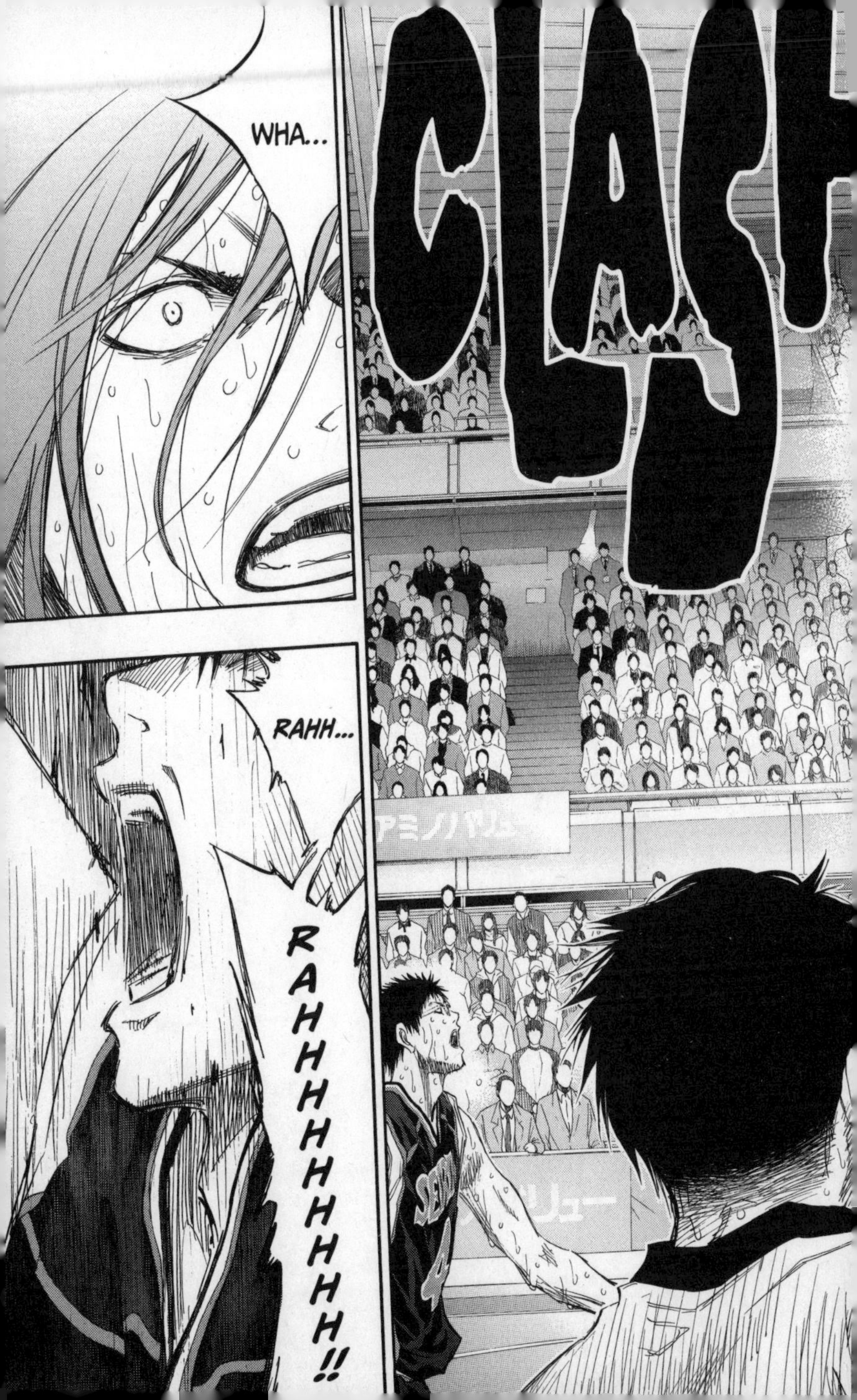
CLAS
WHA...
RAHH...
RAHHHHHHHHH!!

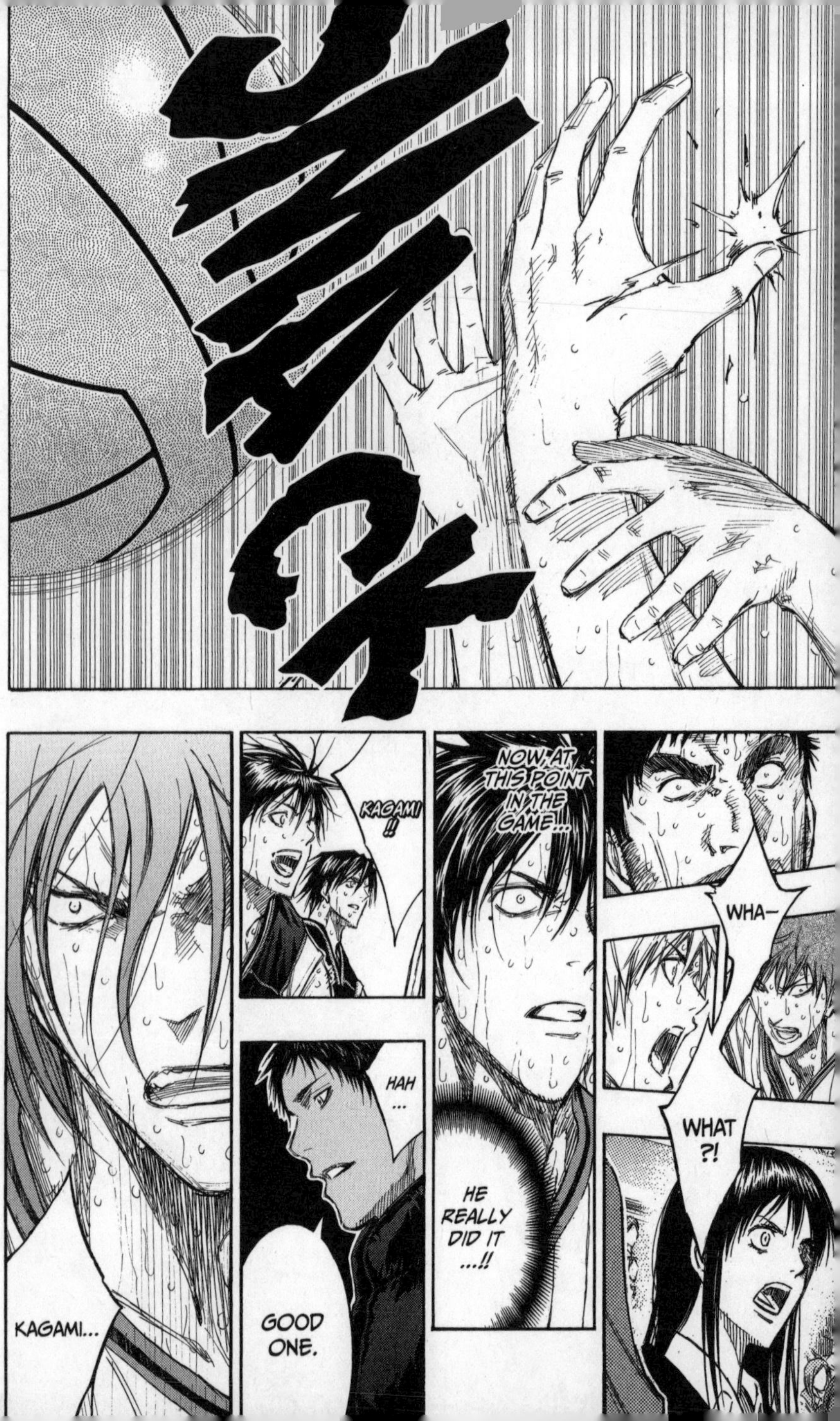
WHA—
WHAT ?!
NOW, AT THIS POINT IN THE GAME...
HE REALLY DID IT ...!!
KAGAMI !!
HAH ...
GOOD ONE.
KAGAMI...

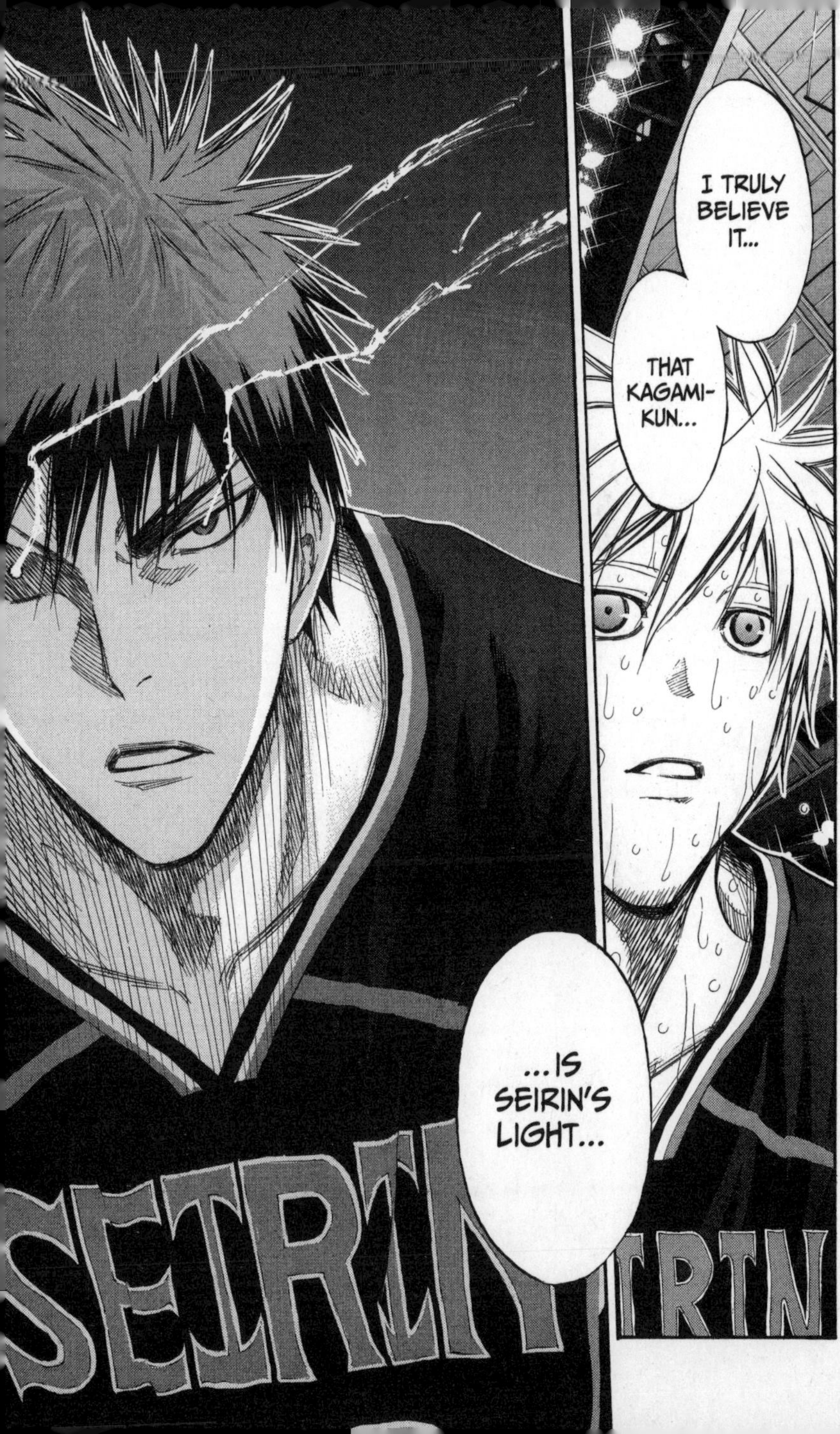
I TRULY BELIEVE IT...
THAT KAGAMI-KUN...
...IS SEIRIN'S LIGHT...
SEIRIN
IRIN

KUROKO'S BASKETBALL BLOOPERS

TAKE 2

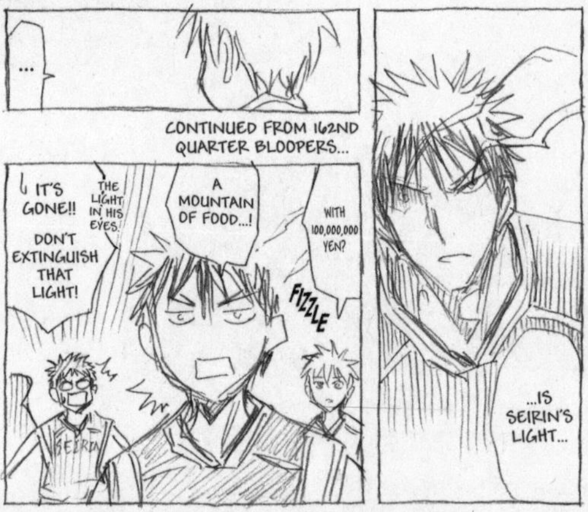
CONTINUED FROM 162ND QUARTER BLOOPERS...
...IS SEIRIN'S LIGHT...
...
A MOUNTAIN OF FOOD...!
WITH 100,000,000 YEN?
FIZZLE
THE LIGHT IN HIS EYES!
IT'S GONE!!
DON'T EXTINGUISH THAT LIGHT!
SEIRIN

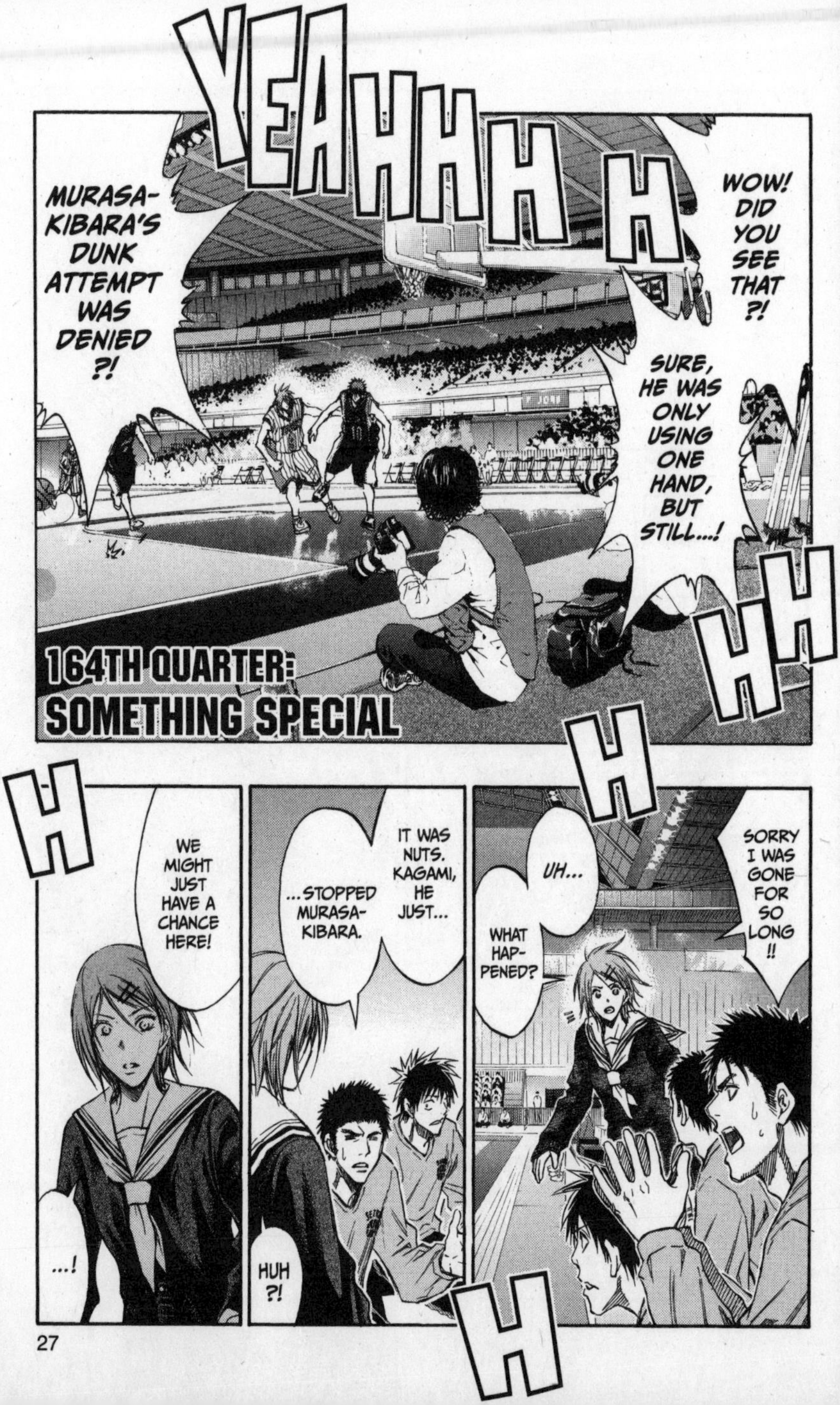
YEAHHHHHHHHHH
WOW! DID YOU SEE THAT?!
MURASA-KIBARA'S DUNK ATTEMPT WAS DENIED?!
SURE, HE WAS ONLY USING ONE HAND, BUT STILL...!
164TH QUARTER:
SOMETHING SPECIAL
SORRY I WAS GONE FOR SO LONG!!
UH...
WHAT HAP-PENED?
IT WAS NUTS. KAGAMI, HE JUST...
...STOPPED MURASA-KIBARA.
HUH?!
WE MIGHT JUST HAVE A CHANCE HERE!
...!

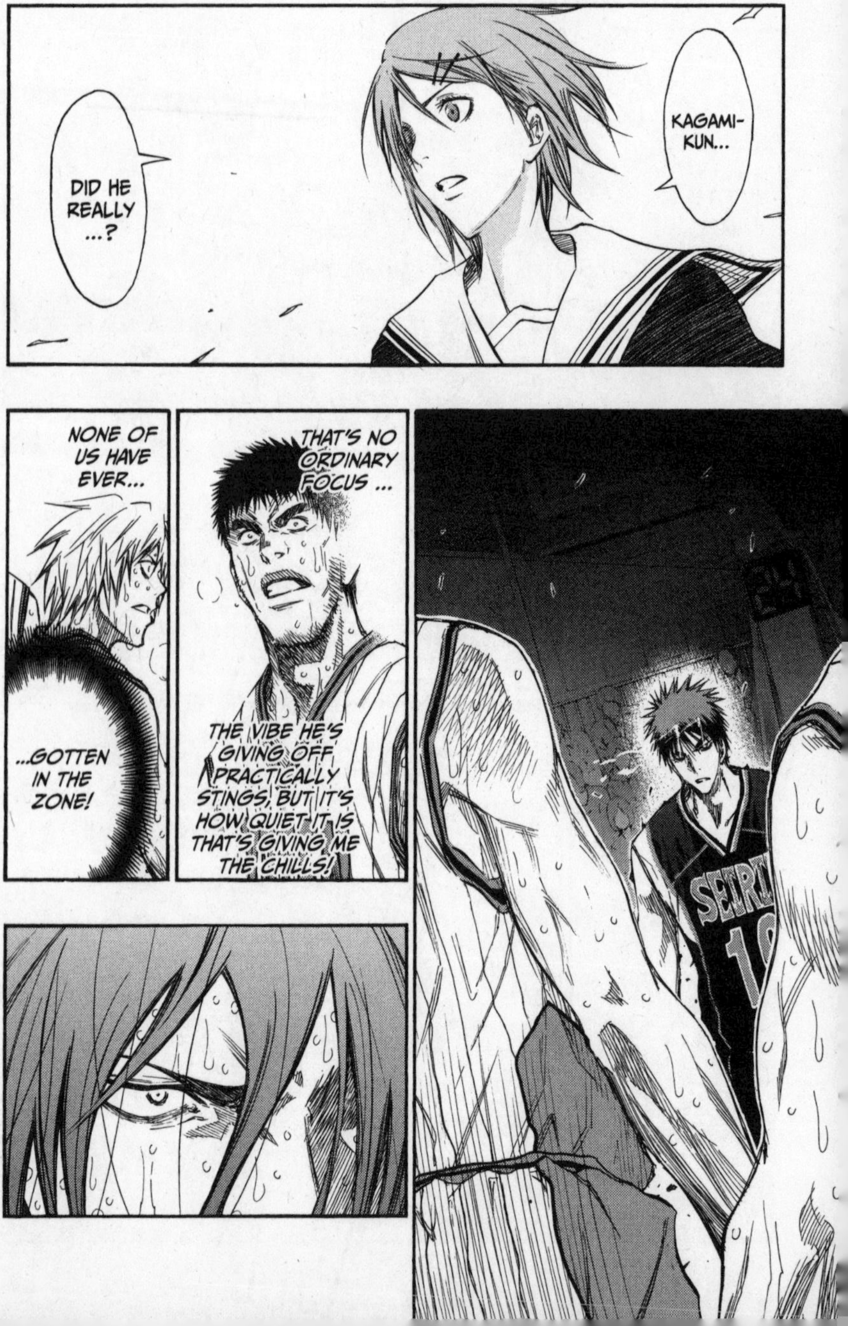
KAGAMI-KUN...
DID HE REALLY ...?
THAT'S NO ORDINARY FOCUS ...
THE VIBE HE'S GIVING OFF PRACTICALLY STINGS, BUT IT'S HOW QUIET IT IS THAT'S GIVING ME THE CHILLS!
NONE OF US HAVE EVER...
...GOTTEN IN THE ZONE!

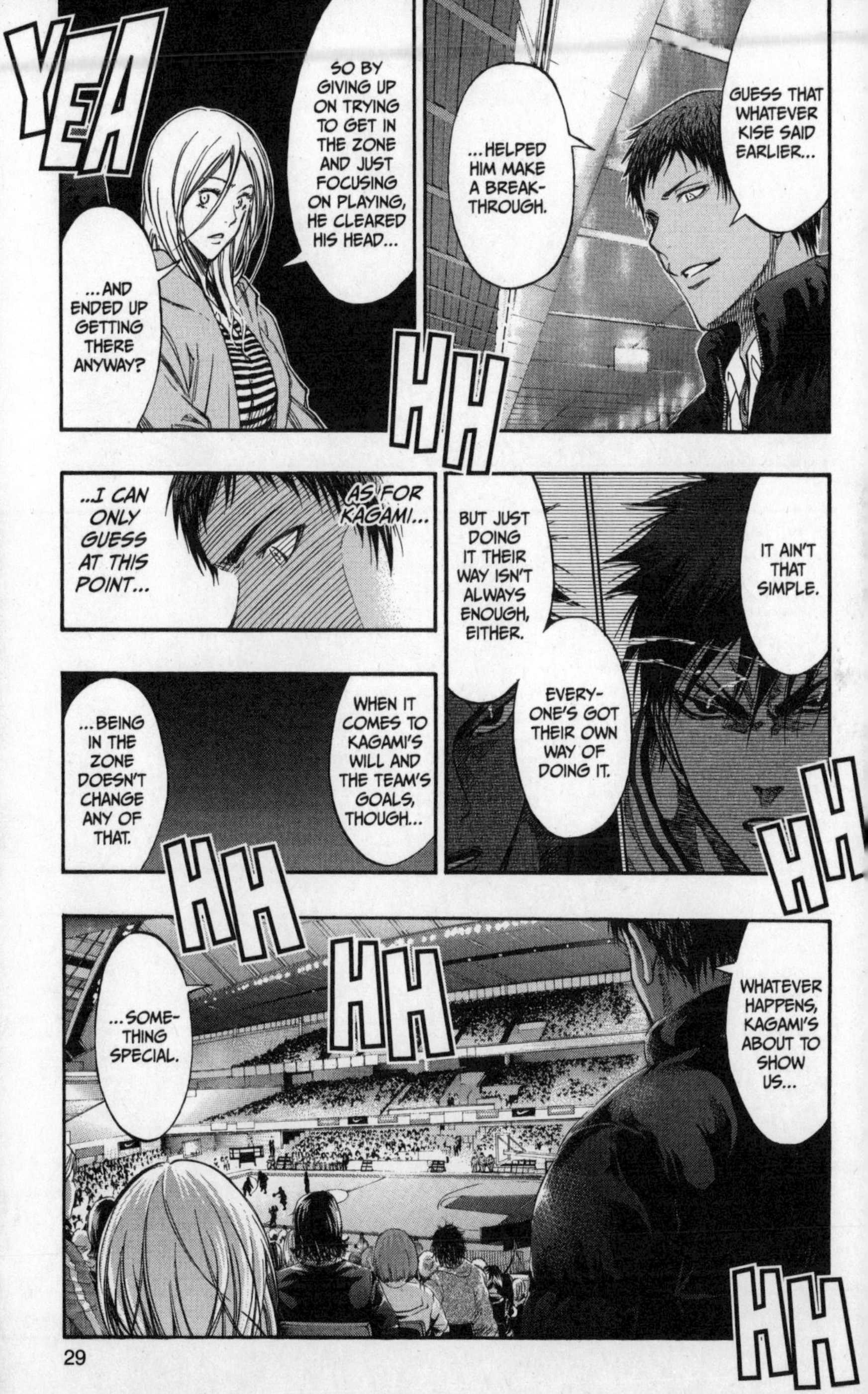
YEA
GUESS THAT WHATEVER KISE SAID EARLIER...
...HELPED HIM MAKE A BREAK-THROUGH.
SO BY GIVING UP ON TRYING TO GET IN THE ZONE AND JUST FOCUSING ON PLAYING, HE CLEARED HIS HEAD...
...AND ENDED UP GETTING THERE ANYWAY?
HH
IT AIN'T THAT SIMPLE.
BUT JUST DOING IT THEIR WAY ISN'T ALWAYS ENOUGH, EITHER.
EVERY-ONE'S GOT THEIR OWN WAY OF DOING IT.
HH
AS FOR KAGAMI...
...I CAN ONLY GUESS AT THIS POINT...
WHEN IT COMES TO KAGAMI'S WILL AND THE TEAM'S GOALS, THOUGH...
...BEING IN THE ZONE DOESN'T CHANGE ANY OF THAT.
HH
WHATEVER HAPPENS, KAGAMI'S ABOUT TO SHOW US...
...SOME-THING SPECIAL.
HH
HH

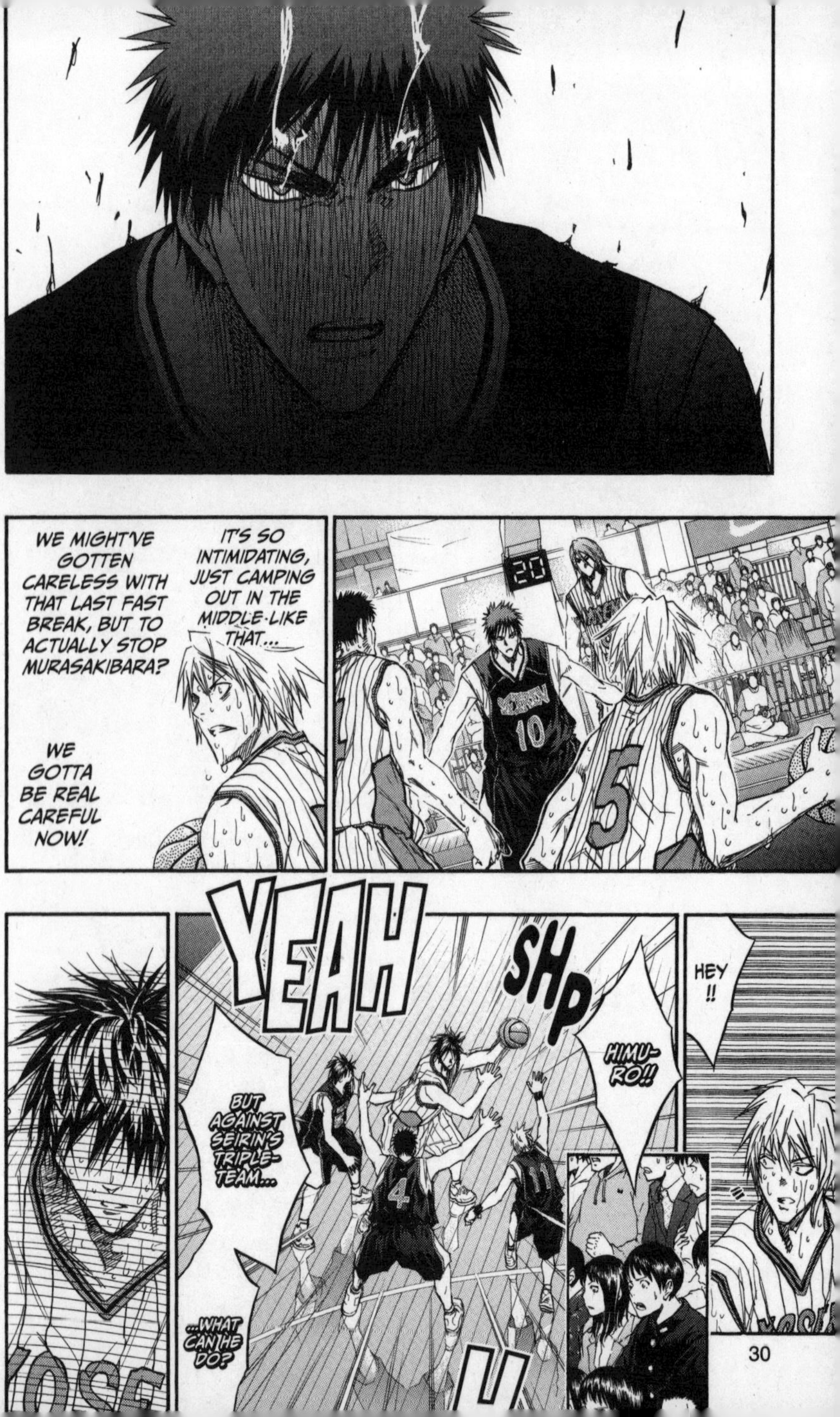
IT'S SO INTIMIDATING, JUST CAMPING OUT IN THE MIDDLE LIKE THAT...
WE MIGHT'VE GOTTEN CARELESS WITH THAT LAST FAST BREAK, BUT TO ACTUALLY STOP MURASAKIBARA?
WE GOTTA BE REAL CAREFUL NOW!
HEY!!
YEAH
SHP
HIMURO!!
BUT AGAINST SEIRIN'S TRIPLE-TEAM...
...WHAT CAN HE DO?

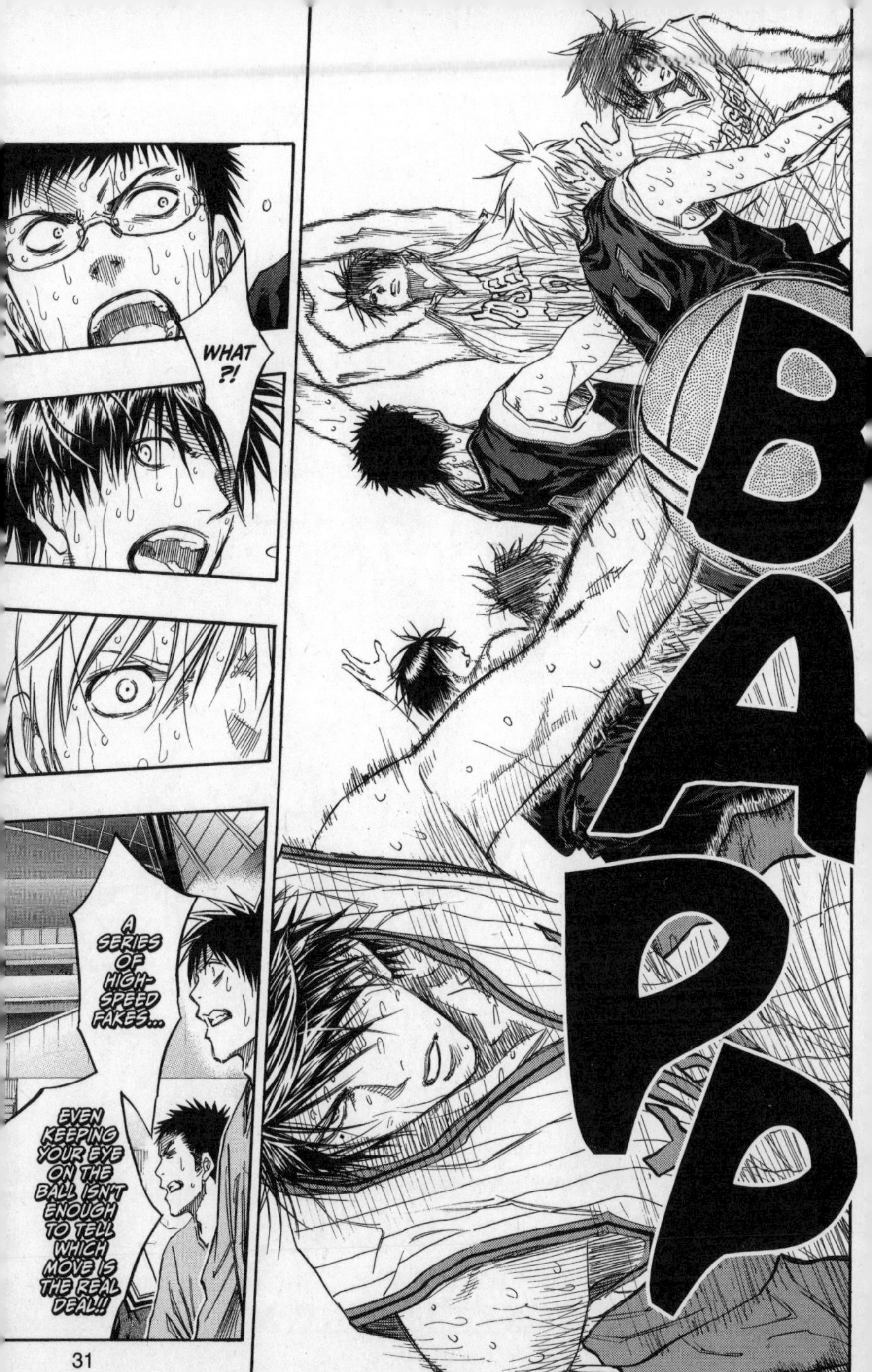
BAM
WHAT ?!
A SERIES OF HIGH-SPEED FAKES...
EVEN KEEPING YOUR EYE ON THE BALL ISN'T ENOUGH TO TELL WHICH MOVE IS THE REAL DEAL!!

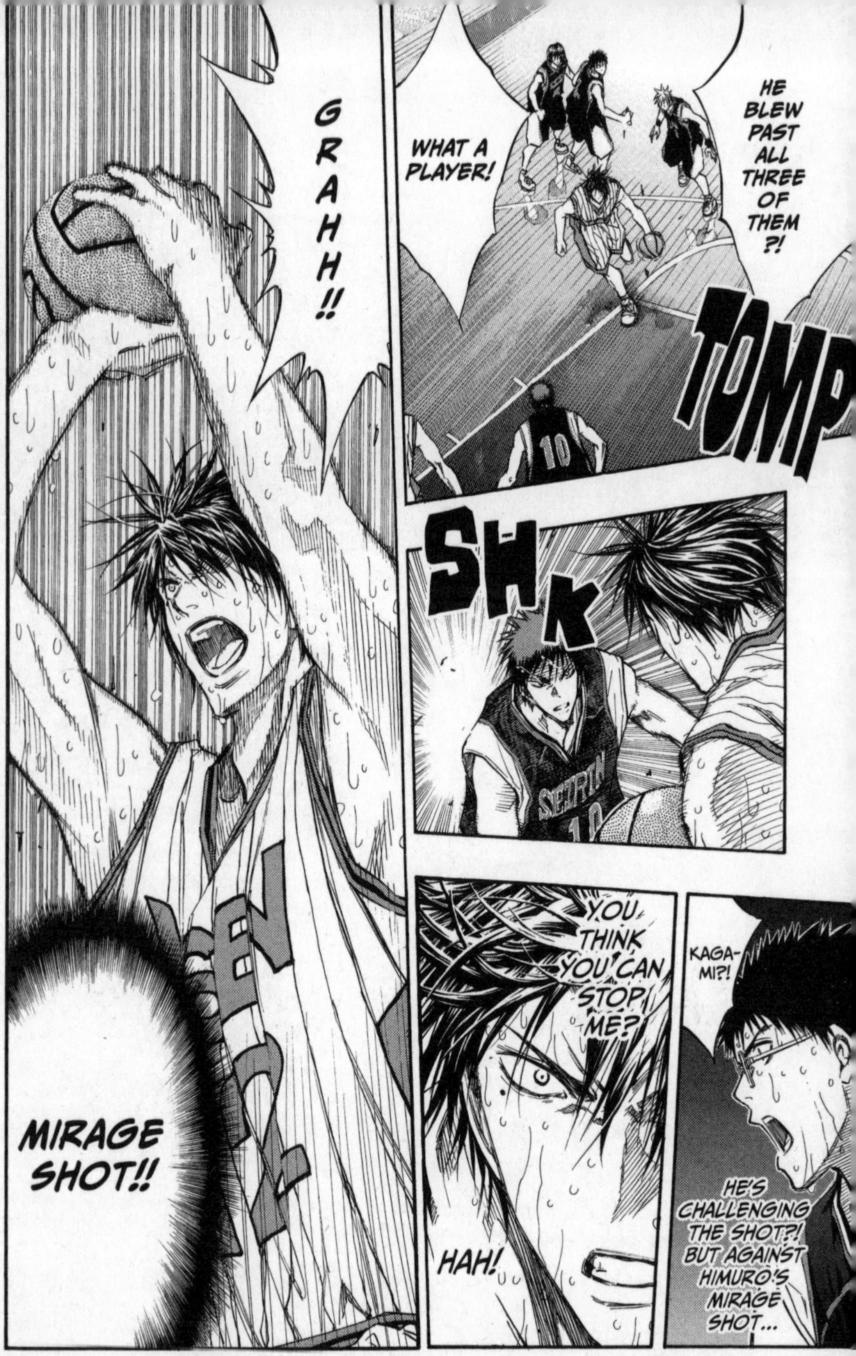
HE BLEW PAST ALL THREE OF THEM?!
WHAT A PLAYER!
TOMP
SHK
KAGA-MI?!
HE'S CHALLENGING THE SHOT?! BUT AGAINST HIMURO'S MIRAGE SHOT...
YOU THINK YOU CAN STOP ME?
HAH!
GRAHHH!!
MIRAGE SHOT!!

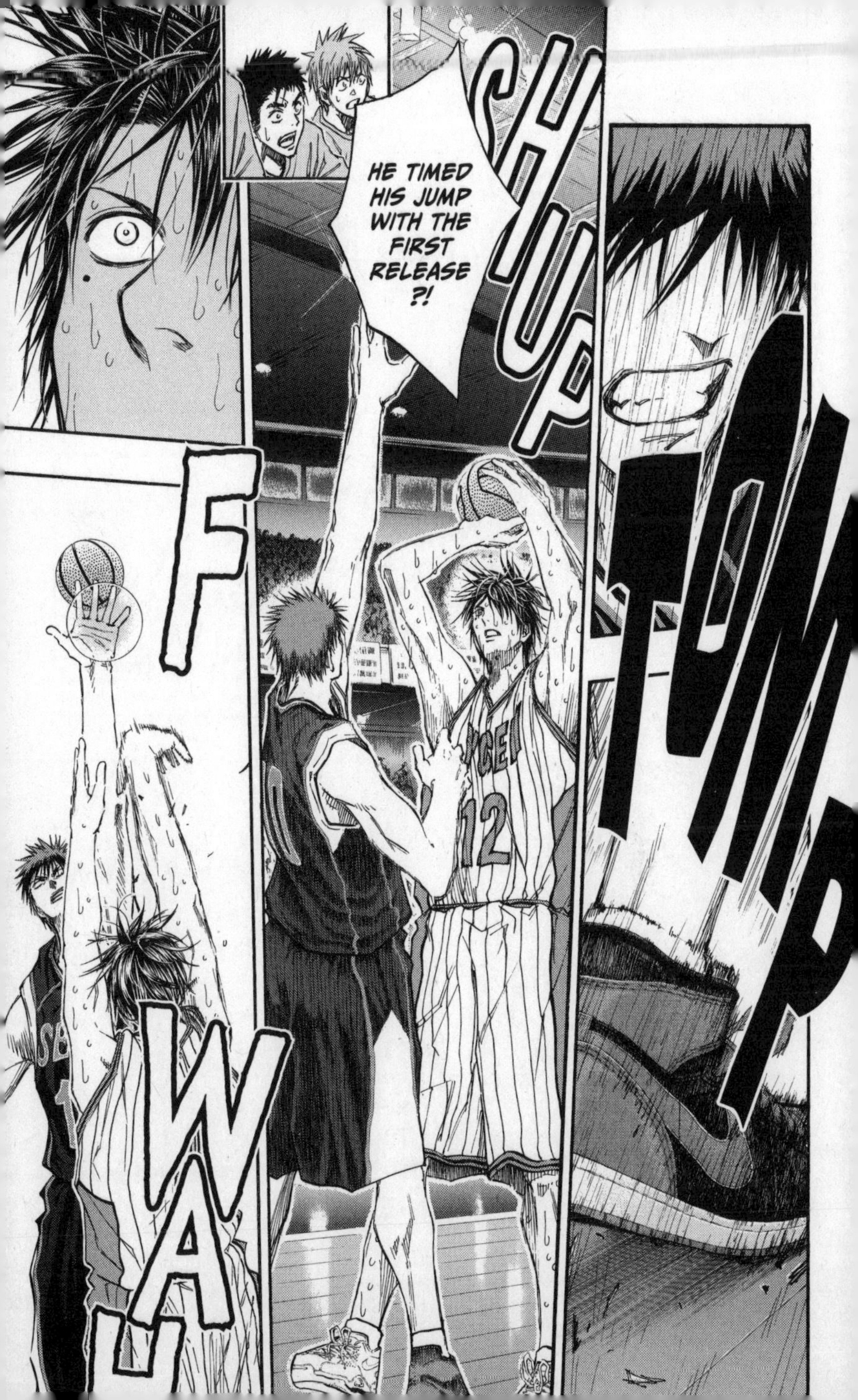
CHUP
HE TIMED HIS JUMP WITH THE FIRST RELEASE ?!
TUMP
FWA

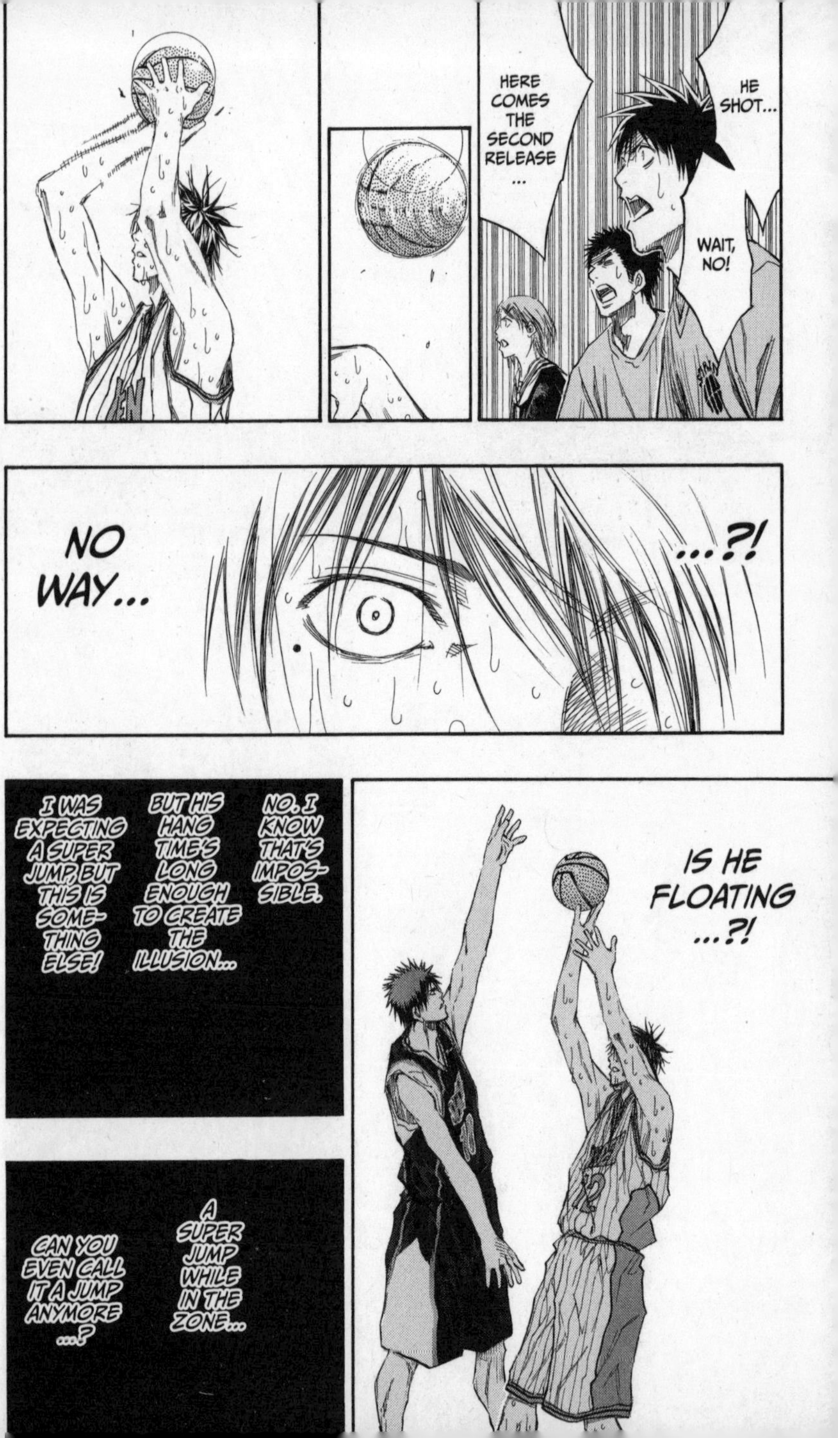
HE SHOT...
HERE COMES THE SECOND RELEASE...
WAIT, NO!
...?!
NO WAY...
IS HE FLOATING...?!
NO. I KNOW THAT'S IMPOSSIBLE.
BUT HIS HANG TIME'S LONG ENOUGH TO CREATE THE ILLUSION...
I WAS EXPECTING A SUPER JUMP, BUT THIS IS SOMETHING ELSE!
A SUPER JUMP WHILE IN THE ZONE...
CAN YOU EVEN CALL IT A JUMP ANYMORE...?

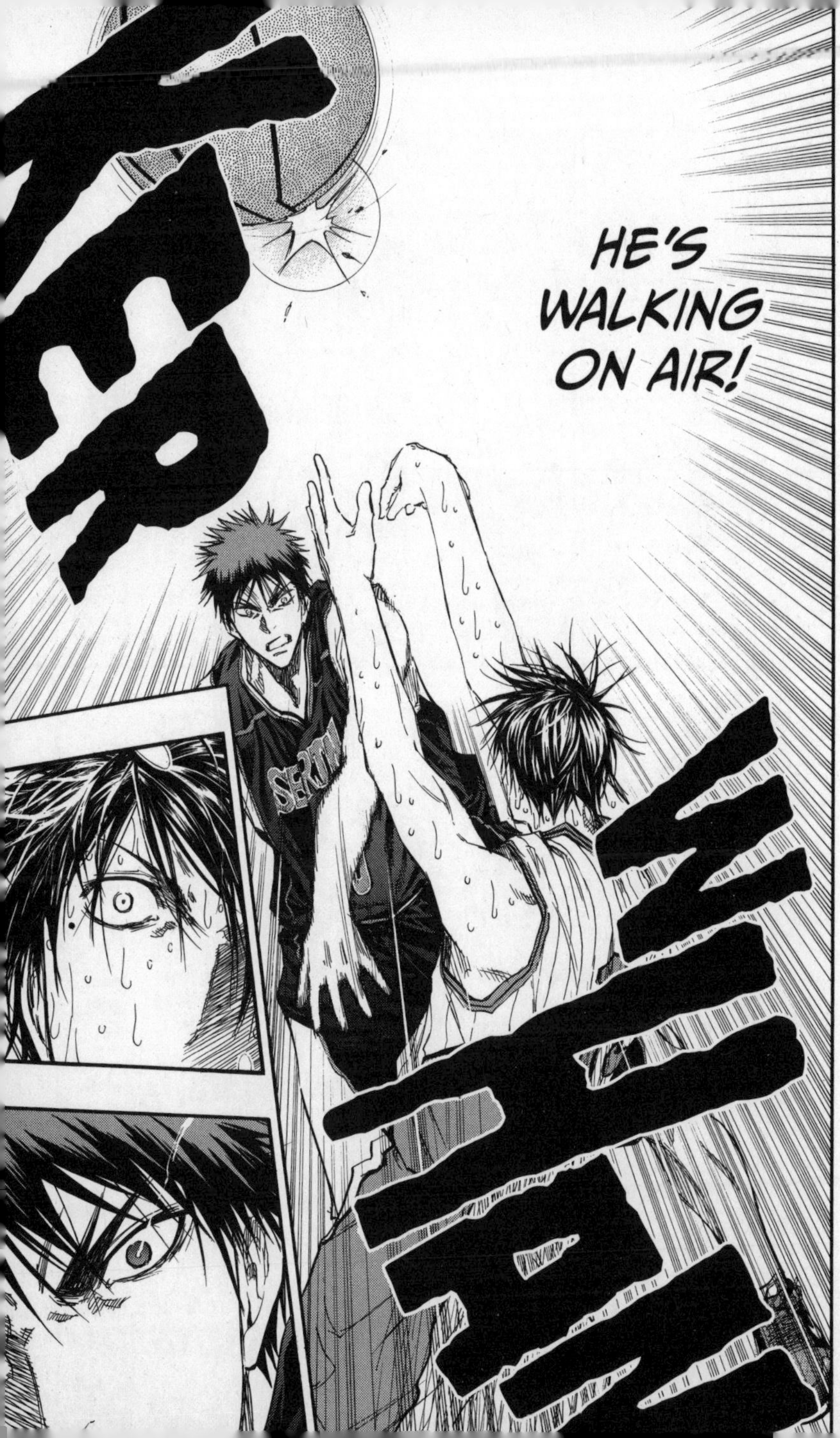
HE'S WALKING ON AIR!

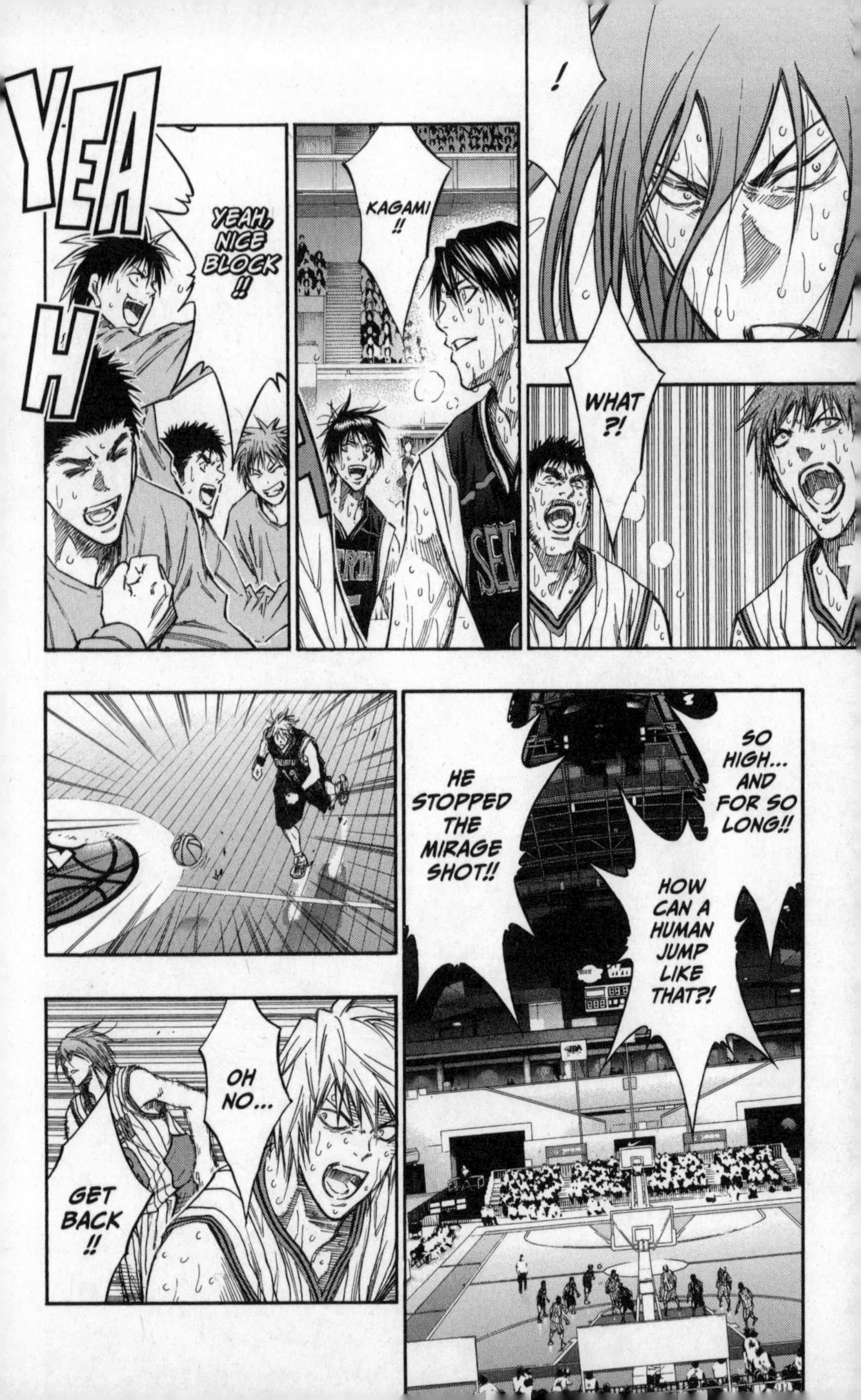
!
WHAT?!
KAGAMI!!
YEAH, NICE BLOCK!!
YEAHH
SO HIGH... AND FOR SO LONG!!
HE STOPPED THE MIRAGE SHOT!!
HOW CAN A HUMAN JUMP LIKE THAT?!
OH NO...
GET BACK!!

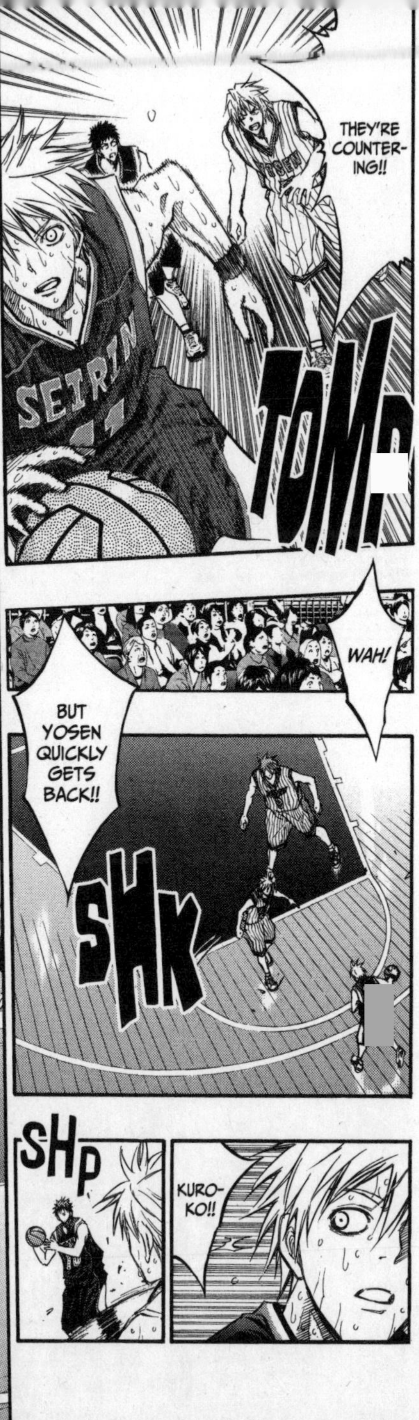
THEY'RE COUNTERING!!
TOMP
WAH!
BUT YOSEN QUICKLY GETS BACK!!
SHK
KURO-KO!!
SHP

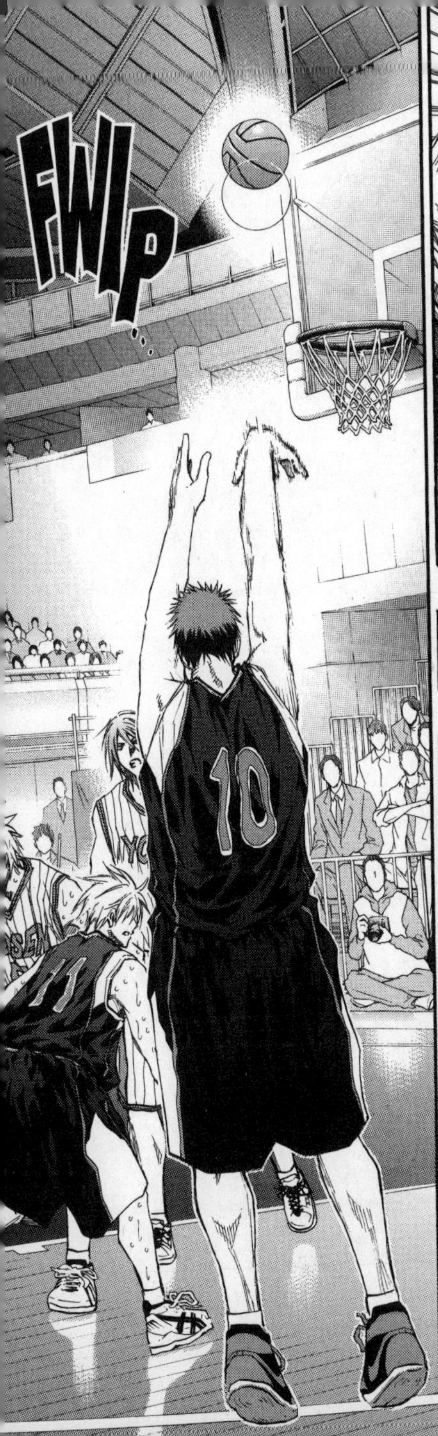
FWIP

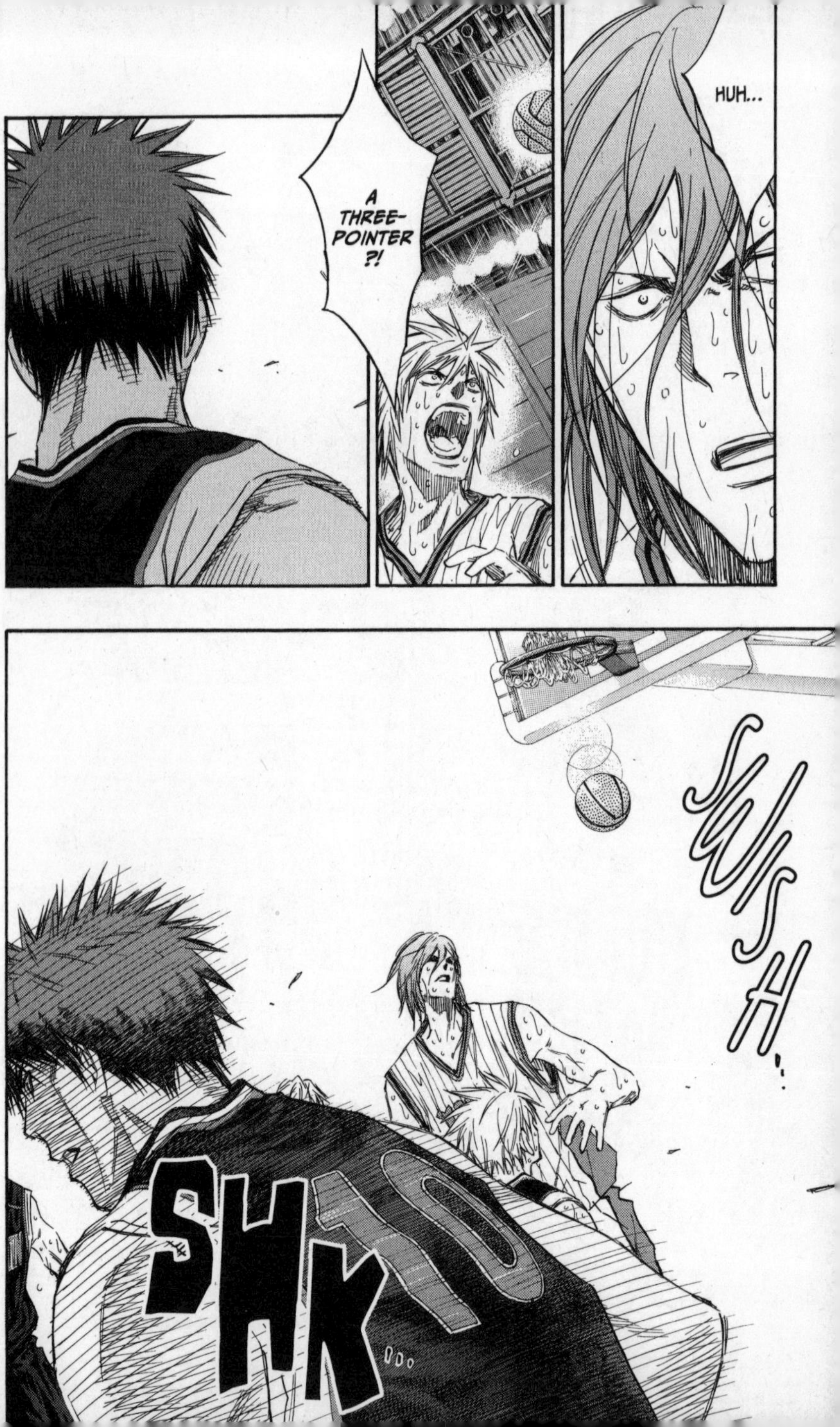
HUH...
A THREE-POINTER?!
SWISH..
SHK

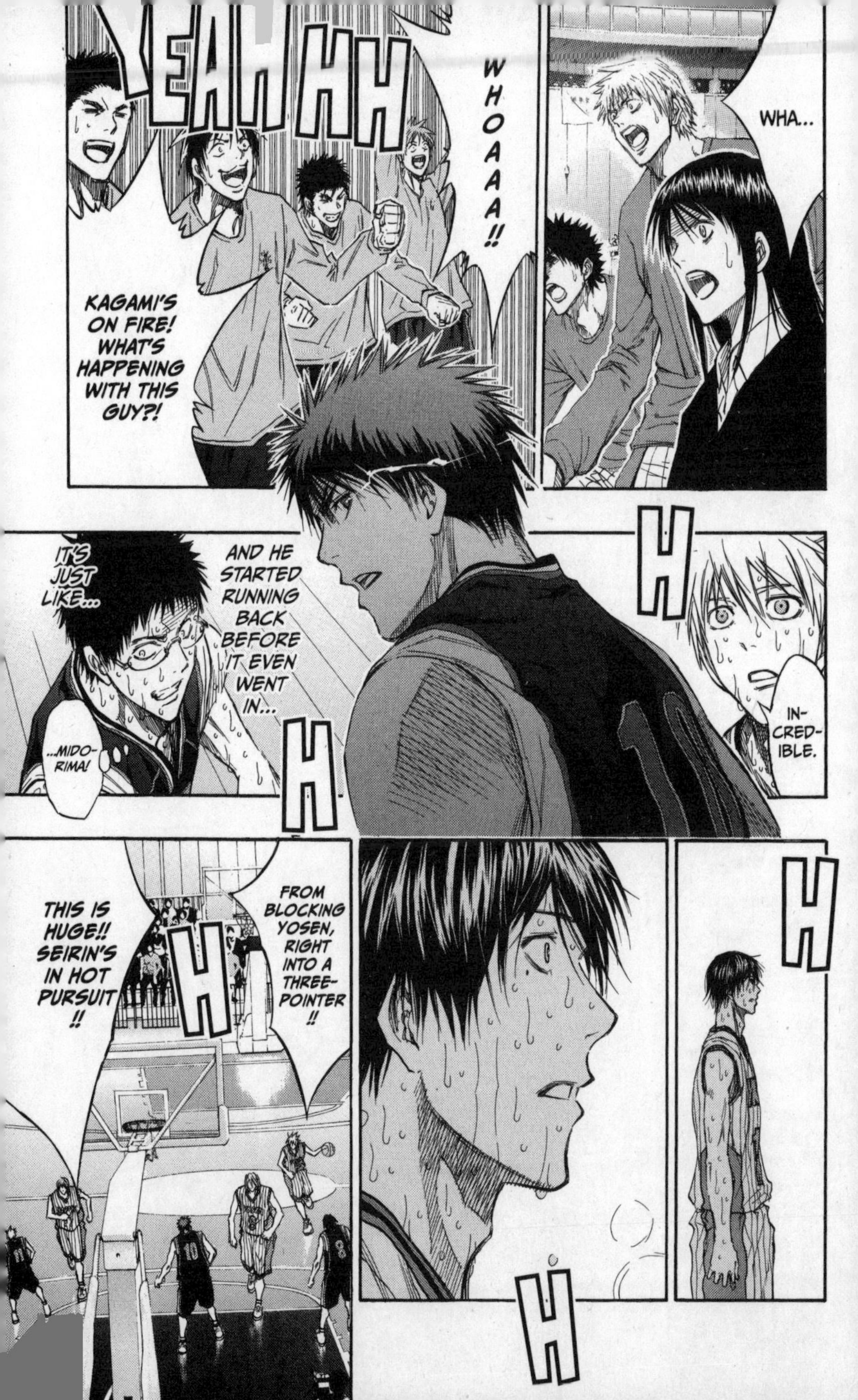
WHA...
YEAHHH
WHOAAAA!!
KAGAMI'S ON FIRE! WHAT'S HAPPENING WITH THIS GUY?!
INCREDIBLE.
H
H
AND HE STARTED RUNNING BACK BEFORE IT EVEN WENT IN...
IT'S JUST LIKE...
...MIDORIMA!
H
H
FROM BLOCKING YOSEN, RIGHT INTO A THREE-POINTER!!
H
THIS IS HUGE!! SEIRIN'S IN HOT PURSUIT!!

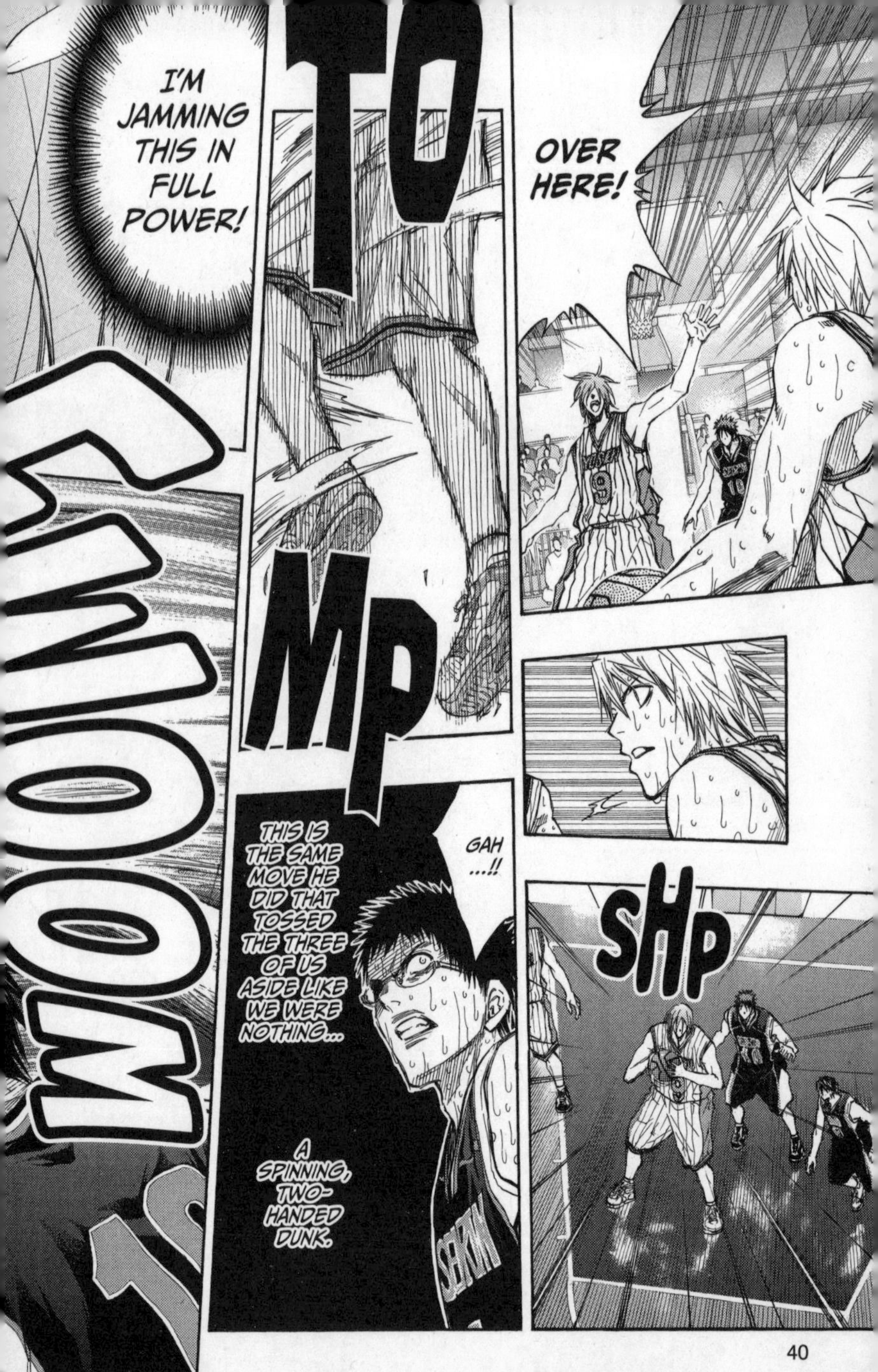
OVER HERE!
TO
MP
I'M JAMMING THIS IN FULL POWER!
SHP
GAH ...!!
THIS IS THE SAME MOVE HE DID THAT TOSSED THE THREE OF US ASIDE LIKE WE WERE NOTHING...
A SPINNING, TWO-HANDED DUNK.

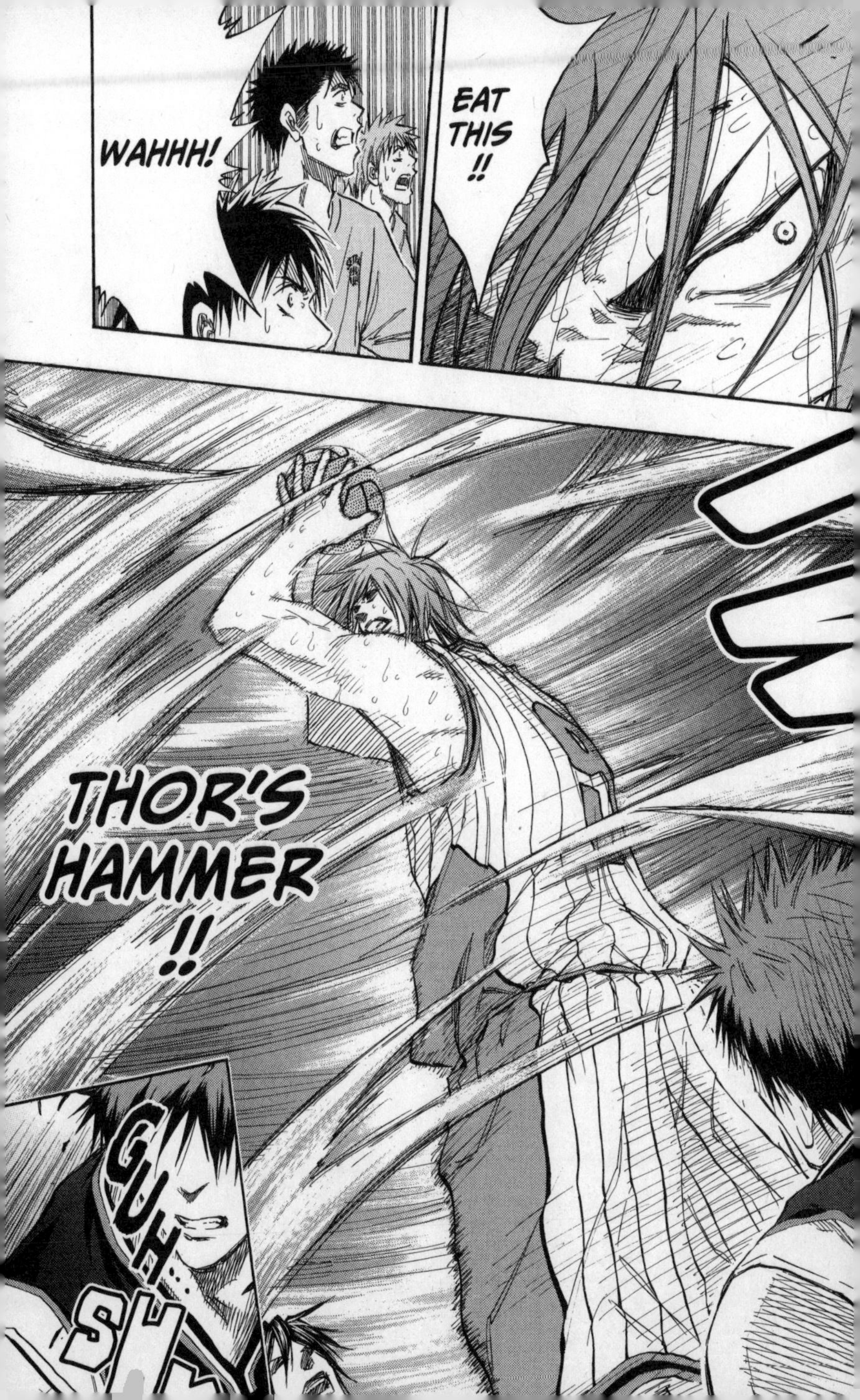
EAT THIS!!
WAHHH!
THOR'S HAMMER!!
GUH...

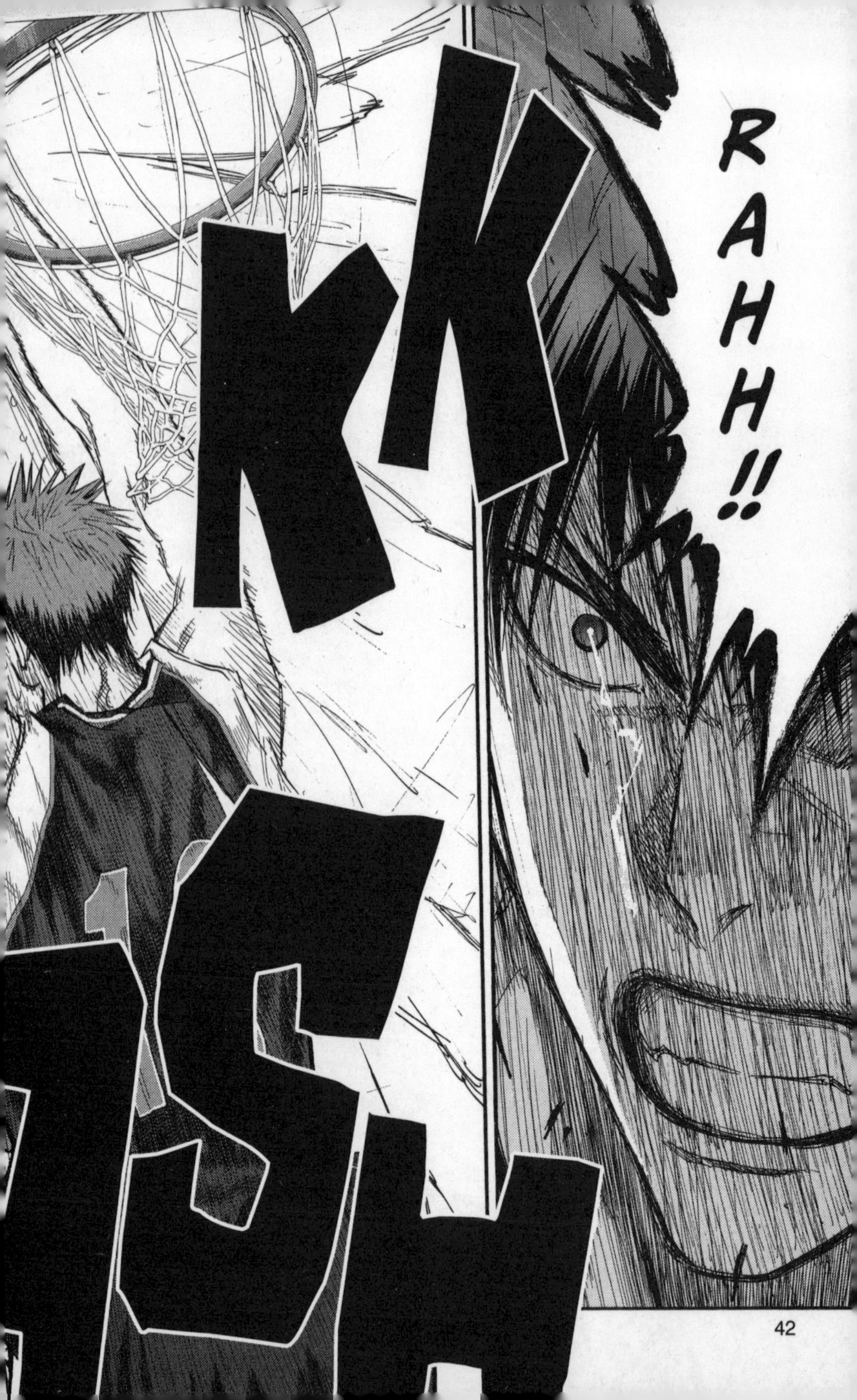
RAHH!!

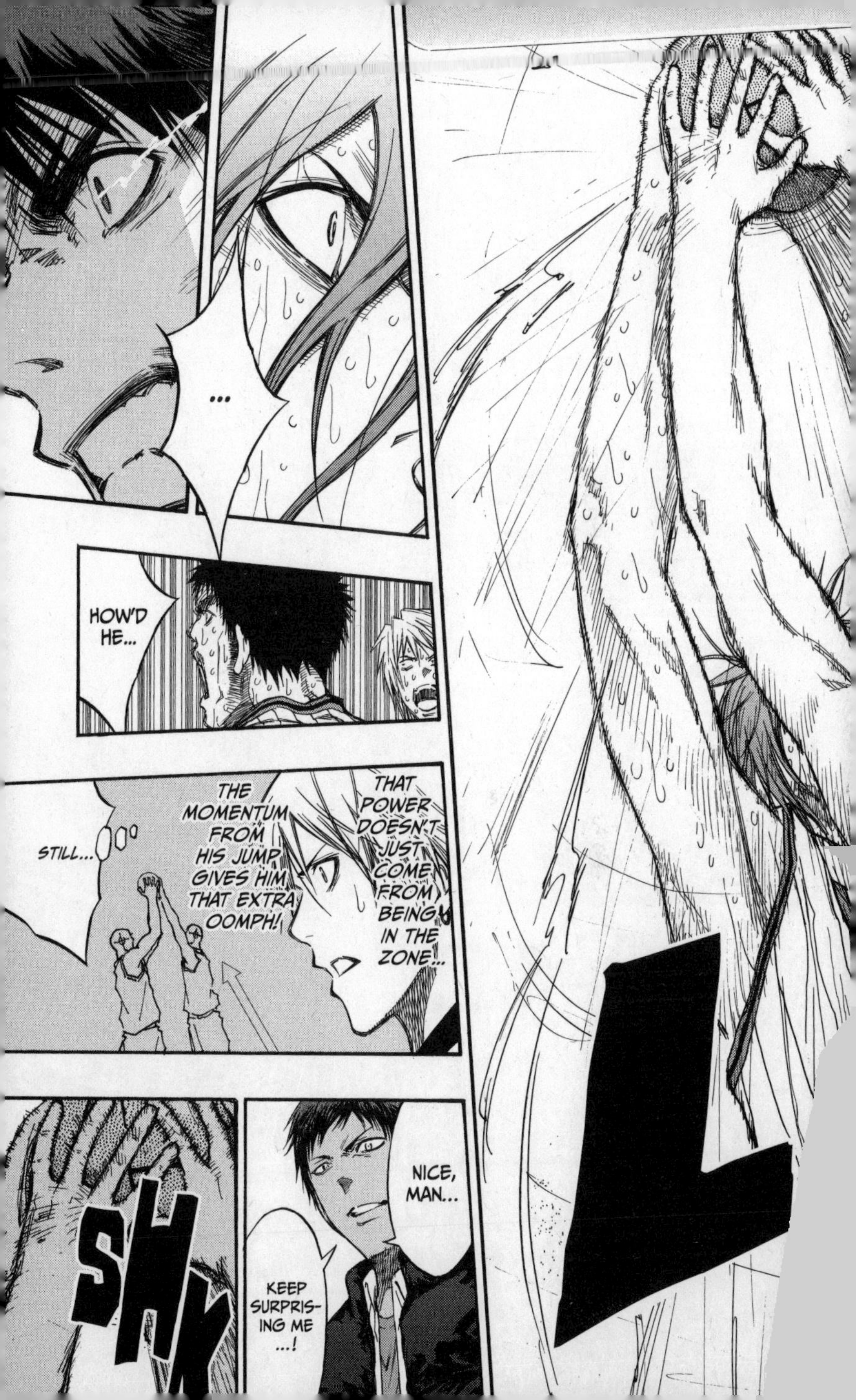
...
HOW'D HE...
THAT POWER DOESN'T JUST COME FROM BEING IN THE ZONE...
THE MOMENTUM FROM HIS JUMP GIVES HIM THAT EXTRA OOMPH!
STILL...
NICE, MAN...
KEEP SURPRIS-ING ME ...!
SHK

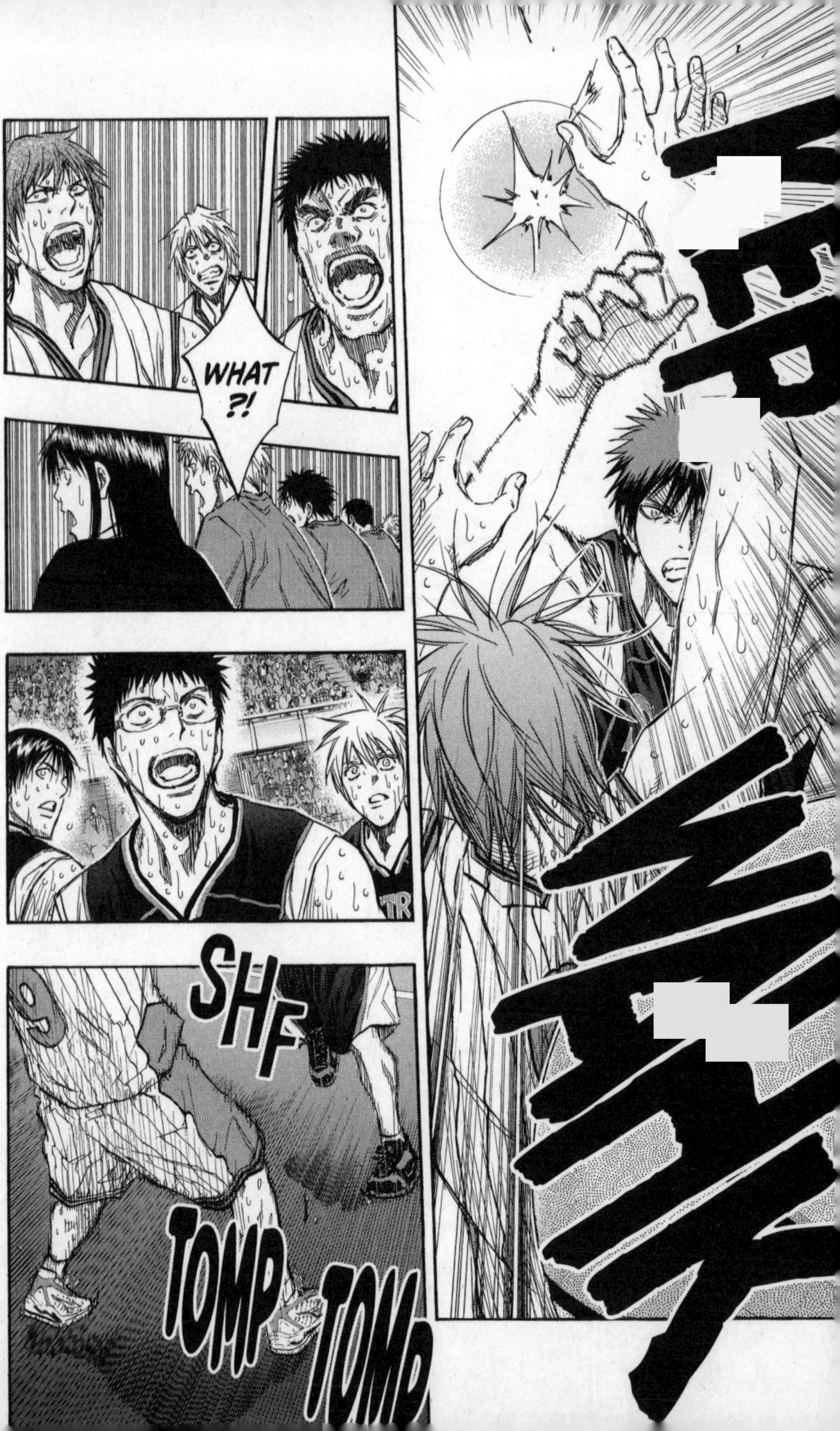
WHAT ?!
SHF
TOMP
TOMP

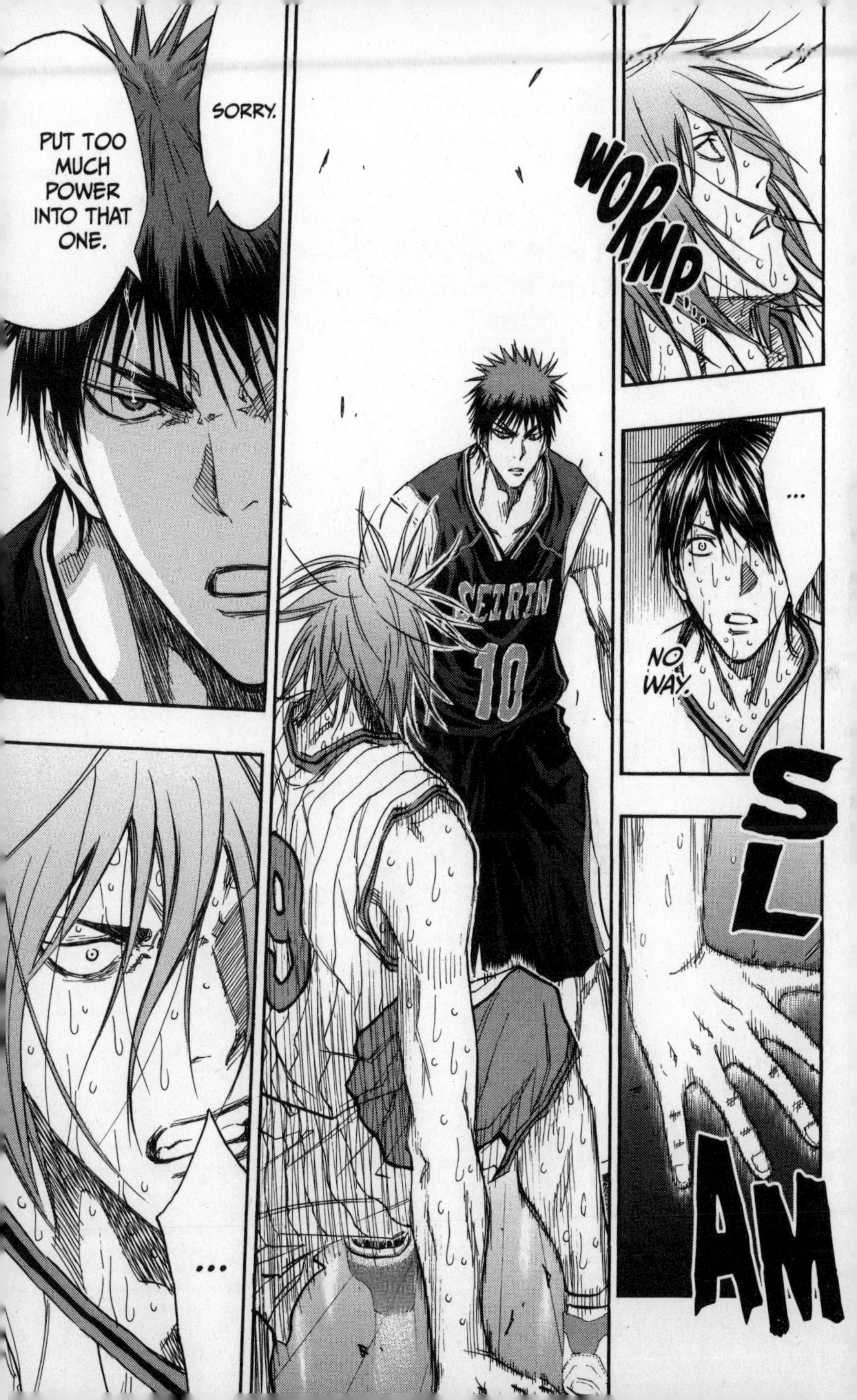
WORMP...
...
NO WAY.
SLAM
SORRY.
PUT TOO MUCH POWER INTO THAT ONE.
...

KUROKO'S BASKETBALL Q&A (W/ HALFWAY-DECENT ANSWERS)

Q. QUESTION FOR WAKAMATSU-KUN! WHAT'S YOUR FAVORITE BATTLE CRY?
(I LIKE "HIYAHH"! from CHIBA PREFECTURE)

A. RAWRRRRR!!!!

KUROKO'S BASKETBALL BLOOPERS

TAKE 1

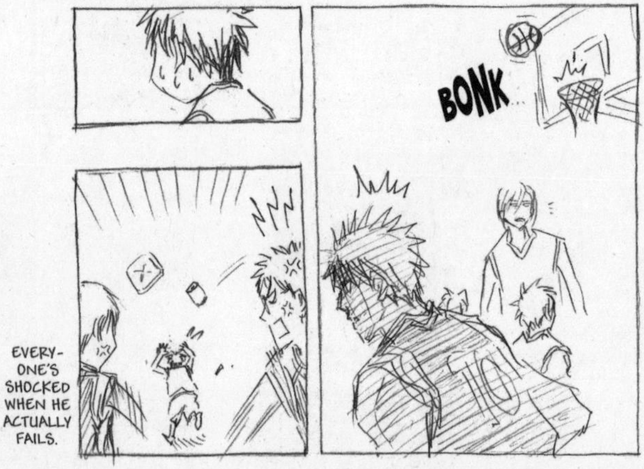
BONK...
EVERY-ONE'S SHOCKED WHEN HE ACTUALLY FAILS.

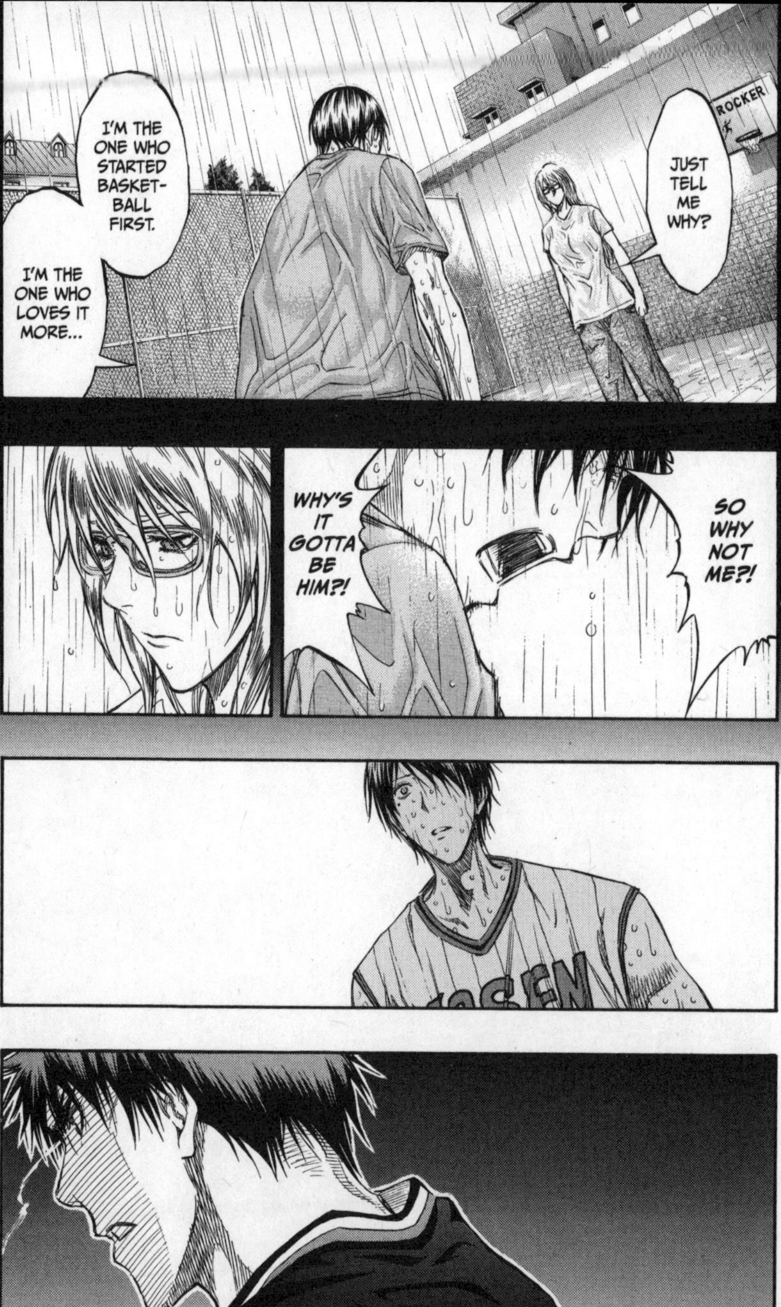
ROCKER
JUST TELL ME WHY?
I'M THE ONE WHO STARTED BASKETBALL FIRST.
I'M THE ONE WHO LOVES IT MORE...
SO WHY NOT ME?!
WHY'S IT GOTTA BE HIM?!

165TH QUARTER: I'VE HAD ENOUGH

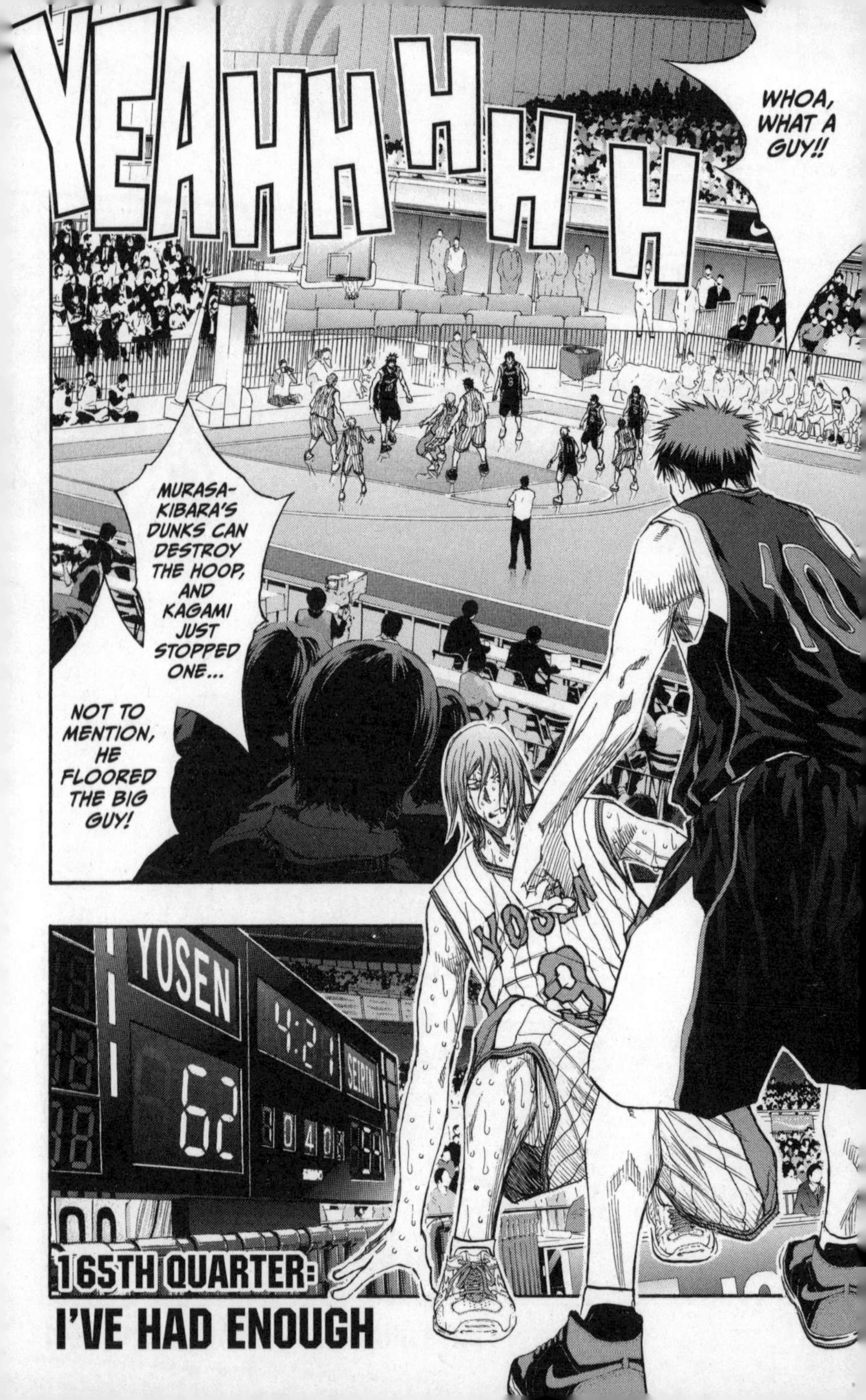

YEAHHHHHH
WHOA, WHAT A GUY!!
MURASA-KIBARA'S DUNKS CAN DESTROY THE HOOP, AND KAGAMI JUST STOPPED ONE...
NOT TO MENTION, HE FLOORED THE BIG GUY!
YOSEN
4:21
SEIRIN
62
165TH QUARTER:
I'VE HAD ENOUGH

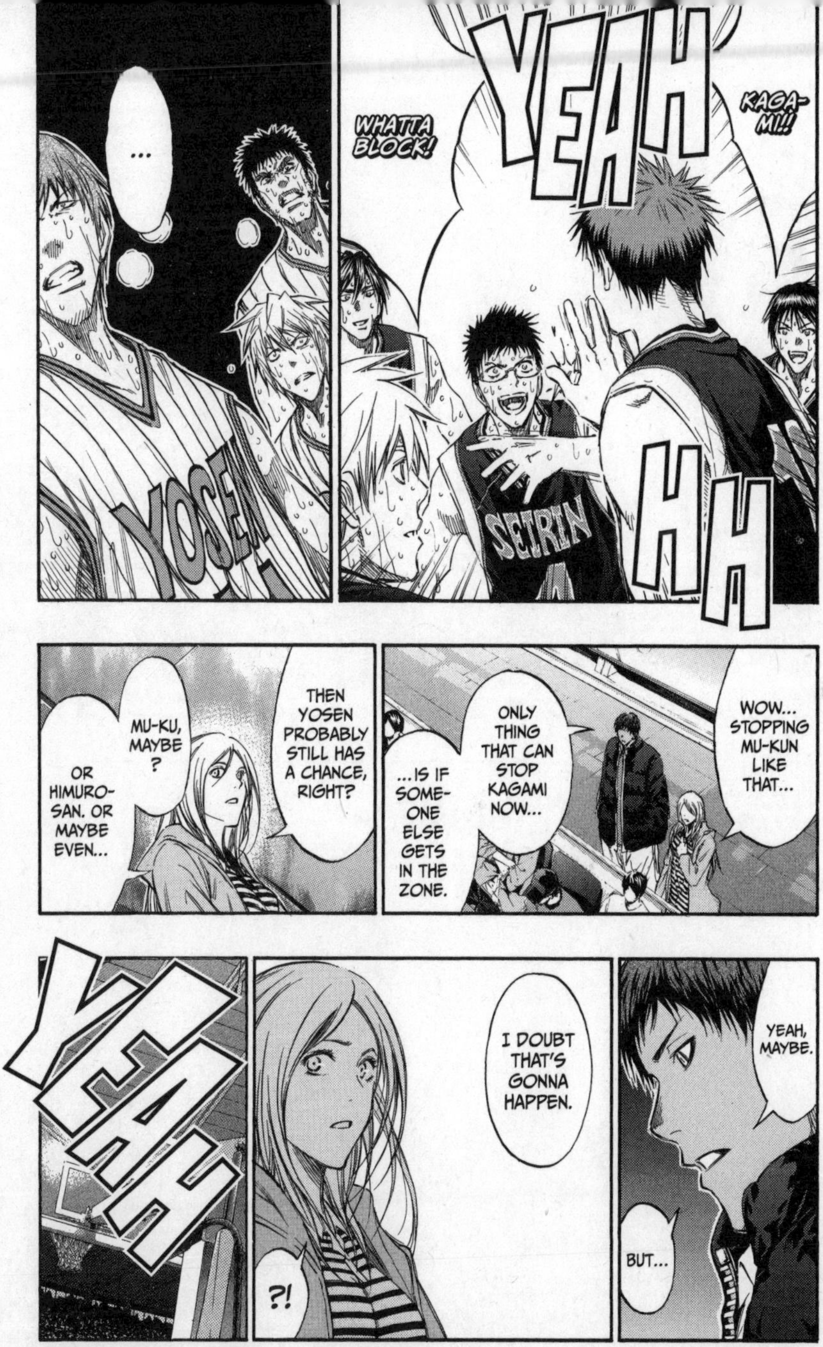
YEAH
KAGA-MI!!
WHATTA BLOCK!
HHH
...
WOW... STOPPING MU-KUN LIKE THAT...
ONLY THING THAT CAN STOP KAGAMI NOW...
...IS IF SOME-ONE ELSE GETS IN THE ZONE.
THEN YOSEN PROBABLY STILL HAS A CHANCE, RIGHT?
MU-KU, MAYBE?
OR HIMURO-SAN. OR MAYBE EVEN...
YEAH, MAYBE.
BUT...
I DOUBT THAT'S GONNA HAPPEN.
?!
YEAH

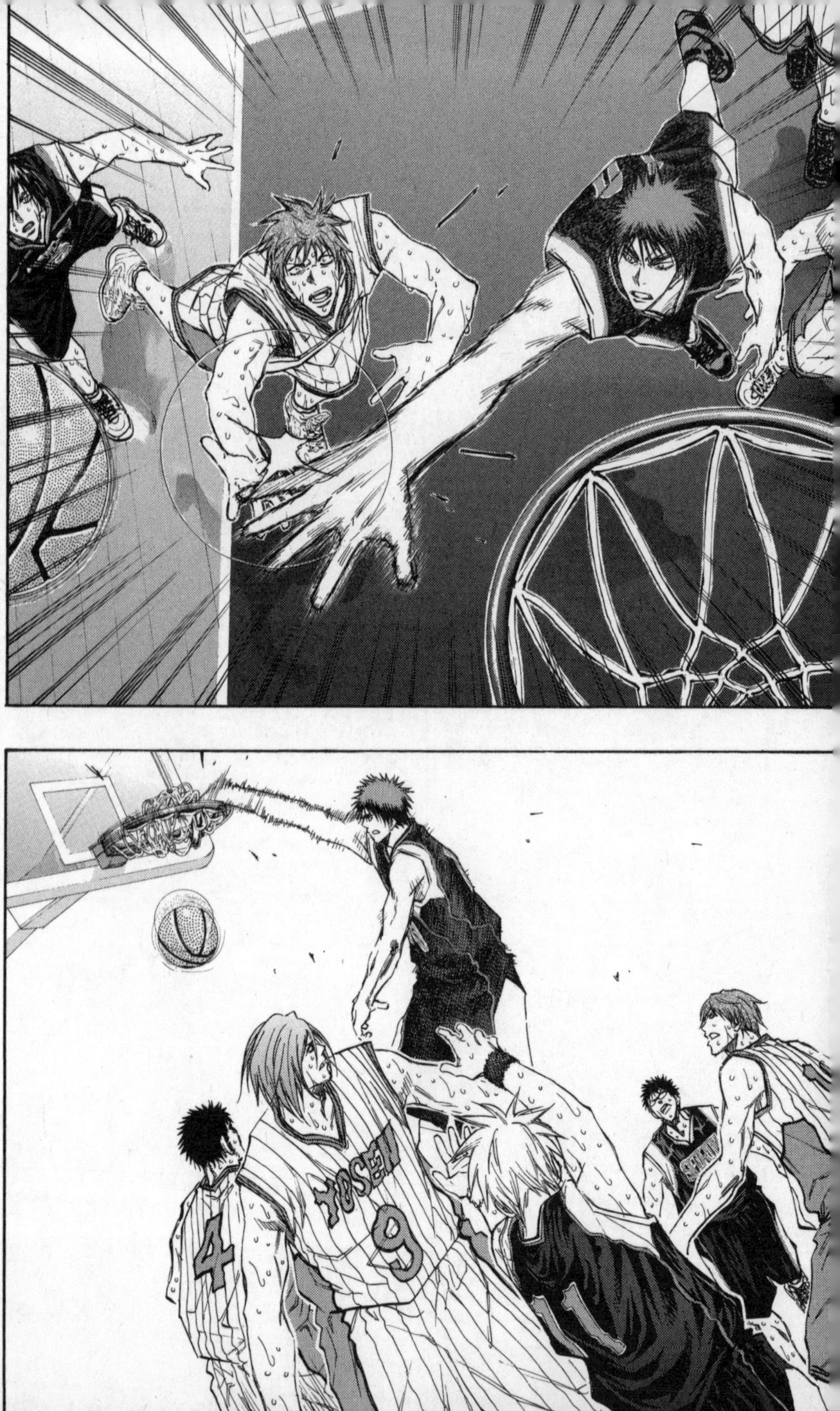
YOSEN

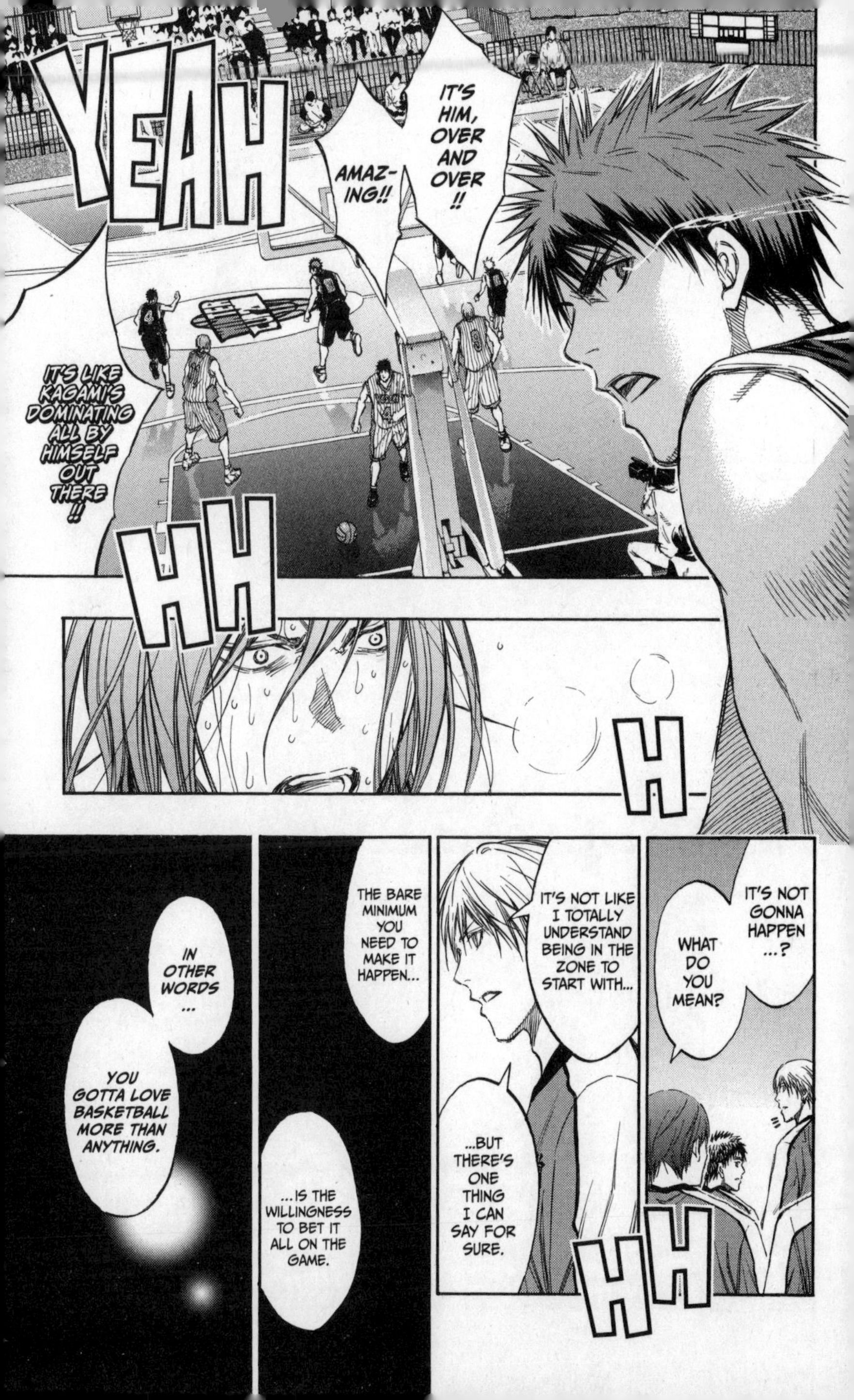
YEAH
IT'S HIM, OVER AND OVER!!
AMAZ-ING!!
IT'S LIKE KAGAMI'S DOMINATING ALL BY HIMSELF OUT THERE!!
HH
H
IT'S NOT GONNA HAPPEN...?
WHAT DO YOU MEAN?
HH
IT'S NOT LIKE I TOTALLY UNDERSTAND BEING IN THE ZONE TO START WITH...
...BUT THERE'S ONE THING I CAN SAY FOR SURE.
THE BARE MINIMUM YOU NEED TO MAKE IT HAPPEN...
...IS THE WILLINGNESS TO BET IT ALL ON THE GAME.
IN OTHER WORDS...
YOU GOTTA LOVE BASKETBALL MORE THAN ANYTHING.

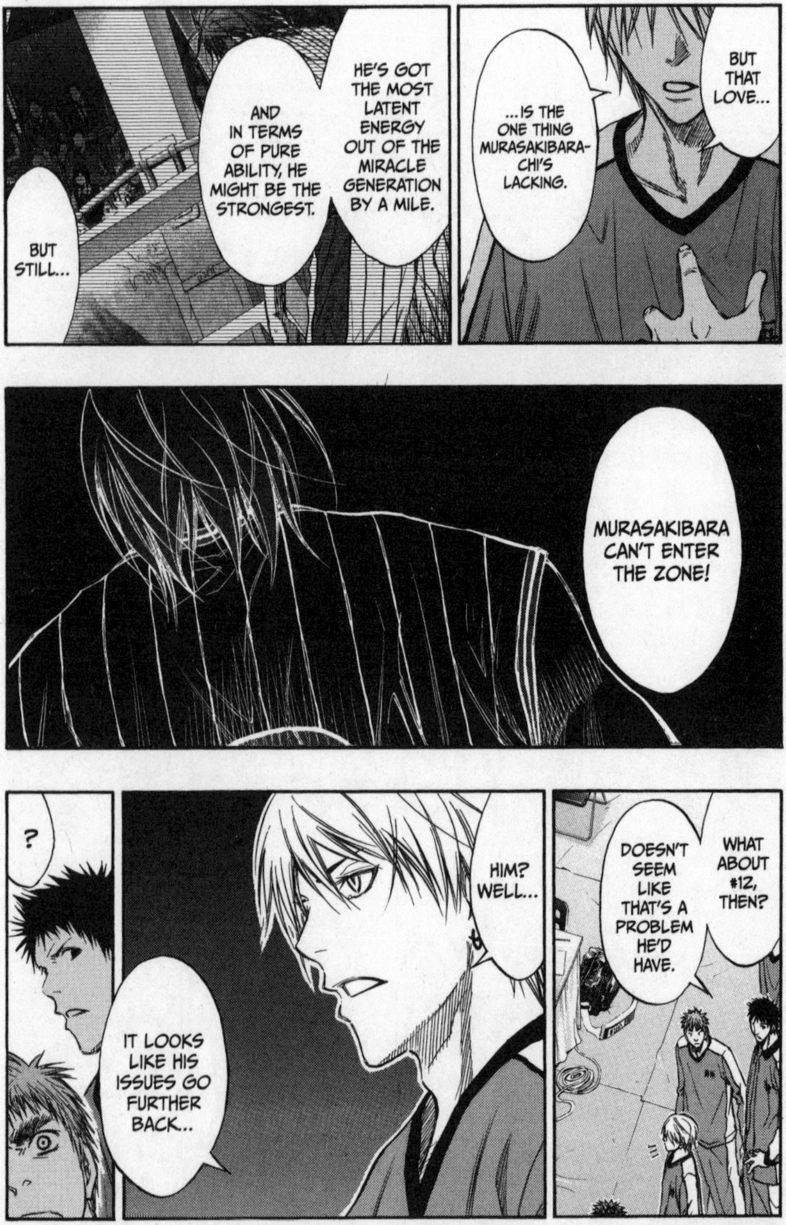
BUT THAT LOVE...
...IS THE ONE THING MURASAKIBARA-CHI'S LACKING.
HE'S GOT THE MOST LATENT ENERGY OUT OF THE MIRACLE GENERATION BY A MILE.
AND IN TERMS OF PURE ABILITY, HE MIGHT BE THE STRONGEST.
BUT STILL...
MURASAKIBARA CAN'T ENTER THE ZONE!
WHAT ABOUT #12, THEN?
DOESN'T SEEM LIKE THAT'S A PROBLEM HE'D HAVE.
HIM? WELL...
IT LOOKS LIKE HIS ISSUES GO FURTHER BACK...
?

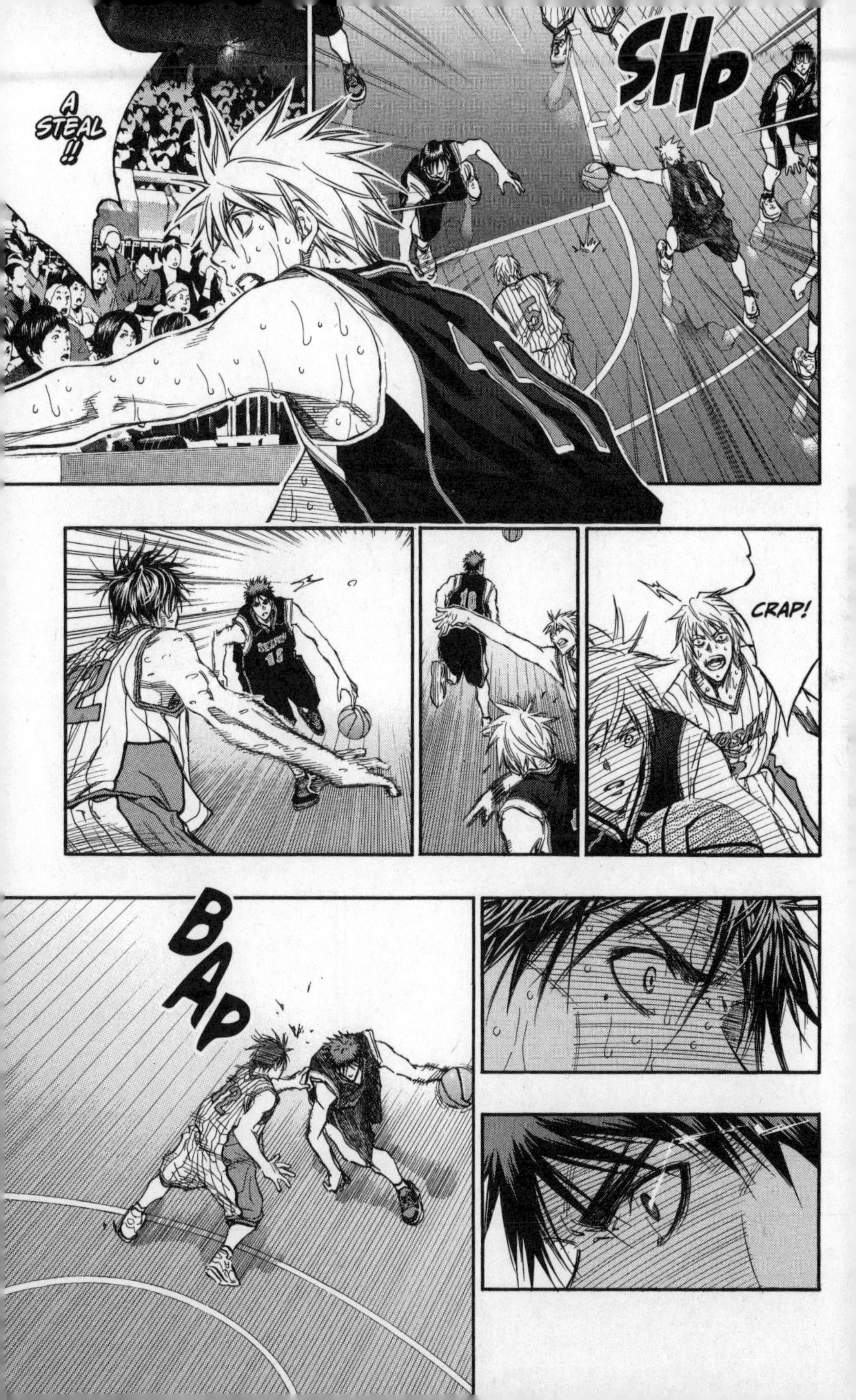
SHP
A STEAL!!
CRAP!
BAP

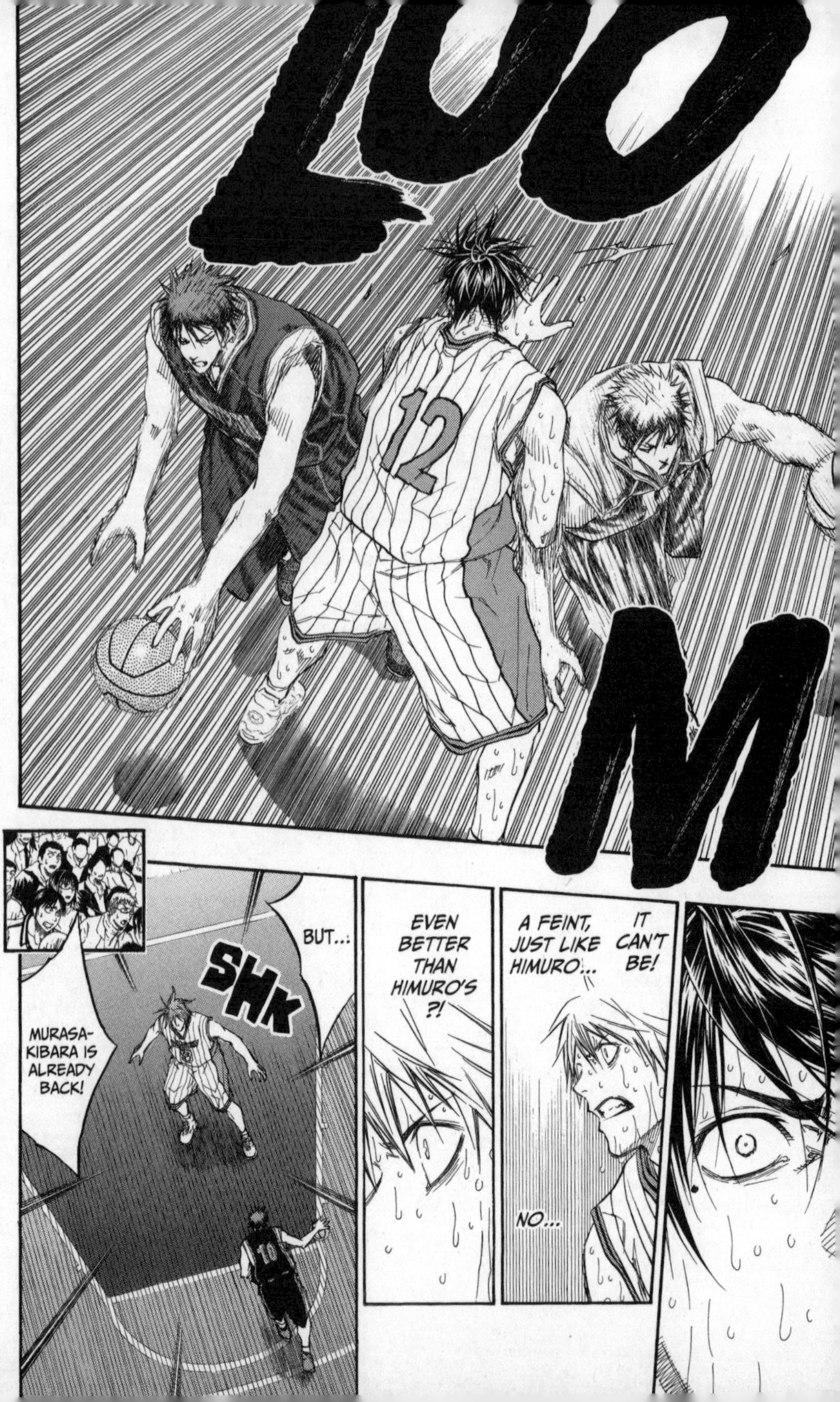
ZOOM
IT CAN'T BE!
A FEINT, JUST LIKE HIMURO...
NO...
EVEN BETTER THAN HIMURO'S ?!
BUT...:
SHK
MURASAKIBARA IS ALREADY BACK!

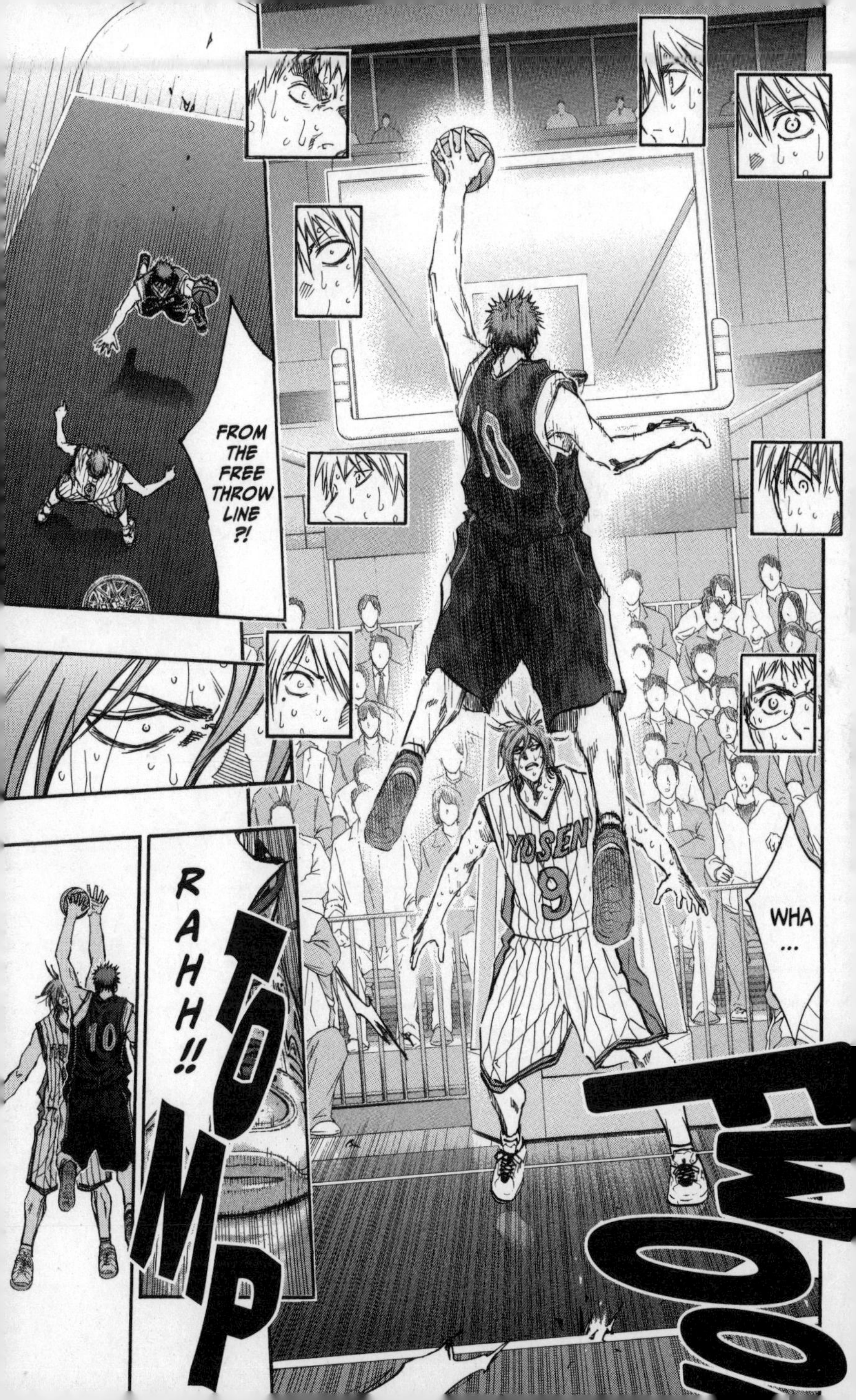
FROM THE FREE THROW LINE ?!
WHA ...
FWOOO
RAHH!!
TOMP

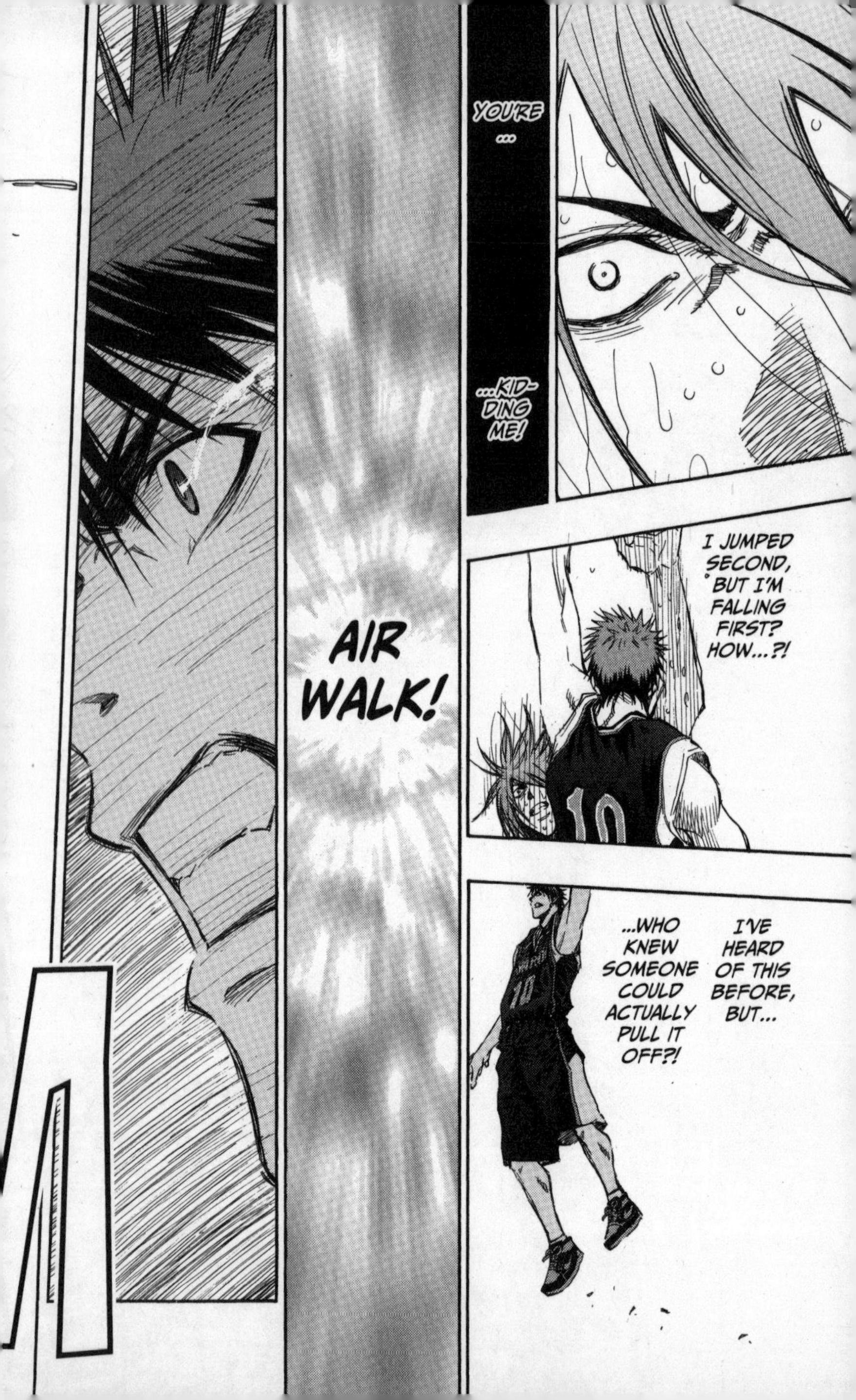
YOU'RE ...
...KID-DING ME!
I JUMPED SECOND, BUT I'M FALLING FIRST? HOW...?!
I'VE HEARD OF THIS BEFORE, BUT...
...WHO KNEW SOMEONE COULD ACTUALLY PULL IT OFF?!
AIR WALK!

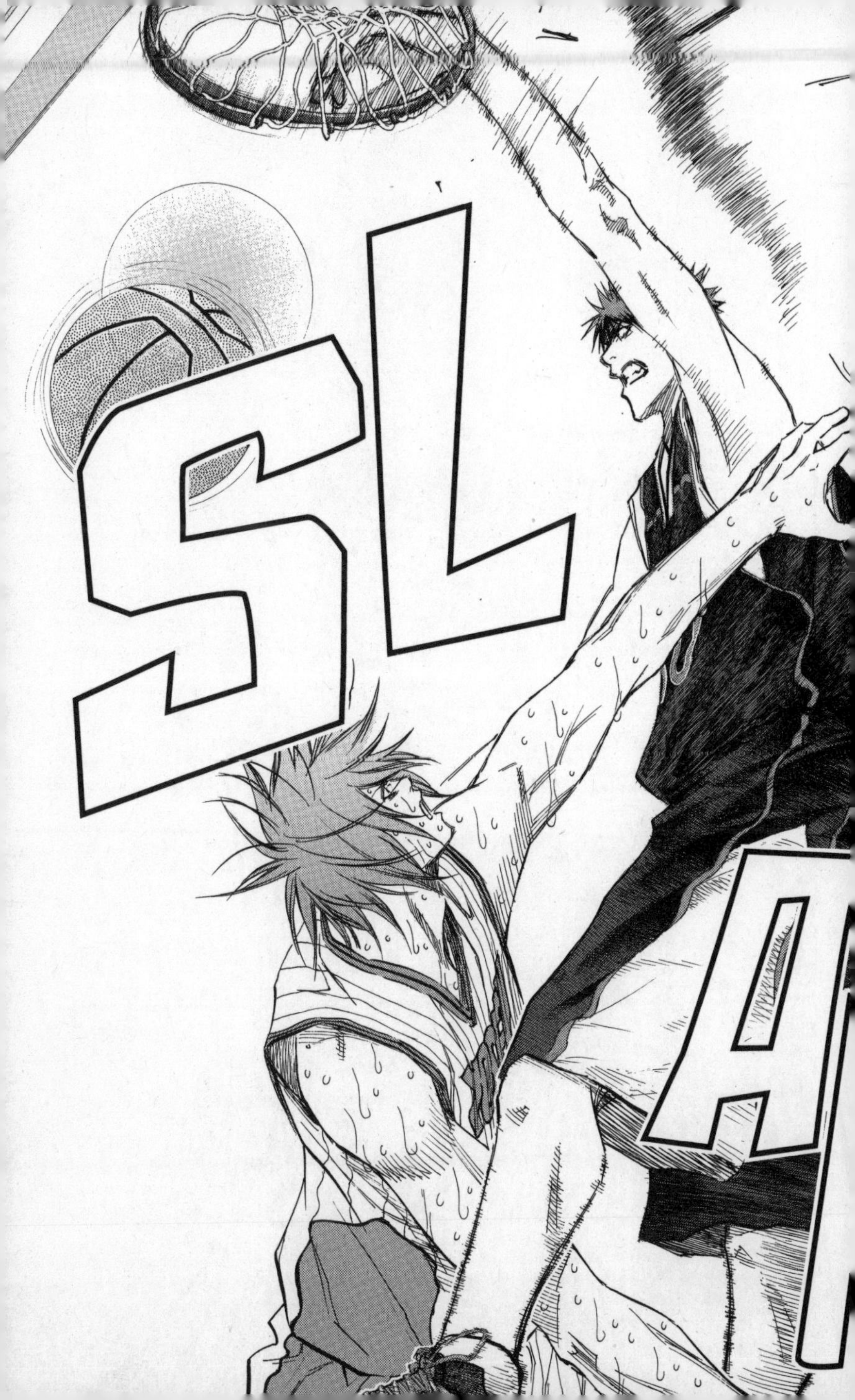
SL
A

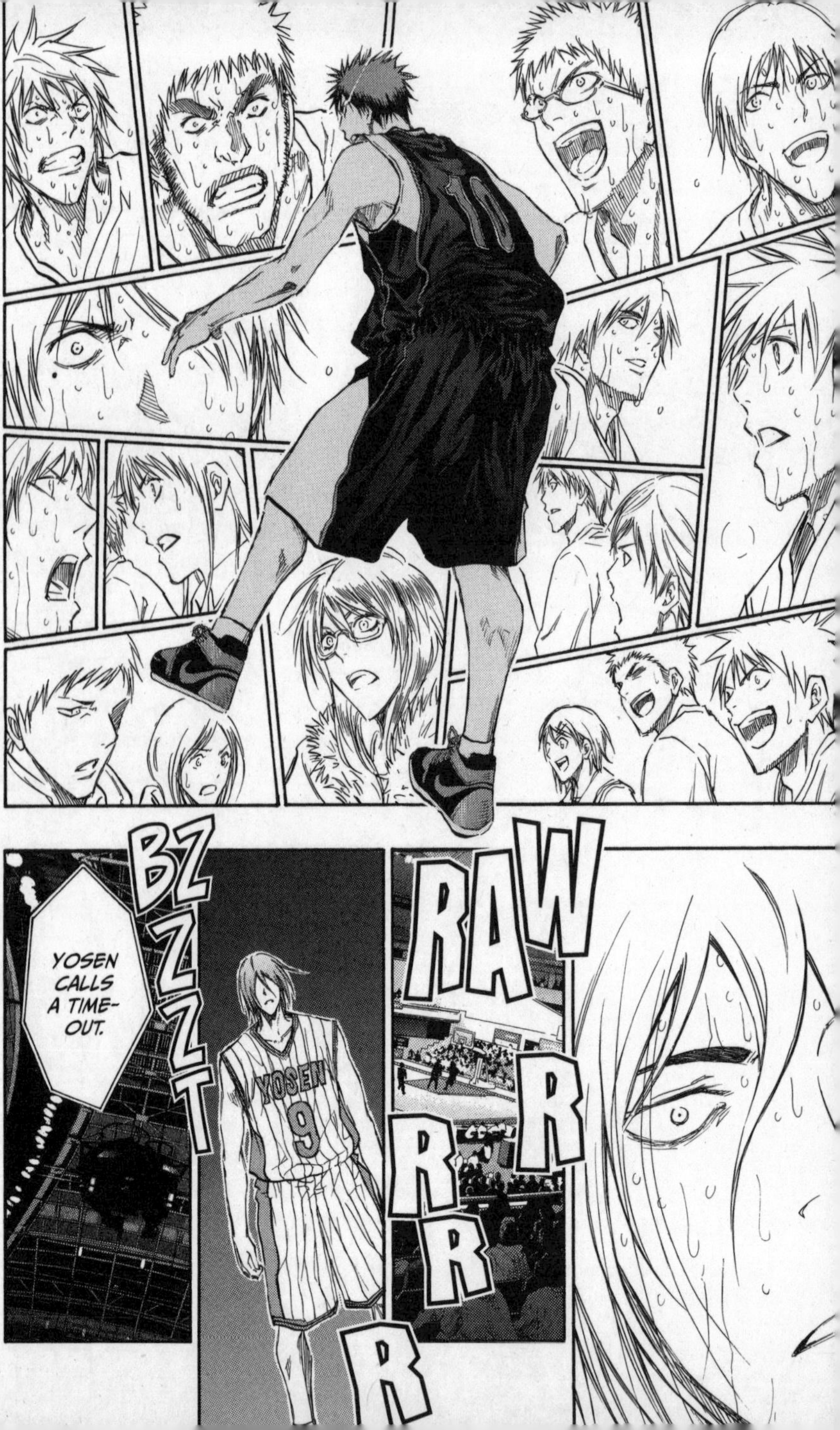
RAWRRRR
BZZZT
YOSEN CALLS A TIME-OUT.

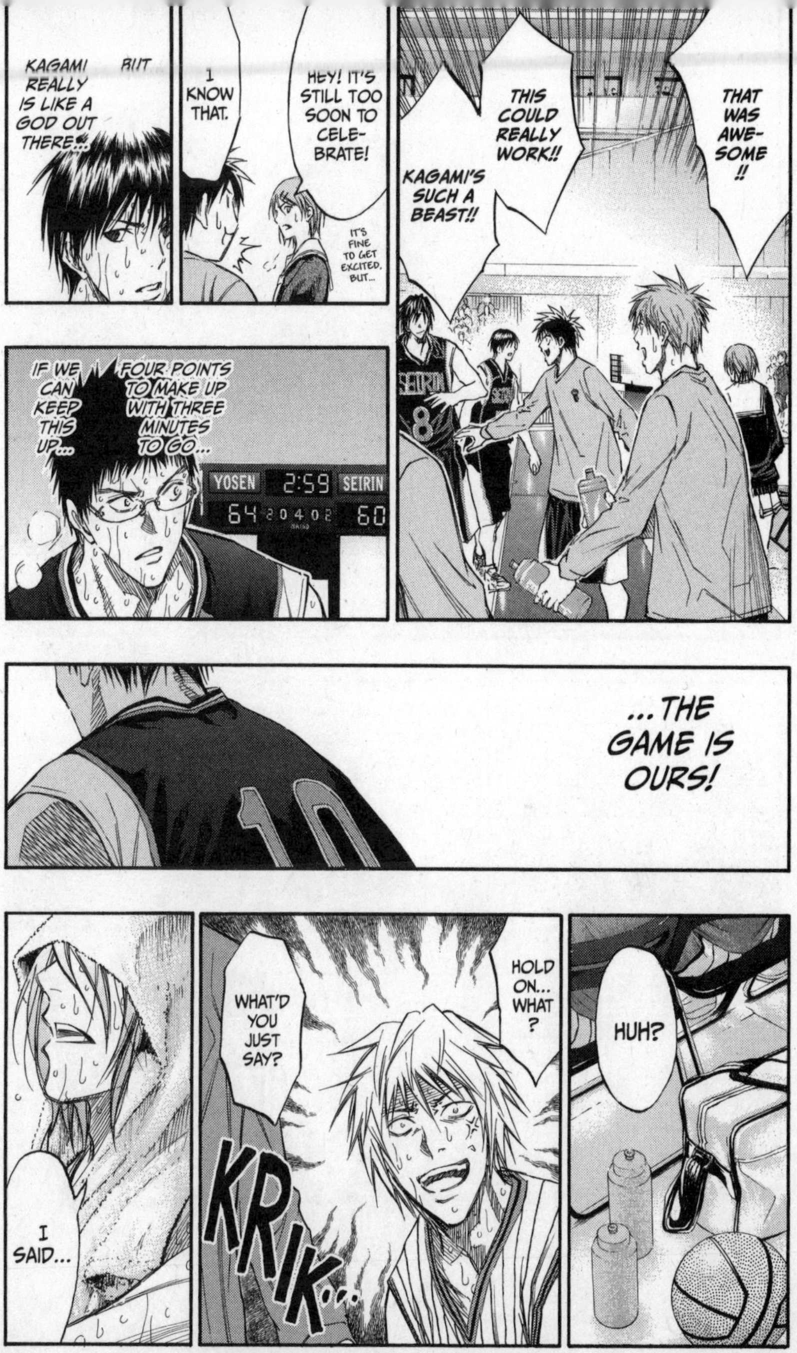
THAT WAS AWE-SOME!!
THIS COULD REALLY WORK!!
KAGAMI'S SUCH A BEAST!!
HEY! IT'S STILL TOO SOON TO CELE-BRATE!
I KNOW THAT.
IT'S FINE TO GET EXCITED, BUT...
BUT KAGAMI REALLY IS LIKE A GOD OUT THERE...
YOSEN 2:59 SEIRIN
64 60
FOUR POINTS TO MAKE UP WITH THREE MINUTES TO GO...
IF WE CAN KEEP THIS UP...
...THE GAME IS OURS!
HUH?
HOLD ON... WHAT?
WHAT'D YOU JUST SAY?
KRIK...
I SAID...

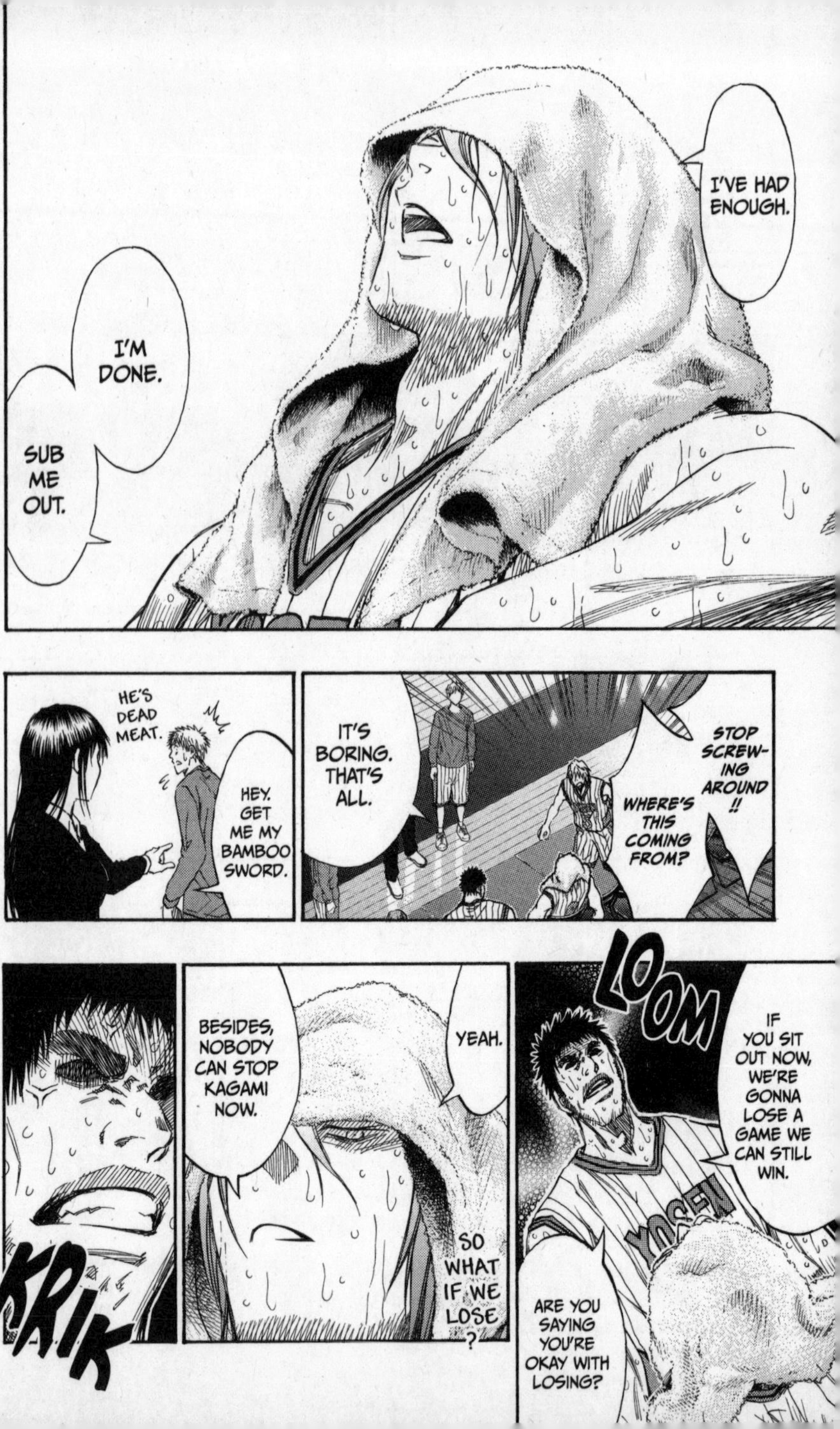
I'VE HAD ENOUGH.
I'M DONE.
SUB ME OUT.
STOP SCREWING AROUND!!
WHERE'S THIS COMING FROM?
IT'S BORING. THAT'S ALL.
HE'S DEAD MEAT.
HEY. GET ME MY BAMBOO SWORD.
LOOM
IF YOU SIT OUT NOW, WE'RE GONNA LOSE A GAME WE CAN STILL WIN.
ARE YOU SAYING YOU'RE OKAY WITH LOSING?
YEAH.
BESIDES, NOBODY CAN STOP KAGAMI NOW.
SO WHAT IF WE LOSE?
KRIK

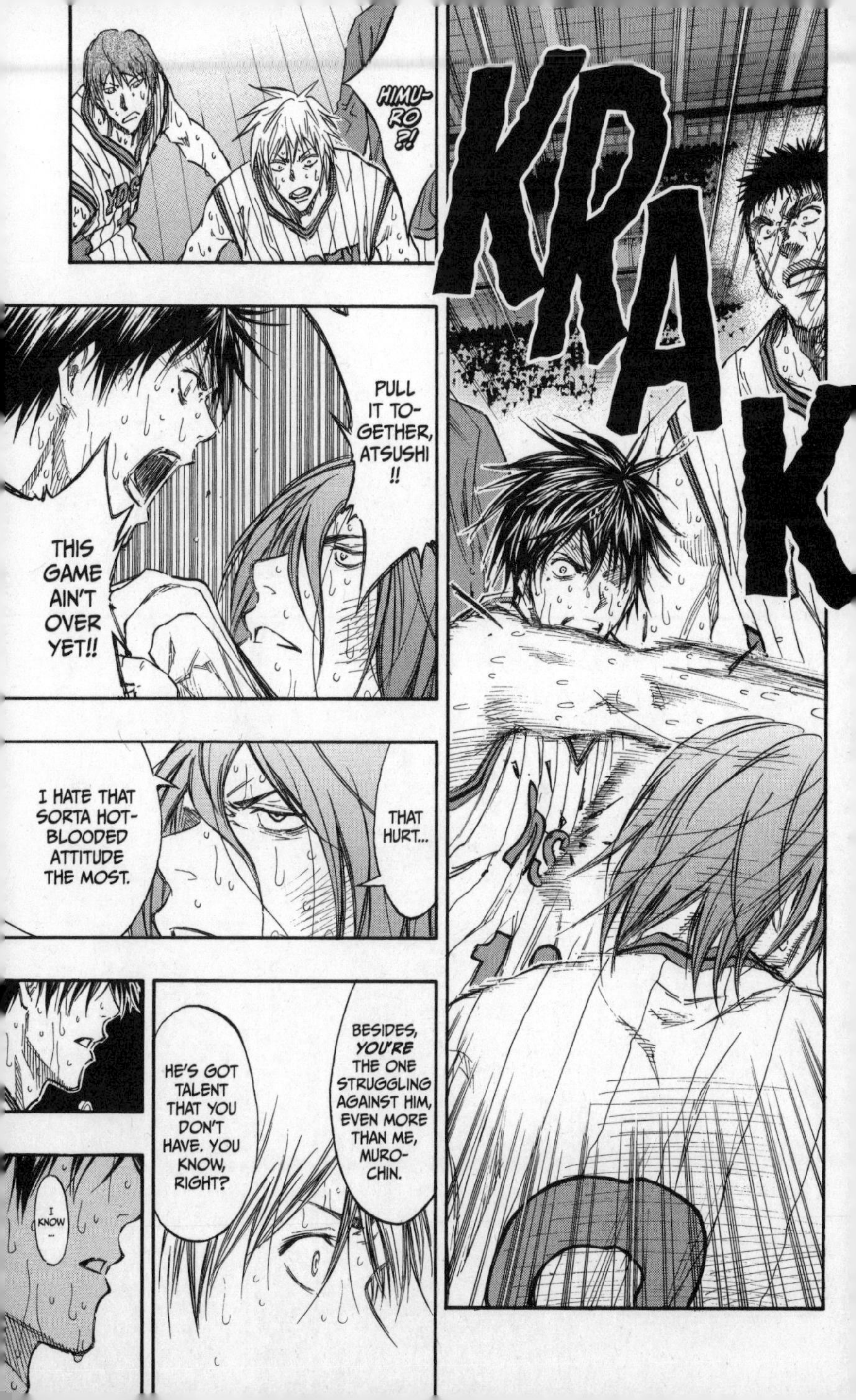
KRAAK
HIMURO?!
PULL IT TOGETHER, ATSUSHI!!
THIS GAME AIN'T OVER YET!!
THAT HURT...
I HATE THAT SORTA HOT-BLOODED ATTITUDE THE MOST.
BESIDES, *YOU'RE* THE ONE STRUGGLING AGAINST HIM, EVEN MORE THAN ME, MURO-CHIN.
HE'S GOT TALENT THAT YOU DON'T HAVE. YOU KNOW, RIGHT?
I KNOW...

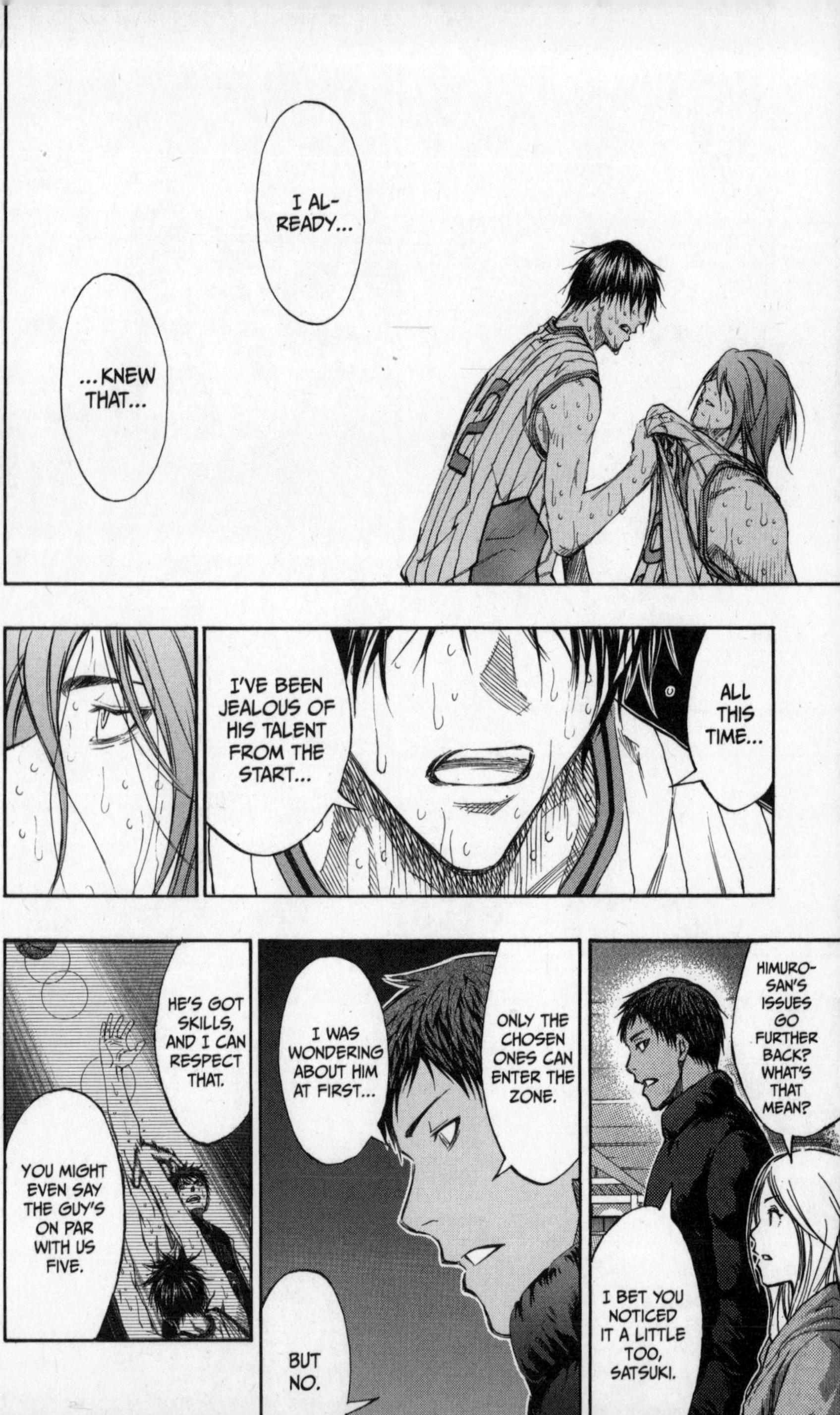
I AL-READY...
...KNEW THAT...
ALL THIS TIME...
I'VE BEEN JEALOUS OF HIS TALENT FROM THE START...
HIMURO-SAN'S ISSUES GO FURTHER BACK? WHAT'S THAT MEAN?
I BET YOU NOTICED IT A LITTLE TOO, SATSUKI.
ONLY THE CHOSEN ONES CAN ENTER THE ZONE.
I WAS WONDERING ABOUT HIM AT FIRST...
BUT NO.
HE'S GOT SKILLS, AND I CAN RESPECT THAT.
YOU MIGHT EVEN SAY THE GUY'S ON PAR WITH US FIVE.

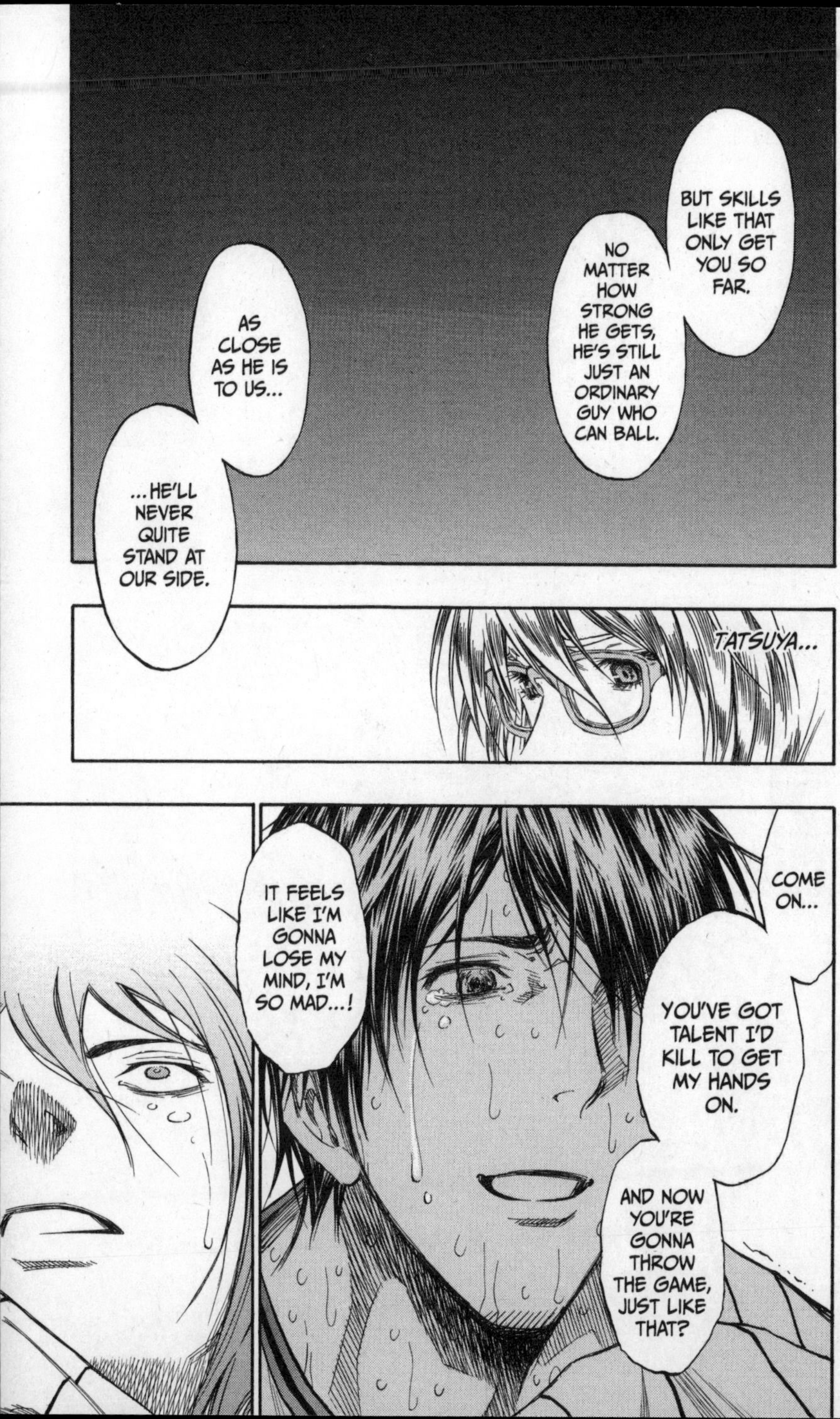
BUT SKILLS LIKE THAT ONLY GET YOU SO FAR.
NO MATTER HOW STRONG HE GETS, HE'S STILL JUST AN ORDINARY GUY WHO CAN BALL.
AS CLOSE AS HE IS TO US...
...HE'LL NEVER QUITE STAND AT OUR SIDE.
TATSUYA...
COME ON...
YOU'VE GOT TALENT I'D KILL TO GET MY HANDS ON.
AND NOW YOU'RE GONNA THROW THE GAME, JUST LIKE THAT?
IT FEELS LIKE I'M GONNA LOSE MY MIND, I'M SO MAD...!

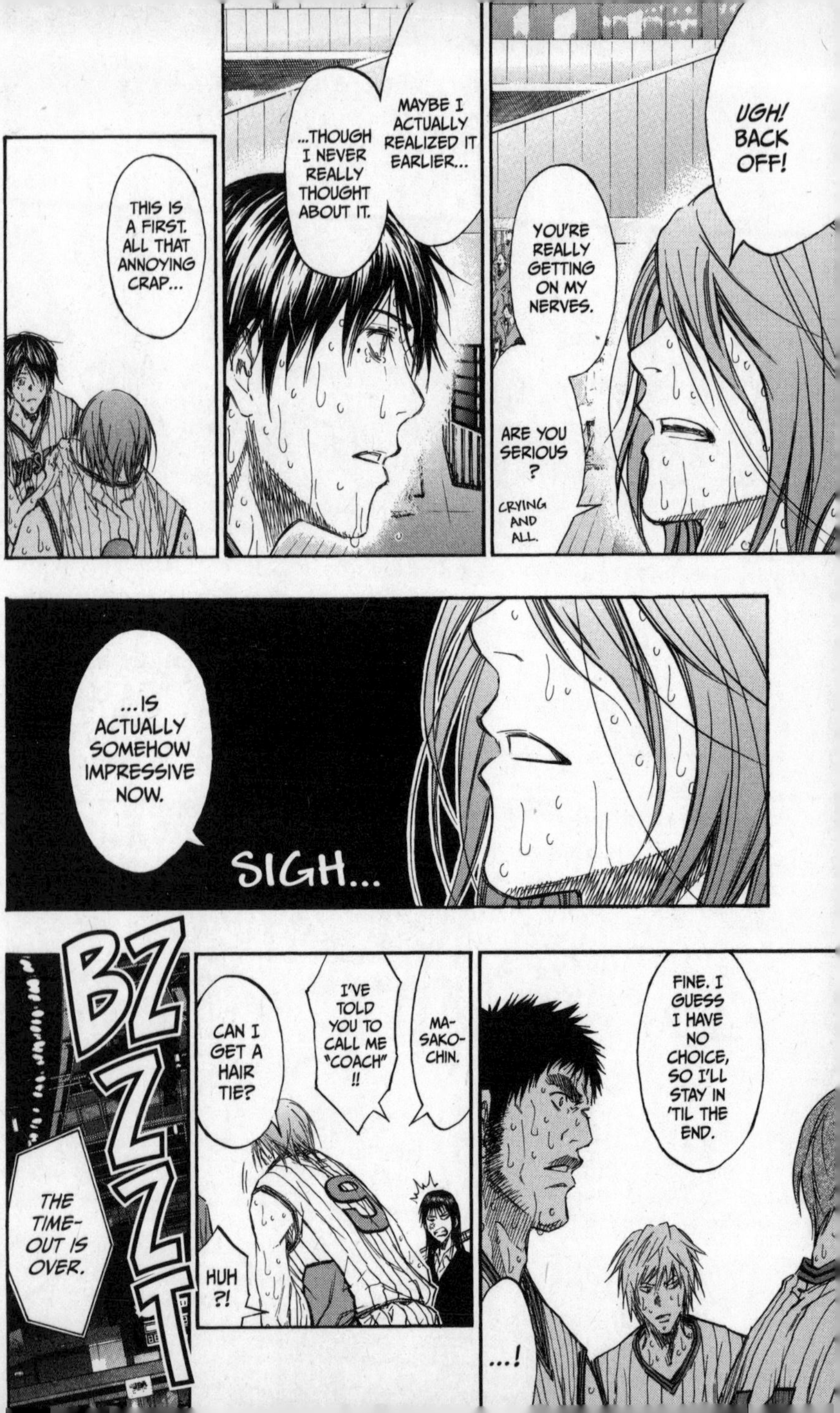
UGH! BACK OFF!
YOU'RE REALLY GETTING ON MY NERVES.
ARE YOU SERIOUS?
CRYING AND ALL.
MAYBE I ACTUALLY REALIZED IT EARLIER...
...THOUGH I NEVER REALLY THOUGHT ABOUT IT.
THIS IS A FIRST. ALL THAT ANNOYING CRAP...
...IS ACTUALLY SOMEHOW IMPRESSIVE NOW.
SIGH...
FINE. I GUESS I HAVE NO CHOICE, SO I'LL STAY IN 'TIL THE END.
...!
MA-SAKO-CHIN.
I'VE TOLD YOU TO CALL ME "COACH" !!
CAN I GET A HAIR TIE?
HUH ?!
BZZZT
THE TIME-OUT IS OVER.

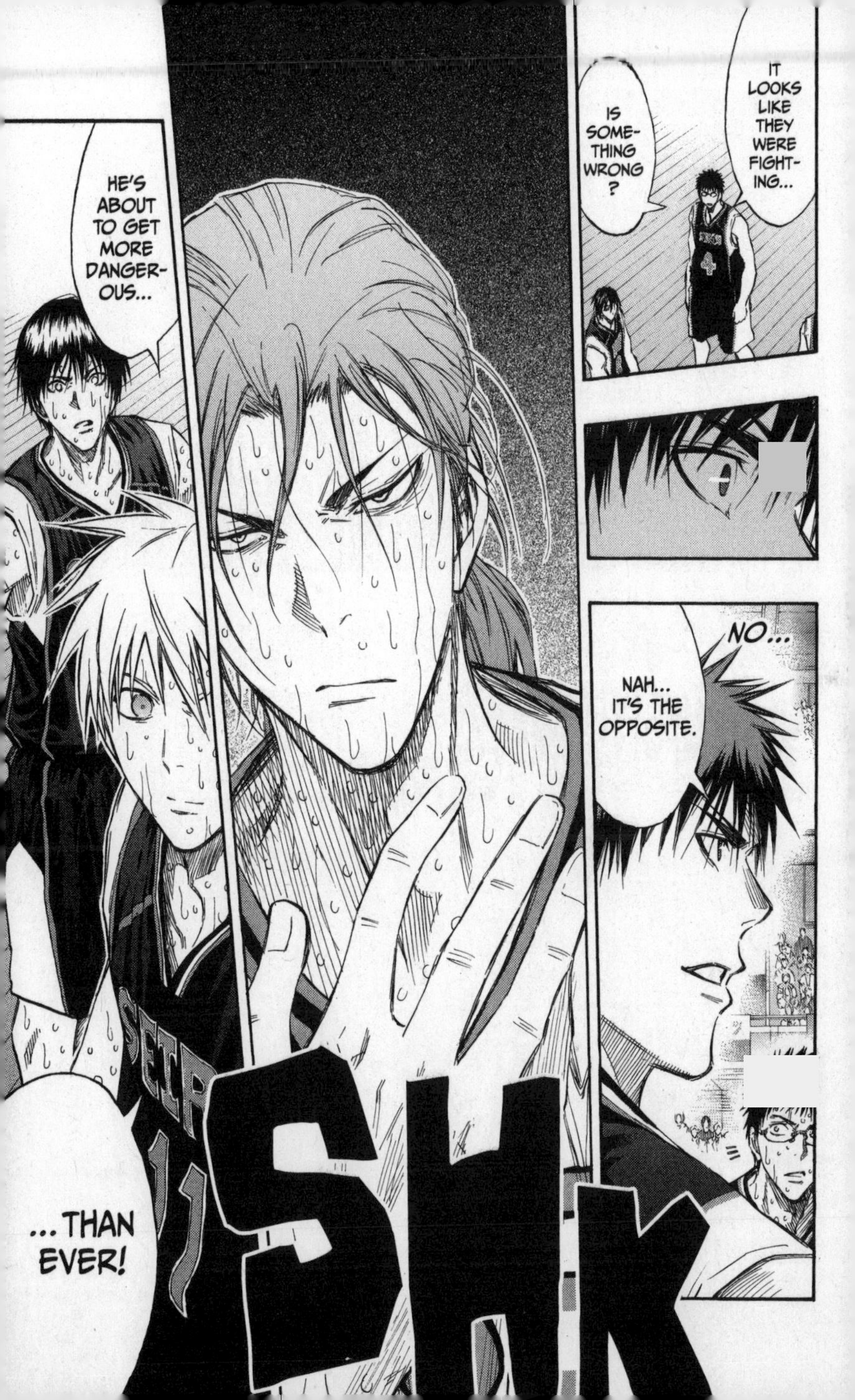
IT LOOKS LIKE THEY WERE FIGHTING...
IS SOMETHING WRONG?
NO...
NAH... IT'S THE OPPOSITE.
SHK
HE'S ABOUT TO GET MORE DANGEROUS...
...THAN EVER!

KUROKO'S BASKETBALL BLOOPERS

TAKE 4

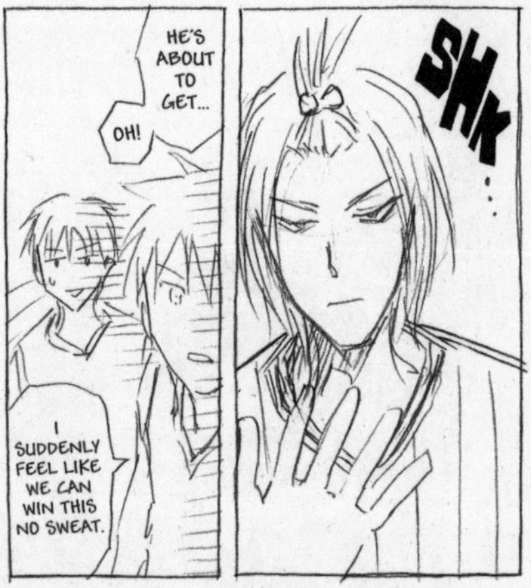
SHK...
HE'S ABOUT TO GET...
OH!
I SUDDENLY FEEL LIKE WE CAN WIN THIS NO SWEAT.

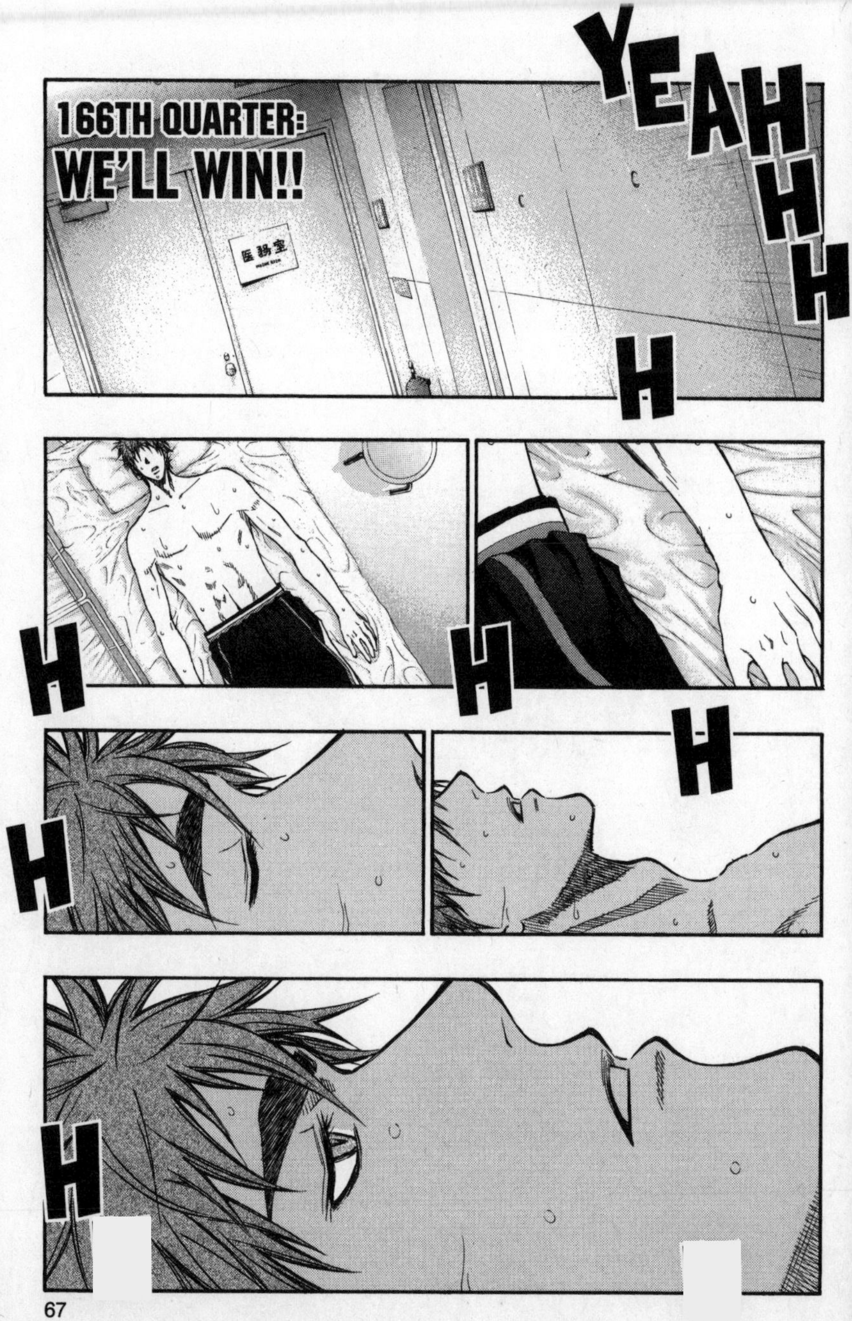

YEAHHHH
166TH QUARTER:
WE'LL WIN!!
H
H
H
H
H
H

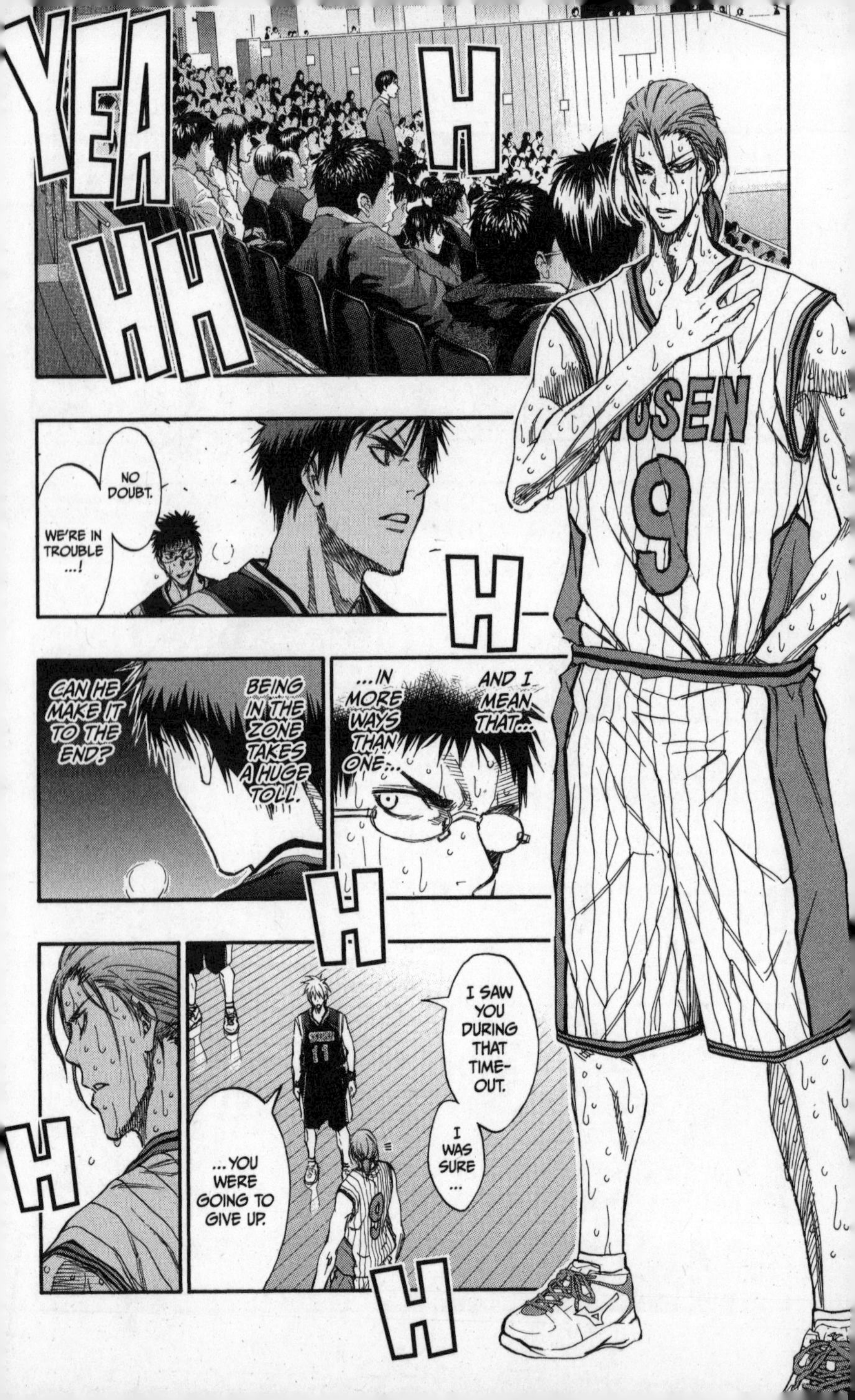
YEAHHHHHHH
NO DOUBT.
WE'RE IN TROUBLE ...!
AND I MEAN THAT...
...IN MORE WAYS THAN ONE...
BEING IN THE ZONE TAKES A HUGE TOLL.
CAN HE MAKE IT TO THE END?
I SAW YOU DURING THAT TIME-OUT.
I WAS SURE ...
...YOU WERE GOING TO GIVE UP.

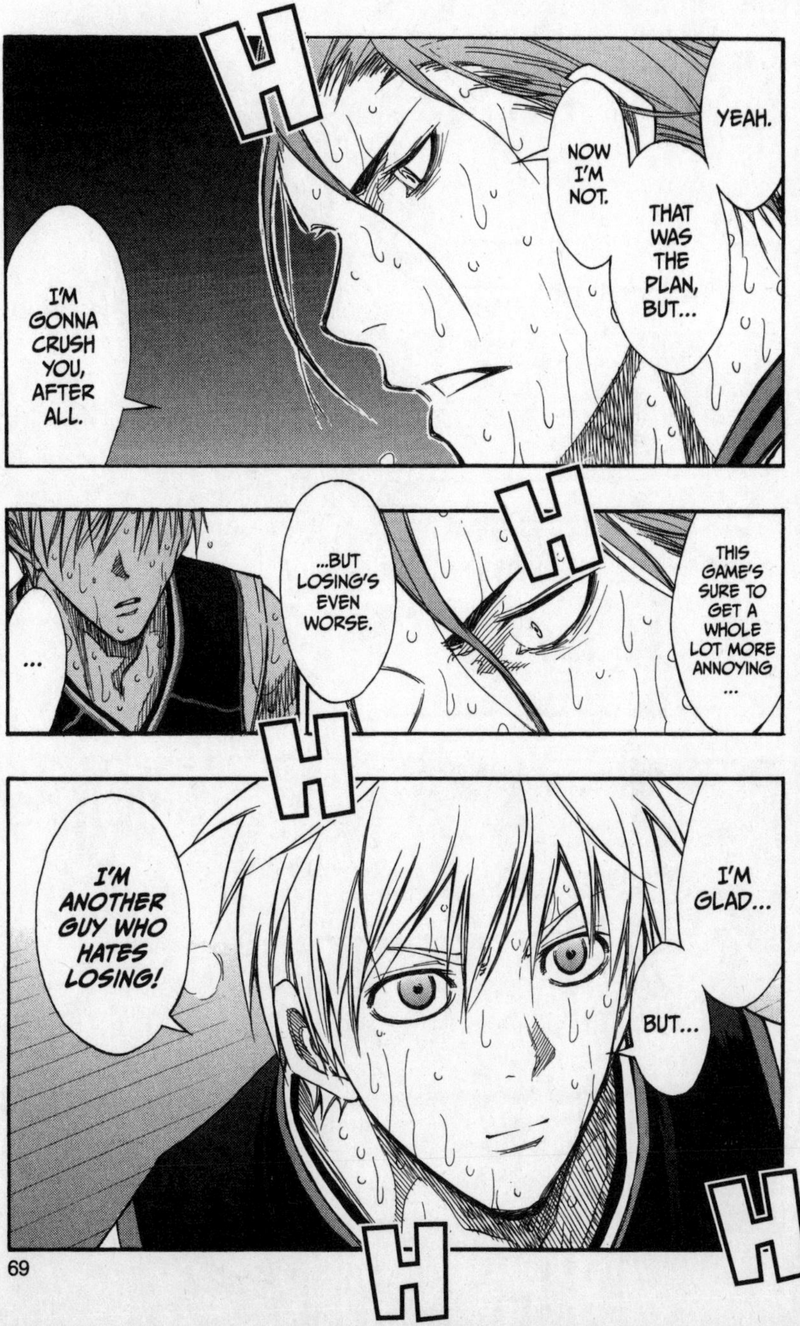
H
YEAH.
THAT WAS THE PLAN, BUT...
NOW I'M NOT.
I'M GONNA CRUSH YOU, AFTER ALL.
H
THIS GAME'S SURE TO GET A WHOLE LOT MORE ANNOYING...
...BUT LOSING'S EVEN WORSE.
...
H
I'M GLAD...
BUT...
I'M ANOTHER GUY WHO HATES LOSING!
H
H

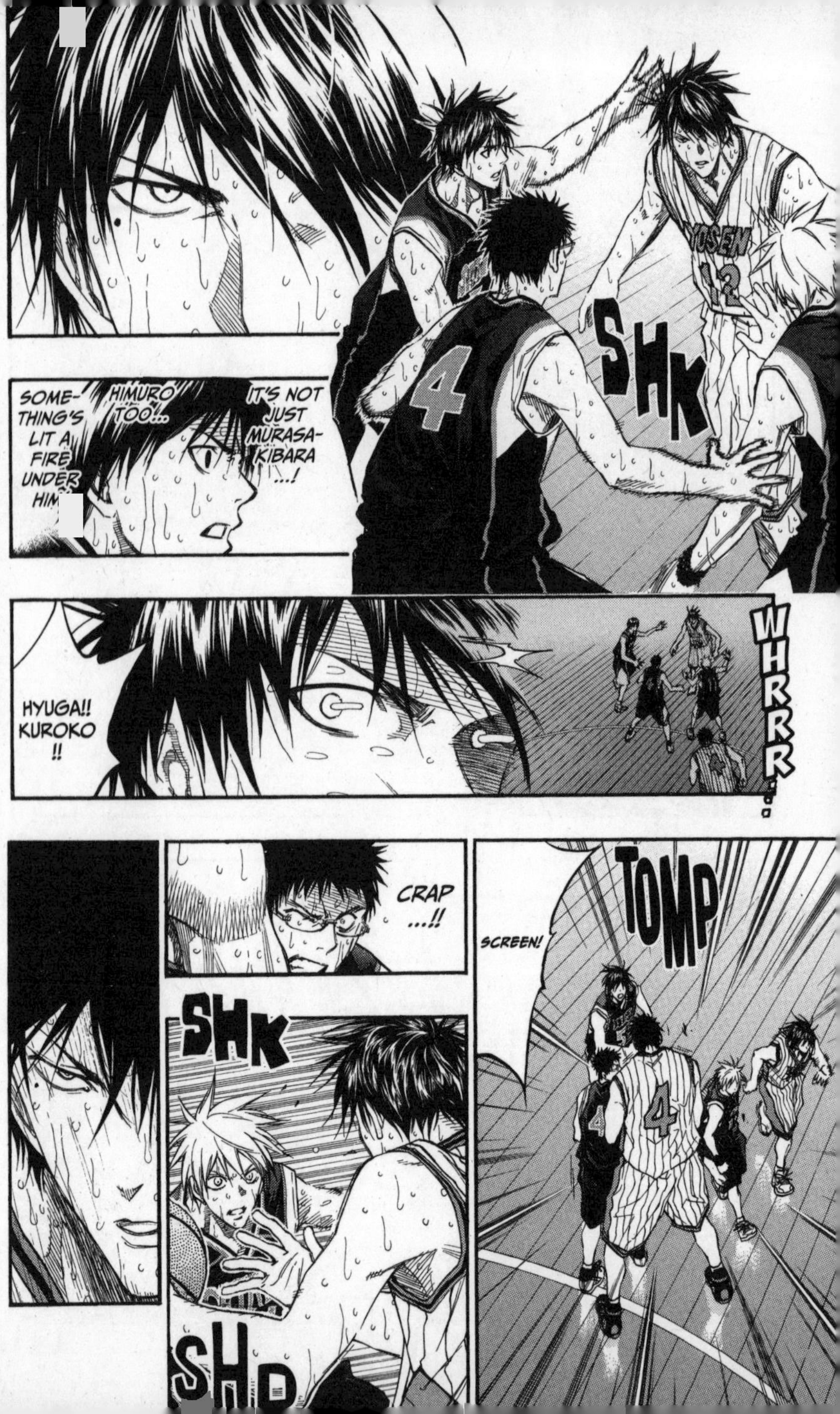
SHK
IT'S NOT JUST MURASA-KIBARA ...!
HIMURO TOO...
SOME-THING'S LIT A FIRE UNDER HIM
WHRRR...
HYUGA!! KUROKO !!
TOMP
SCREEN!
CRAP ...!!
SHK
SHD

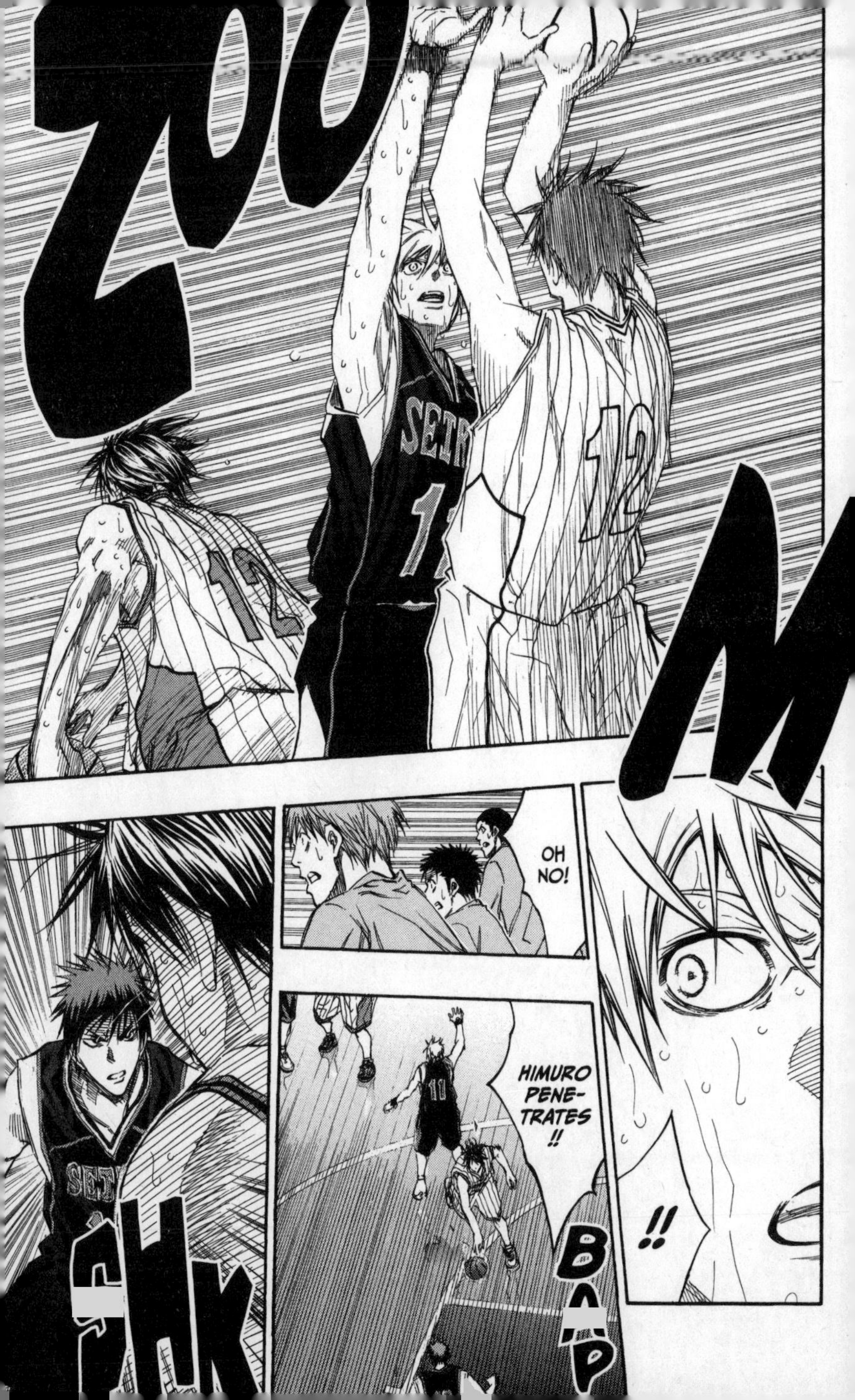
ZOOM
!!
OH NO!
HIMURO PENETRATES !!
BAP
SHK

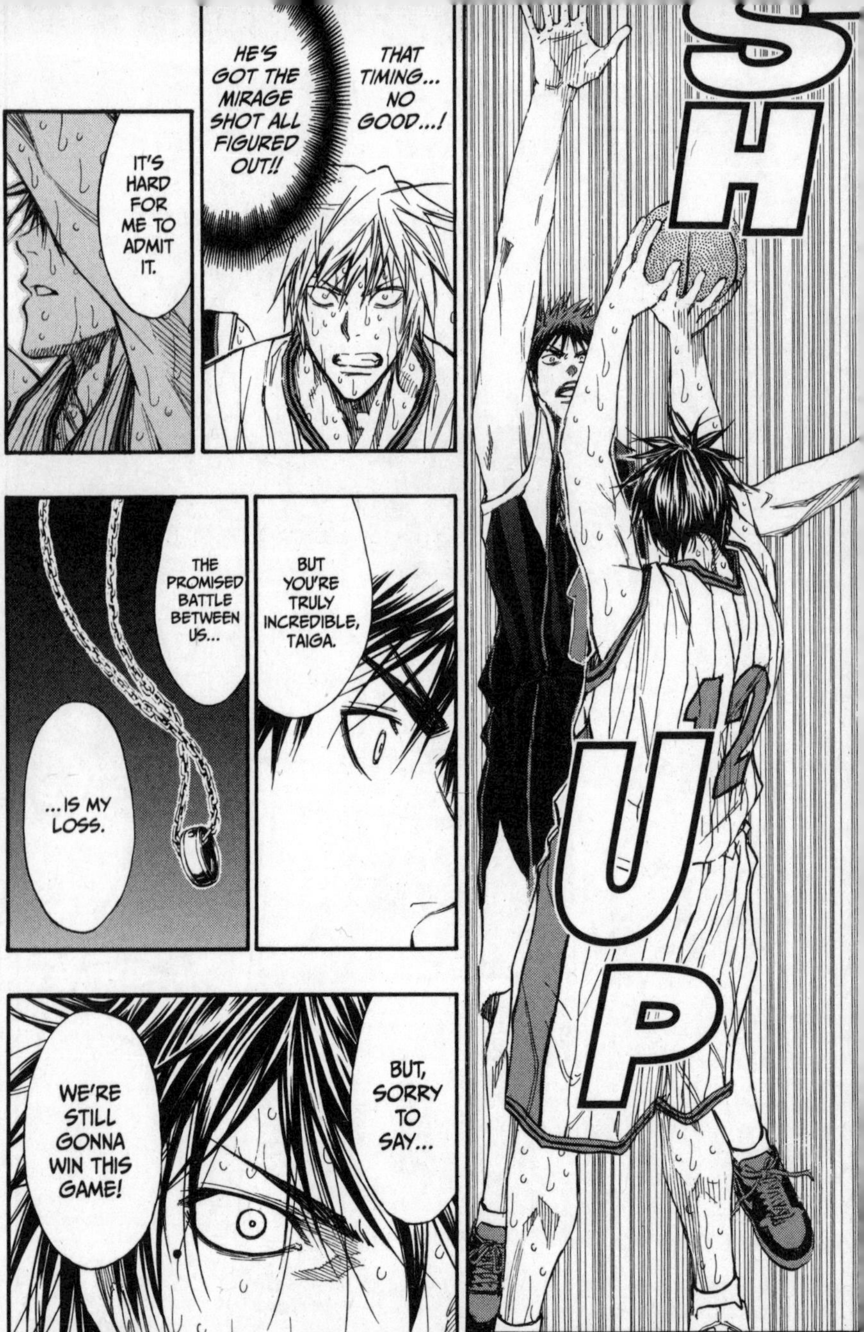
SHUP
THAT TIMING... NO GOOD...!
HE'S GOT THE MIRAGE SHOT ALL FIGURED OUT!!
IT'S HARD FOR ME TO ADMIT IT.
BUT YOU'RE TRULY INCREDIBLE, TAIGA.
THE PROMISED BATTLE BETWEEN US...
...IS MY LOSS.
BUT, SORRY TO SAY...
WE'RE STILL GONNA WIN THIS GAME!

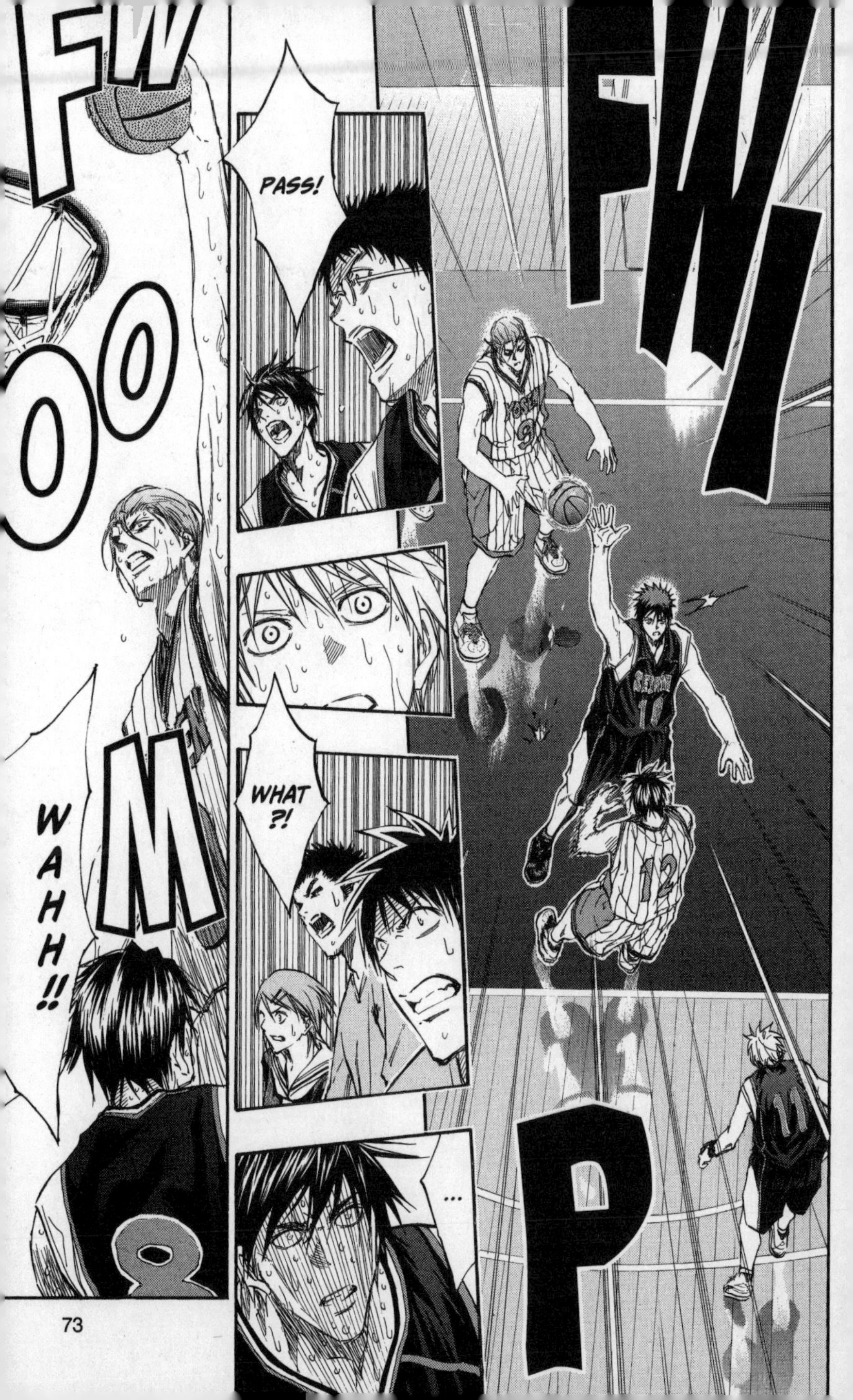
FW
P
PASS!
WHAT ?!
...
FW
OO
M
WAHHH!!

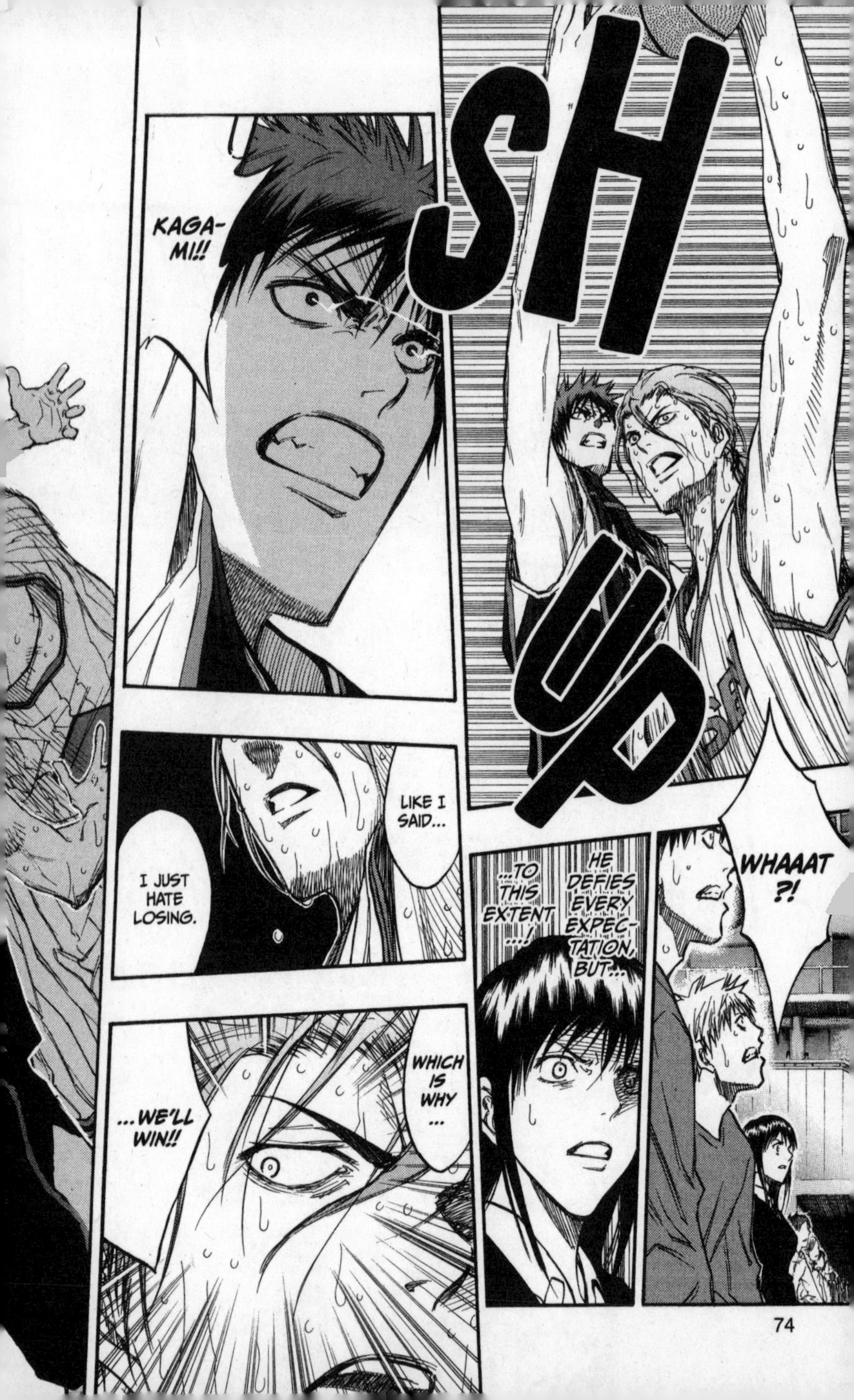
SHUP
KAGA-MI!!
WHAAAT?!
HE DEFIES EVERY EXPECTATION, BUT...
...TO THIS EXTENT...!
LIKE I SAID...
I JUST HATE LOSING.
WHICH IS WHY...
...WE'LL WIN!!

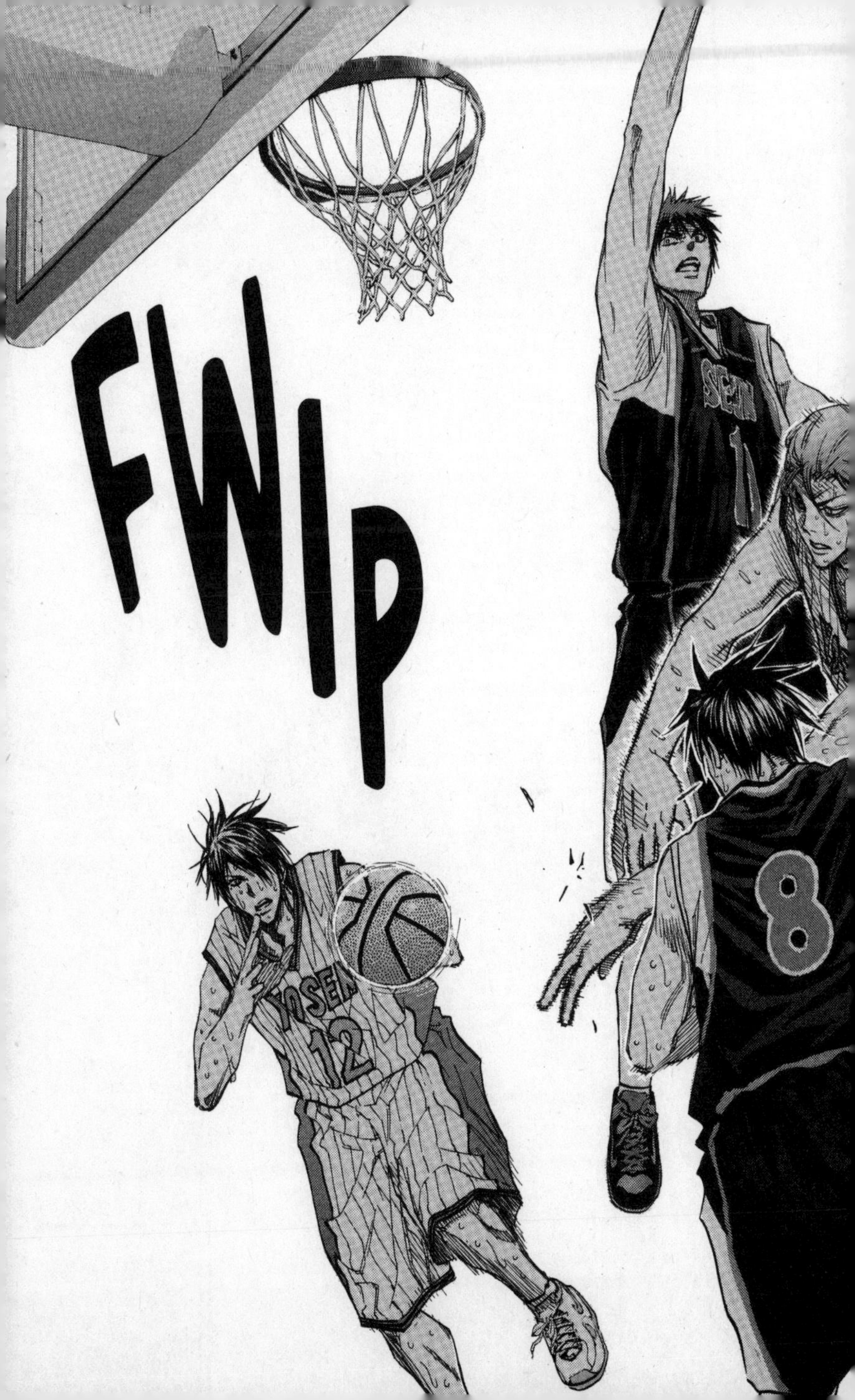
FWIP

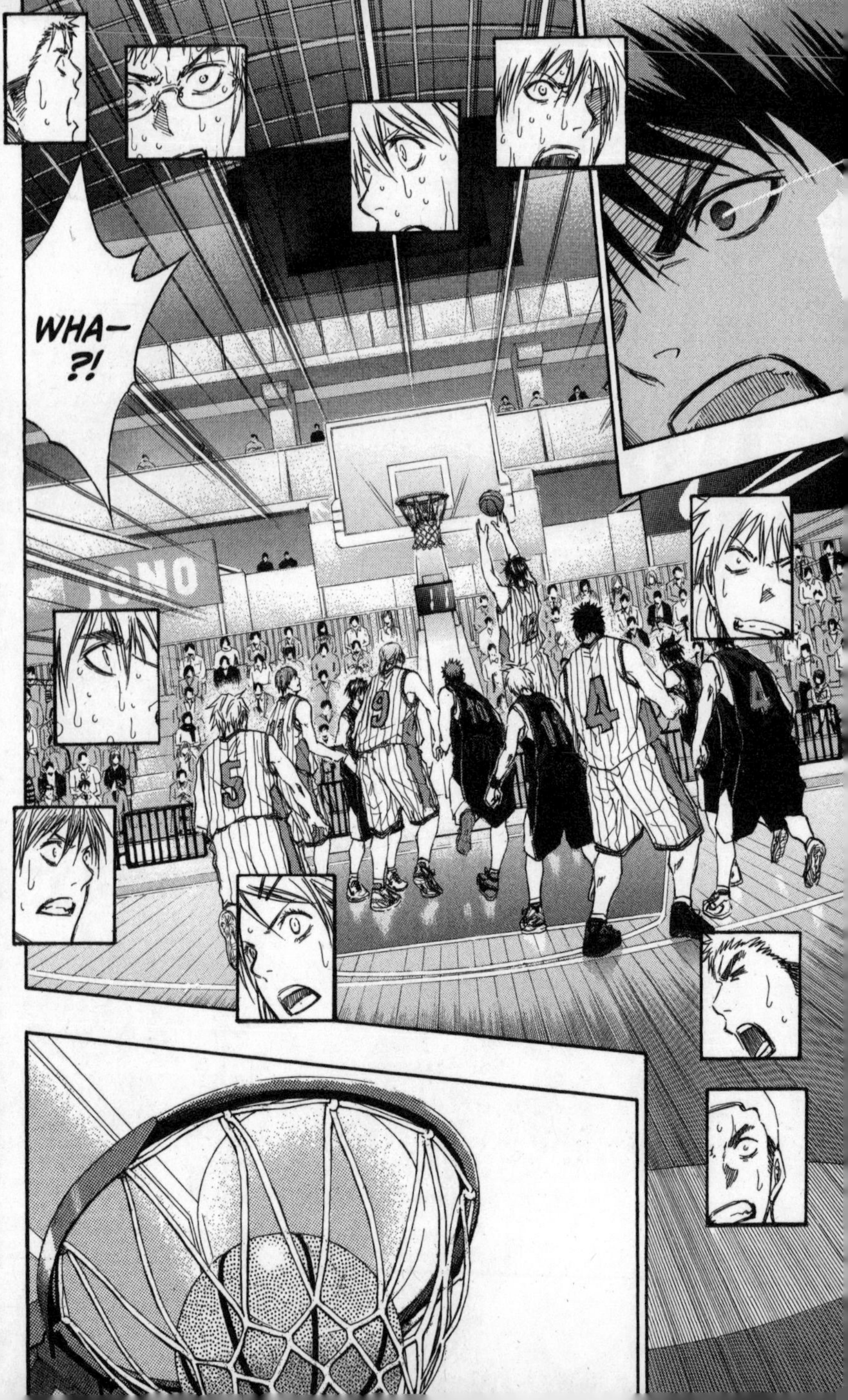
WHA- ?!
ONO

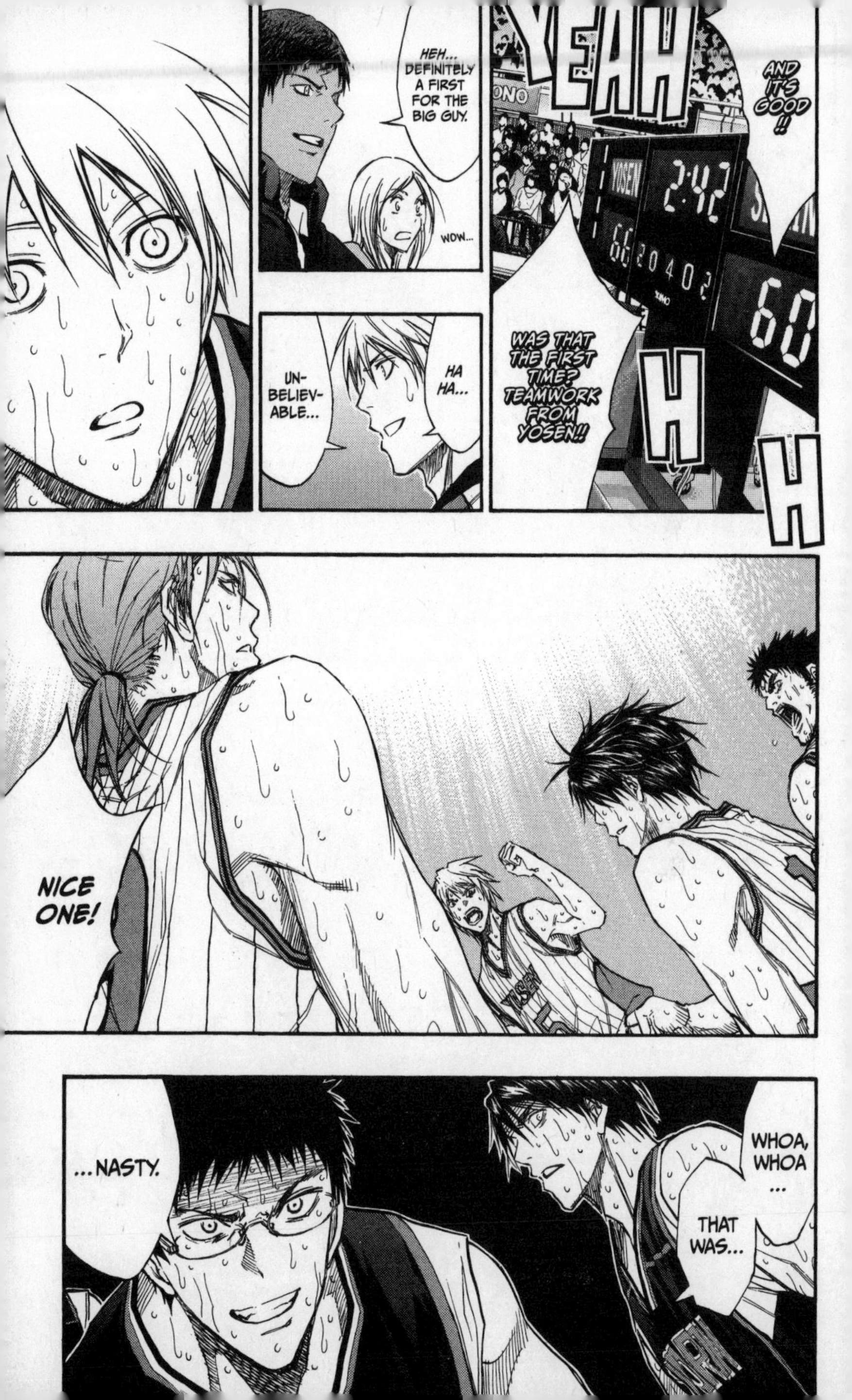
YEAH
AND IT'S GOOD!!
WAS THAT THE FIRST TIME? TEAMWORK FROM YOSEN!!
HH
HEH... DEFINITELY A FIRST FOR THE BIG GUY.
WOW...
HA HA...
UN-BELIEVABLE...
NICE ONE!
WHOA, WHOA...
THAT WAS...
...NASTY.

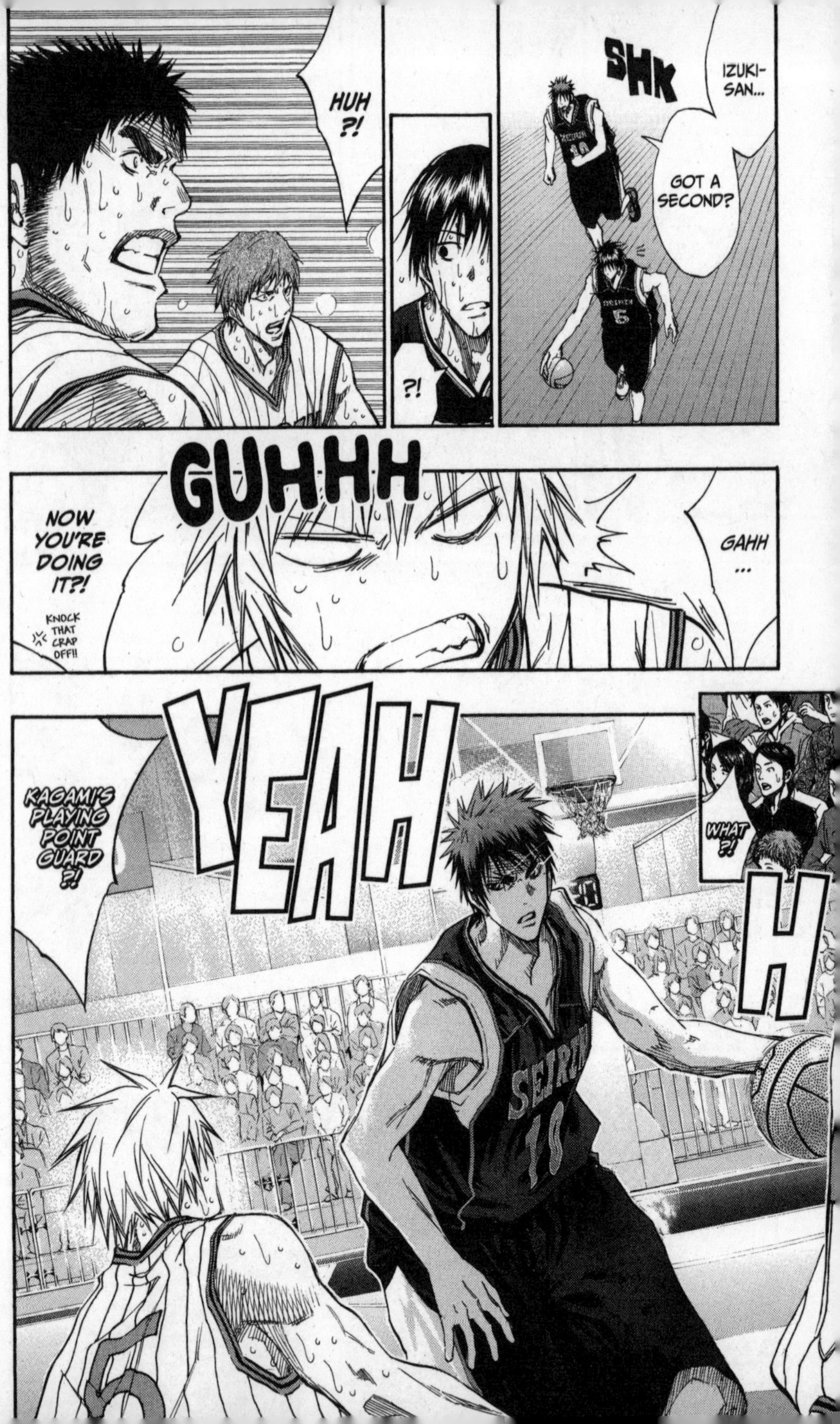
SHK
IZUKI-SAN...
GOT A SECOND?
?!
HUH ?!
GAHH ...
GUHHH
NOW YOU'RE DOING IT?!
KNOCK THAT CRAP OFF!!
WHAT ?!
YEAH
H
KAGAMI'S PLAYING POINT GUARD ?!

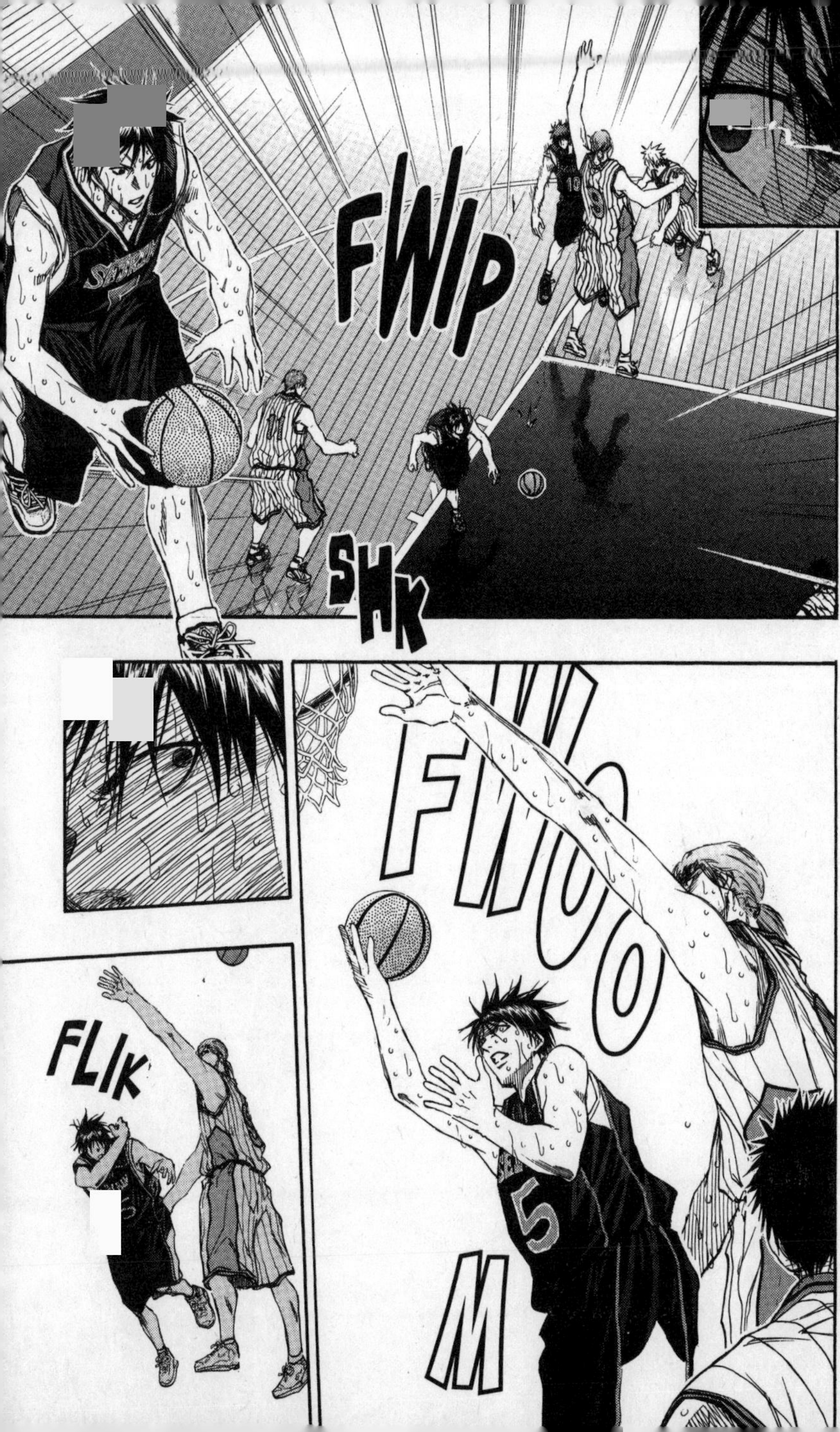
FWIP
SHK
FWOOOM
FLIK

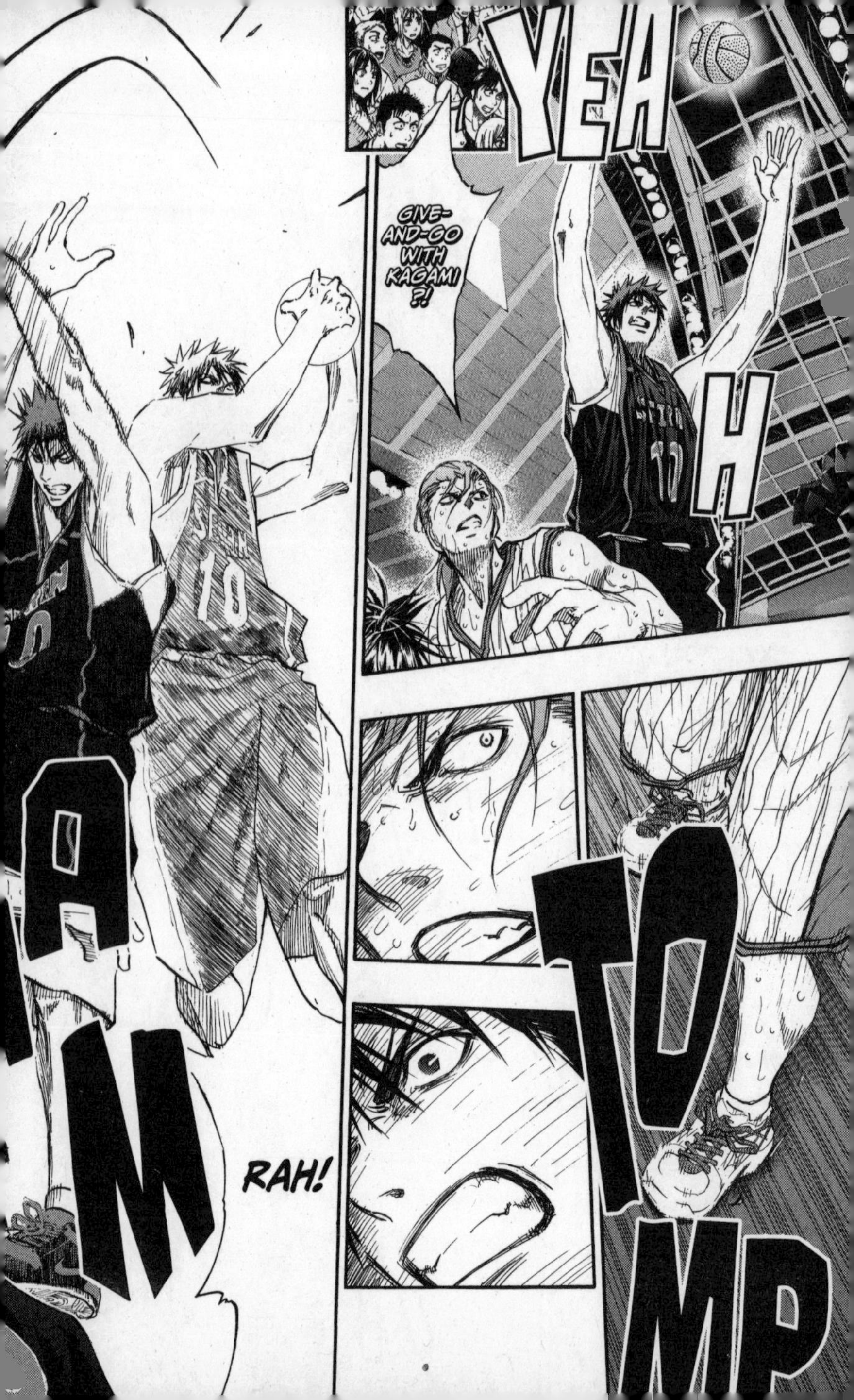
YEAH
GIVE-AND-GO WITH KAGAMI?!
RAH!

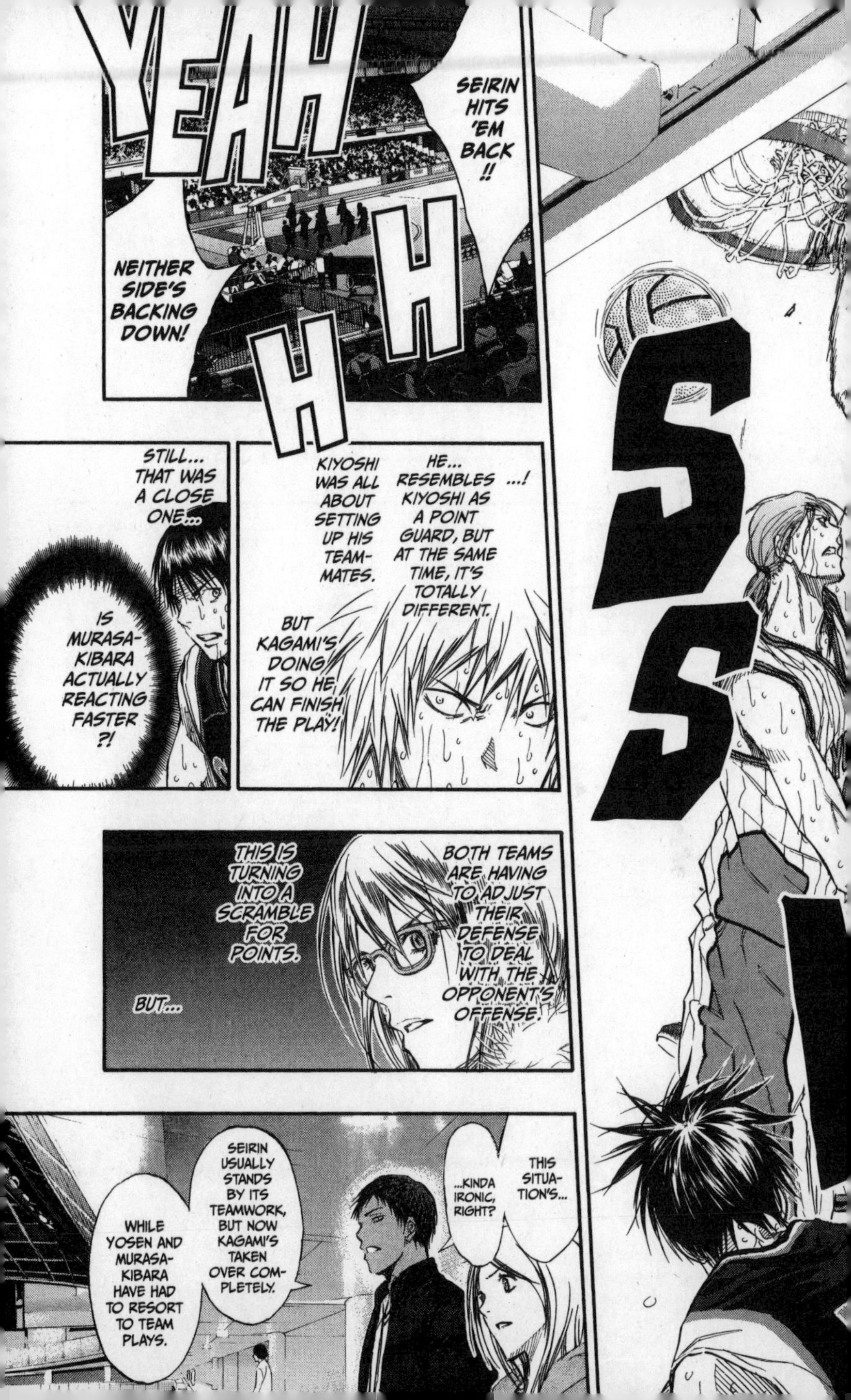
SSS
YEAHHH
SEIRIN HITS 'EM BACK!!
NEITHER SIDE'S BACKING DOWN!
...!
HE... RESEMBLES KIYOSHI AS A POINT GUARD, BUT AT THE SAME TIME, IT'S TOTALLY DIFFERENT.
KIYOSHI WAS ALL ABOUT SETTING UP HIS TEAMMATES.
BUT KAGAMI'S DOING IT SO HE CAN FINISH THE PLAY!
STILL... THAT WAS A CLOSE ONE...
IS MURASAKIBARA ACTUALLY REACTING FASTER?!
BOTH TEAMS ARE HAVING TO ADJUST THEIR DEFENSE TO DEAL WITH THE OPPONENT'S OFFENSE.
THIS IS TURNING INTO A SCRAMBLE FOR POINTS.
BUT...
THIS SITUATION'S...
...KINDA IRONIC, RIGHT?
SEIRIN USUALLY STANDS BY ITS TEAMWORK, BUT NOW KAGAMI'S TAKEN OVER COMPLETELY.
WHILE YOSEN AND MURASAKIBARA HAVE HAD TO RESORT TO TEAM PLAYS.

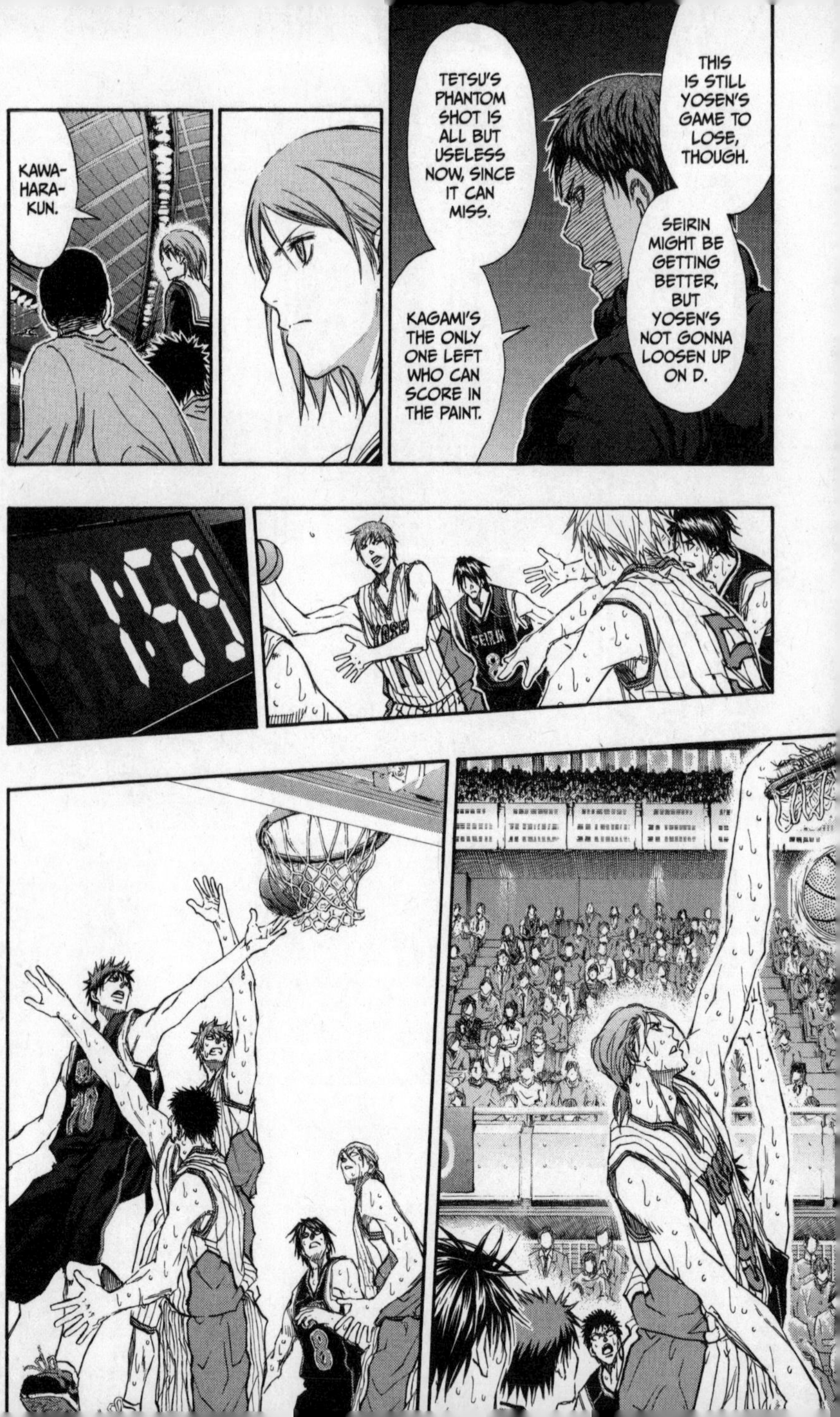
THIS IS STILL YOSEN'S GAME TO LOSE, THOUGH.
SEIRIN MIGHT BE GETTING BETTER, BUT YOSEN'S NOT GONNA LOOSEN UP ON D.
TETSU'S PHANTOM SHOT IS ALL BUT USELESS NOW, SINCE IT CAN MISS.
KAGAMI'S THE ONLY ONE LEFT WHO CAN SCORE IN THE PAINT.
KAWA-HARA-KUN.
1:59
SEIRIN

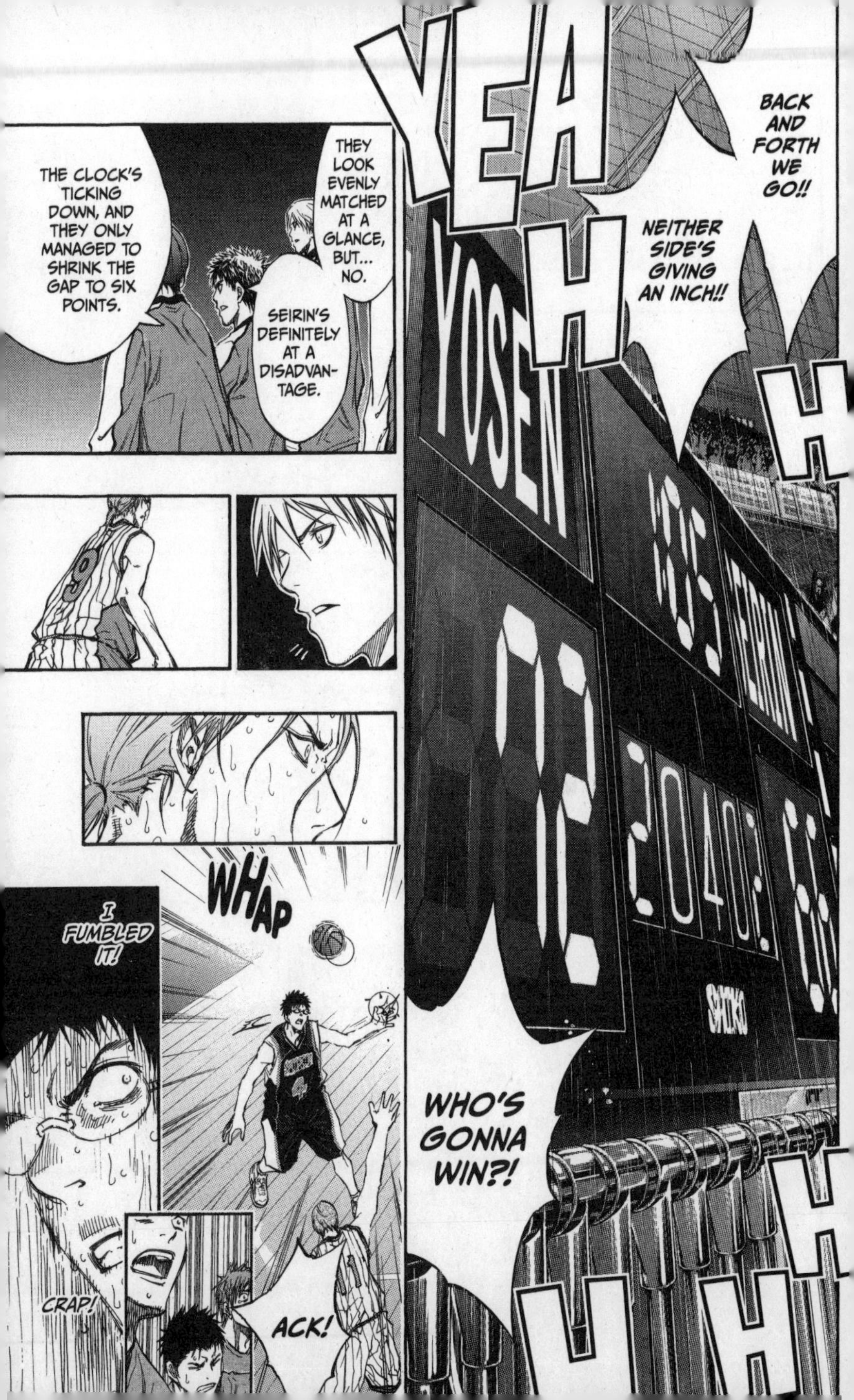
YEAHHHH
BACK AND FORTH WE GO!!
NEITHER SIDE'S GIVING AN INCH!!
YOSEN
WHO'S GONNA WIN?!
THEY LOOK EVENLY MATCHED AT A GLANCE, BUT... NO.
SEIRIN'S DEFINITELY AT A DISADVANTAGE.
THE CLOCK'S TICKING DOWN, AND THEY ONLY MANAGED TO SHRINK THE GAP TO SIX POINTS.
WHAP
I FUMBLED IT!
ACK!
CRAP!

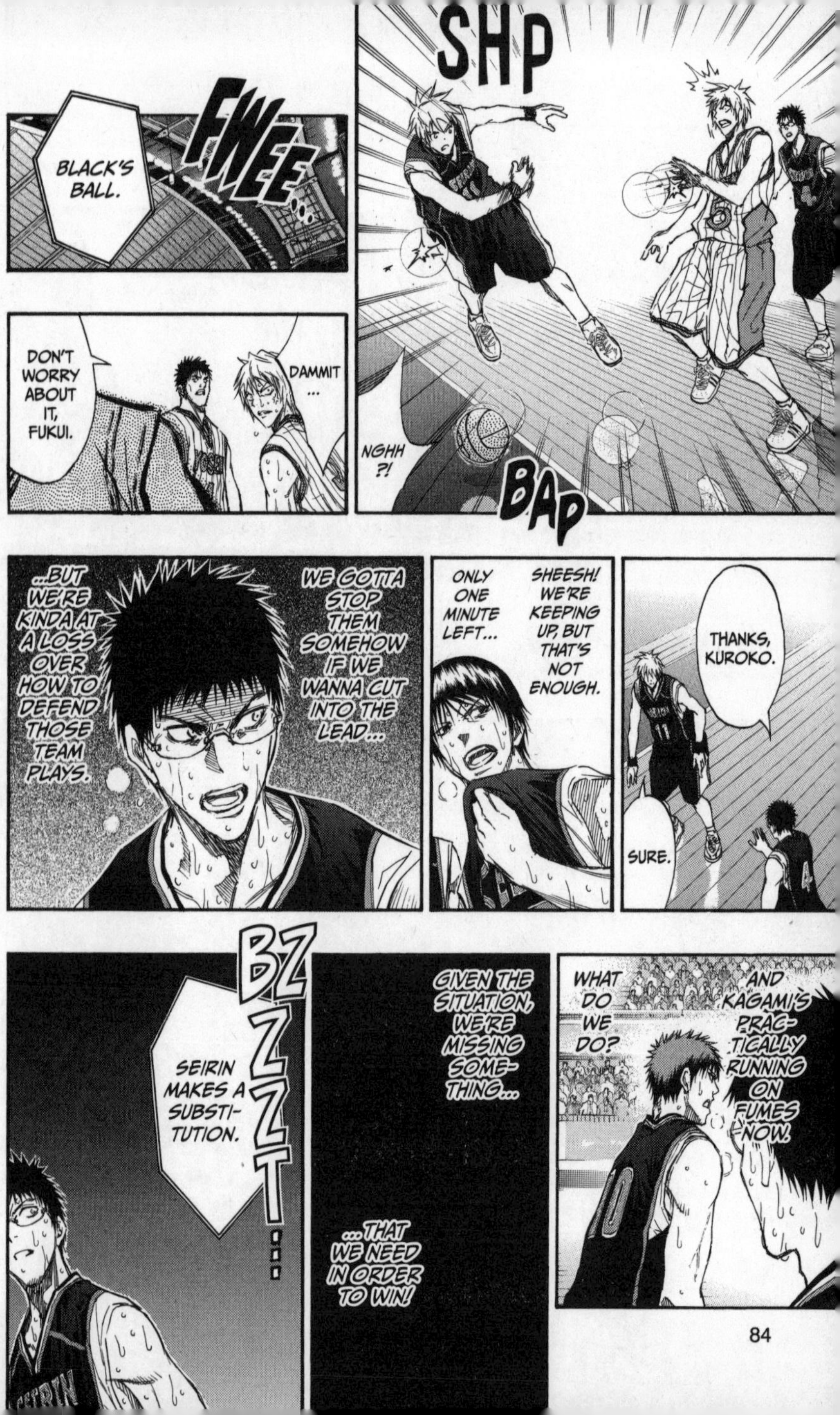
SHP
NGHH ?!
BAP
FWEE...
BLACK'S BALL.
DAMMIT ...
DON'T WORRY ABOUT IT, FUKUI.
THANKS, KUROKO.
SURE.
SHEESH! WE'RE KEEPING UP, BUT THAT'S NOT ENOUGH.
ONLY ONE MINUTE LEFT...
WE GOTTA STOP THEM SOMEHOW IF WE WANNA CUT INTO THE LEAD...
...BUT WE'RE KINDA AT A LOSS OVER HOW TO DEFEND THOSE TEAM PLAYS.
AND KAGAMI'S PRAC-TICALLY RUNNING ON FUMES NOW.
WHAT DO WE DO?
GIVEN THE SITUATION, WE'RE MISSING SOME-THING...
...THAT WE NEED IN ORDER TO WIN!
BZZZT...
SEIRIN MAKES A SUBSTI-TUTION.

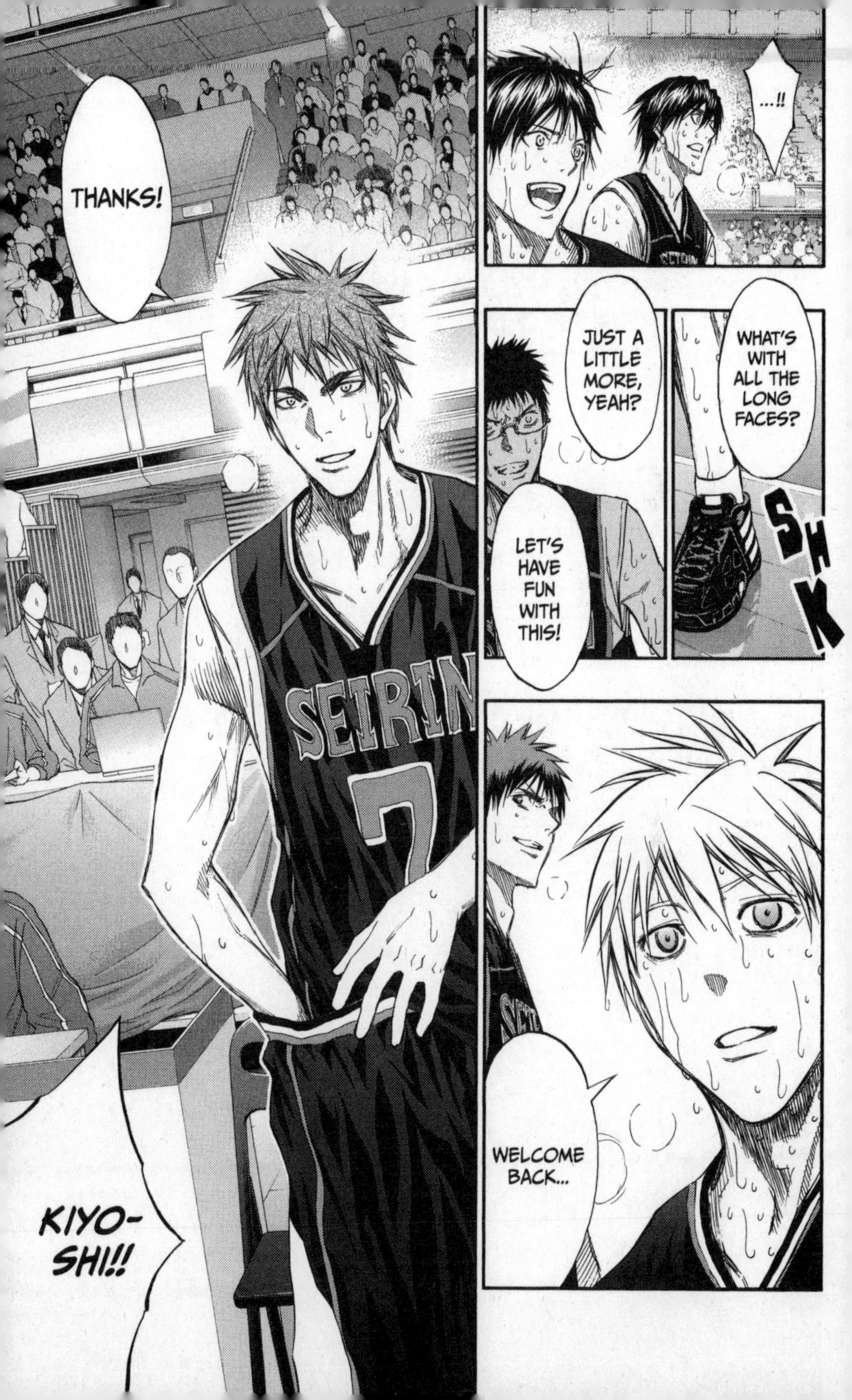

...!!
WHAT'S WITH ALL THE LONG FACES?
SHK
JUST A LITTLE MORE, YEAH?
LET'S HAVE FUN WITH THIS!
WELCOME BACK...
KIYO-SHI!!
THANKS!

KUROKO'S BASKETBALL Q&A (W/ HALFWAY-DECENT ANSWERS)

Q. HOW MANY SENGOKU WARRIOR FIGURES DID HYUGA HAVE? AND HOW MANY HAS RIKO DESTROYED?
(NOTAMAGO from AKITA PREFECTURE)

A. HOW MANY HE HAD: JUST ENOUGH TO RE-CREATE FAMOUS BATTLES.
HOW MANY SHE'S DESTROYED: JUST ENOUGH SO HE CAN'T RE-CREATE THOSE BATTLES.

KUROKO'S BASKETBALL BLOOPERS (TAKE 3)

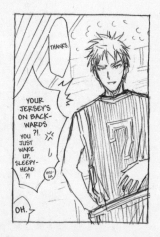

THANKS.
YOUR JERSEY'S ON BACKWARDS ?!
YOU JUST WAKE UP, SLEEPY-HEAD ?!
HYUGA
OH.

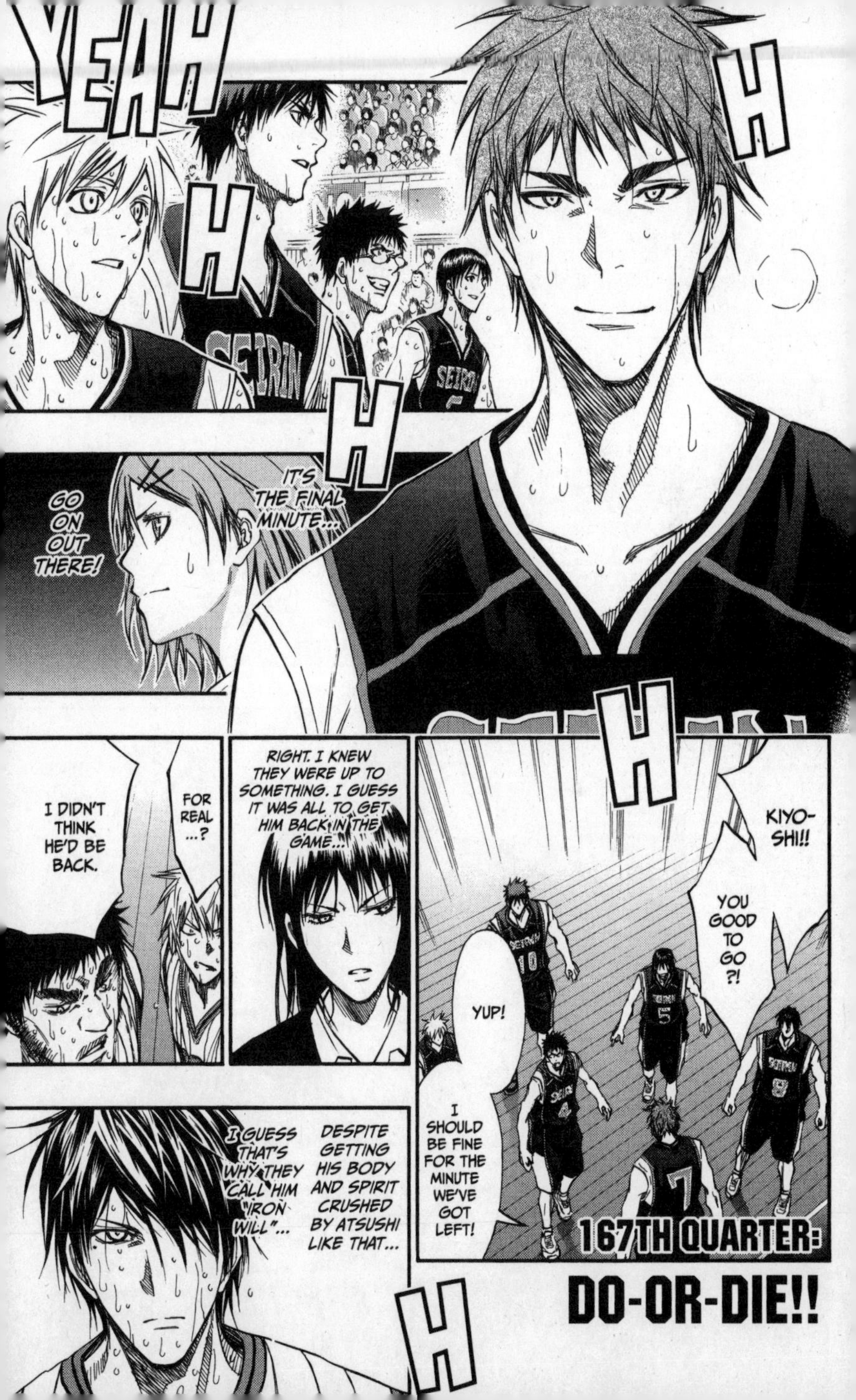
YEAHHHHHH
IT'S THE FINAL MINUTE...
GO ON OUT THERE!
KIYOSHI!!
YOU GOOD TO GO?!
YUP!
I SHOULD BE FINE FOR THE MINUTE WE'VE GOT LEFT!
RIGHT. I KNEW THEY WERE UP TO SOMETHING. I GUESS IT WAS ALL TO GET HIM BACK IN THE GAME...
FOR REAL ...?
I DIDN'T THINK HE'D BE BACK.
167TH QUARTER:
DO-OR-DIE!!
DESPITE GETTING HIS BODY AND SPIRIT CRUSHED BY ATSUSHI LIKE THAT...
I GUESS THAT'S WHY THEY CALL HIM "IRON WILL"...

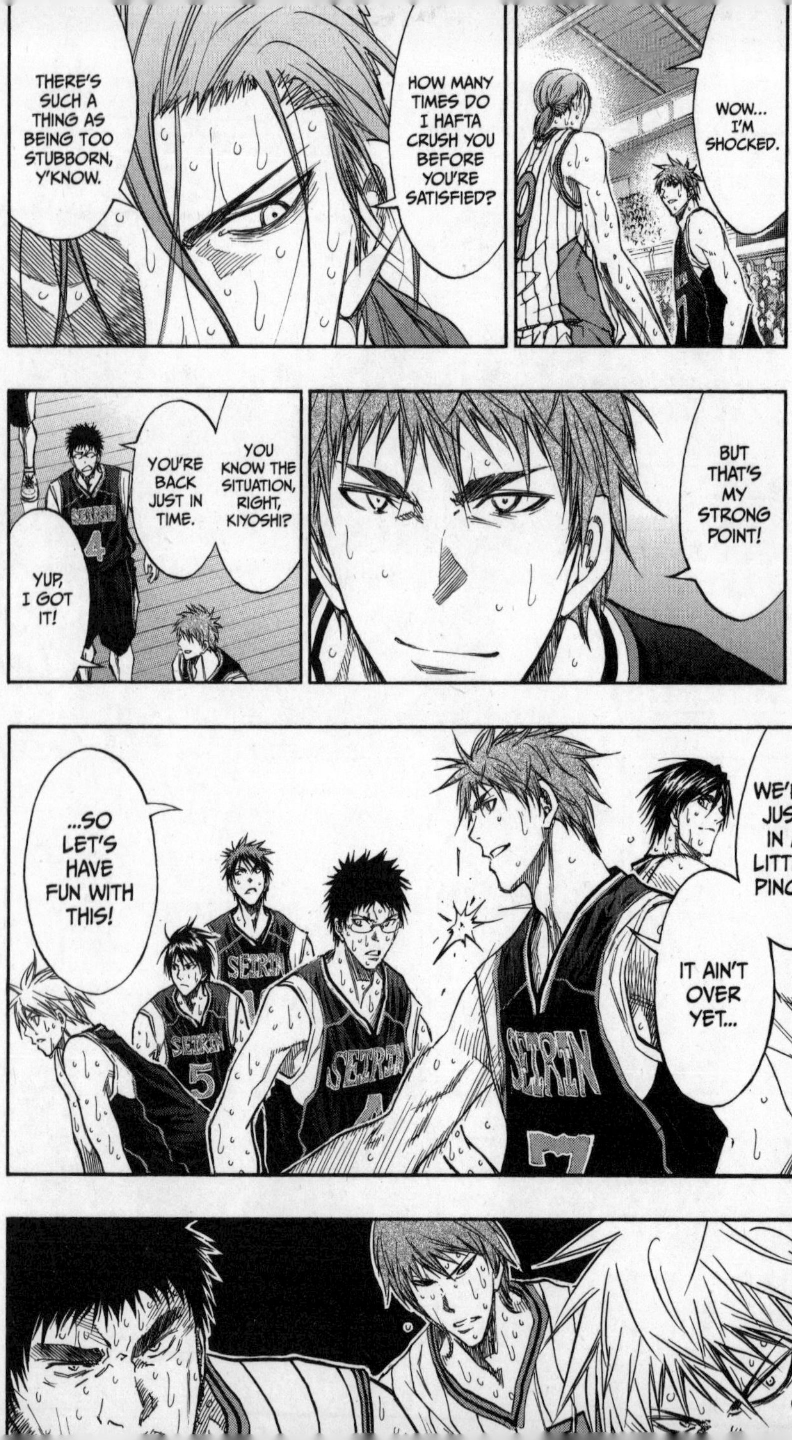
WOW... I'M SHOCKED.
HOW MANY TIMES DO I HAFTA CRUSH YOU BEFORE YOU'RE SATISFIED?
THERE'S SUCH A THING AS BEING TOO STUBBORN, Y'KNOW.
BUT THAT'S MY STRONG POINT!
YOU KNOW THE SITUATION, RIGHT, KIYOSHI?
YOU'RE BACK JUST IN TIME.
YUP, I GOT IT!
WE'RE JUST IN A LITTLE PINCH.
IT AIN'T OVER YET...
...SO LET'S HAVE FUN WITH THIS!

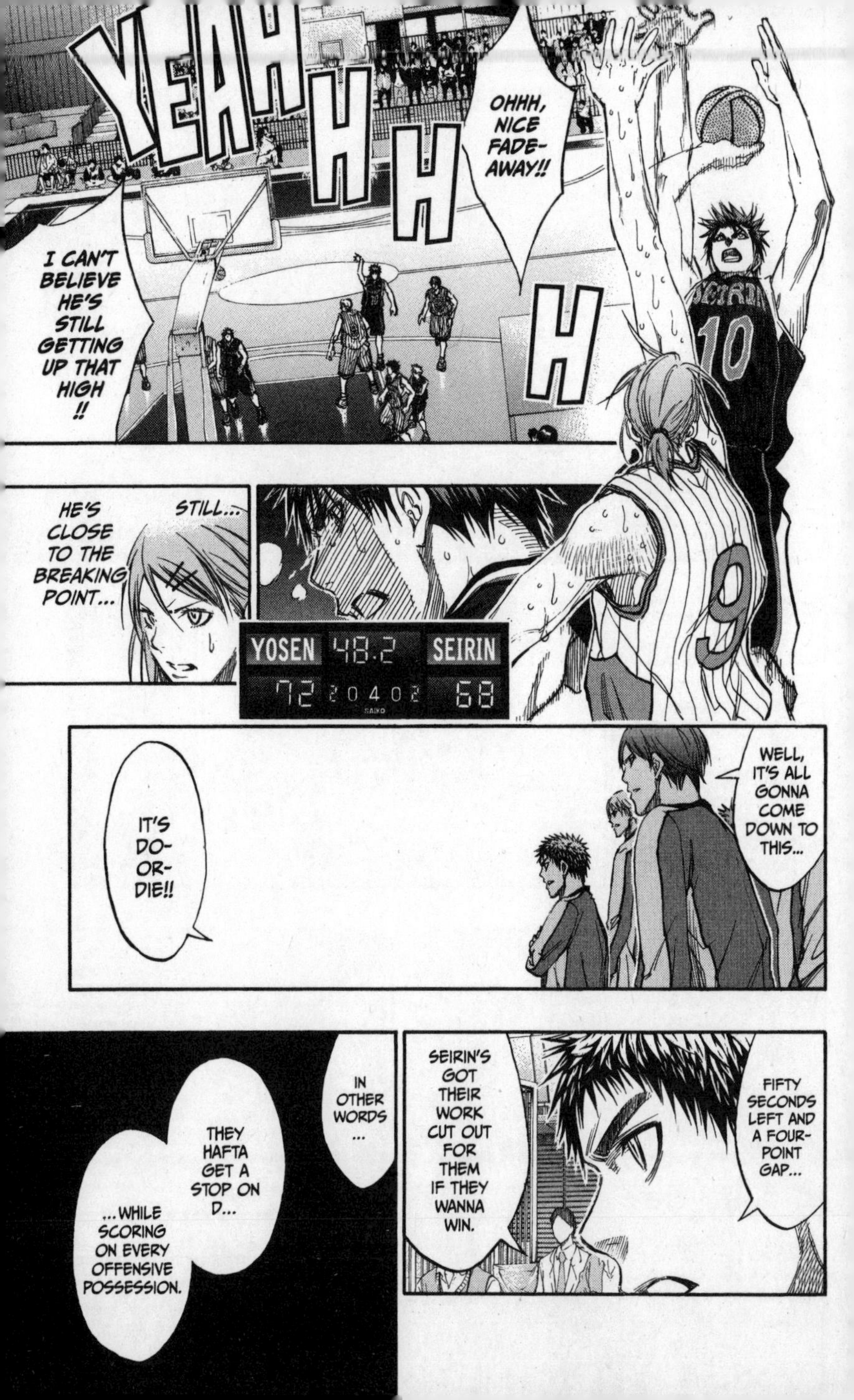
OHHH, NICE FADE-AWAY!!
YEAHHHHH
I CAN'T BELIEVE HE'S STILL GETTING UP THAT HIGH!!
YOSEN 48.2 SEIRIN
72 20402 68
STILL...
HE'S CLOSE TO THE BREAKING POINT...
WELL, IT'S ALL GONNA COME DOWN TO THIS...
IT'S DO-OR-DIE!!
FIFTY SECONDS LEFT AND A FOUR-POINT GAP...
SEIRIN'S GOT THEIR WORK CUT OUT FOR THEM IF THEY WANNA WIN.
IN OTHER WORDS...
THEY HAFTA GET A STOP ON D...
...WHILE SCORING ON EVERY OFFENSIVE POSSESSION.

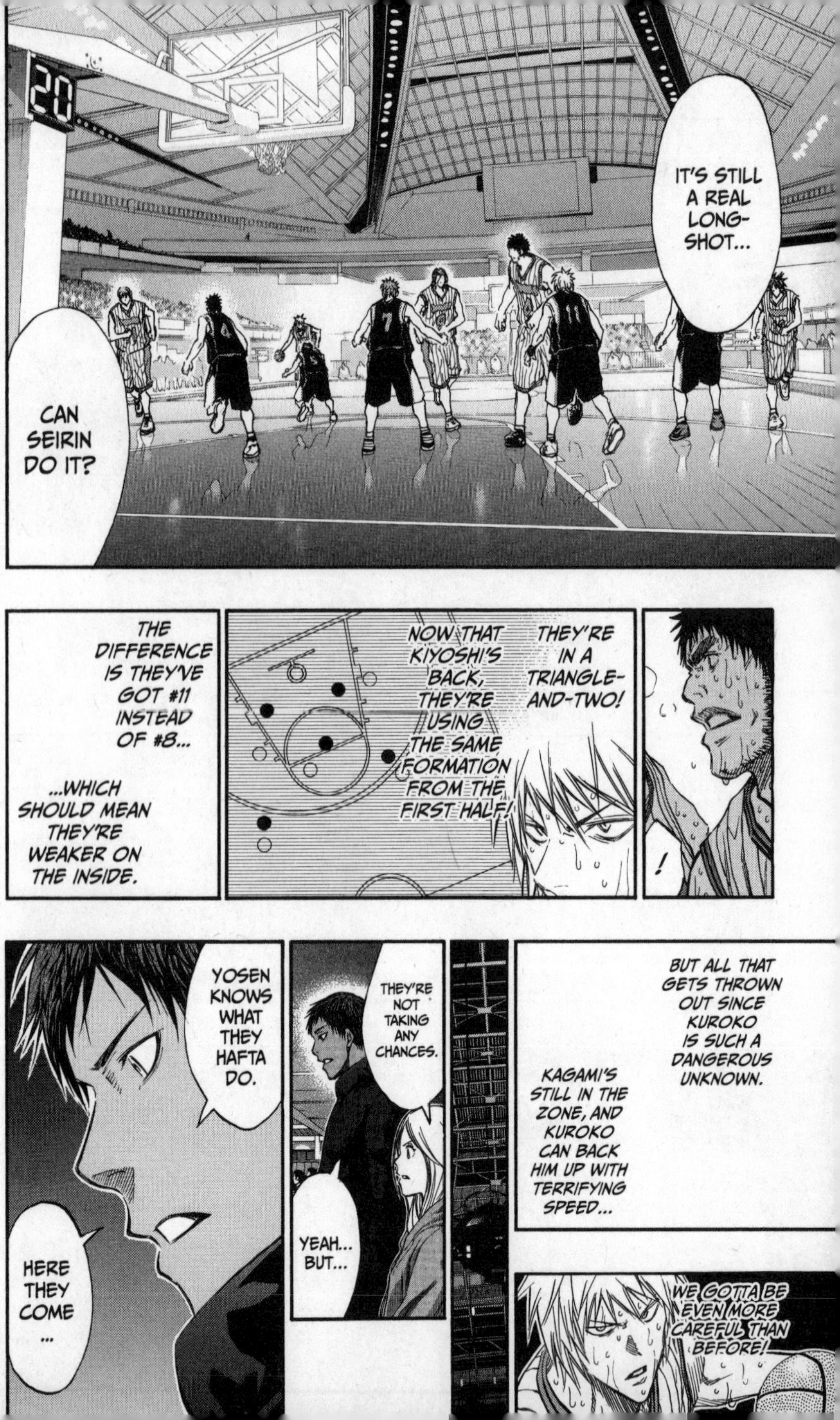

IT'S STILL A REAL LONG-SHOT...
CAN SEIRIN DO IT?
!
THEY'RE IN A TRIANGLE-AND-TWO!
NOW THAT KIYOSHI'S BACK, THEY'RE USING THE SAME FORMATION FROM THE FIRST HALF!
THE DIFFERENCE IS THEY'VE GOT #11 INSTEAD OF #8...
...WHICH SHOULD MEAN THEY'RE WEAKER ON THE INSIDE.
KAGAMI'S STILL IN THE ZONE, AND KUROKO CAN BACK HIM UP WITH TERRIFYING SPEED...
BUT ALL THAT GETS THROWN OUT SINCE KUROKO IS SUCH A DANGEROUS UNKNOWN.
WE GOTTA BE EVEN MORE CAREFUL THAN BEFORE!
THEY'RE NOT TAKING ANY CHANCES.
YEAH... BUT...
YOSEN KNOWS WHAT THEY HAFTA DO.
HERE THEY COME ...

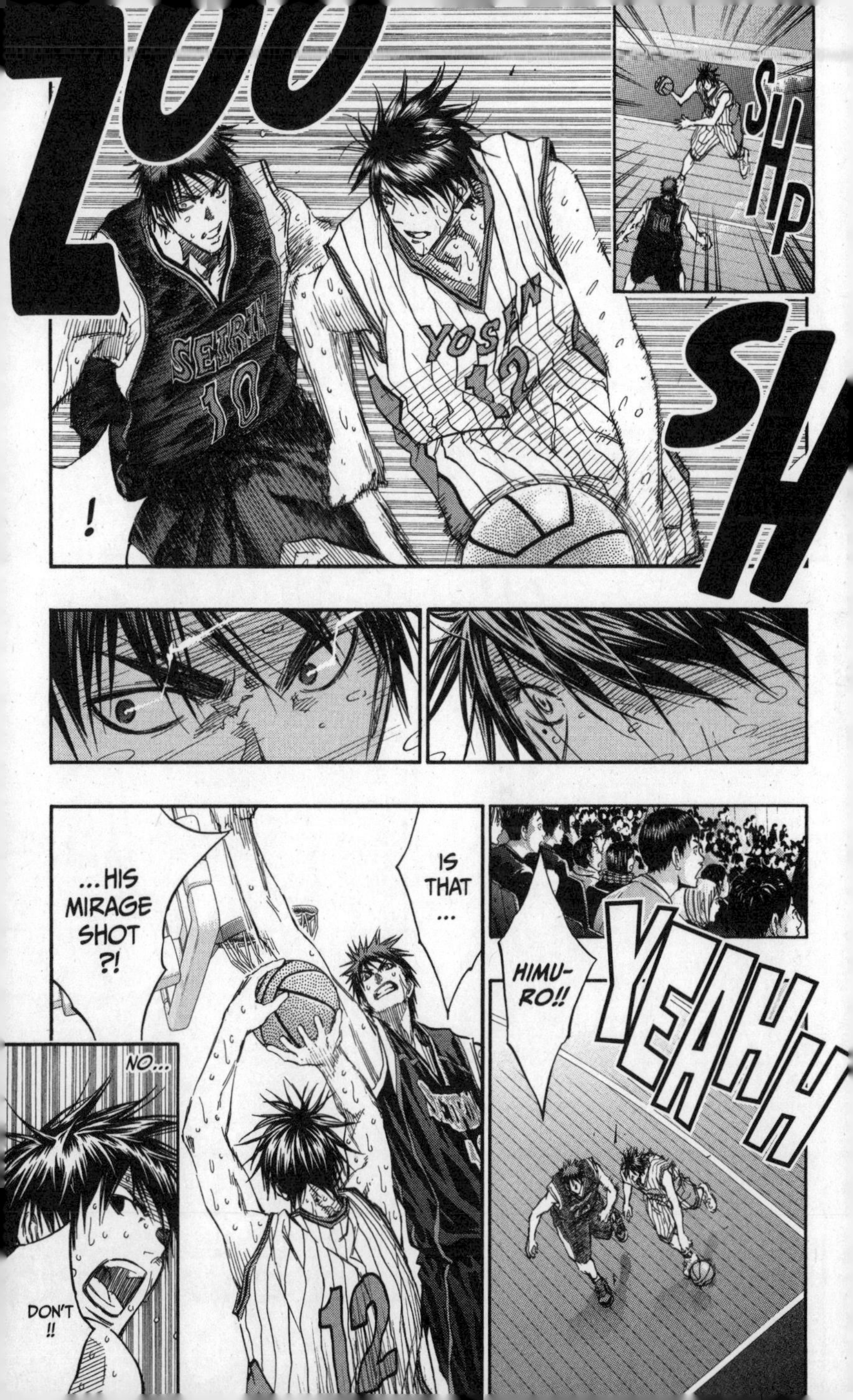
SHP
ZOOO
SH
!
HIMU-RO!!
YEAHH
IS THAT ...
...HIS MIRAGE SHOT ?!
NO...
DON'T !!

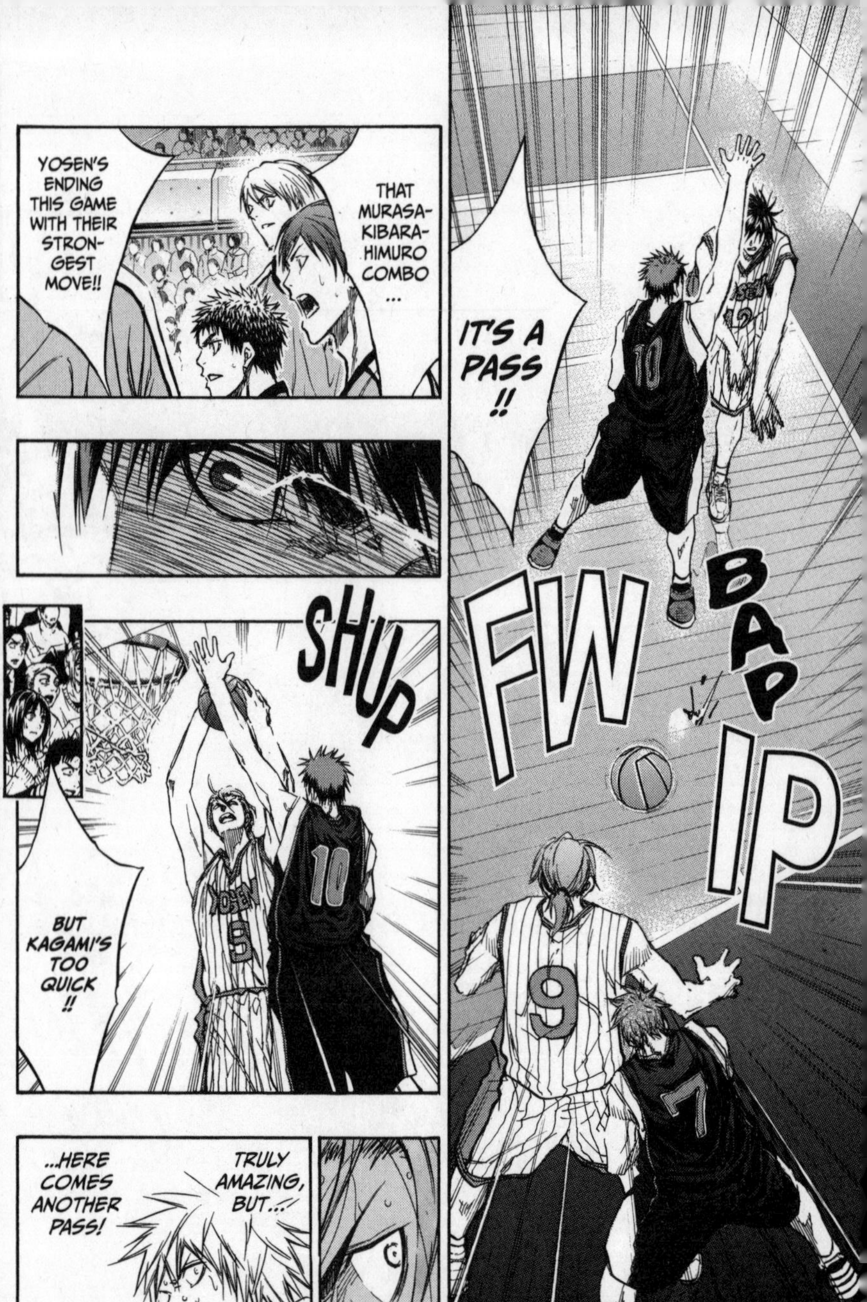
IT'S A PASS!!
FWIP
BAP
THAT MURASA-KIBARA-HIMURO COMBO...
YOSEN'S ENDING THIS GAME WITH THEIR STRONGEST MOVE!!
SHUP
BUT KAGAMI'S TOO QUICK!!
TRULY AMAZING, BUT...
...HERE COMES ANOTHER PASS!

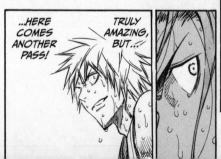

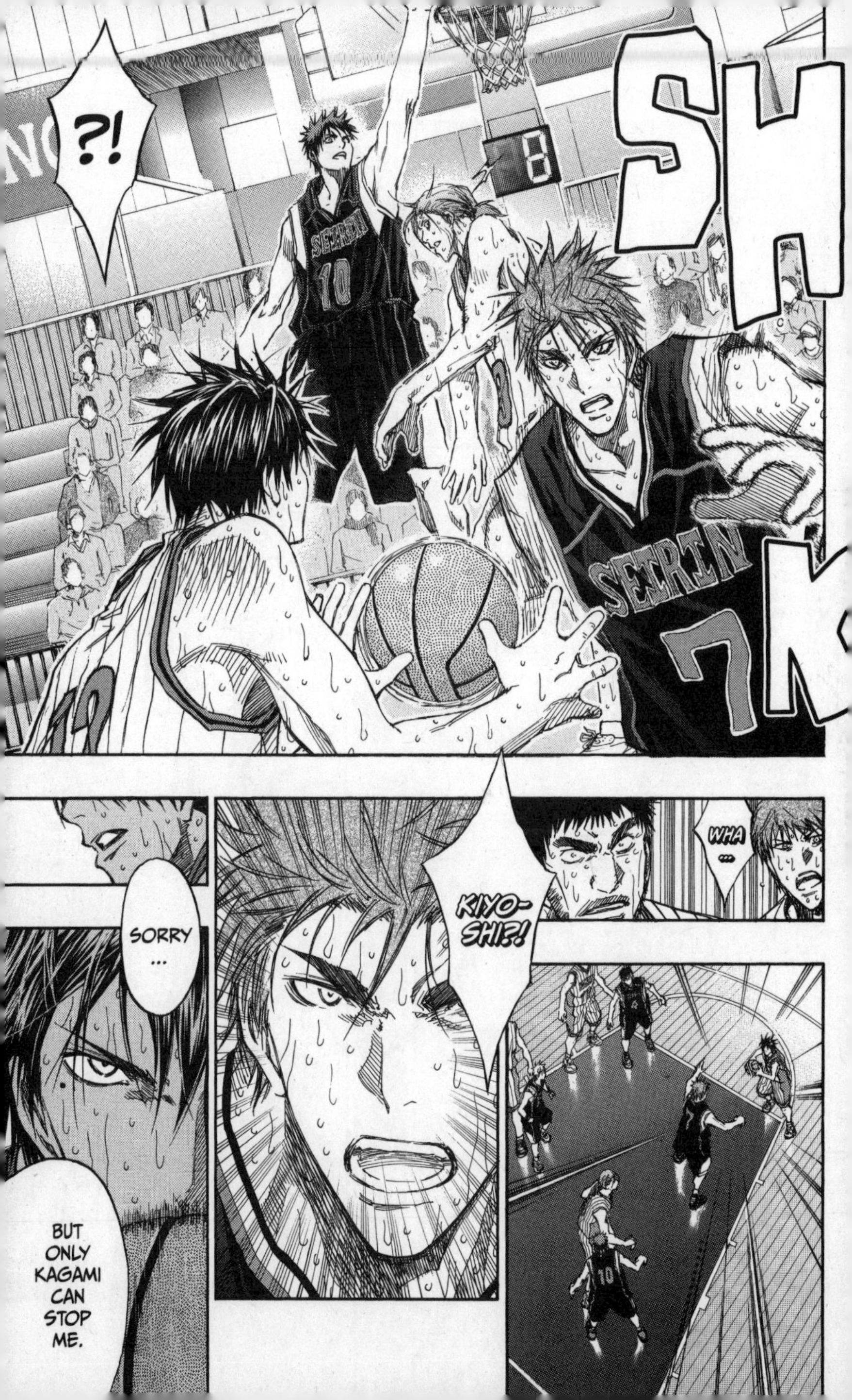
?!
SH
K
WHA ...
KIYO-SHI?!
SORRY ...
BUT ONLY KAGAMI CAN STOP ME.

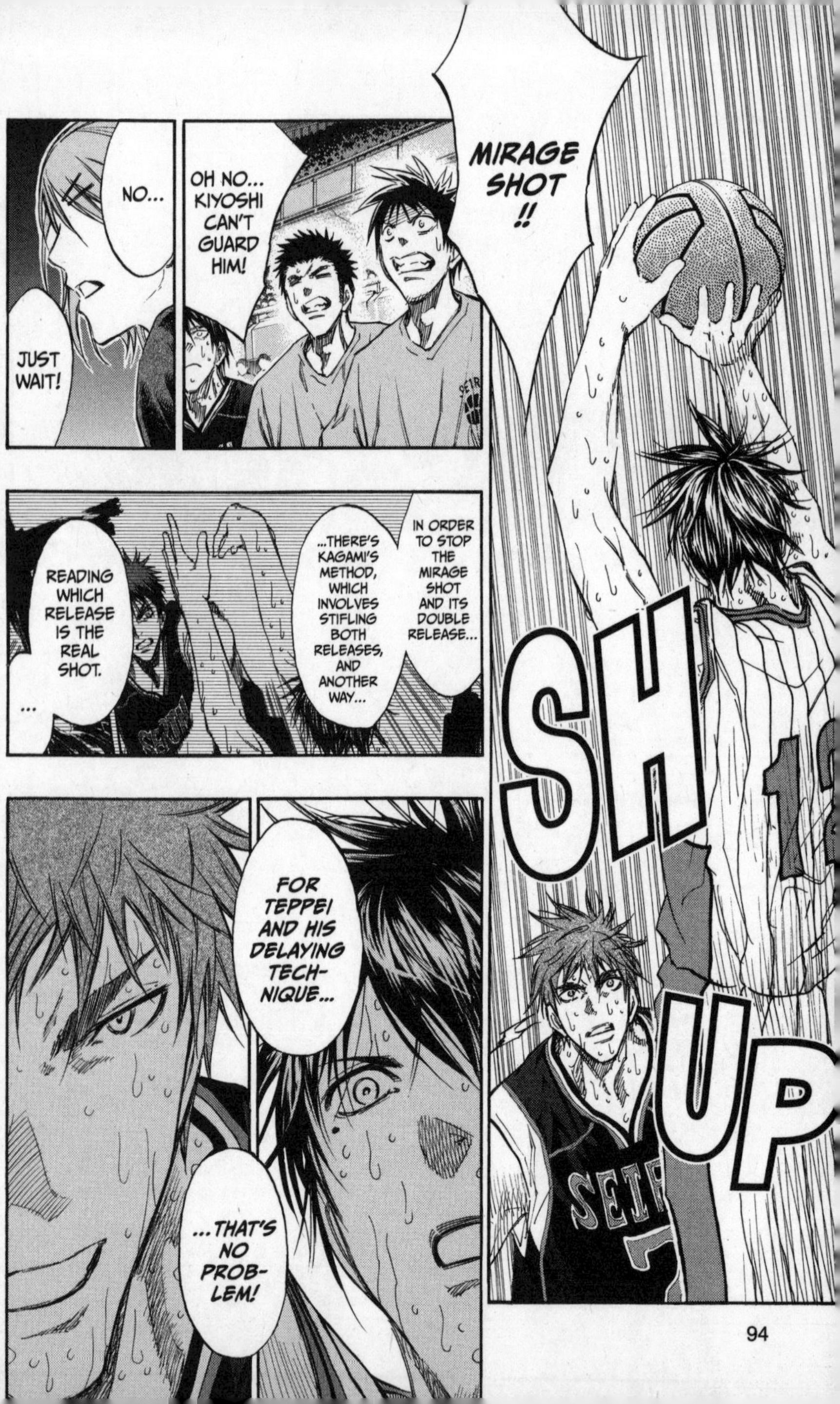
MIRAGE SHOT !!
SHUP
OH NO... KIYOSHI CAN'T GUARD HIM!
NO...
JUST WAIT!
IN ORDER TO STOP THE MIRAGE SHOT AND ITS DOUBLE RELEASE...
...THERE'S KAGAMI'S METHOD, WHICH INVOLVES STIFLING BOTH RELEASES, AND ANOTHER WAY...
READING WHICH RELEASE IS THE REAL SHOT.
...
FOR TEPPEI AND HIS DELAYING TECH-NIQUE...
...THAT'S NO PROB-LEM!

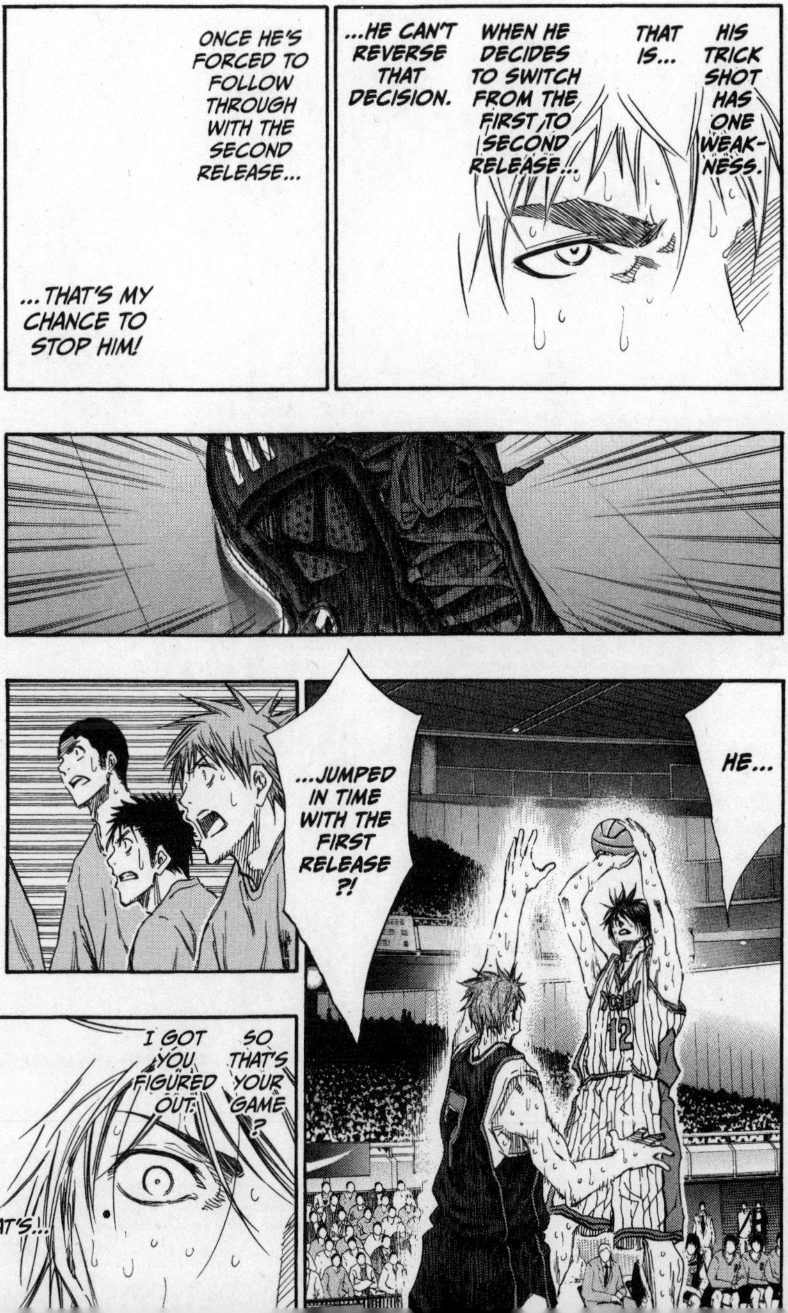
HIS TRICK SHOT HAS ONE WEAKNESS.
THAT IS...
WHEN HE DECIDES TO SWITCH FROM THE FIRST TO SECOND RELEASE...
...HE CAN'T REVERSE THAT DECISION.
ONCE HE'S FORCED TO FOLLOW THROUGH WITH THE SECOND RELEASE...
...THAT'S MY CHANCE TO STOP HIM!
HE...
...JUMPED IN TIME WITH THE FIRST RELEASE ?!
SO THAT'S YOUR GAME?
I GOT YOU FIGURED OUT.
THAT'S...

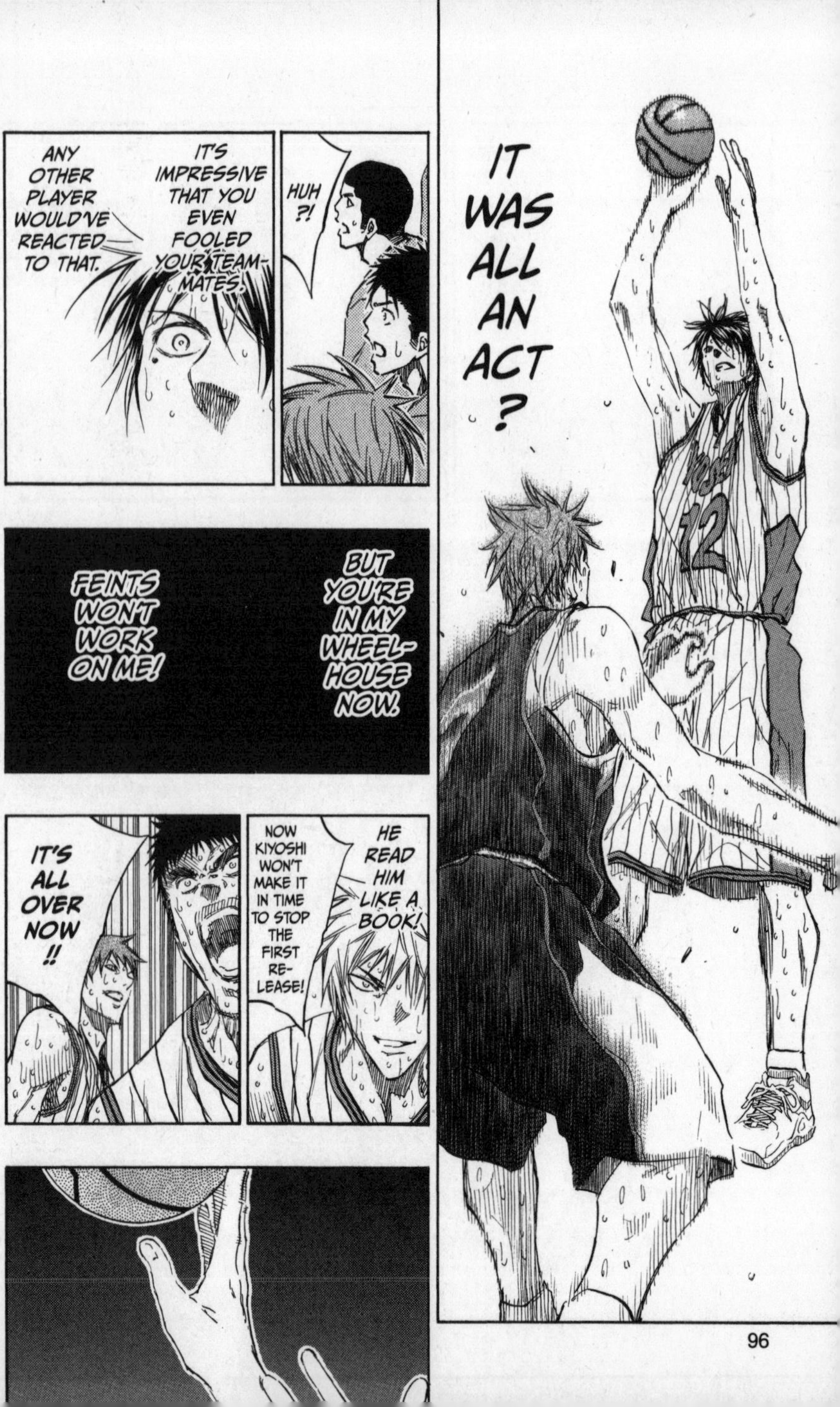
IT WAS ALL AN ACT?
HUH?!
IT'S IMPRESSIVE THAT YOU EVEN FOOLED YOUR TEAM-MATES.
ANY OTHER PLAYER WOULD'VE REACTED TO THAT.
BUT YOU'RE IN MY WHEEL-HOUSE NOW.
FEINTS WON'T WORK ON ME!
HE READ HIM LIKE A BOOK!
NOW KIYOSHI WON'T MAKE IT IN TIME TO STOP THE FIRST RE-LEASE!
IT'S ALL OVER NOW!!

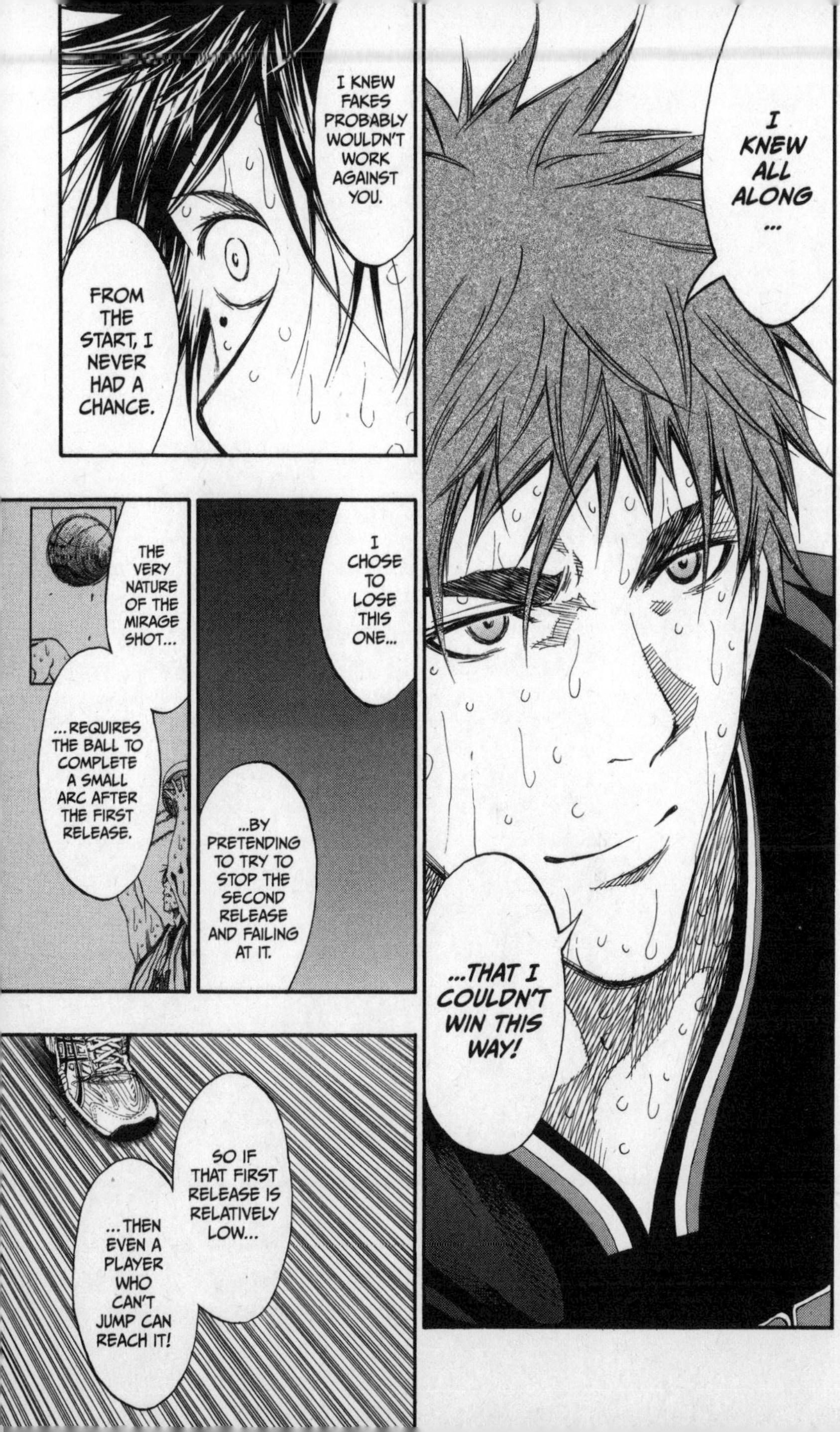
I KNEW ALL ALONG ...
...THAT I COULDN'T WIN THIS WAY!
I KNEW FAKES PROBABLY WOULDN'T WORK AGAINST YOU.
FROM THE START, I NEVER HAD A CHANCE.
I CHOSE TO LOSE THIS ONE...
...BY PRETENDING TO TRY TO STOP THE SECOND RELEASE AND FAILING AT IT.
THE VERY NATURE OF THE MIRAGE SHOT...
...REQUIRES THE BALL TO COMPLETE A SMALL ARC AFTER THE FIRST RELEASE.
SO IF THAT FIRST RELEASE IS RELATIVELY LOW...
...THEN EVEN A PLAYER WHO CAN'T JUMP CAN REACH IT!

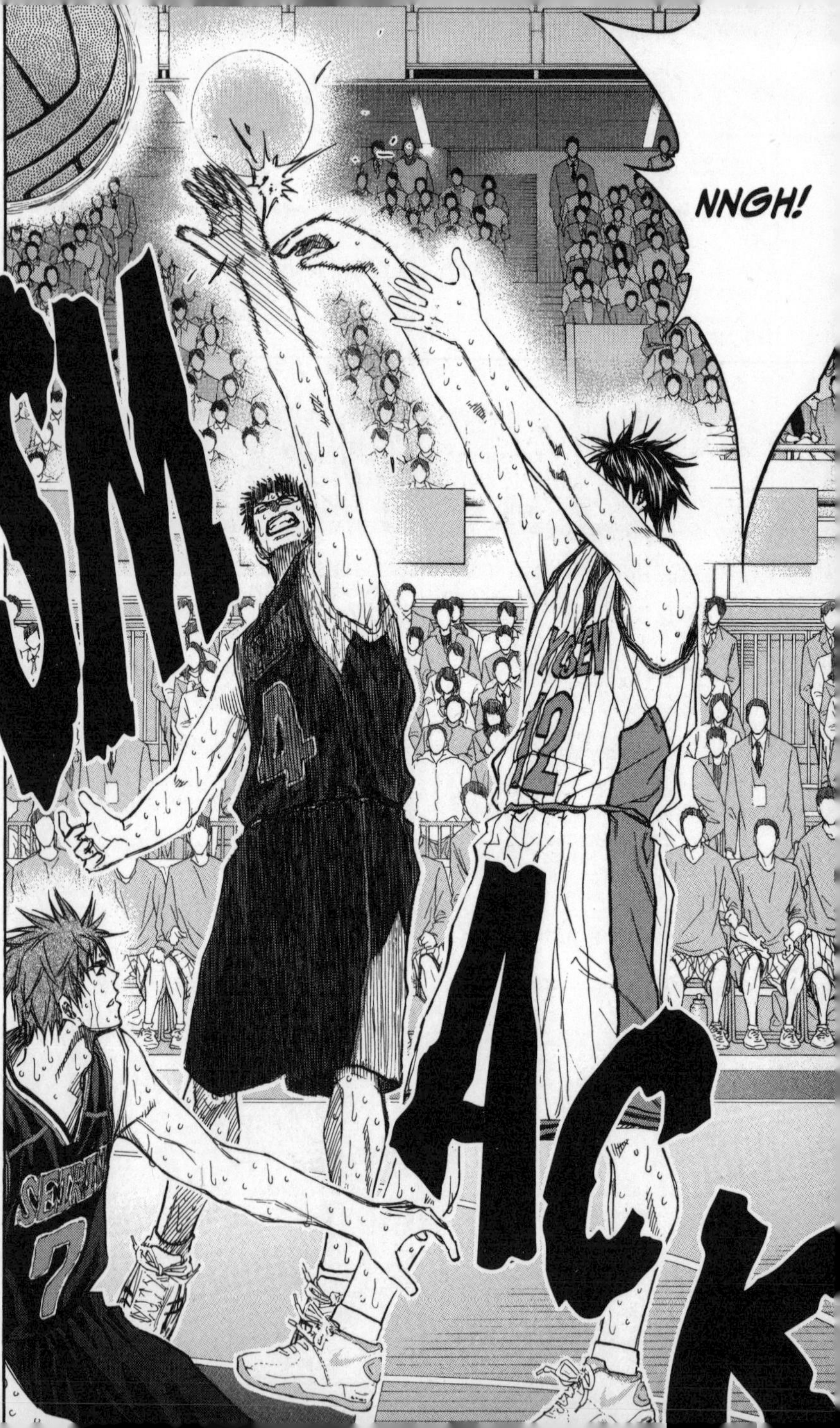
NNGH!
SMACK

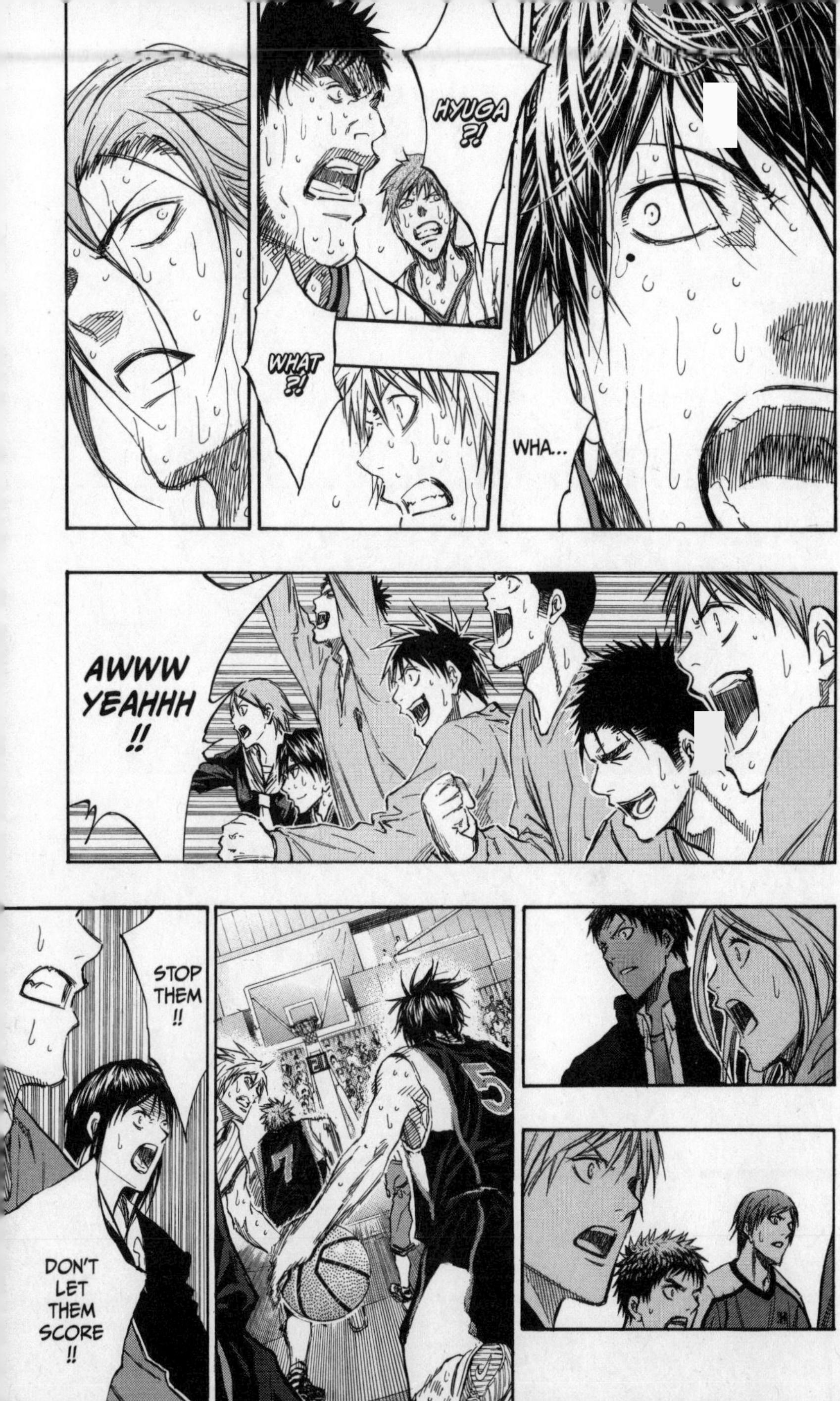
WHA...
HYUGA ?!
WHAT ?!
AWWW YEAHHH !!
STOP THEM !!
DON'T LET THEM SCORE !!

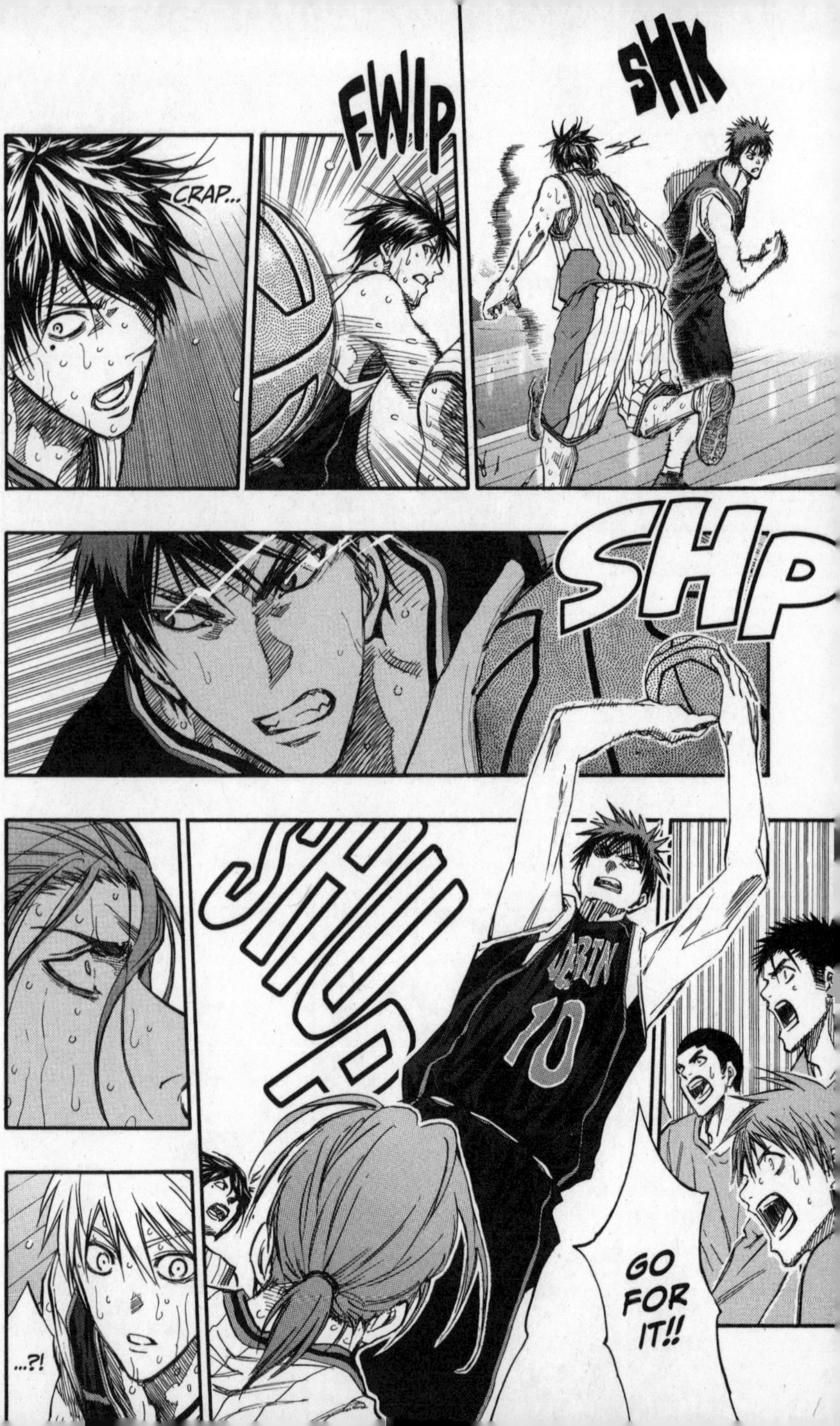
SHK
FWIP
CRAP...
SHP
GO FOR IT!!
...?!

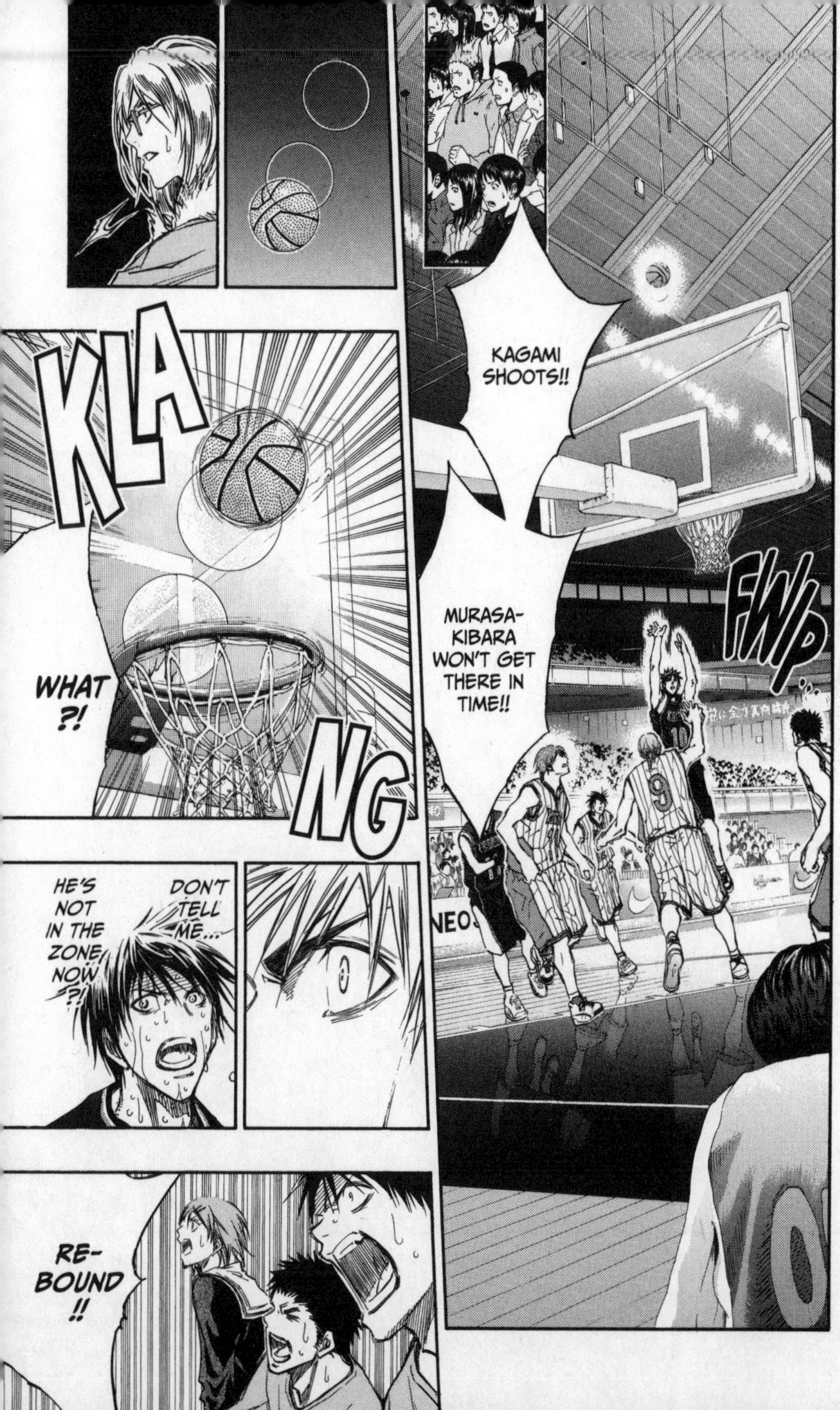
KAGAMI SHOOTS!!
MURASA-KIBARA WON'T GET THERE IN TIME!!
FWIP...
KLANG
WHAT?!
DON'T TELL ME...
HE'S NOT IN THE ZONE NOW?!
RE-BOUND!!

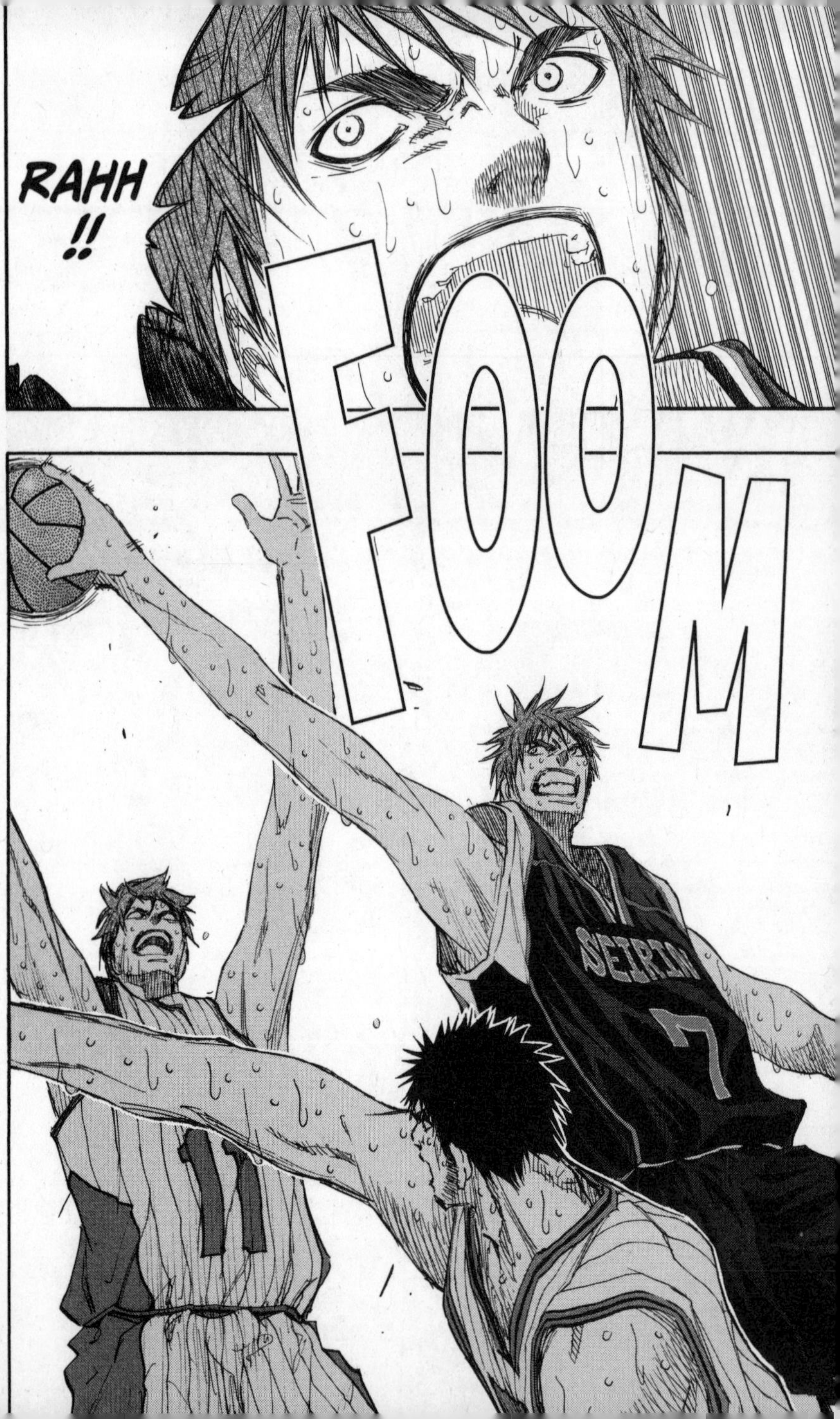
RAHH!!
FOOM
SEIRIN
7

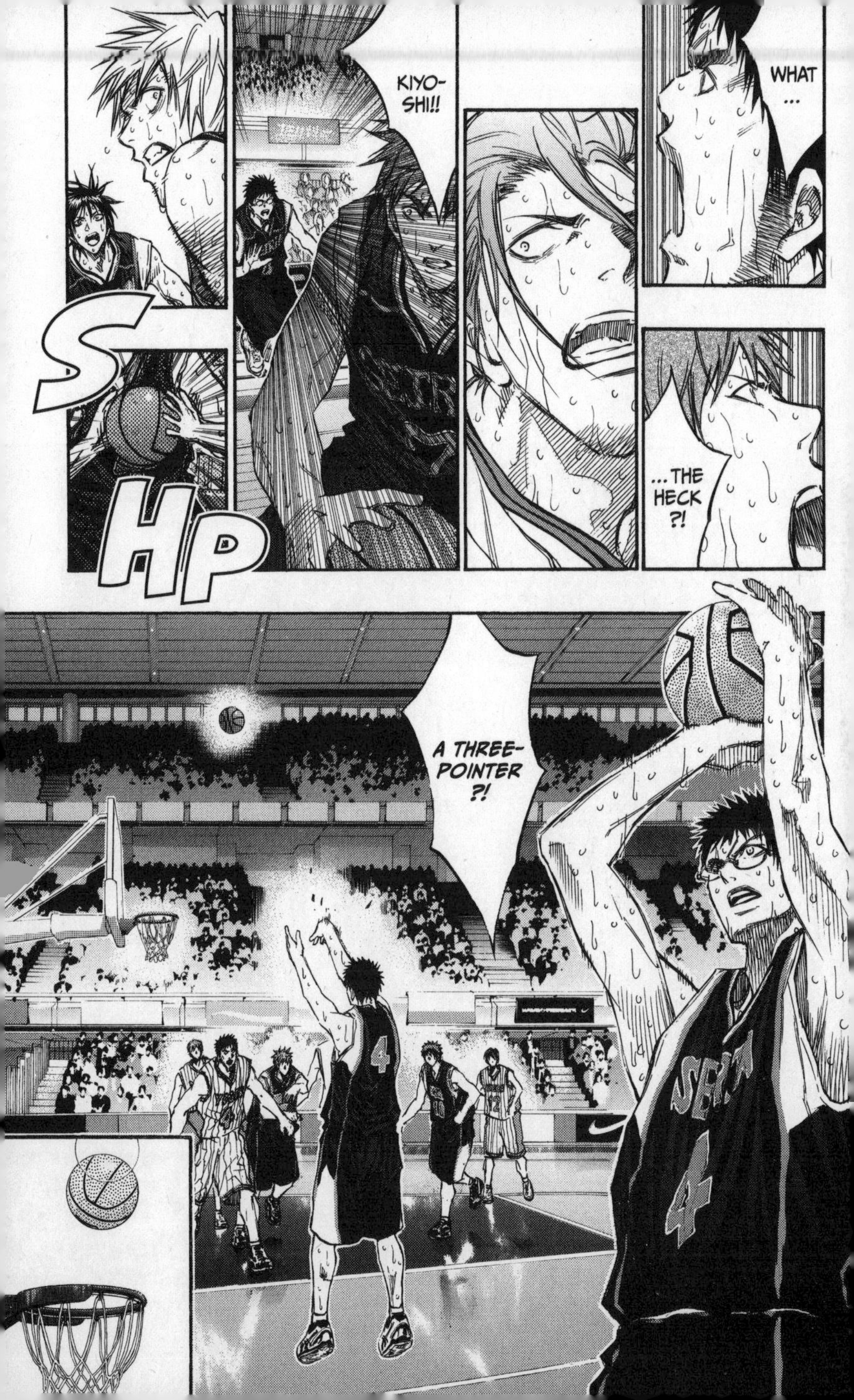
WHAT ...
...THE HECK ?!
KIYO-SHI!!
SHP
A THREE-POINTER ?!

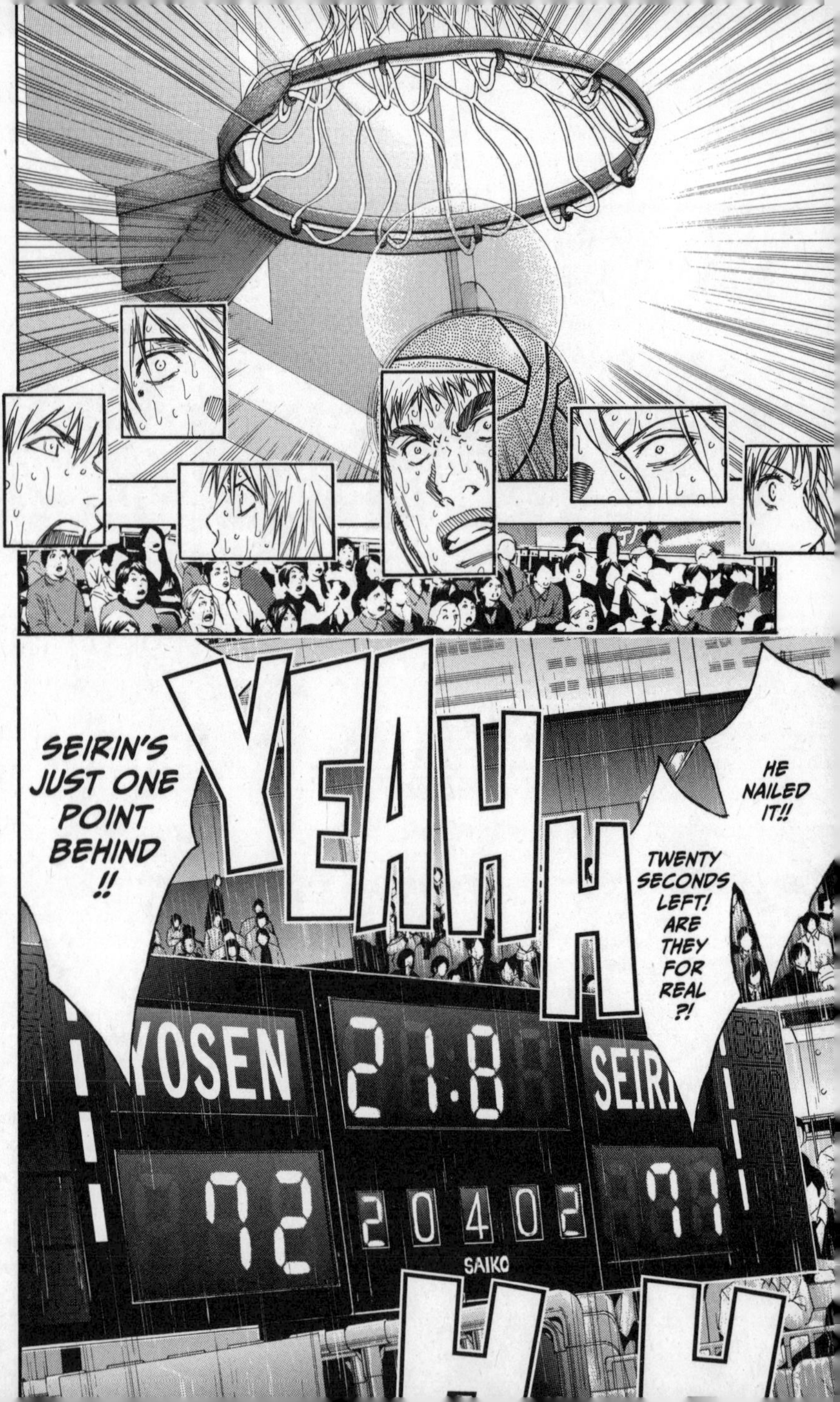
HE NAILED IT!!
TWENTY SECONDS LEFT! ARE THEY FOR REAL?!
YEAHH
SEIRIN'S JUST ONE POINT BEHIND!!
YOSEN
21.8
72
71
SAIKO

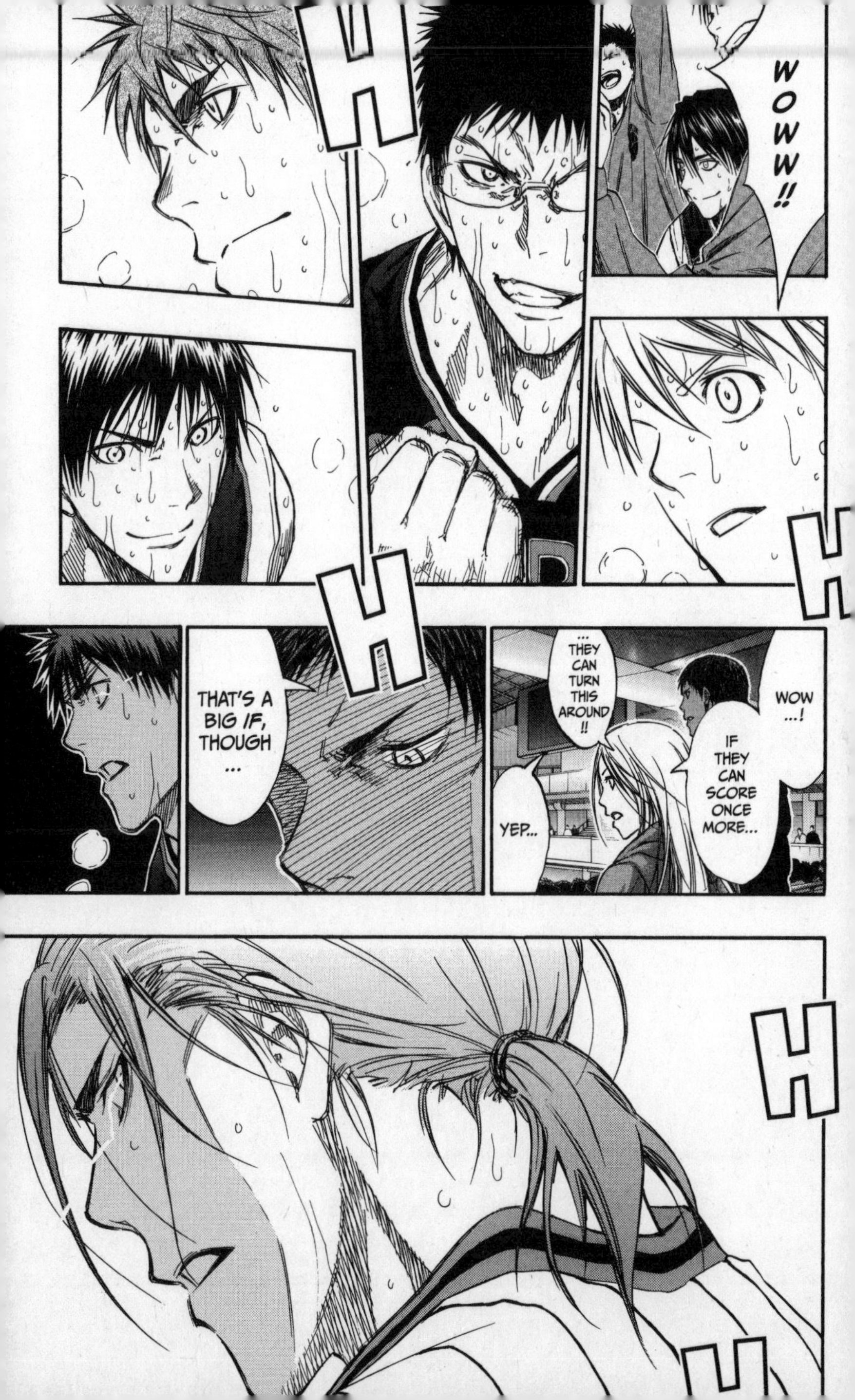
WOWWW!!
WOW ...!
IF THEY CAN SCORE ONCE MORE...
... THEY CAN TURN THIS AROUND!!
YEP...
THAT'S A BIG IF, THOUGH ...

KUROKO'S BASKETBALL BLOOPERS TAKE 1

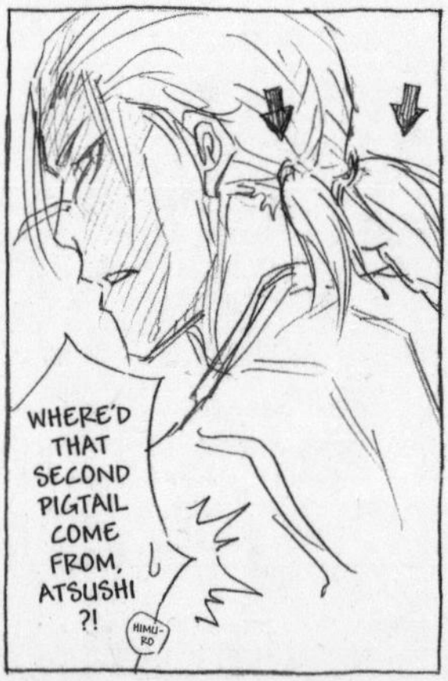
WHERE'D THAT SECOND PIGTAIL COME FROM, ATSUSHI ?!
HIMU-RO

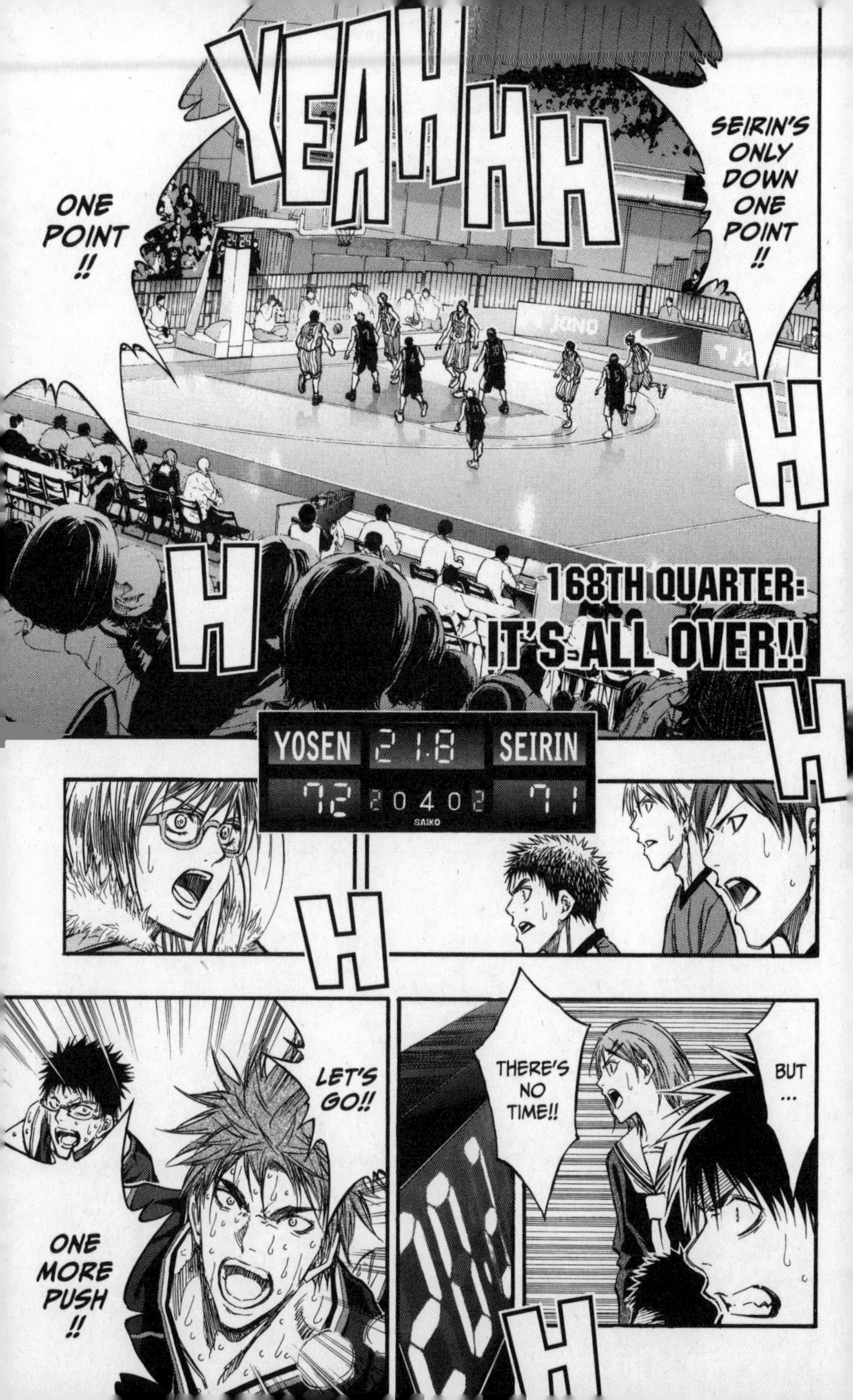
YEAHHH
SEIRIN'S ONLY DOWN ONE POINT!!
ONE POINT!!
HHHH
168TH QUARTER:
IT'S ALL OVER!!
YOSEN 21.8 SEIRIN
72 2 0 4 0 2 71
SAIKO
BUT ...
THERE'S NO TIME!!
LET'S GO!!
ONE MORE PUSH!!

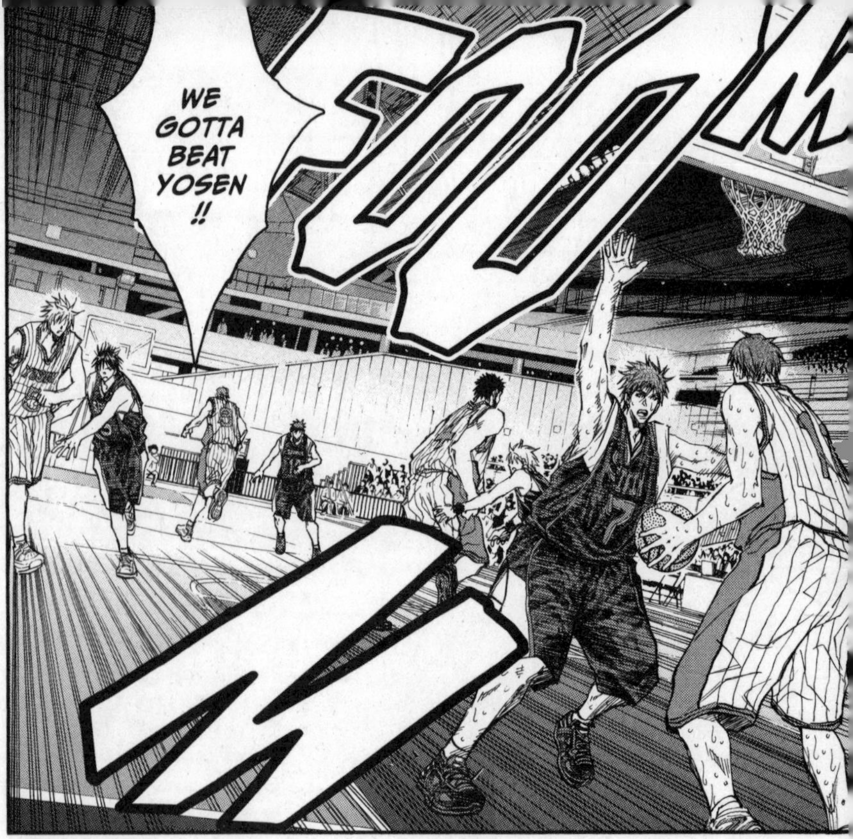
WE GOTTA BEAT YOSEN !!

*The inbounding team must pass the ball in play within five seconds.

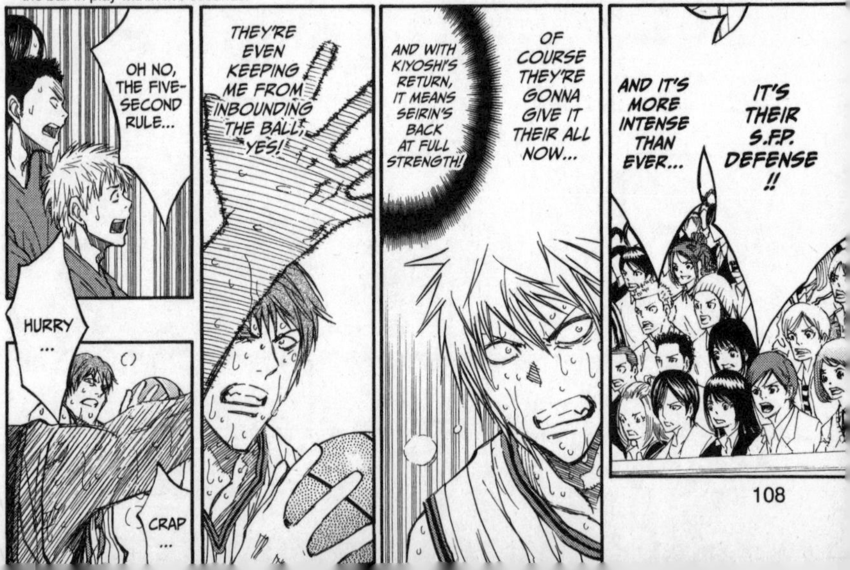
IT'S THEIR S.F.P. DEFENSE !!
AND IT'S MORE INTENSE THAN EVER...
OF COURSE THEY'RE GONNA GIVE IT THEIR ALL NOW...
AND WITH KIYOSHI'S RETURN, IT MEANS SEIRIN'S BACK AT FULL STRENGTH!
THEY'RE EVEN KEEPING ME FROM INBOUNDING THE BALL, YES!
OH NO, THE FIVE-SECOND RULE...
HURRY ...
CRAP ...

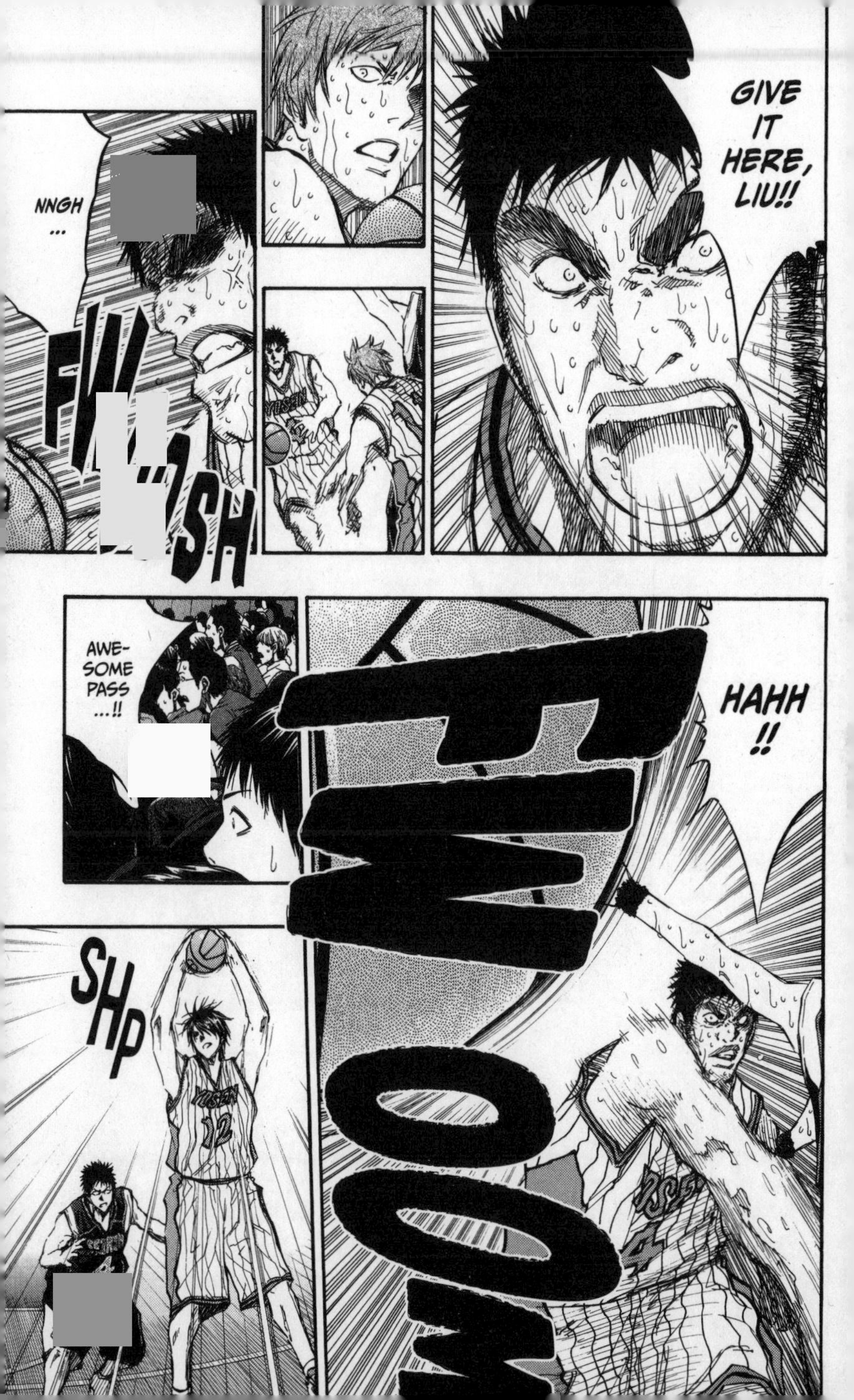
GIVE IT HERE, LIU!!
NNGH ...
HAHH !!
AWE-SOME PASS ...!!
SHP

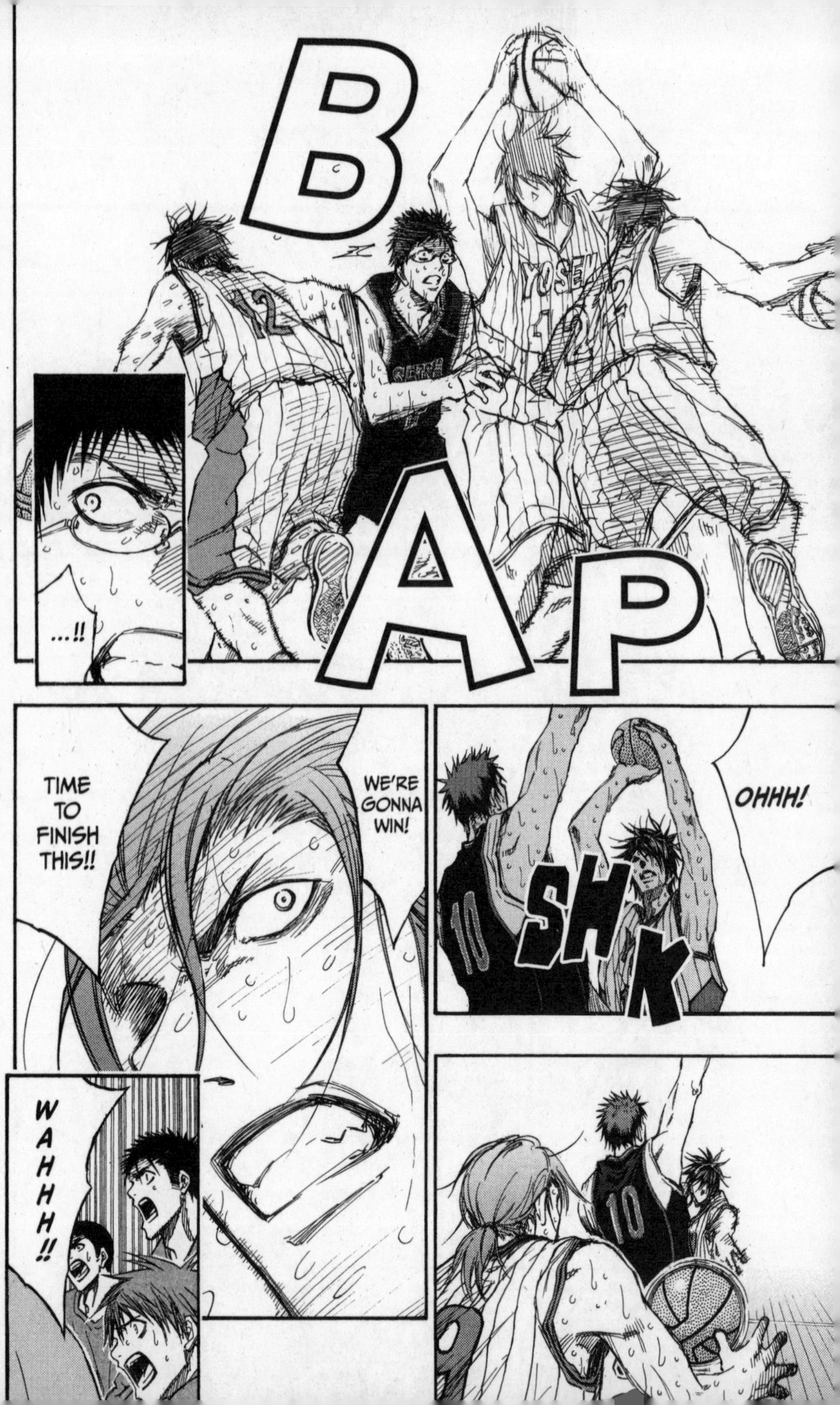
BAP
...!!
OHHH!
SHK
WE'RE GONNA WIN!
TIME TO FINISH THIS!!
WAHHHH!!

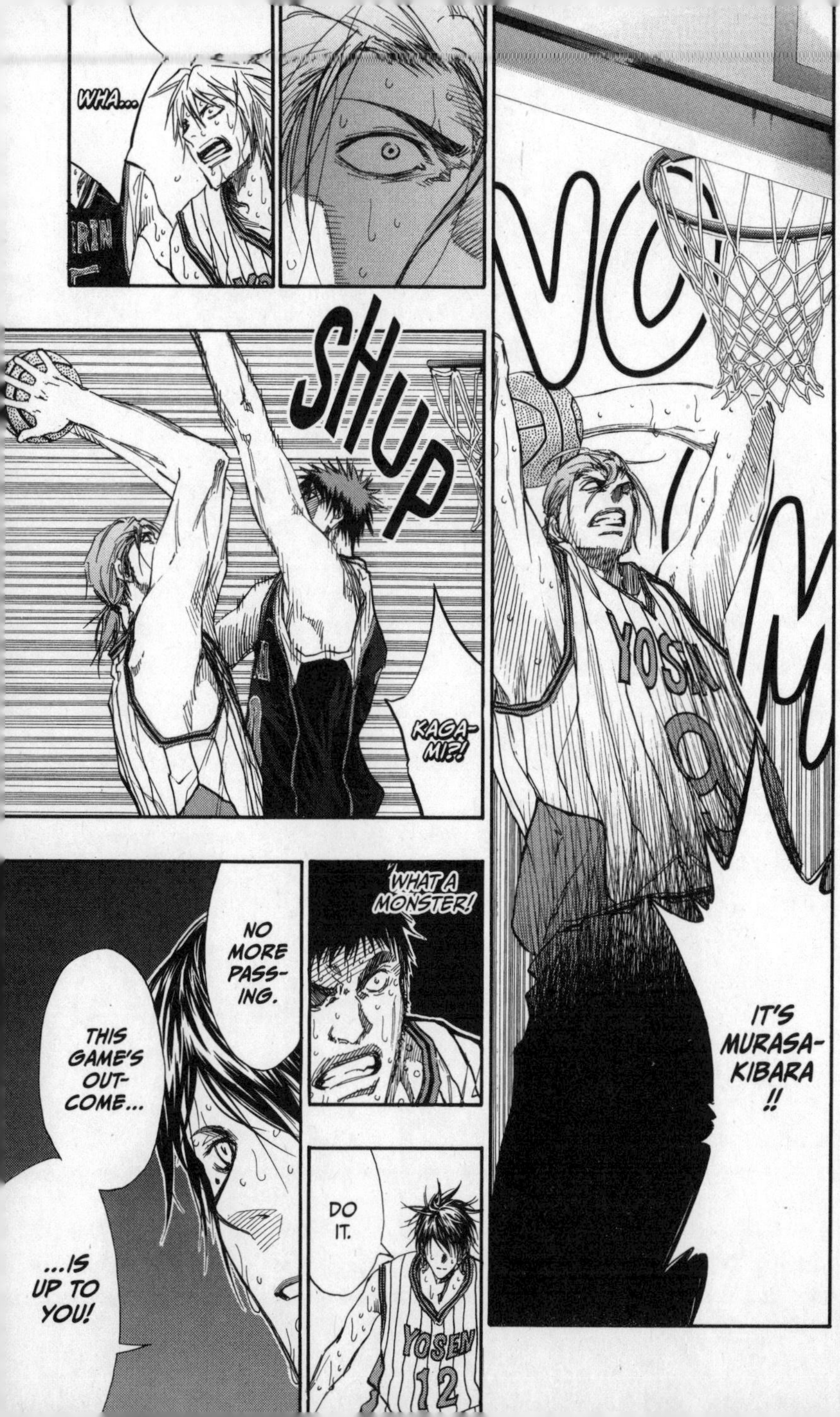

IT'S MURASAKIBARA!!
WHA...
SHUP
KAGAMI?!
WHAT A MONSTER!
DO IT.
NO MORE PASSING.
THIS GAME'S OUTCOME...
...IS UP TO YOU!

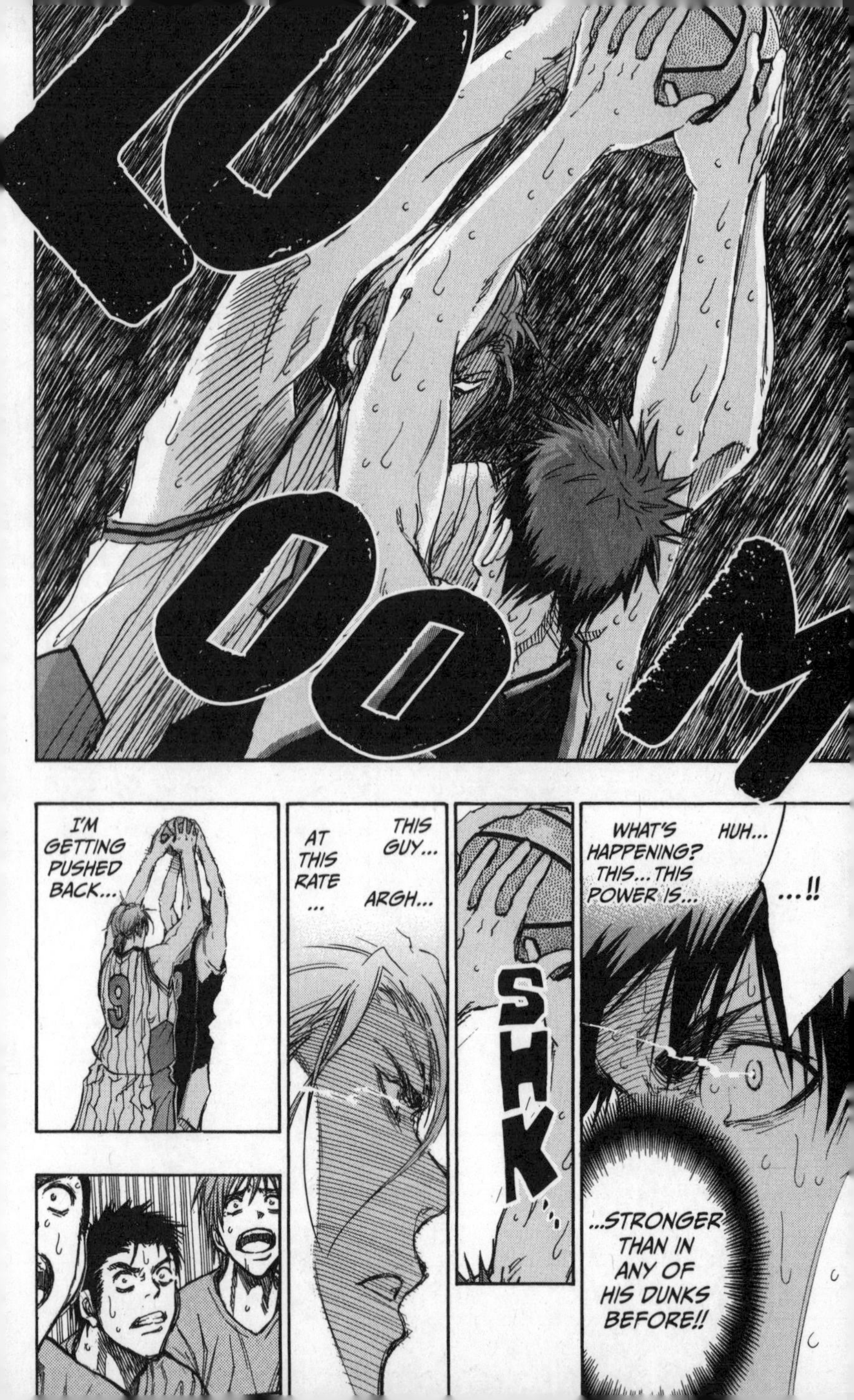
DOOM
HUH...
...!!
WHAT'S HAPPENING? THIS...THIS POWER IS...
...STRONGER THAN IN ANY OF HIS DUNKS BEFORE!!
SHK...
THIS GUY...
ARGH...
AT THIS RATE...
I'M GETTING PUSHED BACK...

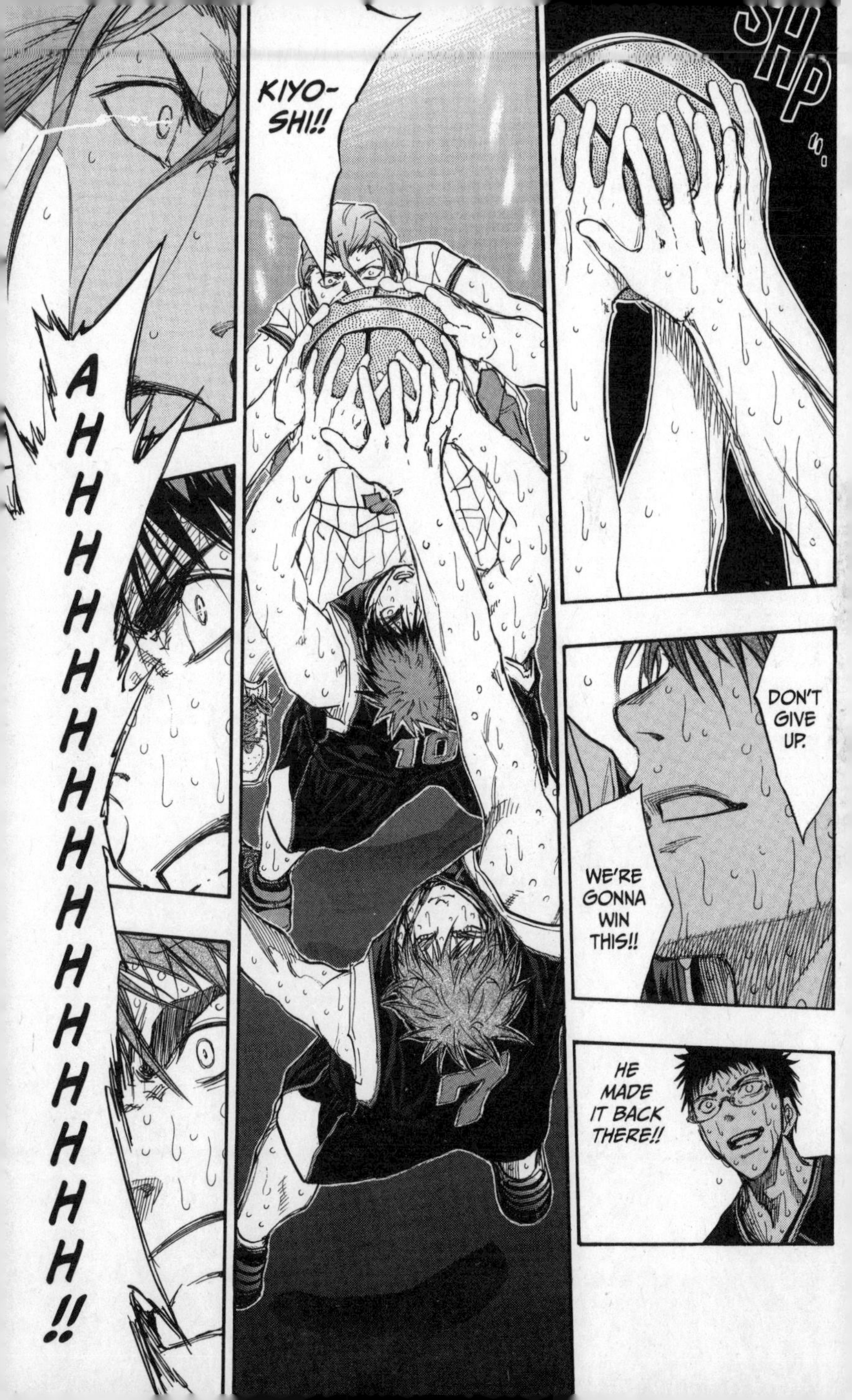
SHP
DON'T GIVE UP.
WE'RE GONNA WIN THIS!!
HE MADE IT BACK THERE!!
KIYO-SHI!!
AHHHHHHHHHHHHHHHHH!!

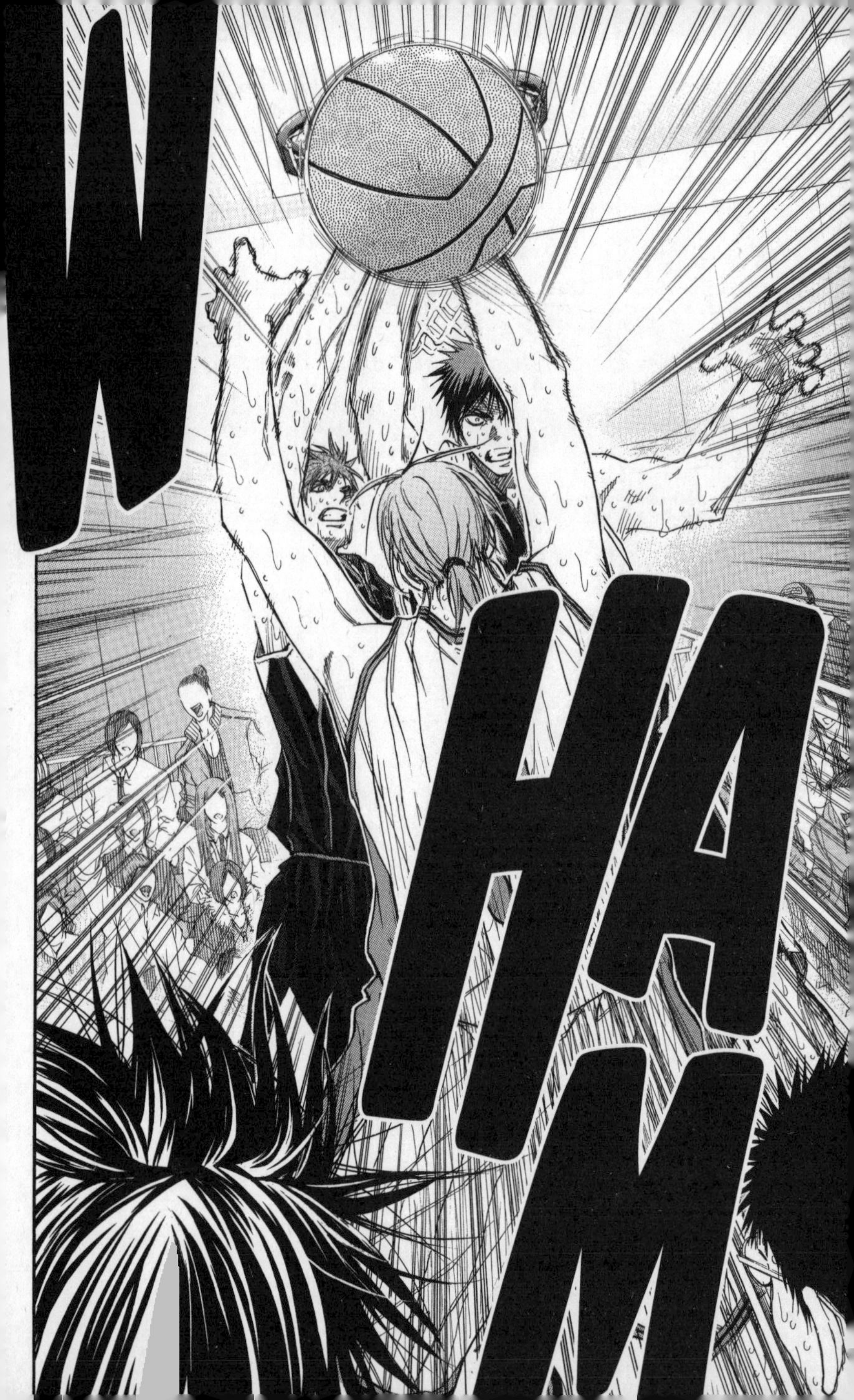
WHAM

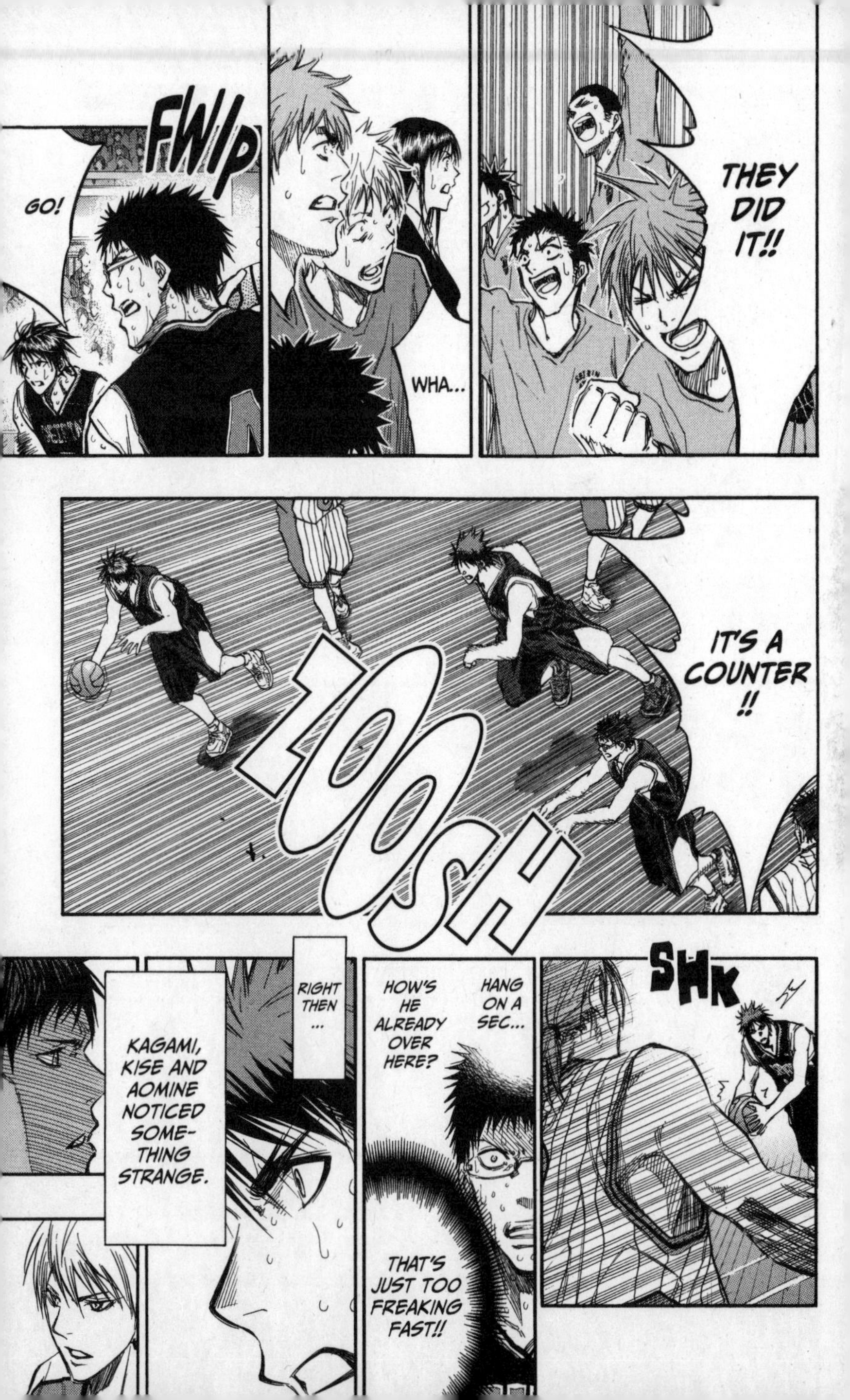
THEY DID IT!!
WHA...
FWIP
GO!
IT'S A COUNTER !!
ZOOSH
SHK
HANG ON A SEC...
HOW'S HE ALREADY OVER HERE?
THAT'S JUST TOO FREAKING FAST!!
RIGHT THEN ...
KAGAMI, KISE AND AOMINE NOTICED SOMETHING STRANGE.

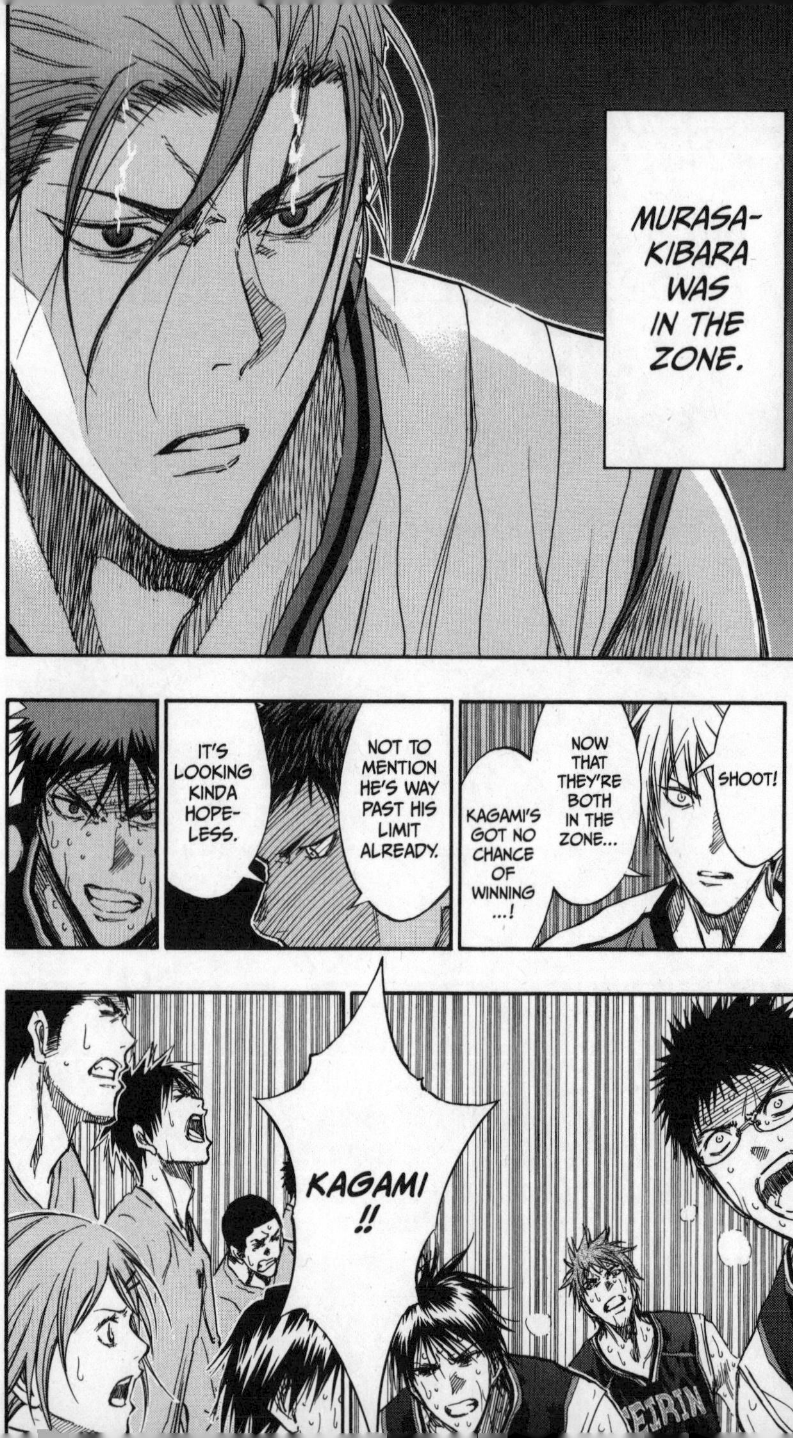
MURASAKIBARA WAS IN THE ZONE.
SHOOT!
NOW THAT THEY'RE BOTH IN THE ZONE...
KAGAMI'S GOT NO CHANCE OF WINNING ...!
NOT TO MENTION HE'S WAY PAST HIS LIMIT ALREADY.
IT'S LOOKING KINDA HOPELESS.
KAGAMI !!

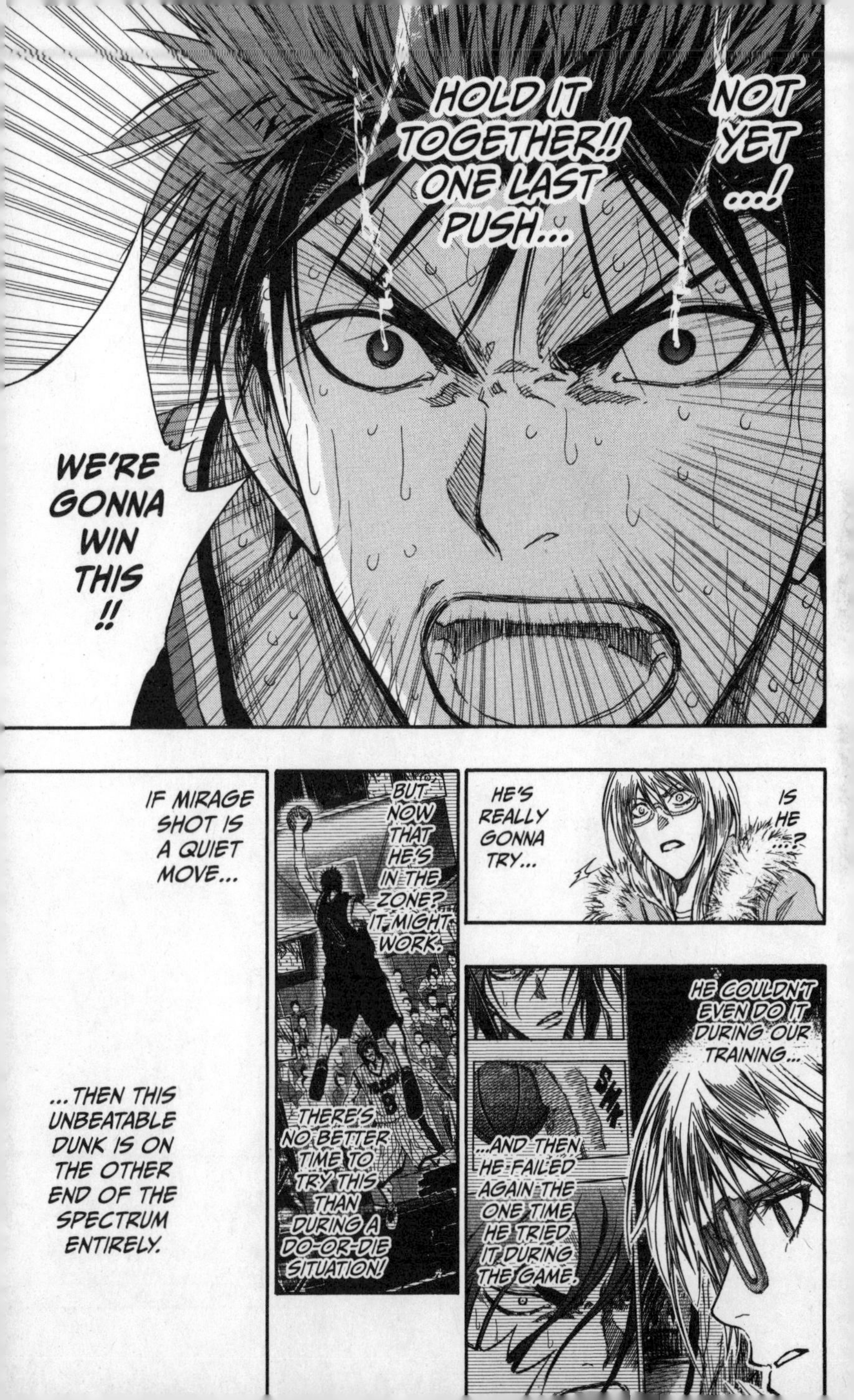
NOT YET ...!
HOLD IT TOGETHER!! ONE LAST PUSH...
WE'RE GONNA WIN THIS !!
IS HE ...?
HE'S REALLY GONNA TRY...
HE COULDN'T EVEN DO IT DURING OUR TRAINING...
SHK
...AND THEN HE FAILED AGAIN THE ONE TIME HE TRIED IT DURING THE GAME.
BUT NOW THAT HE'S IN THE ZONE? IT MIGHT WORK.
THERE'S NO BETTER TIME TO TRY THIS THAN DURING A DO-OR-DIE SITUATION!
IF MIRAGE SHOT IS A QUIET MOVE...
...THEN THIS UNBEATABLE DUNK IS ON THE OTHER END OF THE SPECTRUM ENTIRELY.

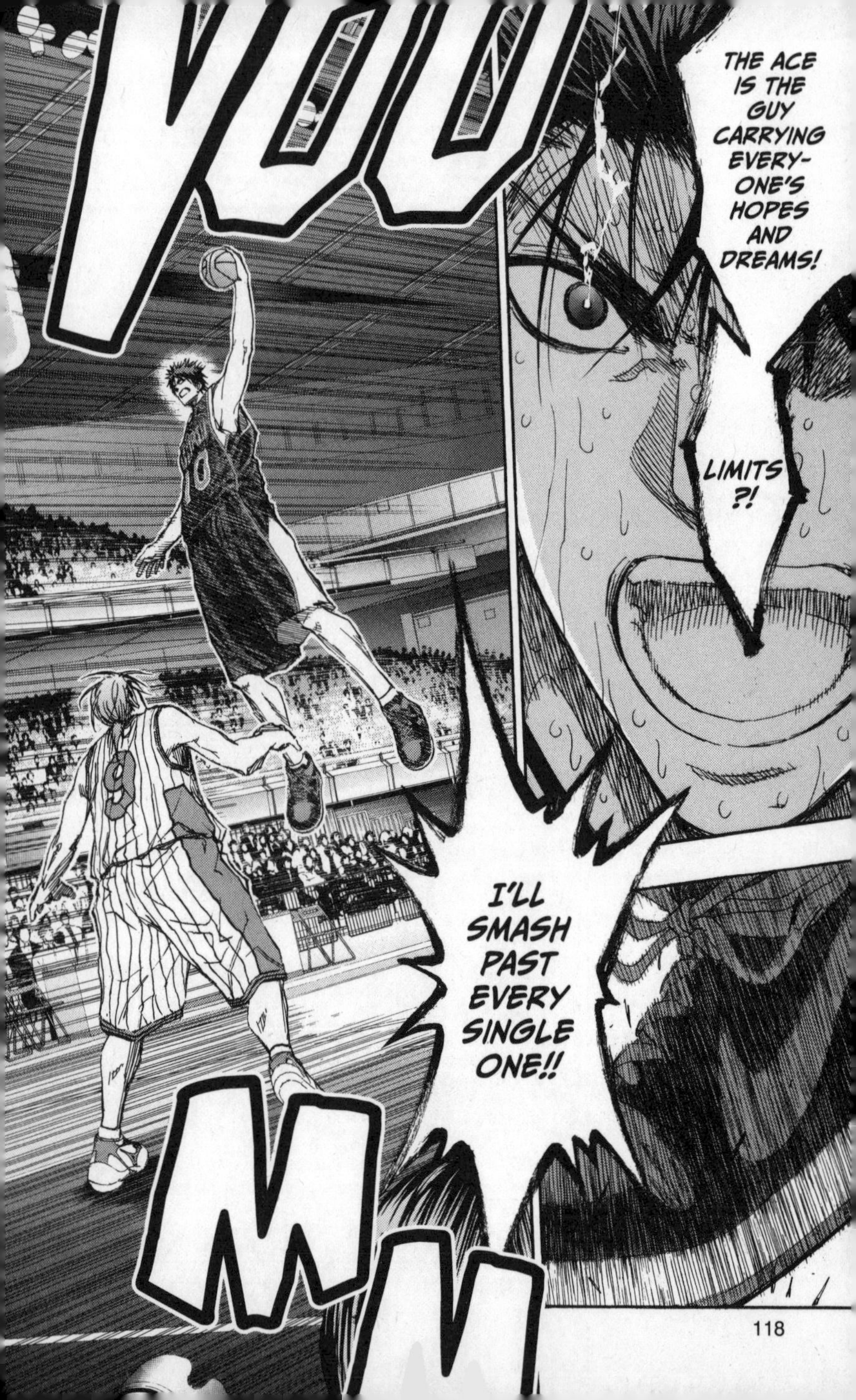
THE ACE IS THE GUY CARRYING EVERY-ONE'S HOPES AND DREAMS!
LIMITS?!
I'LL SMASH PAST EVERY SINGLE ONE!!

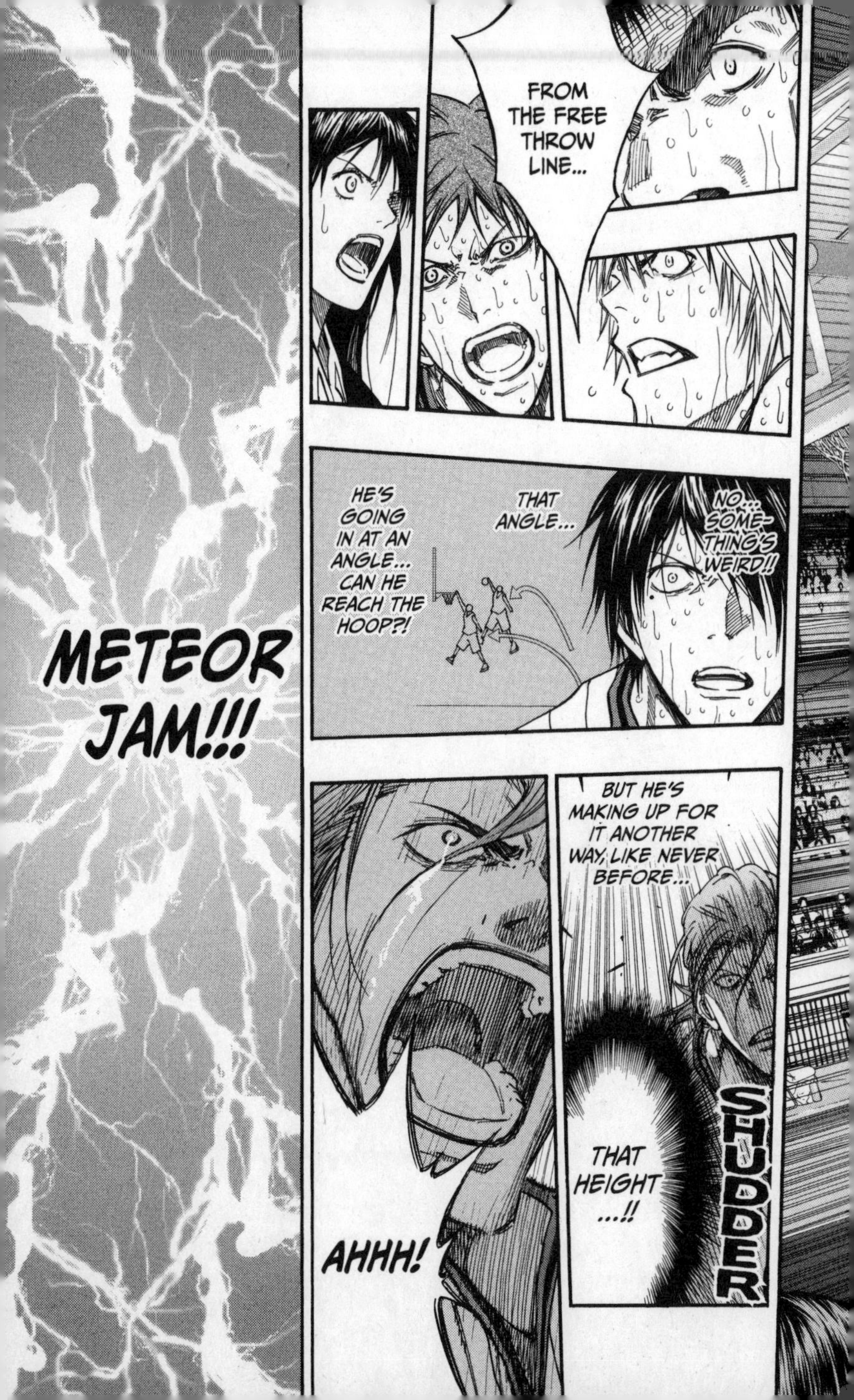
FROM THE FREE THROW LINE...
NO... SOME-THING'S WEIRD!!
THAT ANGLE...
HE'S GOING IN AT AN ANGLE... CAN HE REACH THE HOOP?!
BUT HE'S MAKING UP FOR IT ANOTHER WAY, LIKE NEVER BEFORE...
SHUDDER
THAT HEIGHT ...!!
AHHH!
METEOR JAM!!!

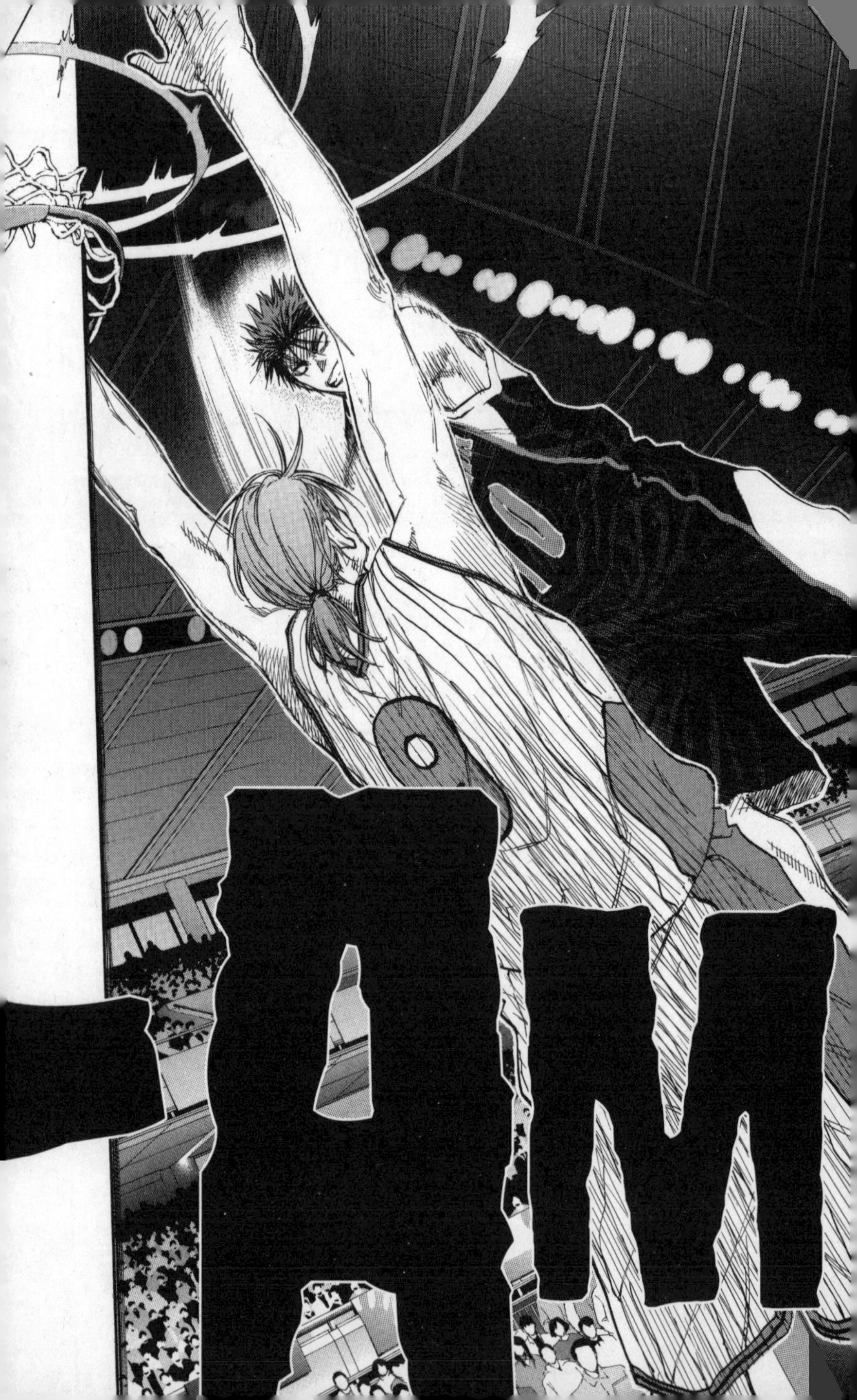
AM

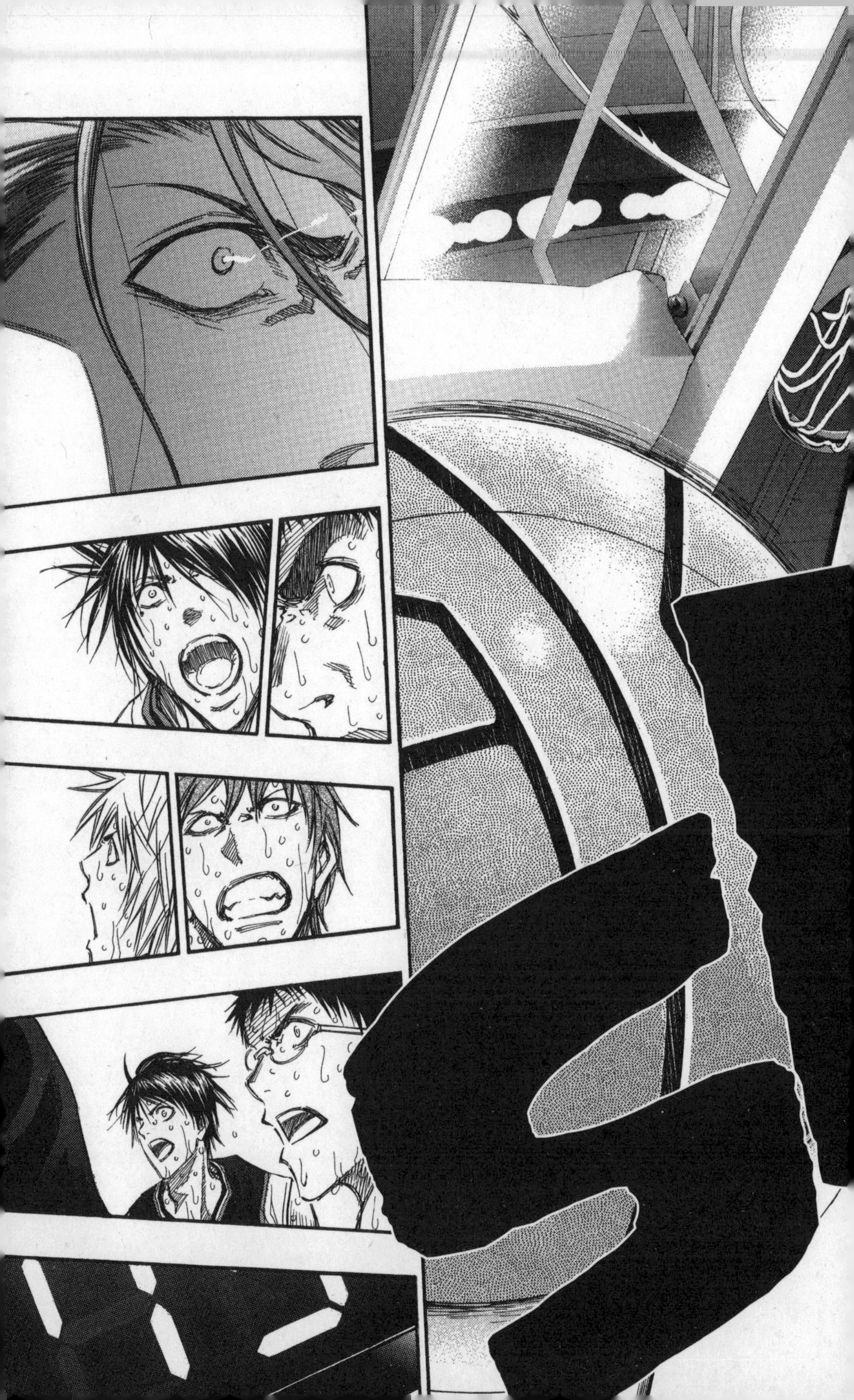

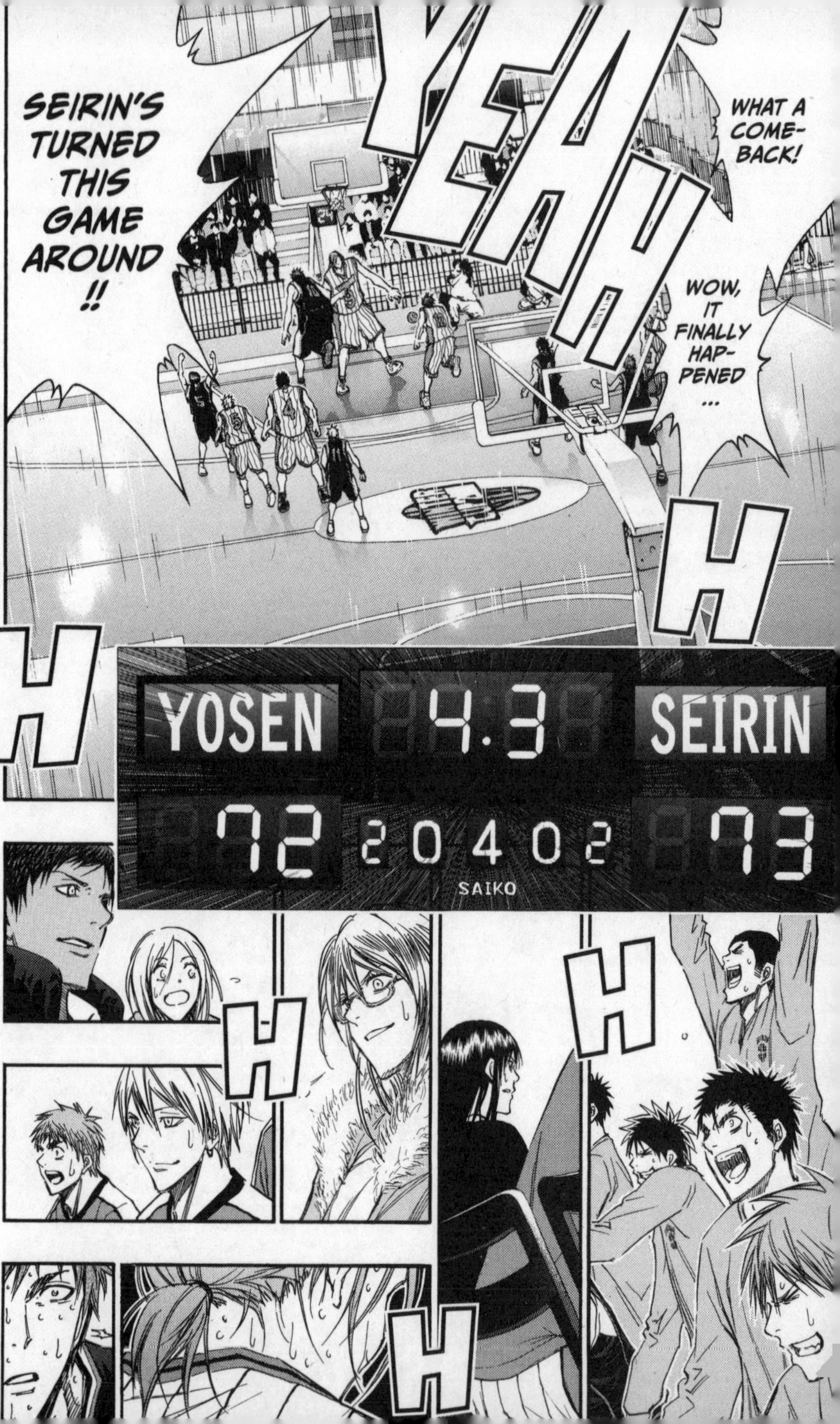
WHAT A COME-BACK!
WOW, IT FINALLY HAP-PENED...
YEAH
SEIRIN'S TURNED THIS GAME AROUND!!
H
H
YOSEN
SEIRIN
72
73
SAIKO
H
H
H

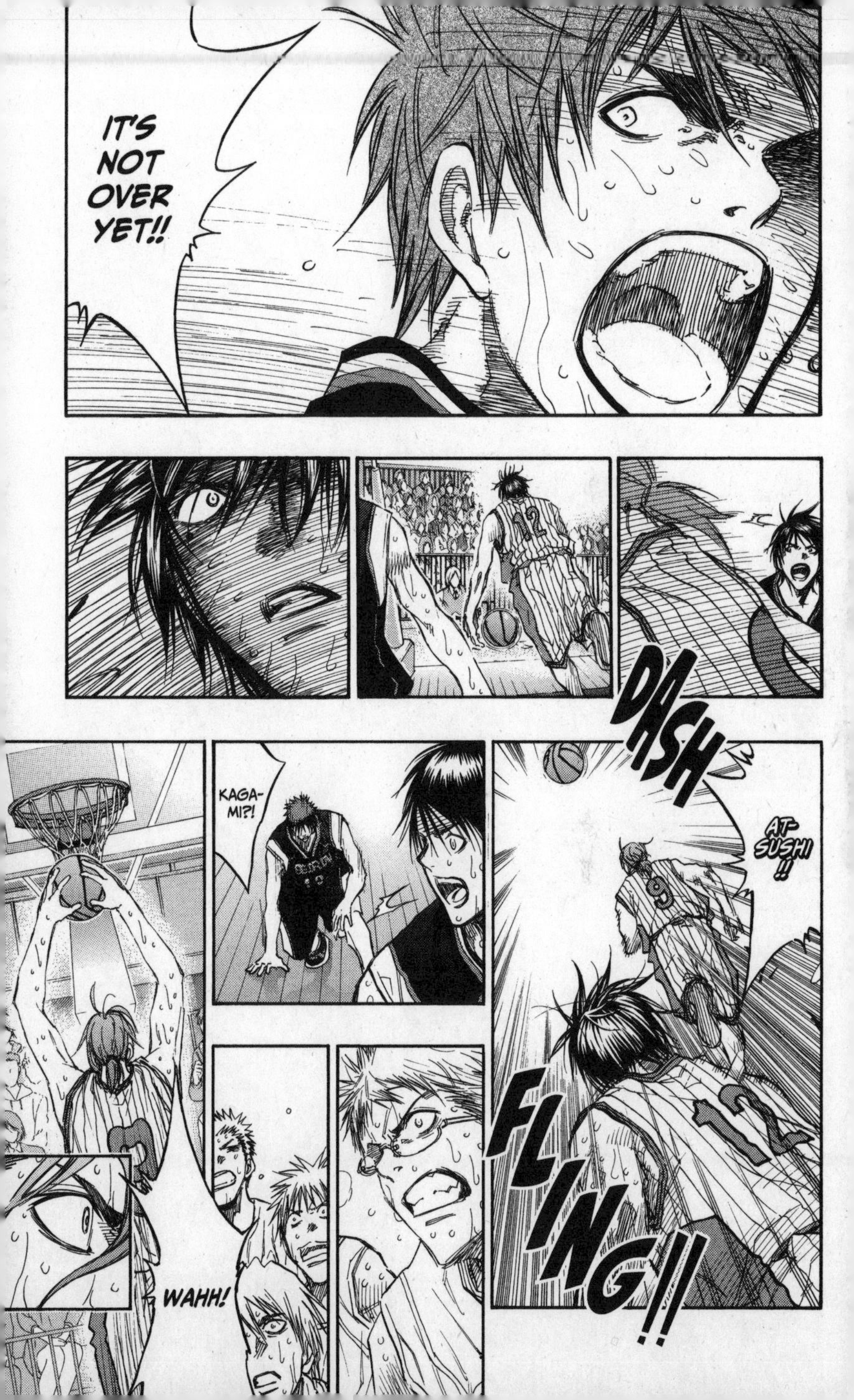
IT'S NOT OVER YET!!
DASH
AT-SUSHI!!
FLING!!
KAGA-MI?!
WAHH!

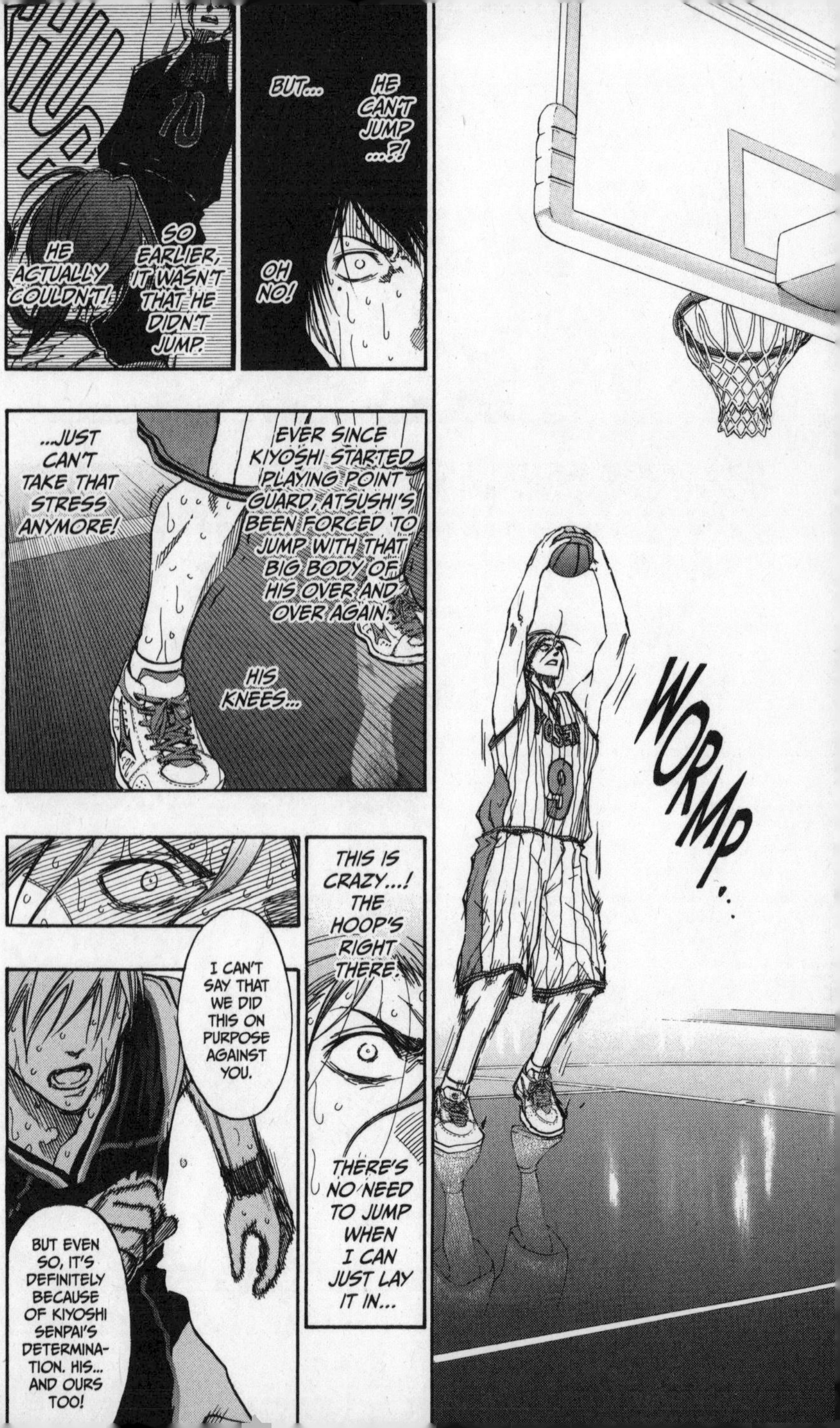
WORMP...
BUT... HE CAN'T JUMP...?!
OH NO!
SO EARLIER, IT WASN'T THAT HE DIDN'T JUMP.
HE ACTUALLY COULDN'T!
EVER SINCE KIYOSHI STARTED PLAYING POINT GUARD, ATSUSHI'S BEEN FORCED TO JUMP WITH THAT BIG BODY OF HIS OVER AND OVER AGAIN.
...JUST CAN'T TAKE THAT STRESS ANYMORE!
HIS KNEES...
THIS IS CRAZY...! THE HOOP'S RIGHT THERE.
THERE'S NO NEED TO JUMP WHEN I CAN JUST LAY IT IN...
I CAN'T SAY THAT WE DID THIS ON PURPOSE AGAINST YOU.
BUT EVEN SO, IT'S DEFINITELY BECAUSE OF KIYOSHI SENPAI'S DETERMINATION. HIS... AND OURS TOO!

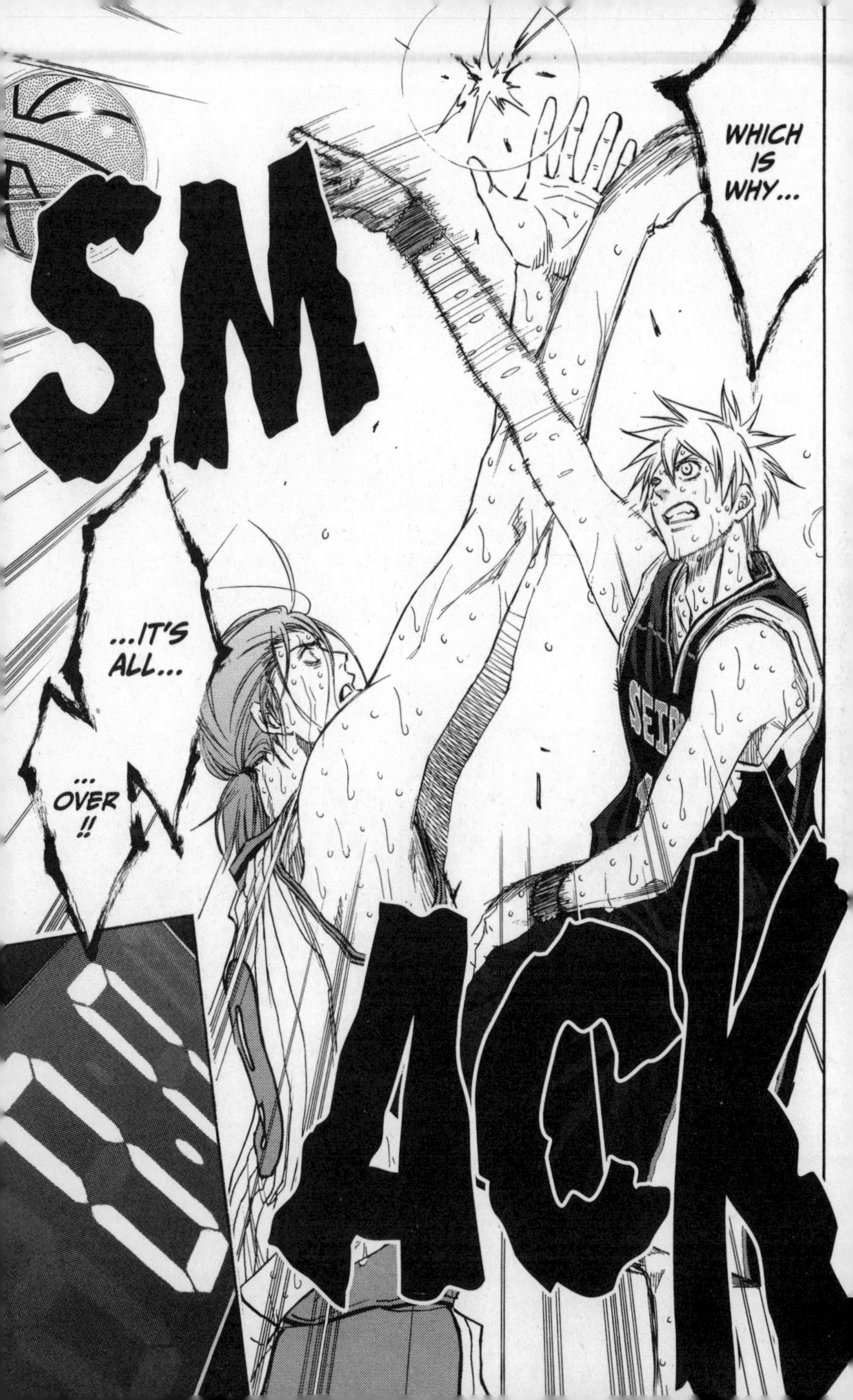
WHICH IS WHY...
SMACK
...IT'S ALL...
...OVER!!

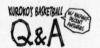

KUROKO'S BASKETBALL Q&A (W/ HALFWAY-DECENT ANSWERS)

Q. CAN YOU TELL US THE BEST PUN IZUKI'S EVER COME UP WITH?
(BOWL CUT BOY from GIFU PREFECTURE)

A. I ONCE BOUGHT A BROKEN TRAFFIC LIGHT FOR A GIRL I WAS DATING, BUT SHE GOT ANGRY AND SAID I WAS GIVING HER MIXED SIGNALS.

KUROKO'S BASKETBALL BLOOPERS (TAKE 9)

METEOR JAM?!
SOUNDS TASTY ...!!
NOT THAT SORTA JAM!!
DROOL...
AND STOP DROOLING!!

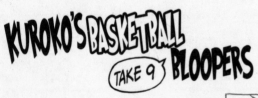

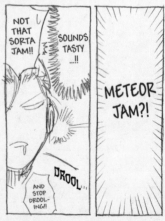

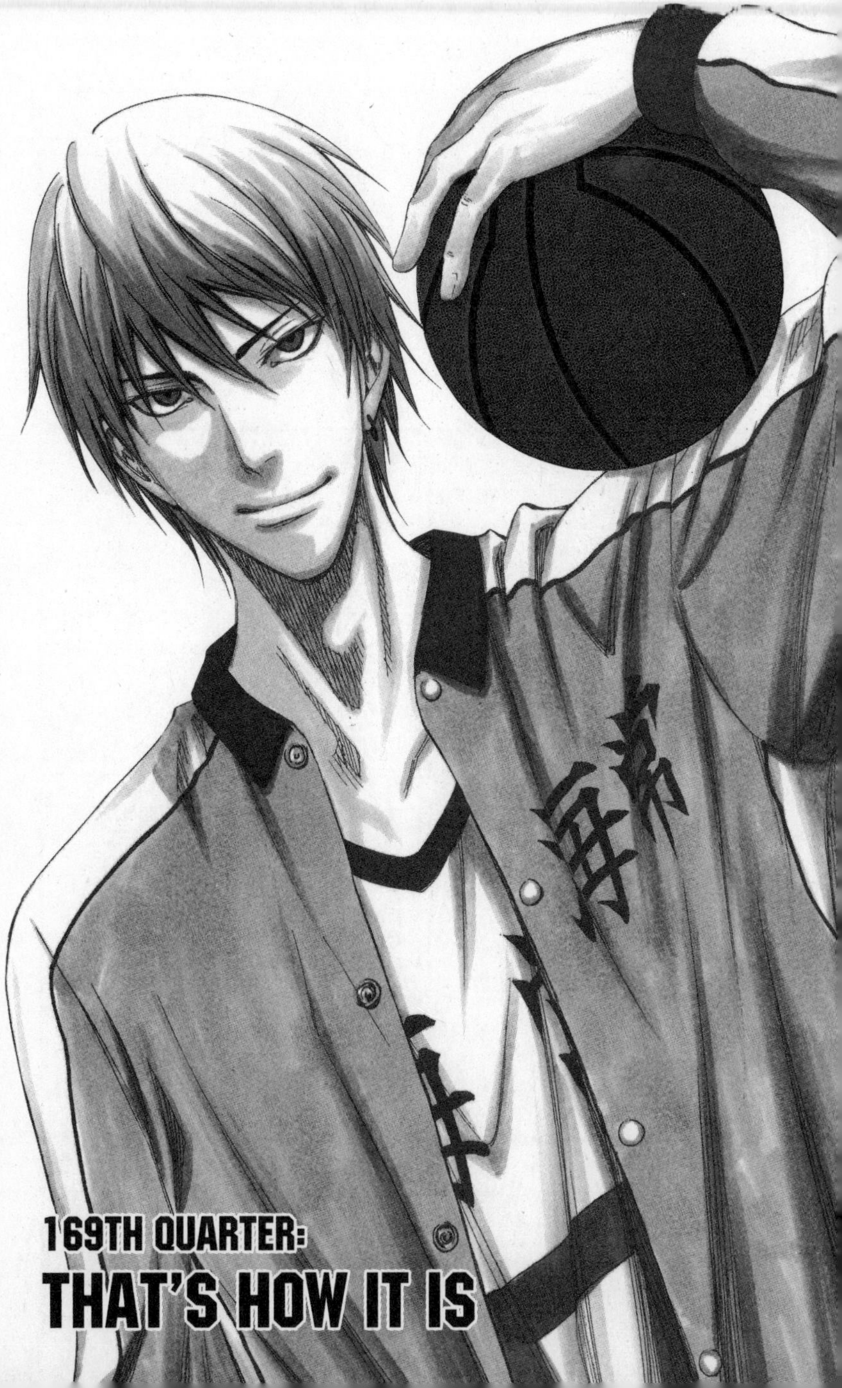

169TH QUARTER:
THAT'S HOW IT IS

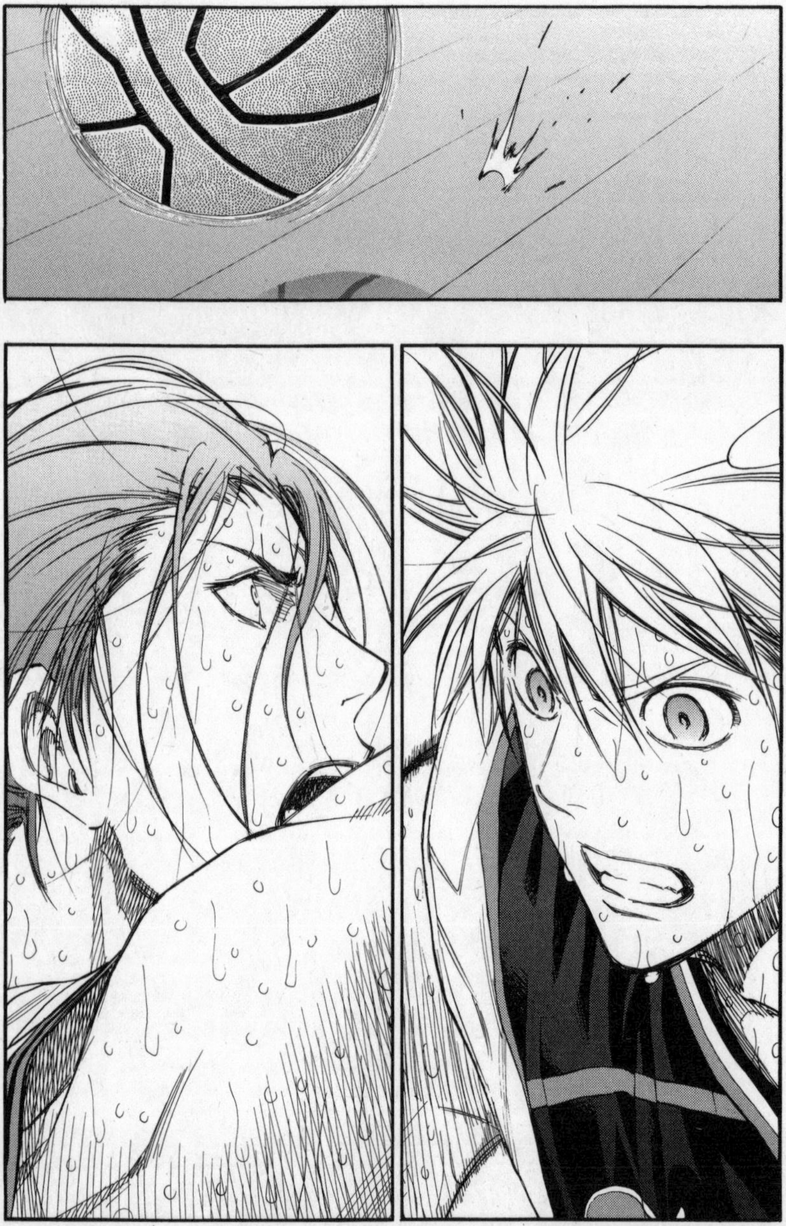

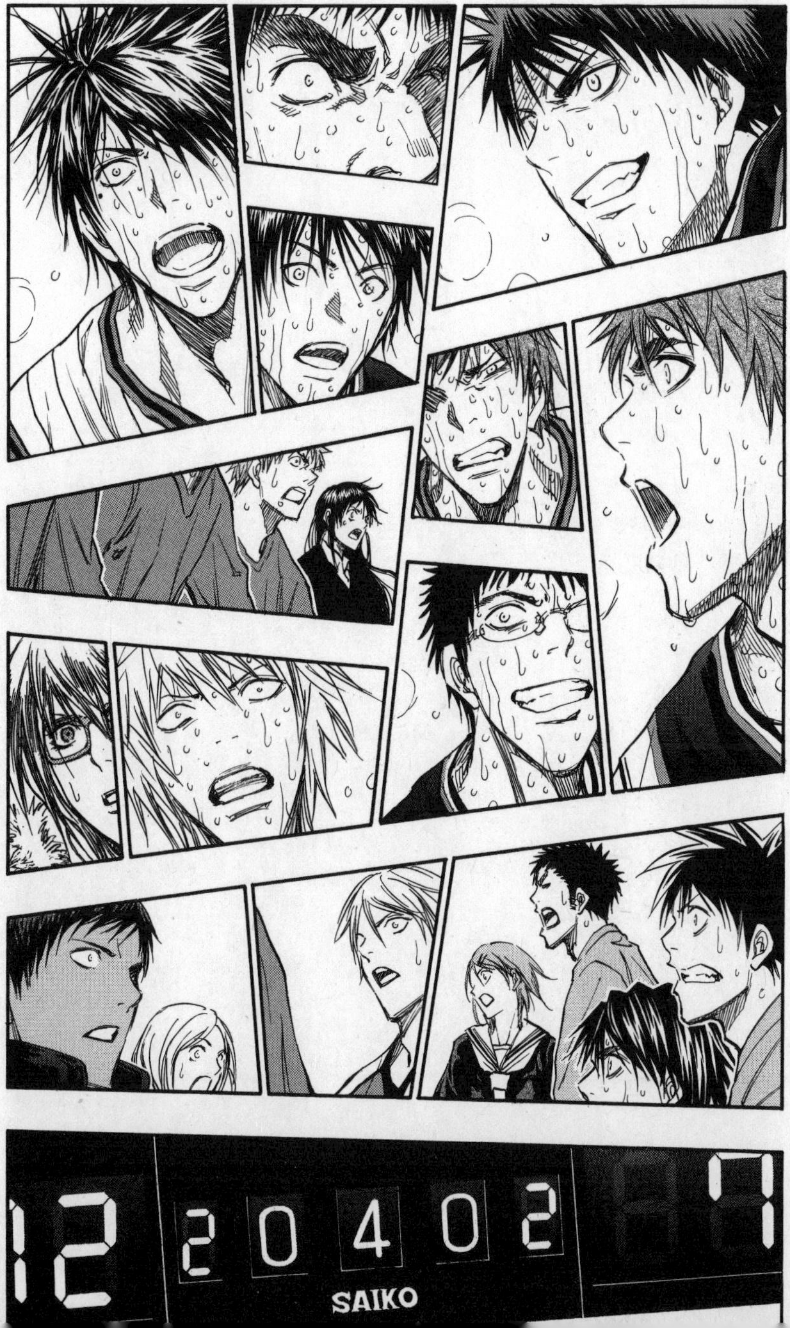
SAIKO

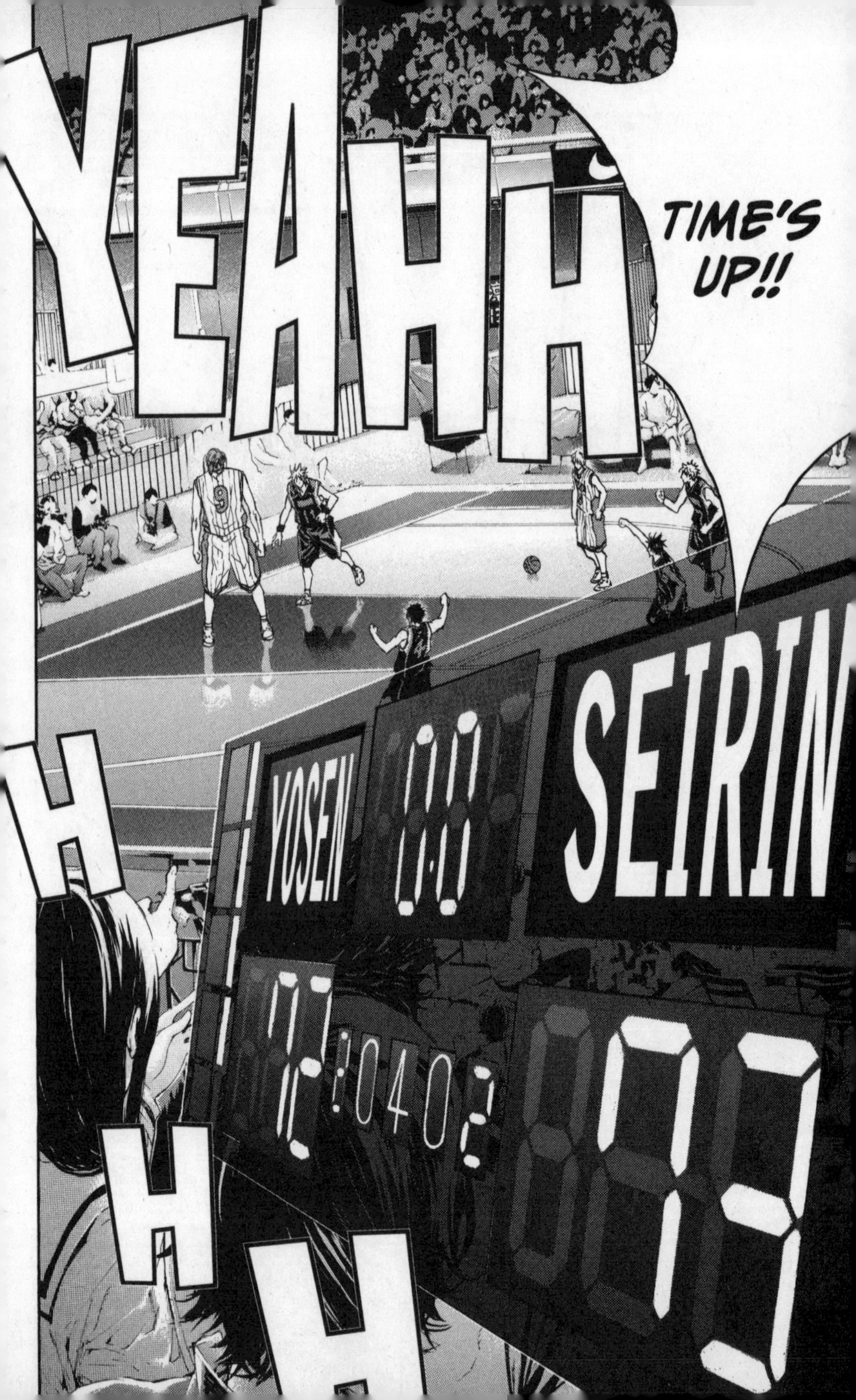
TIME'S UP!!
YEAHHHHH
SEIRIN
YOSEN

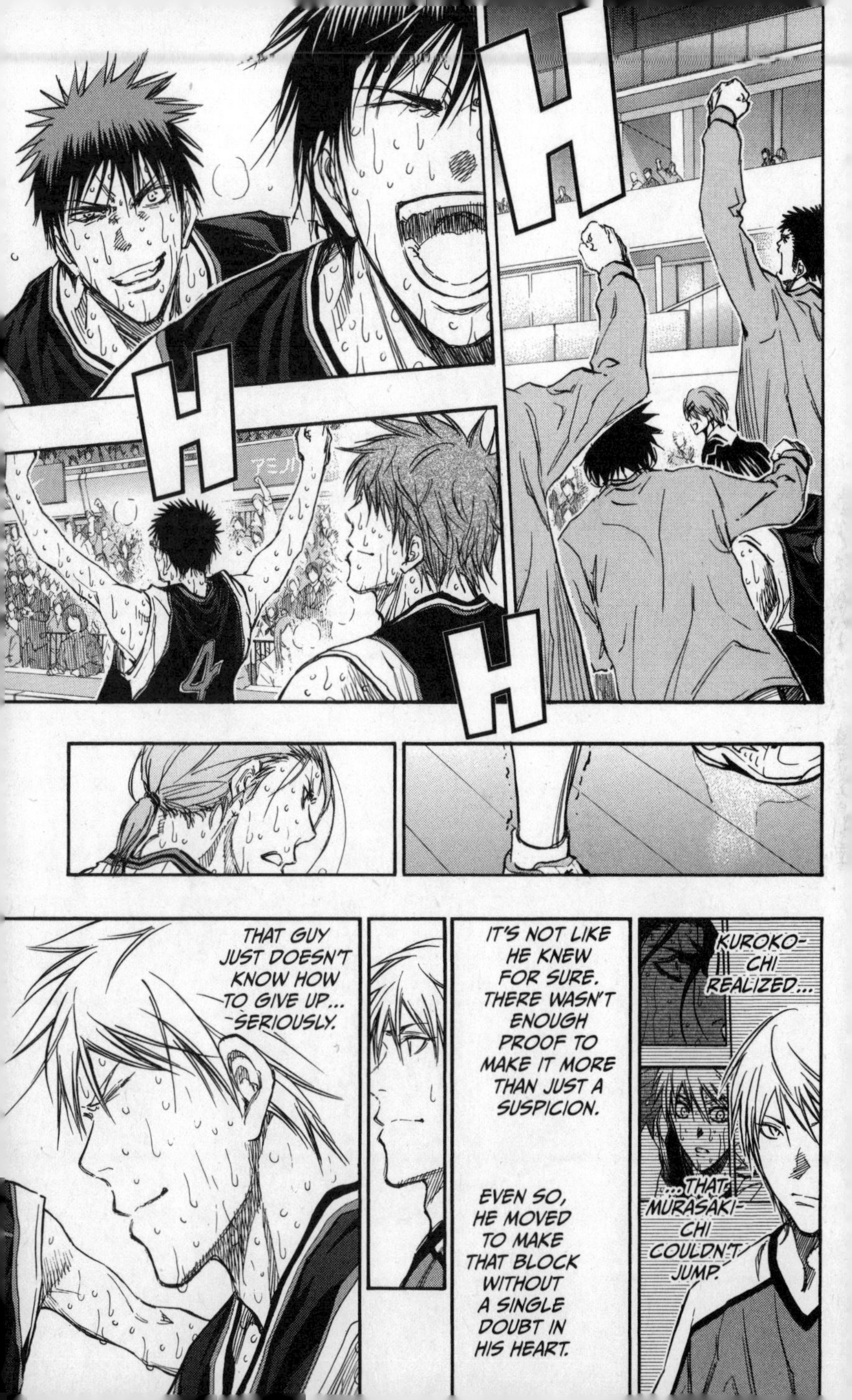
H
H
H
H
KUROKO-CHI REALIZED...
...THAT MURASAKI-CHI COULDN'T JUMP.
IT'S NOT LIKE HE KNEW FOR SURE. THERE WASN'T ENOUGH PROOF TO MAKE IT MORE THAN JUST A SUSPICION.
EVEN SO, HE MOVED TO MAKE THAT BLOCK WITHOUT A SINGLE DOUBT IN HIS HEART.
THAT GUY JUST DOESN'T KNOW HOW TO GIVE UP... SERIOUSLY.

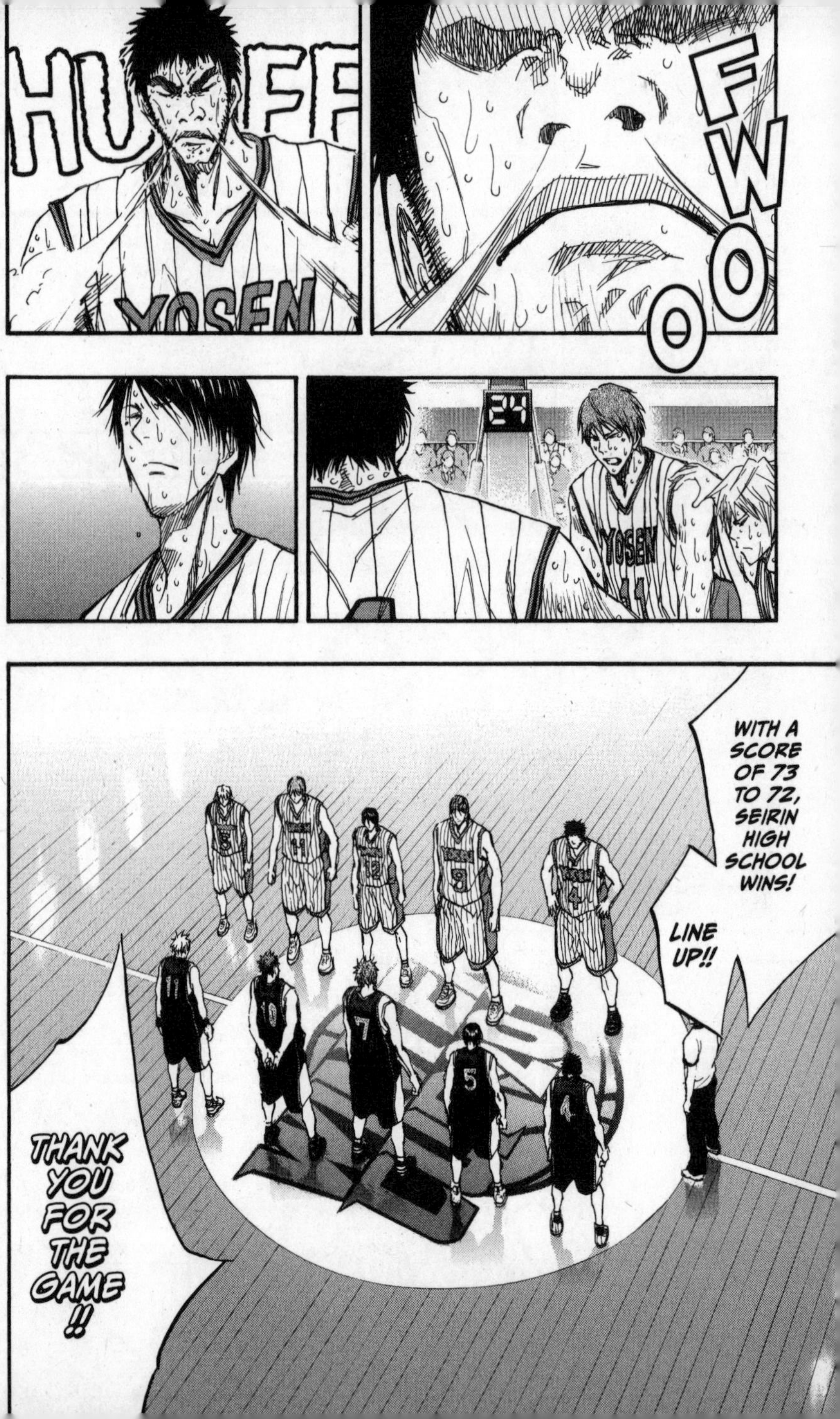
FWOO
HUFF
WITH A SCORE OF 73 TO 72, SEIRIN HIGH SCHOOL WINS!
LINE UP!!
THANK YOU FOR THE GAME!!

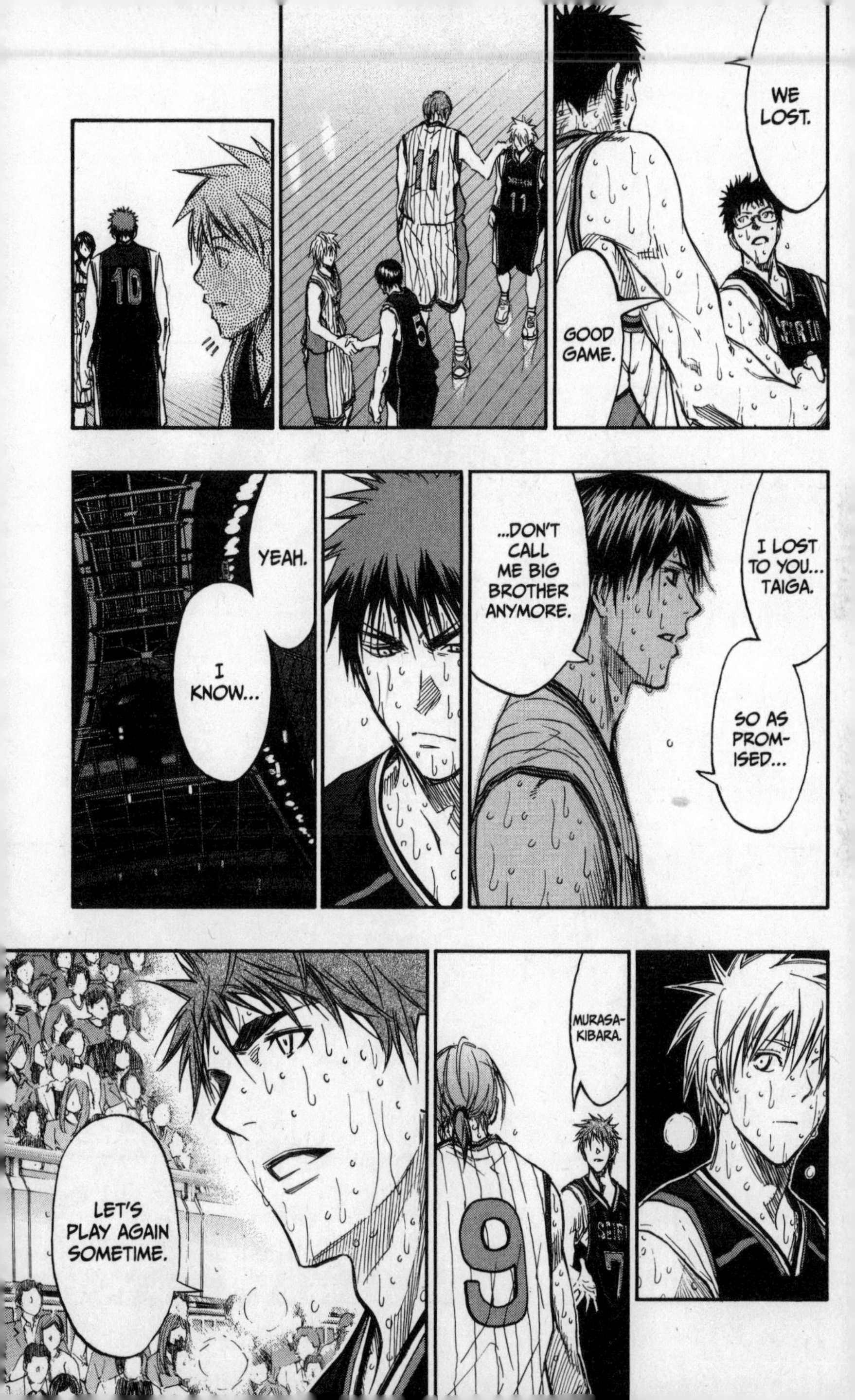
WE LOST.
GOOD GAME.
!!
I LOST TO YOU... TAIGA.
SO AS PROMISED...
...DON'T CALL ME BIG BROTHER ANYMORE.
YEAH.
I KNOW...
MURASA-KIBARA.
LET'S PLAY AGAIN SOMETIME.

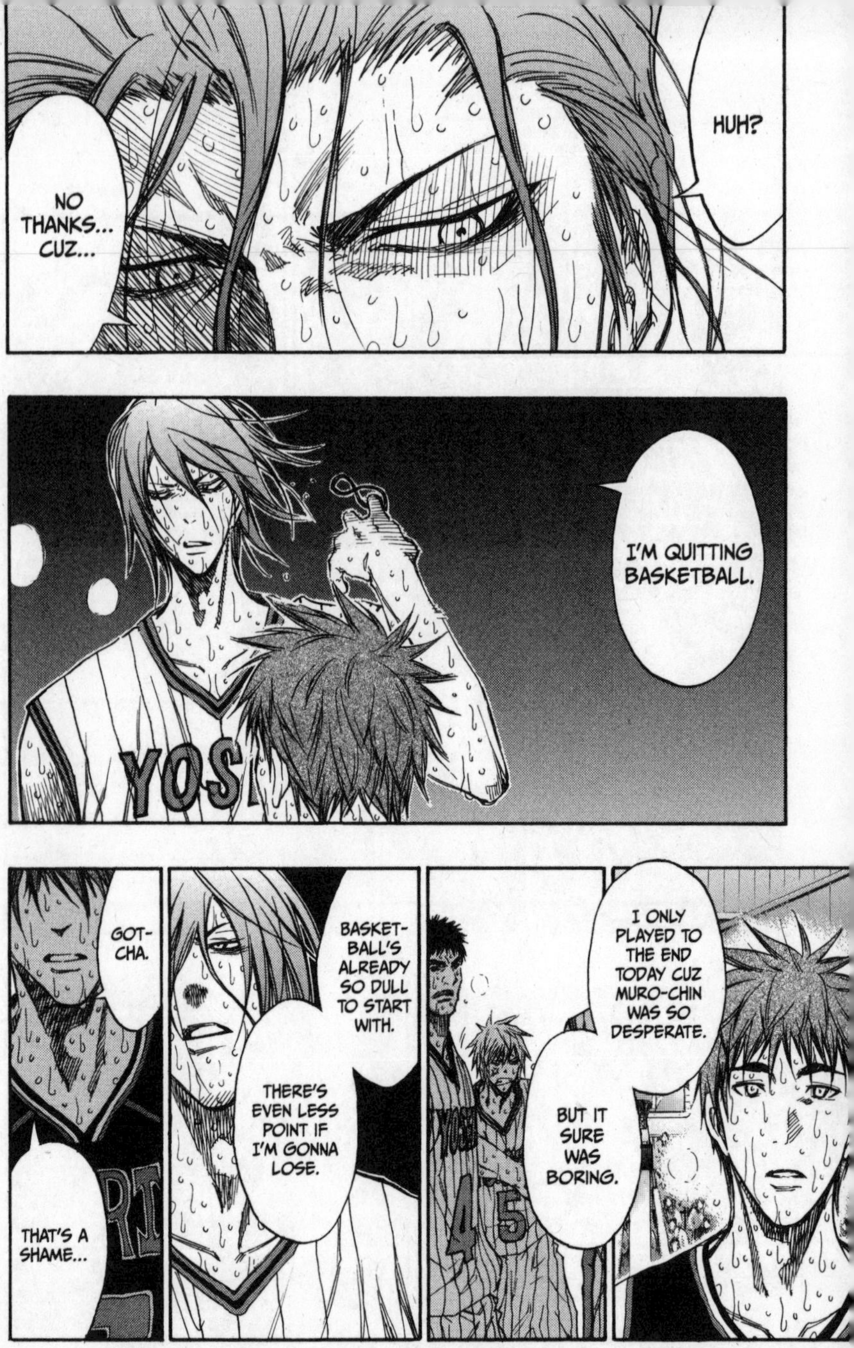
HUH?
NO THANKS... CUZ...
I'M QUITTING BASKETBALL.
I ONLY PLAYED TO THE END TODAY CUZ MURO-CHIN WAS SO DESPERATE.
BUT IT SURE WAS BORING.
BASKET-BALL'S ALREADY SO DULL TO START WITH.
THERE'S EVEN LESS POINT IF I'M GONNA LOSE.
GOT-CHA.
THAT'S A SHAME...

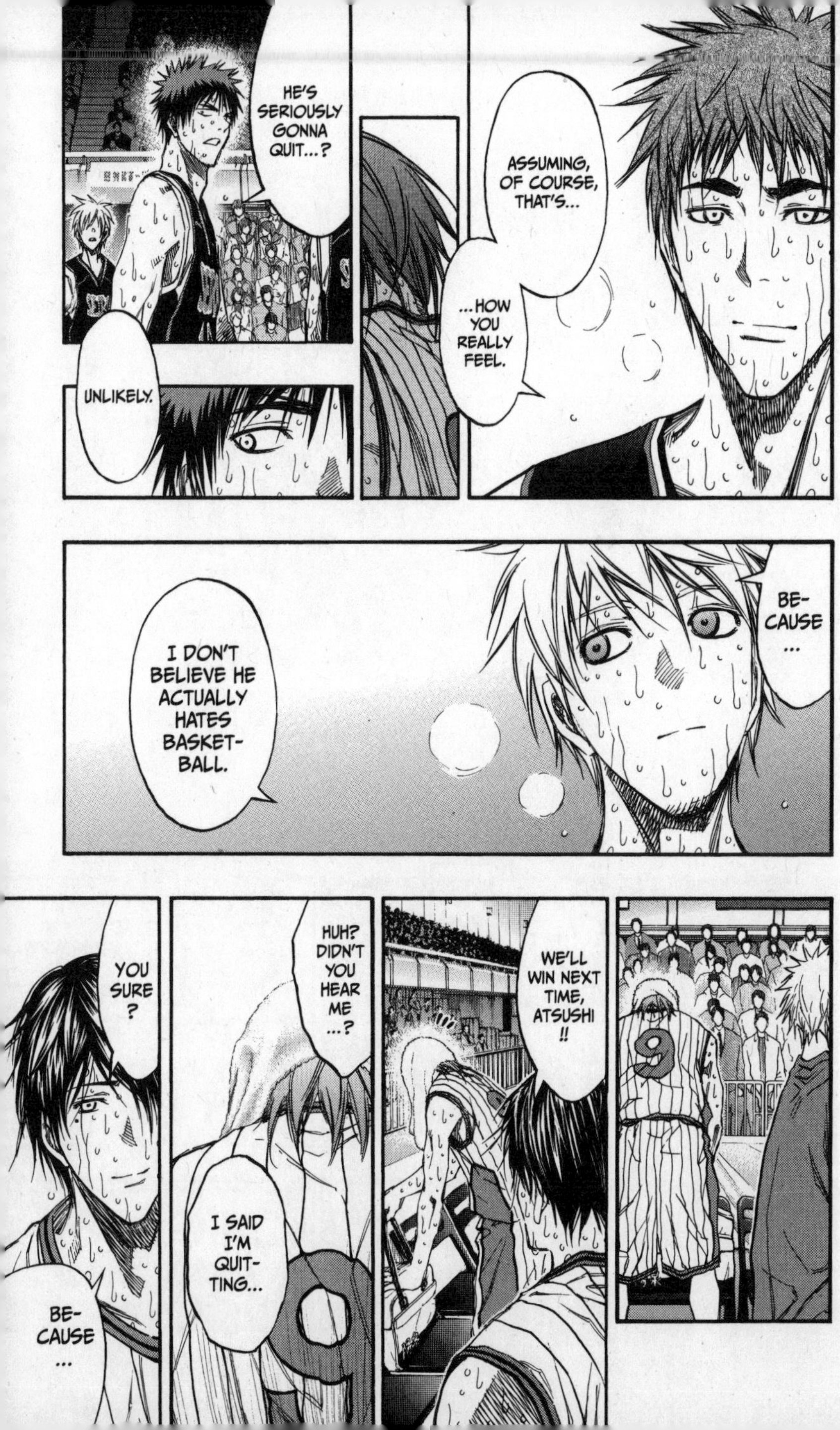
ASSUMING, OF COURSE, THAT'S...
...HOW YOU REALLY FEEL.
HE'S SERIOUSLY GONNA QUIT...?
UNLIKELY.
BE-CAUSE...
I DON'T BELIEVE HE ACTUALLY HATES BASKET-BALL.
WE'LL WIN NEXT TIME, ATSUSHI!!
HUH? DIDN'T YOU HEAR ME...?
I SAID I'M QUIT-TING...
YOU SURE?
BE-CAUSE...

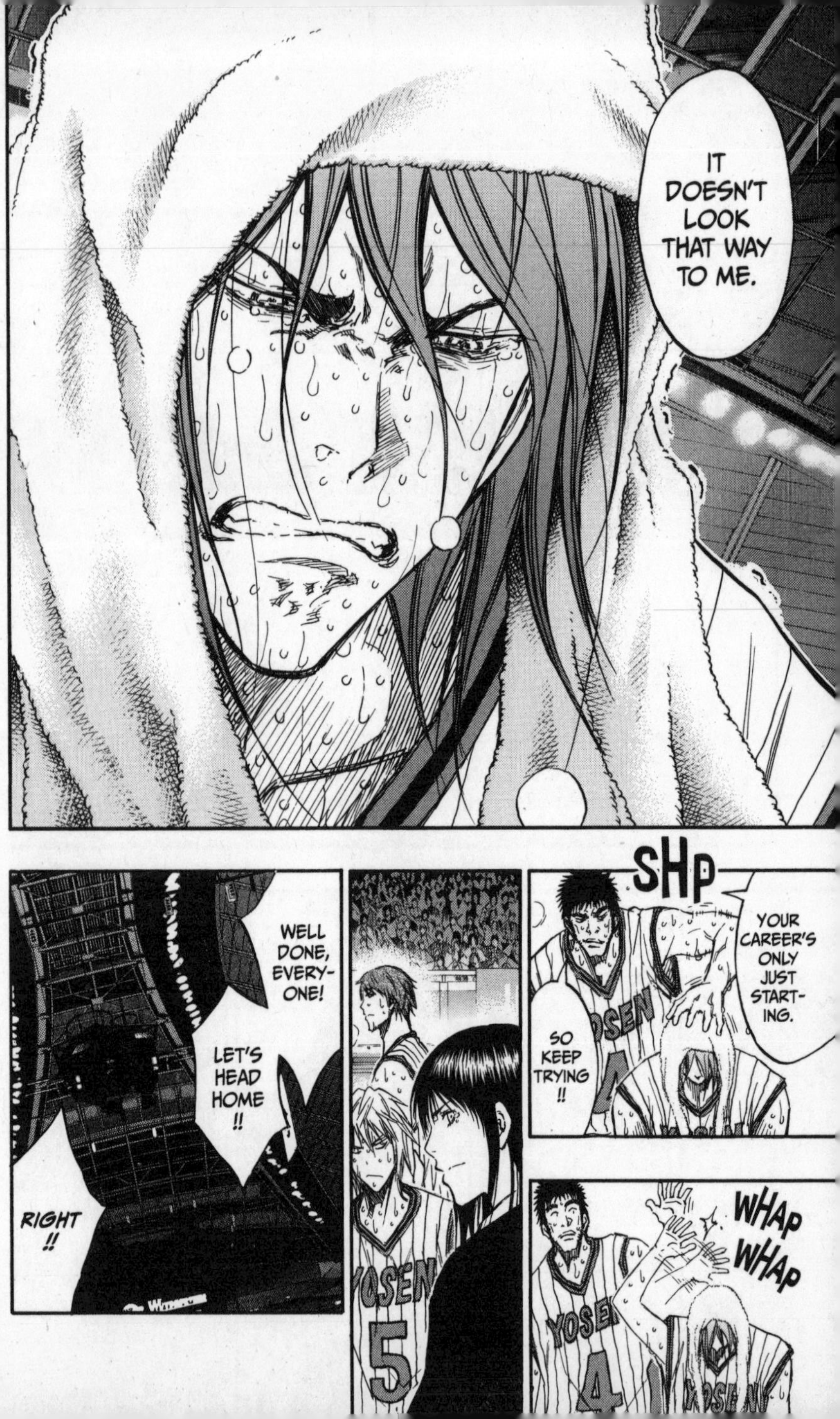
IT DOESN'T LOOK THAT WAY TO ME.
SHP
YOUR CAREER'S ONLY JUST STARTING.
SO KEEP TRYING!!
WHAP WHAP
WELL DONE, EVERYONE!
LET'S HEAD HOME!!
RIGHT!!

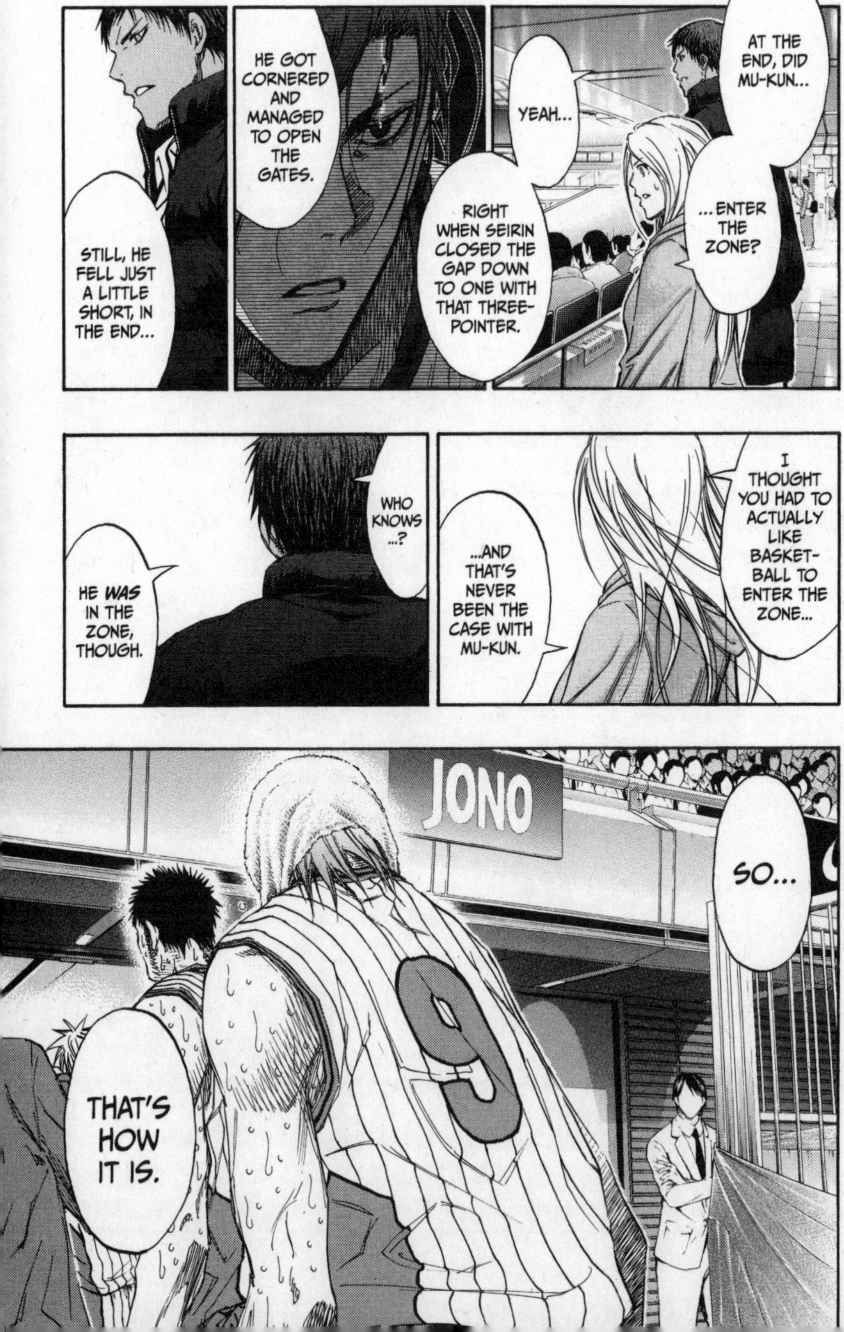
AT THE END, DID MU-KUN...
...ENTER THE ZONE?
YEAH...
RIGHT WHEN SEIRIN CLOSED THE GAP DOWN TO ONE WITH THAT THREE-POINTER.
HE GOT CORNERED AND MANAGED TO OPEN THE GATES.
STILL, HE FELL JUST A LITTLE SHORT, IN THE END...
I THOUGHT YOU HAD TO ACTUALLY LIKE BASKET-BALL TO ENTER THE ZONE...
...AND THAT'S NEVER BEEN THE CASE WITH MU-KUN.
WHO KNOWS ...?
HE *WAS* IN THE ZONE, THOUGH.
JONO
SO...
THAT'S HOW IT IS.

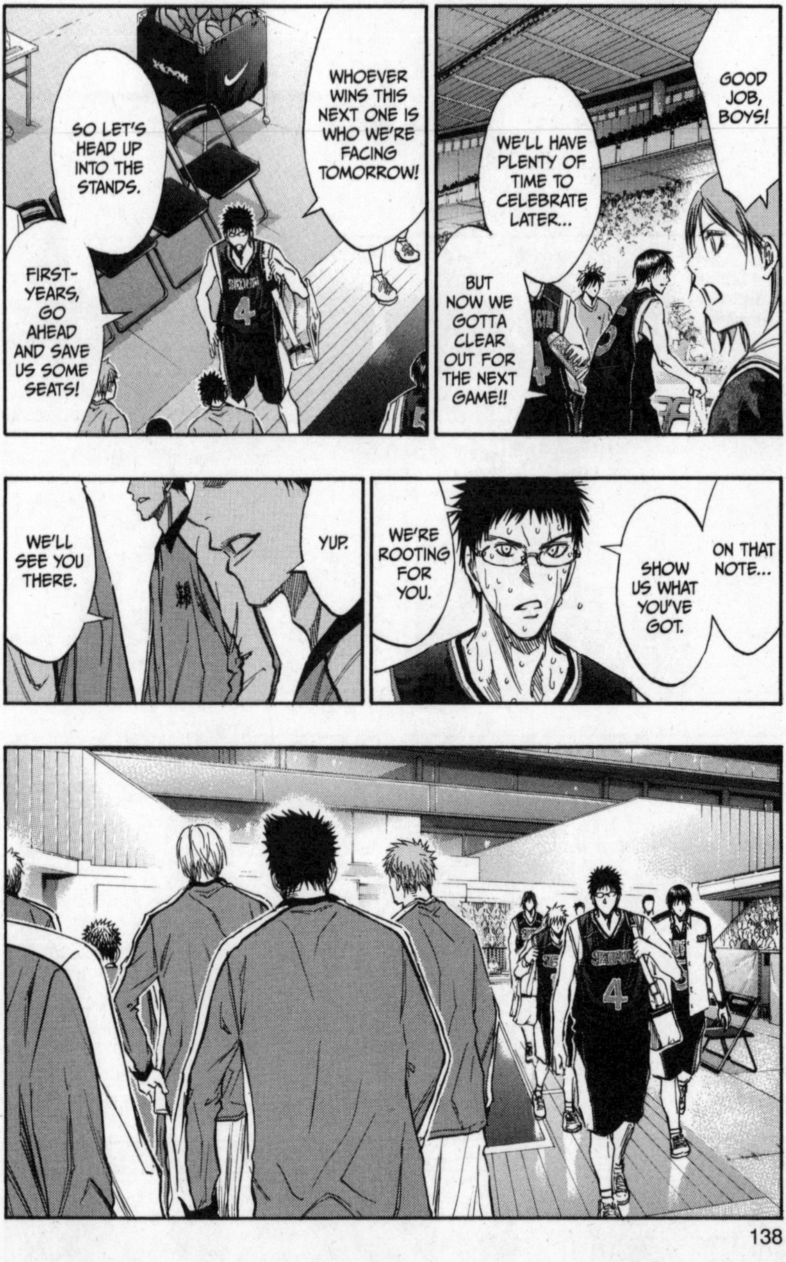
GOOD JOB, BOYS!
WE'LL HAVE PLENTY OF TIME TO CELEBRATE LATER...
BUT NOW WE GOTTA CLEAR OUT FOR THE NEXT GAME!!
WHOEVER WINS THIS NEXT ONE IS WHO WE'RE FACING TOMORROW!
SO LET'S HEAD UP INTO THE STANDS.
FIRST-YEARS, GO AHEAD AND SAVE US SOME SEATS!
ON THAT NOTE...
SHOW US WHAT YOU'VE GOT.
WE'RE ROOTING FOR YOU.
YUP.
WE'LL SEE YOU THERE.

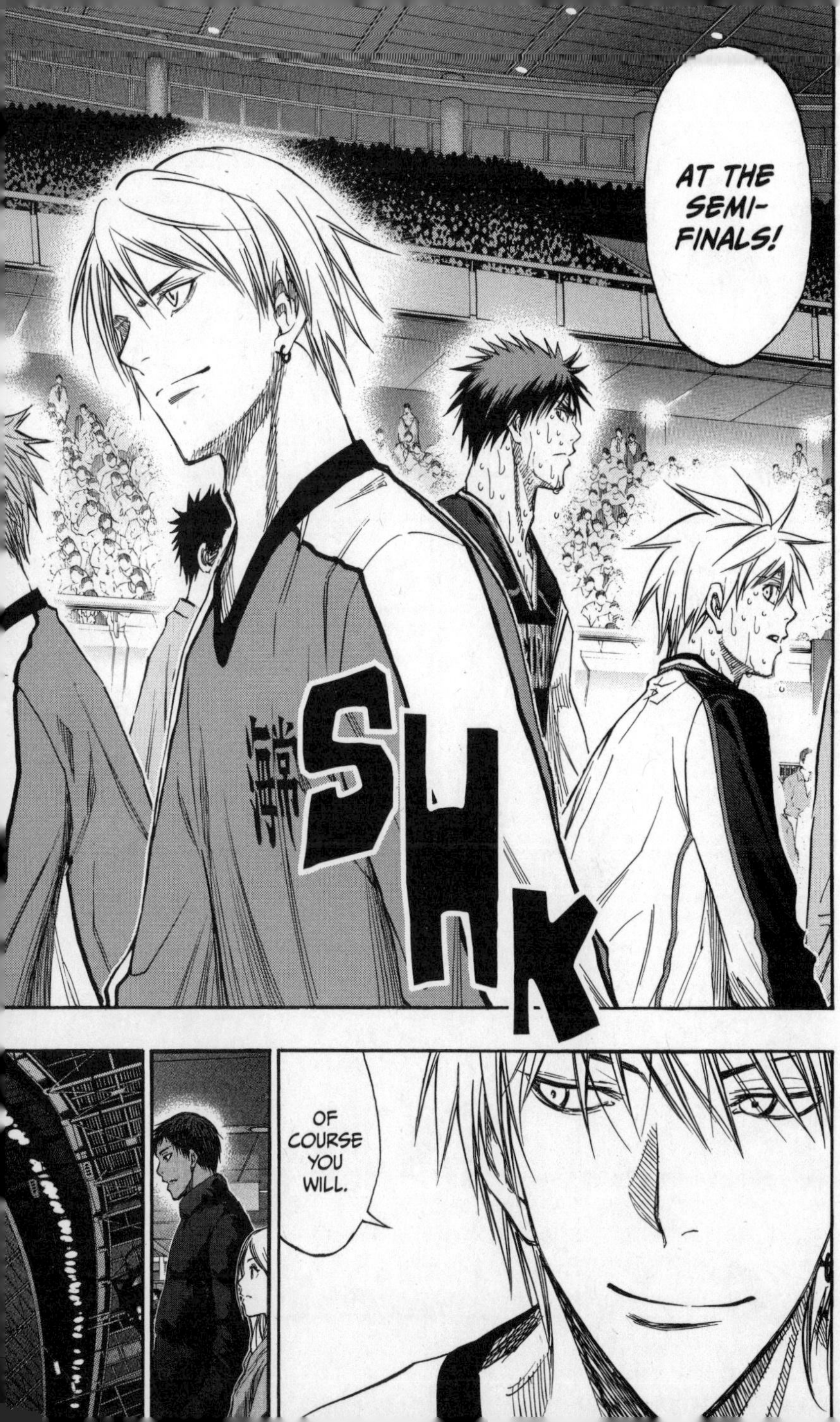
AT THE SEMI-FINALS!
SHK
OF COURSE YOU WILL.

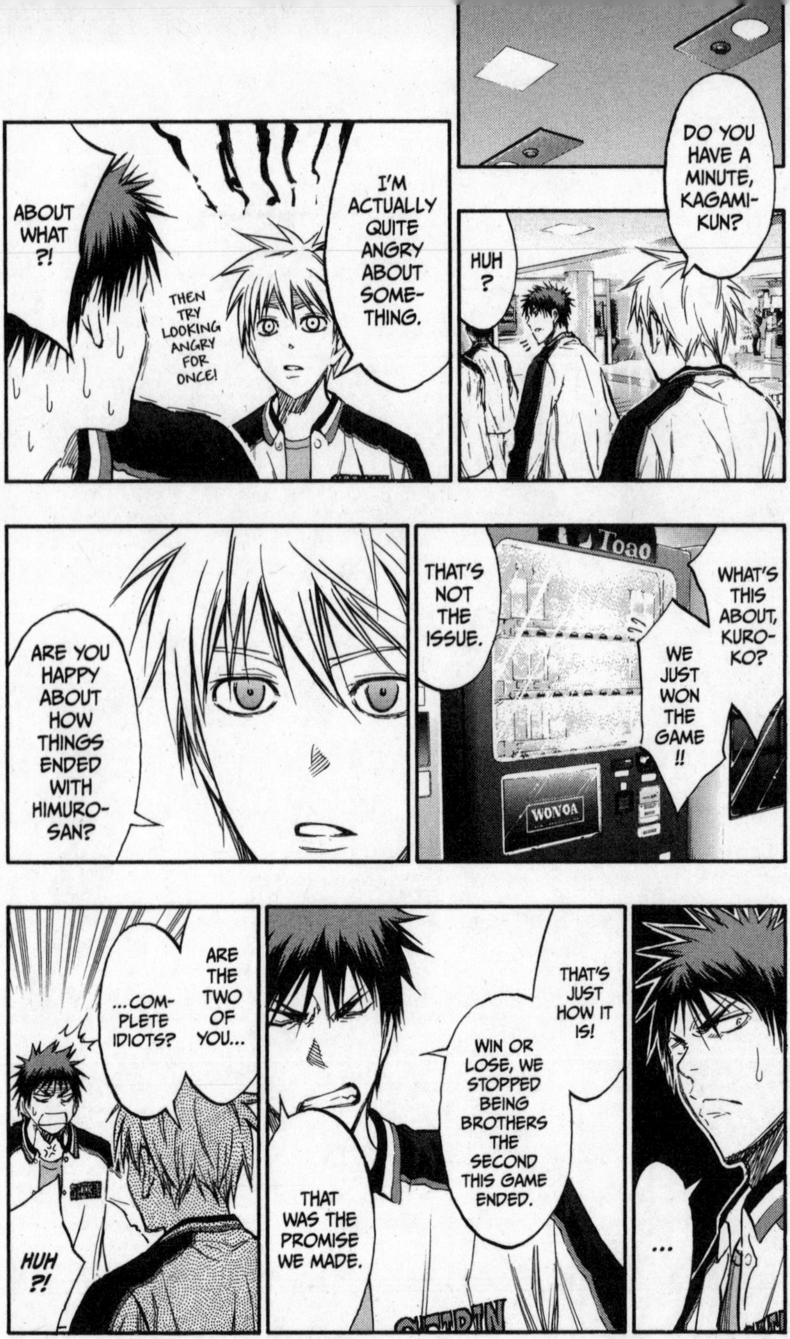
DO YOU HAVE A MINUTE, KAGAMI-KUN?
HUH?
I'M ACTUALLY QUITE ANGRY ABOUT SOME-THING.
ABOUT WHAT?!
THEN TRY LOOKING ANGRY FOR ONCE!
WHAT'S THIS ABOUT, KURO-KO?
WE JUST WON THE GAME!!
THAT'S NOT THE ISSUE.
ARE YOU HAPPY ABOUT HOW THINGS ENDED WITH HIMURO-SAN?
...
THAT'S JUST HOW IT IS!
WIN OR LOSE, WE STOPPED BEING BROTHERS THE SECOND THIS GAME ENDED.
THAT WAS THE PROMISE WE MADE.
ARE THE TWO OF YOU...
...COM-PLETE IDIOTS?
HUH?!

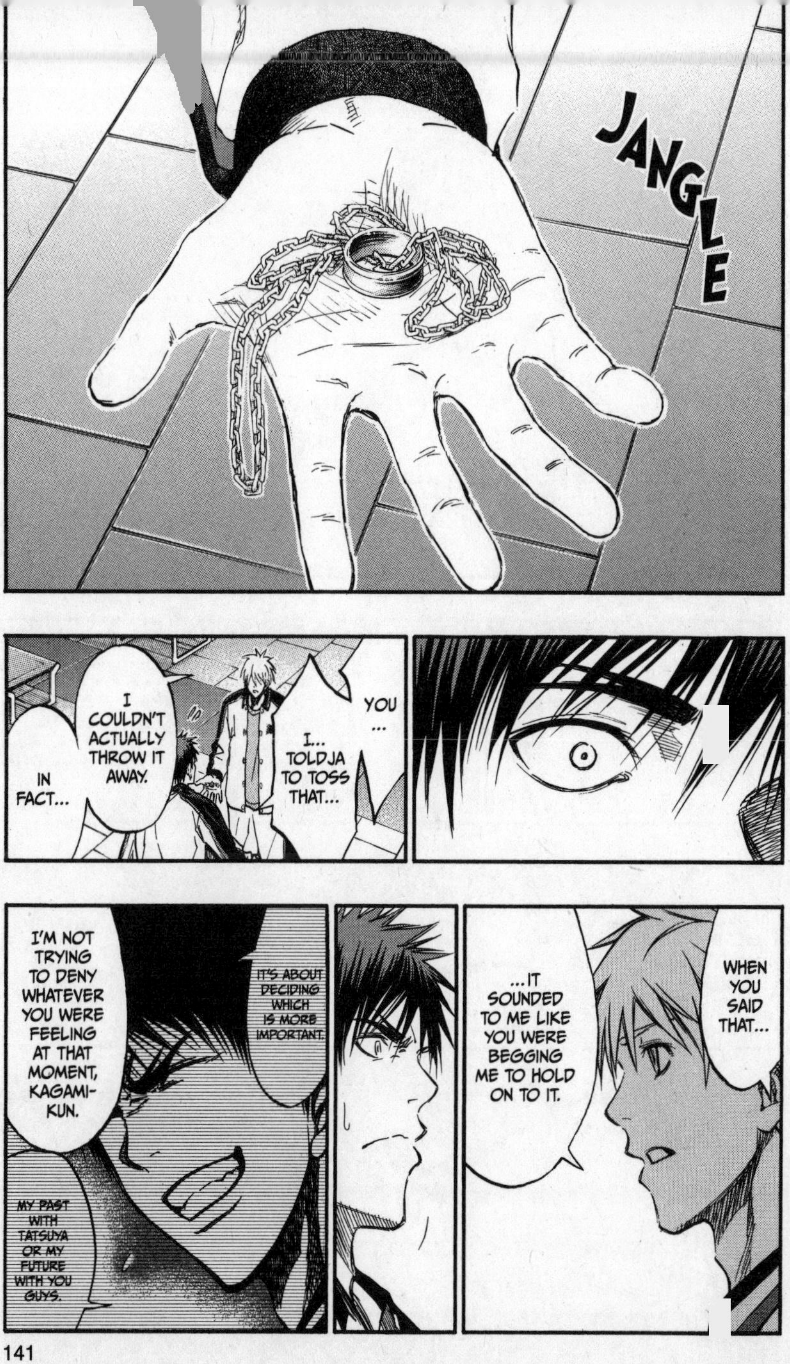
JANGLE
YOU ...
I... TOLDJA TO TOSS THAT...
I COULDN'T ACTUALLY THROW IT AWAY.
IN FACT...
WHEN YOU SAID THAT...
...IT SOUNDED TO ME LIKE YOU WERE BEGGING ME TO HOLD ON TO IT.
IT'S ABOUT DECIDING WHICH IS MORE IMPORTANT.
I'M NOT TRYING TO DENY WHATEVER YOU WERE FEELING AT THAT MOMENT, KAGAMI-KUN.
MY PAST WITH TATSUYA OR MY FUTURE WITH YOU GUYS.

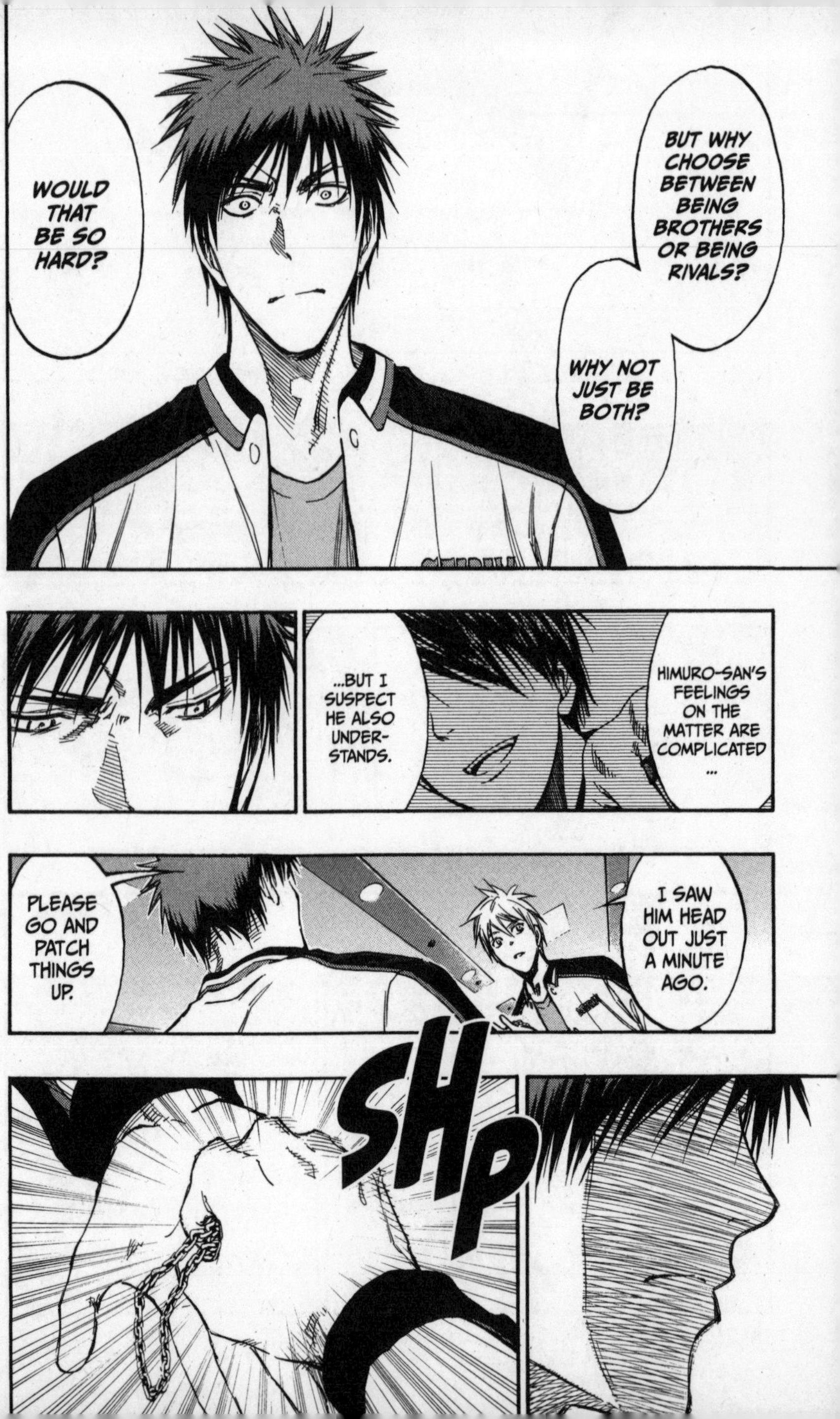
BUT WHY CHOOSE BETWEEN BEING BROTHERS OR BEING RIVALS?
WHY NOT JUST BE BOTH?
WOULD THAT BE SO HARD?
HIMURO-SAN'S FEELINGS ON THE MATTER ARE COMPLICATED ...
...BUT I SUSPECT HE ALSO UNDER- STANDS.
I SAW HIM HEAD OUT JUST A MINUTE AGO.
PLEASE GO AND PATCH THINGS UP.
SHP

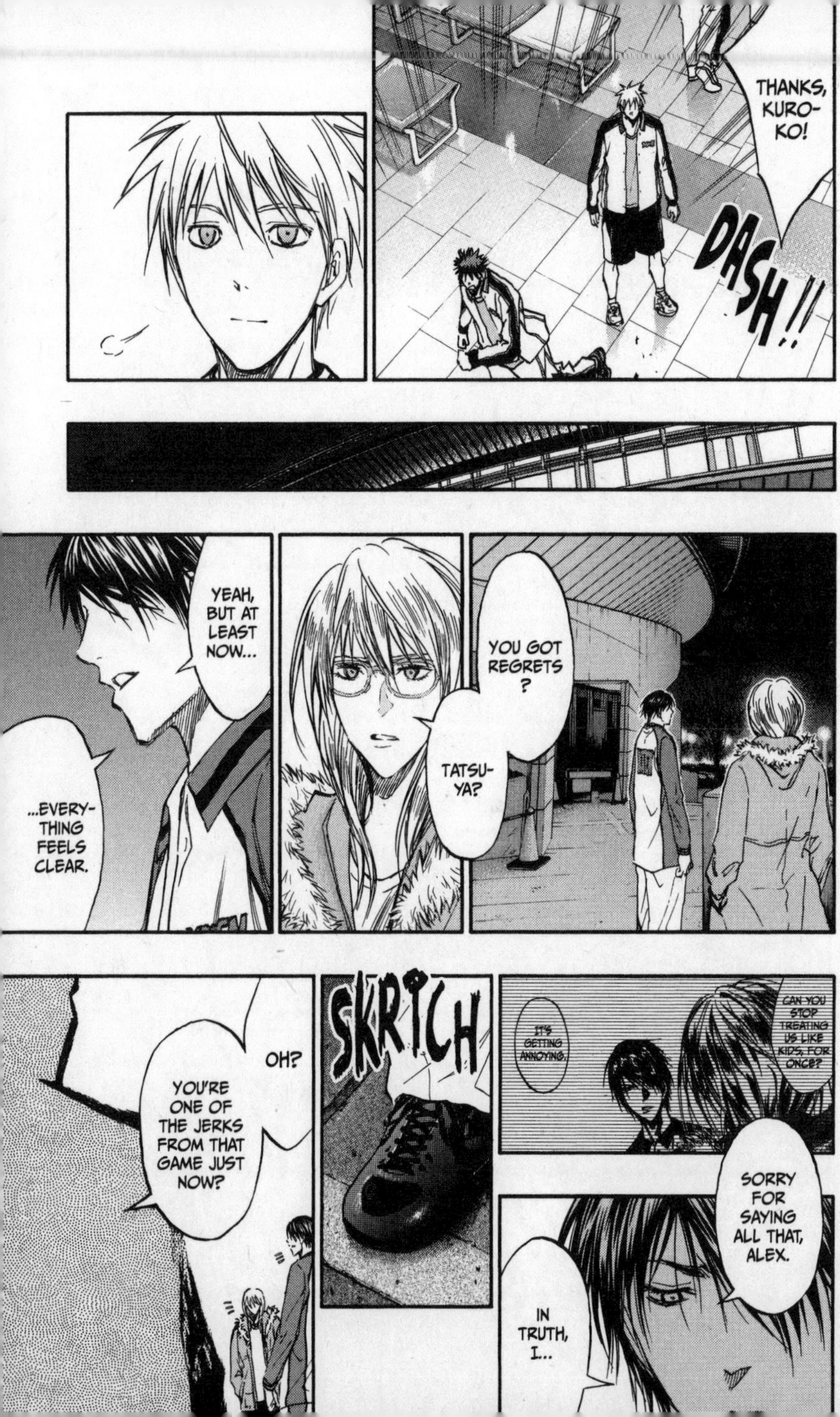
THANKS, KURO-KO!
DASH!!
YOU GOT REGRETS?
TATSU-YA?
YEAH, BUT AT LEAST NOW...
...EVERY-THING FEELS CLEAR.
CAN YOU STOP TREATING US LIKE KIDS, FOR ONCE?
IT'S GETTING ANNOYING.
SORRY FOR SAYING ALL THAT, ALEX.
IN TRUTH, I...
SKRITCH
OH?
YOU'RE ONE OF THE JERKS FROM THAT GAME JUST NOW?

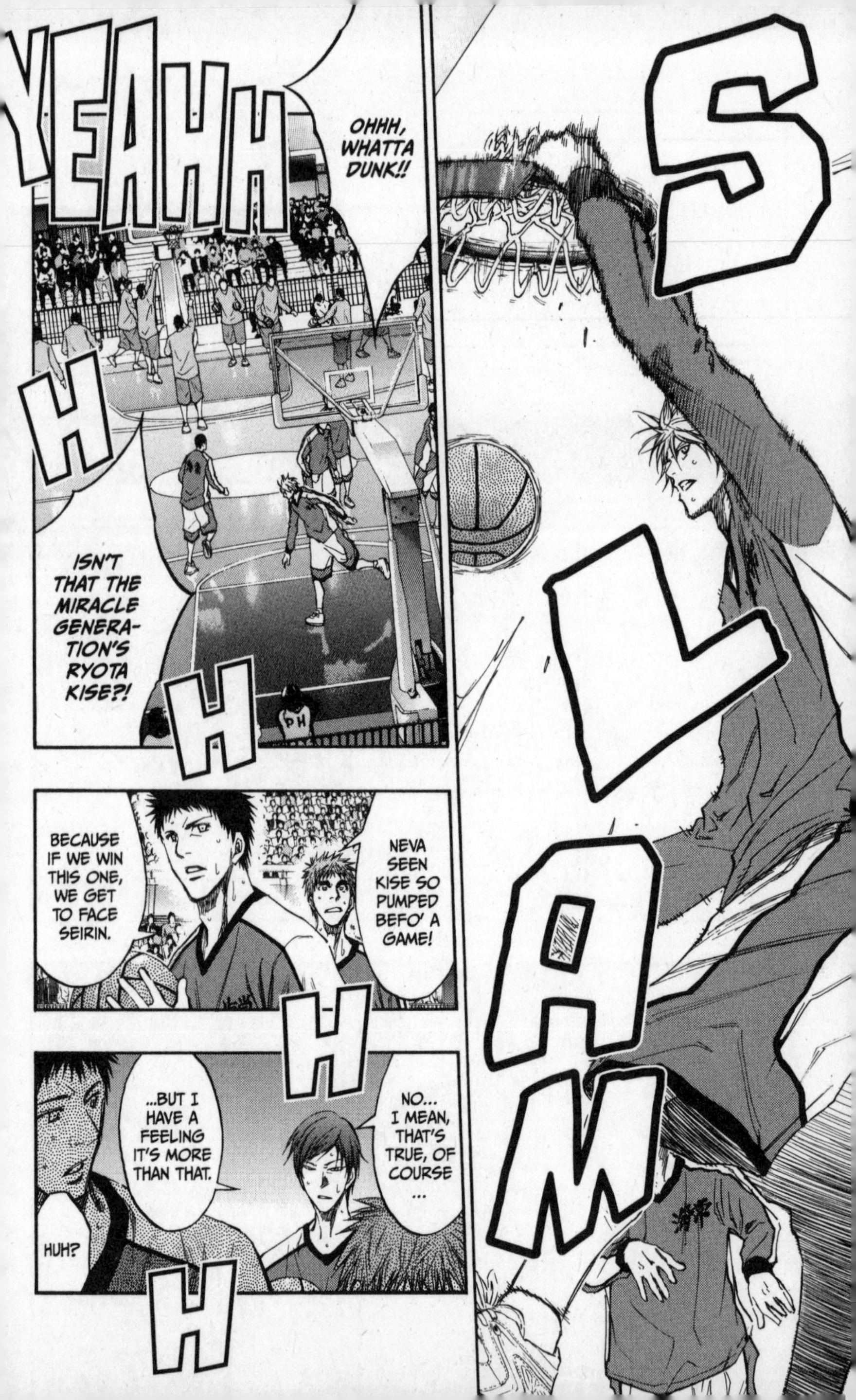
SLAM
YEAHHHHHH
OHHH, WHATTA DUNK!!
ISN'T THAT THE MIRACLE GENERATION'S RYOTA KISE?!
NEVA SEEN KISE SO PUMPED BEFO' A GAME!
BECAUSE IF WE WIN THIS ONE, WE GET TO FACE SEIRIN.
NO... I MEAN, THAT'S TRUE, OF COURSE ...
...BUT I HAVE A FEELING IT'S MORE THAN THAT.
HUH?

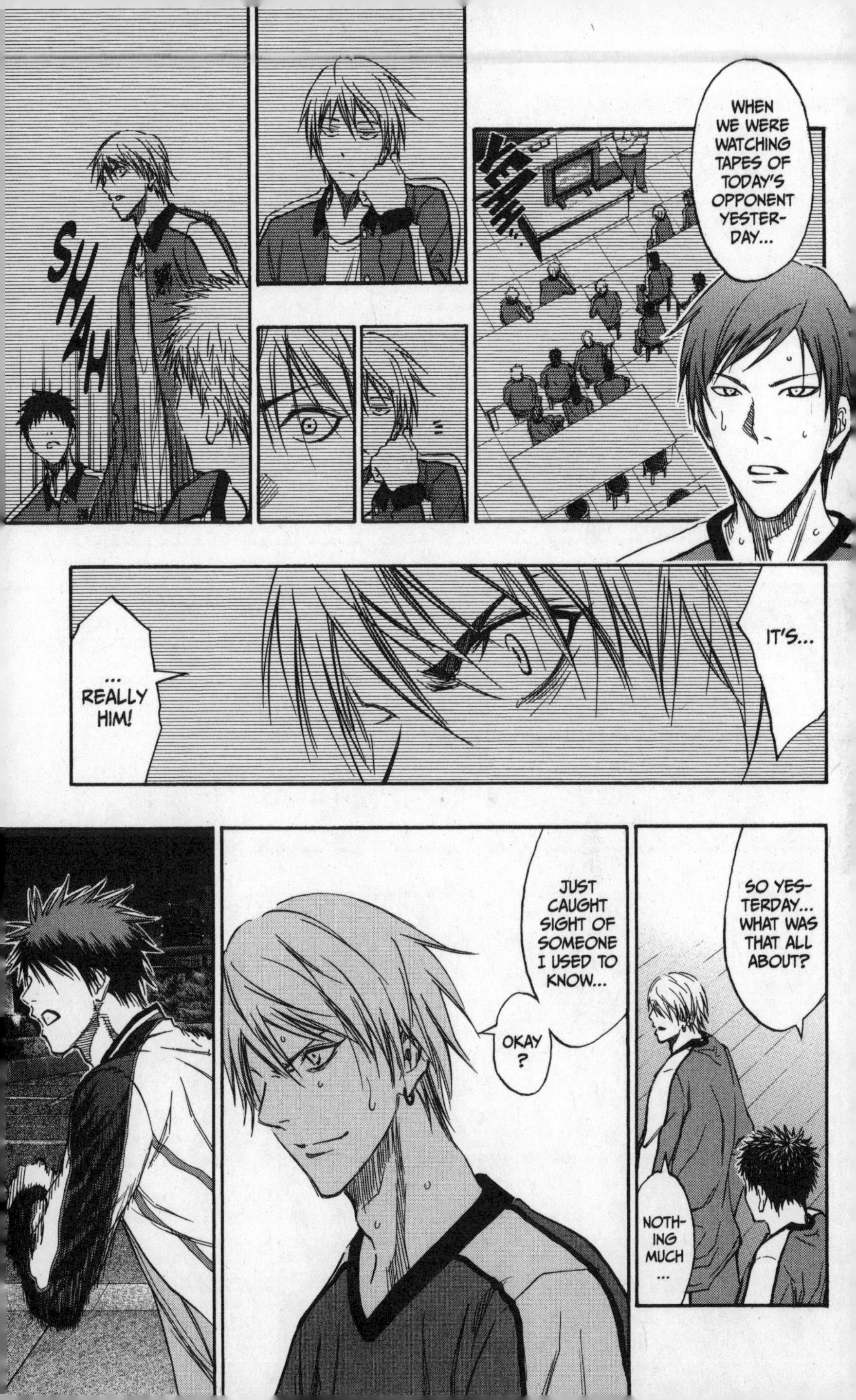
WHEN WE WERE WATCHING TAPES OF TODAY'S OPPONENT YESTER-DAY...
YEAH...
SHAH
IT'S...
... REALLY HIM!
SO YES-TERDAY... WHAT WAS THAT ALL ABOUT?
NOTH-ING MUCH ...
JUST CAUGHT SIGHT OF SOMEONE I USED TO KNOW...
OKAY ?

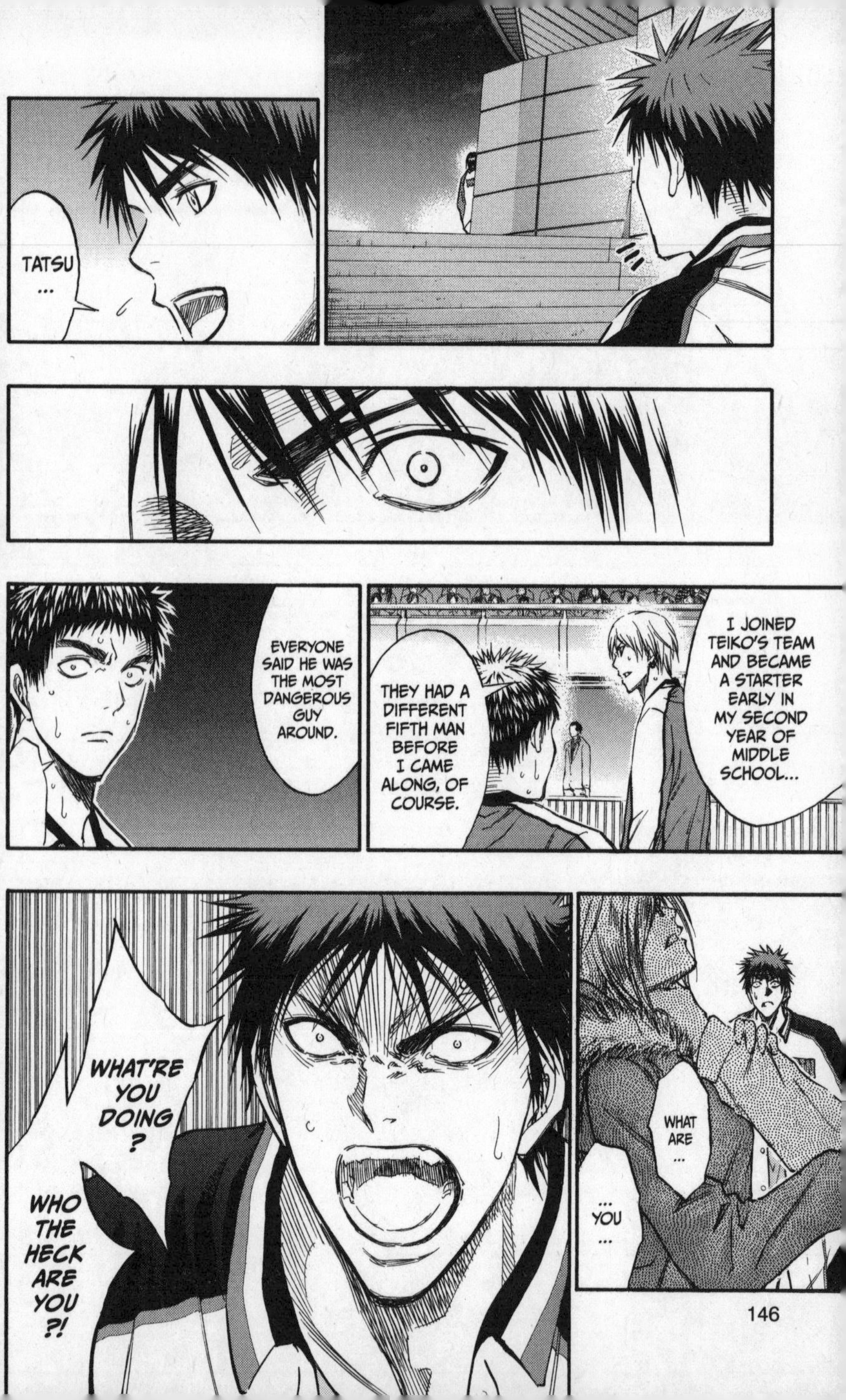
TATSU ...
I JOINED TEIKO'S TEAM AND BECAME A STARTER EARLY IN MY SECOND YEAR OF MIDDLE SCHOOL...
THEY HAD A DIFFERENT FIFTH MAN BEFORE I CAME ALONG, OF COURSE.
EVERYONE SAID HE WAS THE MOST DANGEROUS GUY AROUND.
WHAT ARE ...
... YOU ...
WHAT'RE YOU DOING?
WHO THE HECK ARE YOU?!

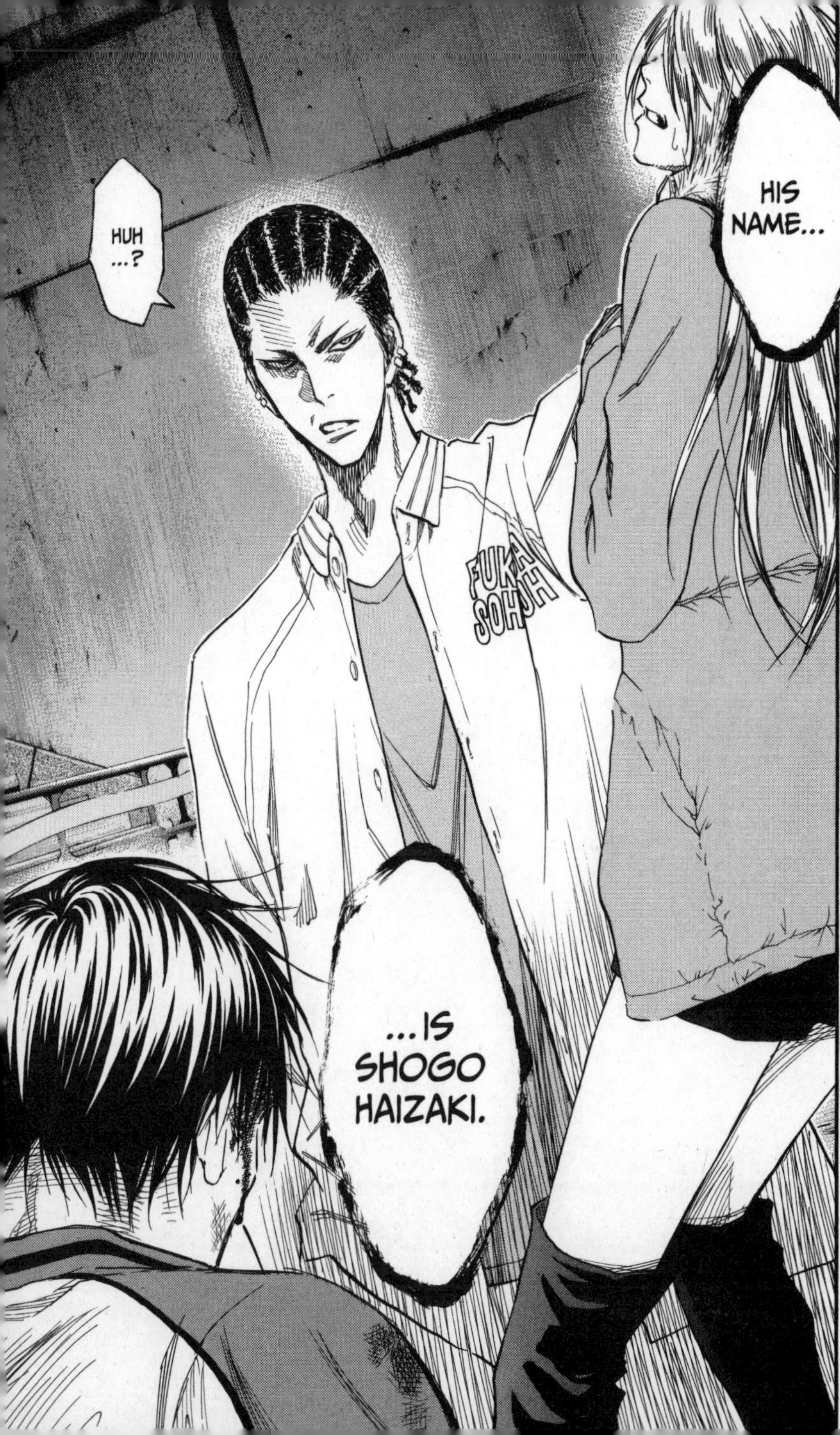
HIS NAME...
HUH ...?
...IS SHOGO HAIZAKI.

KUROKO'S BASKETBALL BLOOPERS

TAKE 7

FROM 76TH QUARTER BLOOPERS

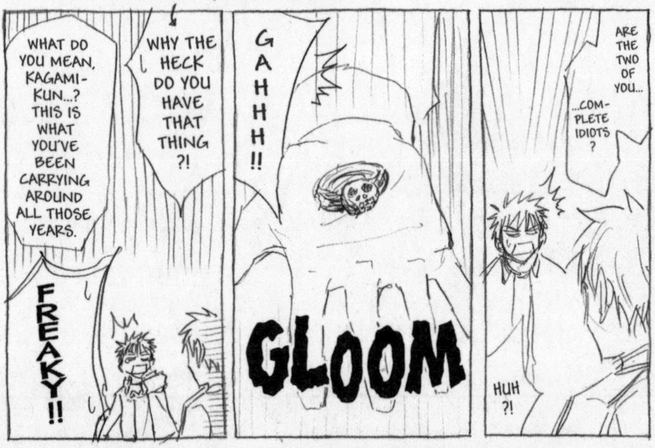
ARE THE TWO OF YOU...
...COMPLETE IDIOTS?
HUH?!
GAHHH!!
GLOOM
WHY THE HECK DO YOU HAVE THAT THING?!
WHAT DO YOU MEAN, KAGAMI-KUN...? THIS IS WHAT YOU'VE BEEN CARRYING AROUND ALL THOSE YEARS.
FREAKY!!

170TH QUARTER: JUST KILLING TIME

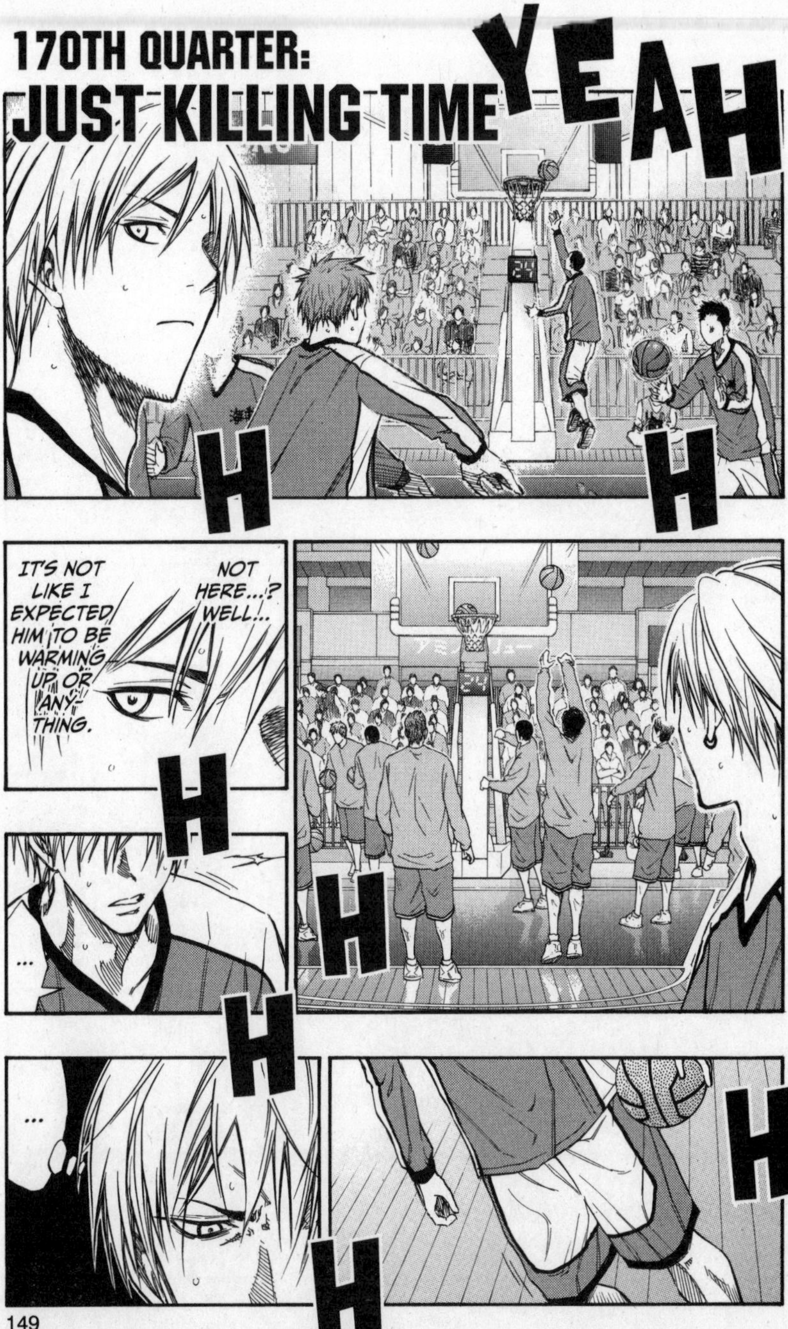
YEAH
H
H
H
NOT HERE...? WELL...
IT'S NOT LIKE I EXPECTED HIM TO BE WARMING UP OR ANYTHING.
H
...
H
H
H
...
H

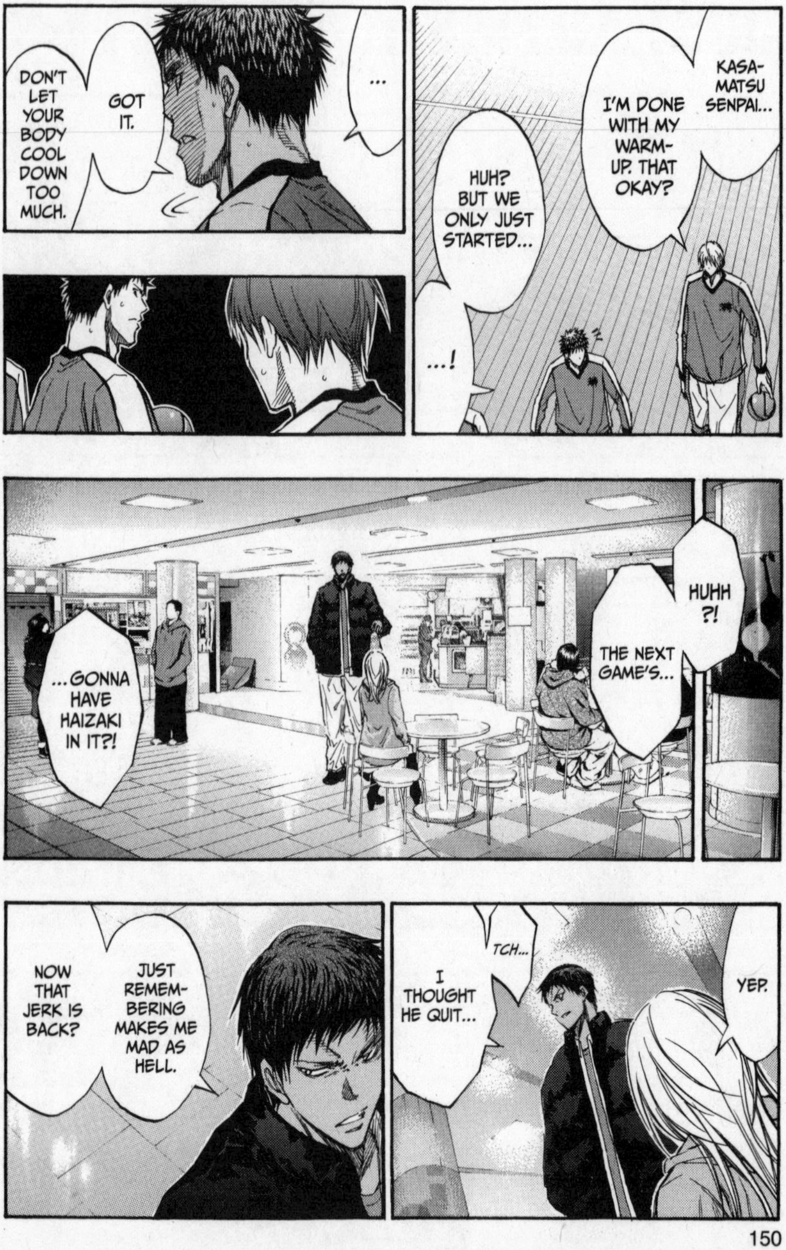
KASA-MATSU SENPAI...
I'M DONE WITH MY WARM-UP. THAT OKAY?
HUH? BUT WE ONLY JUST STARTED...
...!
...
GOT IT.
DON'T LET YOUR BODY COOL DOWN TOO MUCH.
HUHH ?!
THE NEXT GAME'S...
...GONNA HAVE HAIZAKI IN IT?!
YEP.
TCH...
I THOUGHT HE QUIT...
JUST REMEMBERING MAKES ME MAD AS HELL.
NOW THAT JERK IS BACK?

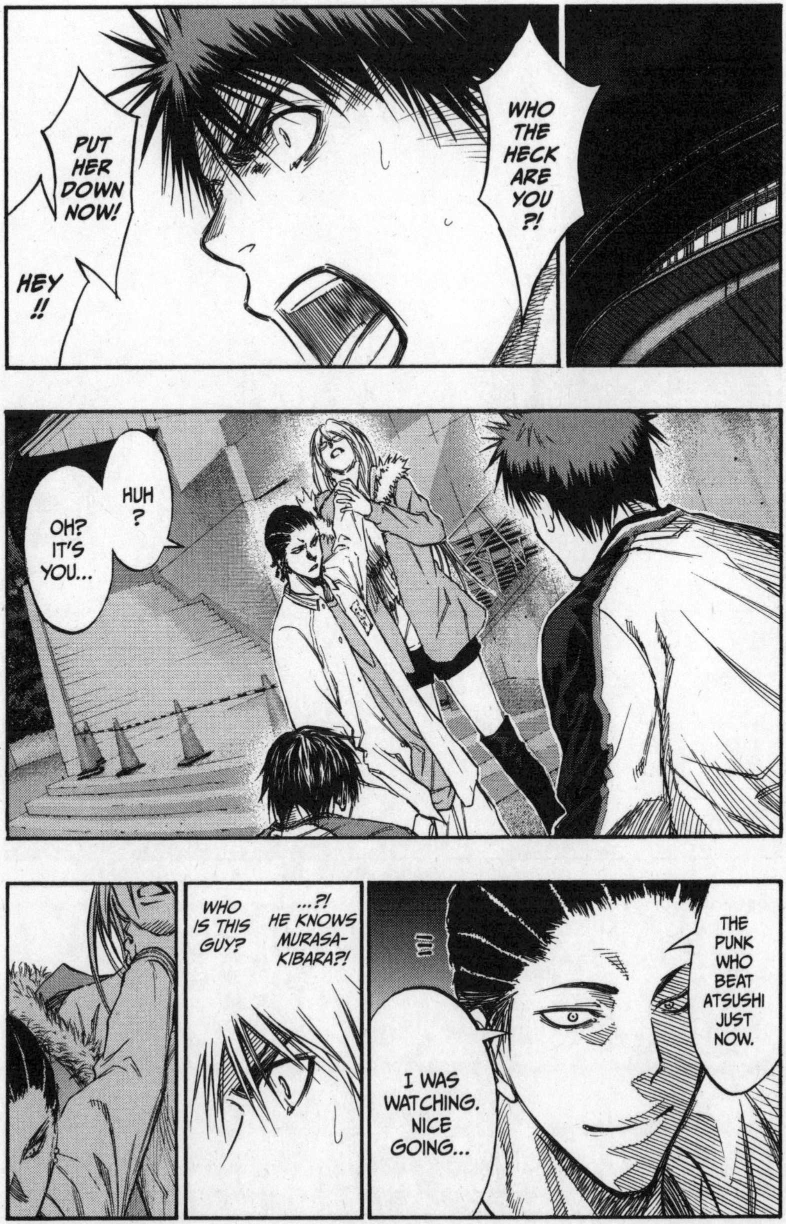
WHO THE HECK ARE YOU?!
PUT HER DOWN NOW!
HEY!!
HUH?
OH? IT'S YOU...
THE PUNK WHO BEAT ATSUSHI JUST NOW.
I WAS WATCHING. NICE GOING...
...?! HE KNOWS MURASA-KIBARA?!
WHO IS THIS GUY?

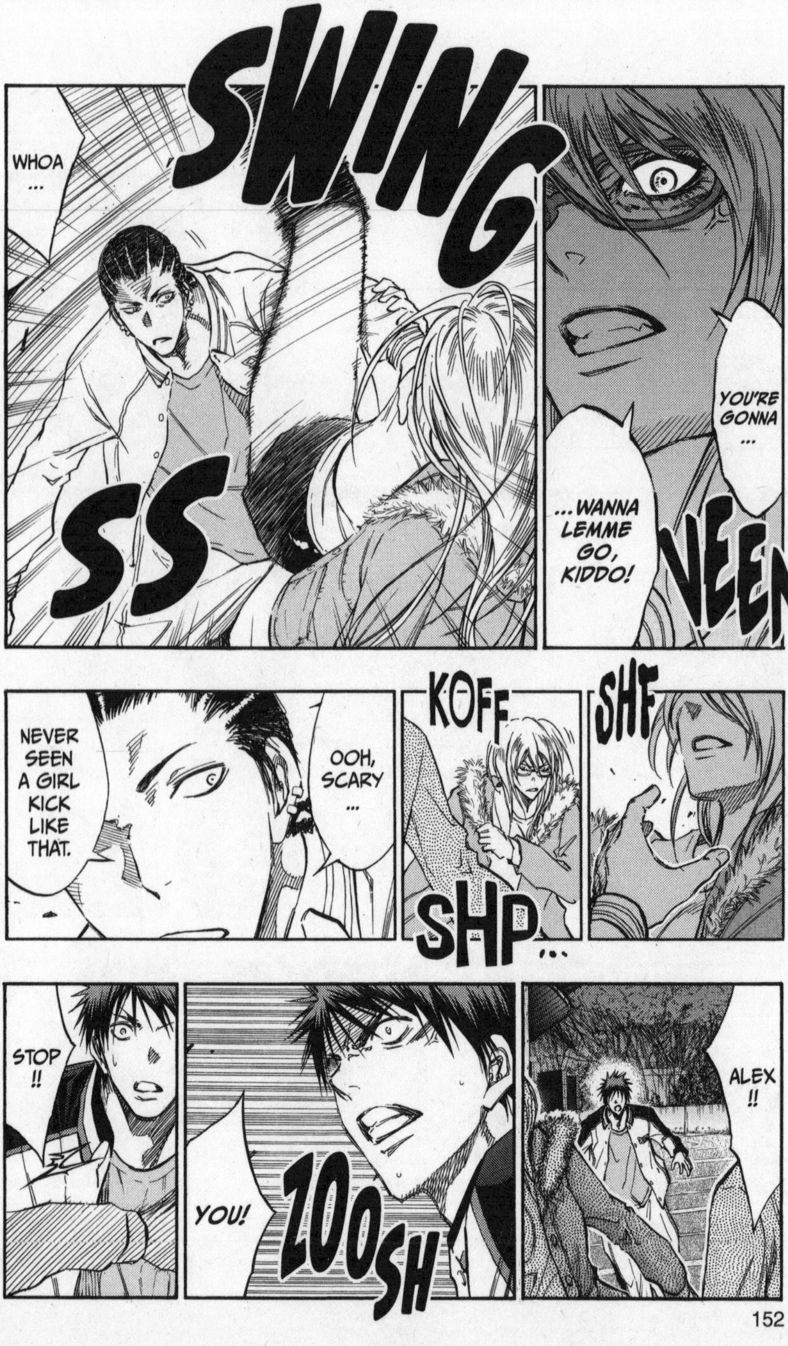
YOU'RE GONNA ...
...WANNA LEMME GO, KIDDO!
VEEN
SWING
WHOA ...
SS
SHF
KOFF
SHP...
OOH, SCARY ...
NEVER SEEN A GIRL KICK LIKE THAT.
ALEX !!
ZOOSH
YOU!
STOP !!

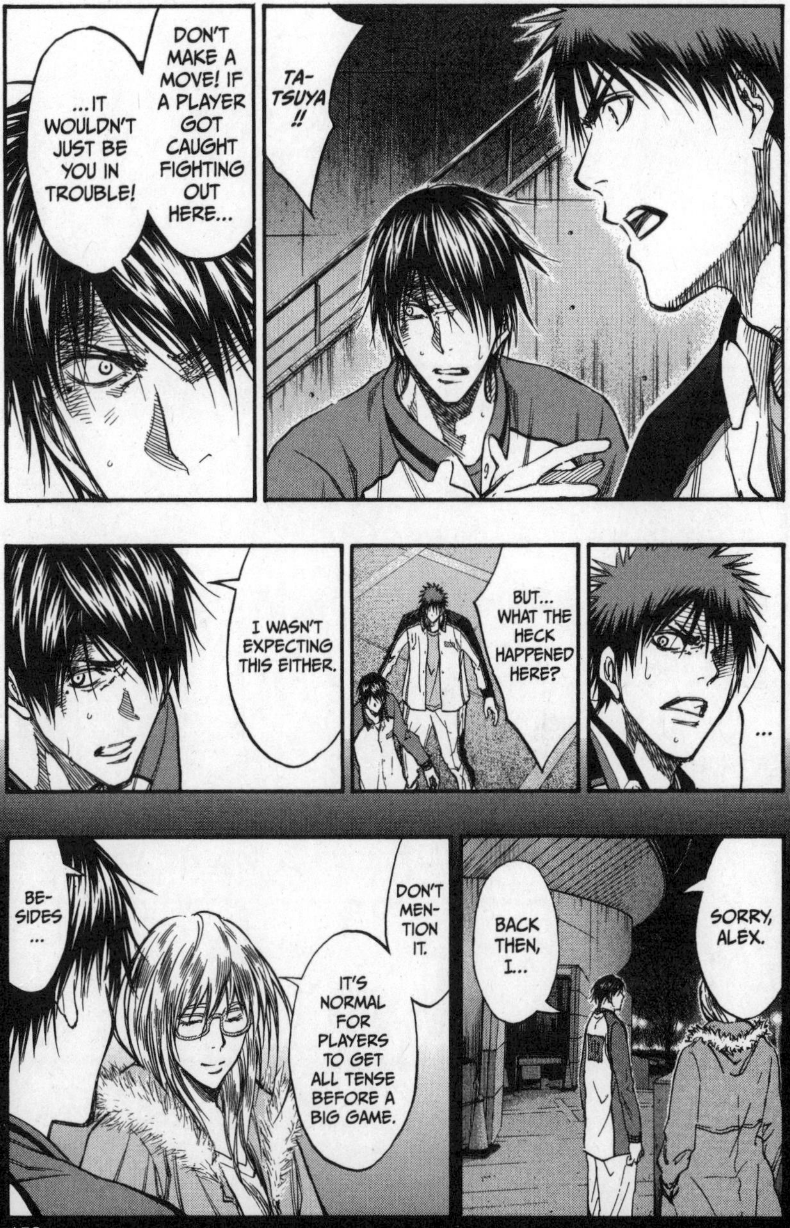
TATSUYA!!
DON'T MAKE A MOVE! IF A PLAYER GOT CAUGHT FIGHTING OUT HERE...
...IT WOULDN'T JUST BE YOU IN TROUBLE!
...
BUT... WHAT THE HECK HAPPENED HERE?
I WASN'T EXPECTING THIS EITHER.
SORRY, ALEX.
BACK THEN, I...
DON'T MENTION IT.
IT'S NORMAL FOR PLAYERS TO GET ALL TENSE BEFORE A BIG GAME.
BESIDES...

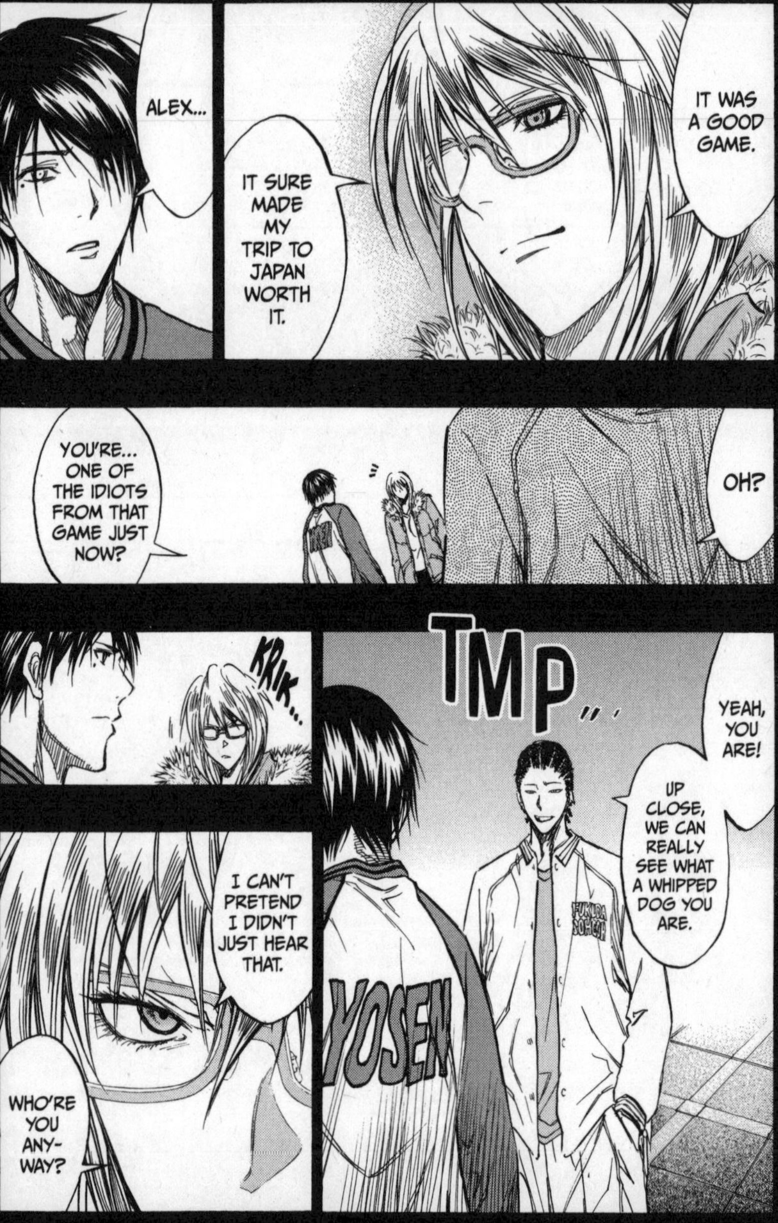
IT WAS A GOOD GAME.
IT SURE MADE MY TRIP TO JAPAN WORTH IT.
ALEX...
OH?
YOU'RE... ONE OF THE IDIOTS FROM THAT GAME JUST NOW?
TMP...
YEAH, YOU ARE!
UP CLOSE, WE CAN REALLY SEE WHAT A WHIPPED DOG YOU ARE.
YOSEN
KRIK...
I CAN'T PRETEND I DIDN'T JUST HEAR THAT.
WHO'RE YOU ANY-WAY?

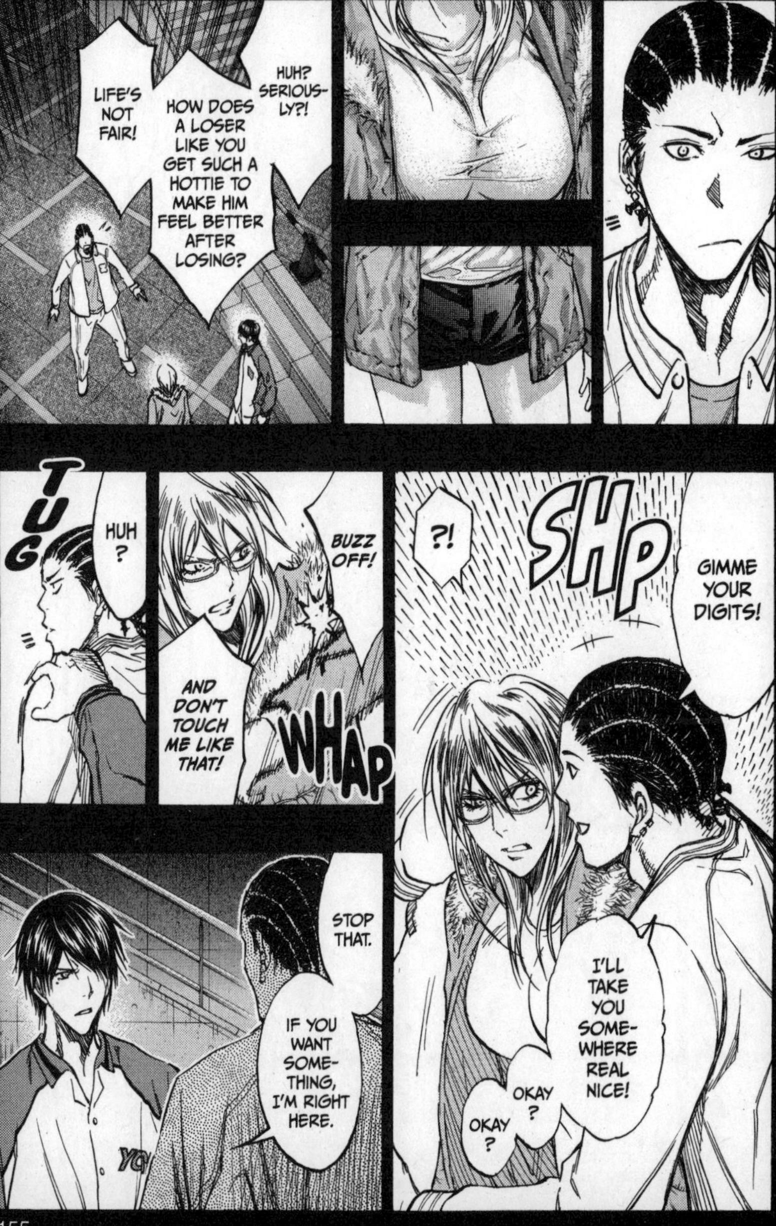
HUH? SERIOUS-LY?!
HOW DOES A LOSER LIKE YOU GET SUCH A HOTTIE TO MAKE HIM FEEL BETTER AFTER LOSING?
LIFE'S NOT FAIR!
GIMME YOUR DIGITS!
SHP
?!
I'LL TAKE YOU SOME-WHERE REAL NICE!
OKAY ?
OKAY ?
BUZZ OFF!
AND DON'T TOUCH ME LIKE THAT!
WHAP
TUG
HUH ?
STOP THAT.
IF YOU WANT SOME-THING, I'M RIGHT HERE.

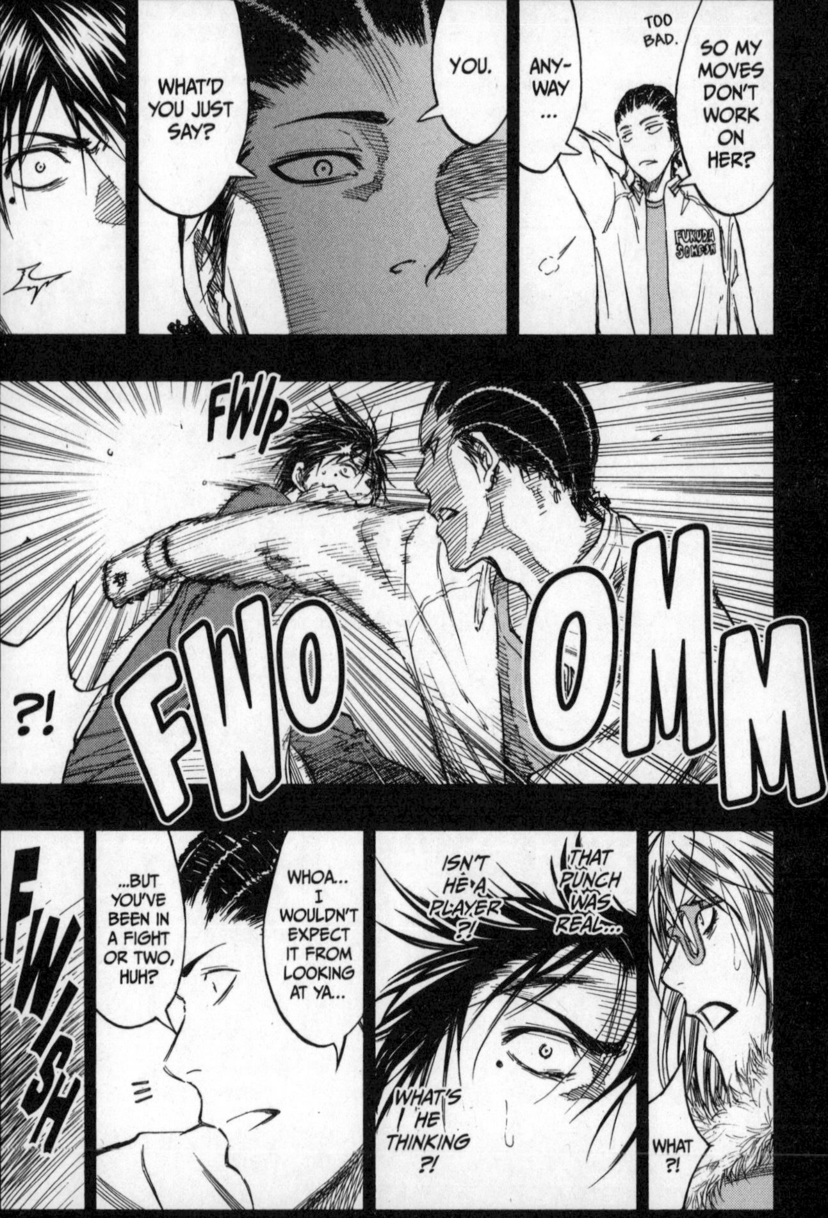
SO MY MOVES DON'T WORK ON HER?
TOO BAD.
ANY-WAY ...
FUKUDA SOMEN
YOU.
WHAT'D YOU JUST SAY?
FWIP
FWOOMM
?!
WHAT ?!
THAT PUNCH WAS REAL...
ISN'T HE A PLAYER ?!
WHAT'S HE THINKING ?!
WHOA... I WOULDN'T EXPECT IT FROM LOOKING AT YA...
...BUT YOU'VE BEEN IN A FIGHT OR TWO, HUH?
FWISH

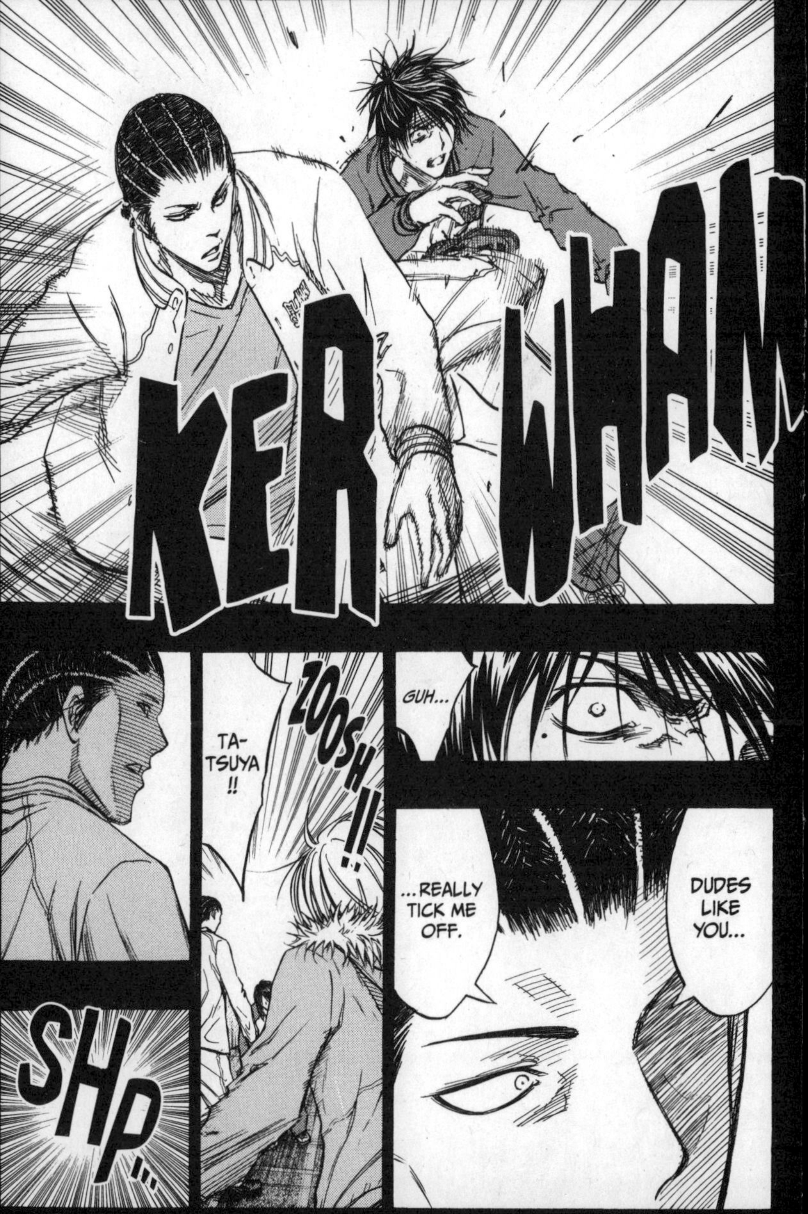
KER
WHAM
GUH...
DUDES LIKE YOU...
...REALLY TICK ME OFF.
ZOOSH!!
TA-TSUYA!!
SHP...

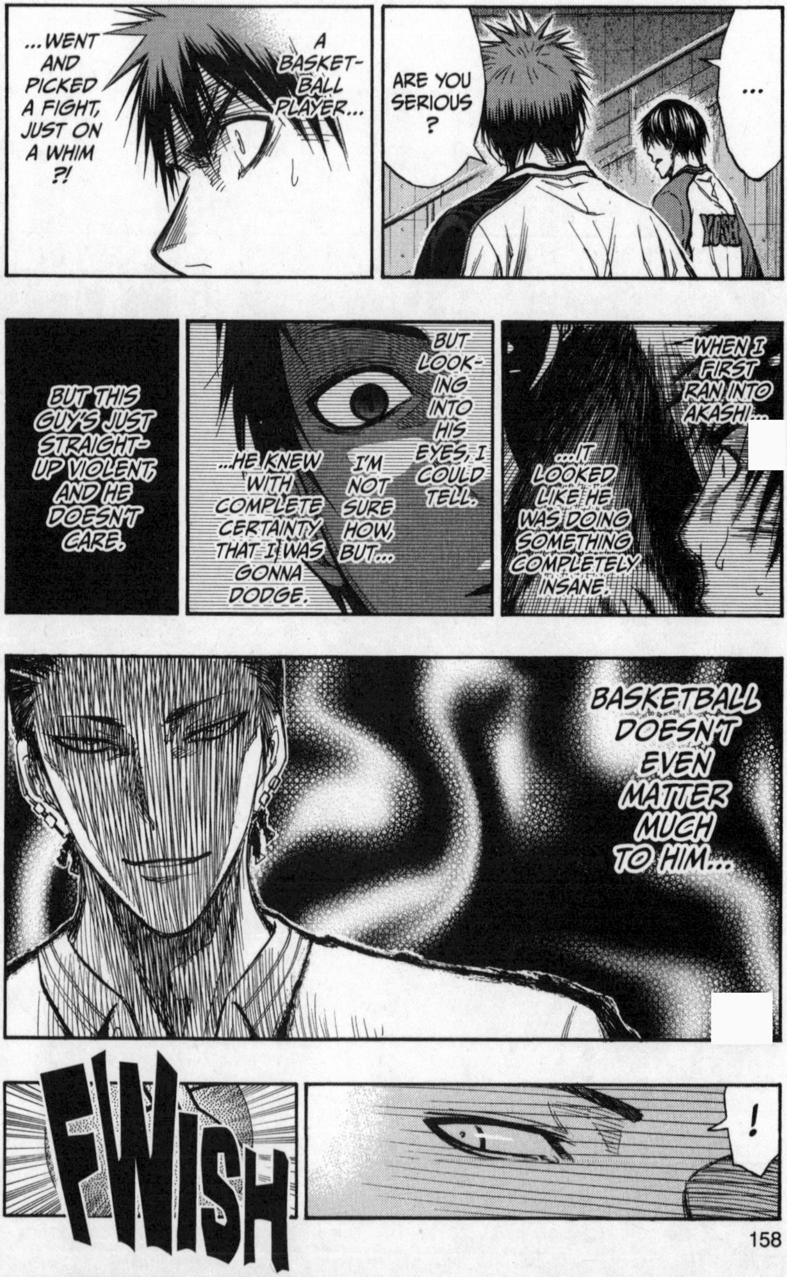
...
ARE YOU SERIOUS?
A BASKET-BALL PLAYER...
...WENT AND PICKED A FIGHT, JUST ON A WHIM?!
WHEN I FIRST RAN INTO AKASHI...
...IT LOOKED LIKE HE WAS DOING SOMETHING COMPLETELY INSANE.
BUT LOOKING INTO HIS EYES, I COULD TELL.
I'M NOT SURE HOW, BUT...
...HE KNEW WITH COMPLETE CERTAINTY THAT I WAS GONNA DODGE.
BUT THIS GUY'S JUST STRAIGHT-UP VIOLENT, AND HE DOESN'T CARE.
BASKETBALL DOESN'T EVEN MATTER MUCH TO HIM...
!
FWISH

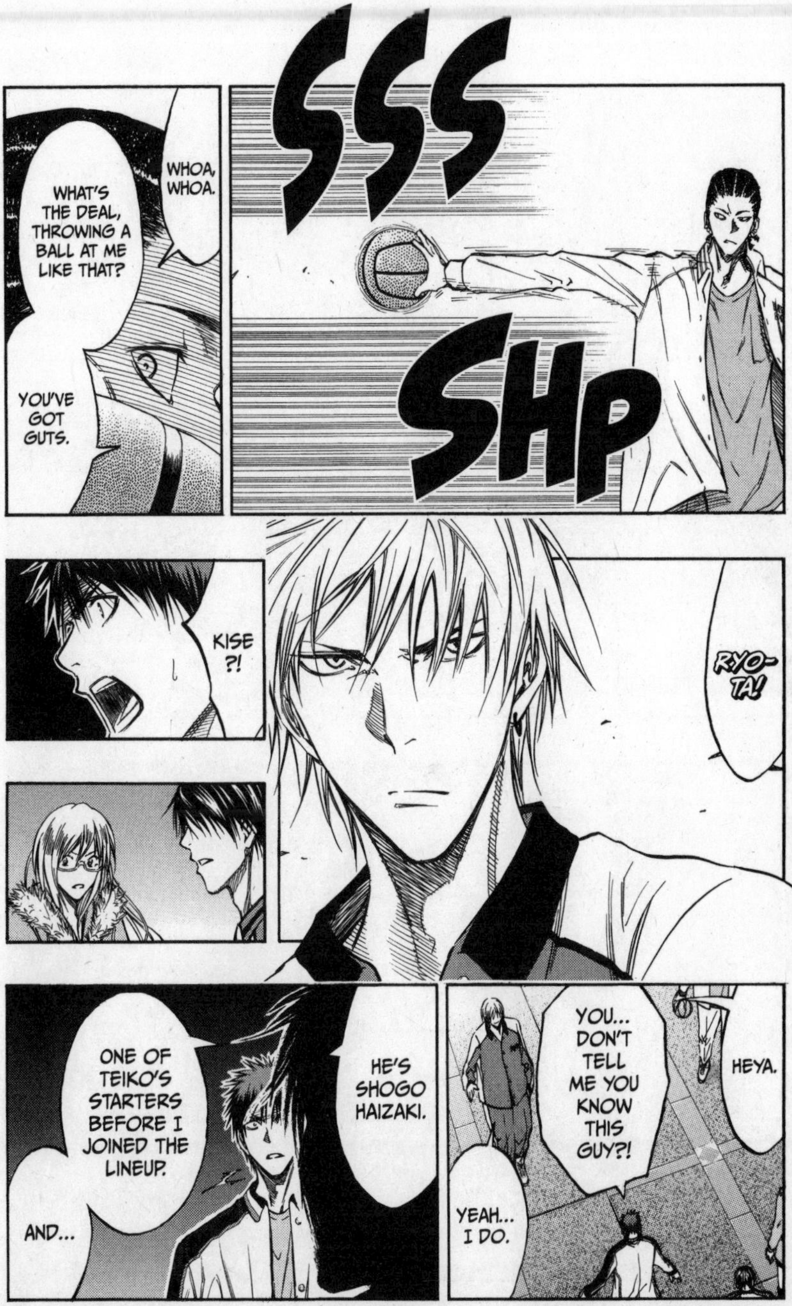
SSS
SHP
WHOA, WHOA.
WHAT'S THE DEAL, THROWING A BALL AT ME LIKE THAT?
YOU'VE GOT GUTS.
RYO-TA!
KISE ?!
HEYA.
YOU... DON'T TELL ME YOU KNOW THIS GUY?!
YEAH... I DO.
HE'S SHOGO HAIZAKI.
ONE OF TEIKO'S STARTERS BEFORE I JOINED THE LINEUP.
AND...

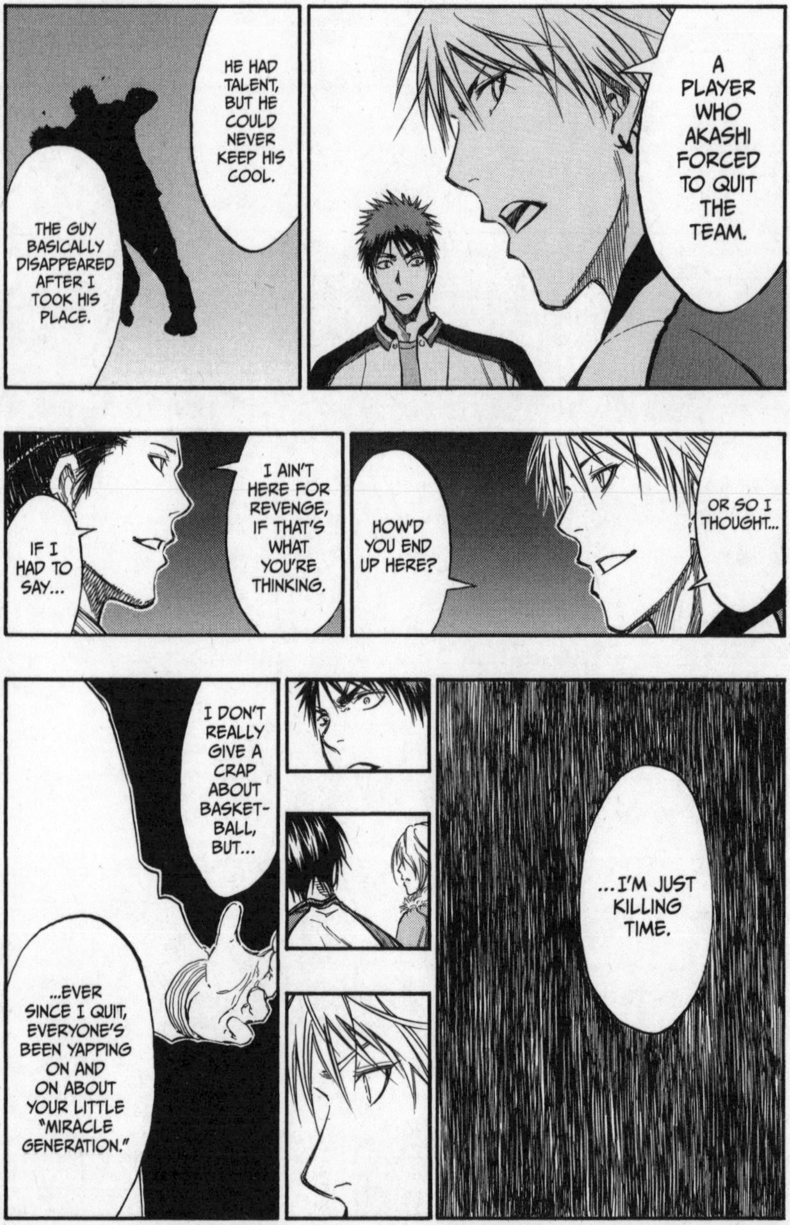
A PLAYER WHO AKASHI FORCED TO QUIT THE TEAM.
HE HAD TALENT, BUT HE COULD NEVER KEEP HIS COOL.
THE GUY BASICALLY DISAPPEARED AFTER I TOOK HIS PLACE.
OR SO I THOUGHT...
HOW'D YOU END UP HERE?
I AIN'T HERE FOR REVENGE, IF THAT'S WHAT YOU'RE THINKING.
IF I HAD TO SAY...
...I'M JUST KILLING TIME.
I DON'T REALLY GIVE A CRAP ABOUT BASKET-BALL, BUT...
...EVER SINCE I QUIT, EVERYONE'S BEEN YAPPING ON AND ON ABOUT YOUR LITTLE "MIRACLE GENERATION."

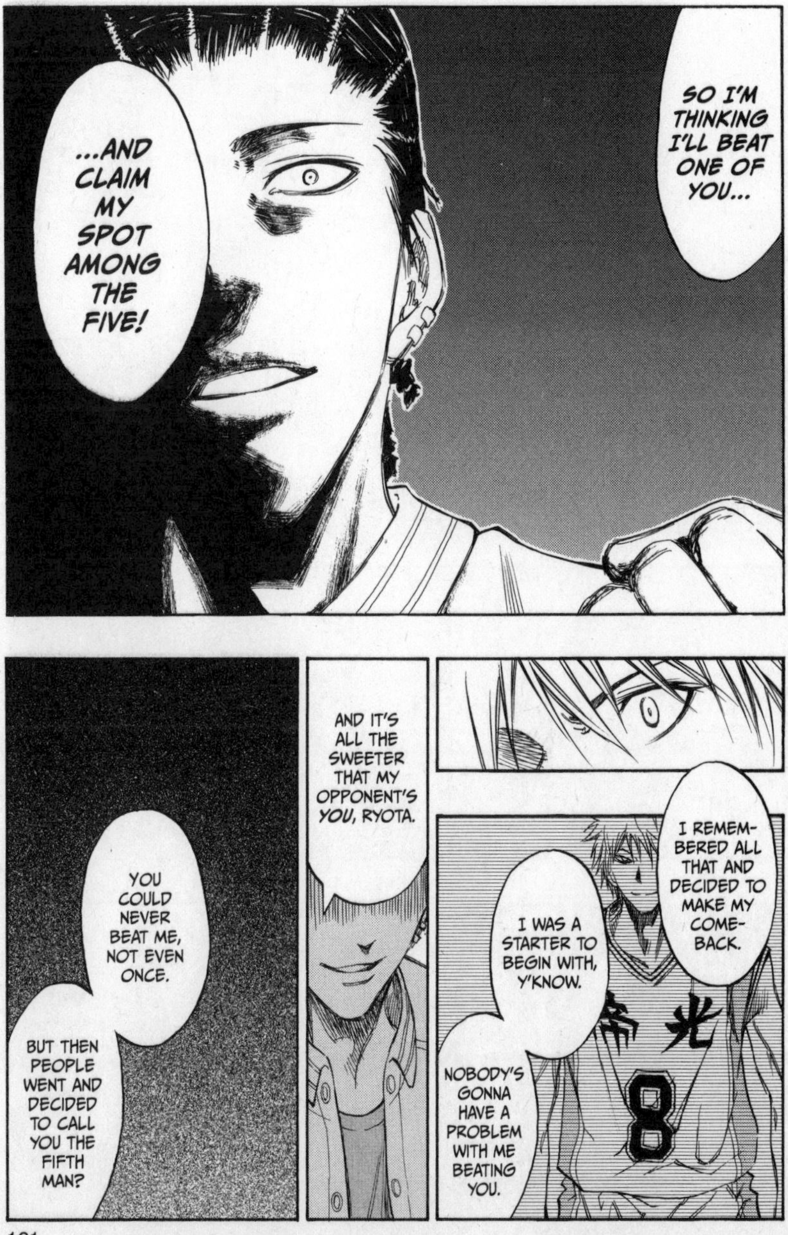
SO I'M THINKING I'LL BEAT ONE OF YOU...
...AND CLAIM MY SPOT AMONG THE FIVE!
I REMEMBERED ALL THAT AND DECIDED TO MAKE MY COMEBACK.
I WAS A STARTER TO BEGIN WITH, Y'KNOW.
NOBODY'S GONNA HAVE A PROBLEM WITH ME BEATING YOU.
AND IT'S ALL THE SWEETER THAT MY OPPONENT'S *YOU*, RYOTA.
YOU COULD NEVER BEAT ME, NOT EVEN ONCE.
BUT THEN PEOPLE WENT AND DECIDED TO CALL YOU THE FIFTH MAN?

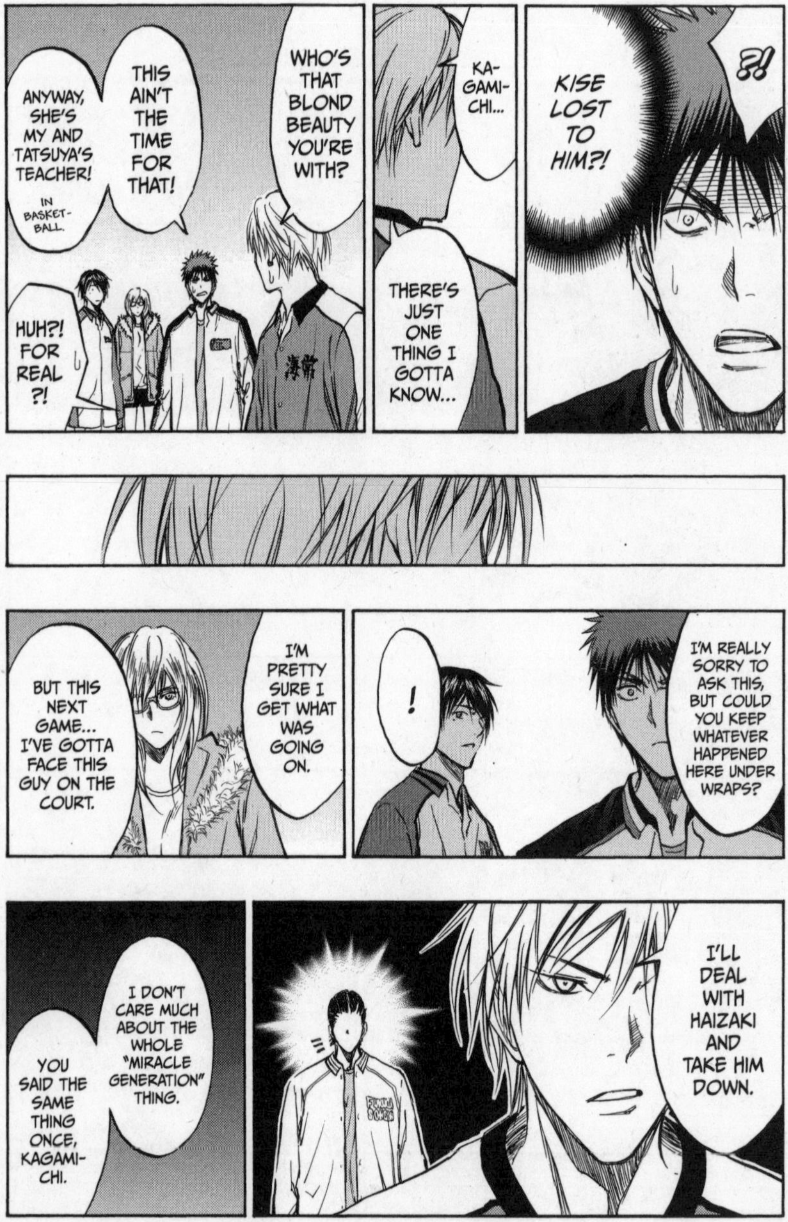
?!
KISE LOST TO HIM?!
KA-GAMI-CHI...
THERE'S JUST ONE THING I GOTTA KNOW...
WHO'S THAT BLOND BEAUTY YOU'RE WITH?
THIS AIN'T THE TIME FOR THAT!
ANYWAY, SHE'S MY AND TATSUYA'S TEACHER!
IN BASKET-BALL.
HUH?! FOR REAL?!
I'M REALLY SORRY TO ASK THIS, BUT COULD YOU KEEP WHATEVER HAPPENED HERE UNDER WRAPS?
!
I'M PRETTY SURE I GET WHAT WAS GOING ON.
BUT THIS NEXT GAME... I'VE GOTTA FACE THIS GUY ON THE COURT.
I'LL DEAL WITH HAIZAKI AND TAKE HIM DOWN.
I DON'T CARE MUCH ABOUT THE WHOLE "MIRACLE GENERATION" THING.
YOU SAID THE SAME THING ONCE, KAGAMI-CHI.

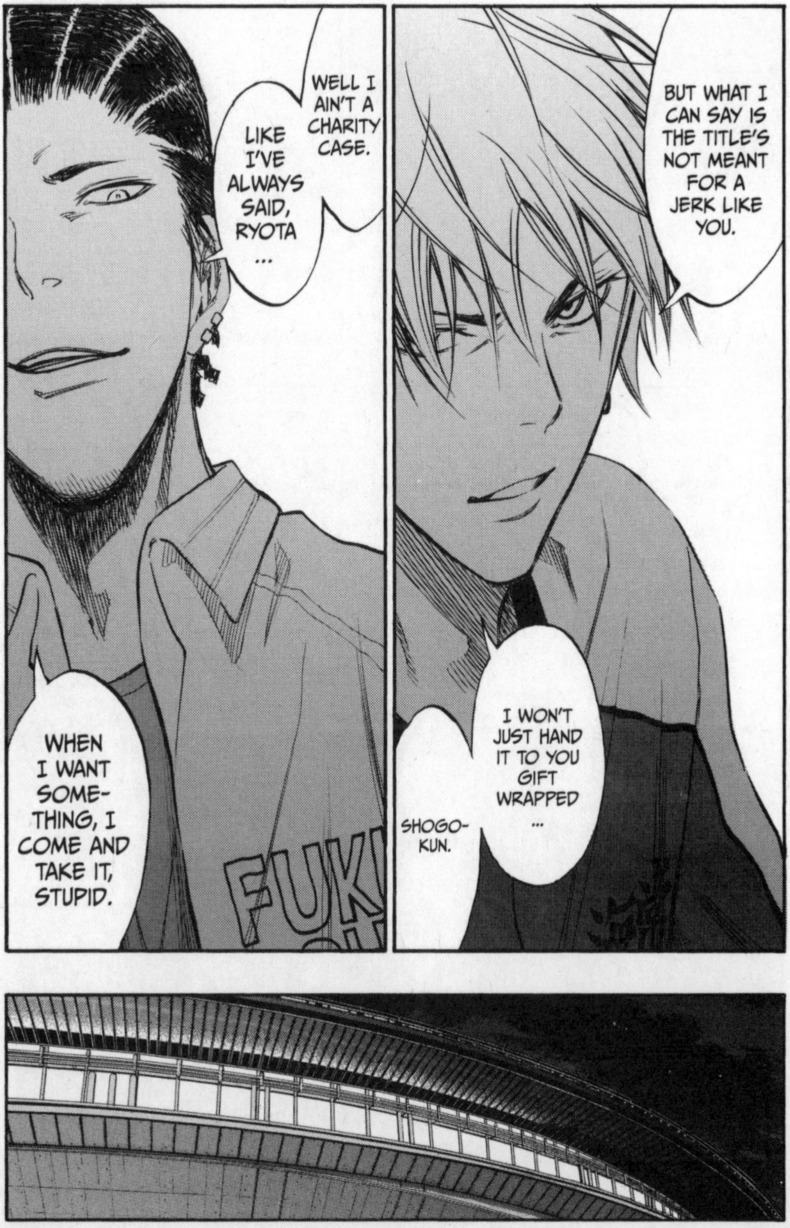
BUT WHAT I CAN SAY IS THE TITLE'S NOT MEANT FOR A JERK LIKE YOU.
I WON'T JUST HAND IT TO YOU GIFT WRAPPED ...
SHOGO-KUN.
WELL I AIN'T A CHARITY CASE.
LIKE I'VE ALWAYS SAID, RYOTA ...
WHEN I WANT SOME-THING, I COME AND TAKE IT, STUPID.

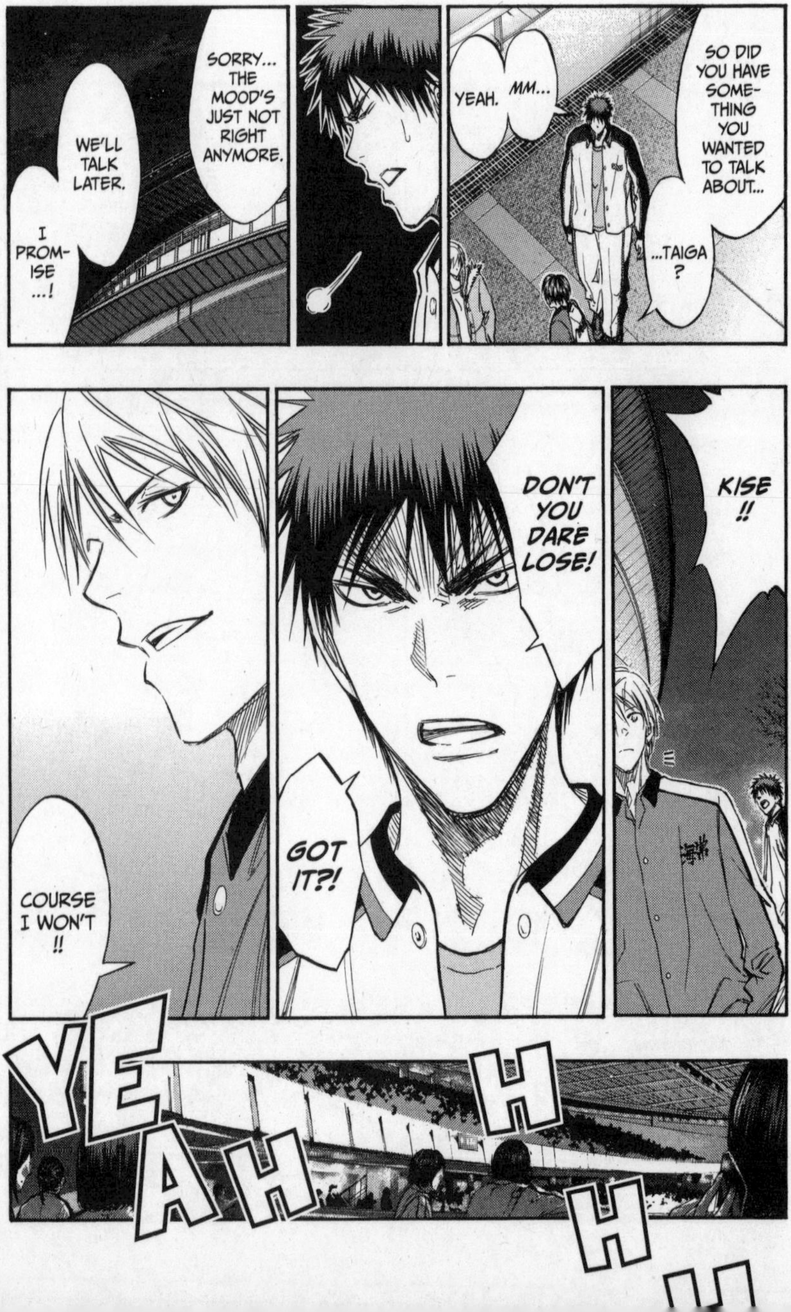
SO DID YOU HAVE SOME-THING YOU WANTED TO TALK ABOUT...
...TAIGA?
MM...
YEAH.
SORRY... THE MOOD'S JUST NOT RIGHT ANYMORE.
WE'LL TALK LATER.
I PROM-ISE ...!
KISE!!
DON'T YOU DARE LOSE!
GOT IT?!
COURSE I WON'T!!
YEAHHHH

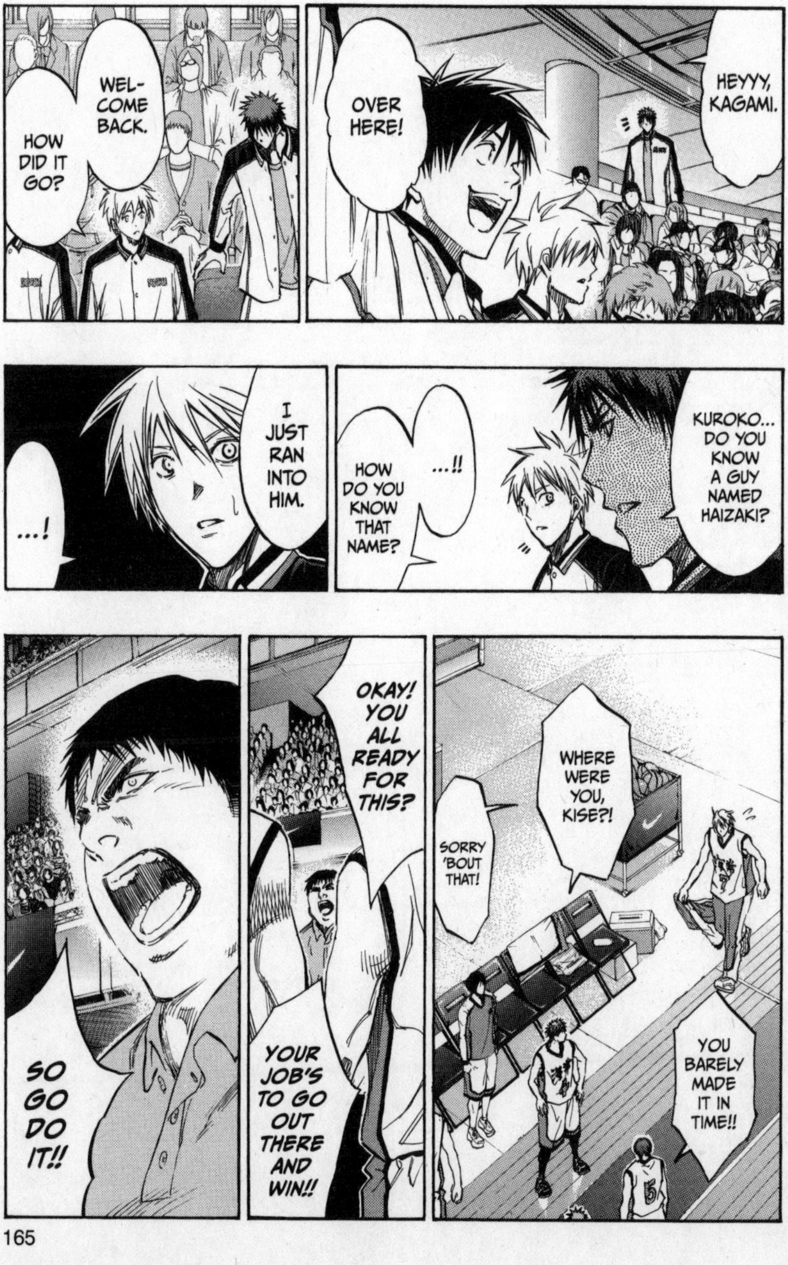
HEYYY, KAGAMI.
OVER HERE!
WEL-COME BACK.
HOW DID IT GO?
KUROKO... DO YOU KNOW A GUY NAMED HAIZAKI?
...!!
HOW DO YOU KNOW THAT NAME?
I JUST RAN INTO HIM.
...!
WHERE WERE YOU, KISE?!
SORRY 'BOUT THAT!
YOU BARELY MADE IT IN TIME!!
OKAY! YOU ALL READY FOR THIS?
YOUR JOB'S TO GO OUT THERE AND WIN!!
SO GO DO IT!!

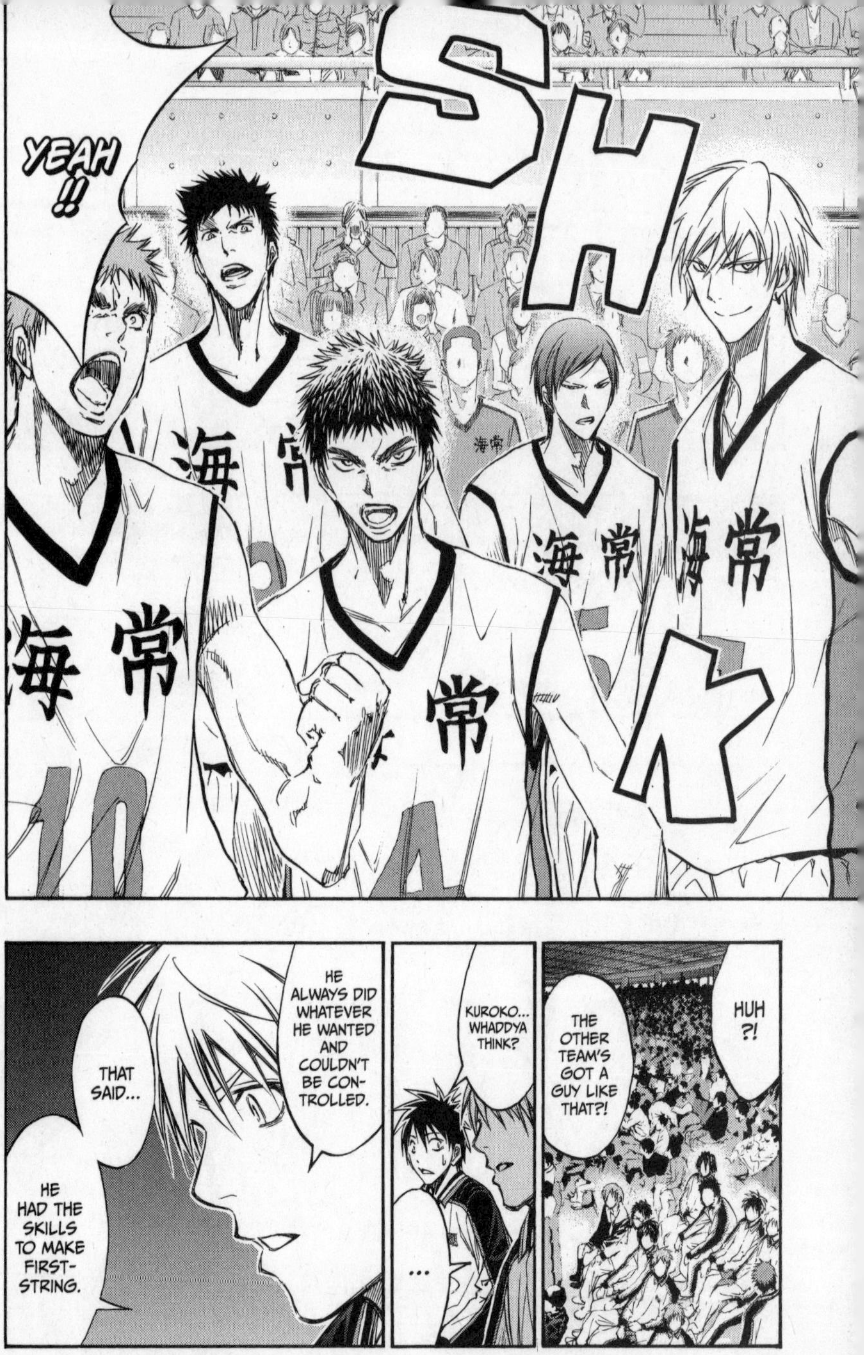
SHK
YEAH!!
HUH?!
THE OTHER TEAM'S GOT A GUY LIKE THAT?!
KUROKO... WHADDYA THINK?
...
HE ALWAYS DID WHATEVER HE WANTED AND COULDN'T BE CON-TROLLED.
THAT SAID...
HE HAD THE SKILLS TO MAKE FIRST-STRING.

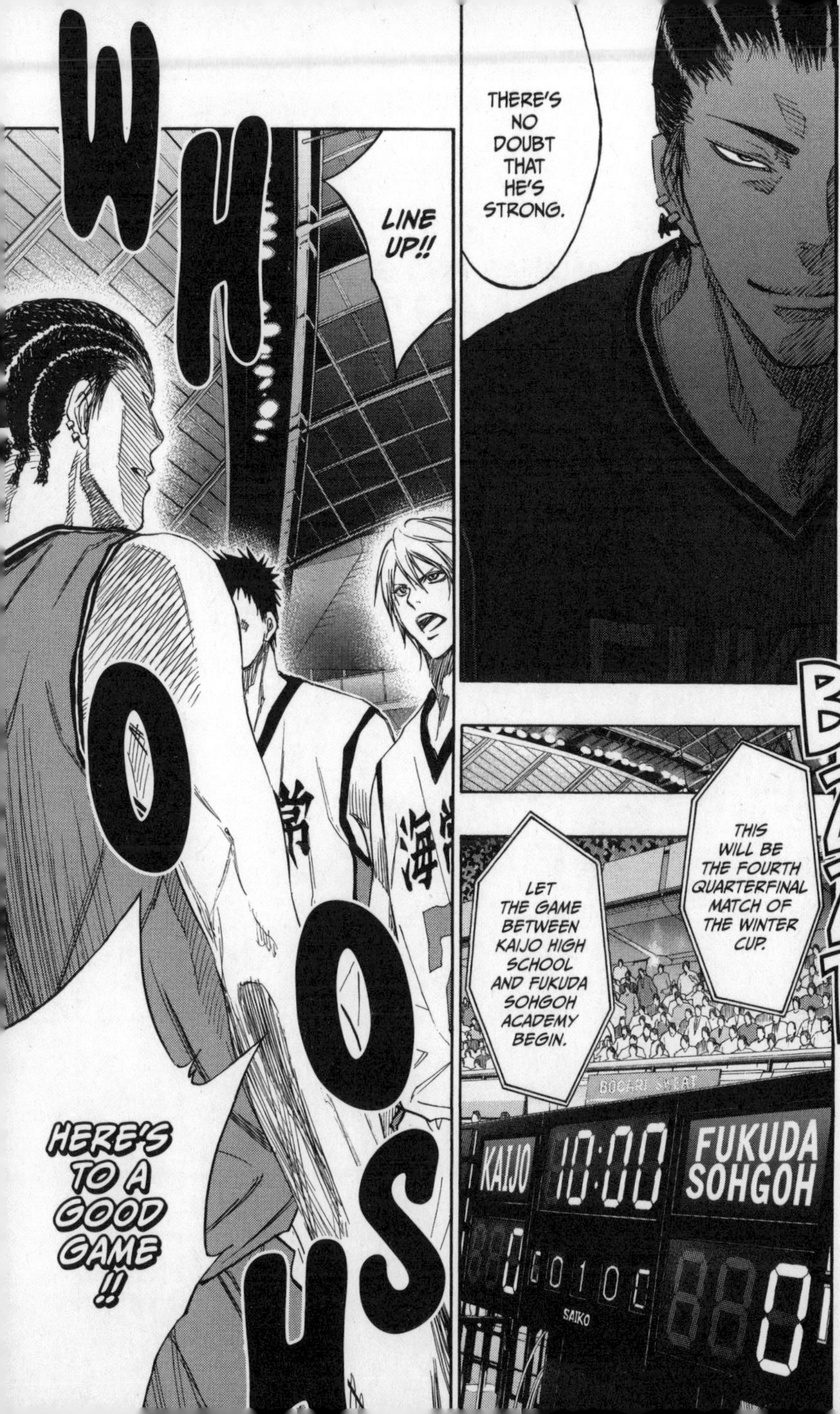
THERE'S NO DOUBT THAT HE'S STRONG.
BZZT
THIS WILL BE THE FOURTH QUARTERFINAL MATCH OF THE WINTER CUP.
LET THE GAME BETWEEN KAIJO HIGH SCHOOL AND FUKUDA SOHGOH ACADEMY BEGIN.
KAIJO
10:00
FUKUDA SOHGOH
SAIKO
LINE UP!!
WHOOSH
HERE'S TO A GOOD GAME!!

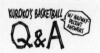

KUROKO'S BASKETBALL
Q&A
W/ HALFWAY-DECENT ANSWERS

Q. BESIDES BANANAS AND STRAWBERRIES, WHAT OTHER FRUIT DID RIKO PUT INTO THAT STEW SHE MADE?
(THE GENERAL from TOKYO)

A. CASTELLA CAKE.

KUROKO'S BASKETBALL BLOOPERS
TAKE 5

YOU'RE GONNA...
...WANNA LEMME GO, KIDDO!
BWAH!
WHAM
OH!
VIC-TORY!!
NO, THAT'S NOT GOOD AT ALL!!
WE NEED HIM FOR THE PLOT!!
IT'S JUST... THAT FELT REFRESHING!
SHF
HEY!
HAIZAKI
FSSHH...

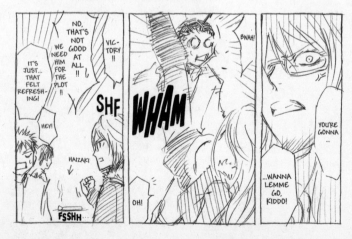

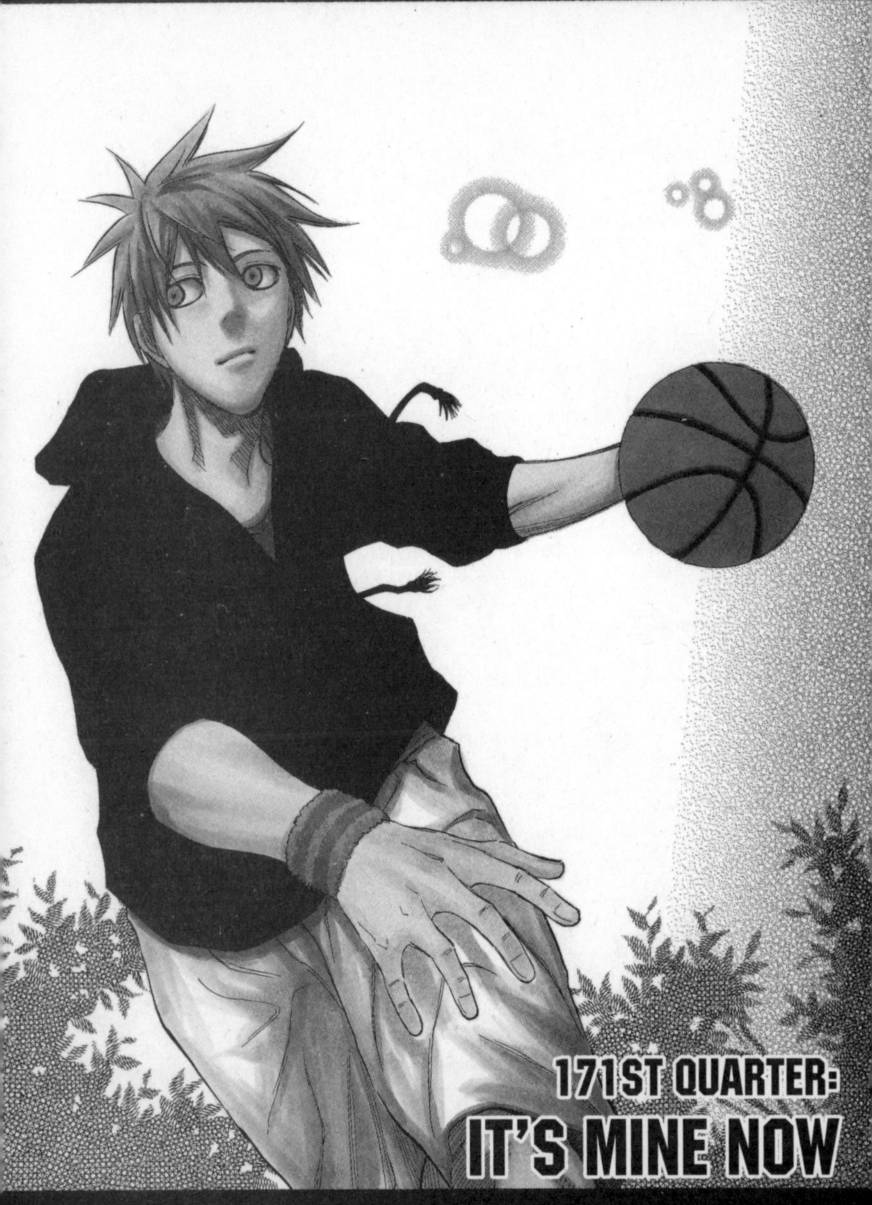
171ST QUARTER:
IT'S MINE NOW

Kuroko's BASKETBALL

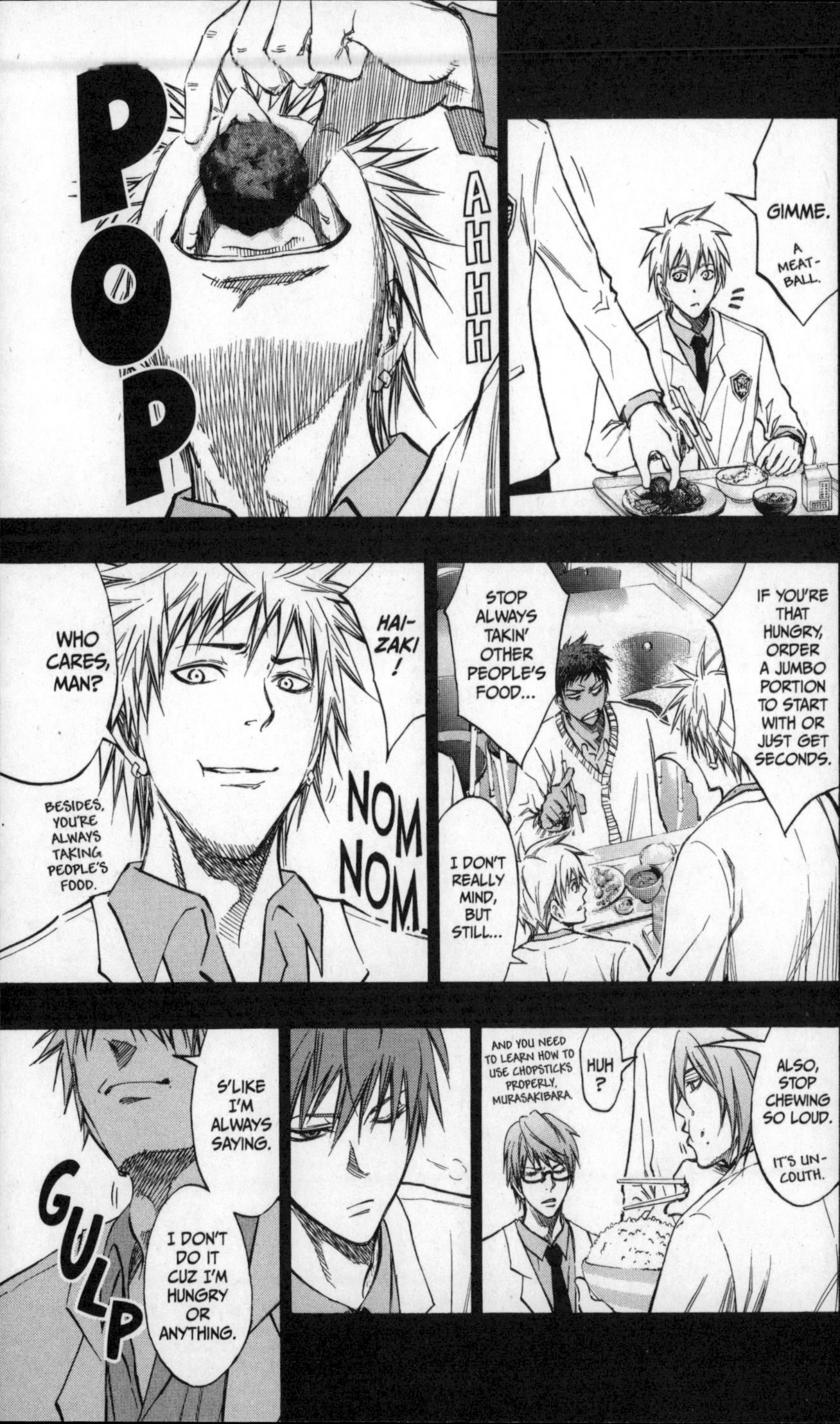
GIMME.
A MEAT-BALL.
AHHHH
POP
IF YOU'RE THAT HUNGRY, ORDER A JUMBO PORTION TO START WITH OR JUST GET SECONDS.
STOP ALWAYS TAKIN' OTHER PEOPLE'S FOOD...
I DON'T REALLY MIND, BUT STILL...
HAI-ZAKI!
WHO CARES, MAN?
NOM NOM
BESIDES, YOU'RE ALWAYS TAKING PEOPLE'S FOOD.
ALSO, STOP CHEWING SO LOUD.
IT'S UN-COUTH.
HUH?
AND YOU NEED TO LEARN HOW TO USE CHOPSTICKS PROPERLY, MURASAKIBARA
S'LIKE I'M ALWAYS SAYING.
GULP
I DON'T DO IT CUZ I'M HUNGRY OR ANYTHING.

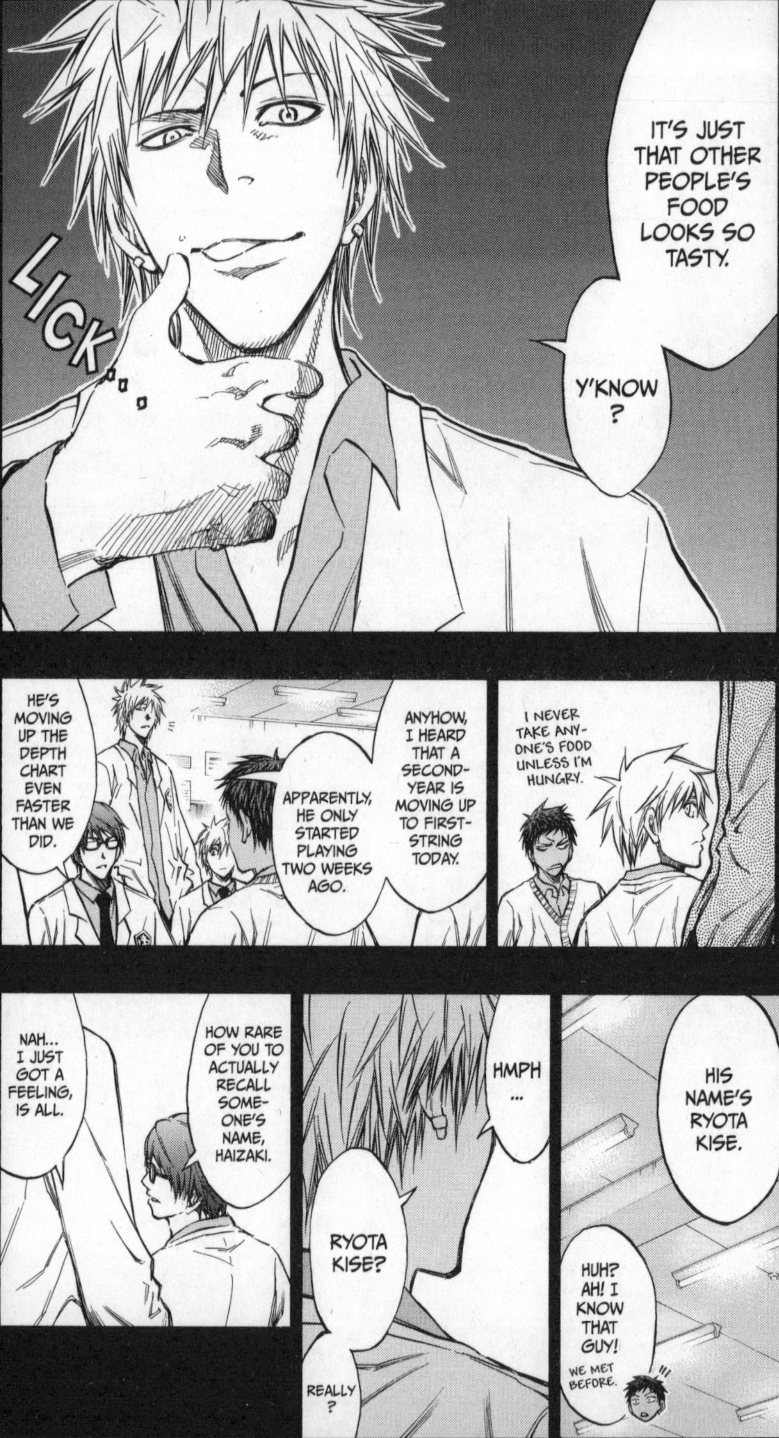
IT'S JUST THAT OTHER PEOPLE'S FOOD LOOKS SO TASTY.
Y'KNOW?
LICK
I NEVER TAKE ANYONE'S FOOD UNLESS I'M HUNGRY.
ANYHOW, I HEARD THAT A SECOND-YEAR IS MOVING UP TO FIRST-STRING TODAY.
APPARENTLY, HE ONLY STARTED PLAYING TWO WEEKS AGO.
HE'S MOVING UP THE DEPTH CHART EVEN FASTER THAN WE DID.
HIS NAME'S RYOTA KISE.
HUH? AH! I KNOW THAT GUY!
WE MET BEFORE.
HMPH...
RYOTA KISE?
REALLY?
HOW RARE OF YOU TO ACTUALLY RECALL SOMEONE'S NAME, HAIZAKI.
NAH... I JUST GOT A FEELING, IS ALL.

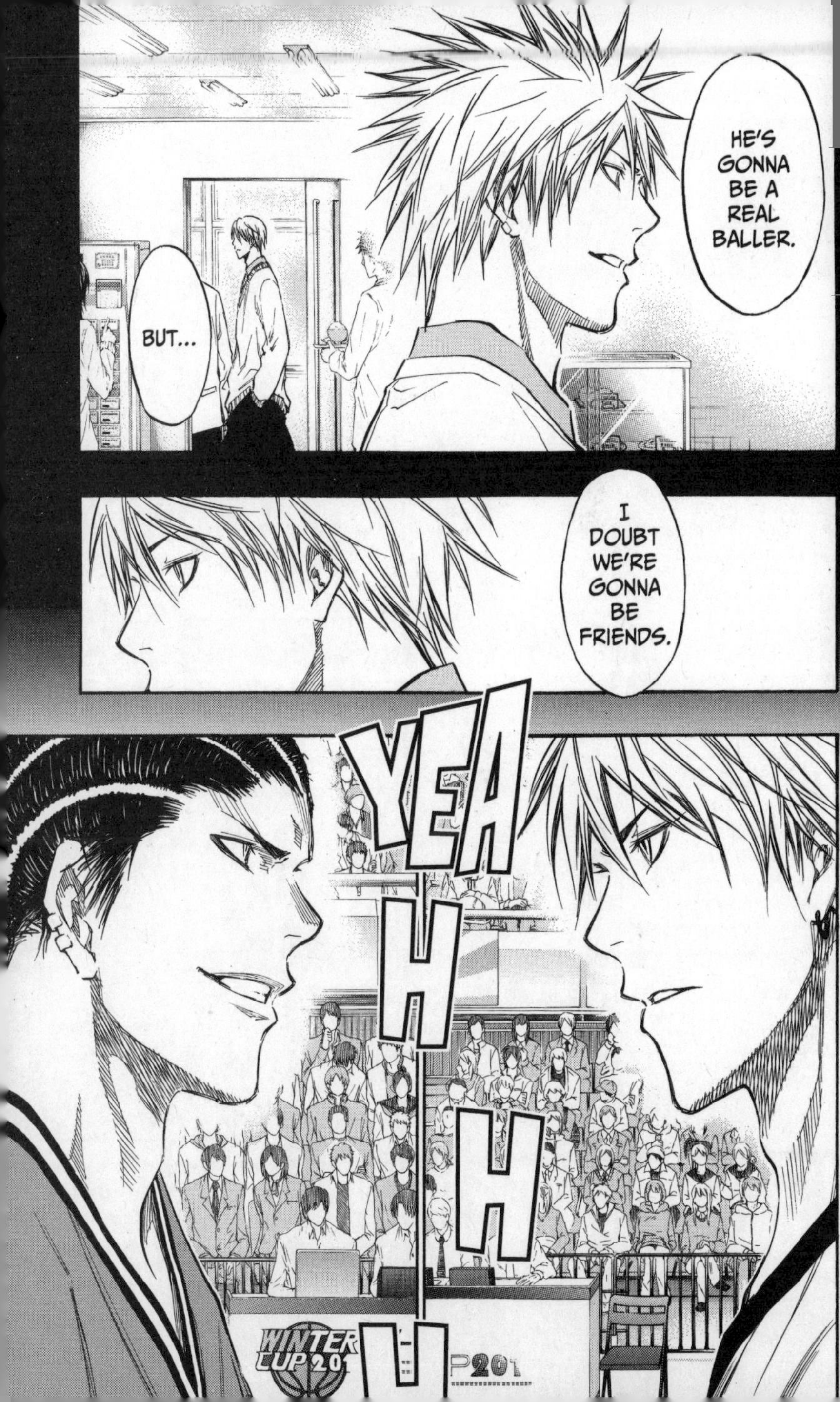
HE'S GONNA BE A REAL BALLER.
BUT...
I DOUBT WE'RE GONNA BE FRIENDS.
YEAHHHH
WINTER CUP 201

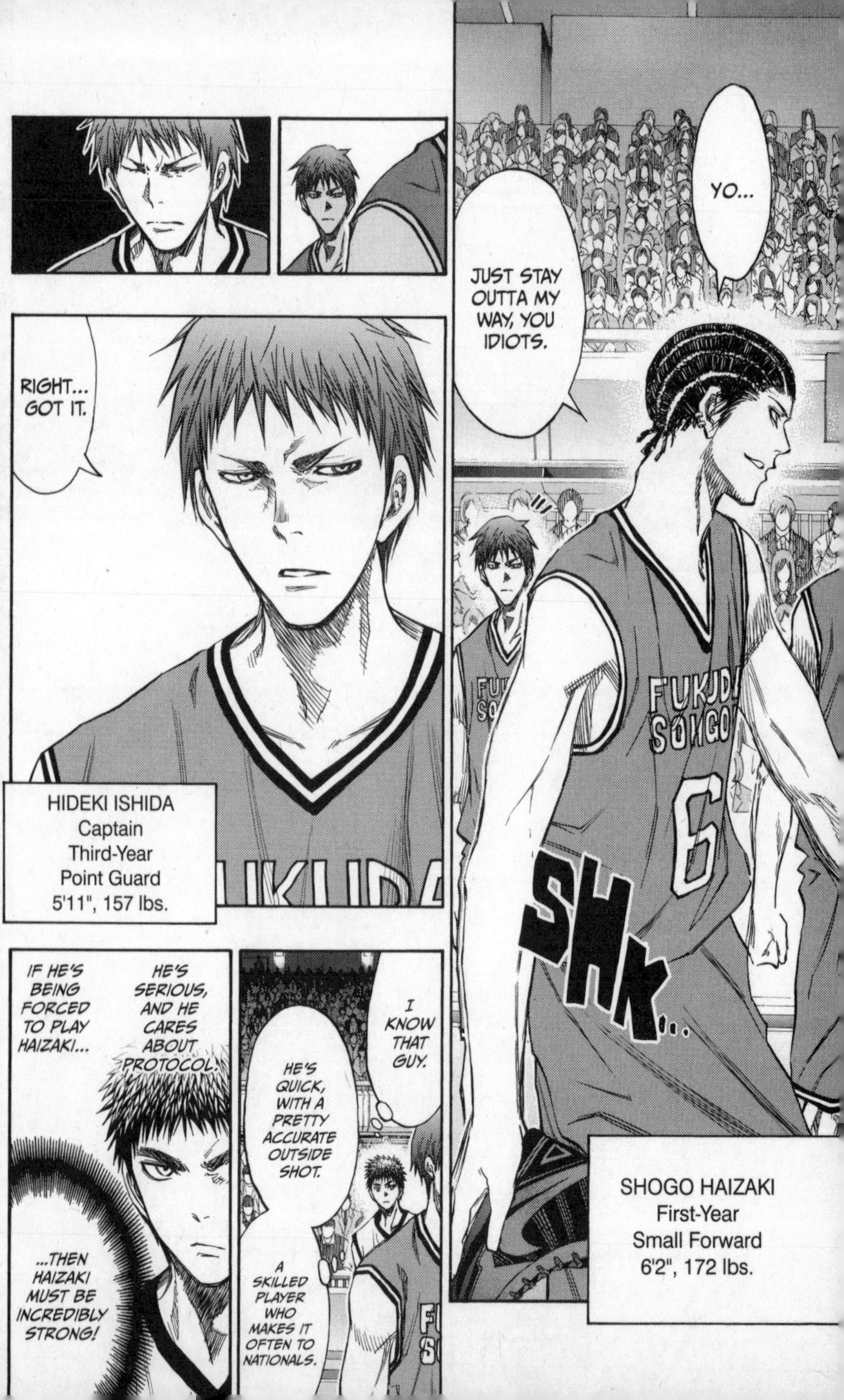
YO...
JUST STAY OUTTA MY WAY, YOU IDIOTS.
SHK...
SHOGO HAIZAKI
First-Year
Small Forward
6'2", 172 lbs.
RIGHT... GOT IT.
HIDEKI ISHIDA
Captain
Third-Year
Point Guard
5'11", 157 lbs.
I KNOW THAT GUY.
HE'S QUICK, WITH A PRETTY ACCURATE OUTSIDE SHOT.
A SKILLED PLAYER WHO MAKES IT OFTEN TO NATIONALS.
HE'S SERIOUS, AND HE CARES ABOUT PROTOCOL.
IF HE'S BEING FORCED TO PLAY HAIZAKI...
...THEN HAIZAKI MUST BE INCREDIBLY STRONG!

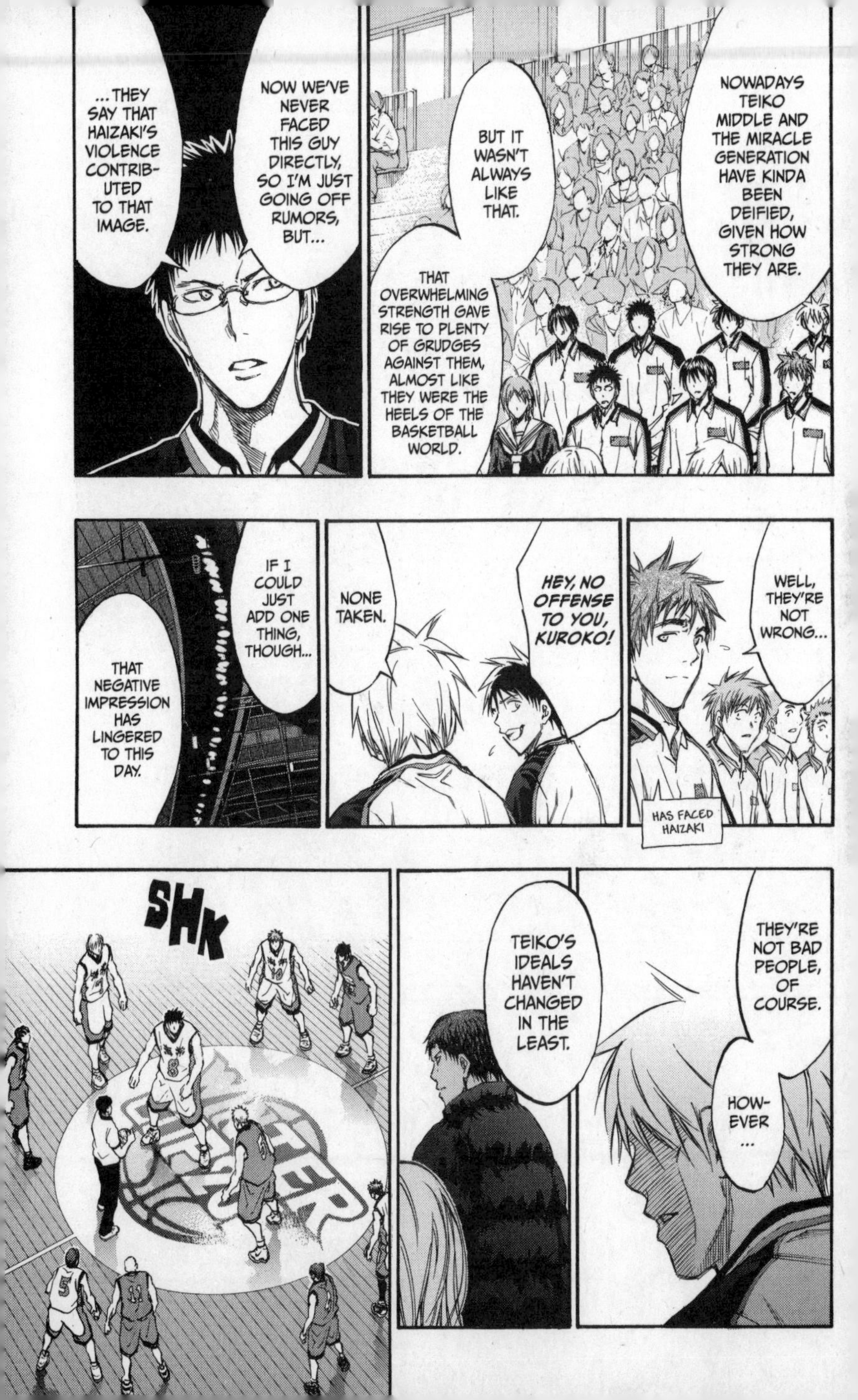
NOWADAYS TEIKO MIDDLE AND THE MIRACLE GENERATION HAVE KINDA BEEN DEIFIED, GIVEN HOW STRONG THEY ARE.
BUT IT WASN'T ALWAYS LIKE THAT.
THAT OVERWHELMING STRENGTH GAVE RISE TO PLENTY OF GRUDGES AGAINST THEM, ALMOST LIKE THEY WERE THE HEELS OF THE BASKETBALL WORLD.
NOW WE'VE NEVER FACED THIS GUY DIRECTLY, SO I'M JUST GOING OFF RUMORS, BUT...
...THEY SAY THAT HAIZAKI'S VIOLENCE CONTRIBUTED TO THAT IMAGE.
WELL, THEY'RE NOT WRONG...
HAS FACED HAIZAKI
HEY, NO OFFENSE TO YOU, KUROKO!
NONE TAKEN.
IF I COULD JUST ADD ONE THING, THOUGH...
THAT NEGATIVE IMPRESSION HAS LINGERED TO THIS DAY.
THEY'RE NOT BAD PEOPLE, OF COURSE.
HOWEVER...
TEIKO'S IDEALS HAVEN'T CHANGED IN THE LEAST.
SHK

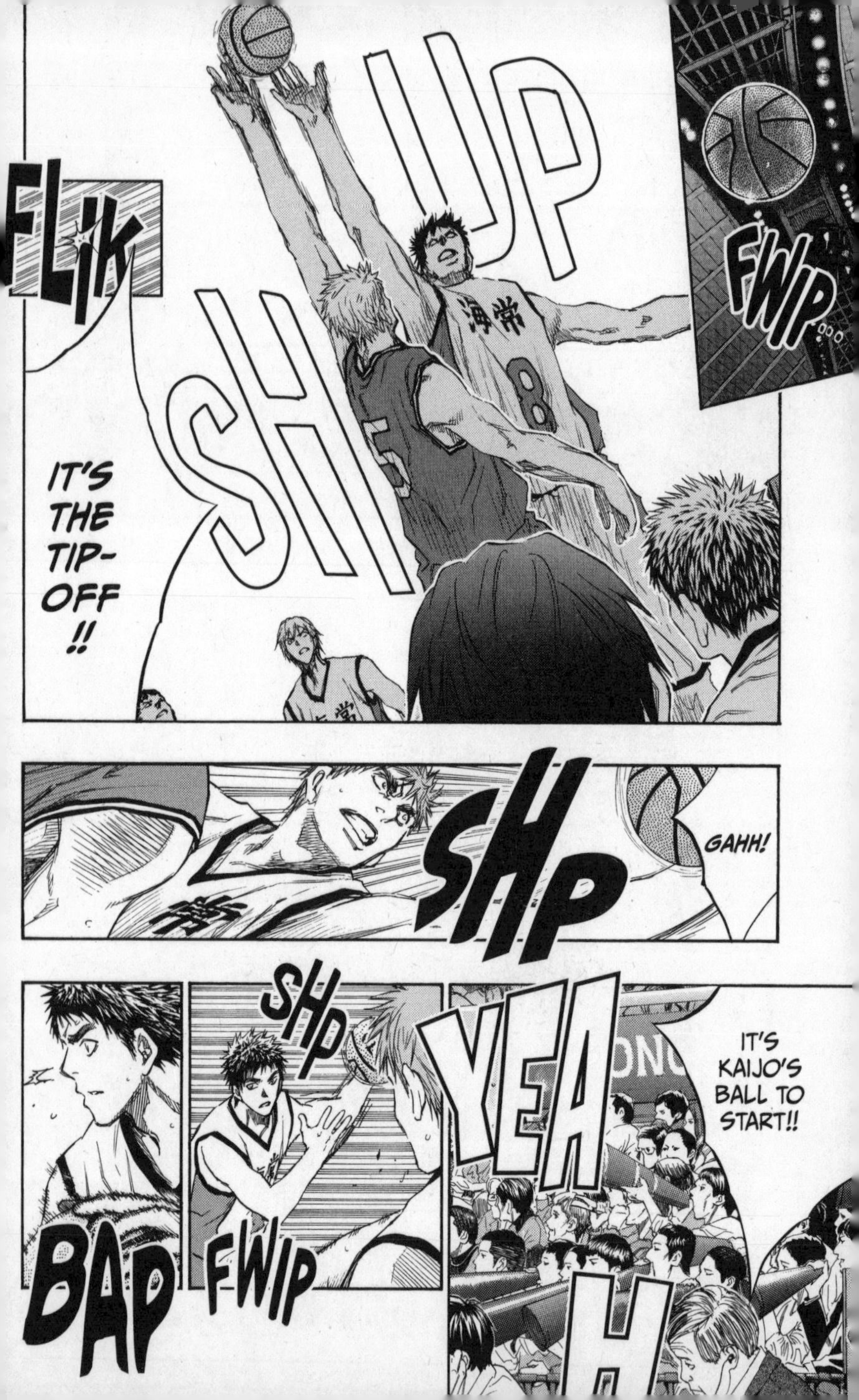
FWIP...
UP
SH
FLIK
IT'S THE TIP-OFF!!
GAHH!
SHP
IT'S KAIJO'S BALL TO START!!
YEAH
SHP
FWIP
BAP

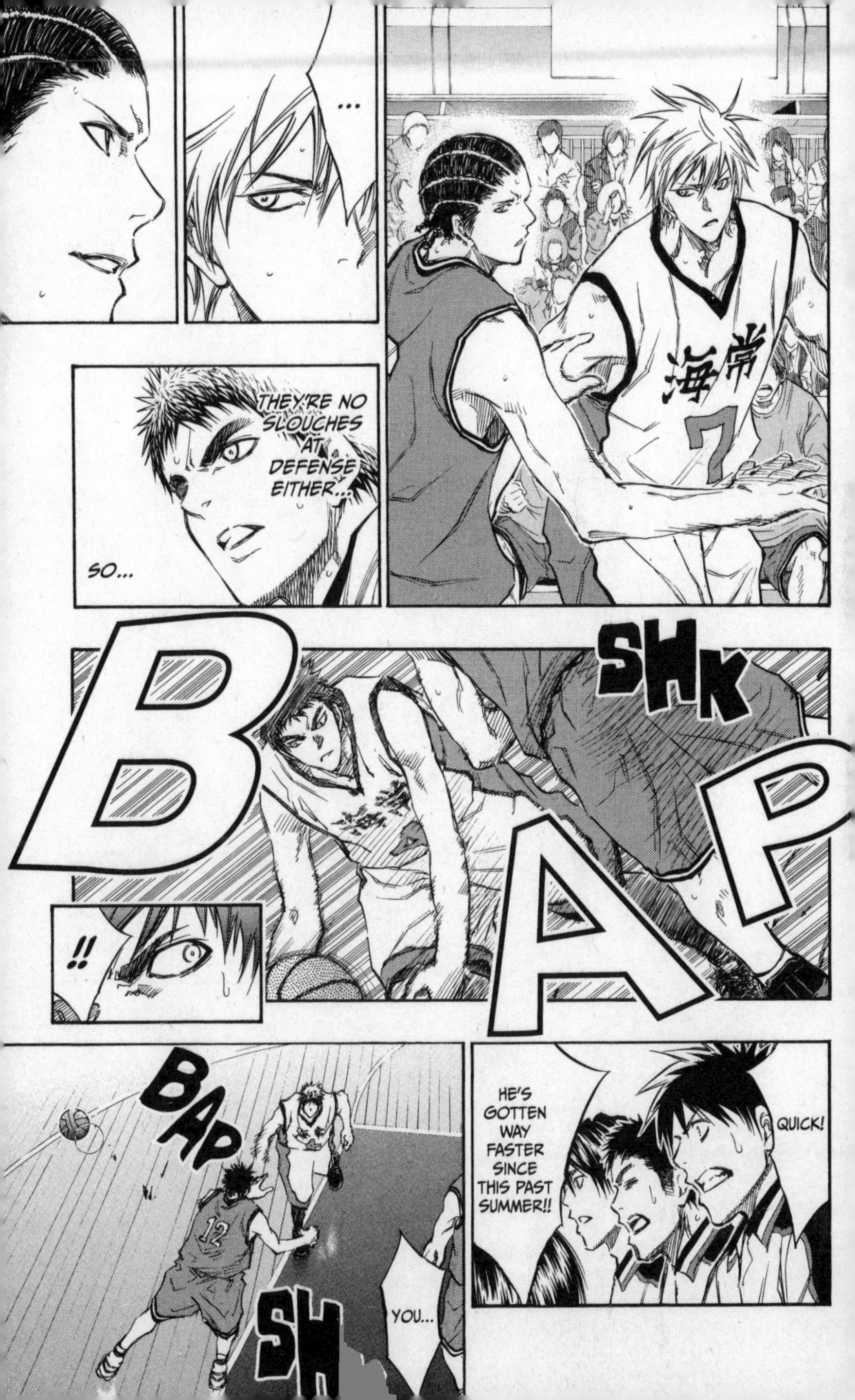
...
THEY'RE NO SLOUCHES AT DEFENSE EITHER...
SO...
海常
7
SHK
BAP
!!
QUICK!
HE'S GOTTEN WAY FASTER SINCE THIS PAST SUMMER!!
BAP
12
YOU...
SH

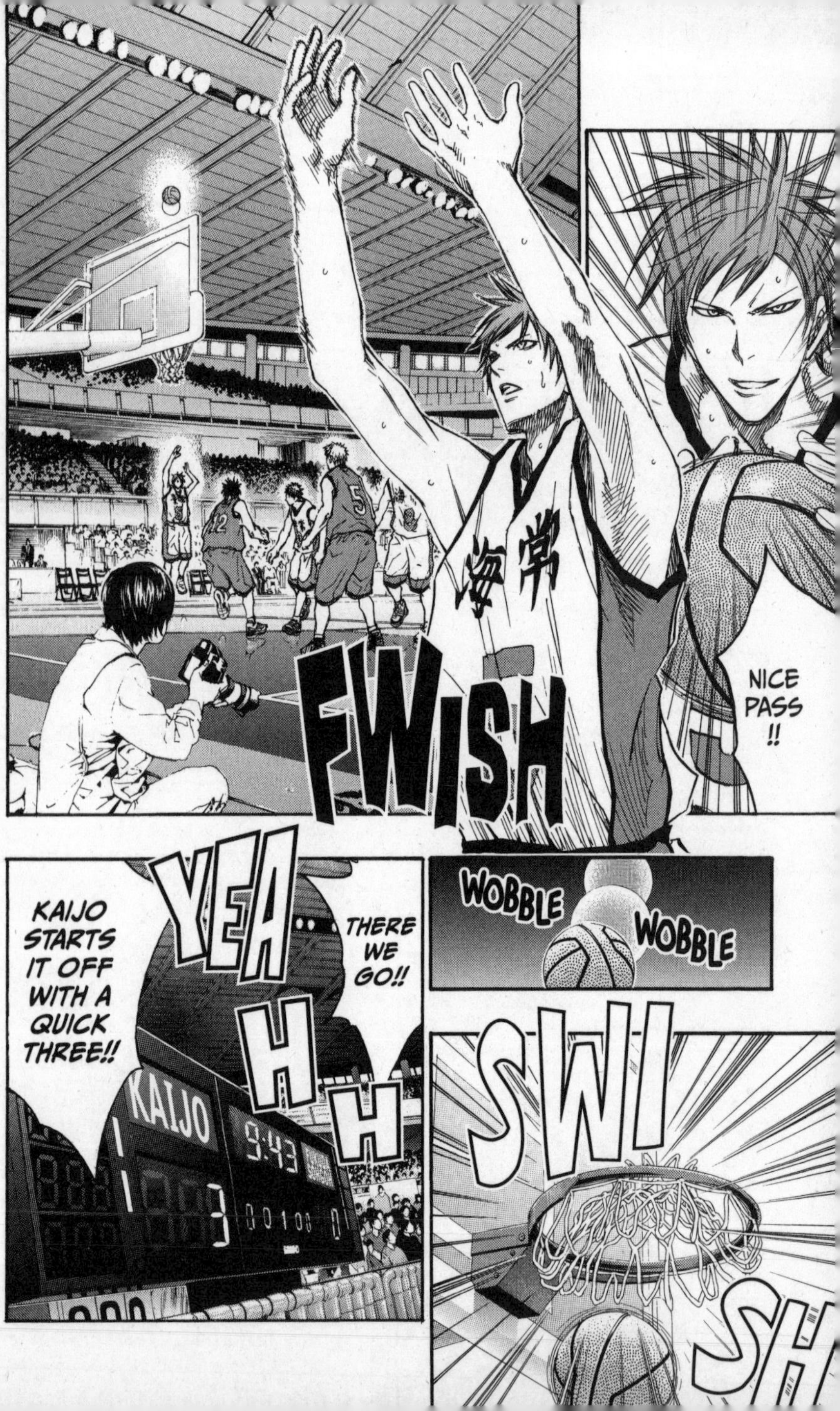
NICE PASS!!
海常
FWISH
WOBBLE
WOBBLE
SWISH
YEAHHH
THERE WE GO!!
KAIJO STARTS IT OFF WITH A QUICK THREE!!
KAIJO
9:43

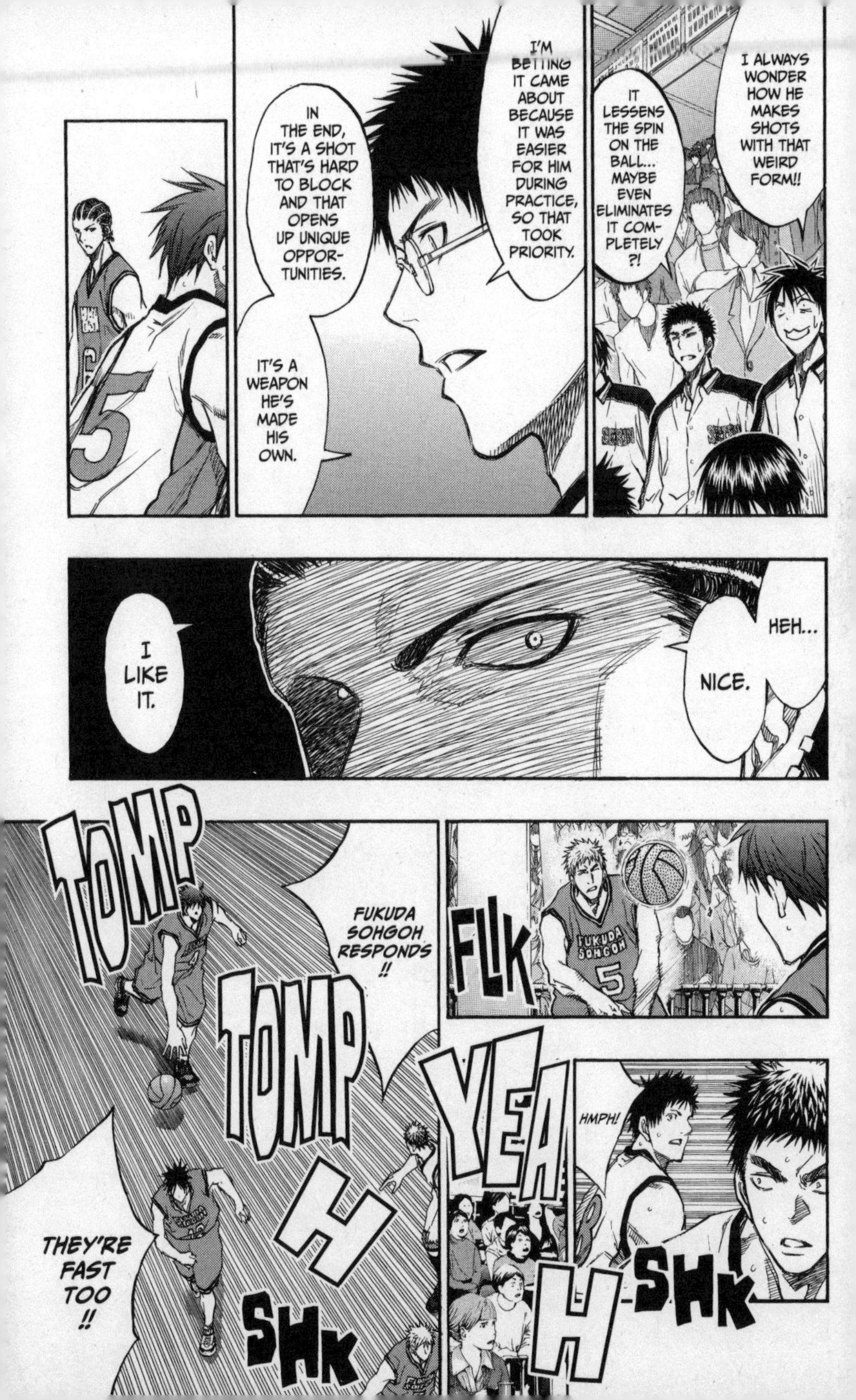
I ALWAYS WONDER HOW HE MAKES SHOTS WITH THAT WEIRD FORM!!
IT LESSENS THE SPIN ON THE BALL... MAYBE EVEN ELIMINATES IT COMPLETELY?!
I'M BETTING IT CAME ABOUT BECAUSE IT WAS EASIER FOR HIM DURING PRACTICE, SO THAT TOOK PRIORITY.
IN THE END, IT'S A SHOT THAT'S HARD TO BLOCK AND THAT OPENS UP UNIQUE OPPORTUNITIES.
IT'S A WEAPON HE'S MADE HIS OWN.
HEH...
NICE.
I LIKE IT.
FLIK
FUKUDA SOHGOH
FUKUDA SOHGOH RESPONDS!!
TOMP
TOMP
YEAH
HMPH!
SHK
H-SHK
SHK
THEY'RE FAST TOO!!

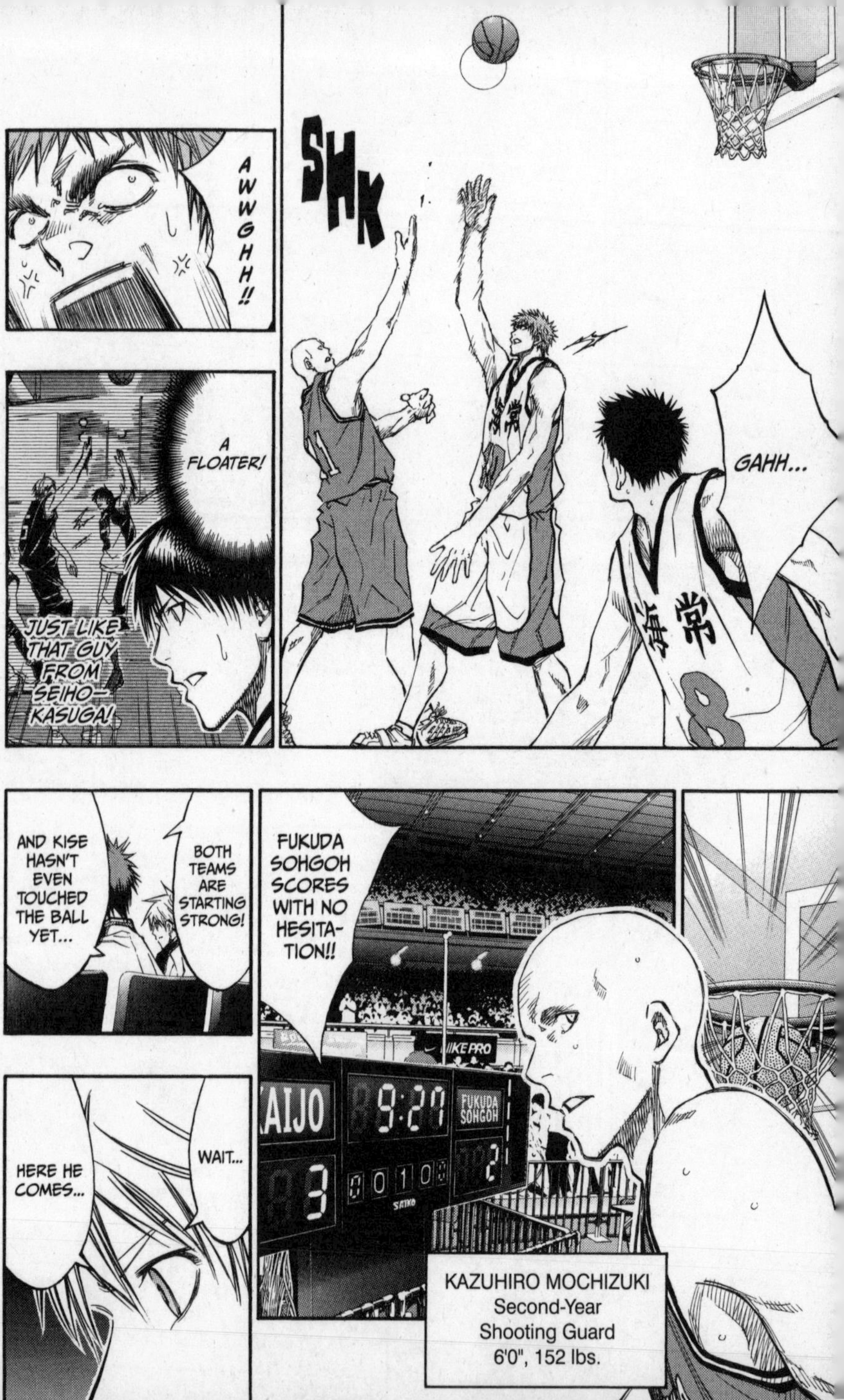
GAHH...
SHK
AWWGHH!!
A FLOATER!
JUST LIKE THAT GUY FROM SEIHO-KASUGA!
KAZUHIRO MOCHIZUKI
Second-Year
Shooting Guard
6'0", 152 lbs.
FUKUDA SOHGOH SCORES WITH NO HESITATION!!
KAIJO
9:27
FUKUDA SOHGOH
3
2
BOTH TEAMS ARE STARTING STRONG!
AND KISE HASN'T EVEN TOUCHED THE BALL YET...
WAIT...
HERE HE COMES...

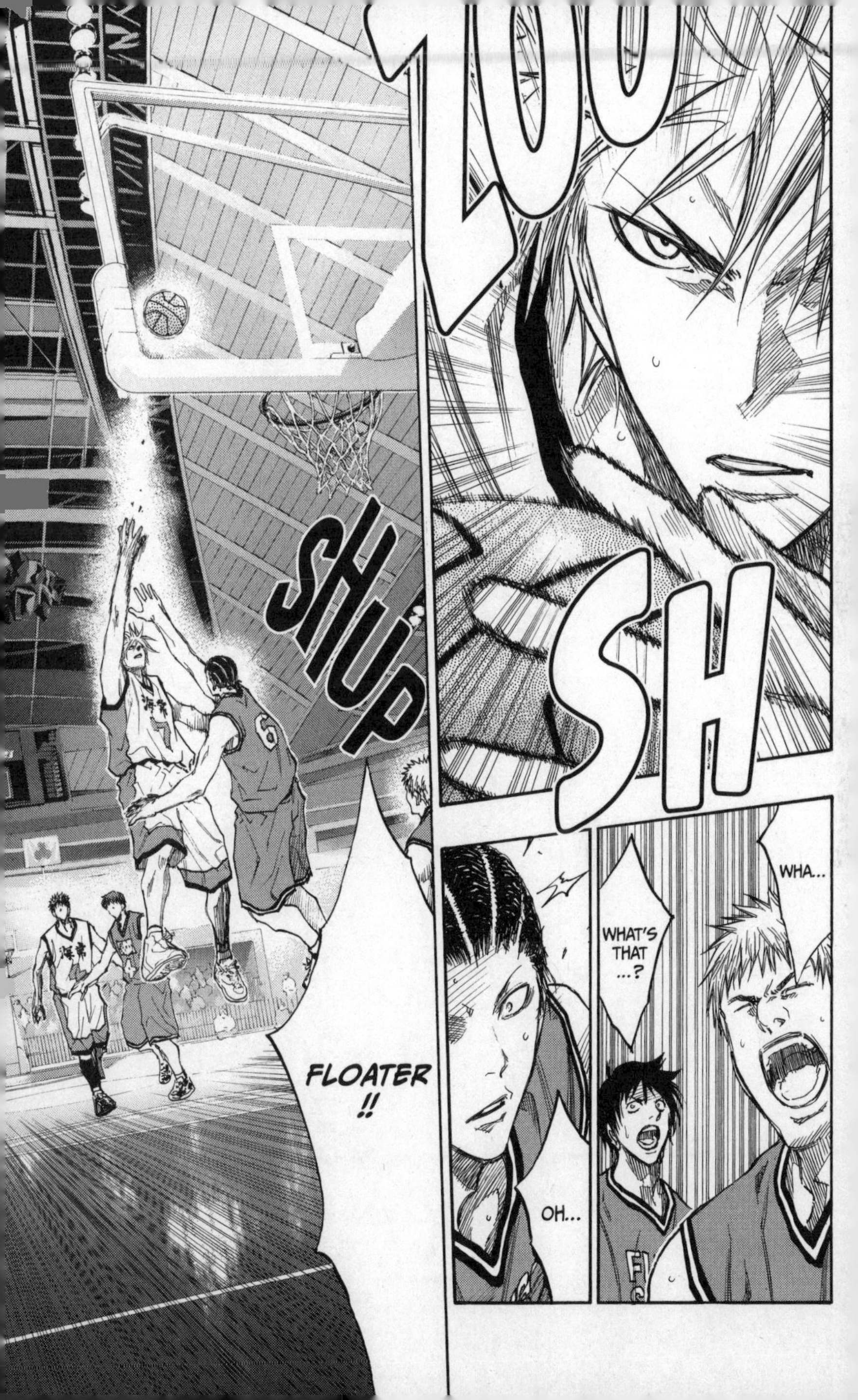

SH
WHA...
WHAT'S THAT ...?
OH...
SHUP
FLOATER !!

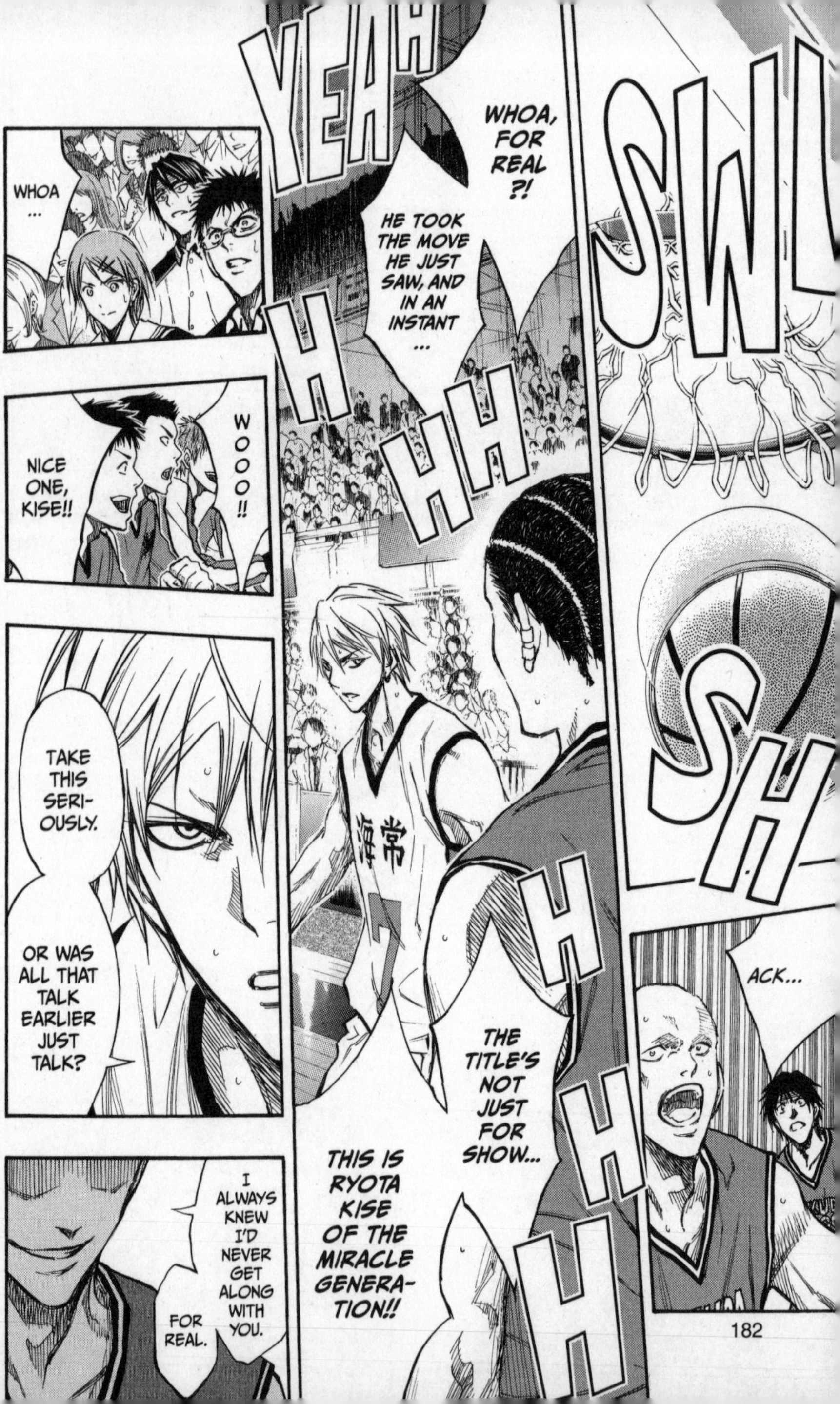
SWISH
ACK...
YEAHHHHHHHH
WHOA, FOR REAL?!
HE TOOK THE MOVE HE JUST SAW, AND IN AN INSTANT...
THE TITLE'S NOT JUST FOR SHOW...
THIS IS RYOTA KISE OF THE MIRACLE GENERATION!!
WHOA...
WOOOO!!
NICE ONE, KISE!!
TAKE THIS SERIOUSLY.
OR WAS ALL THAT TALK EARLIER JUST TALK?
I ALWAYS KNEW I'D NEVER GET ALONG WITH YOU.
FOR REAL.

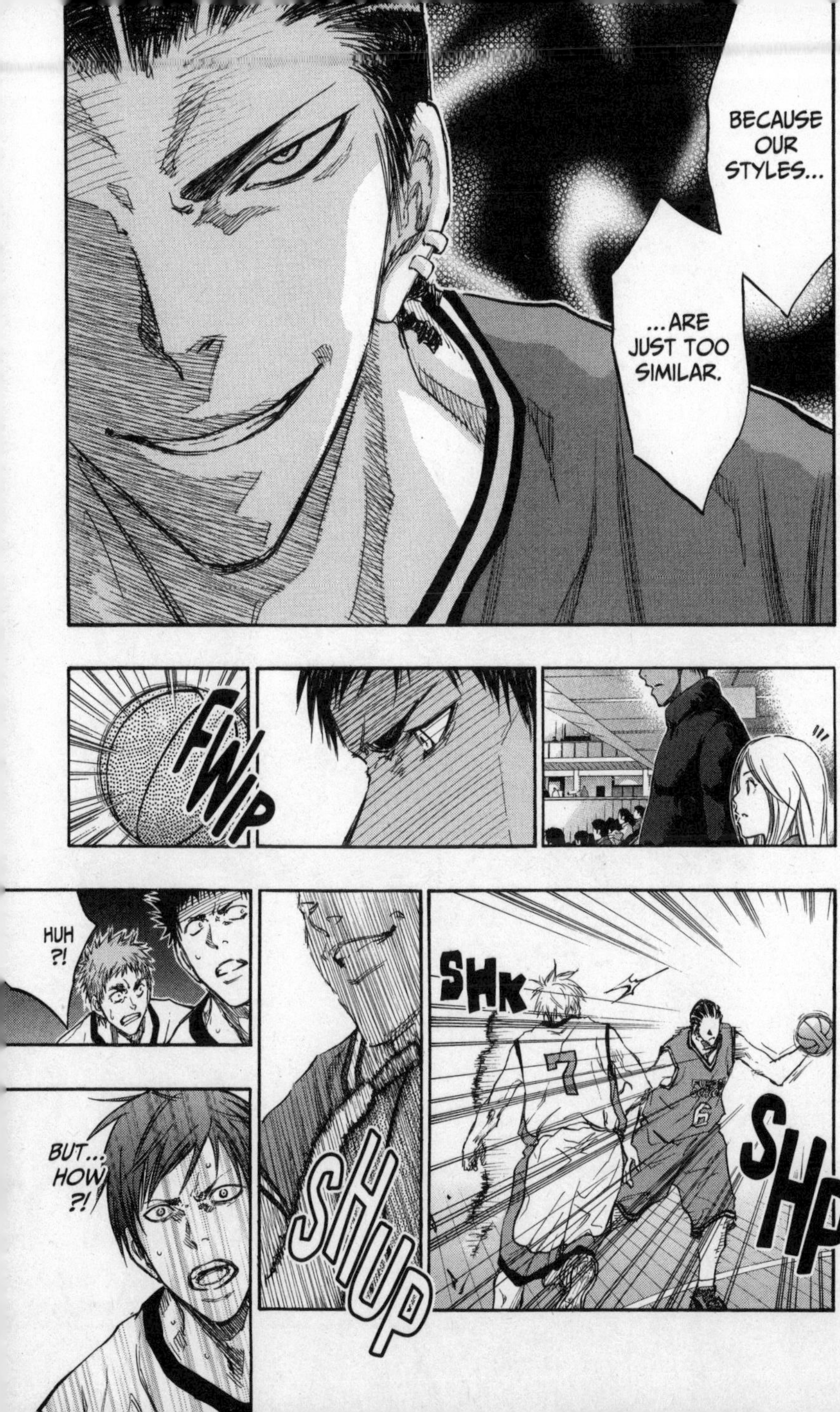
BECAUSE OUR STYLES...
...ARE JUST TOO SIMILAR.
FWIP
SHK
SHP
SHUP
HUH ?!
BUT... HOW ?!

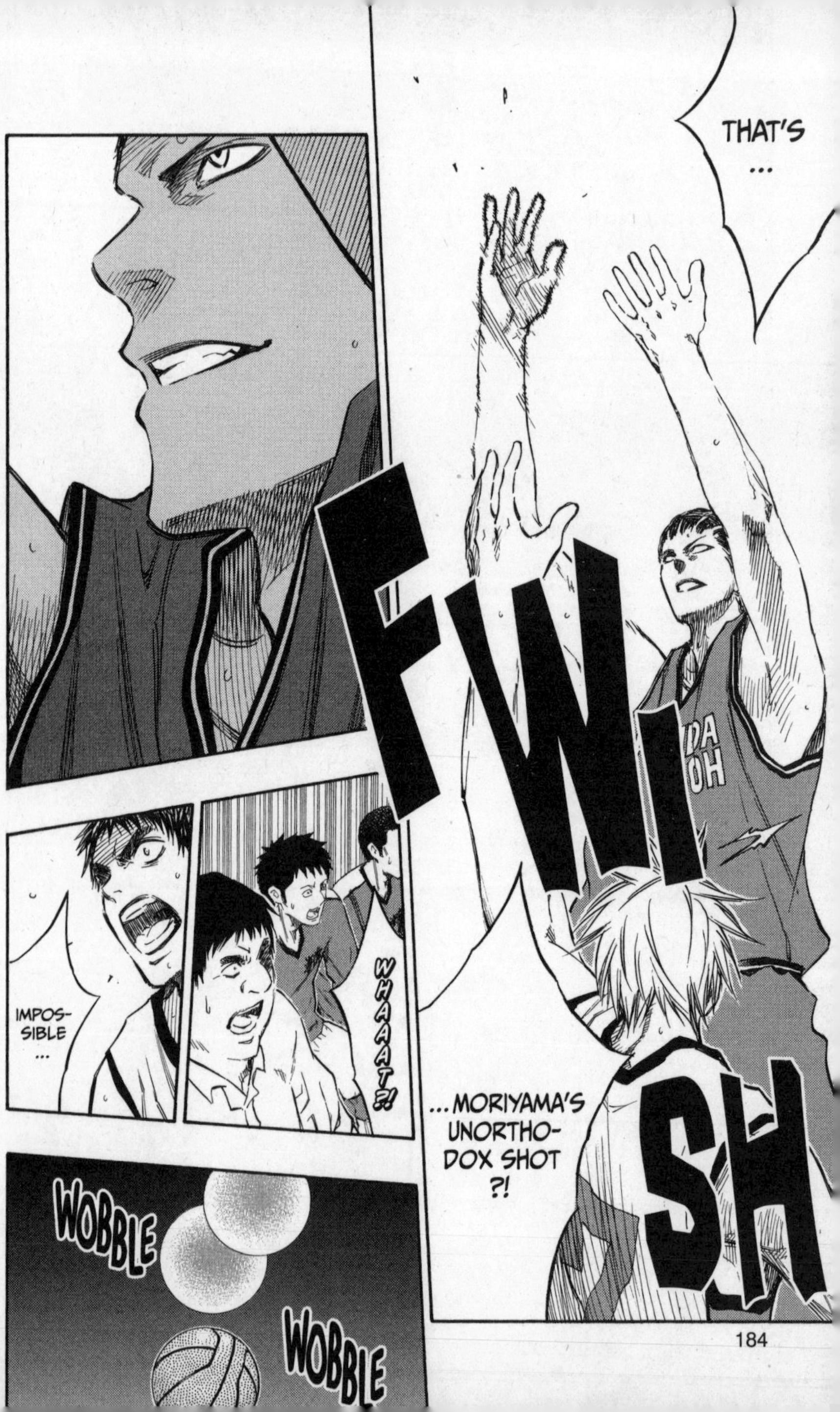
THAT'S ...
FWISH
...MORIYAMA'S UNORTHODOX SHOT ?!
WHAAAAT?!
IMPOSSIBLE ...
WOBBLE
WOBBLE

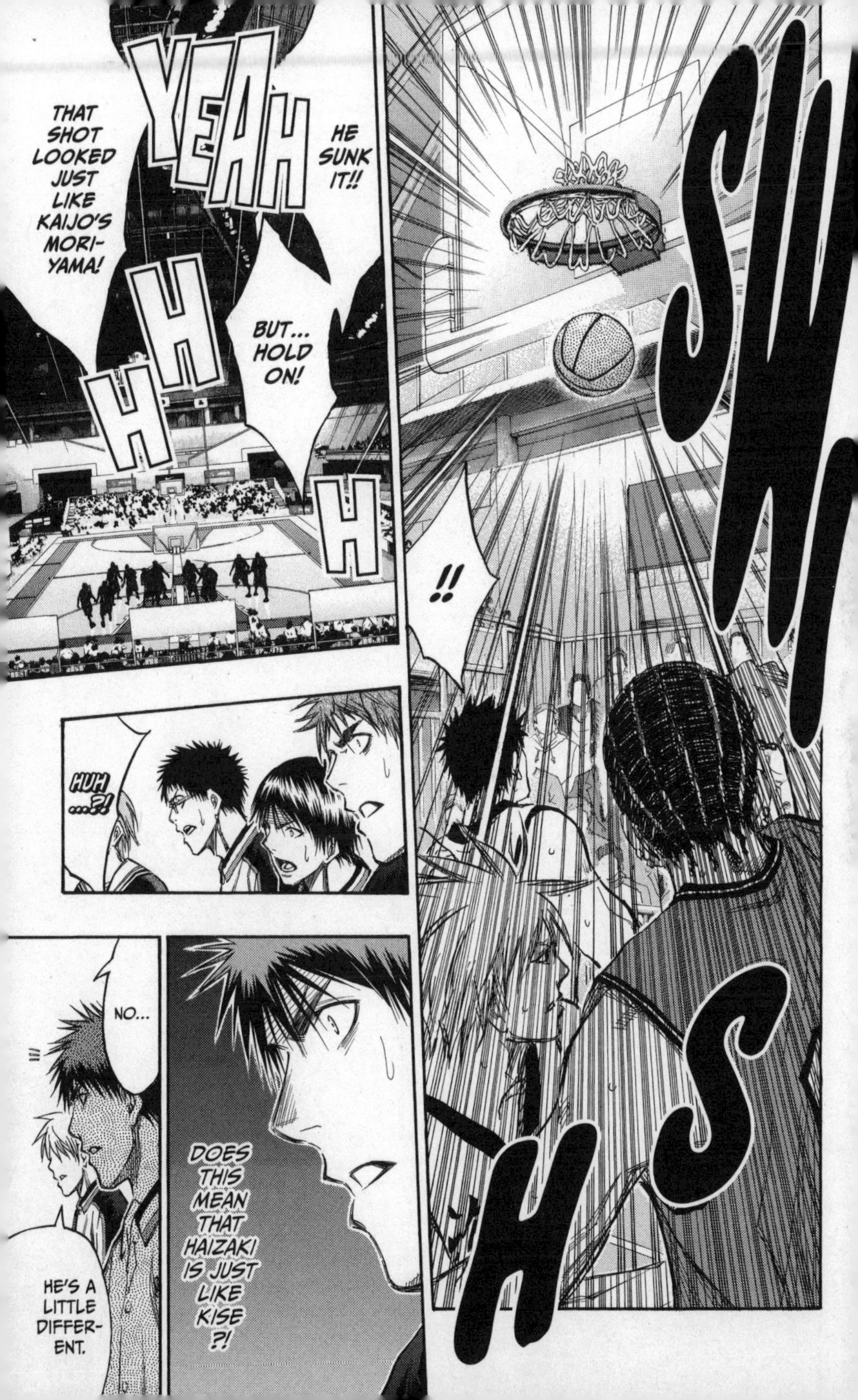
SH
!!
HE SUNK IT!!
YEAHHHH
BUT... HOLD ON!
THAT SHOT LOOKED JUST LIKE KAIJO'S MORI-YAMA!
HUH ...?!
DOES THIS MEAN THAT HAIZAKI IS JUST LIKE KISE?!
NO...
!!!
HE'S A LITTLE DIFFER-ENT.

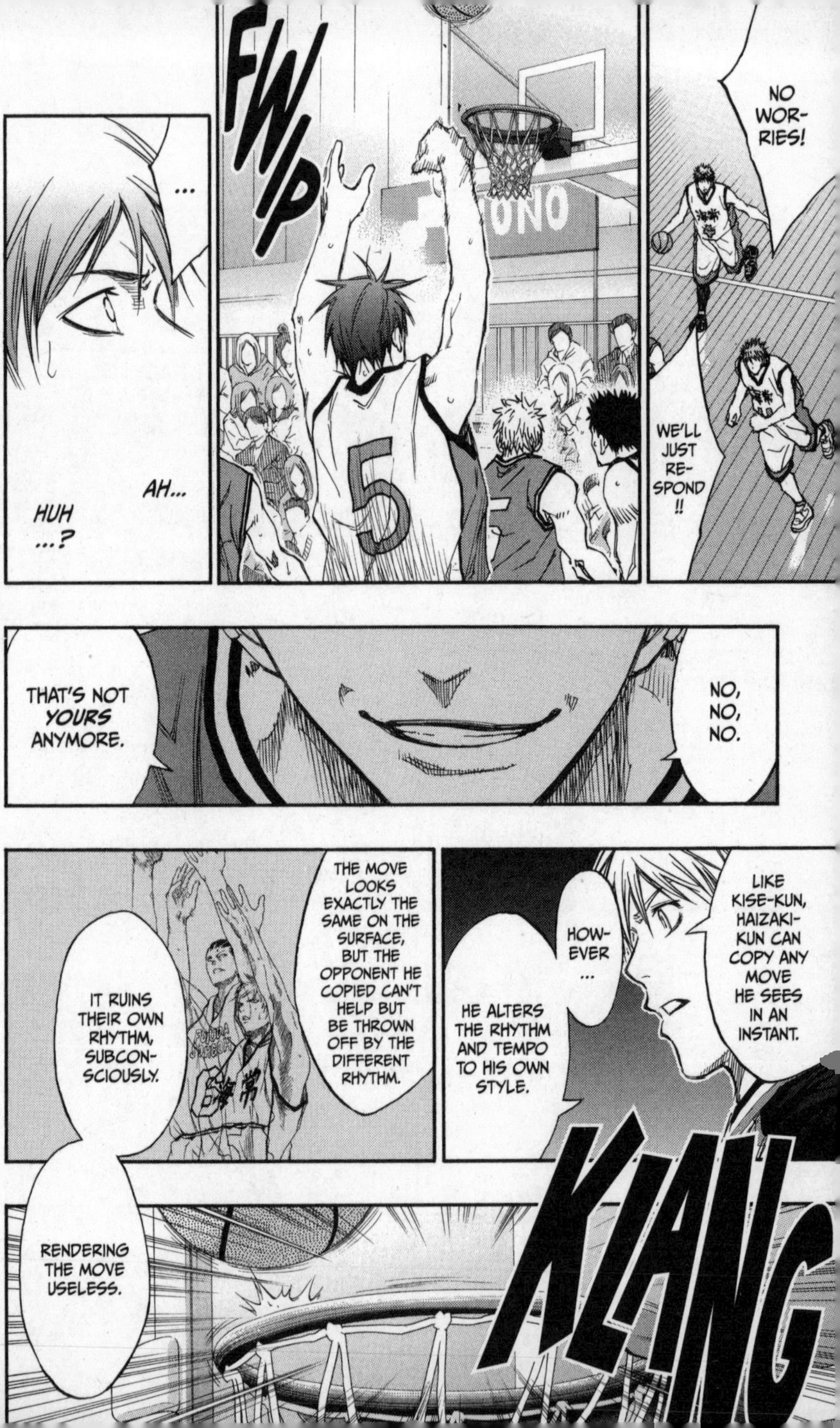

NO WORRIES!
WE'LL JUST RESPOND!!
FWIP
...
AH...
HUH...?
NO, NO, NO.
THAT'S NOT *YOURS* ANYMORE.
LIKE KISE-KUN, HAIZAKI-KUN CAN COPY ANY MOVE HE SEES IN AN INSTANT.
HOWEVER...
HE ALTERS THE RHYTHM AND TEMPO TO HIS OWN STYLE.
THE MOVE LOOKS EXACTLY THE SAME ON THE SURFACE, BUT THE OPPONENT HE COPIED CAN'T HELP BUT BE THROWN OFF BY THE DIFFERENT RHYTHM.
IT RUINS THEIR OWN RHYTHM, SUBCONSCIOUSLY.
KLANG
RENDERING THE MOVE USELESS.

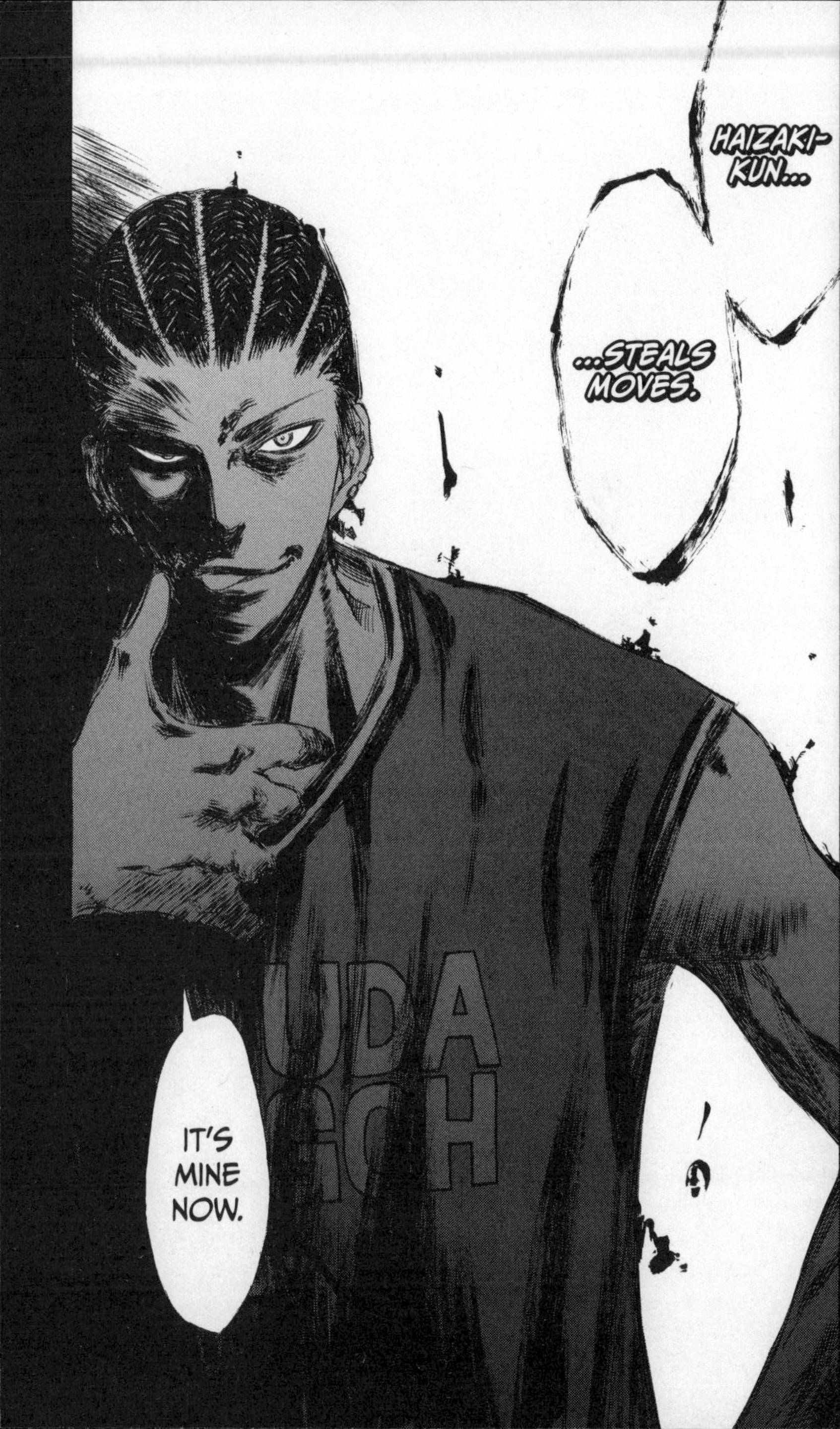
HAIZAKI-KUN...
...STEALS MOVES.
IT'S MINE NOW.

KUROKO'S BASKETBALL BLOOPERS

TAKE 6

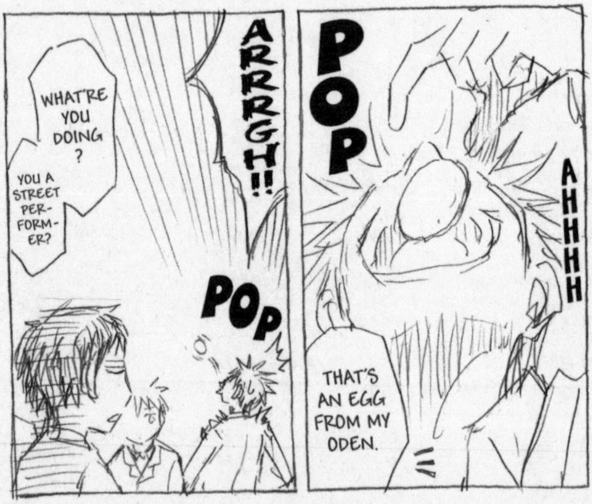
POP
AHHHH
THAT'S AN EGG FROM MY ODEN.
ARRRGH!!
WHAT'RE YOU DOING?
YOU A STREET PER-FORM-ER?
POP

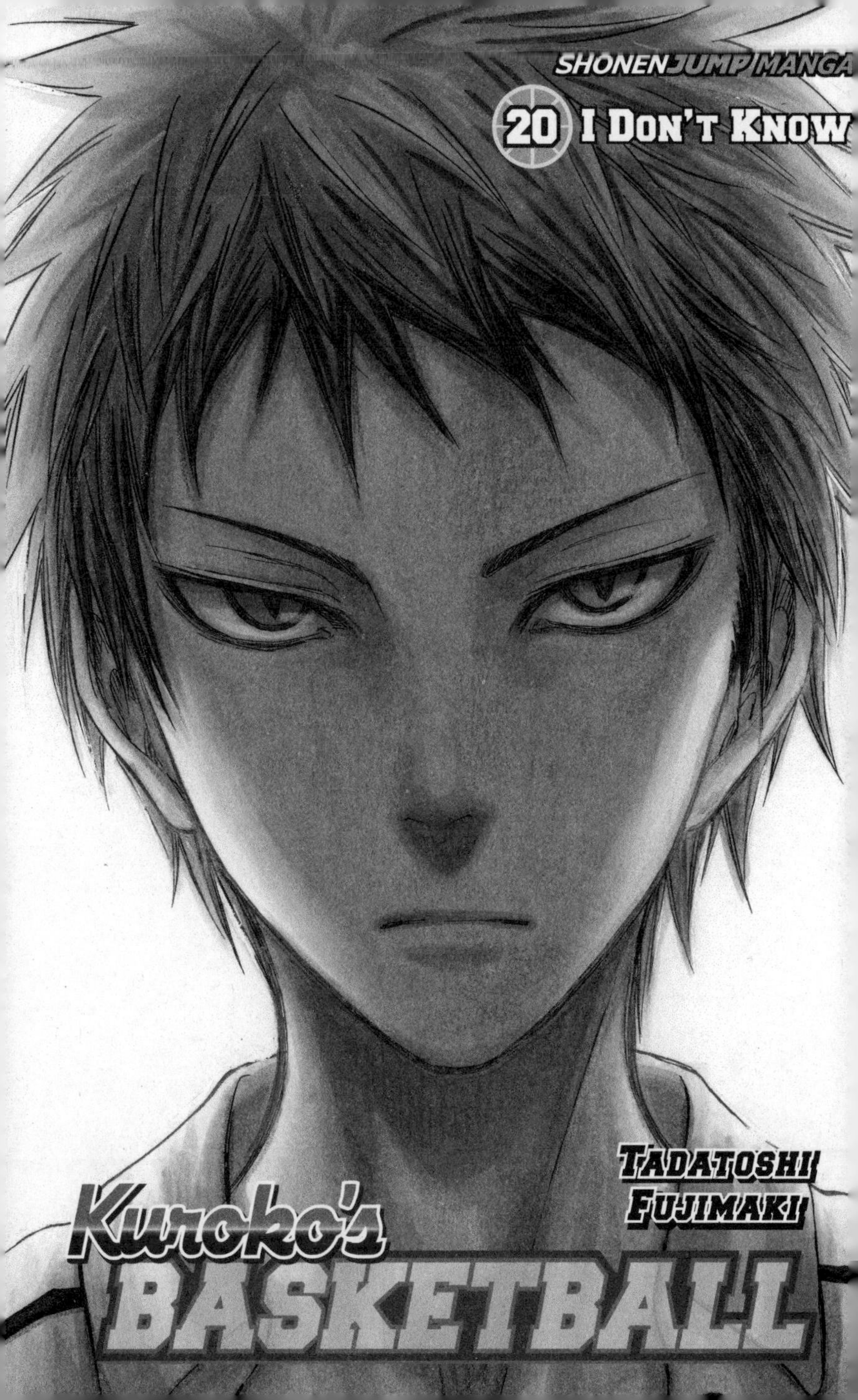
SHONEN JUMP MANGA
20 I Don't Know
Tadatoshi Fujimaki
Kuroko's
BASKETBALL

TADATOSHI FUJIMAKI

Putting your money where your mouth is? Supercool. Acting without the need to talk about it? Refined and elegant. No talk, no action? No opinion. All talk, no action? Get outta here.

—2012

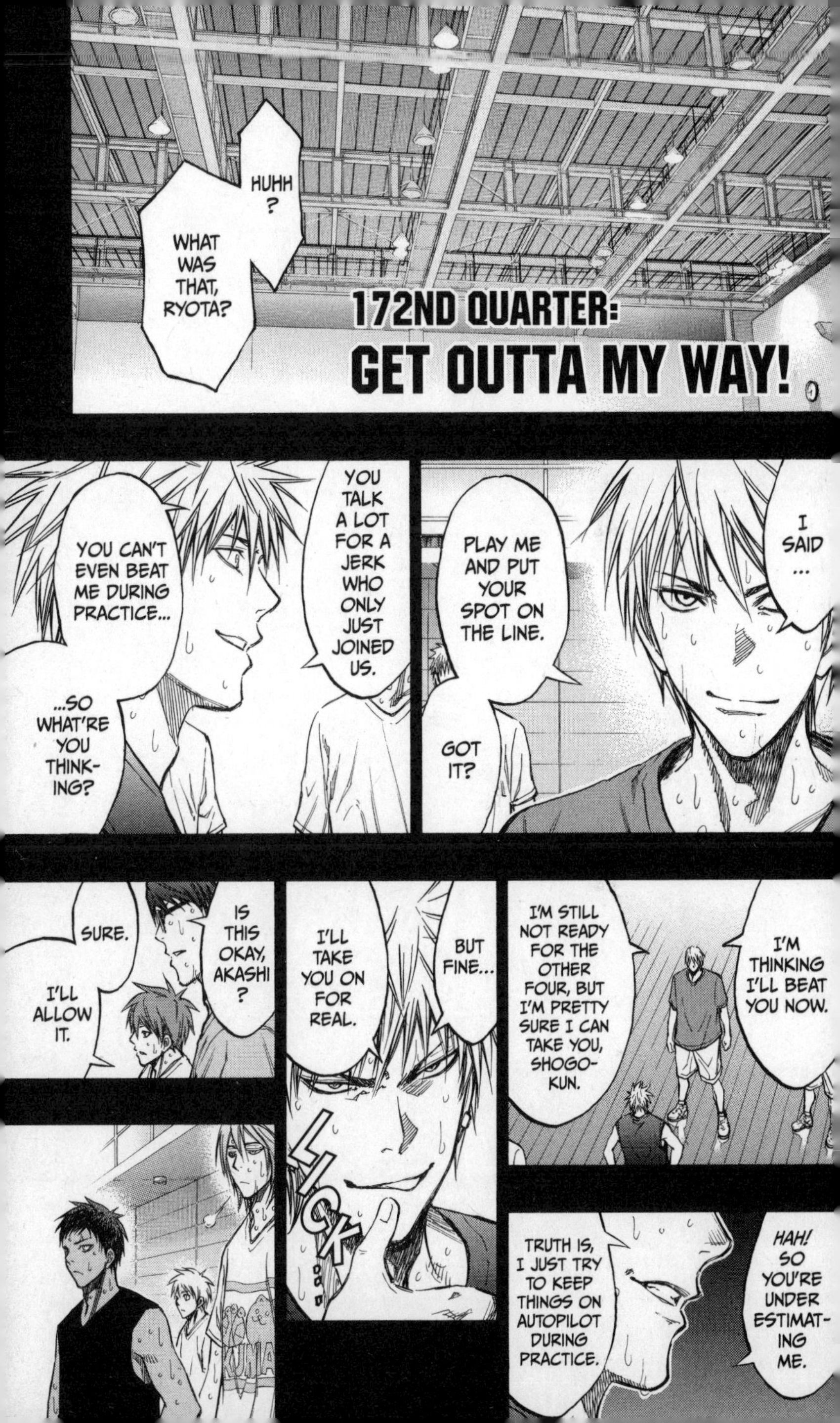
HUHH?
WHAT WAS THAT, RYOTA?
172ND QUARTER:
GET OUTTA MY WAY!
I SAID...
PLAY ME AND PUT YOUR SPOT ON THE LINE.
GOT IT?
YOU TALK A LOT FOR A JERK WHO ONLY JUST JOINED US.
YOU CAN'T EVEN BEAT ME DURING PRACTICE...
...SO WHAT'RE YOU THINKING?
I'M THINKING I'LL BEAT YOU NOW.
I'M STILL NOT READY FOR THE OTHER FOUR, BUT I'M PRETTY SURE I CAN TAKE YOU, SHOGO-KUN.
HAH! SO YOU'RE UNDERESTIMATING ME.
TRUTH IS, I JUST TRY TO KEEP THINGS ON AUTOPILOT DURING PRACTICE.
BUT FINE...
I'LL TAKE YOU ON FOR REAL.
LICK
IS THIS OKAY, AKASHI?
SURE.
I'LL ALLOW IT.

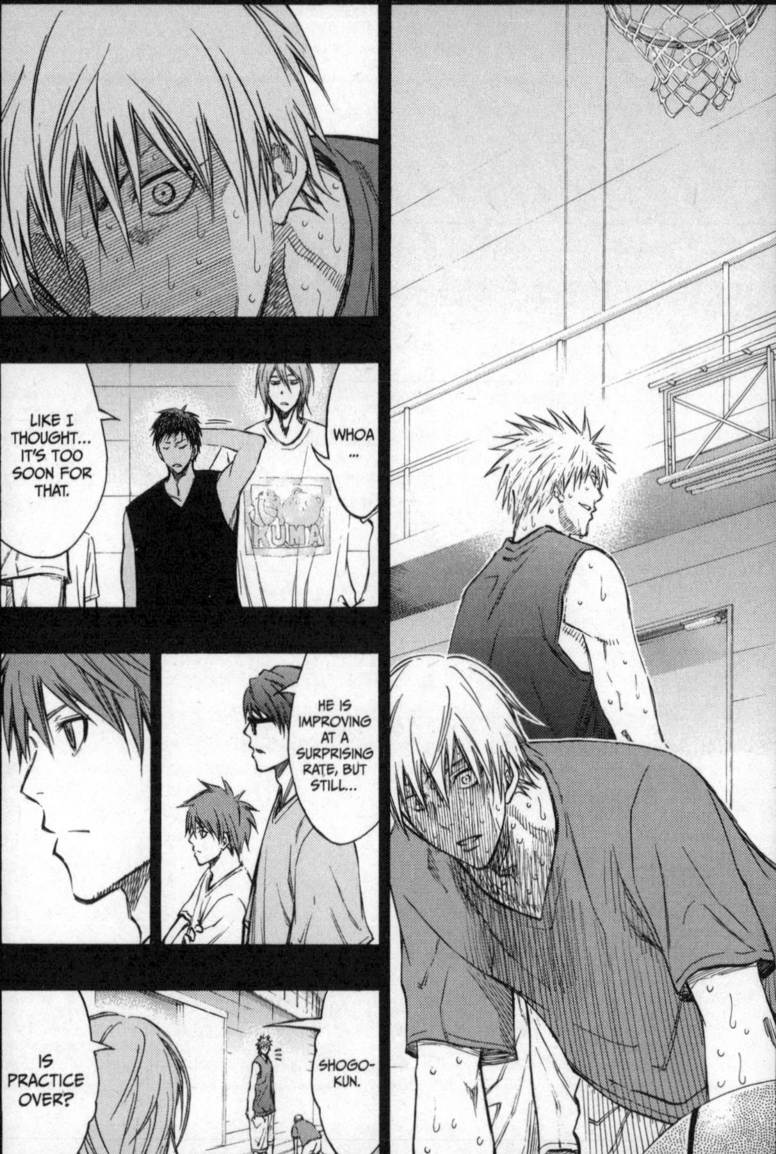
WHOA ...
LIKE I THOUGHT... IT'S TOO SOON FOR THAT.
HE IS IMPROVING AT A SURPRISING RATE, BUT STILL...
SHOGO-KUN.
IS PRACTICE OVER?

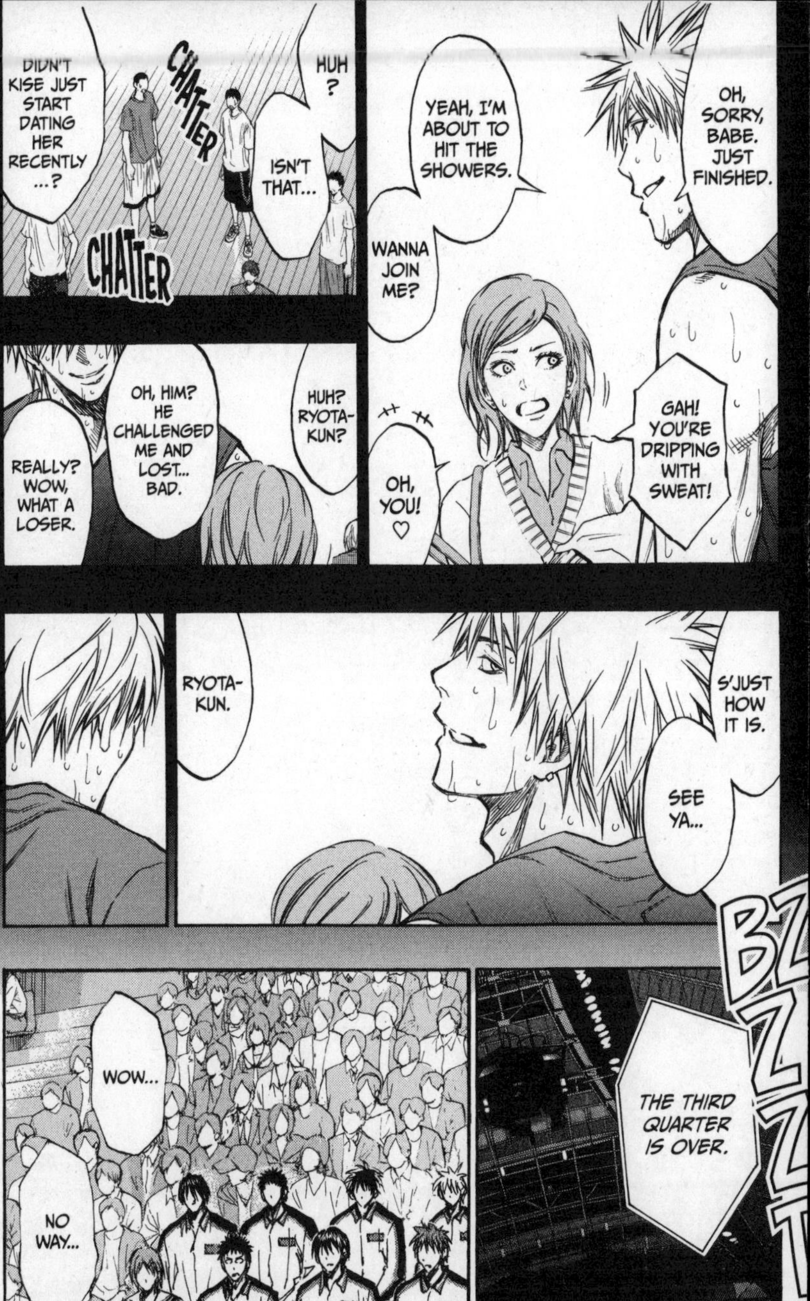
OH, SORRY, BABE. JUST FINISHED.
YEAH, I'M ABOUT TO HIT THE SHOWERS.
WANNA JOIN ME?
GAH! YOU'RE DRIPPING WITH SWEAT!
OH, YOU! ♡
HUH?
ISN'T THAT...
CHATTER
DIDN'T KISE JUST START DATING HER RECENTLY...?
CHATTER
HUH? RYOTA-KUN?
OH, HIM? HE CHALLENGED ME AND LOST... BAD.
REALLY? WOW, WHAT A LOSER.
S'JUST HOW IT IS.
SEE YA...
RYOTA-KUN.
BZZZT
THE THIRD QUARTER IS OVER.
WOW...
NO WAY...

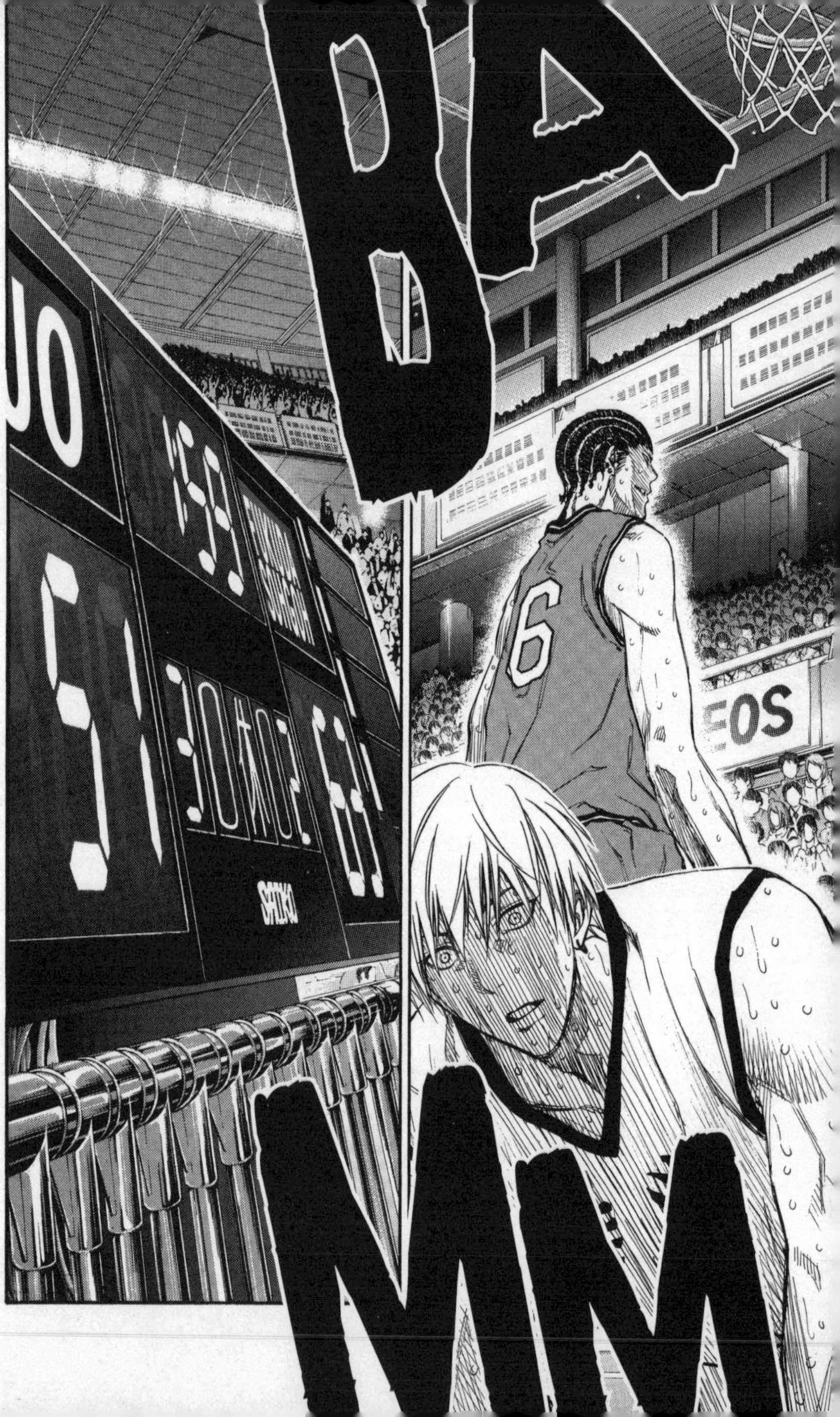
BA
MM
EOS

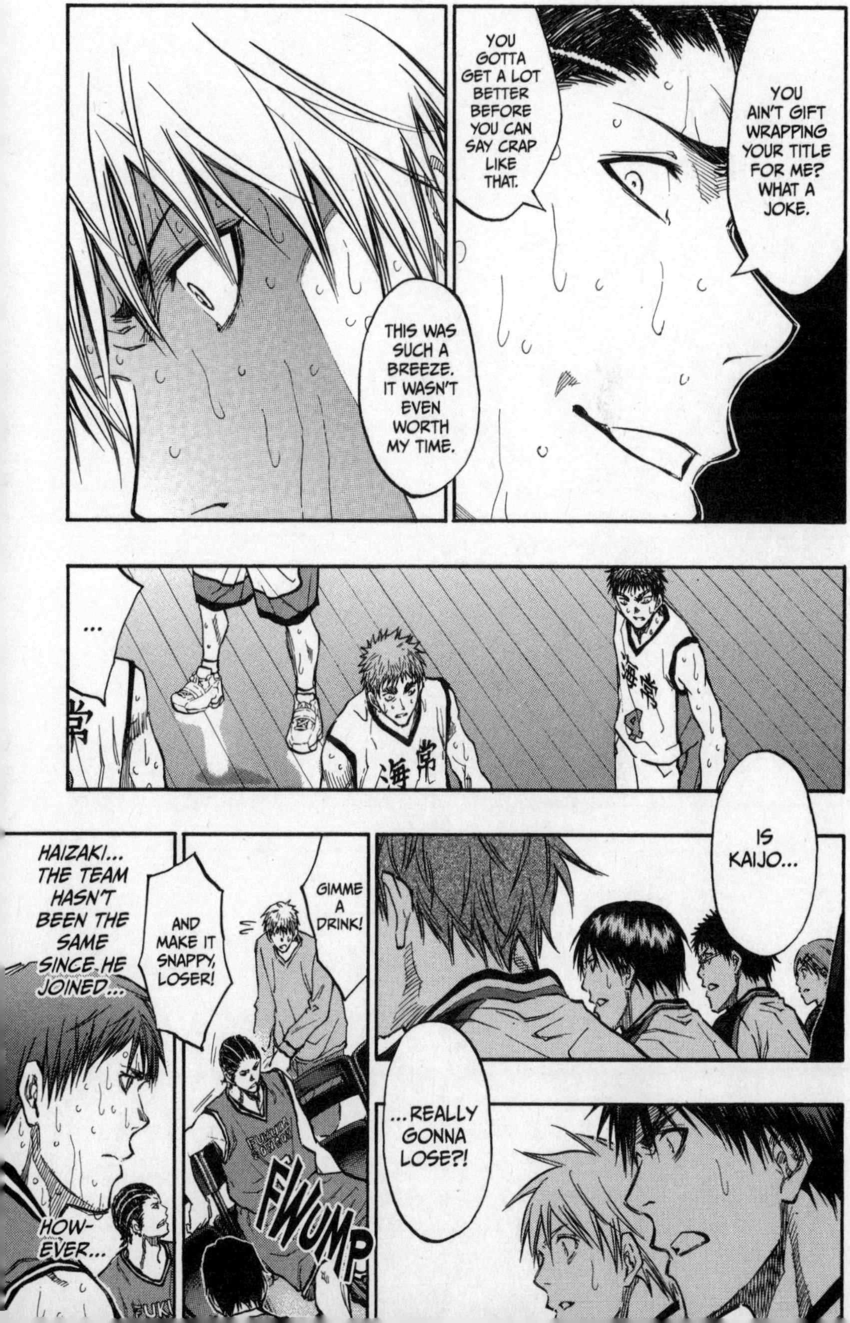
YOU AIN'T GIFT WRAPPING YOUR TITLE FOR ME? WHAT A JOKE.
YOU GOTTA GET A LOT BETTER BEFORE YOU CAN SAY CRAP LIKE THAT.
THIS WAS SUCH A BREEZE. IT WASN'T EVEN WORTH MY TIME.
...
IS KAIJO...
...REALLY GONNA LOSE?!
GIMME A DRINK!
AND MAKE IT SNAPPY, LOSER!
FWUMP
HAIZAKI... THE TEAM HASN'T BEEN THE SAME SINCE HE JOINED...
HOW-EVER...

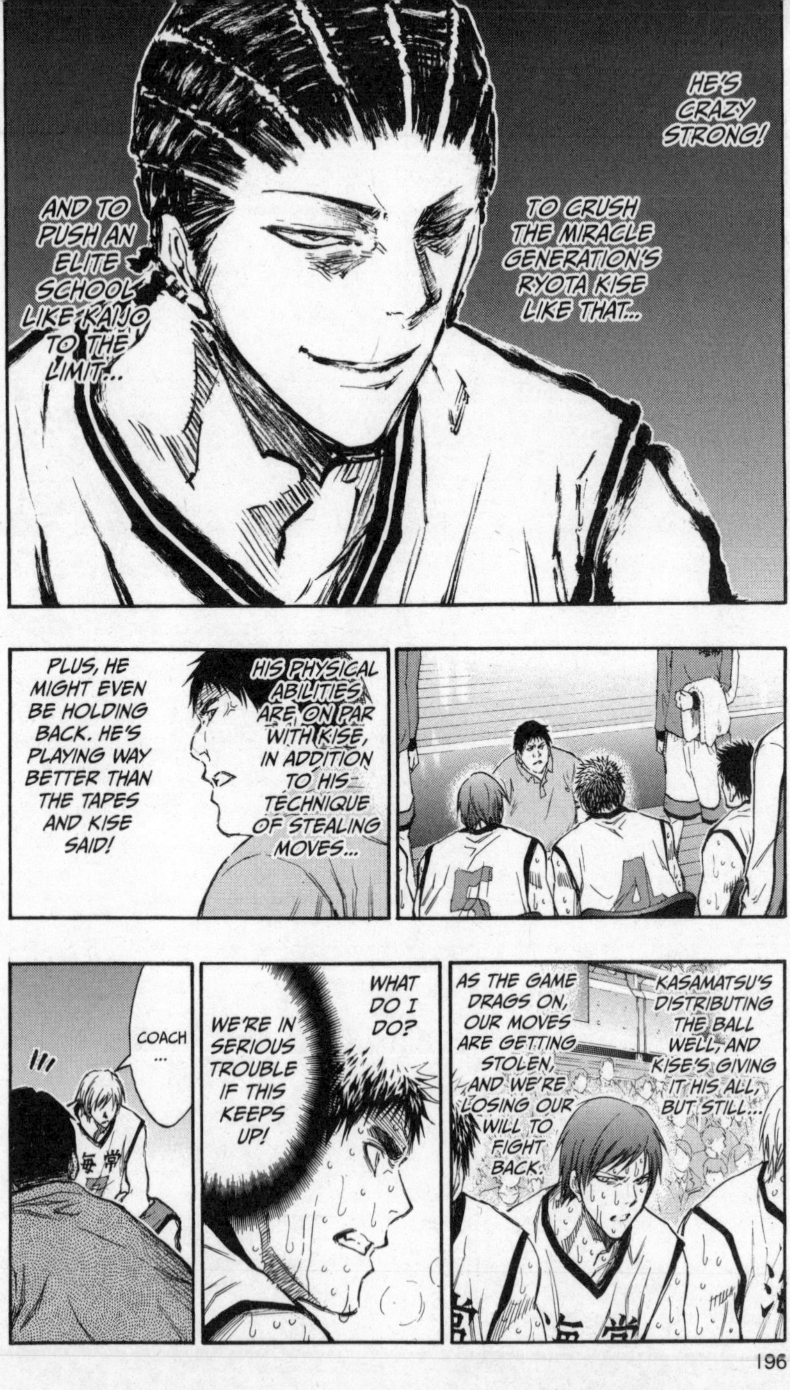
HE'S CRAZY STRONG!
TO CRUSH THE MIRACLE GENERATION'S RYOTA KISE LIKE THAT...
AND TO PUSH AN ELITE SCHOOL LIKE KAIJO TO THE LIMIT...
HIS PHYSICAL ABILITIES ARE ON PAR WITH KISE, IN ADDITION TO HIS TECHNIQUE OF STEALING MOVES...
PLUS, HE MIGHT EVEN BE HOLDING BACK. HE'S PLAYING WAY BETTER THAN THE TAPES AND KISE SAID!
KASAMATSU'S DISTRIBUTING THE BALL WELL, AND KISE'S GIVING IT HIS ALL, BUT STILL...
AS THE GAME DRAGS ON, OUR MOVES ARE GETTING STOLEN, AND WE'RE LOSING OUR WILL TO FIGHT BACK.
WHAT DO I DO?
WE'RE IN SERIOUS TROUBLE IF THIS KEEPS UP!
COACH ...

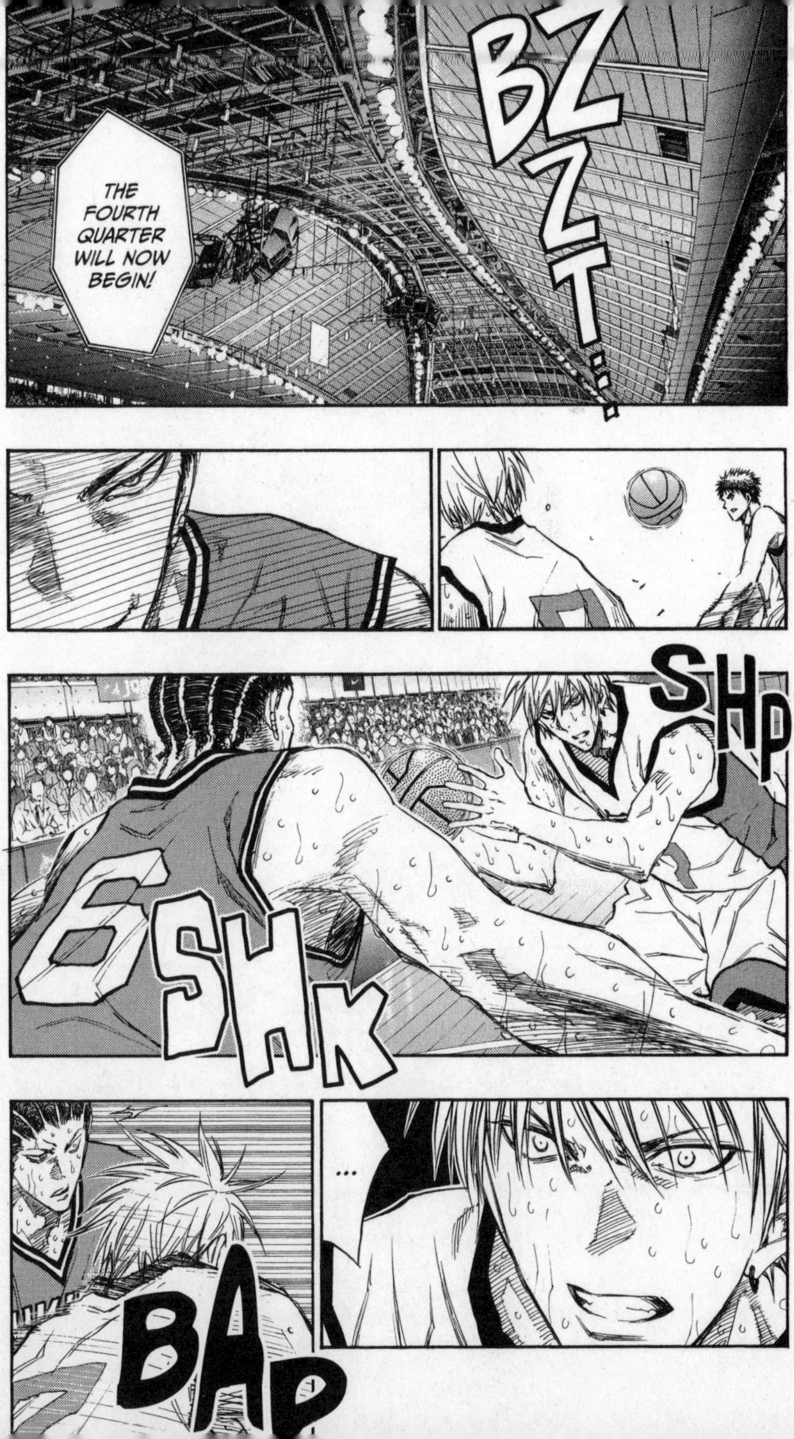
BZZT...
THE FOURTH QUARTER WILL NOW BEGIN!
SHP
SHK
...
BAP

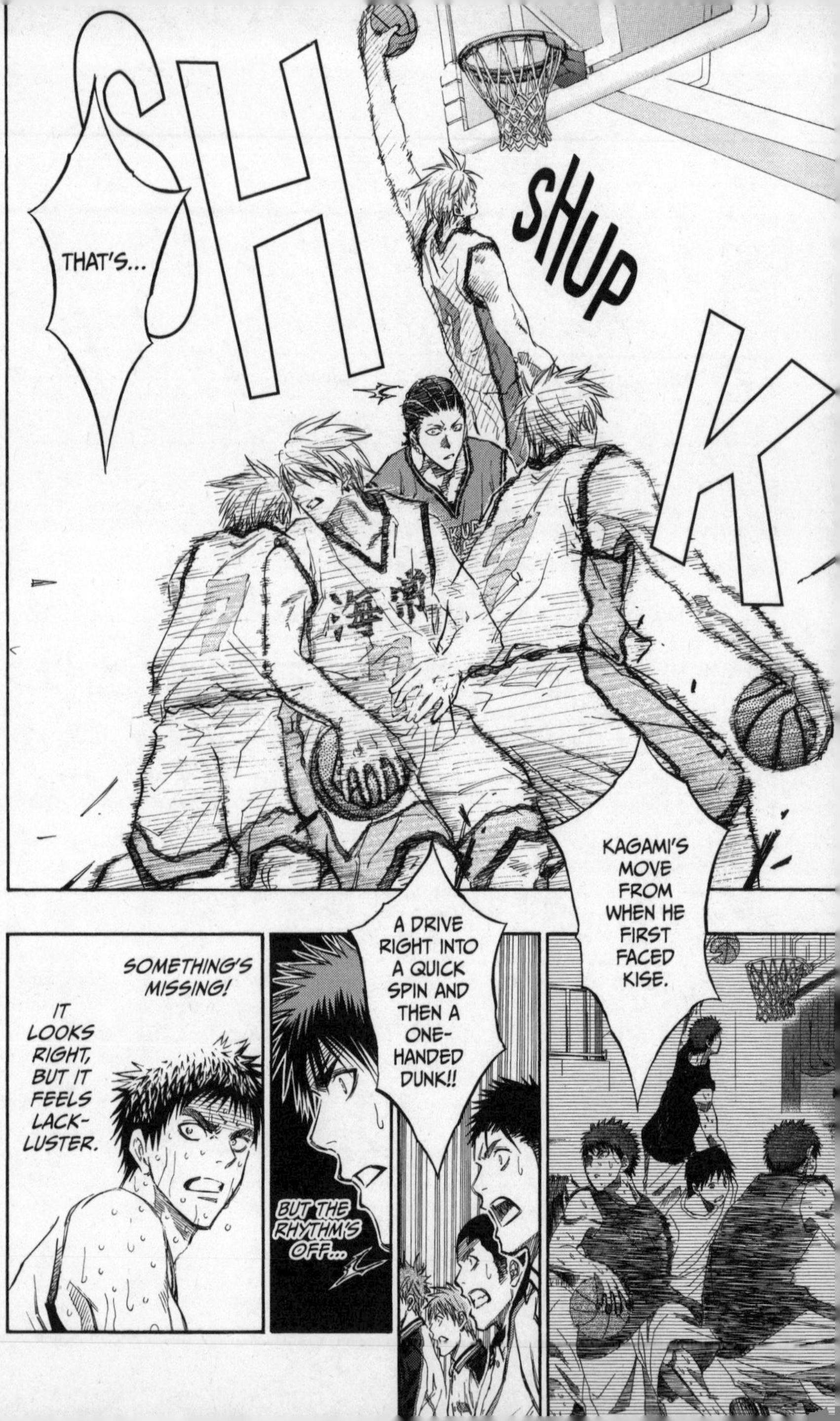
SHUP
SHK
海常
THAT'S...
KAGAMI'S MOVE FROM WHEN HE FIRST FACED KISE.
A DRIVE RIGHT INTO A QUICK SPIN AND THEN A ONE-HANDED DUNK!!
BUT THE RHYTHM'S OFF...
SOMETHING'S MISSING!
IT LOOKS RIGHT, BUT IT FEELS LACK-LUSTER.

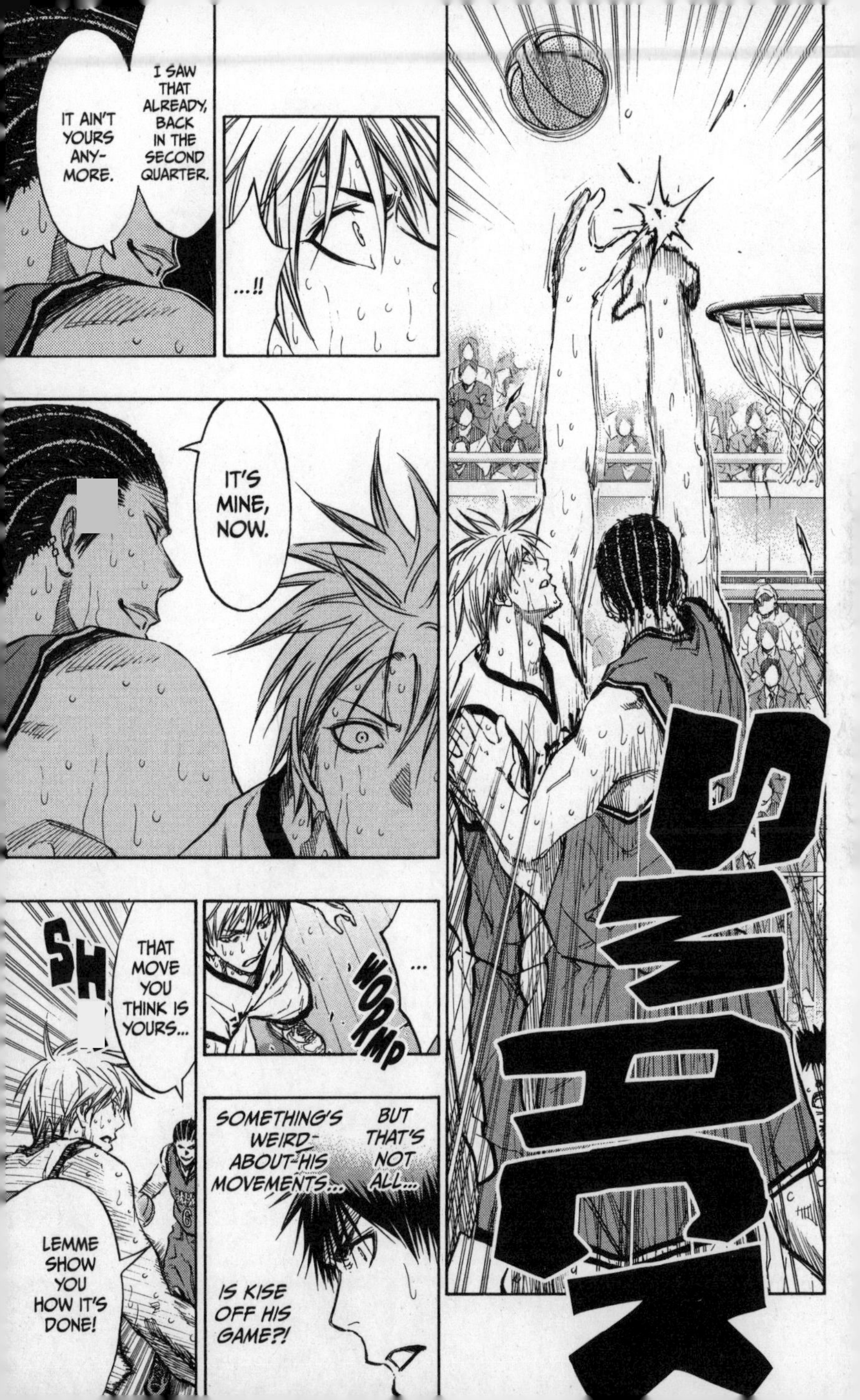
SMACK
I SAW THAT ALREADY, BACK IN THE SECOND QUARTER.
IT AIN'T YOURS ANYMORE.
...!!
IT'S MINE, NOW.
...
WORMP
SOMETHING'S WEIRD ABOUT HIS MOVEMENTS...
BUT THAT'S NOT ALL...
IS KISE OFF HIS GAME?!
SH
THAT MOVE YOU THINK IS YOURS...
LEMME SHOW YOU HOW IT'S DONE!

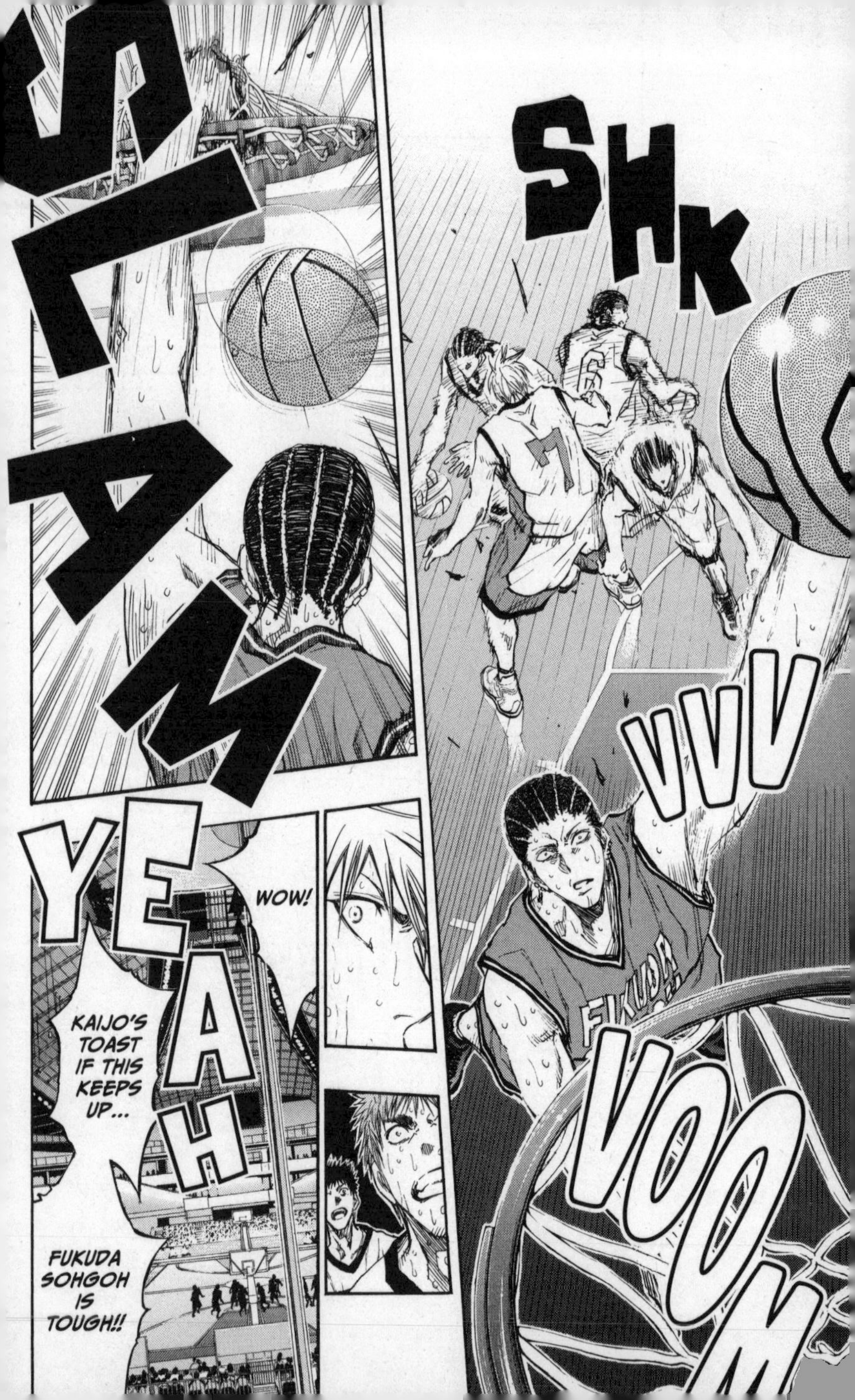
SHK
VVVOOM
SLAM
YEAH
WOW!
KAIJO'S TOAST IF THIS KEEPS UP...
FUKUDA SOHGOH IS TOUGH!!

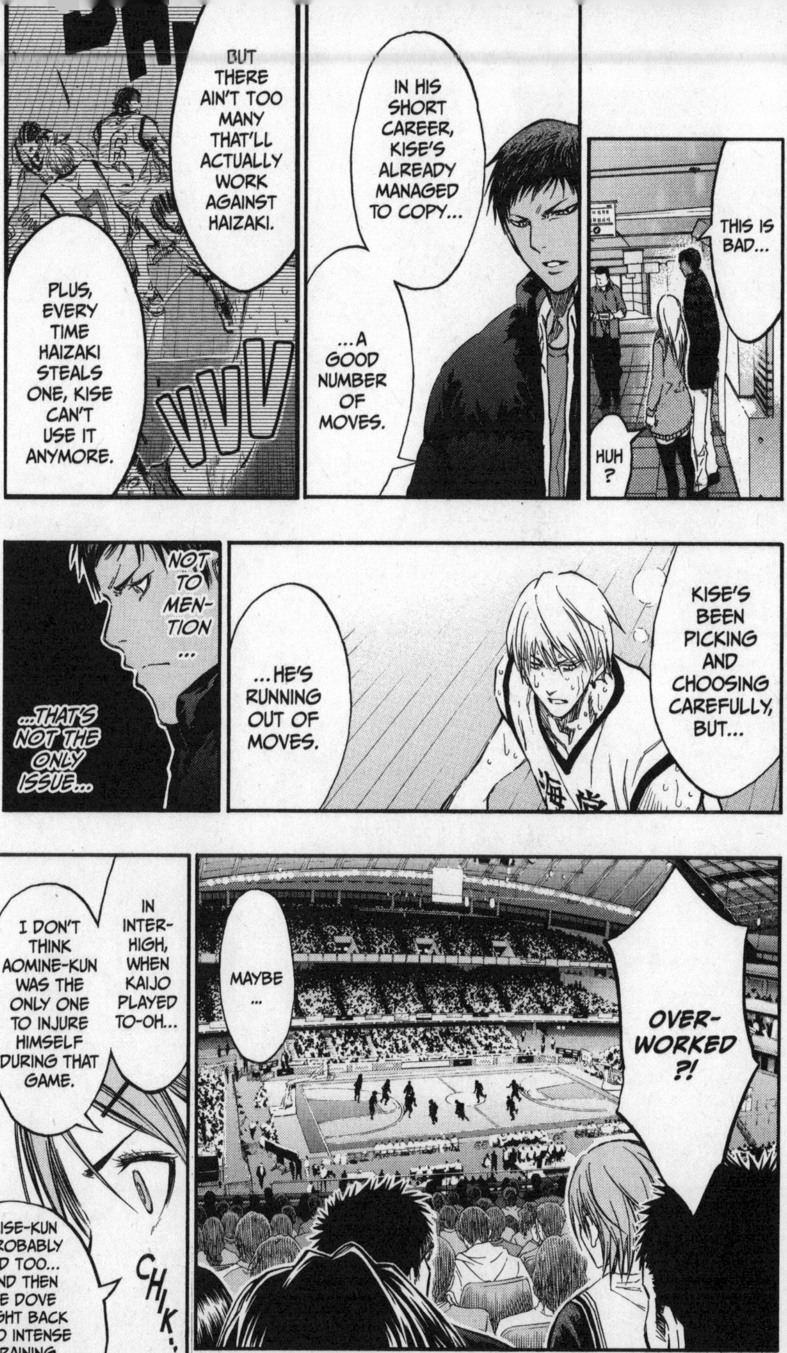
THIS IS BAD...
HUH?
IN HIS SHORT CAREER, KISE'S ALREADY MANAGED TO COPY...
...A GOOD NUMBER OF MOVES.
BUT THERE AIN'T TOO MANY THAT'LL ACTUALLY WORK AGAINST HAIZAKI.
PLUS, EVERY TIME HAIZAKI STEALS ONE, KISE CAN'T USE IT ANYMORE.
KISE'S BEEN PICKING AND CHOOSING CAREFULLY, BUT...
...HE'S RUNNING OUT OF MOVES.
NOT TO MENTION...
...THAT'S NOT THE ONLY ISSUE...
OVER-WORKED?!
MAYBE...
IN INTER-HIGH, WHEN KAIJO PLAYED TO-OH...
I DON'T THINK AOMINE-KUN WAS THE ONLY ONE TO INJURE HIMSELF DURING THAT GAME.
KISE-KUN PROBABLY DID TOO... AND THEN HE DOVE RIGHT BACK INTO INTENSE TRAINING WITHOUT RECOVERING PROPERLY.
CHIK...

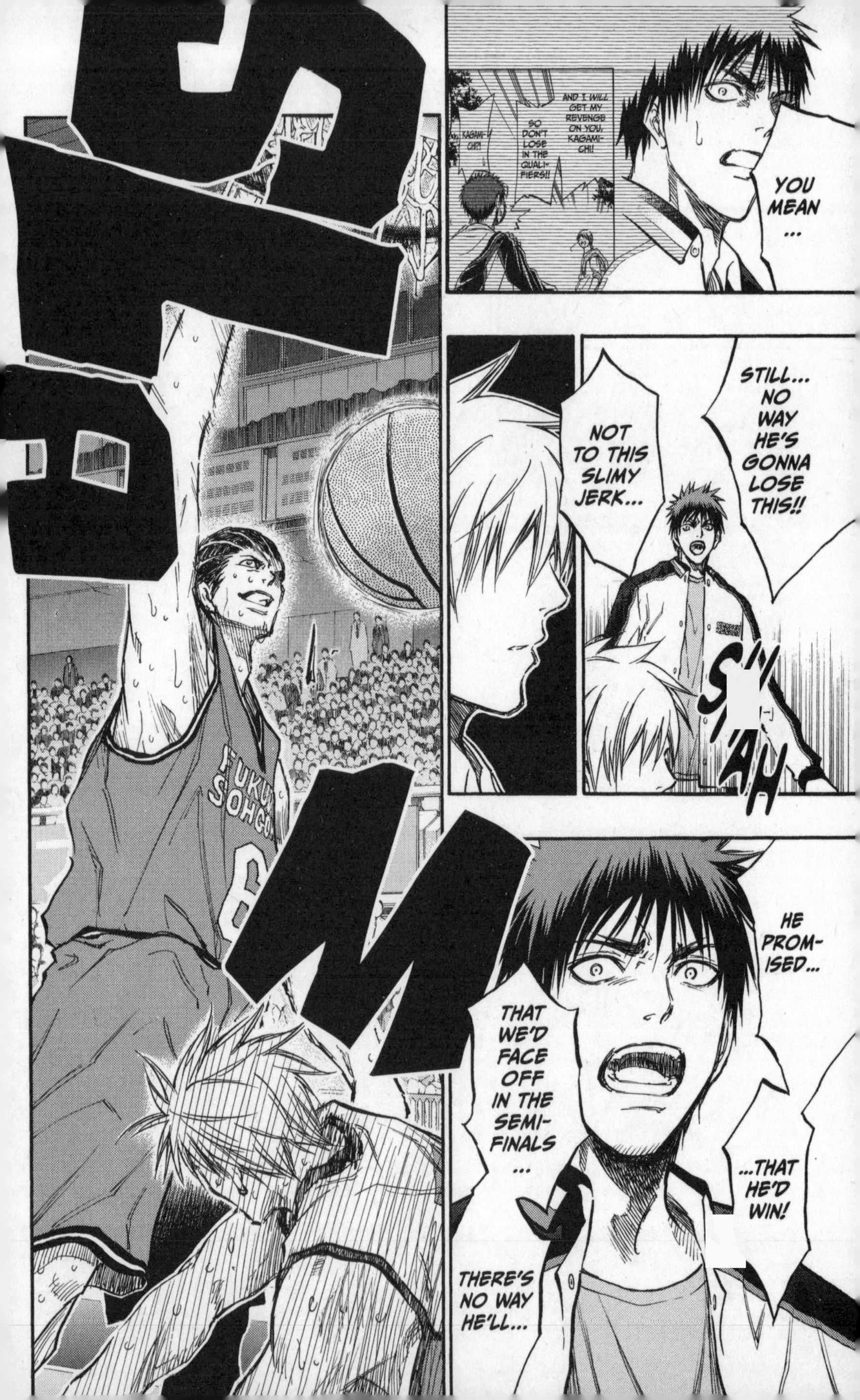
YOU MEAN ...
AND I WILL GET MY REVENGE ON YOU, KAGAMI-CHI!!
SO DON'T LOSE IN THE QUALI-FIERS!!
KAGAMI-CHI?!
STILL... NO WAY HE'S GONNA LOSE THIS!!
NOT TO THIS SLIMY JERK...
HE PROM-ISED...
THAT WE'D FACE OFF IN THE SEMI-FINALS ...
...THAT HE'D WIN!
THERE'S NO WAY HE'LL...
FUKU SOHGO

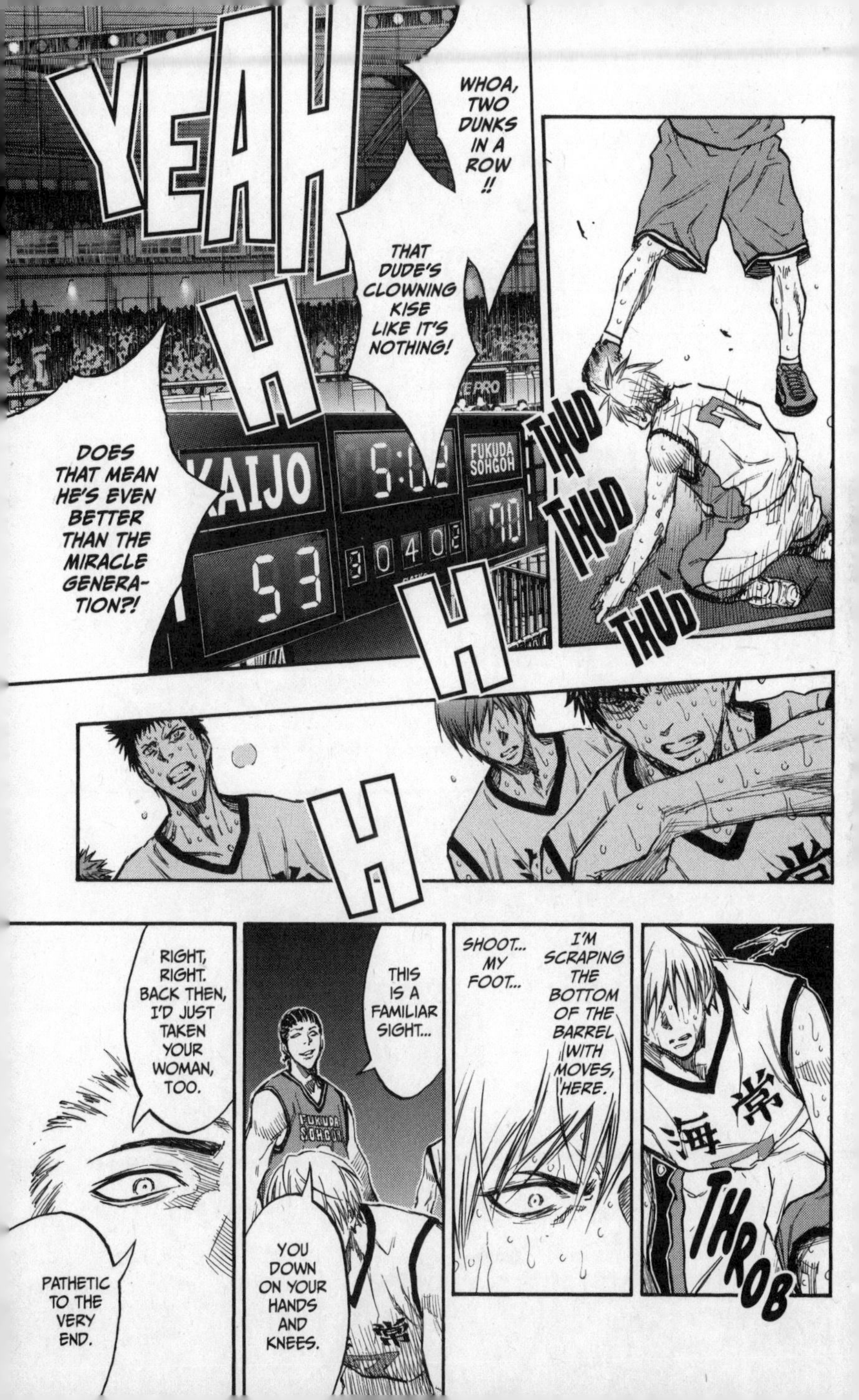
THUD
THUD
THUD
YEAHHHH
WHOA, TWO DUNKS IN A ROW!!
THAT DUDE'S CLOWNING KISE LIKE IT'S NOTHING!
KAIJO
FUKUDA SOHGOH
53
DOES THAT MEAN HE'S EVEN BETTER THAN THE MIRACLE GENERATION?!
THROB
I'M SCRAPING THE BOTTOM OF THE BARREL WITH MOVES, HERE.
SHOOT... MY FOOT...
THIS IS A FAMILIAR SIGHT...
YOU DOWN ON YOUR HANDS AND KNEES.
RIGHT, RIGHT. BACK THEN, I'D JUST TAKEN YOUR WOMAN, TOO.
PATHETIC TO THE VERY END.

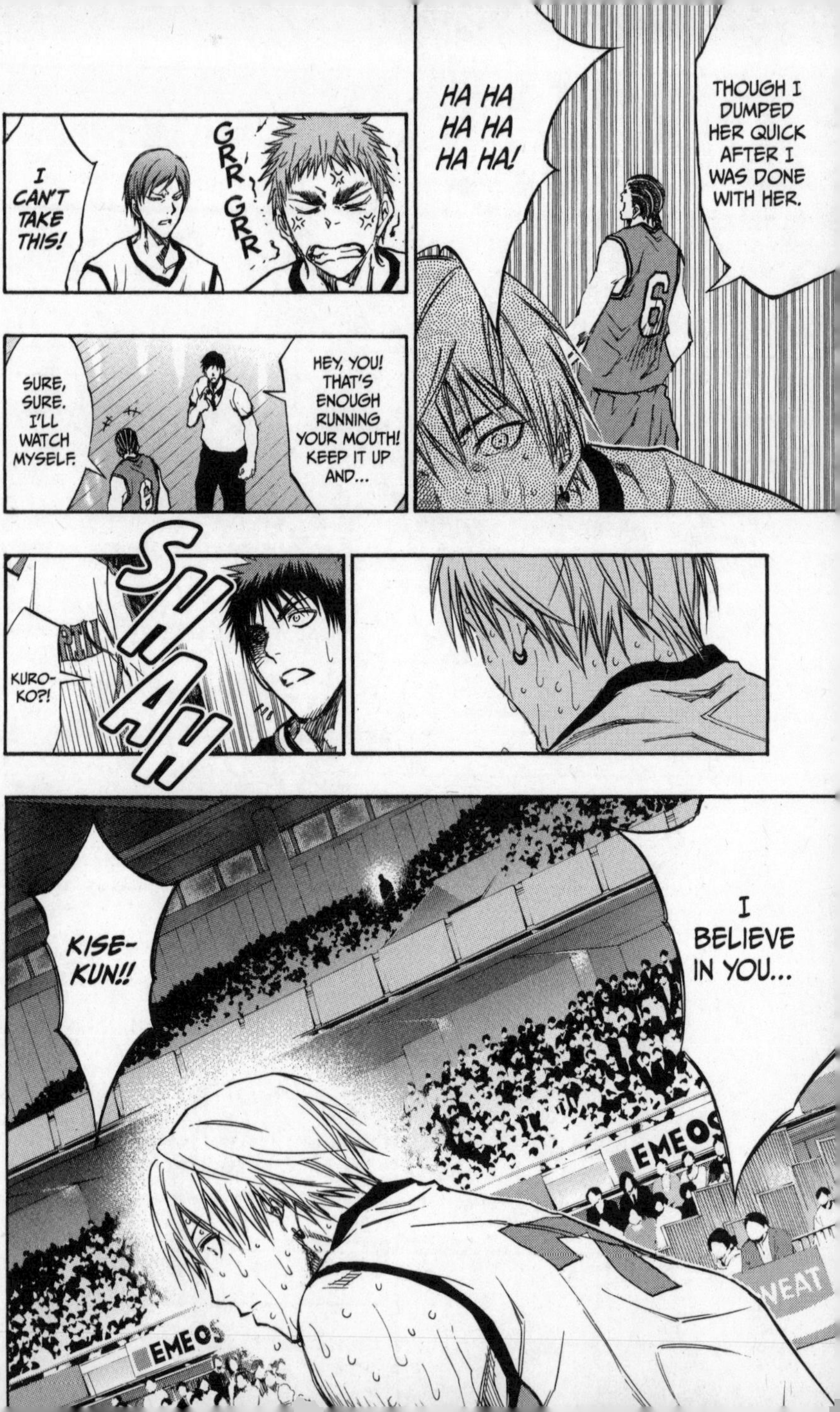
THOUGH I DUMPED HER QUICK AFTER I WAS DONE WITH HER.
HA HA HA HA HA HA!
GRR GRR
I CAN'T TAKE THIS!
HEY, YOU! THAT'S ENOUGH RUNNING YOUR MOUTH! KEEP IT UP AND...
SURE, SURE. I'LL WATCH MYSELF.
SHAAH
KURO-KO?!
I BELIEVE IN YOU...
KISE-KUN!!
EMEOS
NEAT
EMEOS

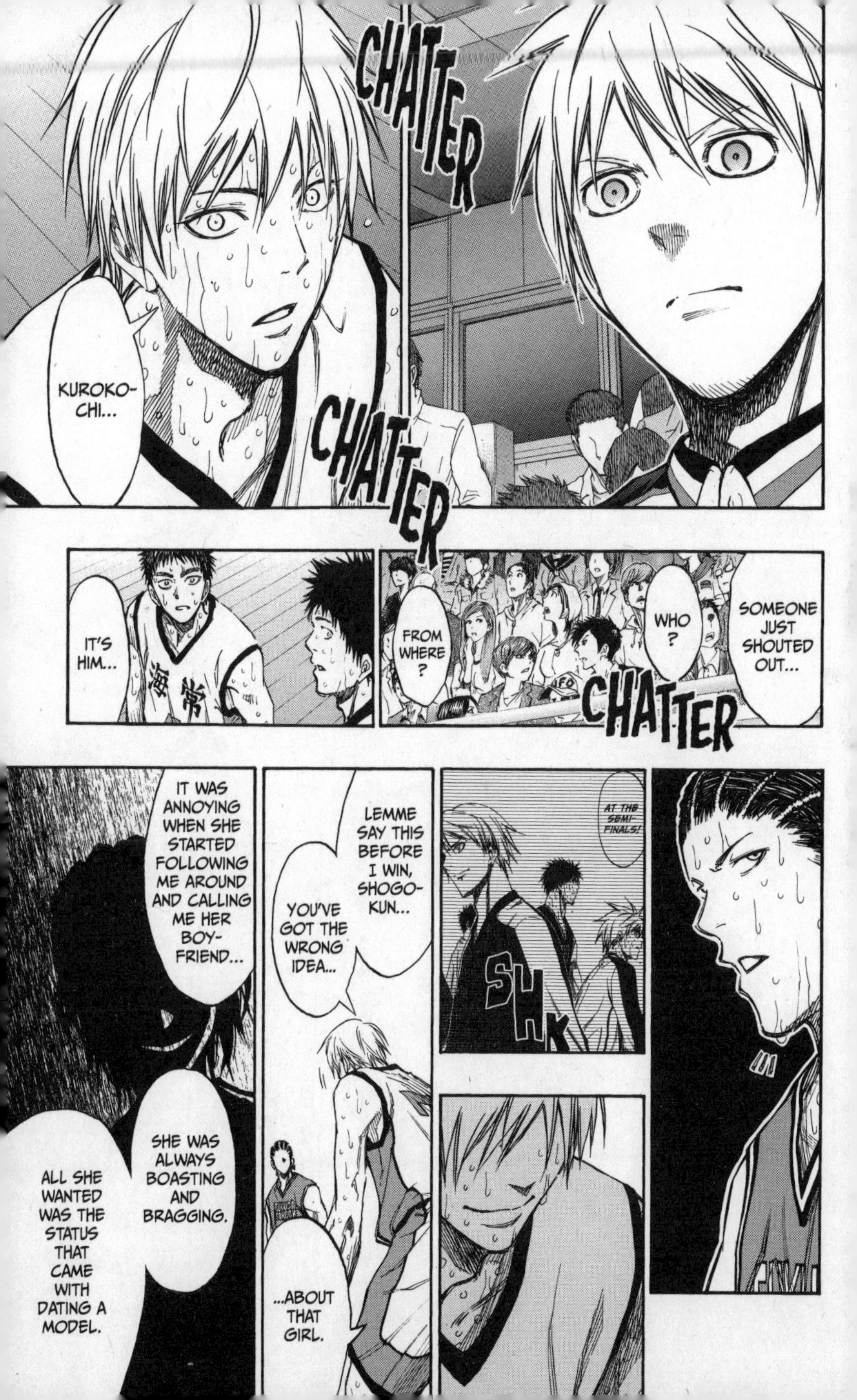
CHATTER
KUROKO-CHI...
CHATTER
SOMEONE JUST SHOUTED OUT...
WHO?
FROM WHERE?
CHATTER
IT'S HIM...
海常
AT THE SEMI-FINALS!
SHK
LEMME SAY THIS BEFORE I WIN, SHOGO-KUN...
YOU'VE GOT THE WRONG IDEA...
...ABOUT THAT GIRL.
IT WAS ANNOYING WHEN SHE STARTED FOLLOWING ME AROUND AND CALLING ME HER BOY-FRIEND...
SHE WAS ALWAYS BOASTING AND BRAGGING.
ALL SHE WANTED WAS THE STATUS THAT CAME WITH DATING A MODEL.

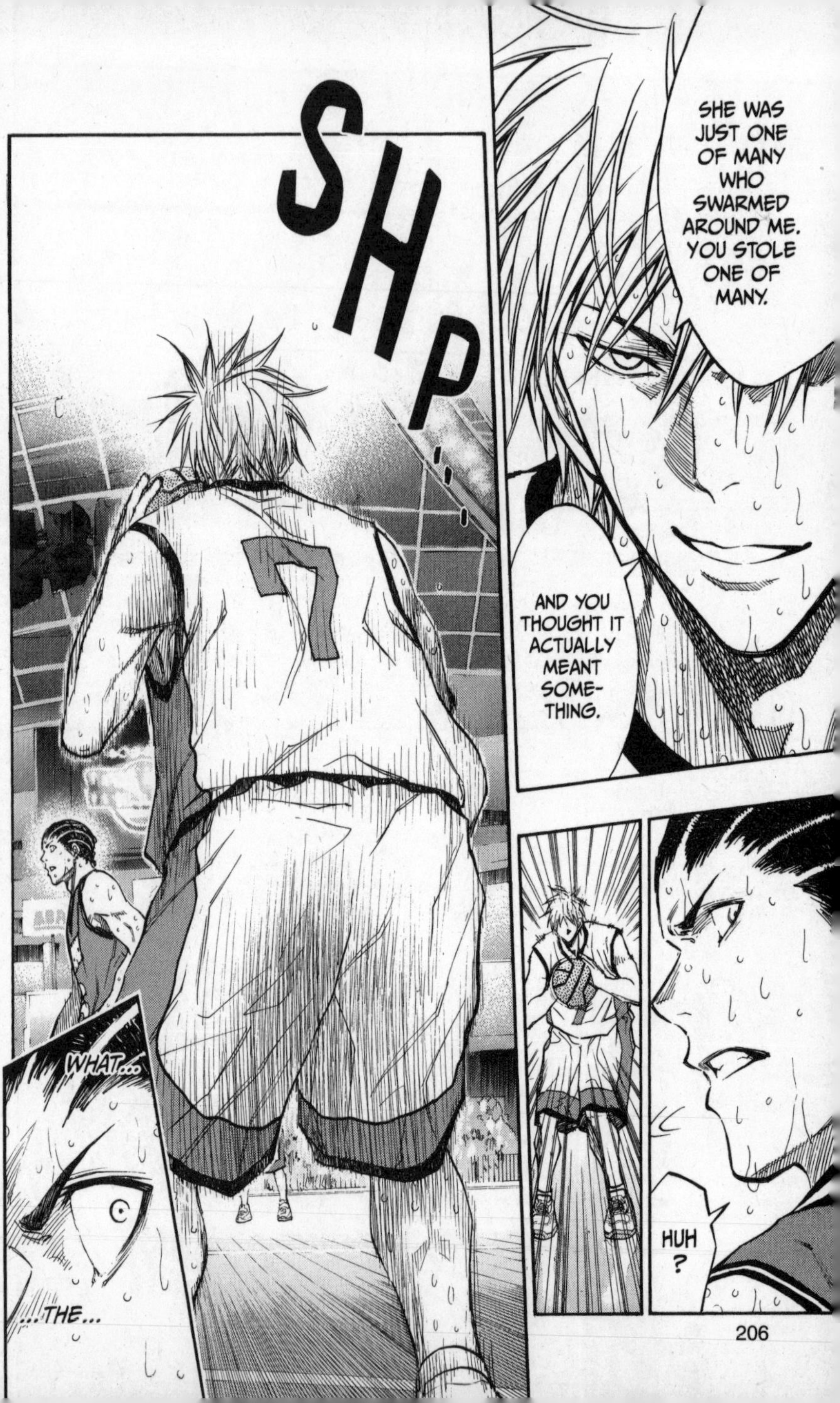
SHE WAS JUST ONE OF MANY WHO SWARMED AROUND ME. YOU STOLE ONE OF MANY.
AND YOU THOUGHT IT ACTUALLY MEANT SOME-THING.
HUH?
SHP...
WHAT...
...THE...

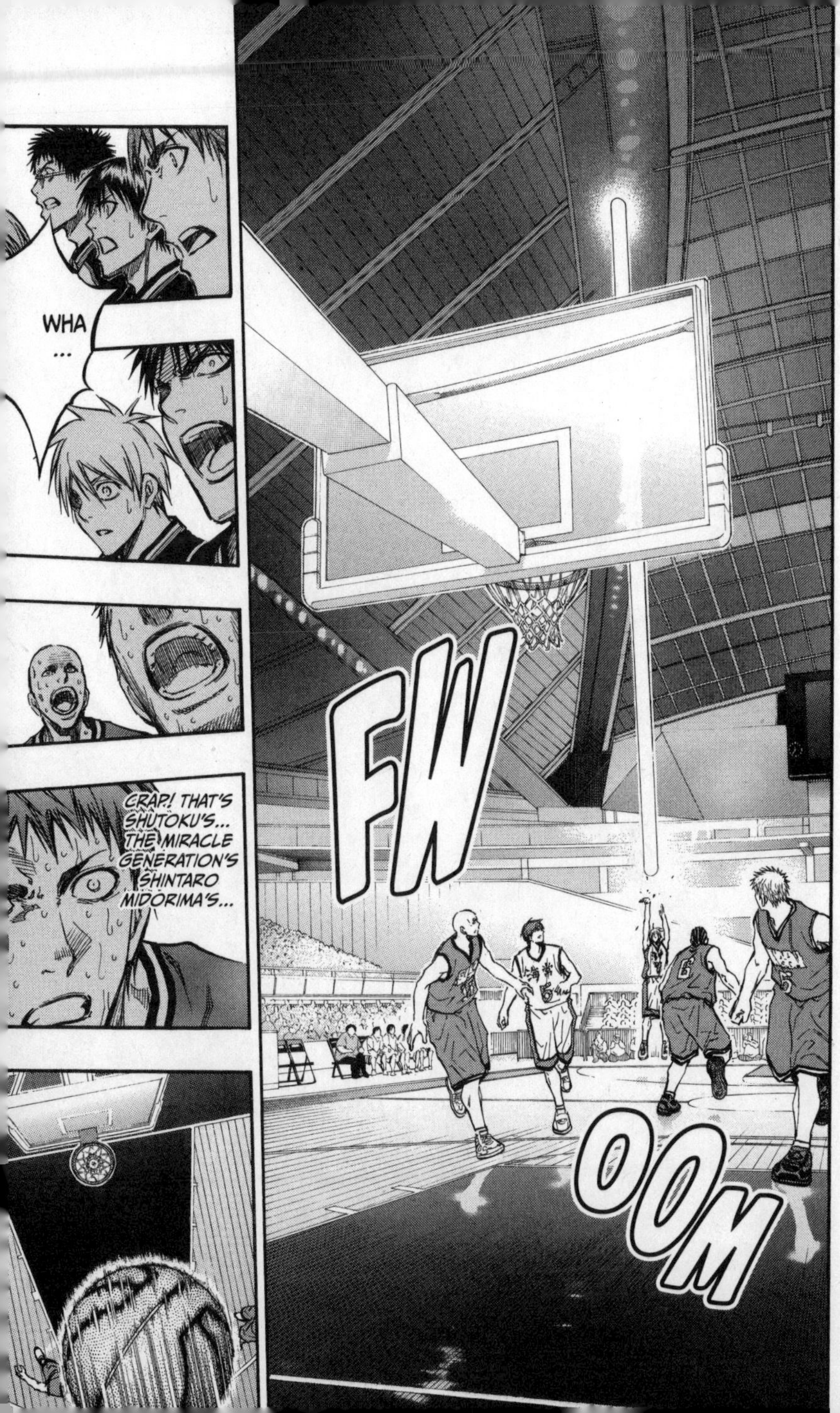
FW
OOM
WHA
...
CRAP! THAT'S SHUTOKU'S... THE MIRACLE GENERATION'S SHINTARO MIDORIMA'S...

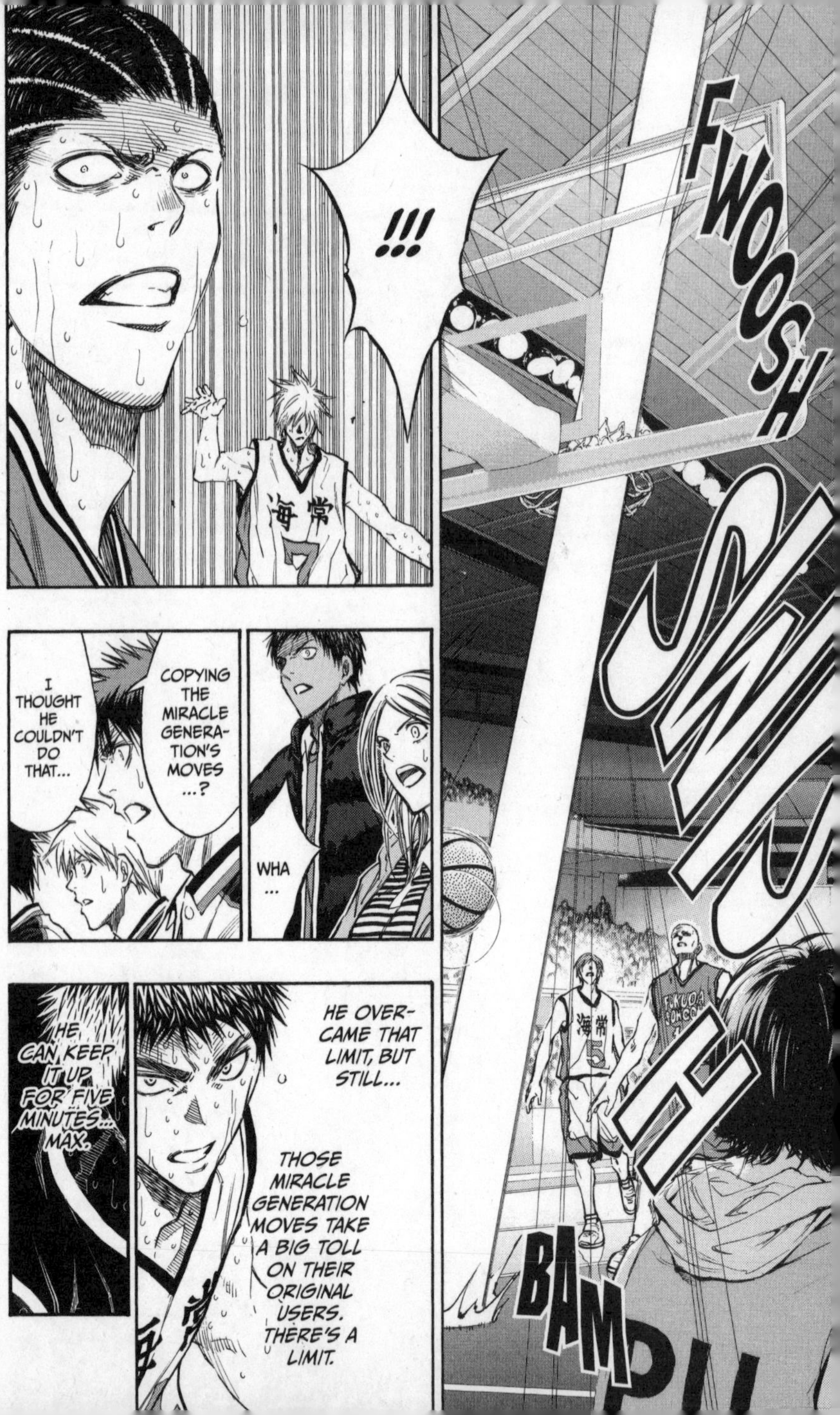
FWOOSH
SWISH
BAM
!!!
WHA...
COPYING THE MIRACLE GENERATION'S MOVES...?
I THOUGHT HE COULDN'T DO THAT...
HE OVERCAME THAT LIMIT, BUT STILL...
THOSE MIRACLE GENERATION MOVES TAKE A BIG TOLL ON THEIR ORIGINAL USERS. THERE'S A LIMIT.
HE CAN KEEP IT UP FOR FIVE MINUTES... MAX.

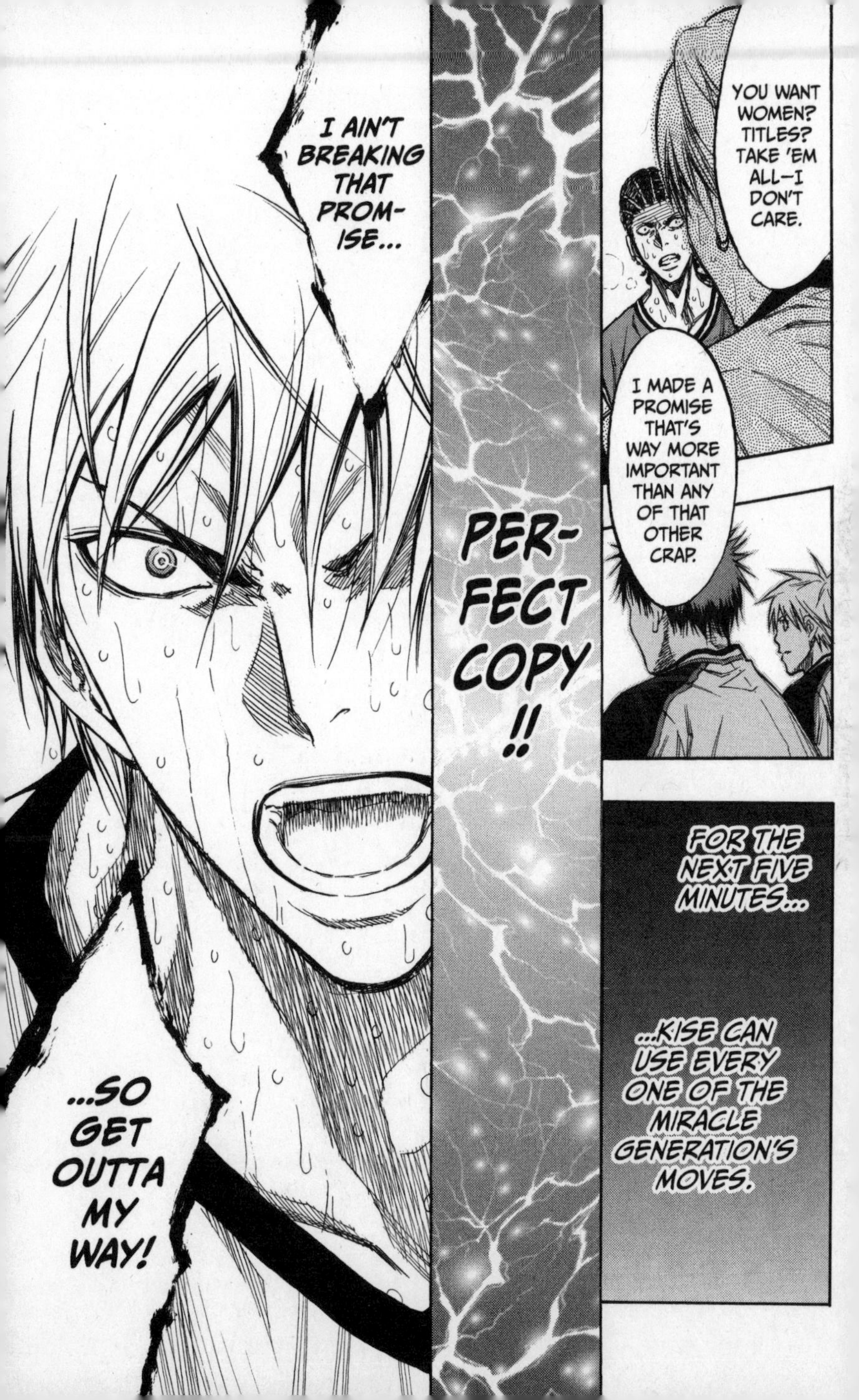
YOU WANT WOMEN? TITLES? TAKE 'EM ALL—I DON'T CARE.
I MADE A PROMISE THAT'S WAY MORE IMPORTANT THAN ANY OF THAT OTHER CRAP.
FOR THE NEXT FIVE MINUTES...
...KISE CAN USE EVERY ONE OF THE MIRACLE GENERATION'S MOVES.
PERFECT COPY!!
I AIN'T BREAKING THAT PROMISE...
...SO GET OUTTA MY WAY!

KUROKO'S BASKETBALL BLOOPERS
TAKE 2

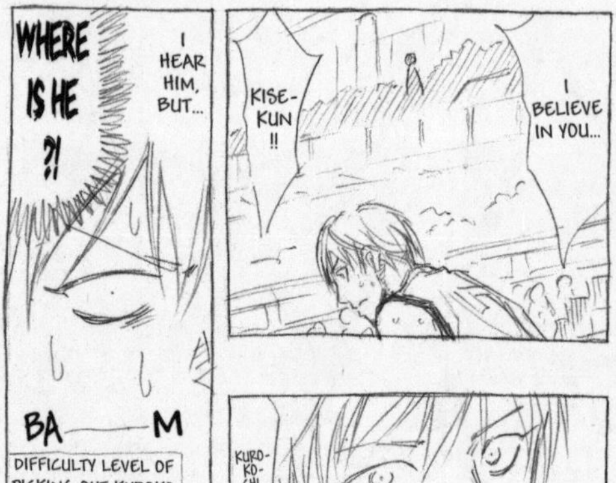
I BELIEVE IN YOU...
KISE-KUN!!
KUROKO-CHI...
I HEAR HIM, BUT...
WHERE IS HE?!
BA——M
DIFFICULTY LEVEL OF PICKING OUT KUROKO FROM A CROWD →MAX

173RD QUARTER: KNOCK IT OFF

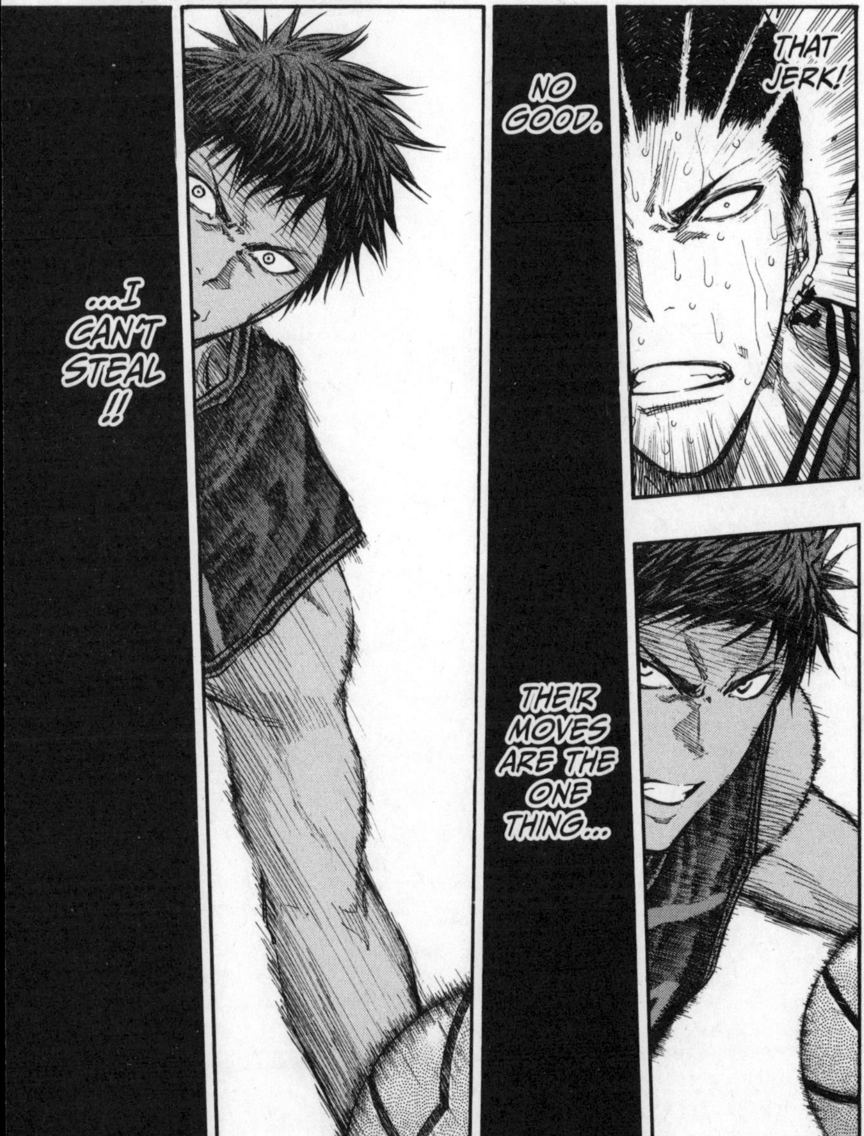
THAT JERK!
NO GOOD.
THEIR MOVES ARE THE ONE THING...
...I CAN'T STEAL!!

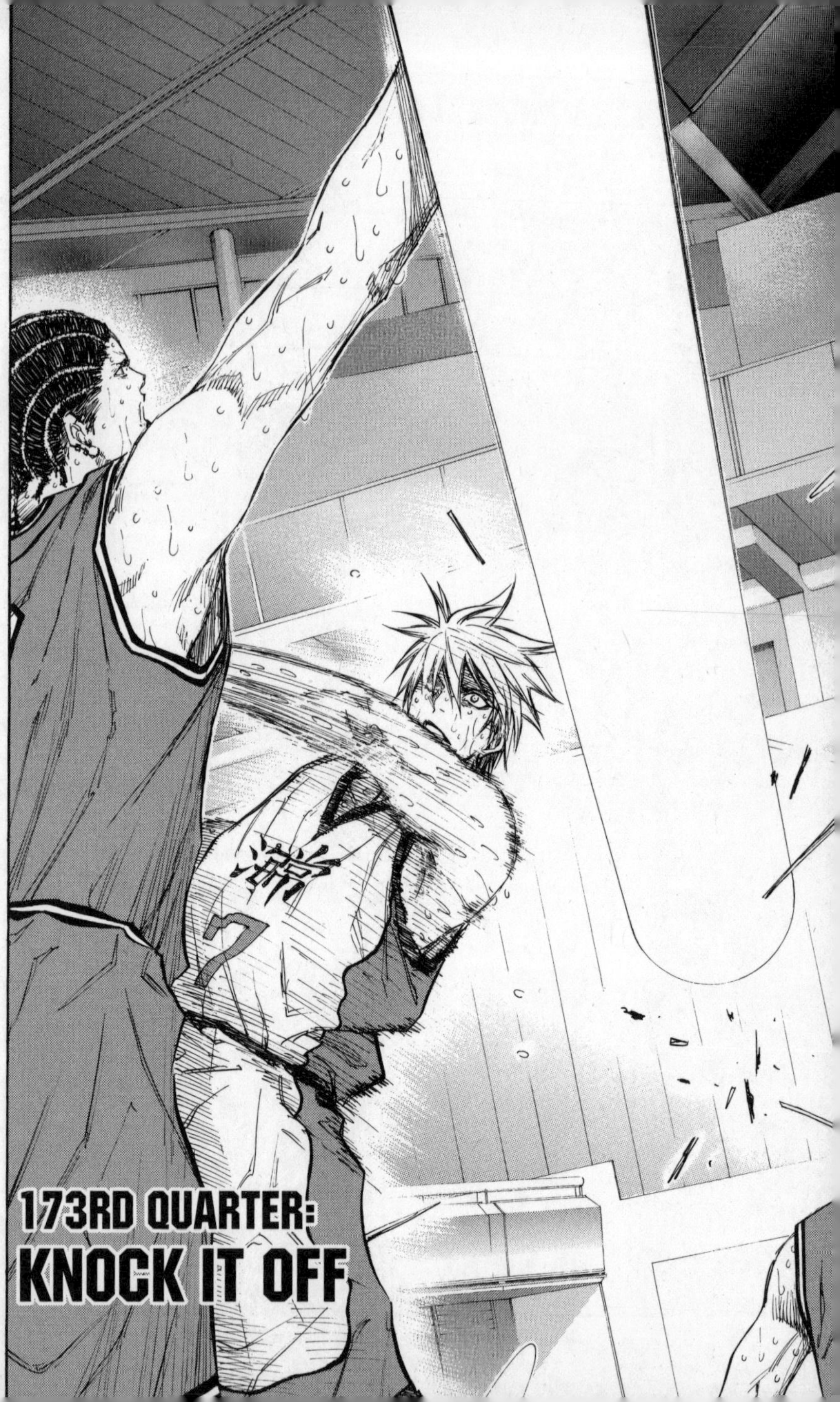
173RD QUARTER:
KNOCK IT OFF

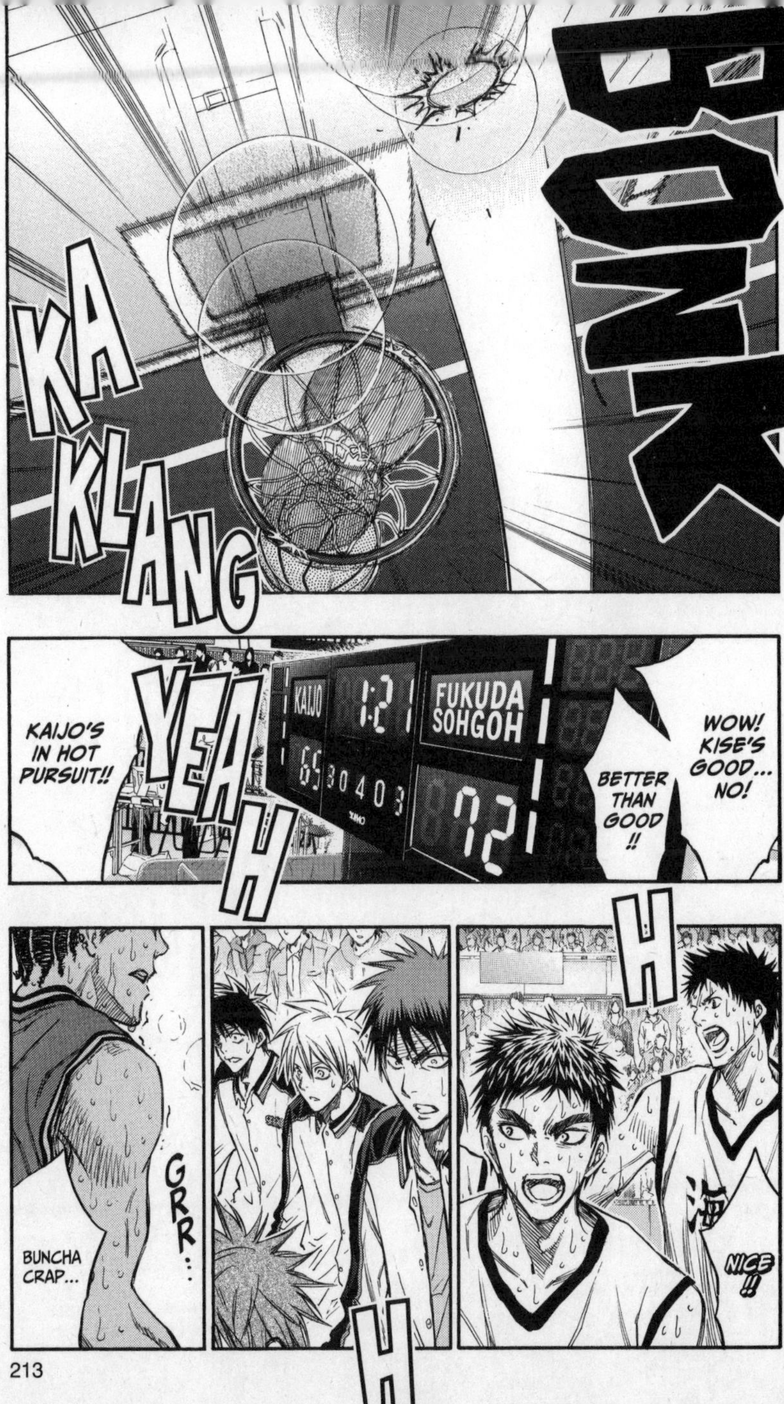
BONK
KA KLANG
WOW! KISE'S GOOD... NO!
BETTER THAN GOOD !!
FUKUDA SOHGOH
KAIJO
1:21
65
72
YEAHHHH
KAIJO'S IN HOT PURSUIT!!
NICE !!
GRR...
BUNCHA CRAP...

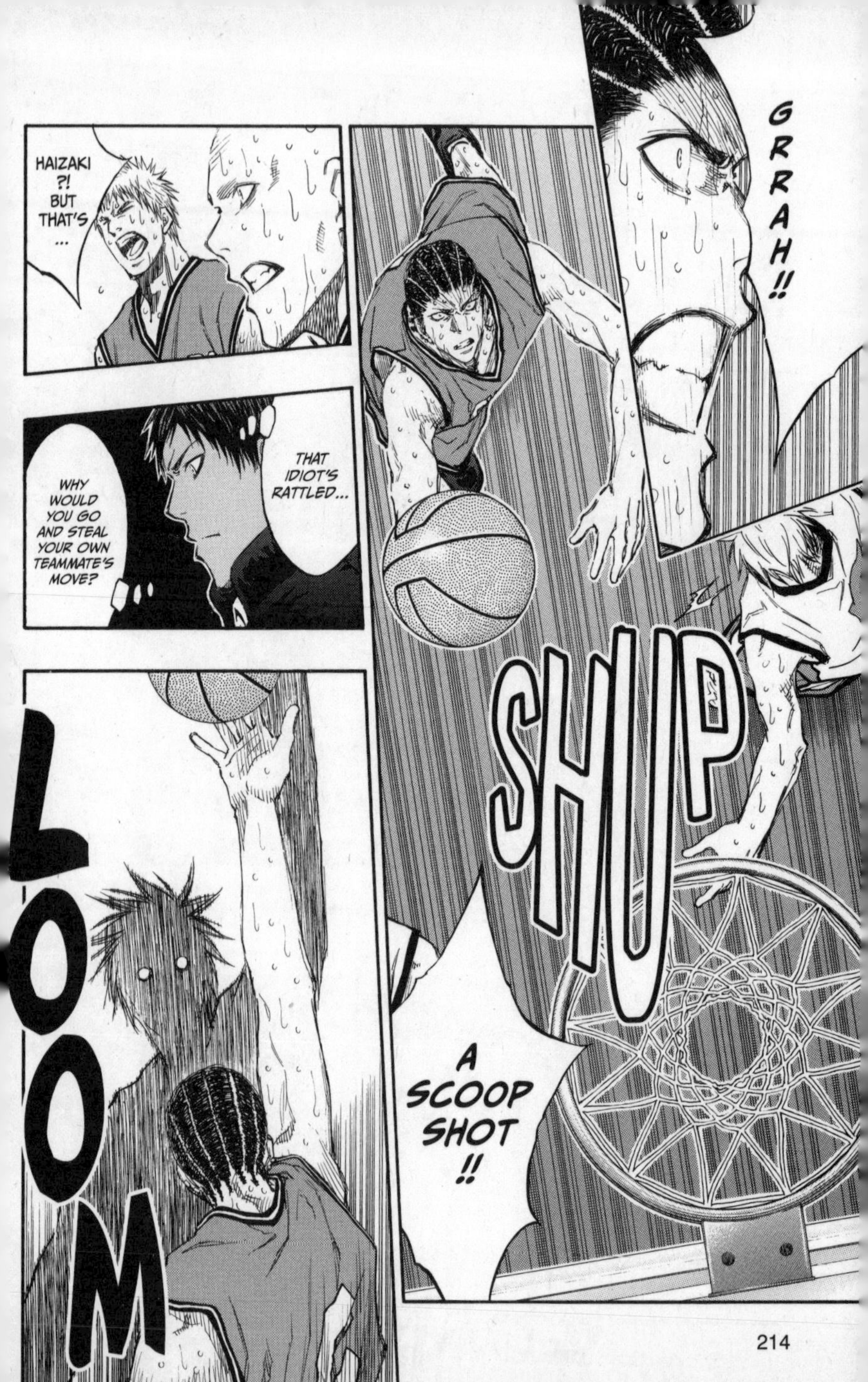
GRRAH!!
SHUP
A SCOOP SHOT!!
HAIZAKI?! BUT THAT'S...
THAT IDIOT'S RATTLED...
WHY WOULD YOU GO AND STEAL YOUR OWN TEAMMATE'S MOVE?
LOOM

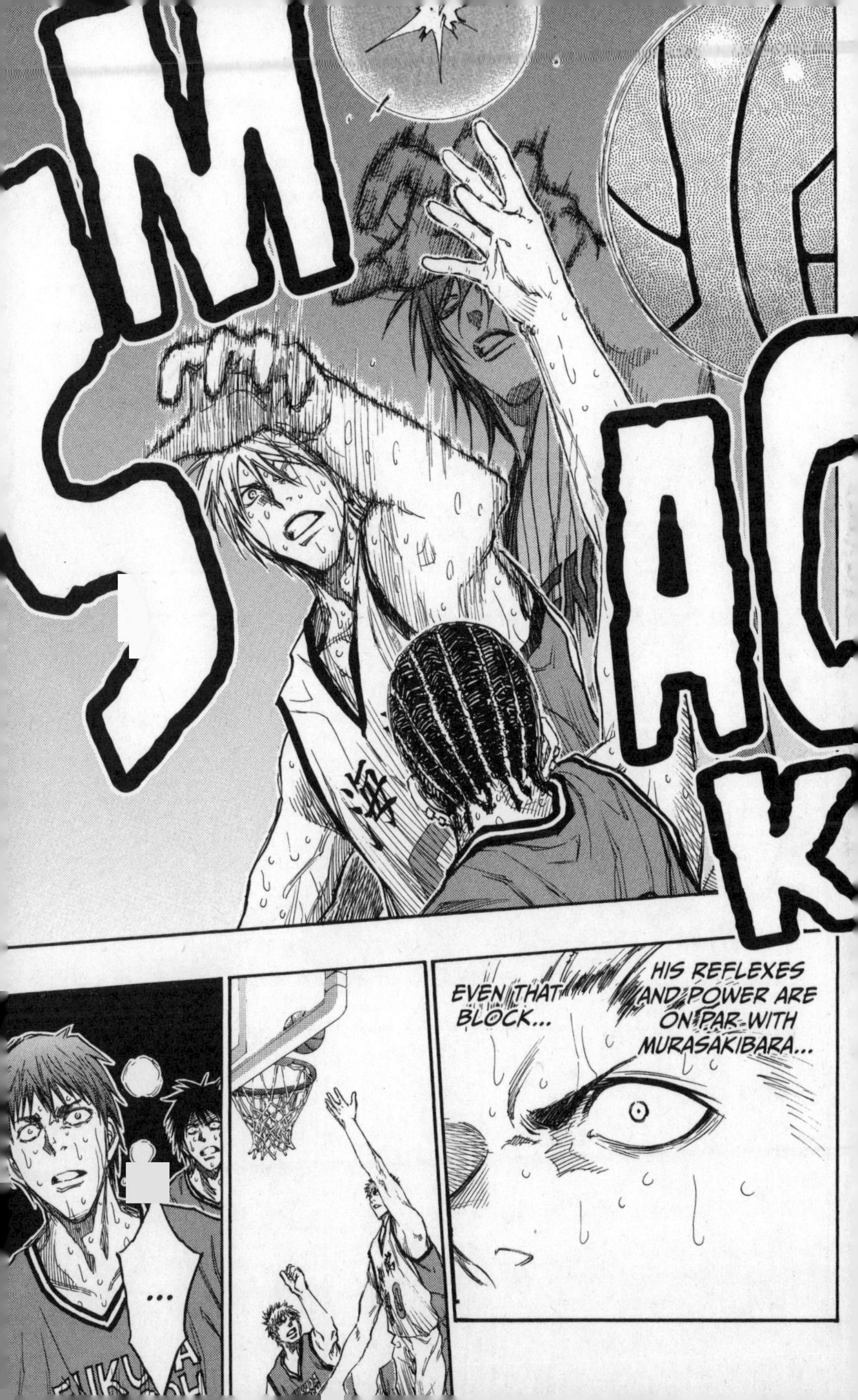
HIS REFLEXES AND POWER ARE ON PAR WITH MURASAKIBARA...
EVEN THAT BLOCK...
...

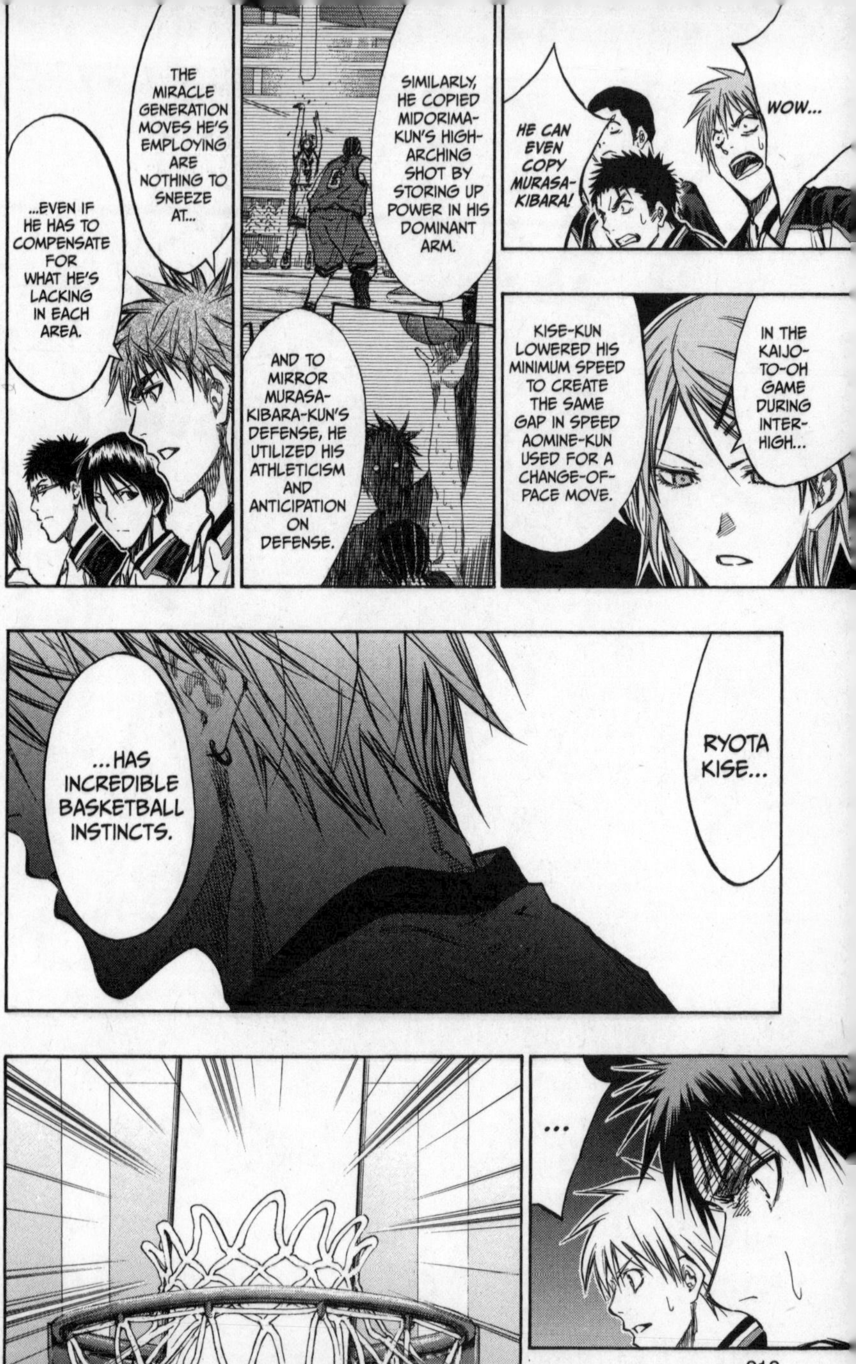
WOW...
HE CAN EVEN COPY MURASAKIBARA!
IN THE KAIJO-TO-OH GAME DURING INTER-HIGH...
KISE-KUN LOWERED HIS MINIMUM SPEED TO CREATE THE SAME GAP IN SPEED AOMINE-KUN USED FOR A CHANGE-OF-PACE MOVE.
SIMILARLY, HE COPIED MIDORIMA-KUN'S HIGH-ARCHING SHOT BY STORING UP POWER IN HIS DOMINANT ARM.
AND TO MIRROR MURASAKIBARA-KUN'S DEFENSE, HE UTILIZED HIS ATHLETICISM AND ANTICIPATION ON DEFENSE.
THE MIRACLE GENERATION MOVES HE'S EMPLOYING ARE NOTHING TO SNEEZE AT...
...EVEN IF HE HAS TO COMPENSATE FOR WHAT HE'S LACKING IN EACH AREA.
RYOTA KISE...
...HAS INCREDIBLE BASKETBALL INSTINCTS.
...

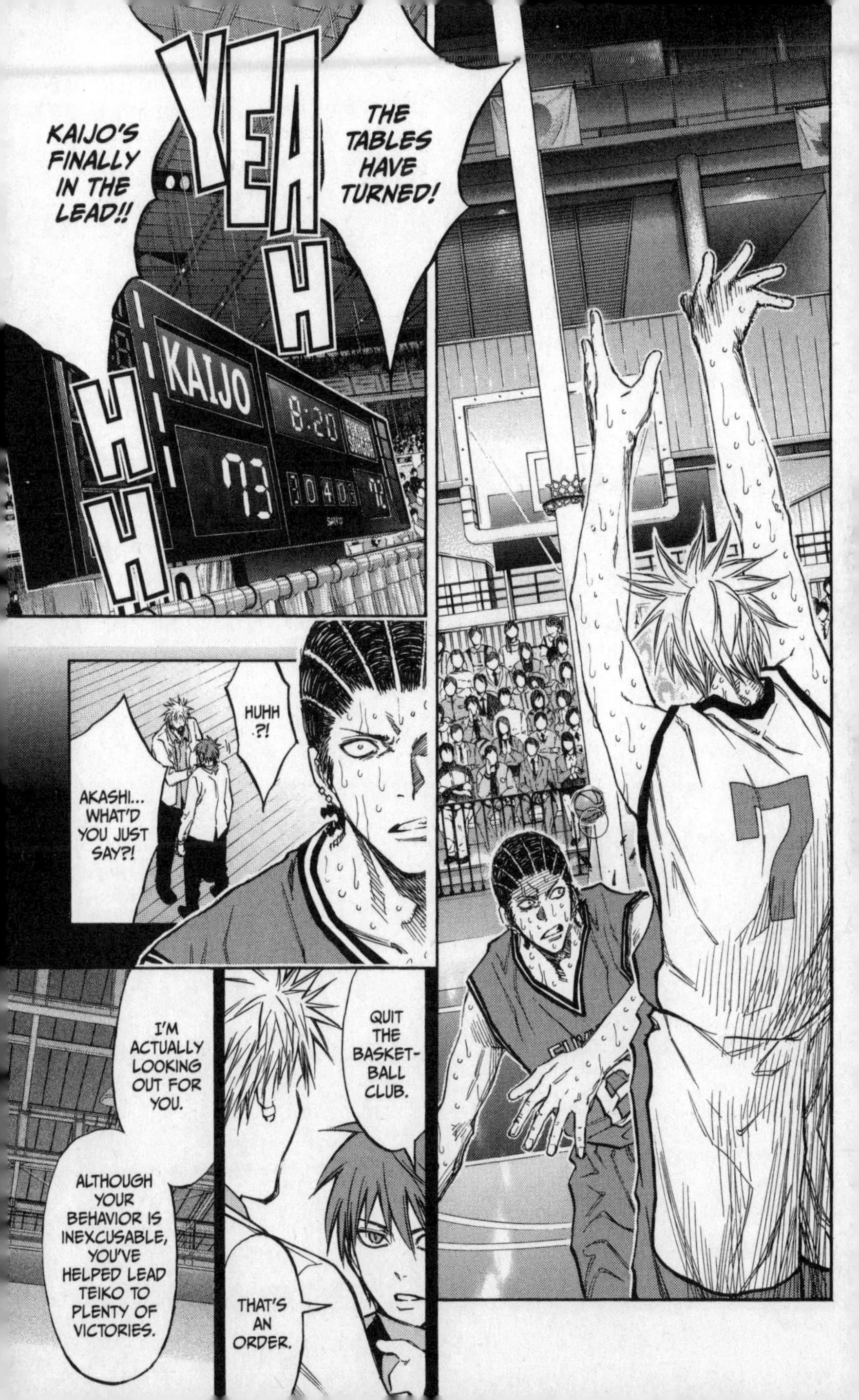
THE TABLES HAVE TURNED!
YEAHHHH
KAIJO'S FINALLY IN THE LEAD!!
KAIJO
8:20
73
HUHH?!
AKASHI... WHAT'D YOU JUST SAY?!
QUIT THE BASKET-BALL CLUB.
THAT'S AN ORDER.
I'M ACTUALLY LOOKING OUT FOR YOU.
ALTHOUGH YOUR BEHAVIOR IS INEXCUSABLE, YOU'VE HELPED LEAD TEIKO TO PLENTY OF VICTORIES.

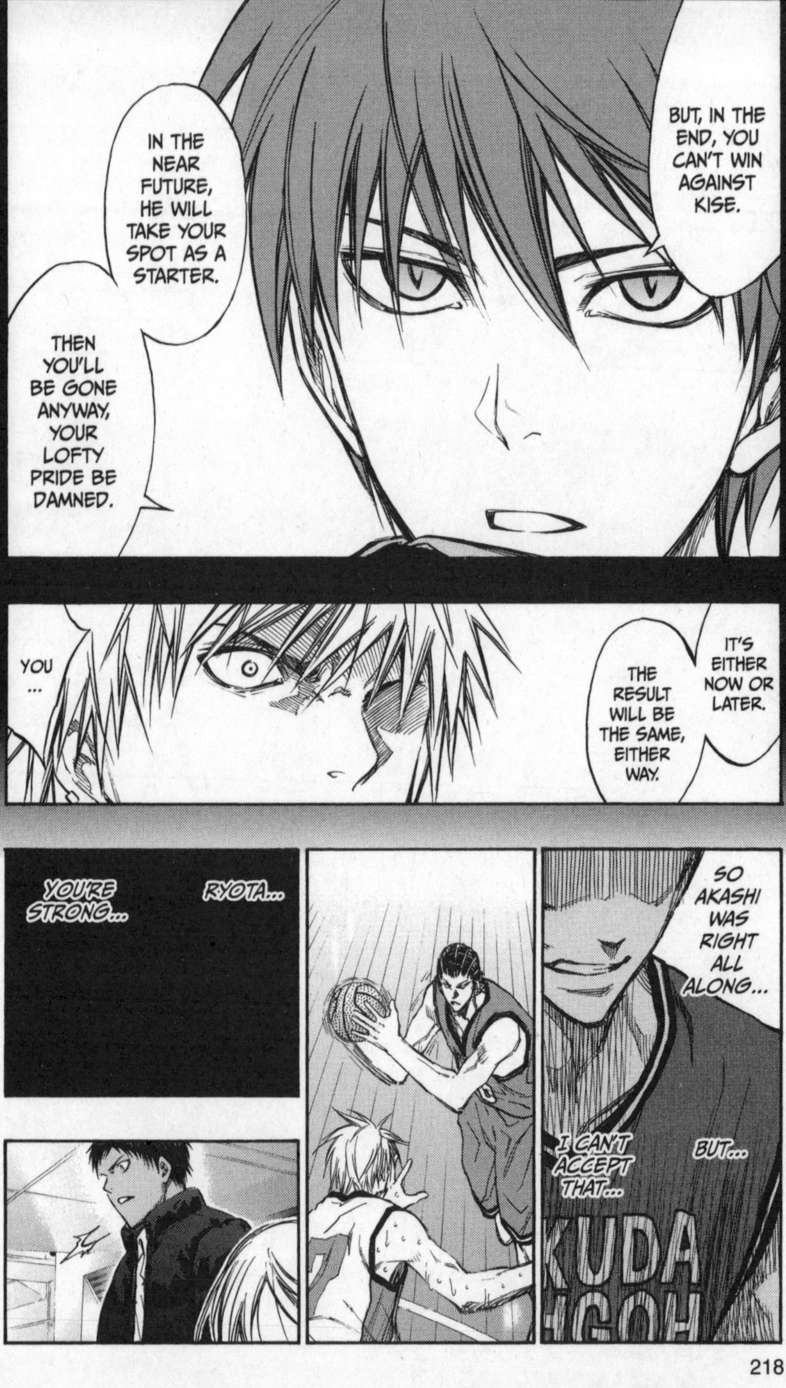
BUT, IN THE END, YOU CAN'T WIN AGAINST KISE.
IN THE NEAR FUTURE, HE WILL TAKE YOUR SPOT AS A STARTER.
THEN YOU'LL BE GONE ANYWAY, YOUR LOFTY PRIDE BE DAMNED.
IT'S EITHER NOW OR LATER.
THE RESULT WILL BE THE SAME, EITHER WAY.
YOU ...
SO AKASHI WAS RIGHT ALL ALONG...
BUT...
I CAN'T ACCEPT THAT...
RYOTA...
YOU'RE STRONG...

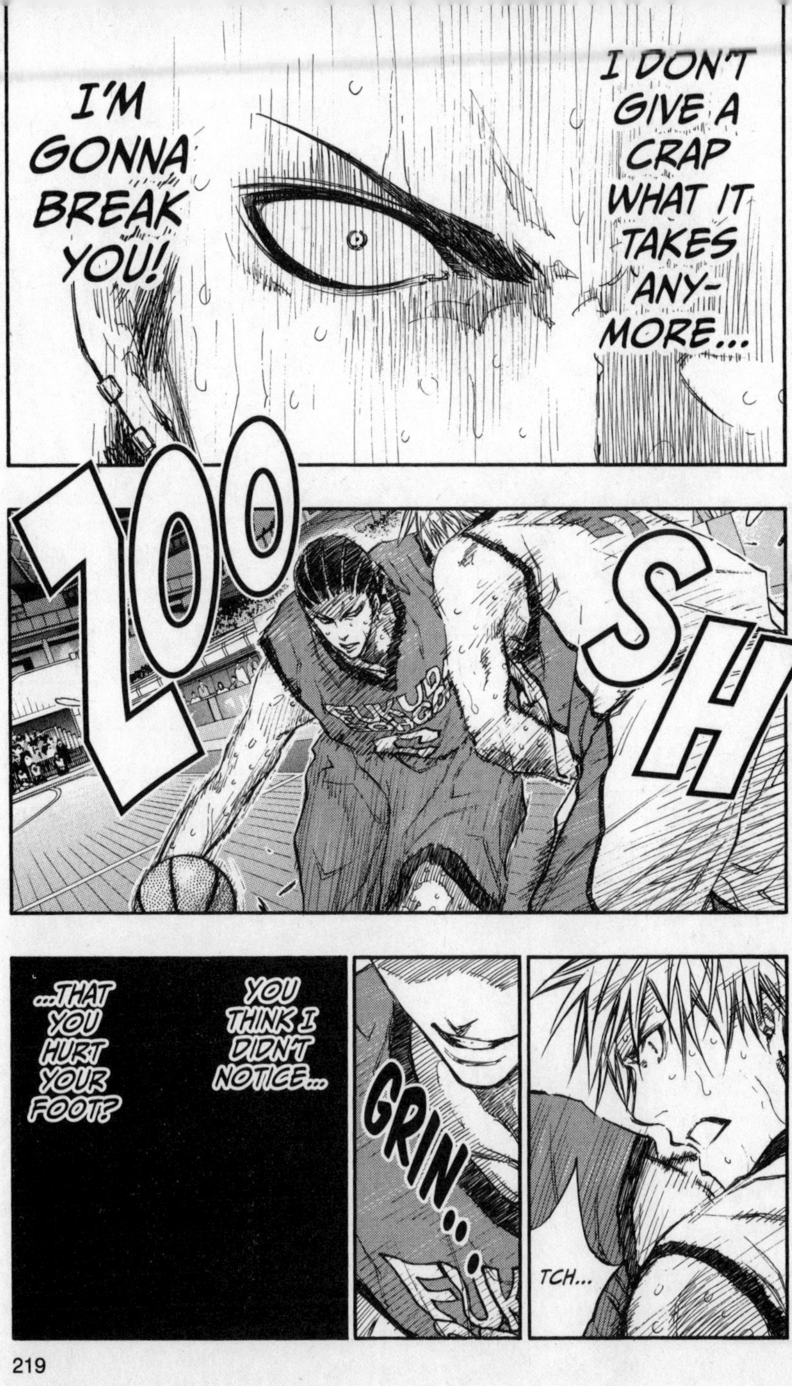
I DON'T GIVE A CRAP WHAT IT TAKES ANYMORE...
I'M GONNA BREAK YOU!
ZOO
SH
TCH...
GRIN...
YOU THINK I DIDN'T NOTICE...
...THAT YOU HURT YOUR FOOT?

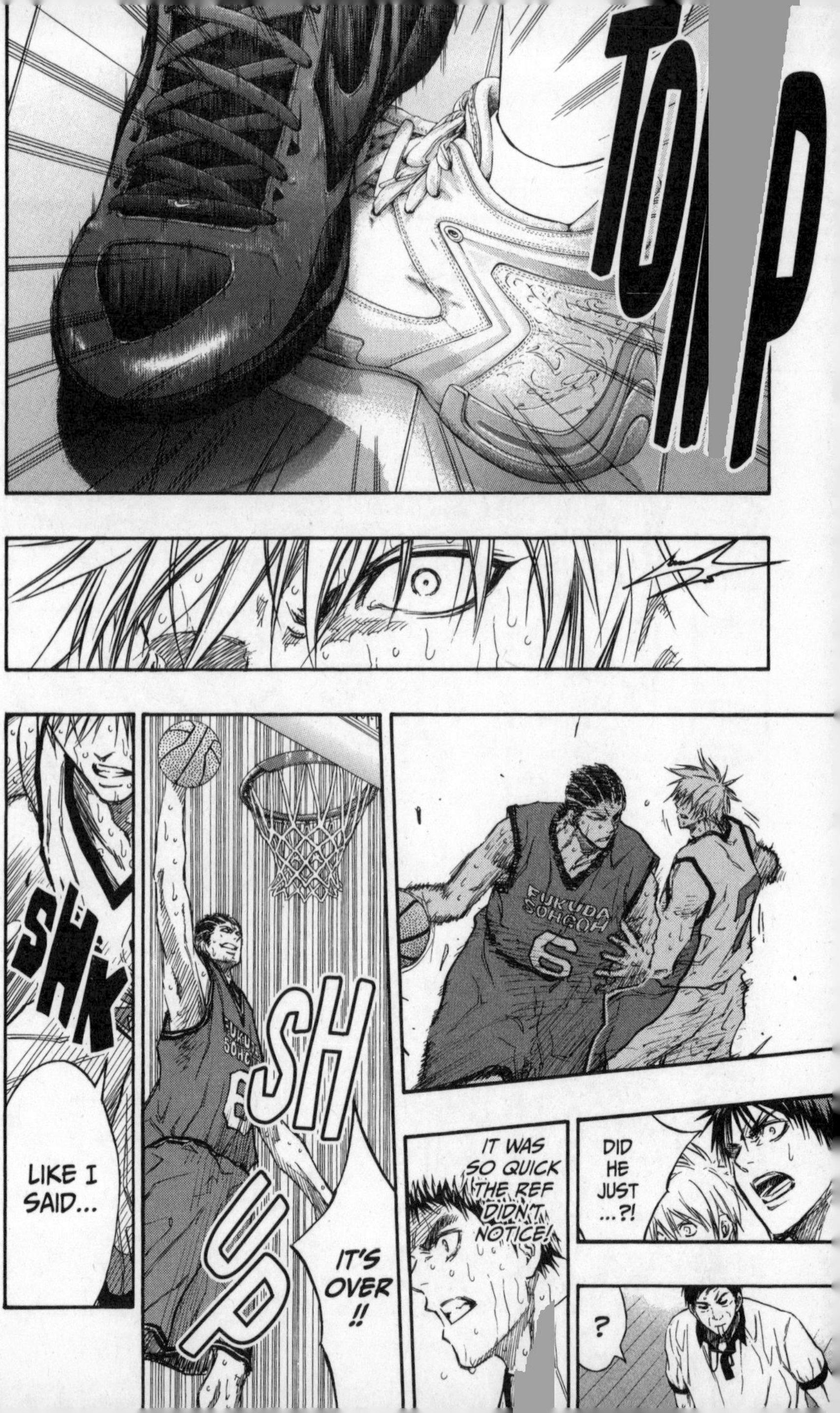
TOMP
DID HE JUST ...?!
IT WAS SO QUICK THE REF DIDN'T NOTICE!
?
SH
UP
IT'S OVER !!
SHK
LIKE I SAID...

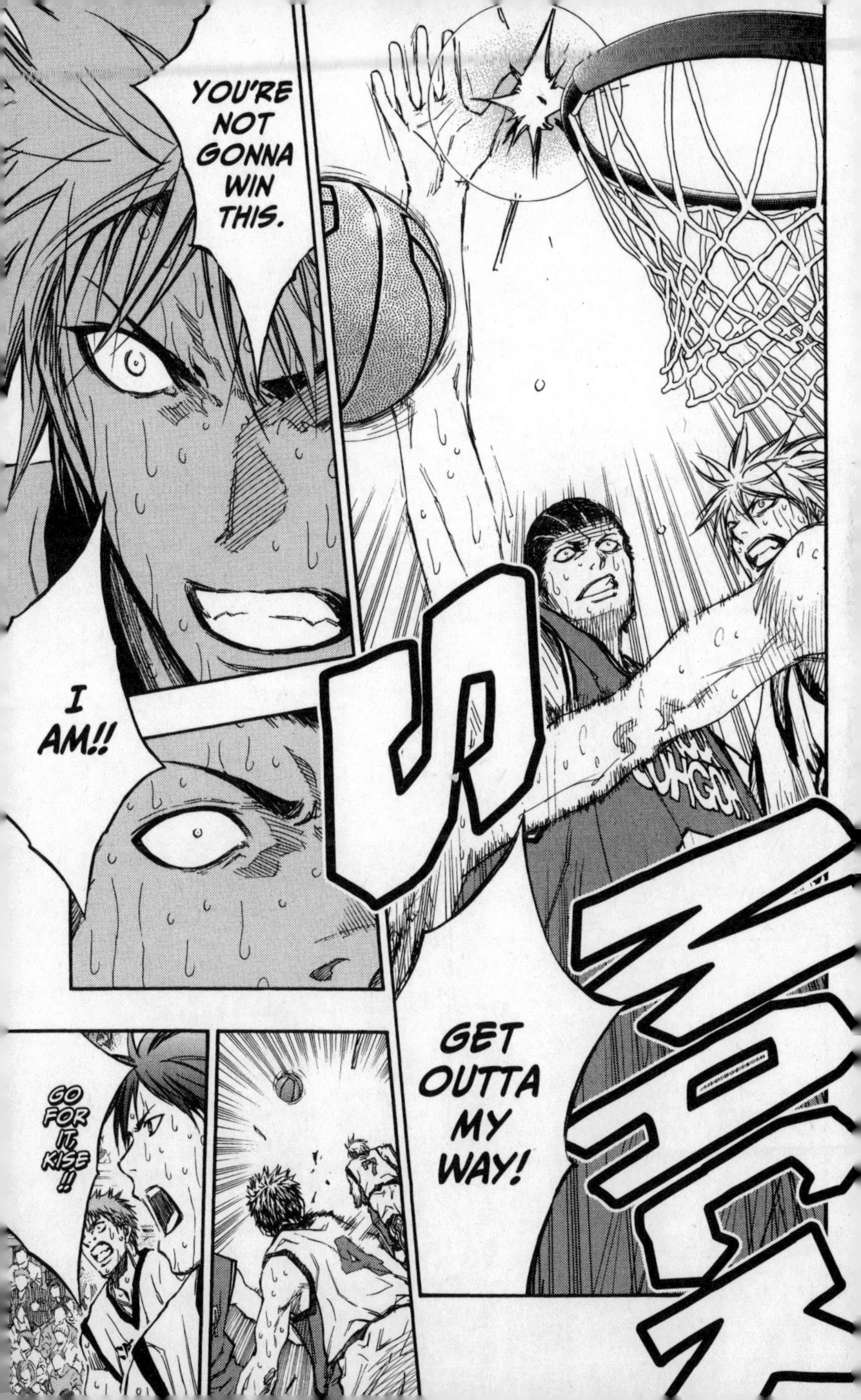
GET OUTTA MY WAY!
YOU'RE NOT GONNA WIN THIS.
I AM!!
GO FOR IT, KISE!!

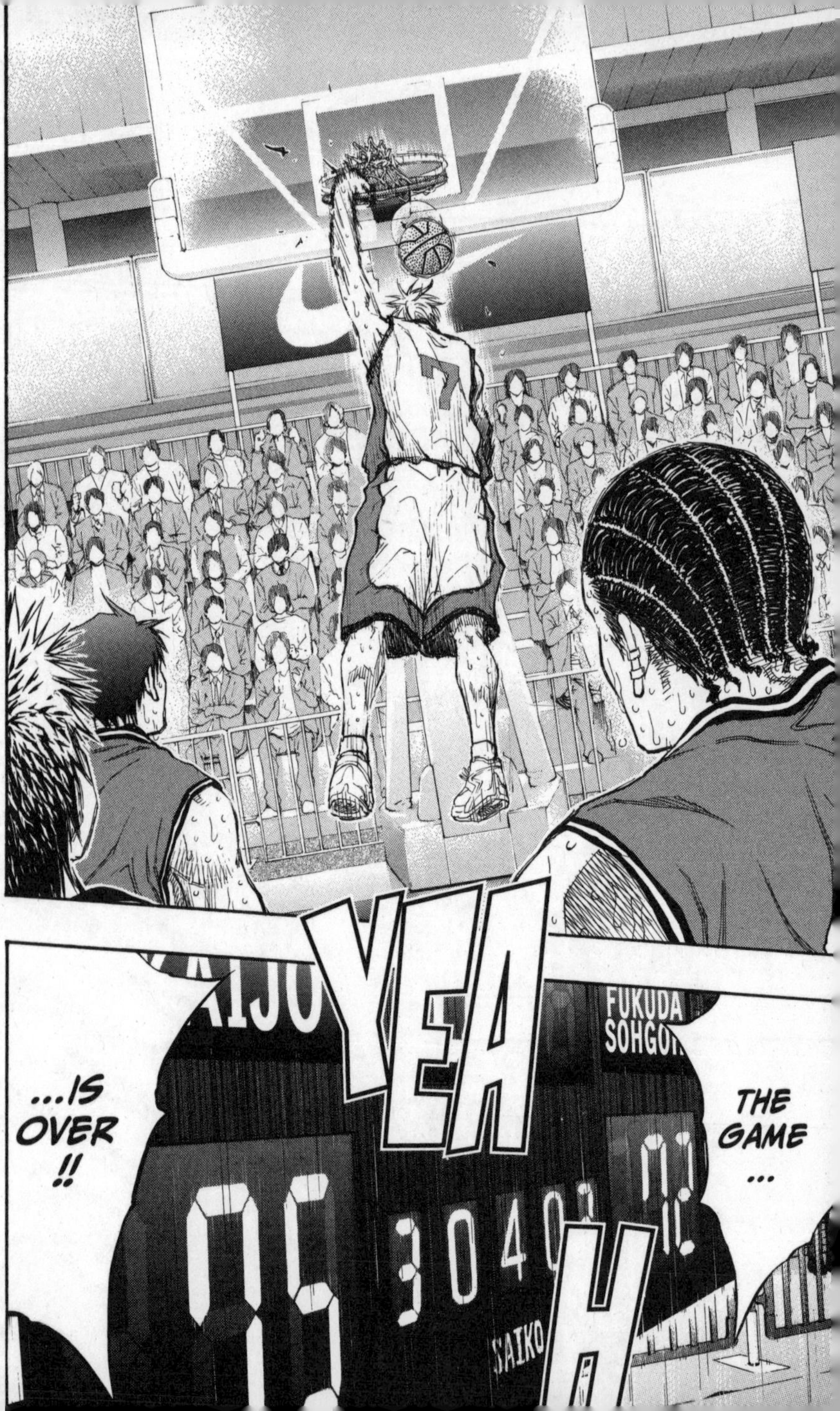
THE GAME ...
...IS OVER !!
YEAH

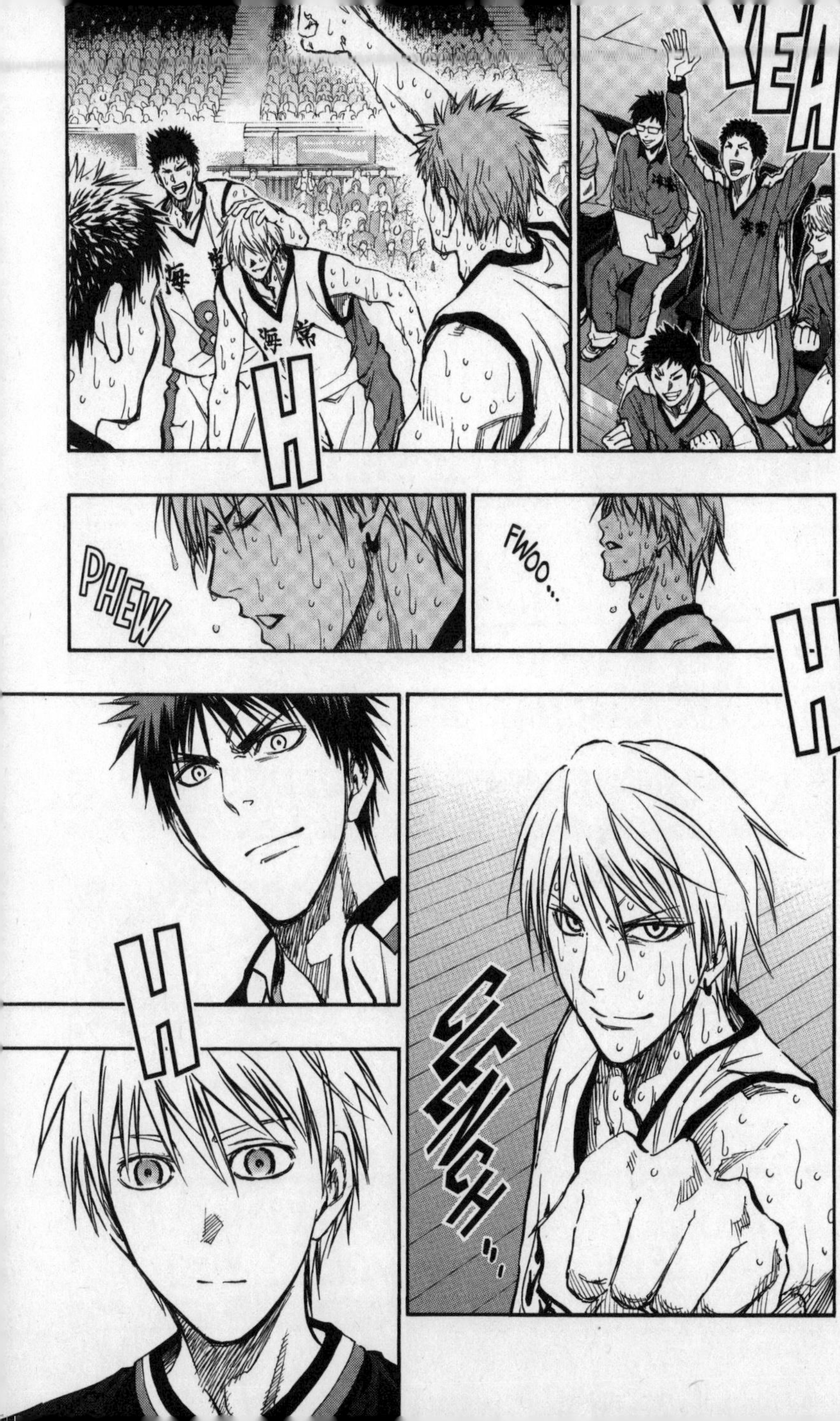

YEA
H
FWOO...
PHEW
H
CLENCH...
H

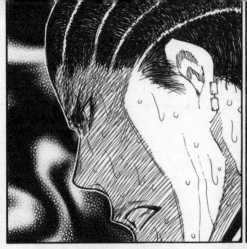

WAIT... DAI-CHAN?!

TMP

I'M LEAVING EARLY, SATSUKI.

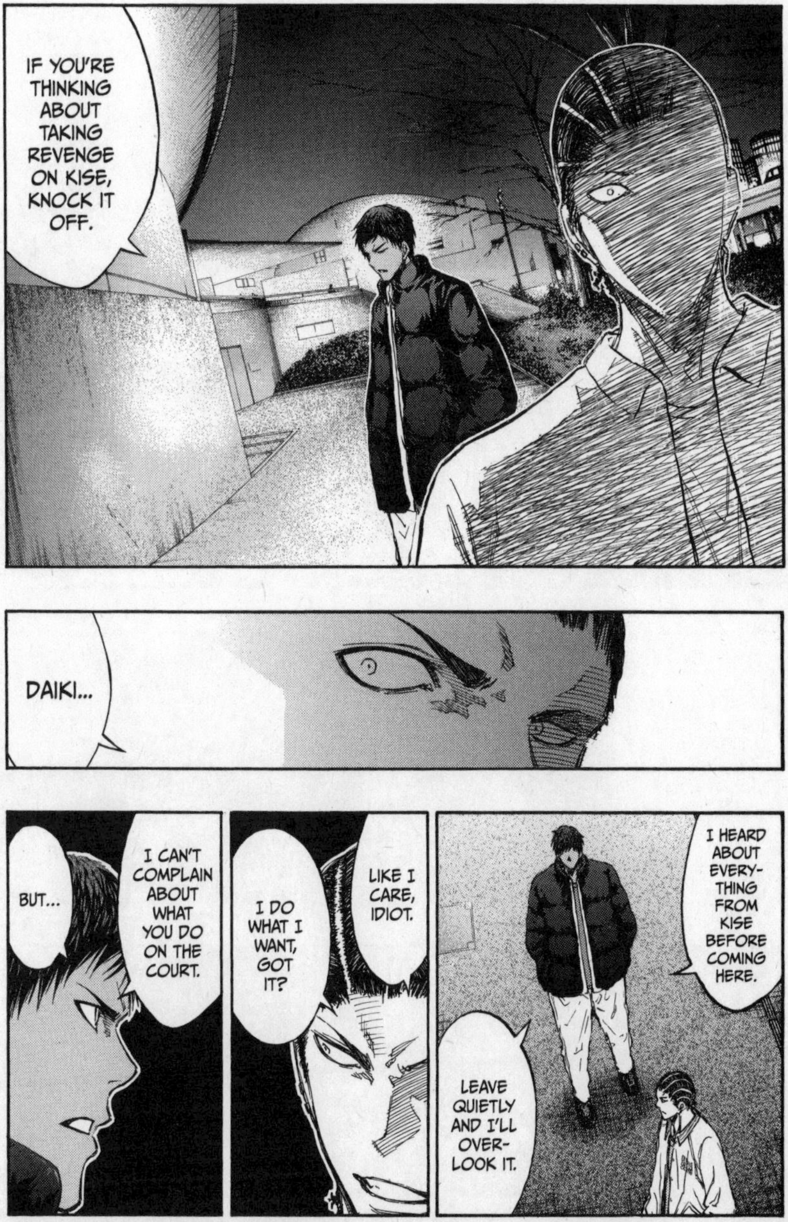
IF YOU'RE THINKING ABOUT TAKING REVENGE ON KISE, KNOCK IT OFF.
DAIKI...
I HEARD ABOUT EVERYTHING FROM KISE BEFORE COMING HERE.
LEAVE QUIETLY AND I'LL OVERLOOK IT.
LIKE I CARE, IDIOT.
I DO WHAT I WANT, GOT IT?
I CAN'T COMPLAIN ABOUT WHAT YOU DO ON THE COURT.
BUT...

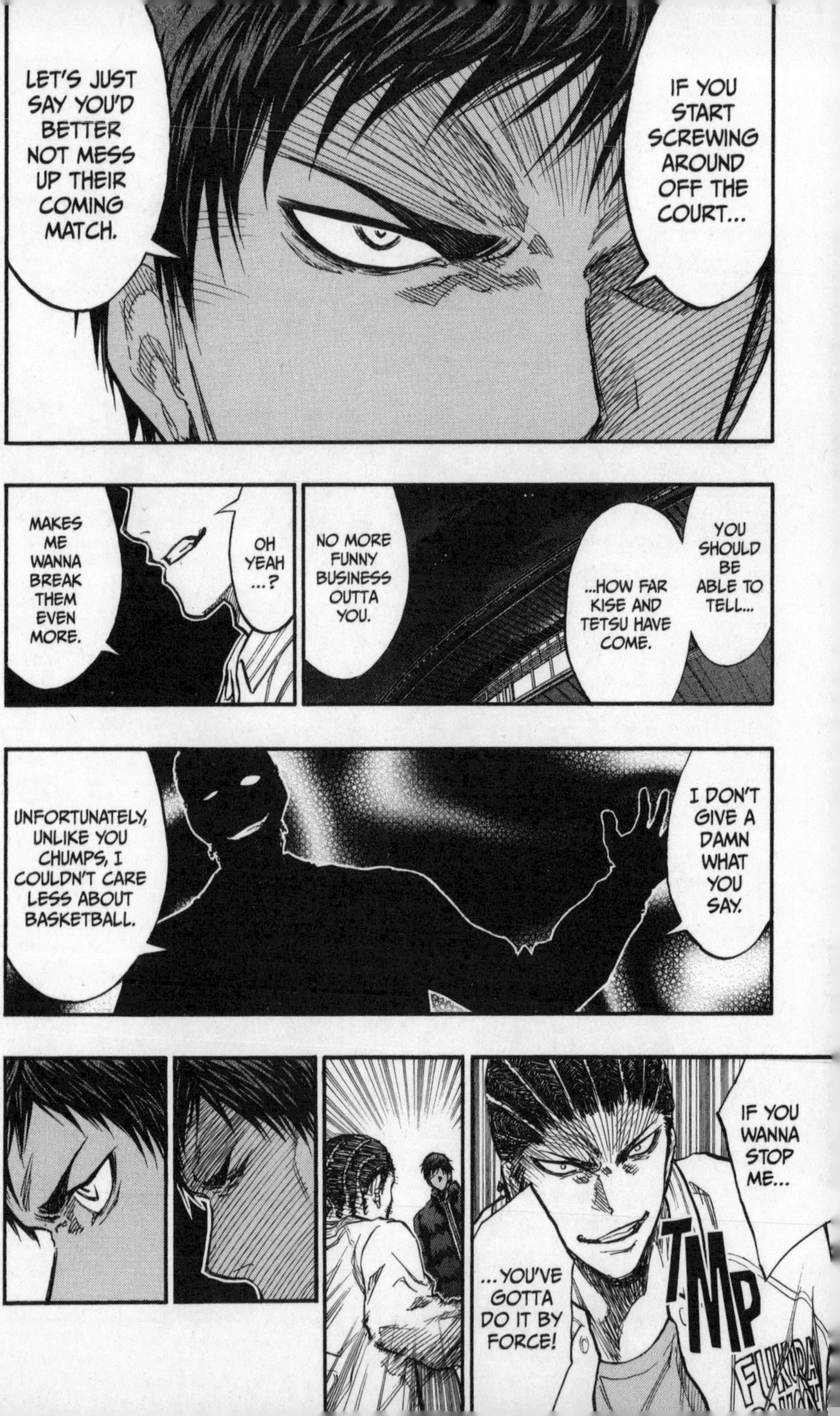
IF YOU START SCREWING AROUND OFF THE COURT...
LET'S JUST SAY YOU'D BETTER NOT MESS UP THEIR COMING MATCH.
YOU SHOULD BE ABLE TO TELL...
...HOW FAR KISE AND TETSU HAVE COME.
NO MORE FUNNY BUSINESS OUTTA YOU.
OH YEAH ...?
MAKES ME WANNA BREAK THEM EVEN MORE.
I DON'T GIVE A DAMN WHAT YOU SAY.
UNFORTUNATELY, UNLIKE YOU CHUMPS, I COULDN'T CARE LESS ABOUT BASKETBALL.
IF YOU WANNA STOP ME...
TMP
...YOU'VE GOTTA DO IT BY FORCE!

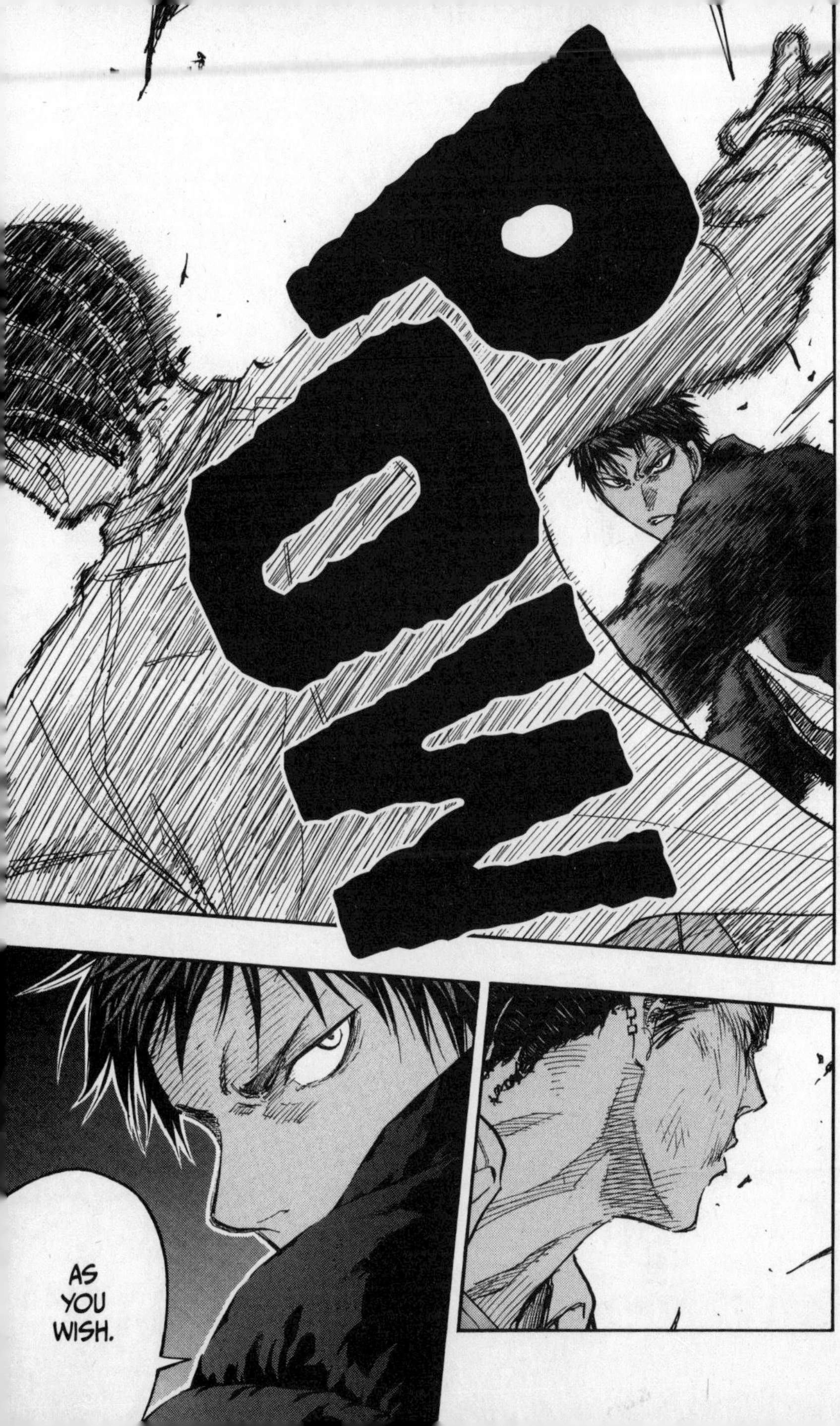
AS YOU WISH.

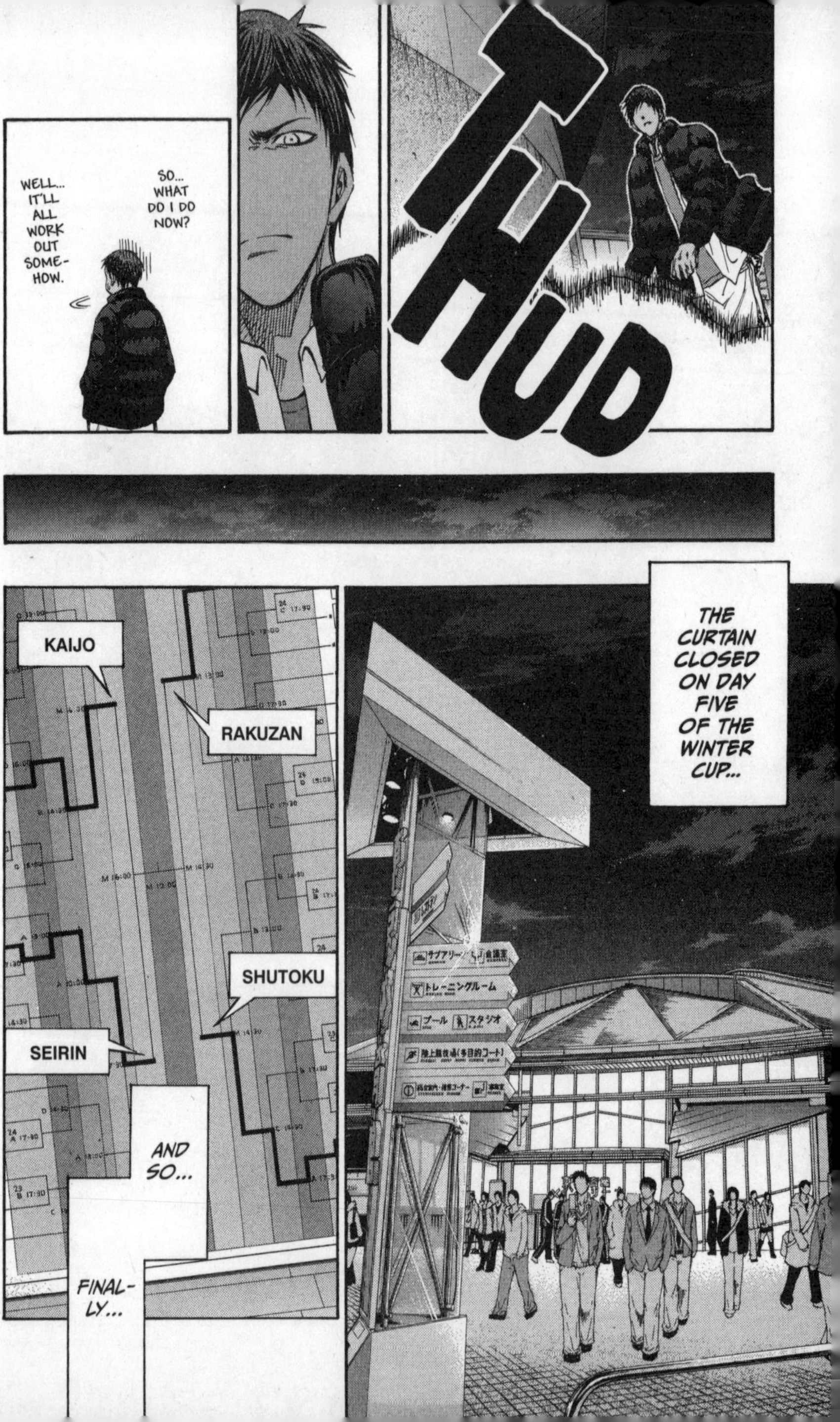
THUD
SO... WHAT DO I DO NOW?
WELL... IT'LL ALL WORK OUT SOME-HOW.
THE CURTAIN CLOSED ON DAY FIVE OF THE WINTER CUP...
KAIJO
RAKUZAN
SHUTOKU
SEIRIN
AND SO...
FINAL-LY...

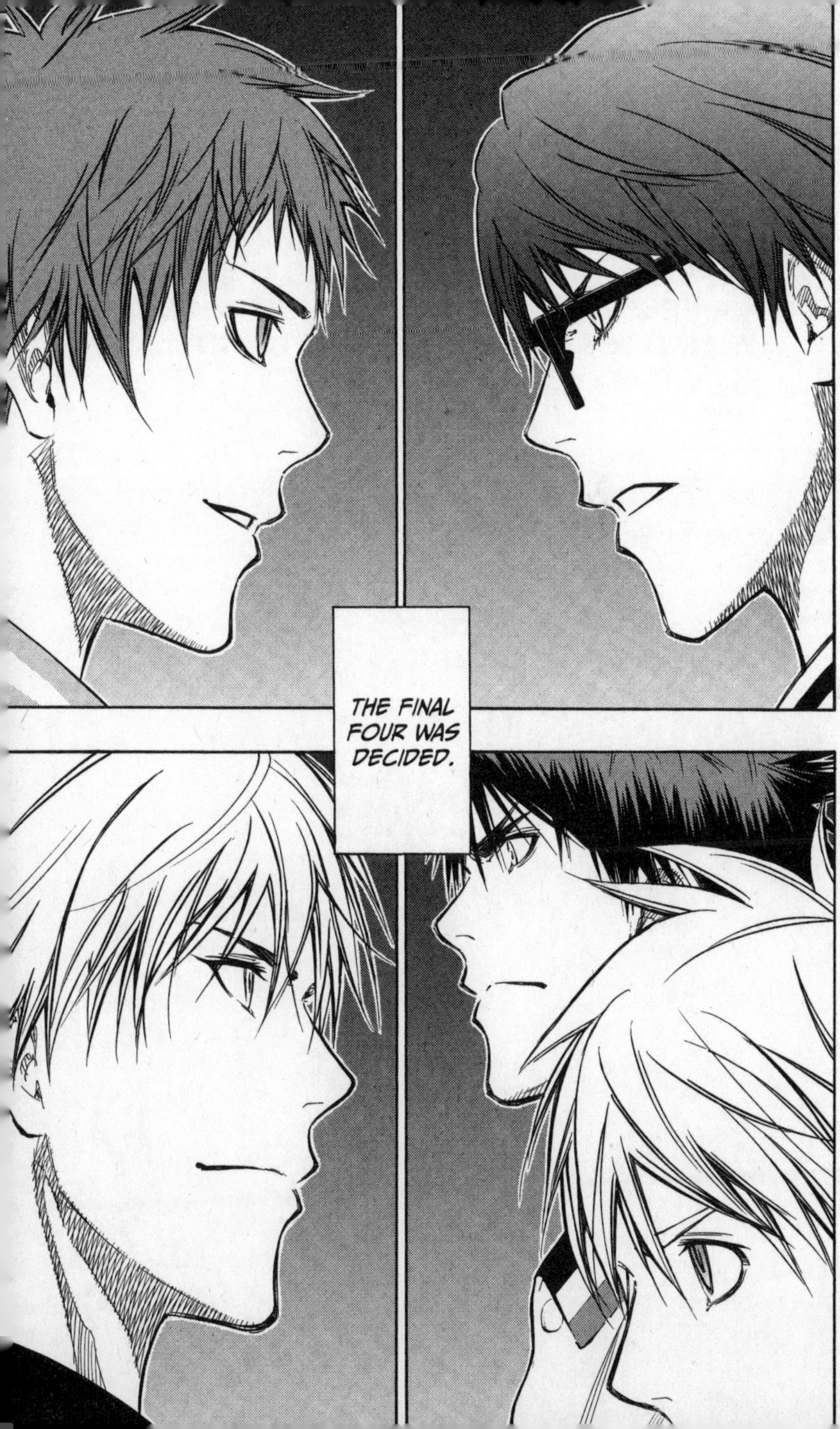
THE FINAL FOUR WAS DECIDED.

KUROKO'S BASKETBALL (W/ HALFWAY-DECENT ANSWERS)

Q&A

Q. YOU KNOW HOW KUROKO GETS THOSE TERRIBLE COWLICKS IN THE MORNING? WHEN DOES HIS HAIR RETURN TO NORMAL?
(KUROKO'S EYEBROWS from TOKYO)

A. AFTER MORNING PRACTICE.

KUROKO'S BASKETBALL BLOOPERS

TAKE 5

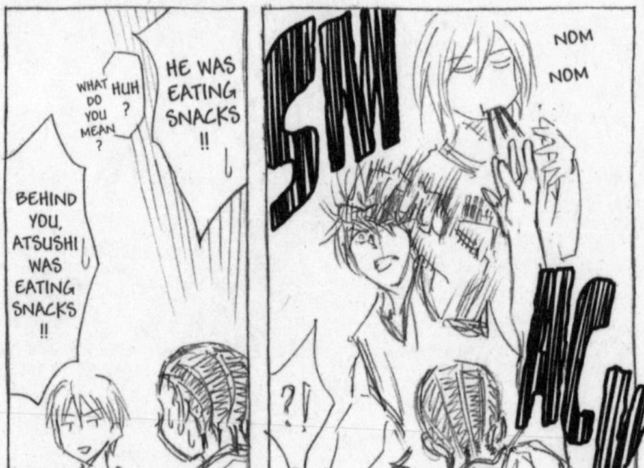

SWACK
NOM NOM
?!
HE WAS EATING SNACKS!!
HUH?
WHAT DO YOU MEAN?
BEHIND YOU, ATSUSHI WAS EATING SNACKS!!

174TH QUARTER: I'LL TAKE 'EM

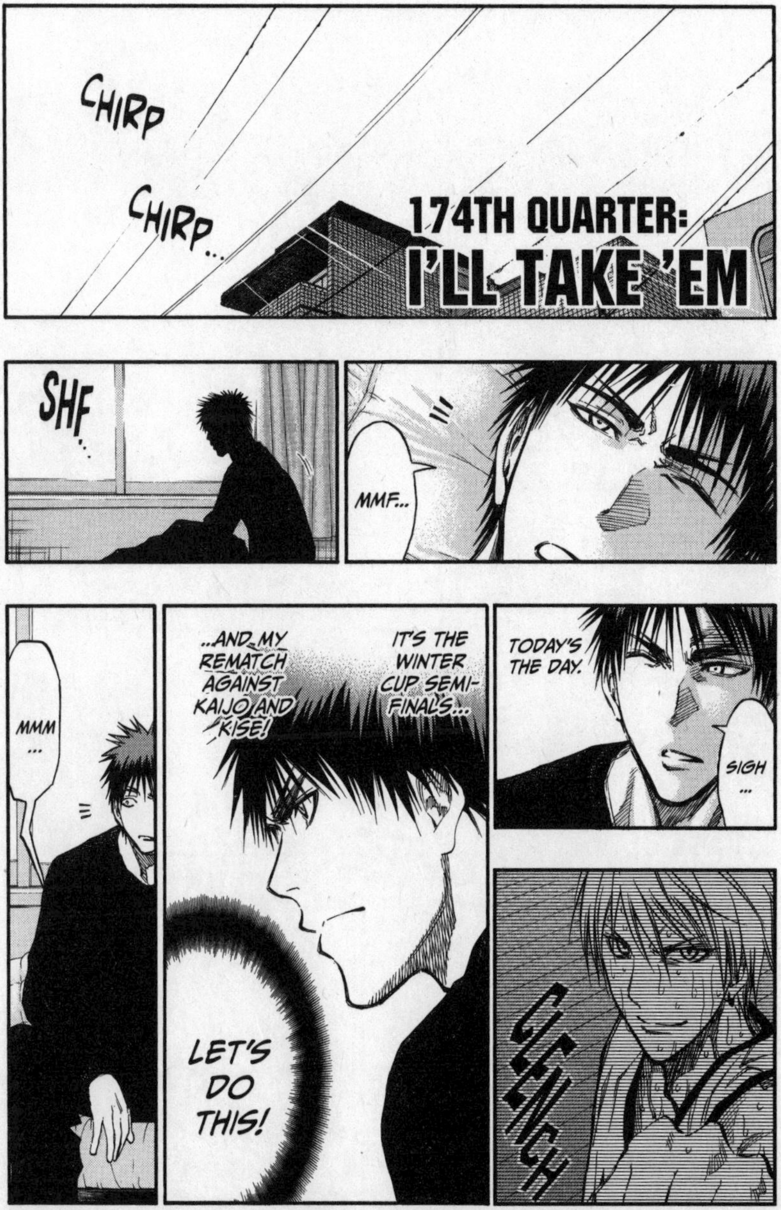
CHIRP
CHIRP...
MMF...
SHF...
TODAY'S THE DAY.
SIGH...
CLENCH
IT'S THE WINTER CUP SEMI-FINALS...
...AND MY REMATCH AGAINST KAIJO AND KISE!
LET'S DO THIS!
MMM...

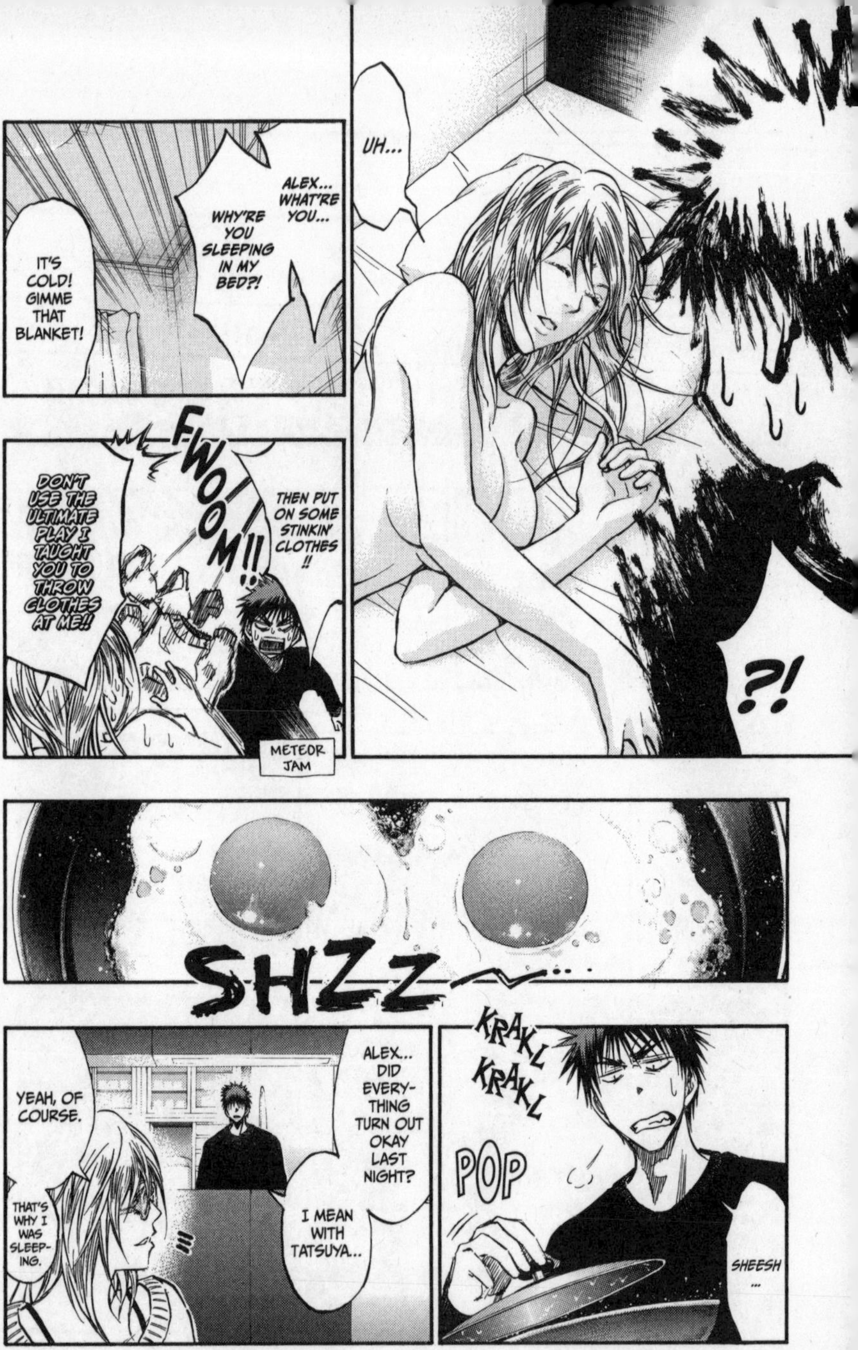
UH...
?!
ALEX... WHAT'RE YOU...
WHY'RE YOU SLEEPING IN MY BED?!
IT'S COLD! GIMME THAT BLANKET!
FWOOM!!
THEN PUT ON SOME STINKIN' CLOTHES!!
DON'T USE THE ULTIMATE PLAY I TAUGHT YOU TO THROW CLOTHES AT ME!!
METEOR JAM
SHZZ
KRAKL KRAKL
POP
SHEESH ...
ALEX... DID EVERYTHING TURN OUT OKAY LAST NIGHT?
I MEAN WITH TATSUYA...
YEAH, OF COURSE.
THAT'S WHY I WAS SLEEPING.

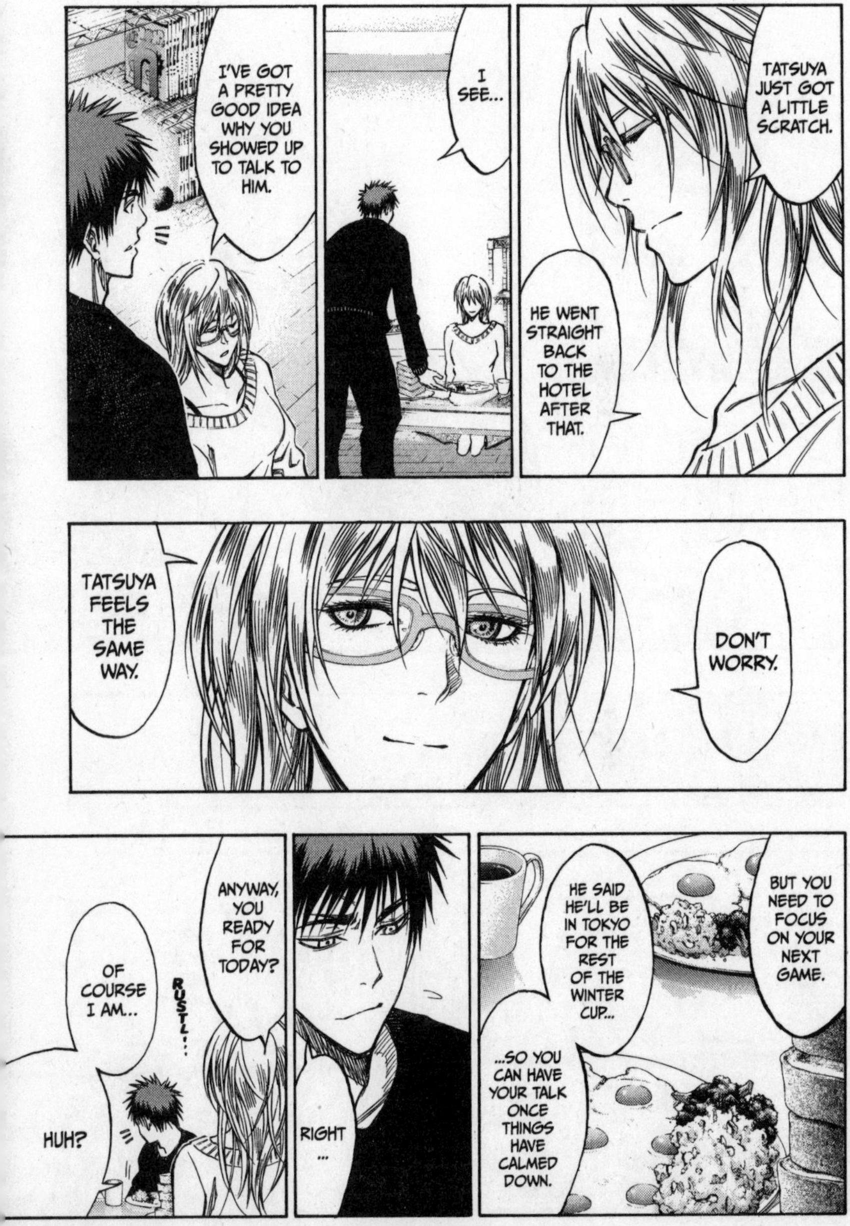
TATSUYA JUST GOT A LITTLE SCRATCH.
HE WENT STRAIGHT BACK TO THE HOTEL AFTER THAT.
I SEE...
I'VE GOT A PRETTY GOOD IDEA WHY YOU SHOWED UP TO TALK TO HIM.
DON'T WORRY.
TATSUYA FEELS THE SAME WAY.
BUT YOU NEED TO FOCUS ON YOUR NEXT GAME.
HE SAID HE'LL BE IN TOKYO FOR THE REST OF THE WINTER CUP...
...SO YOU CAN HAVE YOUR TALK ONCE THINGS HAVE CALMED DOWN.
RIGHT...
ANYWAY, YOU READY FOR TODAY?
OF COURSE I AM...
RUSTL!
HUH?

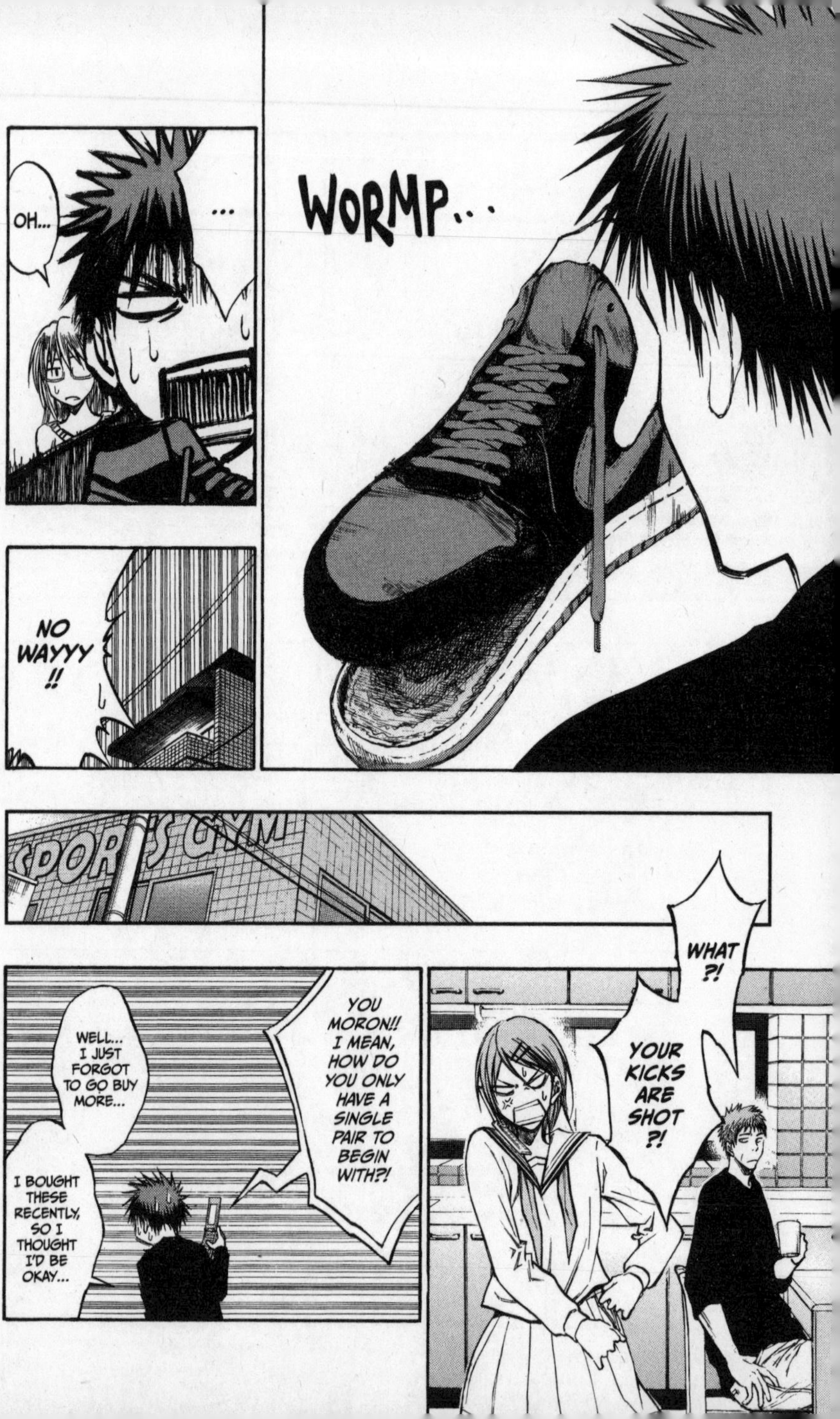
WORMP...
...
OH...
NO WAYYY!!
WHAT?!
YOUR KICKS ARE SHOT?!
YOU MORON!! I MEAN, HOW DO YOU ONLY HAVE A SINGLE PAIR TO BEGIN WITH?!
WELL... I JUST FORGOT TO GO BUY MORE...
I BOUGHT THESE RECENTLY, SO I THOUGHT I'D BE OKAY...

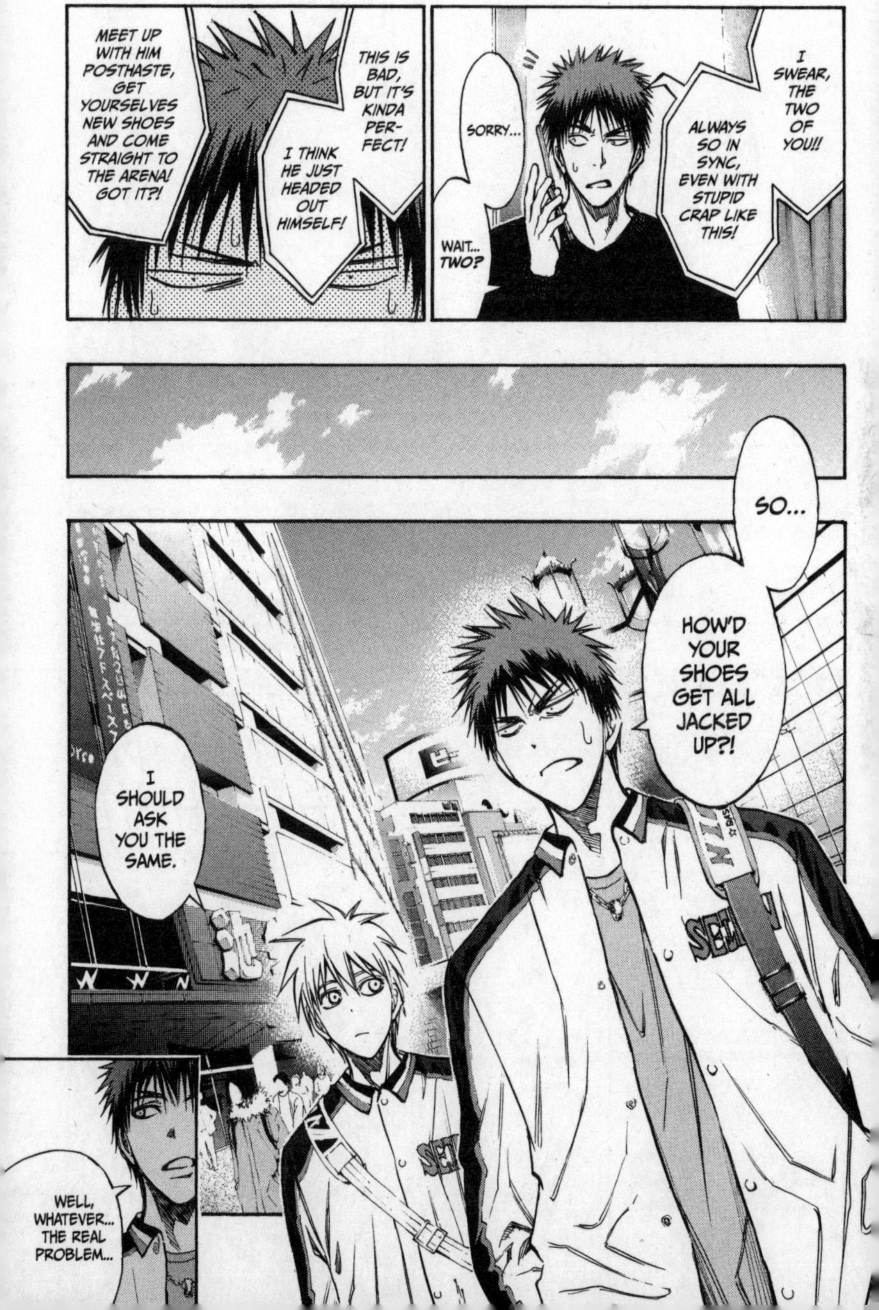
I SWEAR, THE TWO OF YOU!!
ALWAYS SO IN SYNC, EVEN WITH STUPID CRAP LIKE THIS!
SORRY...
WAIT... TWO?
THIS IS BAD, BUT IT'S KINDA PER-FECT!
I THINK HE JUST HEADED OUT HIMSELF!
MEET UP WITH HIM POSTHASTE, GET YOURSELVES NEW SHOES AND COME STRAIGHT TO THE ARENA! GOT IT?!
SO...
HOW'D YOUR SHOES GET ALL JACKED UP?!
I SHOULD ASK YOU THE SAME.
WELL, WHATEVER... THE REAL PROBLEM...

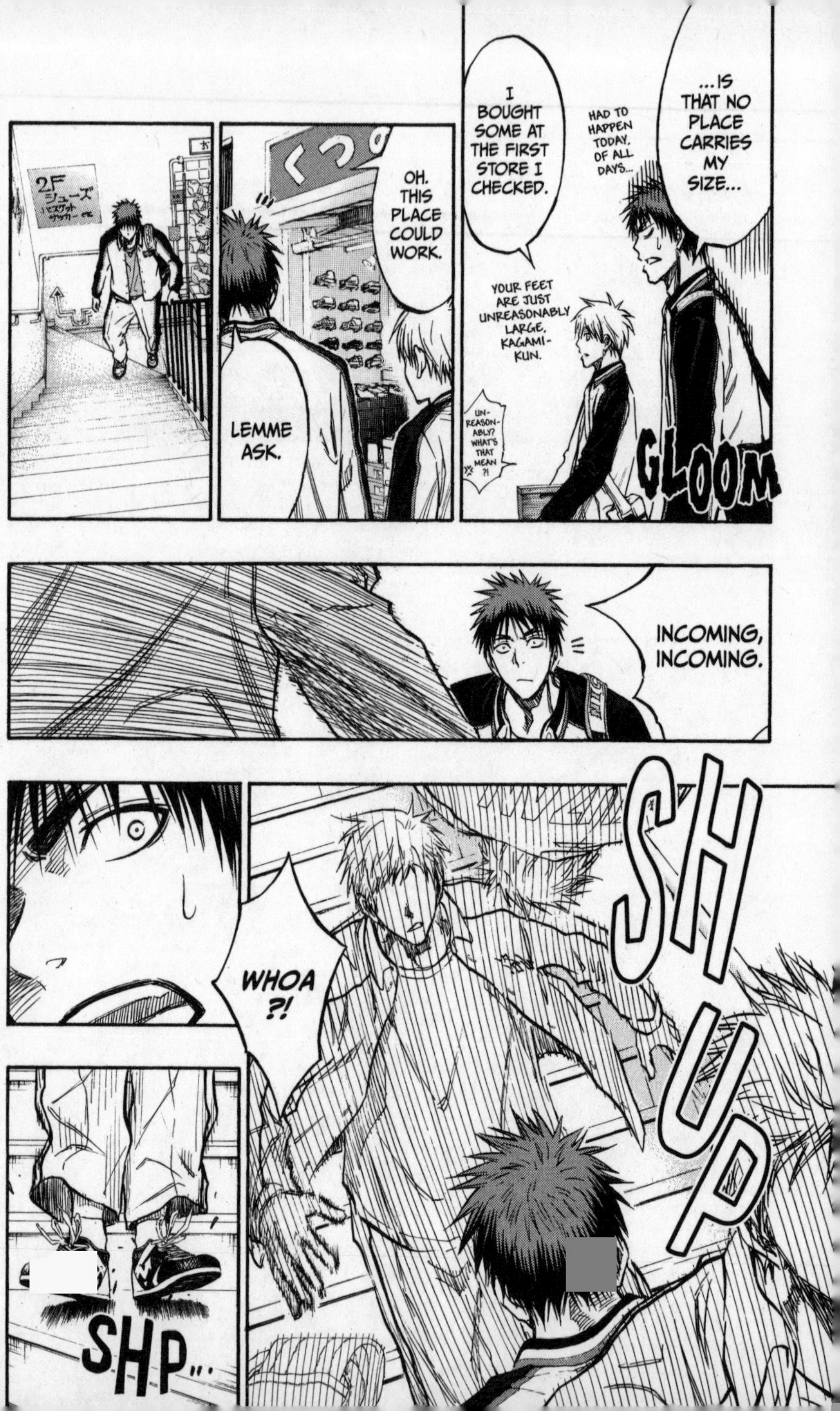
...IS THAT NO PLACE CARRIES MY SIZE...
HAD TO HAPPEN TODAY, OF ALL DAYS...
I BOUGHT SOME AT THE FIRST STORE I CHECKED.
YOUR FEET ARE JUST UNREASONABLY LARGE, KAGAMI-KUN.
UN-REASON-ABLY? WHAT'S THAT MEAN ?!
GLOOM
くつ
OH. THIS PLACE COULD WORK.
LEMME ASK.
2F シューズ
INCOMING, INCOMING.
SHUP
WHOA ?!
SHP..

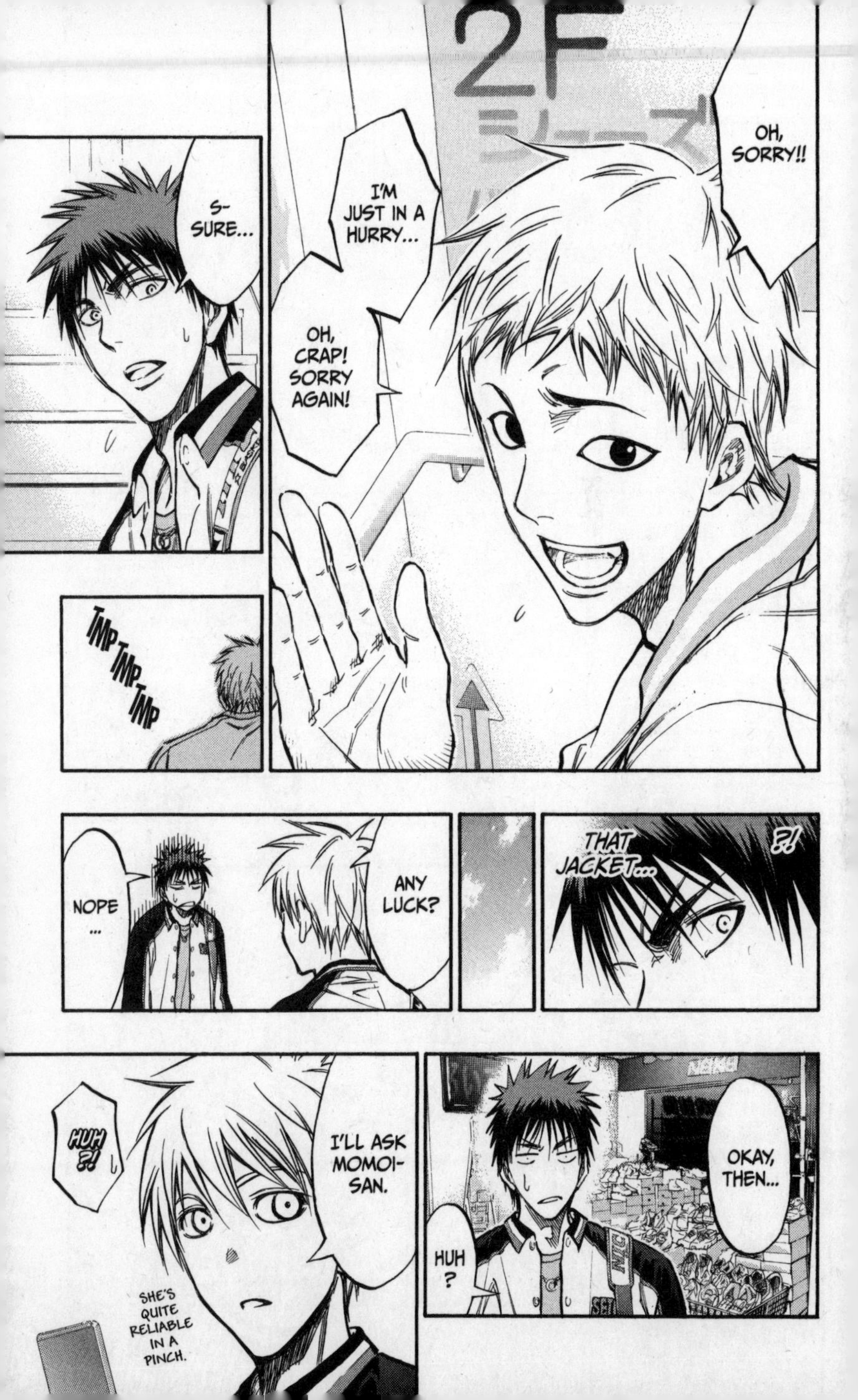

OH, SORRY!!
I'M JUST IN A HURRY...
OH, CRAP! SORRY AGAIN!
S-SURE...
TMP TMP TMP
?!
THAT JACKET...
ANY LUCK?
NOPE ...
OKAY, THEN...
HUH ?
I'LL ASK MOMOI-SAN.
HUH ?!
SHE'S QUITE RELIABLE IN A PINCH.

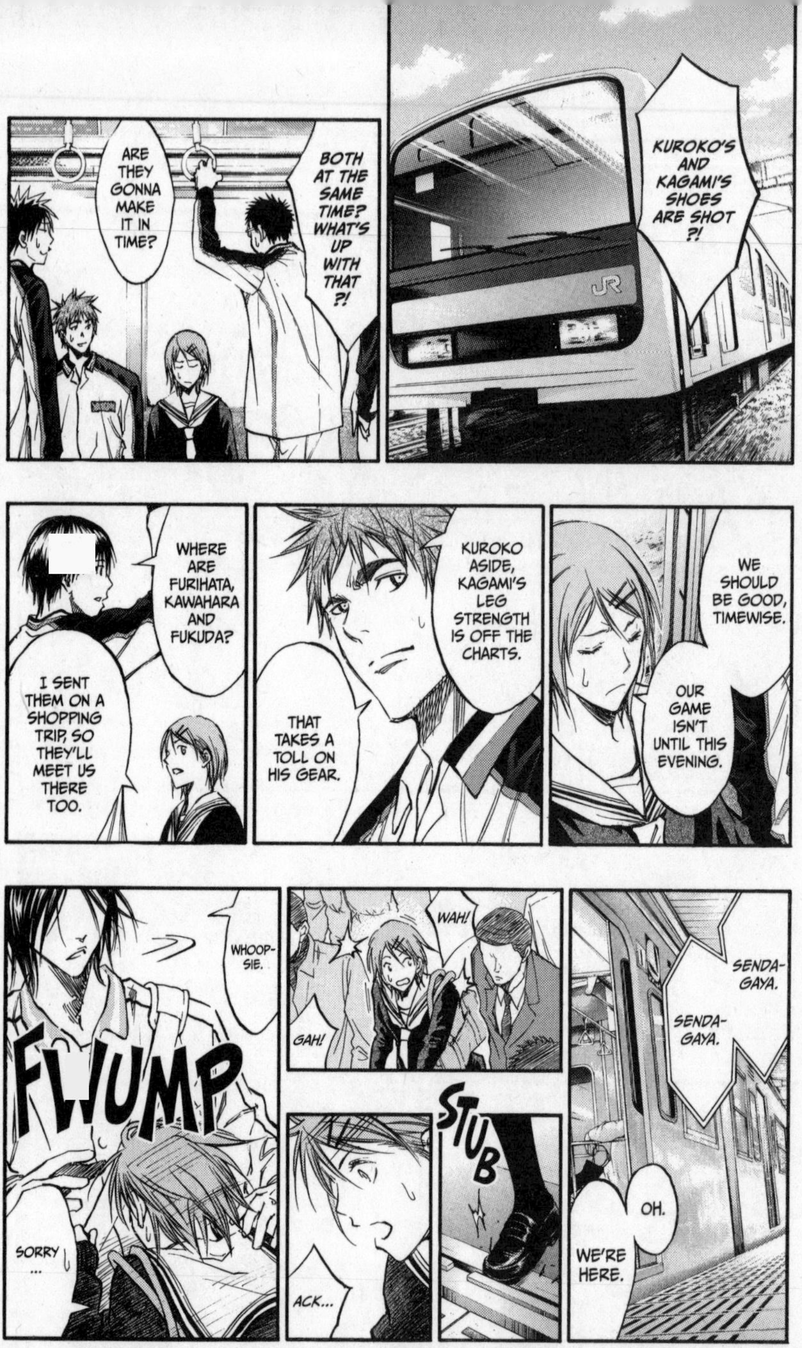
KUROKO'S AND KAGAMI'S SHOES ARE SHOT ?!
BOTH AT THE SAME TIME? WHAT'S UP WITH THAT ?!
ARE THEY GONNA MAKE IT IN TIME?
WE SHOULD BE GOOD, TIMEWISE.
OUR GAME ISN'T UNTIL THIS EVENING.
KUROKO ASIDE, KAGAMI'S LEG STRENGTH IS OFF THE CHARTS.
THAT TAKES A TOLL ON HIS GEAR.
WHERE ARE FURIHATA, KAWAHARA AND FUKUDA?
I SENT THEM ON A SHOPPING TRIP, SO THEY'LL MEET US THERE TOO.
SENDA-GAYA.
SENDA-GAYA.
OH.
WE'RE HERE.
WAH!
GAH!
STUB
ACK...
WHOOP-SIE.
FWUMP
SORRY ...

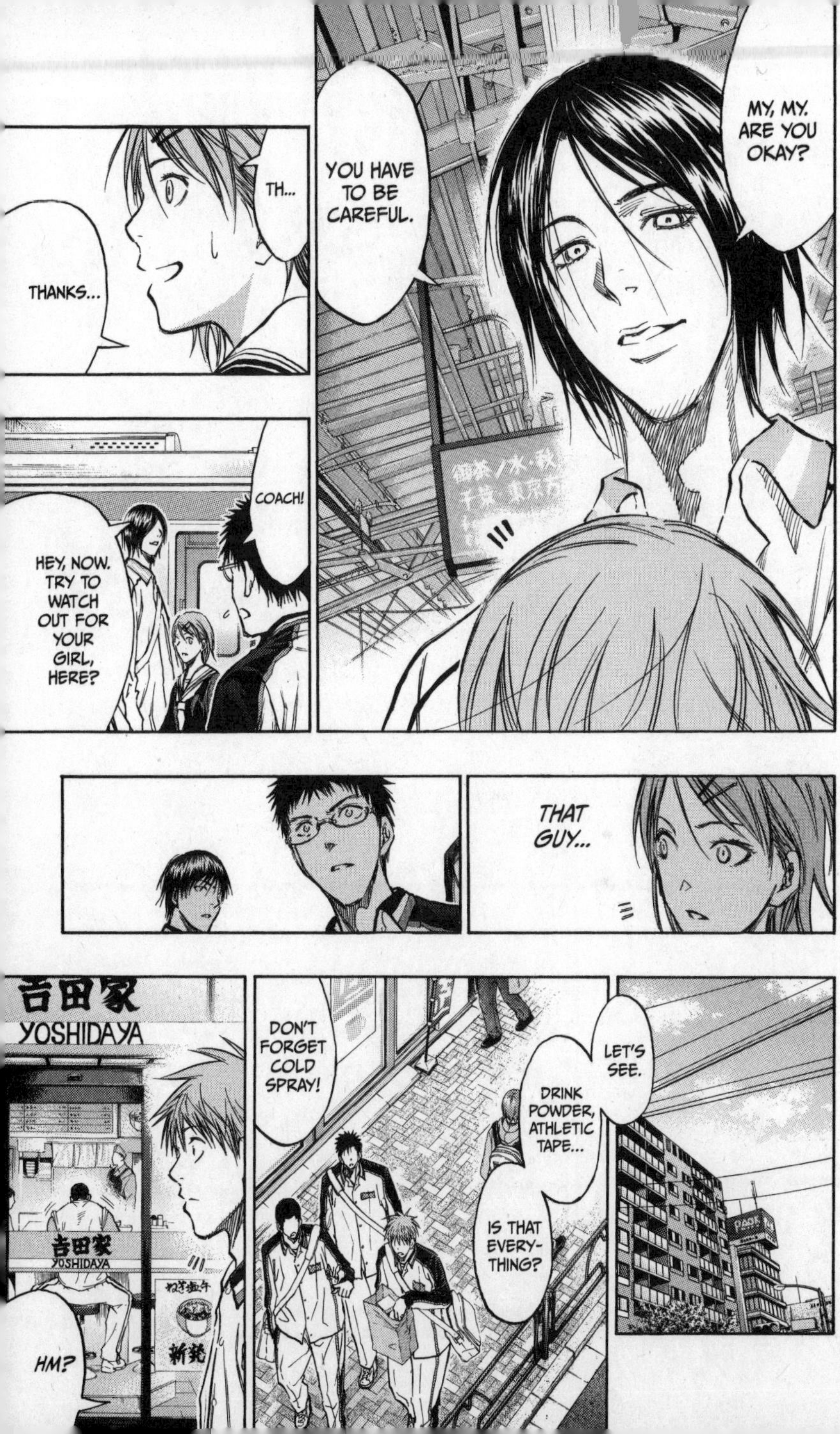
MY, MY. ARE YOU OKAY?
YOU HAVE TO BE CAREFUL.
TH...
THANKS...
COACH!
HEY, NOW. TRY TO WATCH OUT FOR YOUR GIRL, HERE?
THAT GUY...
LET'S SEE.
DRINK POWDER, ATHLETIC TAPE...
IS THAT EVERY-THING?
DON'T FORGET COLD SPRAY!
吉田家
YOSHIDAYA
HM?

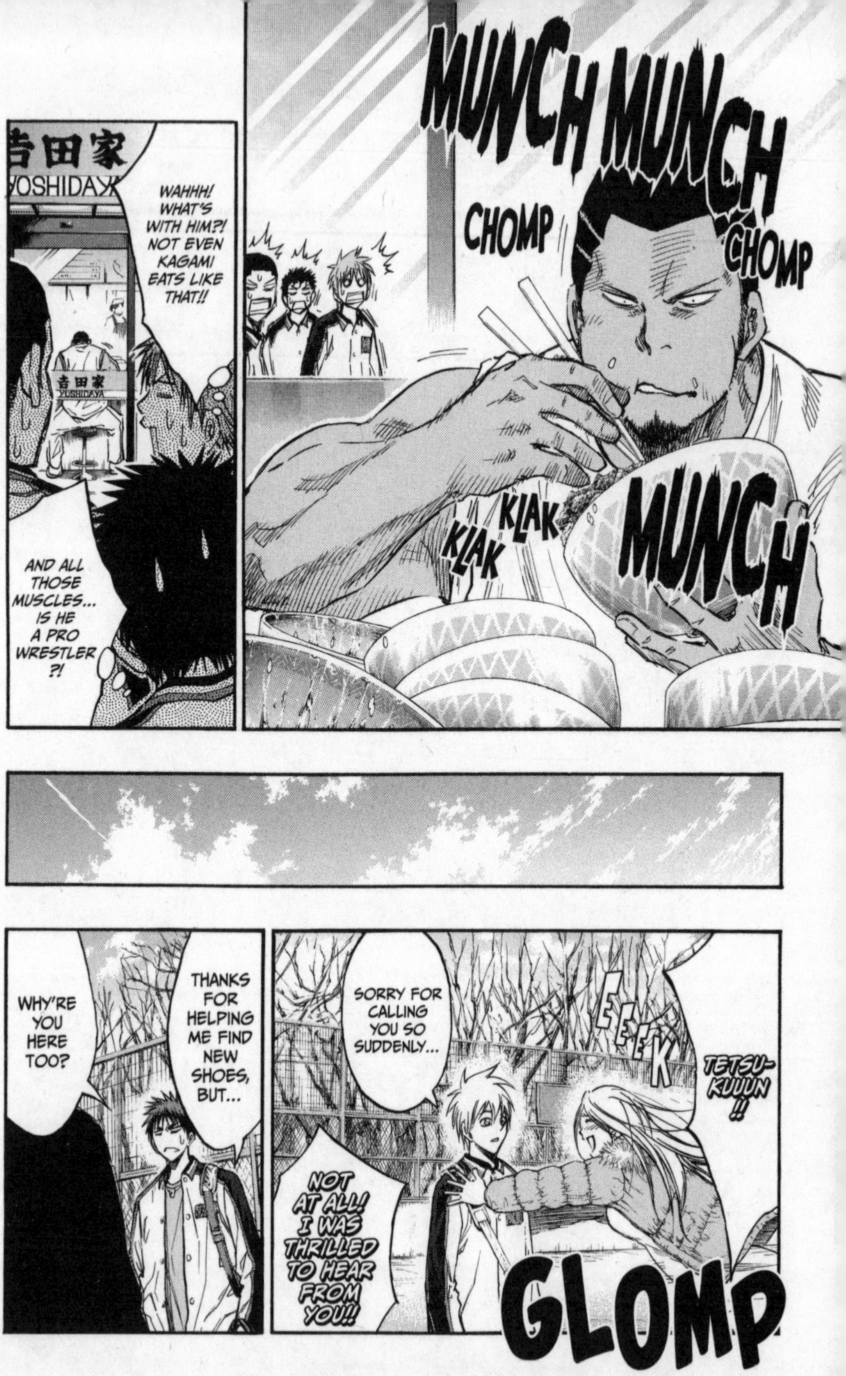

MUNCH MUNCH
CHOMP
CHOMP
KLAK KLAK
MUNCH
吉田家
YOSHIDAYA
WAHHH! WHAT'S WITH HIM?! NOT EVEN KAGAMI EATS LIKE THAT!!
AND ALL THOSE MUSCLES... IS HE A PRO WRESTLER?!
SORRY FOR CALLING YOU SO SUDDENLY...
EEEK
TETSU-KUUUN!!
NOT AT ALL! I WAS THRILLED TO HEAR FROM YOU!!
GLOMP
THANKS FOR HELPING ME FIND NEW SHOES, BUT...
WHY'RE YOU HERE TOO?

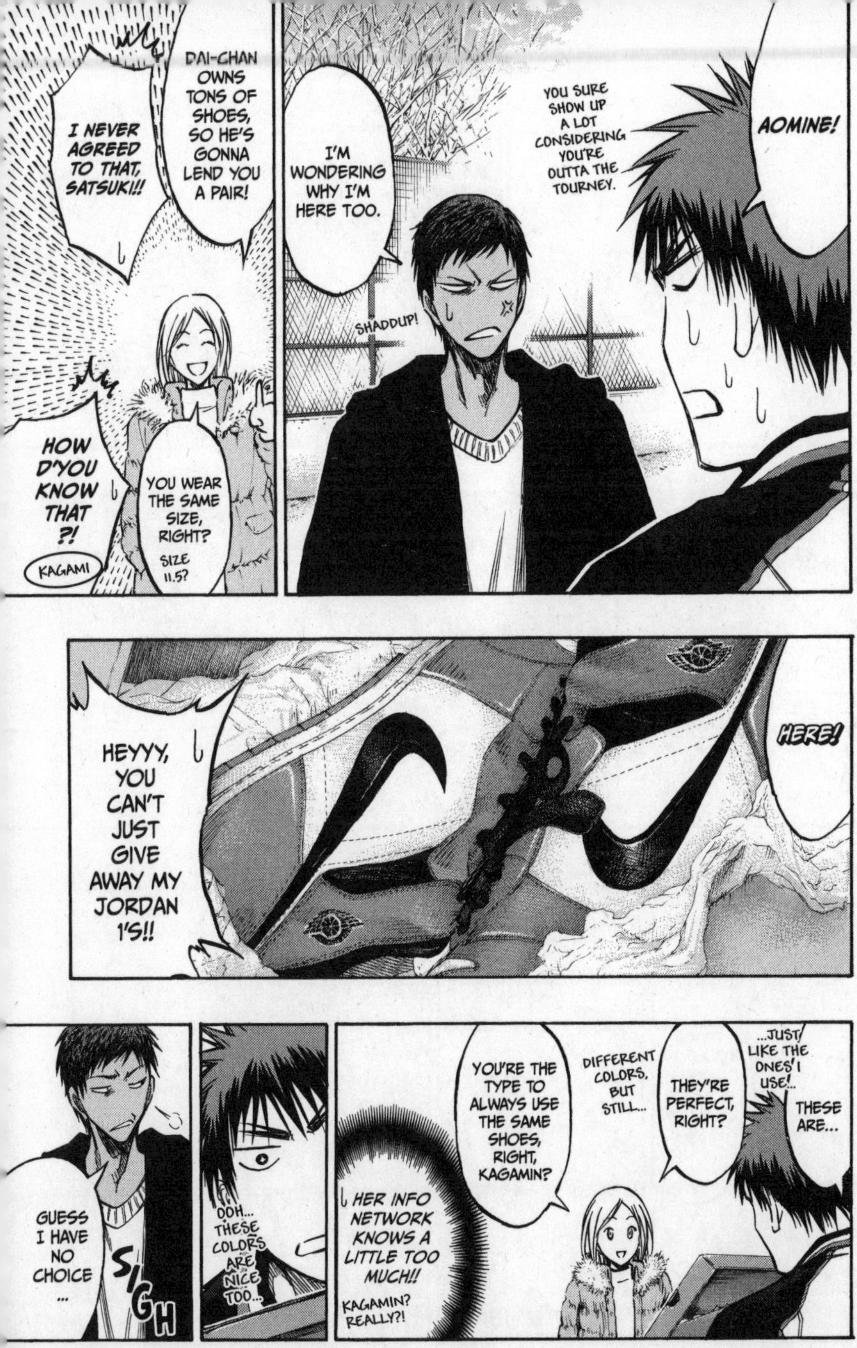
AOMINE!
YOU SURE SHOW UP A LOT CONSIDERING YOU'RE OUTTA THE TOURNEY.
I'M WONDERING WHY I'M HERE TOO.
SHADDUP!
DAI-CHAN OWNS TONS OF SHOES, SO HE'S GONNA LEND YOU A PAIR!
I NEVER AGREED TO THAT, SATSUKI!!
YOU WEAR THE SAME SIZE, RIGHT? SIZE 11.5?
HOW D'YOU KNOW THAT?!
KAGAMI
HERE!
HEYYY, YOU CAN'T JUST GIVE AWAY MY JORDAN 1'S!!
THESE ARE...
...JUST LIKE THE ONES I USE!...
THEY'RE PERFECT, RIGHT?
DIFFERENT COLORS, BUT STILL...
YOU'RE THE TYPE TO ALWAYS USE THE SAME SHOES, RIGHT, KAGAMIN?
HER INFO NETWORK KNOWS A LITTLE TOO MUCH!!
KAGAMIN? REALLY?!
OOH... THESE COLORS ARE NICE TOO...
GUESS I HAVE NO CHOICE...
SIGH

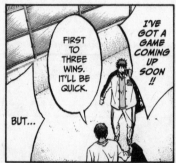

PLAY ME ONE-ON-ONE. IF YOU WIN, THEY'RE YOURS.
WHY'S IT GOTTA BE LIKE THAT?!
I'VE GOT A GAME COMING UP SOON!!
FIRST TO THREE WINS. IT'LL BE QUICK.
BUT...
COME ON, MAN.
MIGHT AS WELL...
I ACTUALLY HAVE SOME-THING I WANNA TEACH YOU.
...?!
AH! AND NO GOING INTO THE ZONE THIS TIME. IT WEARS ME OUT.
WHATEVER! I CAN'T JUST DO IT WHENEVER I WANT, LIKE YOU!
AOMINE-KUN PUNCHED HAIZAKI-KUN...?!
...
AH! BUT IT WAS ALL TO HELP KI-CHAN, RIGHT? HE DIDN'T HAVE A CHOICE...
THERE WOULD BE TROUBLE IF WORD GOT OUT, THOUGH.
YES.

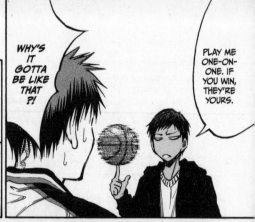

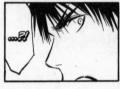

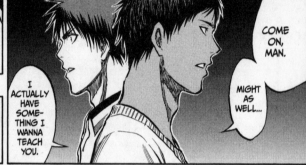

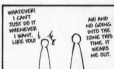

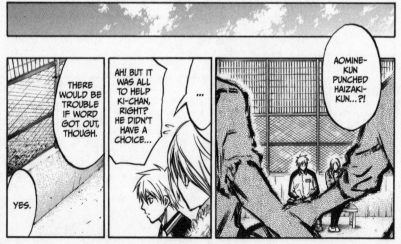

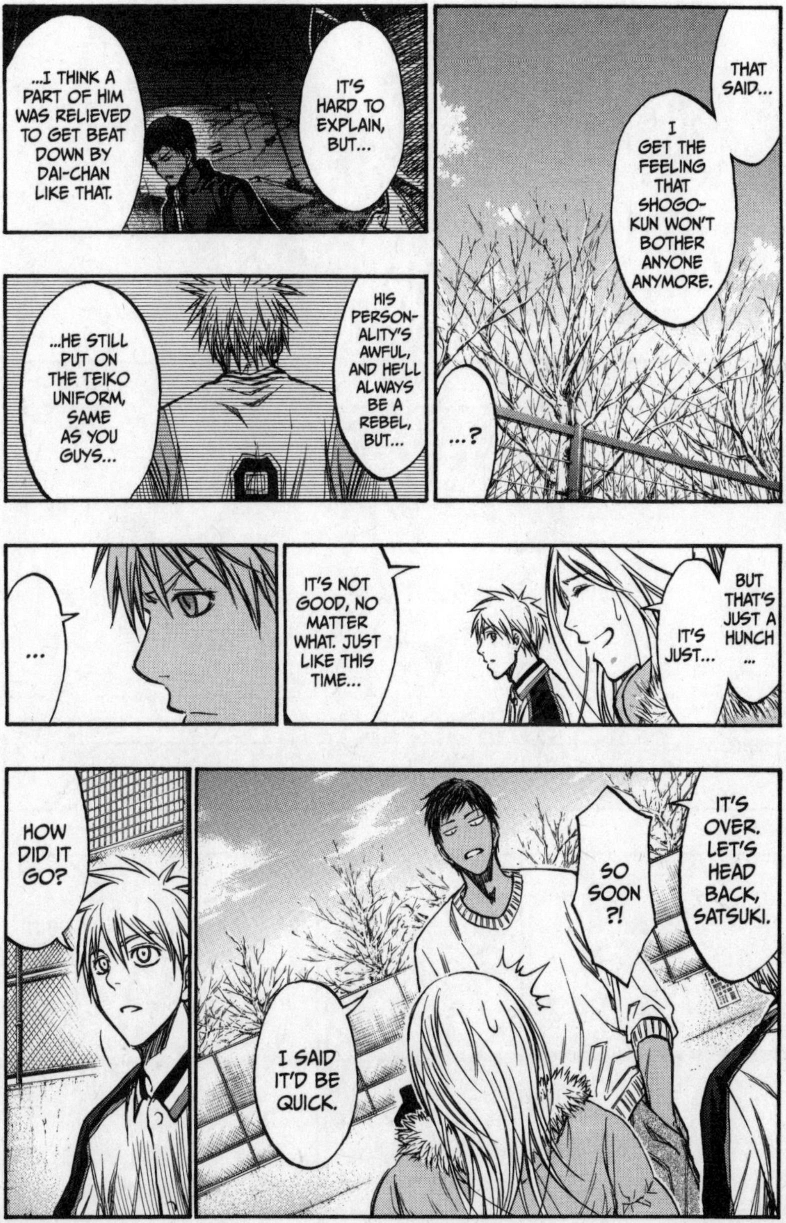

THAT SAID...
I GET THE FEELING THAT SHOGO-KUN WON'T BOTHER ANYONE ANYMORE.
...?
IT'S HARD TO EXPLAIN, BUT...
...I THINK A PART OF HIM WAS RELIEVED TO GET BEAT DOWN BY DAI-CHAN LIKE THAT.
HIS PERSONALITY'S AWFUL, AND HE'LL ALWAYS BE A REBEL, BUT...
...HE STILL PUT ON THE TEIKO UNIFORM, SAME AS YOU GUYS...
BUT THAT'S JUST A HUNCH...
IT'S JUST...
IT'S NOT GOOD, NO MATTER WHAT. JUST LIKE THIS TIME...
...
IT'S OVER. LET'S HEAD BACK, SATSUKI.
SO SOON?!
I SAID IT'D BE QUICK.
HOW DID IT GO?

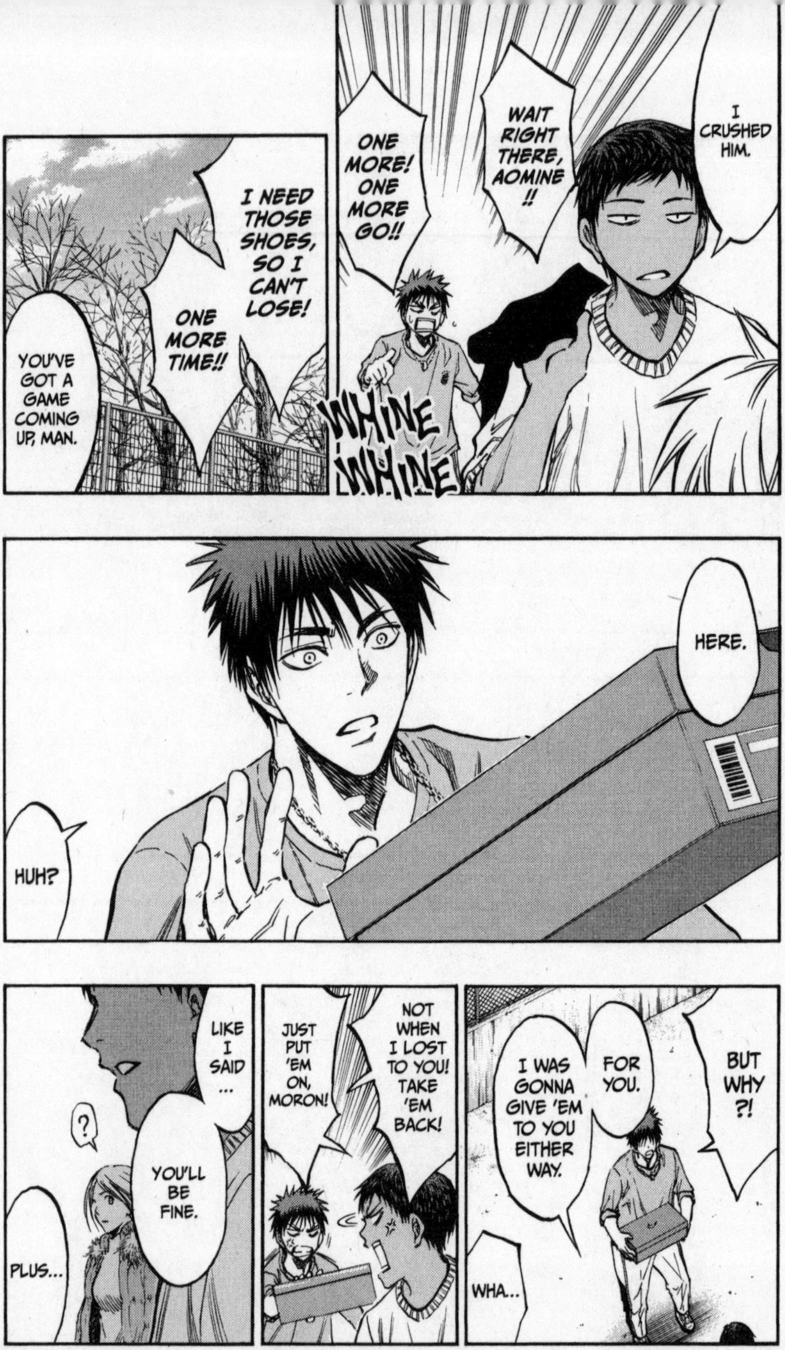
I CRUSHED HIM.
WAIT RIGHT THERE, AOMINE!!
ONE MORE! ONE MORE GO!!
WHINE WHINE
I NEED THOSE SHOES, SO I CAN'T LOSE!
ONE MORE TIME!!
YOU'VE GOT A GAME COMING UP, MAN.
HERE.
HUH?
BUT WHY?!
FOR YOU.
I WAS GONNA GIVE 'EM TO YOU EITHER WAY.
WHA...
NOT WHEN I LOST TO YOU! TAKE 'EM BACK!
JUST PUT 'EM ON, MORON!
LIKE I SAID...
YOU'LL BE FINE.
?
PLUS...

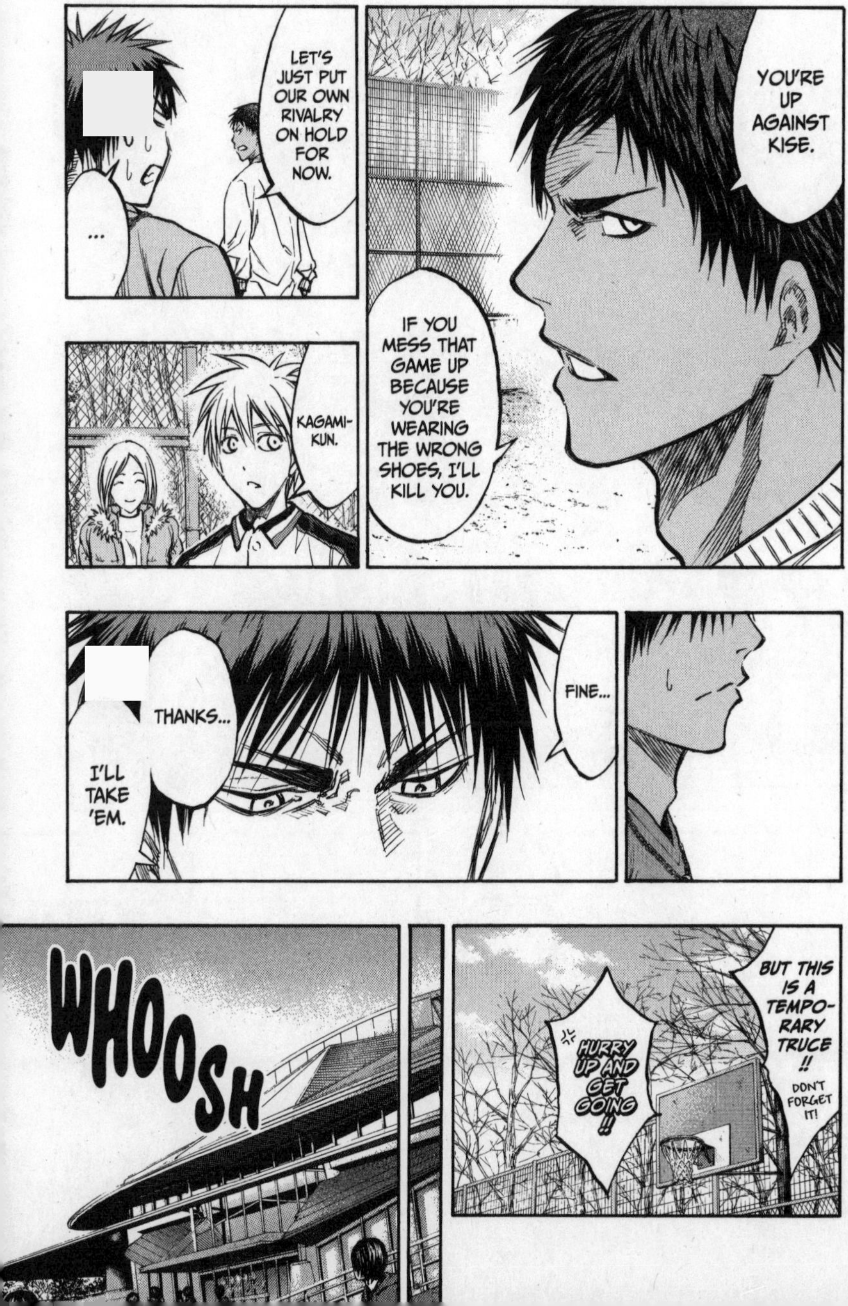
YOU'RE UP AGAINST KISE.
IF YOU MESS THAT GAME UP BECAUSE YOU'RE WEARING THE WRONG SHOES, I'LL KILL YOU.
LET'S JUST PUT OUR OWN RIVALRY ON HOLD FOR NOW.
...
KAGAMI-KUN.
FINE...
THANKS...
I'LL TAKE 'EM.
BUT THIS IS A TEMPO-RARY TRUCE!!
DON'T FORGET IT!
HURRY UP AND GET GOING!!
WHOOSH

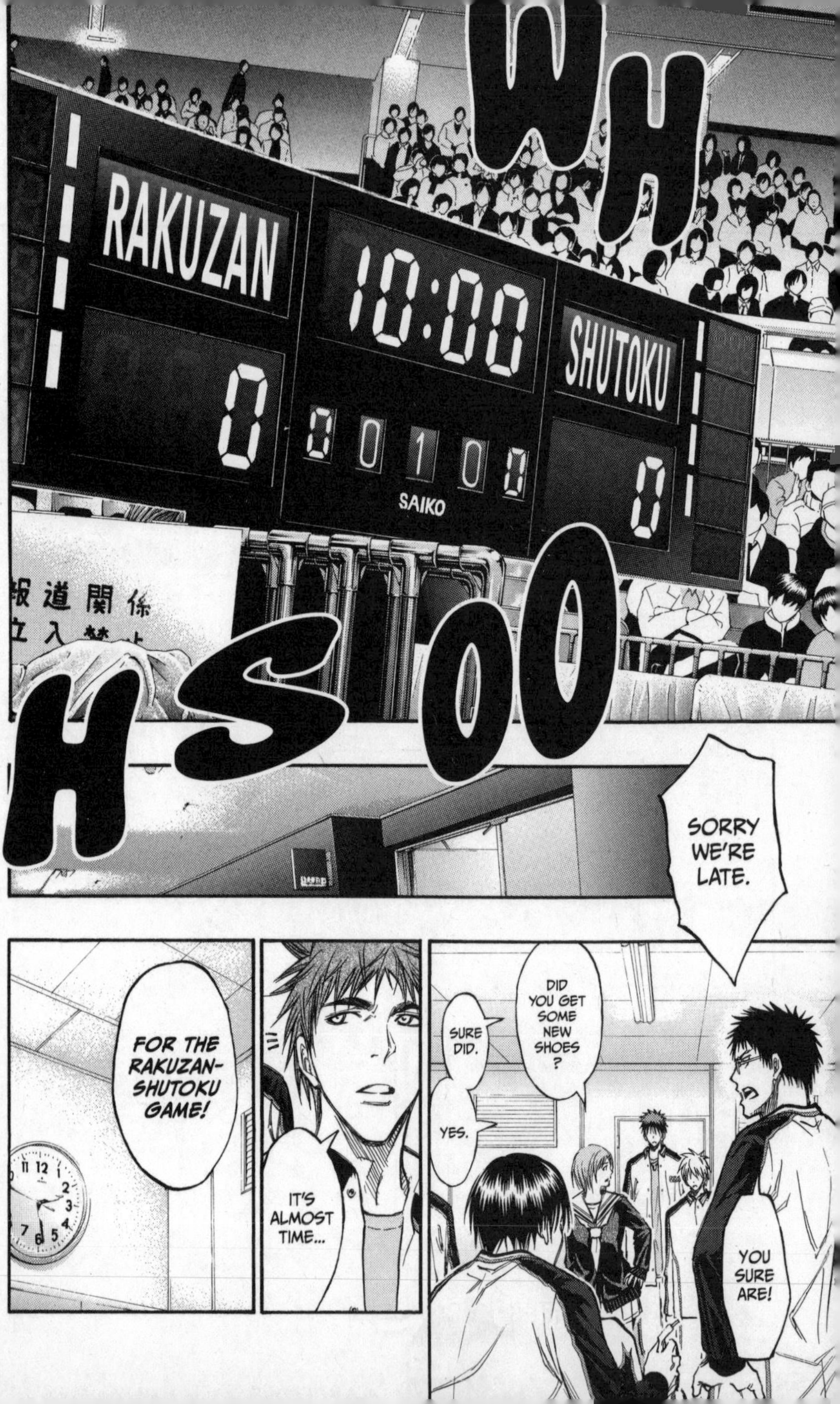
WHSHOO
RAKUZAN
10:00
SHUTOKU
0
0
SAIKO
報道関係
立入禁
SORRY WE'RE LATE.
YOU SURE ARE!
DID YOU GET SOME NEW SHOES?
SURE DID.
YES.
IT'S ALMOST TIME...
FOR THE RAKUZAN-SHUTOKU GAME!

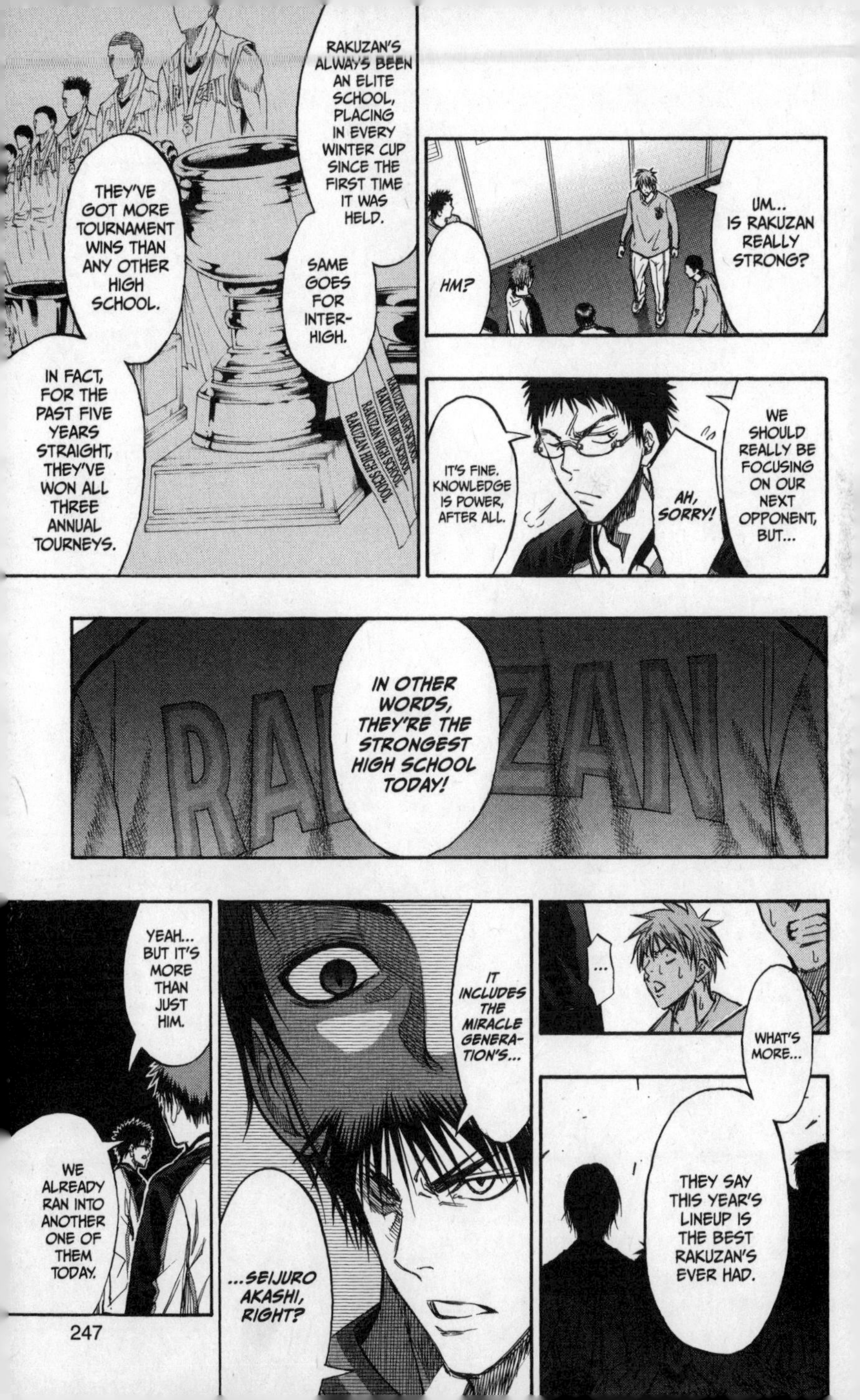
UM... IS RAKUZAN REALLY STRONG?
HM?
WE SHOULD REALLY BE FOCUSING ON OUR NEXT OPPONENT, BUT...
AH, SORRY!
IT'S FINE. KNOWLEDGE IS POWER, AFTER ALL.
RAKUZAN'S ALWAYS BEEN AN ELITE SCHOOL, PLACING IN EVERY WINTER CUP SINCE THE FIRST TIME IT WAS HELD.
THEY'VE GOT MORE TOURNAMENT WINS THAN ANY OTHER HIGH SCHOOL.
SAME GOES FOR INTER-HIGH.
IN FACT, FOR THE PAST FIVE YEARS STRAIGHT, THEY'VE WON ALL THREE ANNUAL TOURNEYS.
RAKUZAN HIGH SCHOOL
RAKUZAN HIGH SCHOOL
RAKUZAN HIGH SCHOOL
RAKUZAN HIGH SCHOOL
IN OTHER WORDS, THEY'RE THE STRONGEST HIGH SCHOOL TODAY!
...
WHAT'S MORE...
THEY SAY THIS YEAR'S LINEUP IS THE BEST RAKUZAN'S EVER HAD.
IT INCLUDES THE MIRACLE GENERATION'S...
...SEIJURO AKASHI, RIGHT?
YEAH... BUT IT'S MORE THAN JUST HIM.
WE ALREADY RAN INTO ANOTHER ONE OF THEM TODAY.

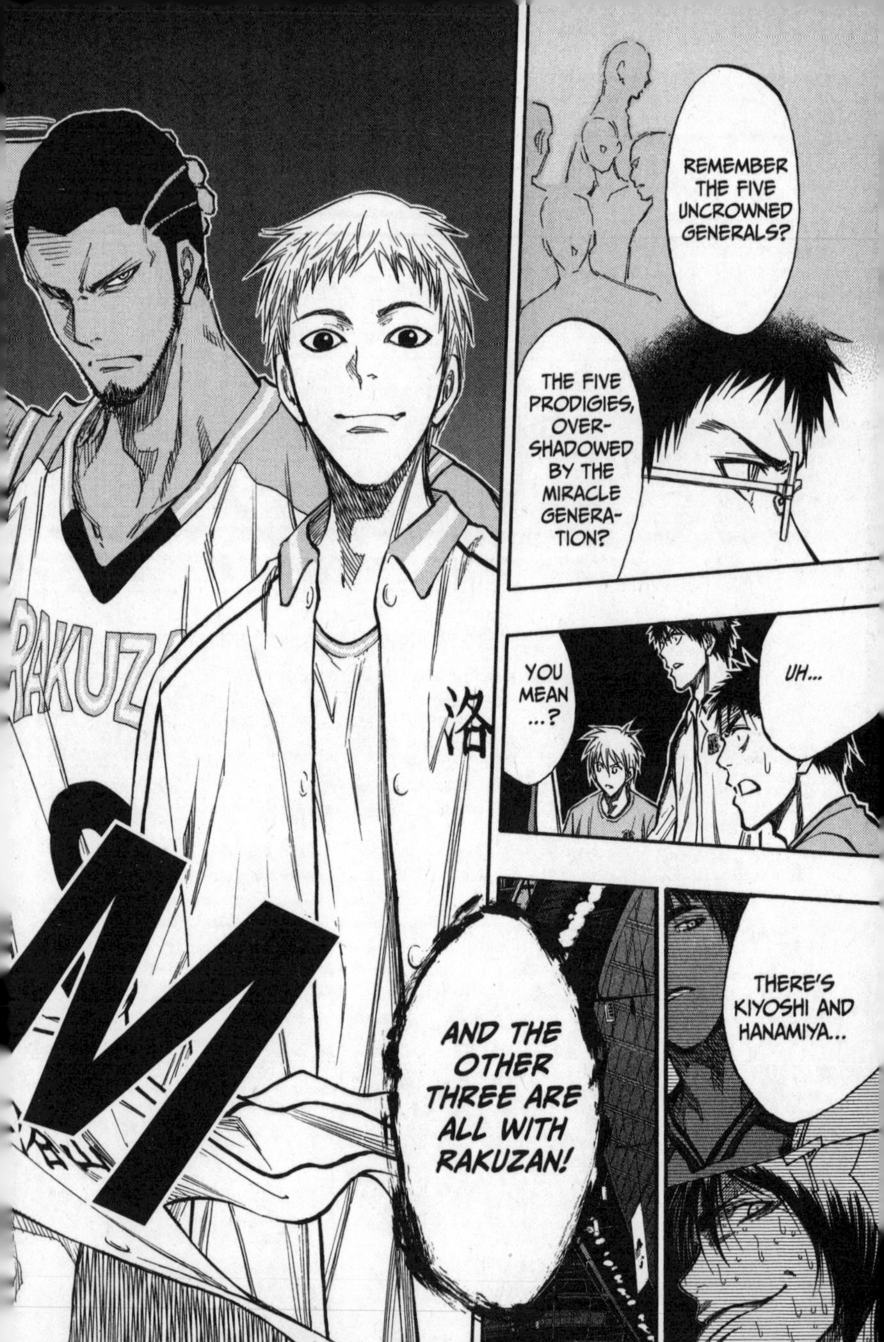
REMEMBER THE FIVE UNCROWNED GENERALS?
THE FIVE PRODIGIES, OVER-SHADOWED BY THE MIRACLE GENERA-TION?
UH...
YOU MEAN ...?
THERE'S KIYOSHI AND HANAMIYA...
AND THE OTHER THREE ARE ALL WITH RAKUZAN!

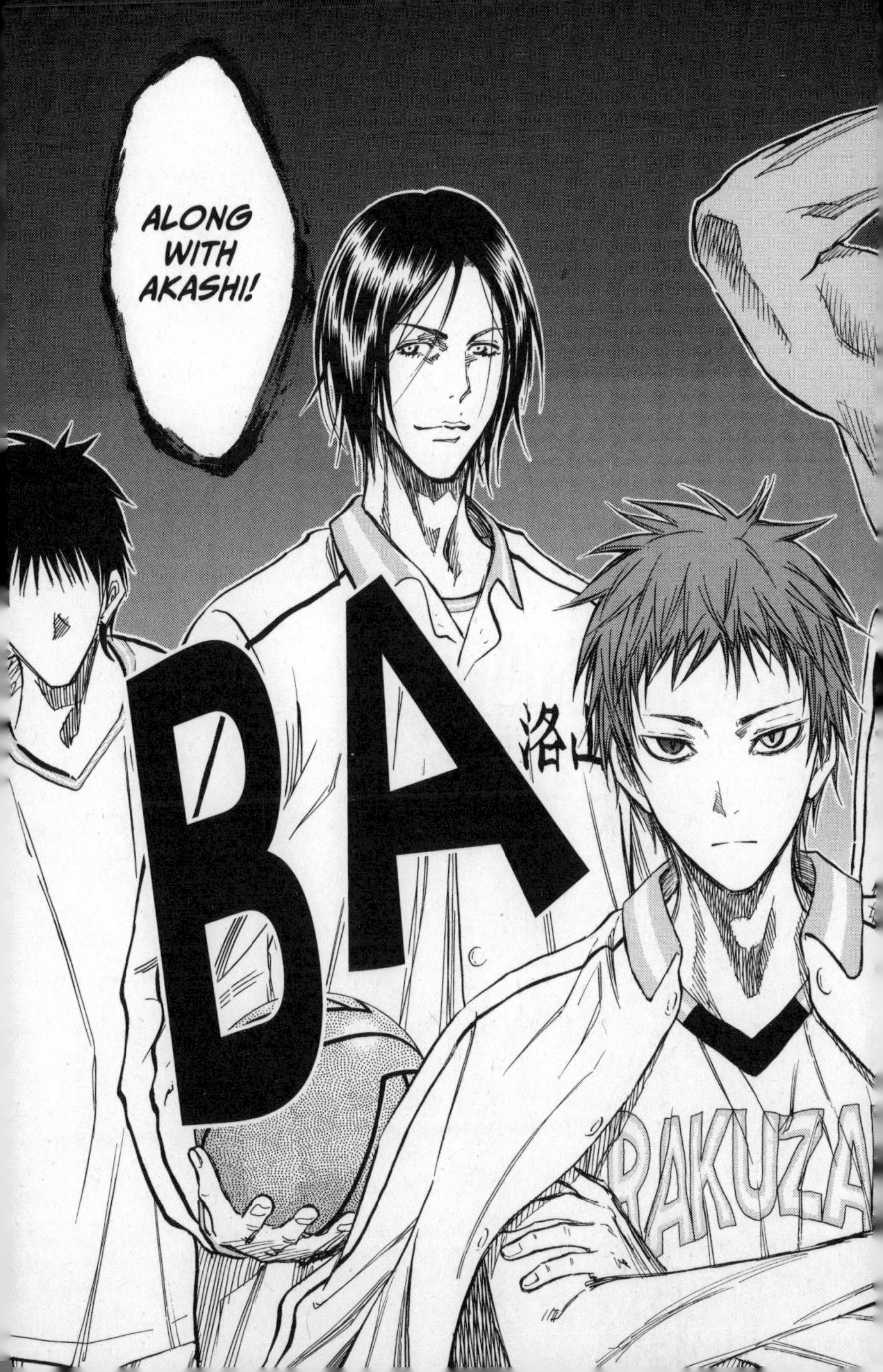
ALONG WITH AKASHI!
BA
洛山
RAKUZAN

KUROKO'S BASKETBALL BLOOPERS

TAKE 1

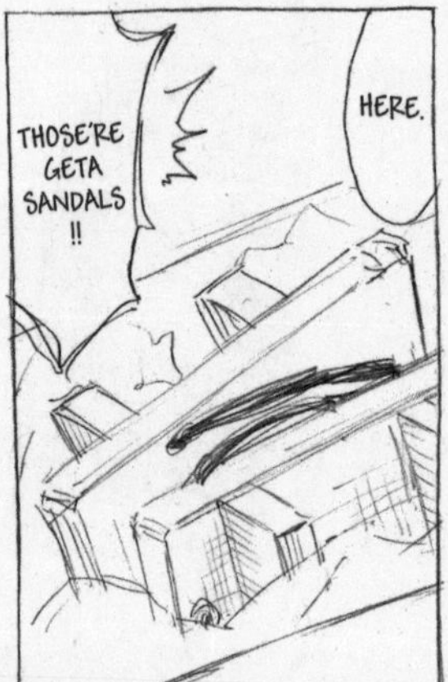
HERE.
THOSE'RE GETA SANDALS !!

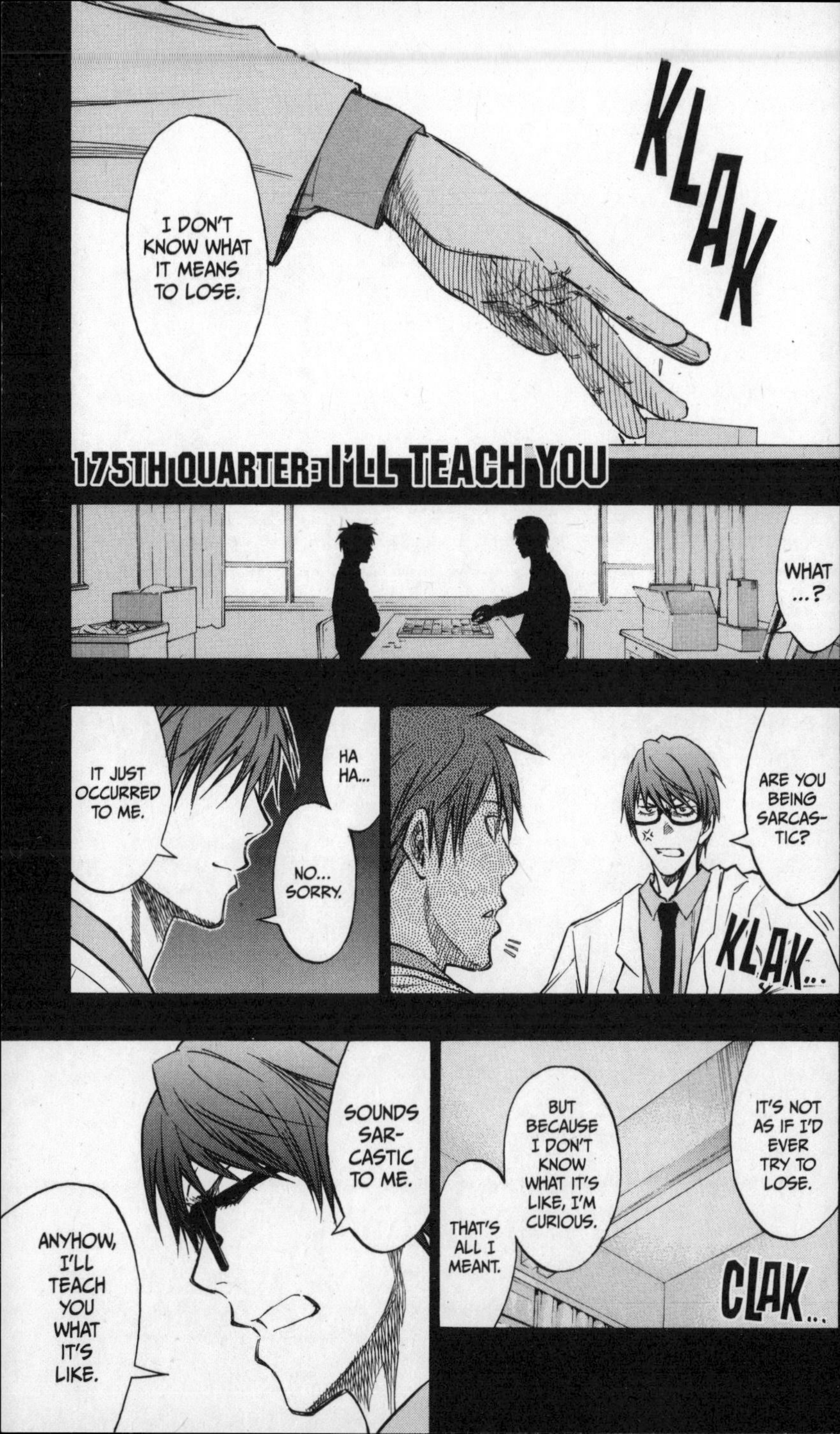
KLAK
I DON'T KNOW WHAT IT MEANS TO LOSE.
175TH QUARTER: I'LL TEACH YOU
WHAT ...?
ARE YOU BEING SARCAS-TIC?
KLAK...
HA HA...
NO... SORRY.
IT JUST OCCURRED TO ME.
IT'S NOT AS IF I'D EVER TRY TO LOSE.
BUT BECAUSE I DON'T KNOW WHAT IT'S LIKE, I'M CURIOUS.
THAT'S ALL I MEANT.
CLAK...
SOUNDS SAR-CASTIC TO ME.
ANYHOW, I'LL TEACH YOU WHAT IT'S LIKE.

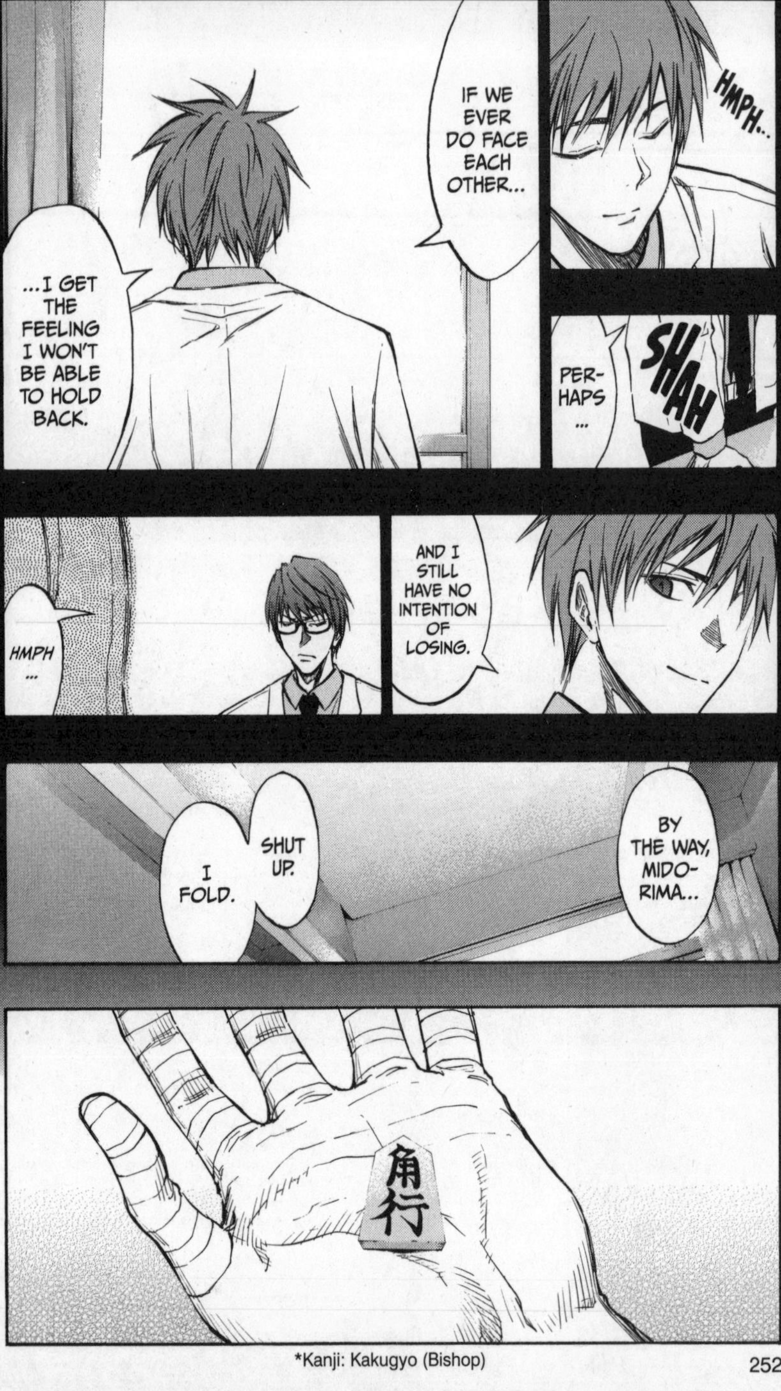
HMPH...
PER-HAPS...
SHAH
IF WE EVER DO FACE EACH OTHER...
...I GET THE FEELING I WON'T BE ABLE TO HOLD BACK.
AND I STILL HAVE NO INTENTION OF LOSING.
HMPH...
BY THE WAY, MIDO-RIMA...
SHUT UP.
I FOLD.
角行

*Kanji: Kakugyo (Bishop)

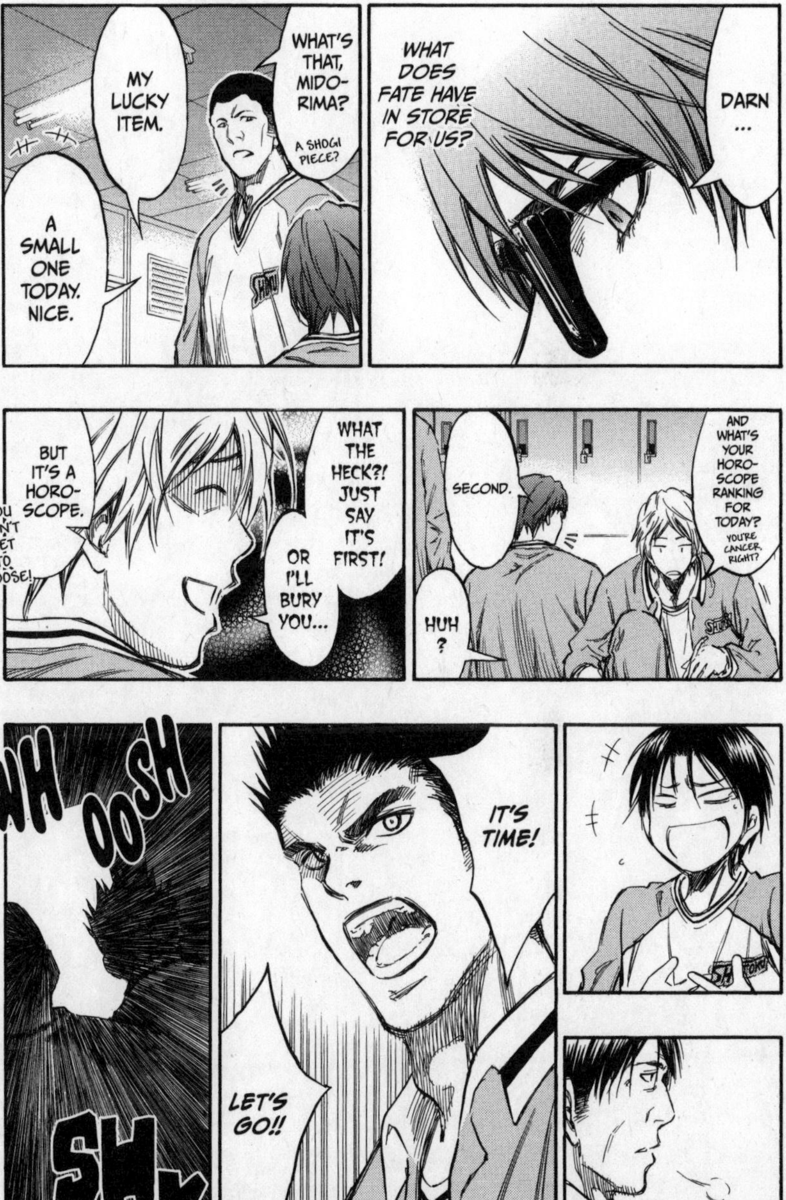
DARN ...
WHAT DOES FATE HAVE IN STORE FOR US?
WHAT'S THAT, MIDORIMA?
A SHOGI PIECE?
MY LUCKY ITEM.
A SMALL ONE TODAY. NICE.
AND WHAT'S YOUR HOROSCOPE RANKING FOR TODAY?
YOU'RE CANCER, RIGHT?
SECOND.
HUH?
WHAT THE HECK?! JUST SAY IT'S FIRST!
OR I'LL BURY YOU...
BUT IT'S A HOROSCOPE.
YOU DON'T GET TO CHOOSE!
IT'S TIME!
LET'S GO!!
WHOOSH
SHK

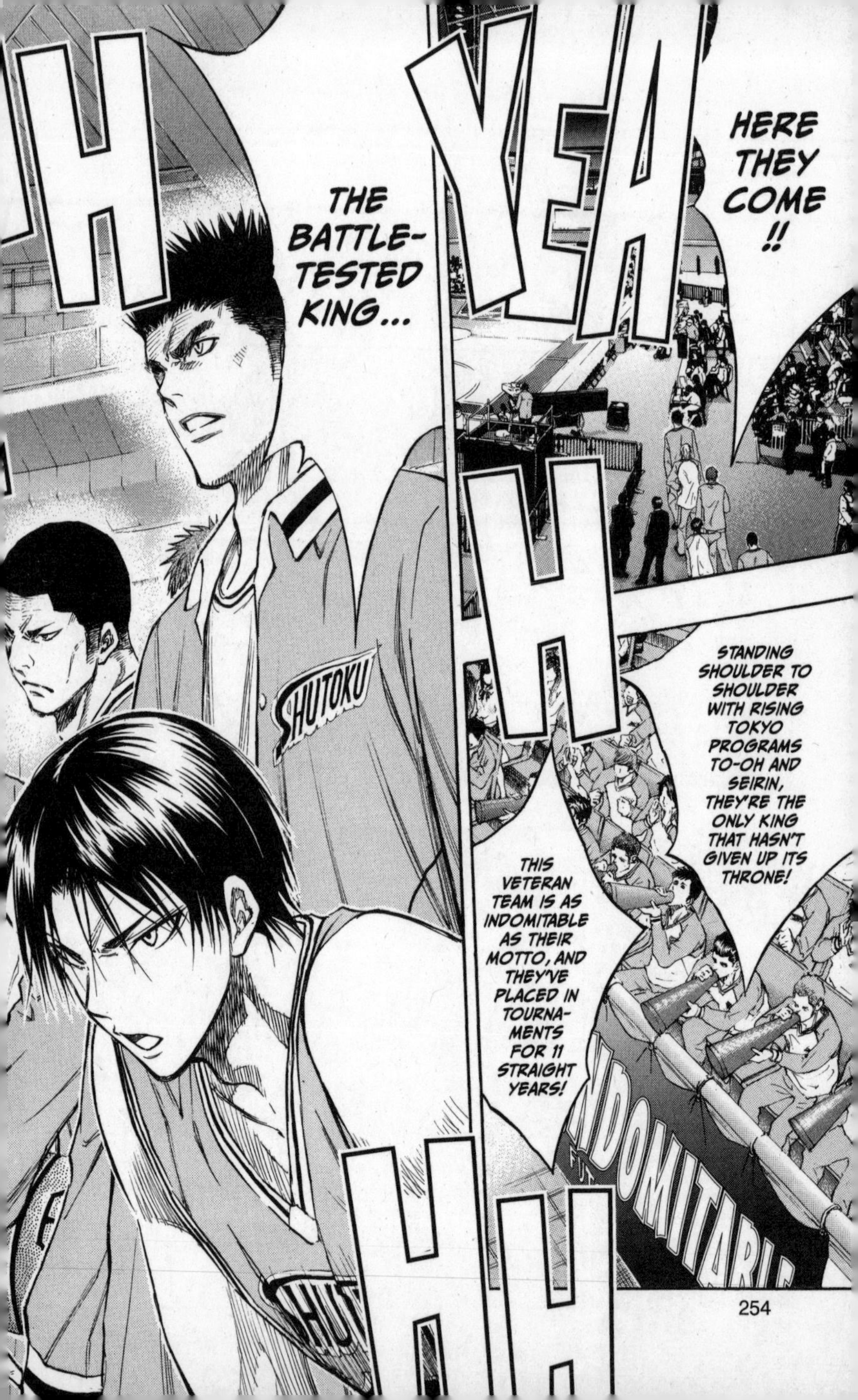
HERE THEY COME!!
YEAHHHH
THE BATTLE-TESTED KING...
STANDING SHOULDER TO SHOULDER WITH RISING TOKYO PROGRAMS TO-OH AND SEIRIN, THEY'RE THE ONLY KING THAT HASN'T GIVEN UP ITS THRONE!
THIS VETERAN TEAM IS AS INDOMITABLE AS THEIR MOTTO, AND THEY'VE PLACED IN TOURNAMENTS FOR 11 STRAIGHT YEARS!
INDOMITABLE
SHUTOKU

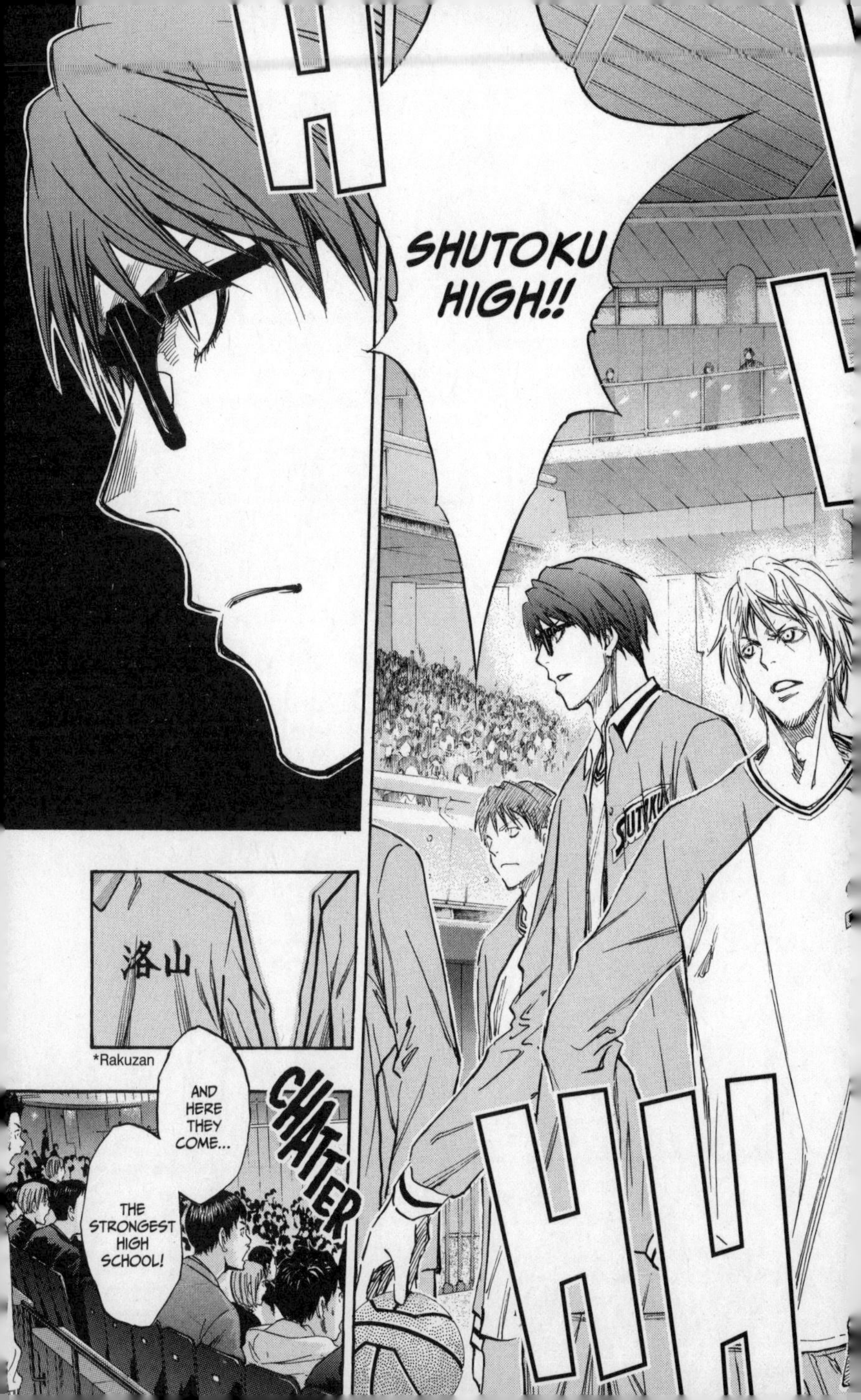
SHUTOKU HIGH!!
洛山
*Rakuzan
AND HERE THEY COME...
THE STRONGEST HIGH SCHOOL!
CHATTER

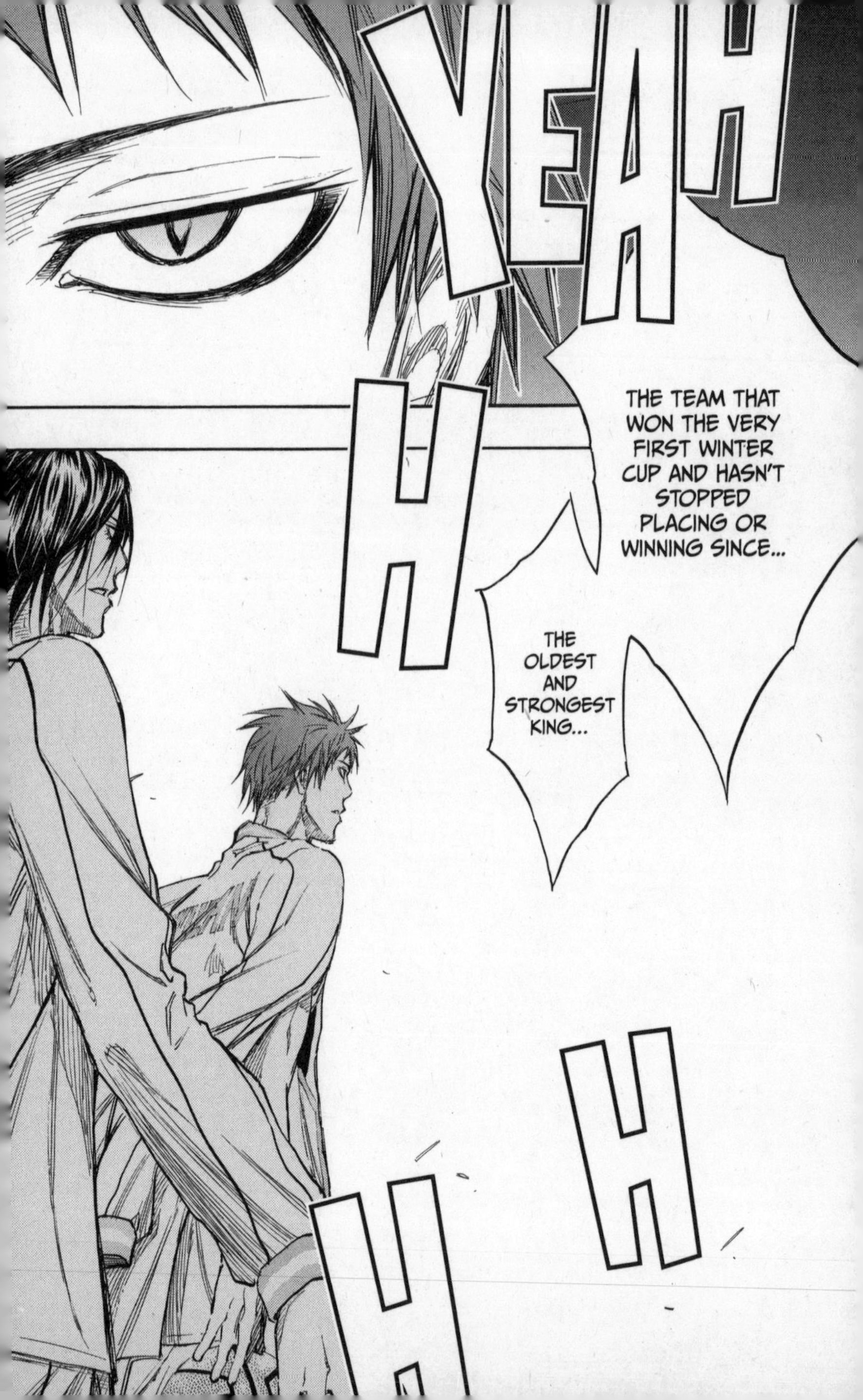

YEAH
THE TEAM THAT WON THE VERY FIRST WINTER CUP AND HASN'T STOPPED PLACING OR WINNING SINCE...
THE OLDEST AND STRONGEST KING...
HHHH

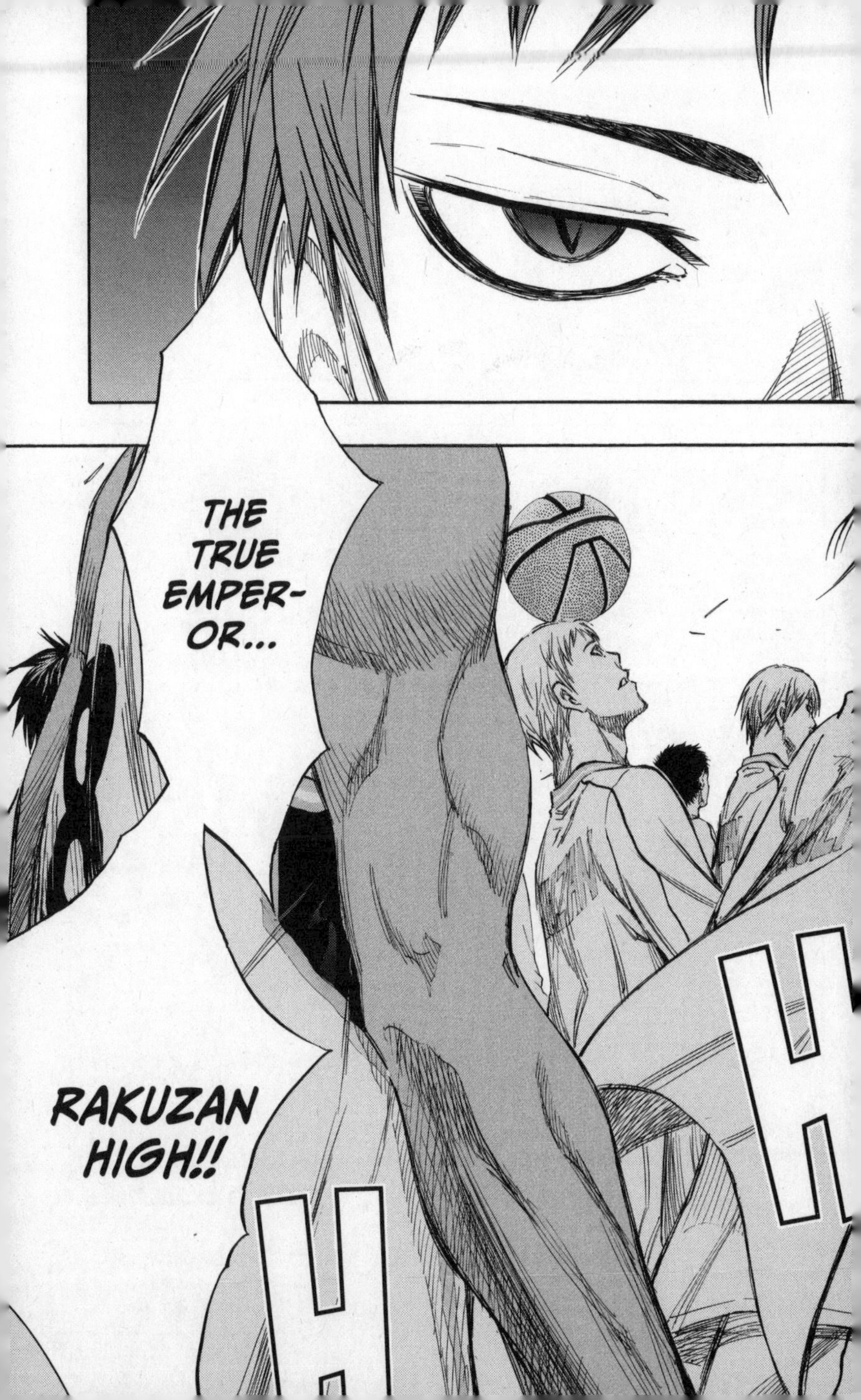
THE TRUE EMPEROR...
RAKUZAN HIGH!!
HH
HH

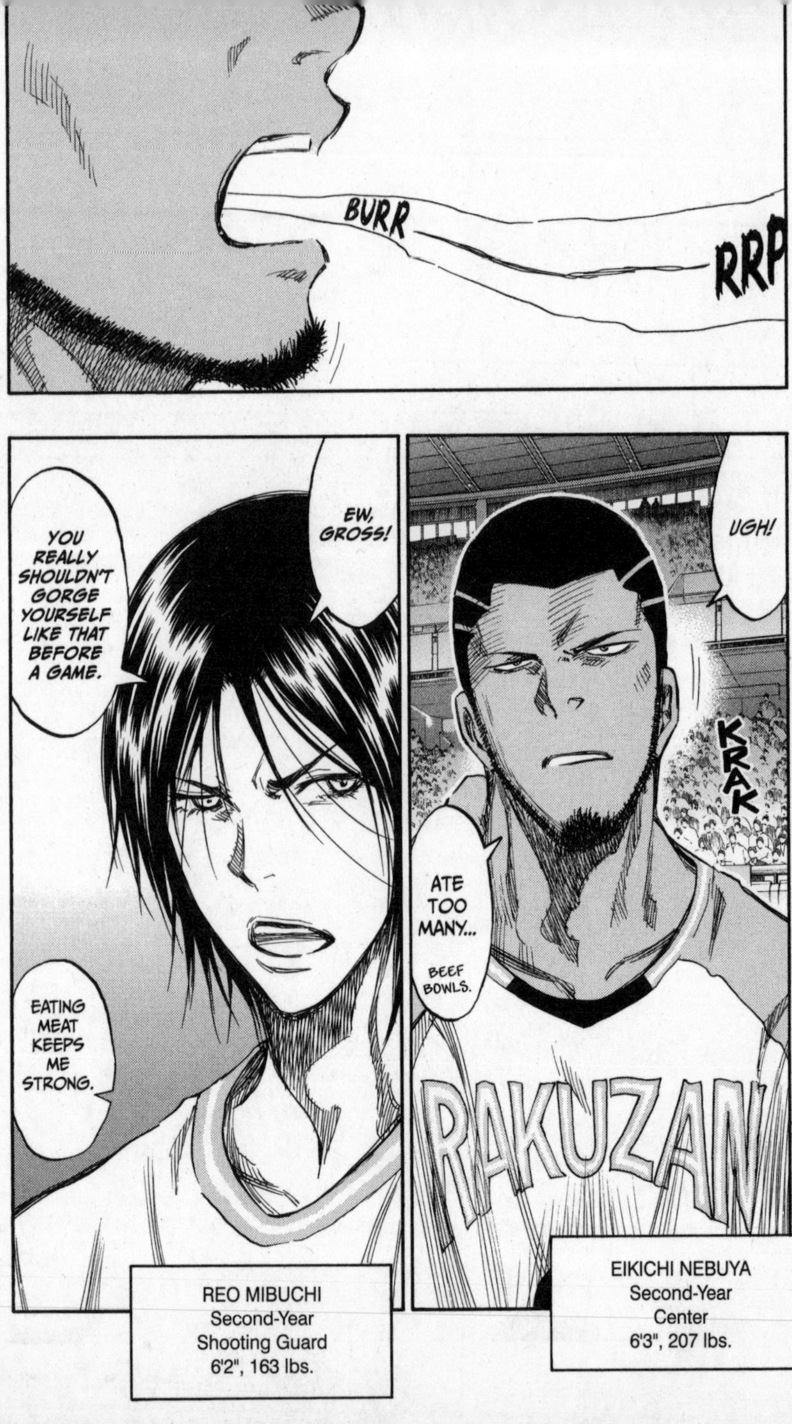
BURR
RRP
UGH!
KRAK
ATE TOO MANY...
BEEF BOWLS.
RAKUZAN
EIKICHI NEBUYA
Second-Year
Center
6'3", 207 lbs.
EW, GROSS!
YOU REALLY SHOULDN'T GORGE YOURSELF LIKE THAT BEFORE A GAME.
EATING MEAT KEEPS ME STRONG.
REO MIBUCHI
Second-Year
Shooting Guard
6'2", 163 lbs.

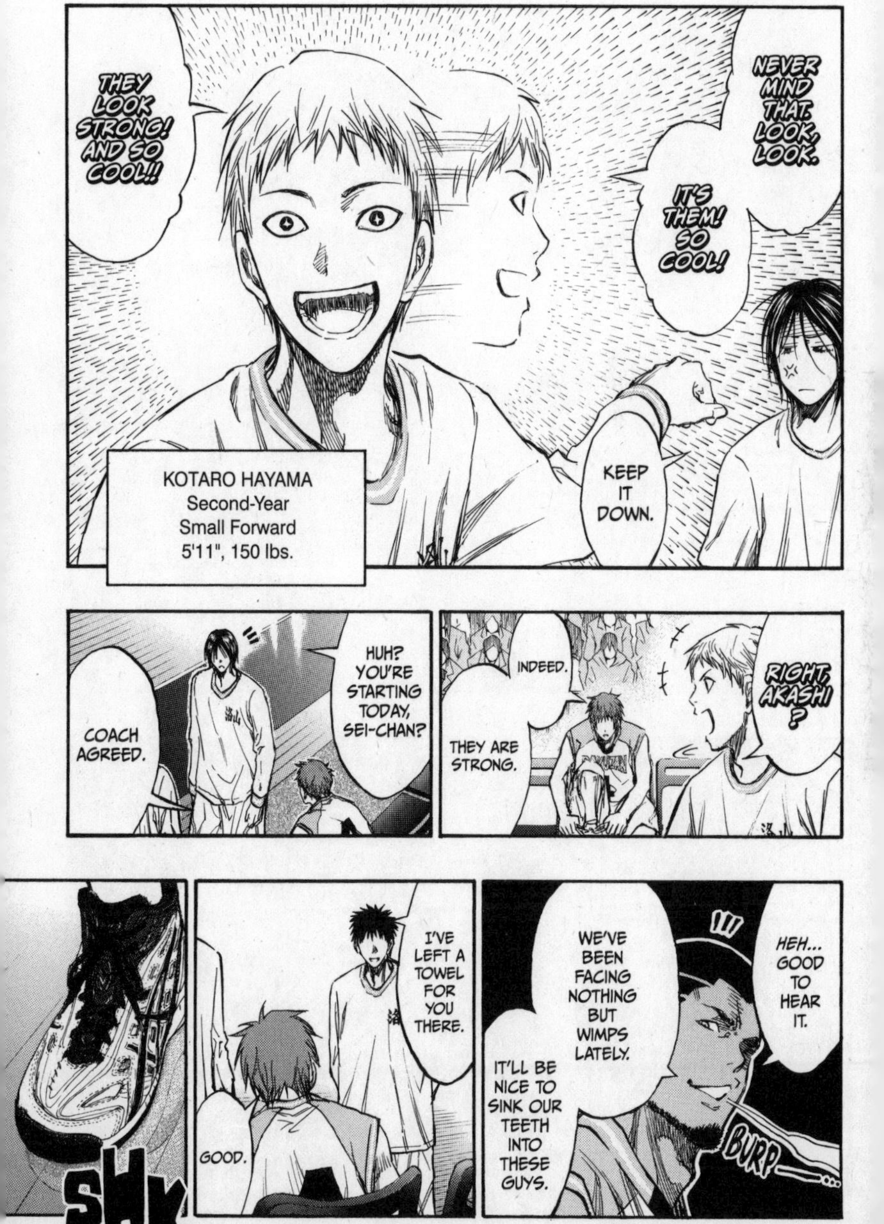
NEVER MIND THAT. LOOK, LOOK.
IT'S THEM! SO COOL!
THEY LOOK STRONG! AND SO COOL!!
KEEP IT DOWN.
KOTARO HAYAMA
Second-Year
Small Forward
5'11", 150 lbs.
RIGHT, AKASHI?
INDEED.
THEY ARE STRONG.
HUH? YOU'RE STARTING TODAY, SEI-CHAN?
COACH AGREED.
HEH... GOOD TO HEAR IT.
WE'VE BEEN FACING NOTHING BUT WIMPS LATELY.
IT'LL BE NICE TO SINK OUR TEETH INTO THESE GUYS.
BURP
I'VE LEFT A TOWEL FOR YOU THERE.
GOOD.
SHK

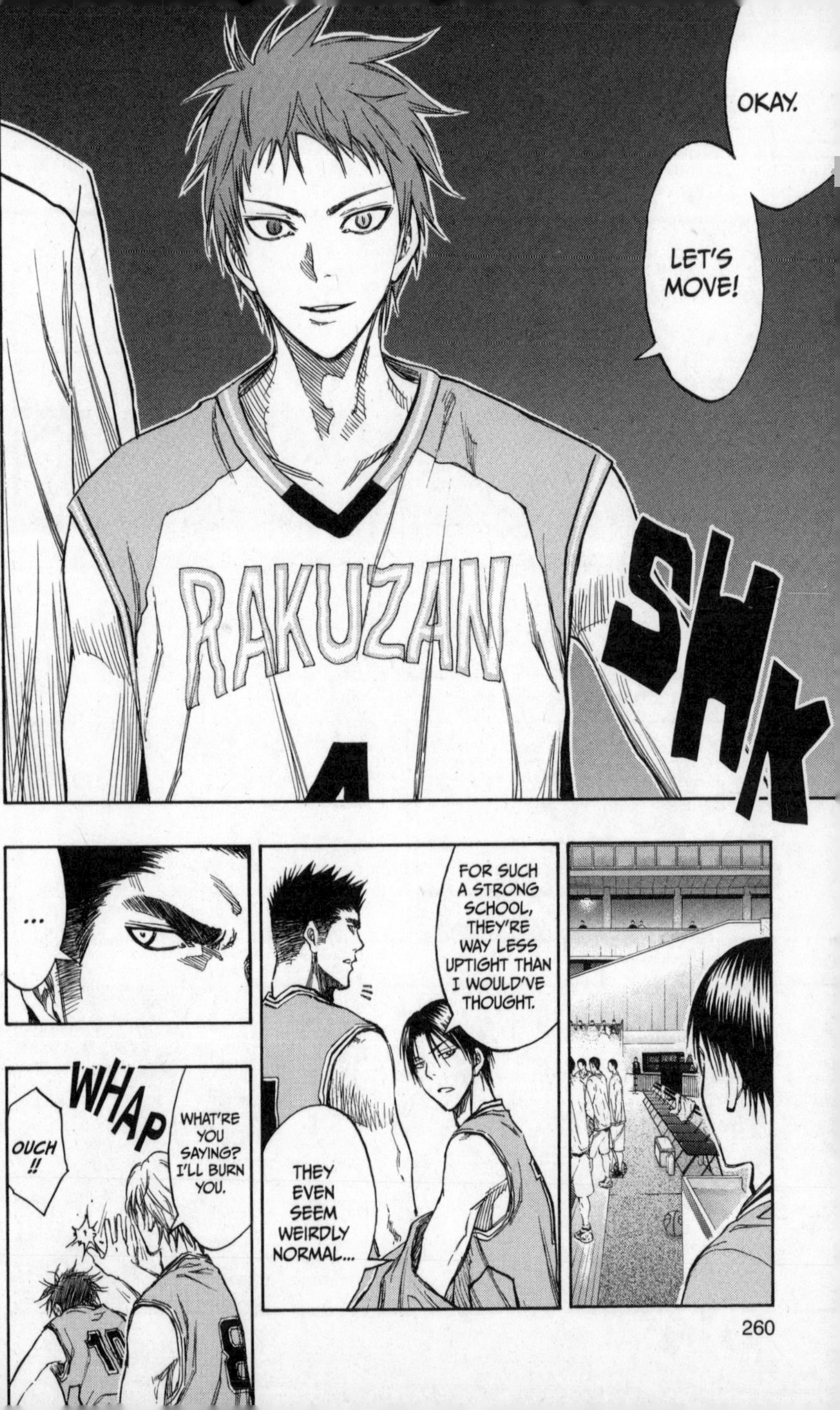
OKAY.
LET'S MOVE!
SHK
FOR SUCH A STRONG SCHOOL, THEY'RE WAY LESS UPTIGHT THAN I WOULD'VE THOUGHT.
THEY EVEN SEEM WEIRDLY NORMAL...
...
WHAT'RE YOU SAYING? I'LL BURN YOU.
WHAP
OUCH!!

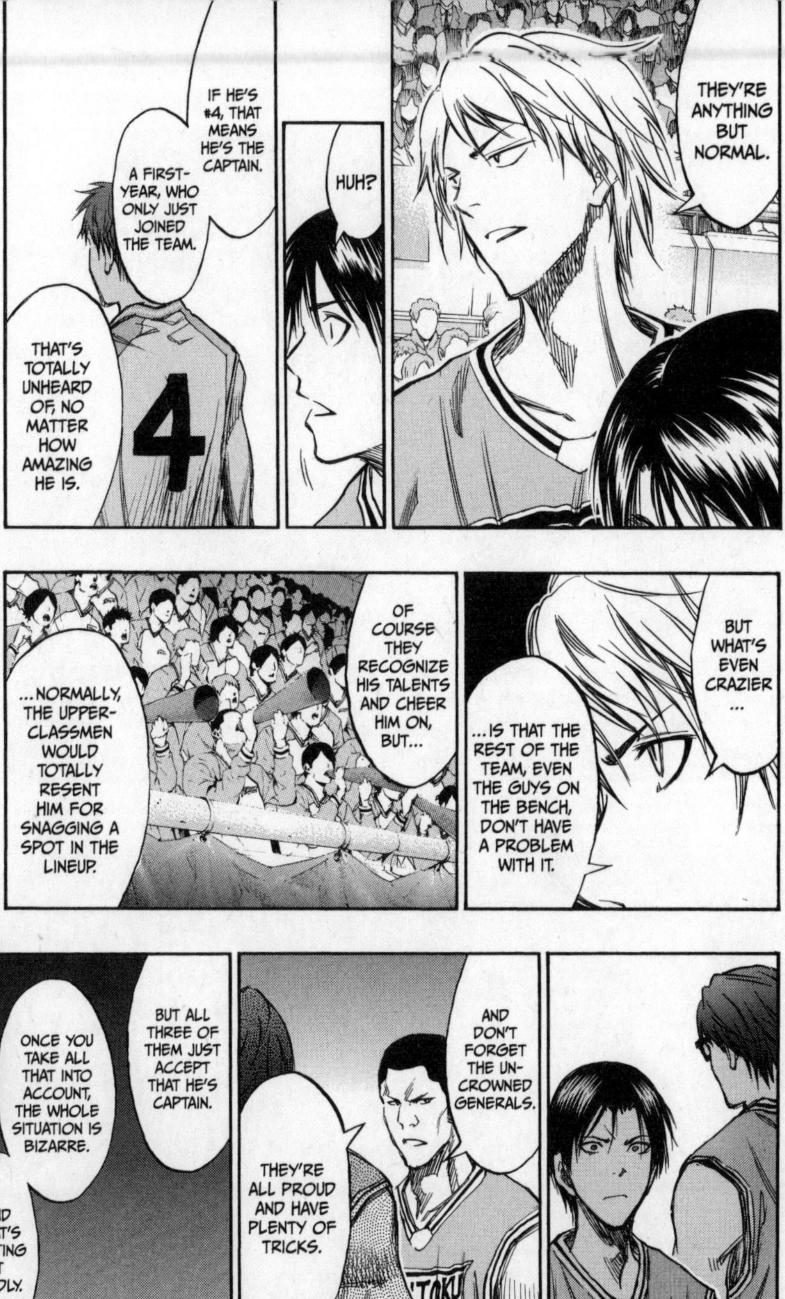
THEY'RE ANYTHING BUT NORMAL.
HUH?
IF HE'S #4, THAT MEANS HE'S THE CAPTAIN.
A FIRST-YEAR, WHO ONLY JUST JOINED THE TEAM.
4
THAT'S TOTALLY UNHEARD OF, NO MATTER HOW AMAZING HE IS.
BUT WHAT'S EVEN CRAZIER...
...IS THAT THE REST OF THE TEAM, EVEN THE GUYS ON THE BENCH, DON'T HAVE A PROBLEM WITH IT.
OF COURSE THEY RECOGNIZE HIS TALENTS AND CHEER HIM ON, BUT...
...NORMALLY, THE UPPER-CLASSMEN WOULD TOTALLY RESENT HIM FOR SNAGGING A SPOT IN THE LINEUP.
AND DON'T FORGET THE UN-CROWNED GENERALS.
THEY'RE ALL PROUD AND HAVE PLENTY OF TRICKS.
BUT ALL THREE OF THEM JUST ACCEPT THAT HE'S CAPTAIN.
ONCE YOU TAKE ALL THAT INTO ACCOUNT, THE WHOLE SITUATION IS BIZARRE.
AND THAT'S PUTTING IT MILDLY.

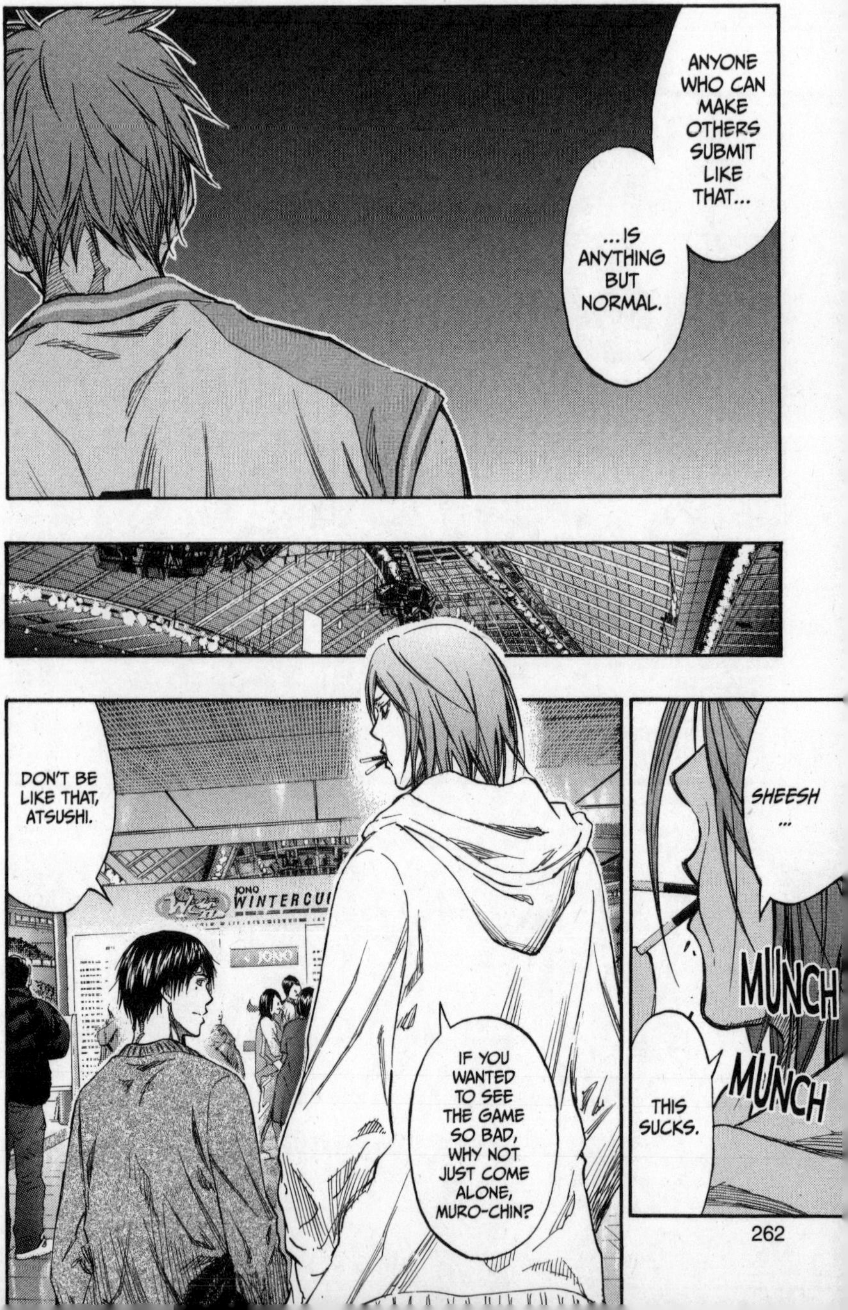
ANYONE WHO CAN MAKE OTHERS SUBMIT LIKE THAT...
...IS ANYTHING BUT NORMAL.
SHEESH ...
MUNCH
MUNCH
THIS SUCKS.
IF YOU WANTED TO SEE THE GAME SO BAD, WHY NOT JUST COME ALONE, MURO-CHIN?
DON'T BE LIKE THAT, ATSUSHI.

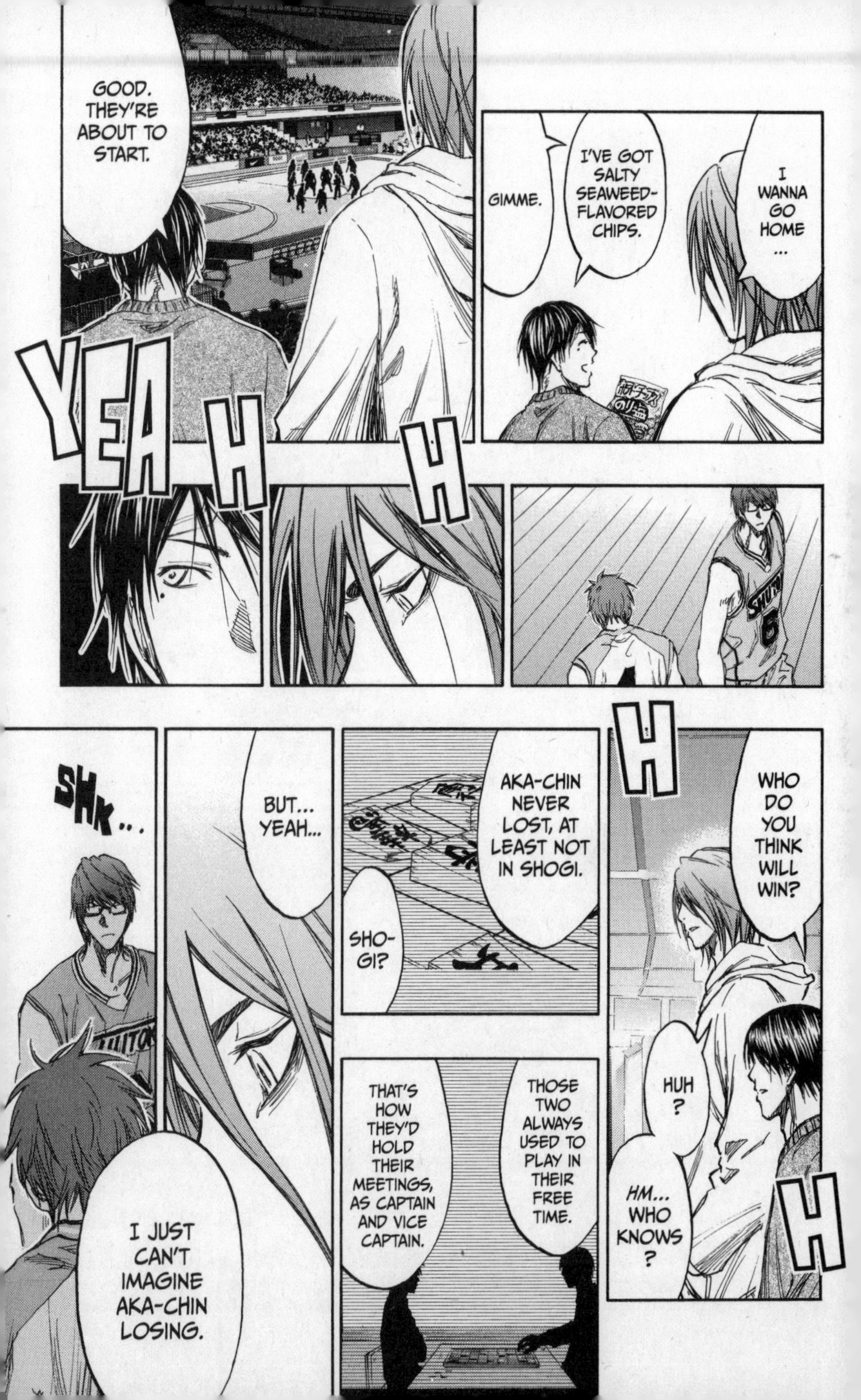
I WANNA GO HOME ...
I'VE GOT SALTY SEAWEED-FLAVORED CHIPS.
GIMME.
GOOD. THEY'RE ABOUT TO START.
YEAHHHH
WHO DO YOU THINK WILL WIN?
HUH?
HM... WHO KNOWS?
H
AKA-CHIN NEVER LOST, AT LEAST NOT IN SHOGI.
SHO-GI?
THOSE TWO ALWAYS USED TO PLAY IN THEIR FREE TIME.
THAT'S HOW THEY'D HOLD THEIR MEETINGS, AS CAPTAIN AND VICE CAPTAIN.
BUT... YEAH...
I JUST CAN'T IMAGINE AKA-CHIN LOSING.
SHK...

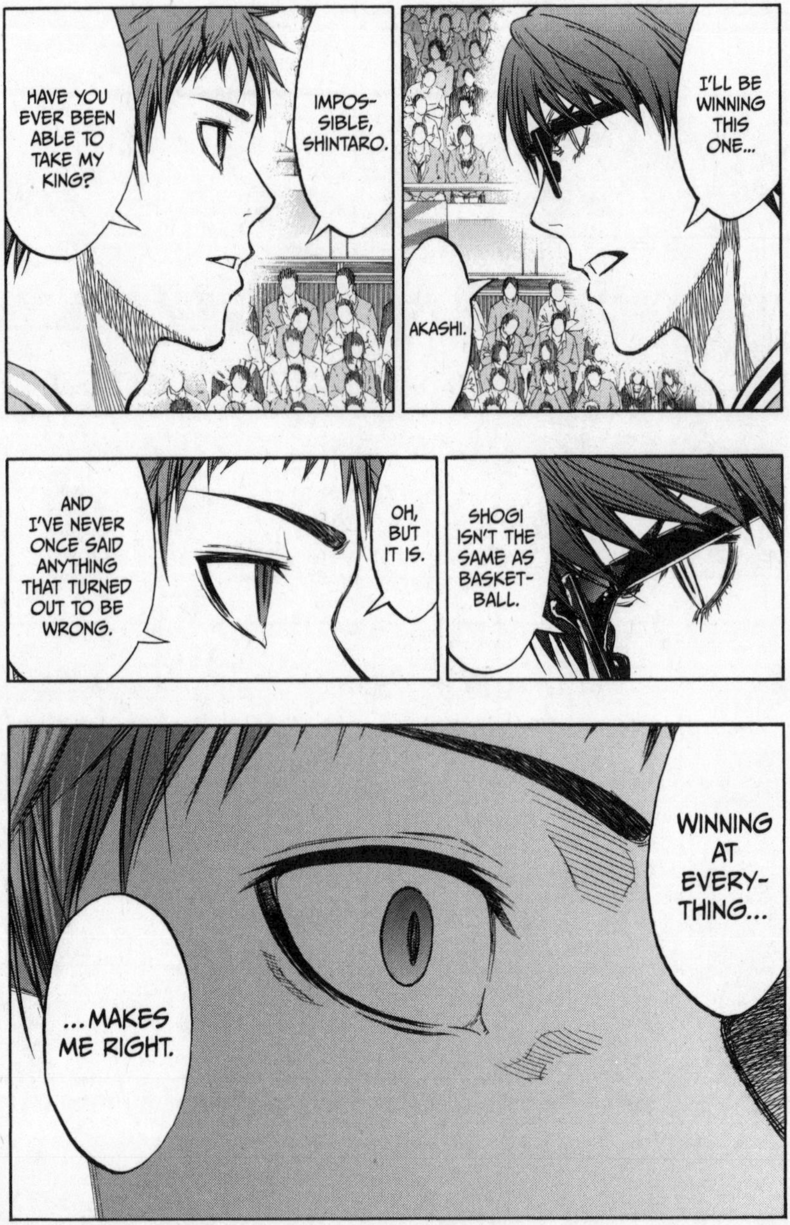
I'LL BE WINNING THIS ONE...
AKASHI.
IMPOSSIBLE, SHINTARO.
HAVE YOU EVER BEEN ABLE TO TAKE MY KING?
SHOGI ISN'T THE SAME AS BASKETBALL.
OH, BUT IT IS.
AND I'VE NEVER ONCE SAID ANYTHING THAT TURNED OUT TO BE WRONG.
WINNING AT EVERYTHING...
...MAKES ME RIGHT.

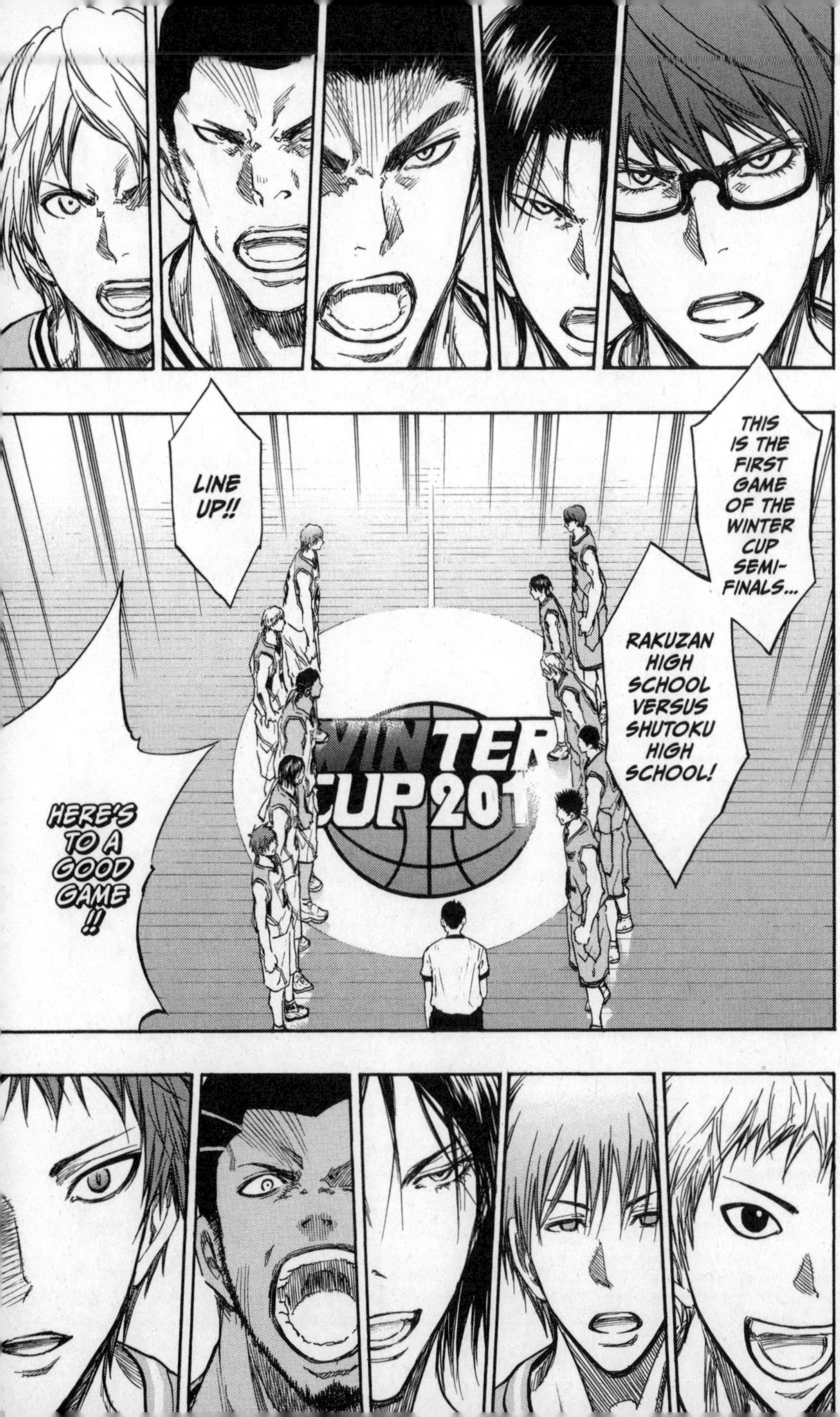
THIS IS THE FIRST GAME OF THE WINTER CUP SEMI-FINALS...
RAKUZAN HIGH SCHOOL VERSUS SHUTOKU HIGH SCHOOL!
LINE UP!!
WINTER CUP 201
HERE'S TO A GOOD GAME!!

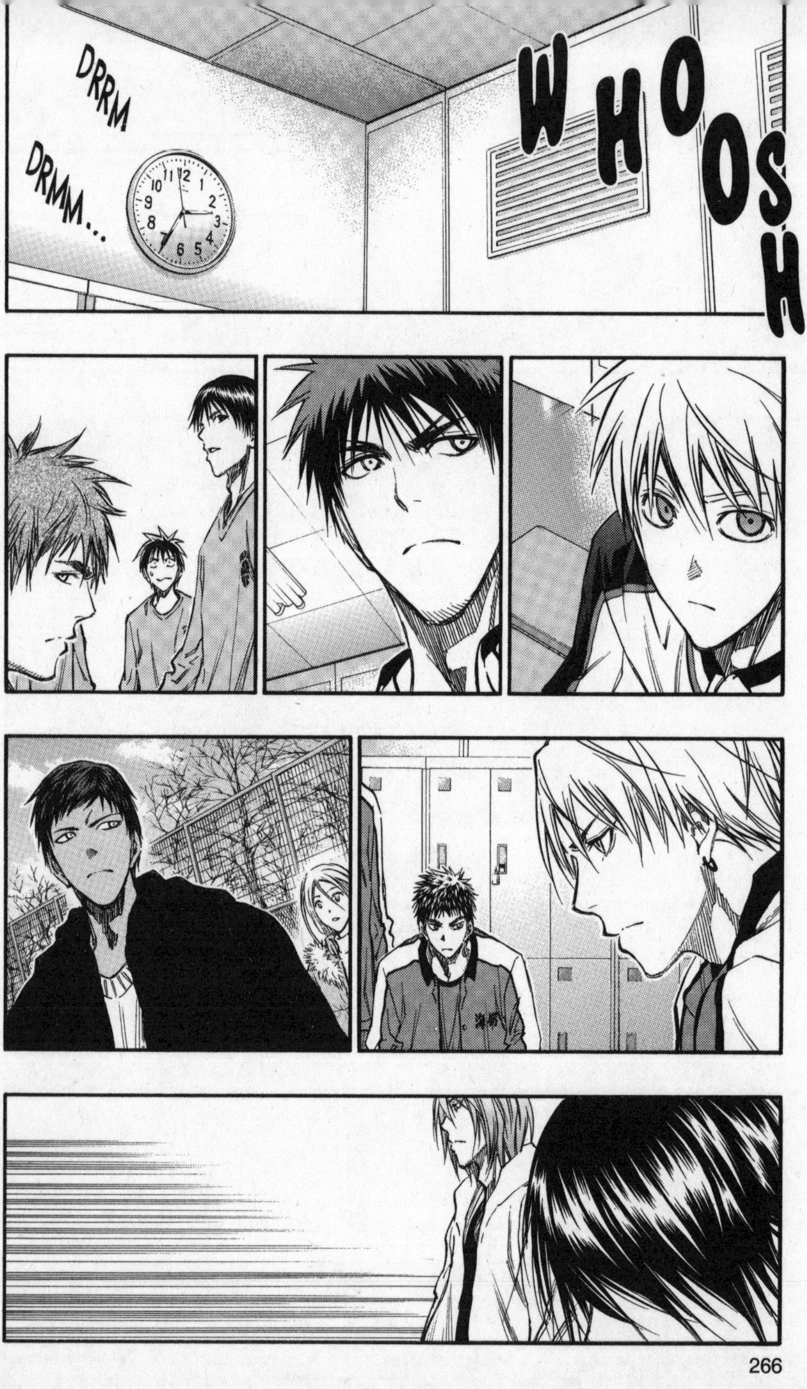
WHOOSH
DRRM
DRMM...

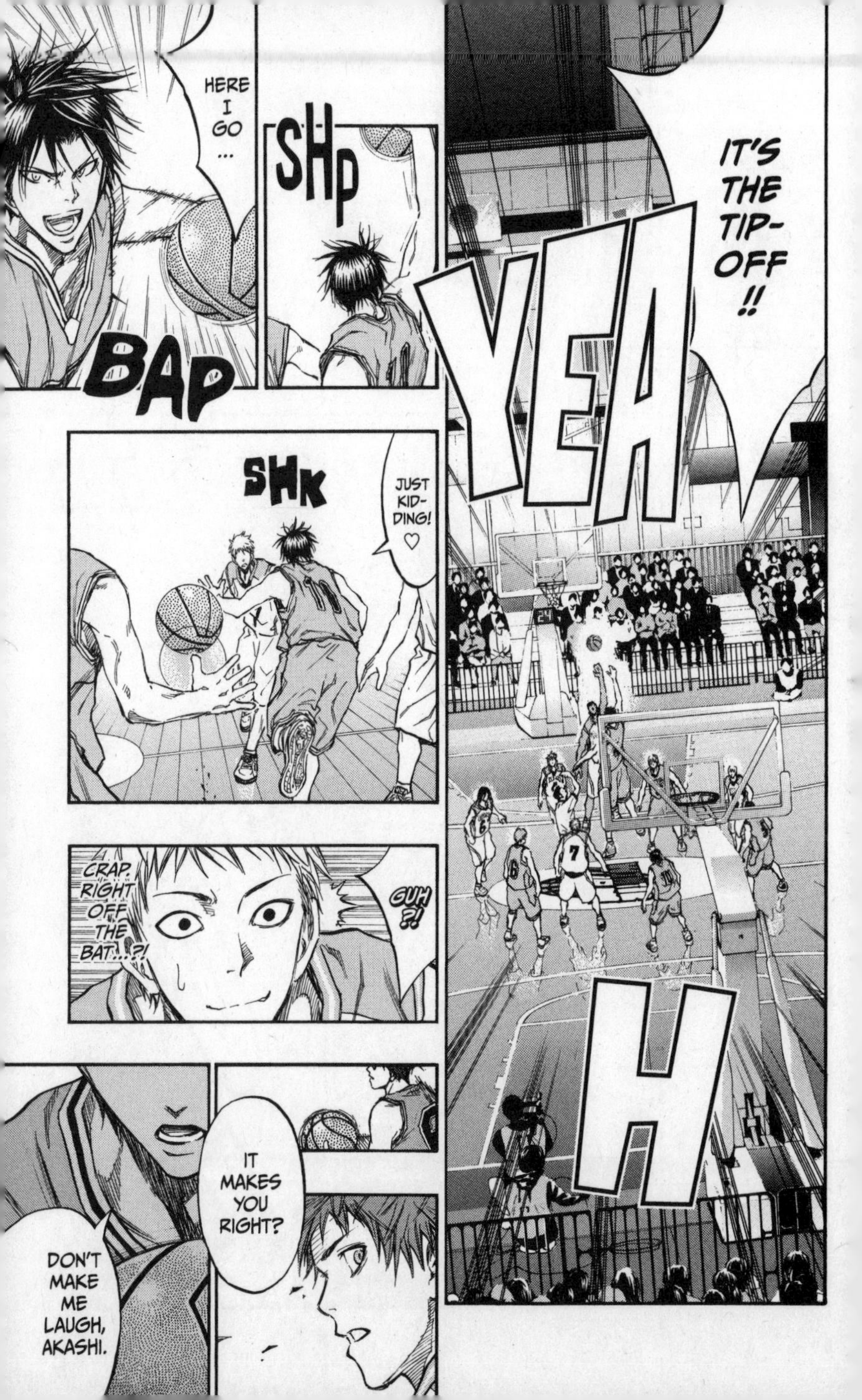

IT'S THE TIP-OFF!!
YEAH
SHP
HERE I GO...
BAP
SHK
JUST KIDDING! ♡
GUH ?!
CRAP. RIGHT OFF THE BAT...?!
IT MAKES YOU RIGHT?
DON'T MAKE ME LAUGH, AKASHI.

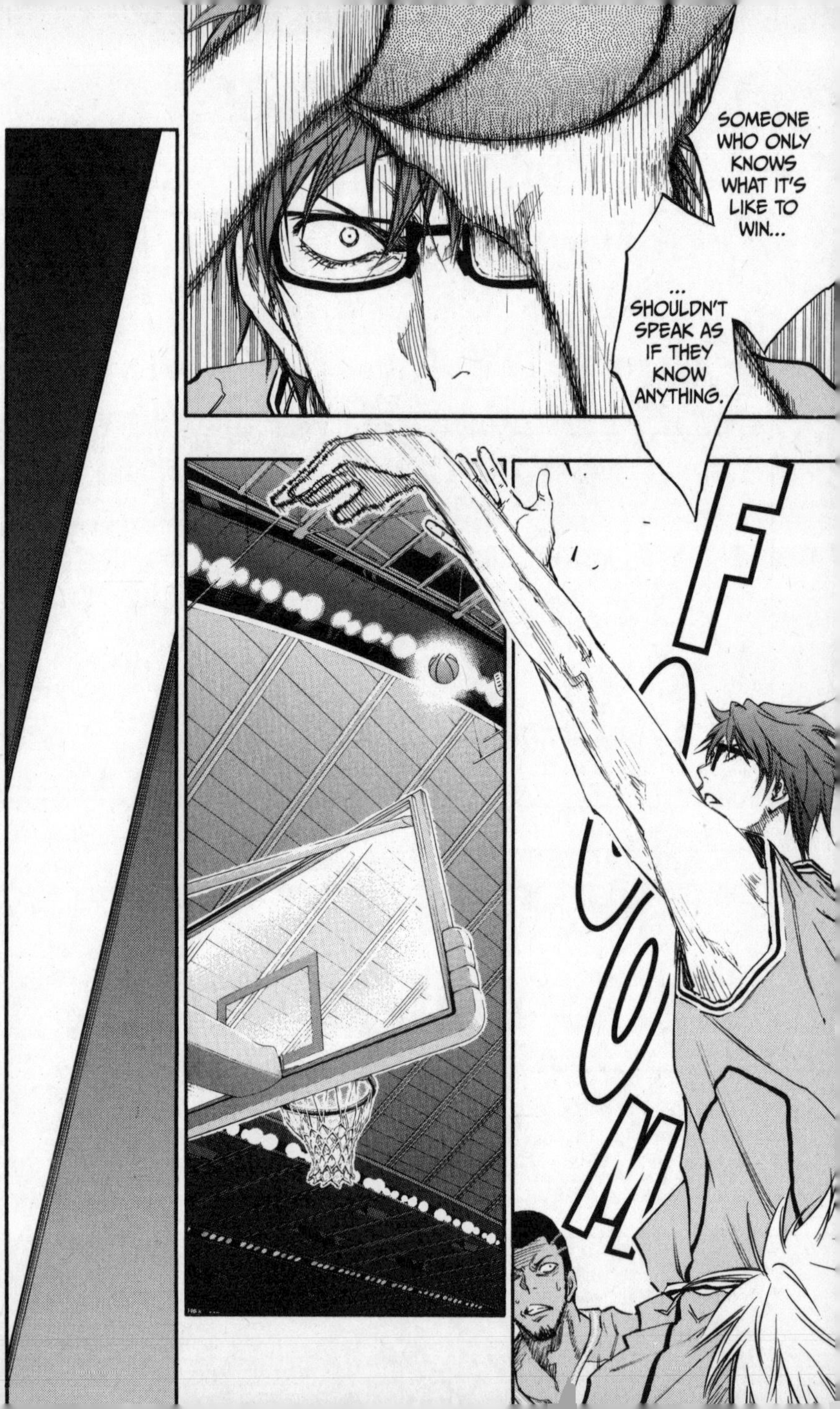
SOMEONE WHO ONLY KNOWS WHAT IT'S LIKE TO WIN...
...SHOULDN'T SPEAK AS IF THEY KNOW ANYTHING.
FWOOM

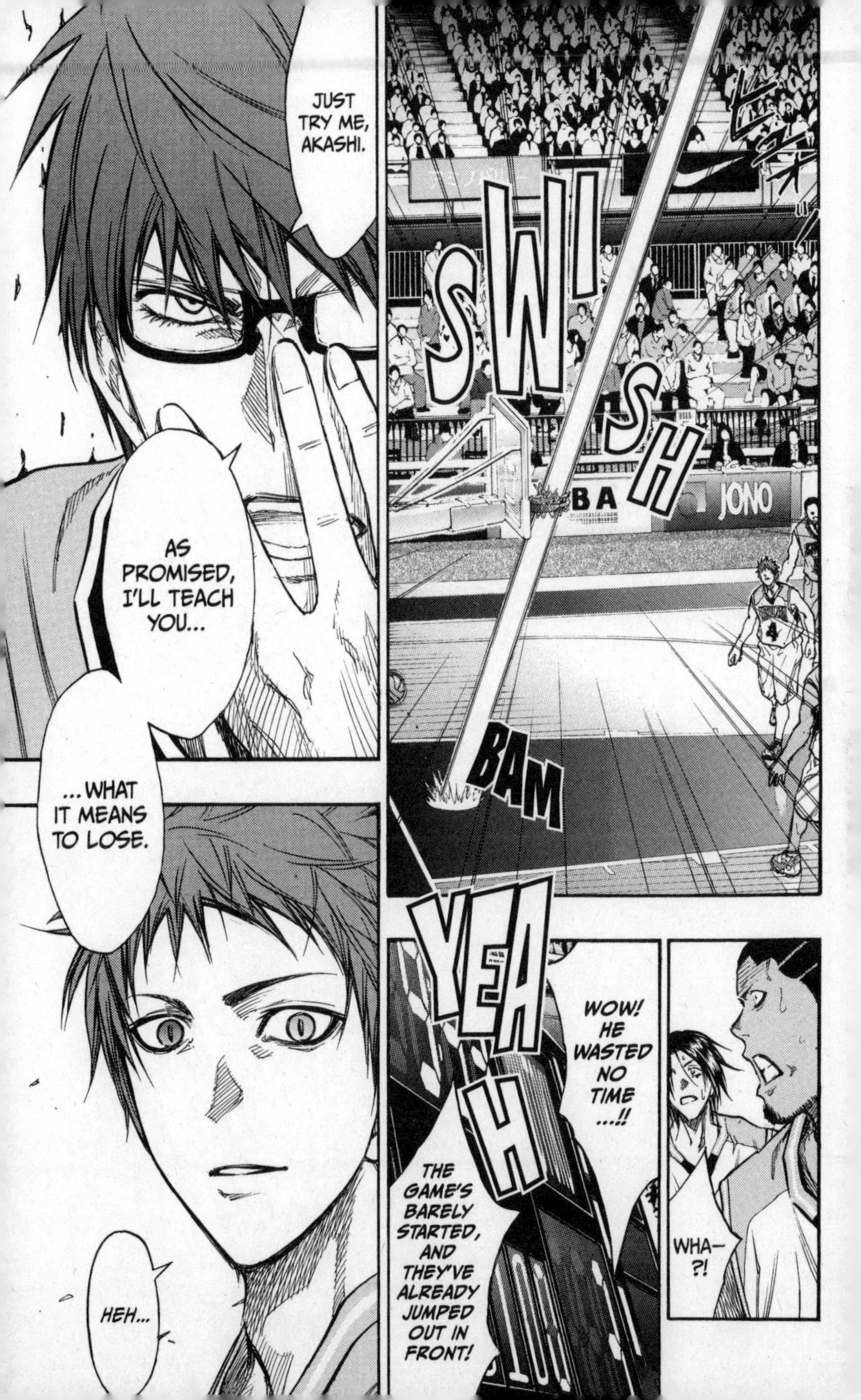
SWISH
BAM
JUST TRY ME, AKASHI.
AS PROMISED, I'LL TEACH YOU...
...WHAT IT MEANS TO LOSE.
WHA—?!
WOW! HE WASTED NO TIME ...!!
THE GAME'S BARELY STARTED, AND THEY'VE ALREADY JUMPED OUT IN FRONT!
YEAH
HEH...

KUROKO'S BASKETBALL Q&A (W/ HALFWAY-DECENT ANSWERS)

Q. WHAT SCHOOL SUBJECTS DO THE COACHES AT SHUTOKU, TO-OH, KAIJO AND YOSEN TEACH? HOW ABOUT RAKUZAN, TOO, IF POSSIBLE?
(BIG BRO from HOKKAIDO)

A. GENTA TAKEUCHI (KAIJO) → JAPANESE HISTORY
MASAAKI NAKATANI (SHUTOKU) → ENGLISH GRAMMAR
KATSUNORI HARASAWA (TO-OH) → CHEMISTRY
MASAKO ARAKI (YOSEN) → GYM
EIJI SHIROGANE (RAKUZAN) → WORLD HISTORY

KUROKO'S BASKETBALL BLOOPERS (TAKE 8)

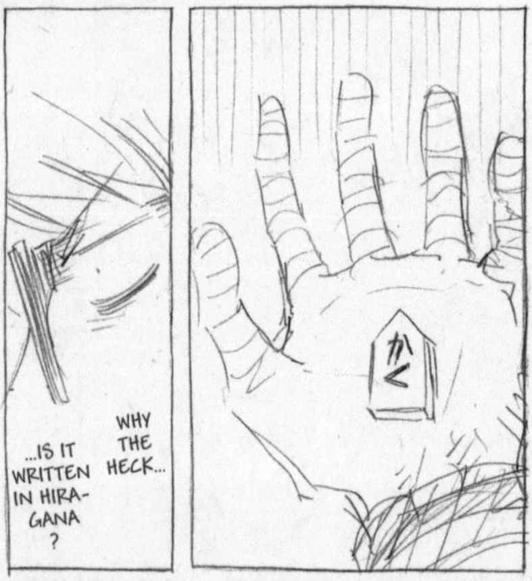
かく
WHY THE HECK...
...IS IT WRITTEN IN HIRAGANA?

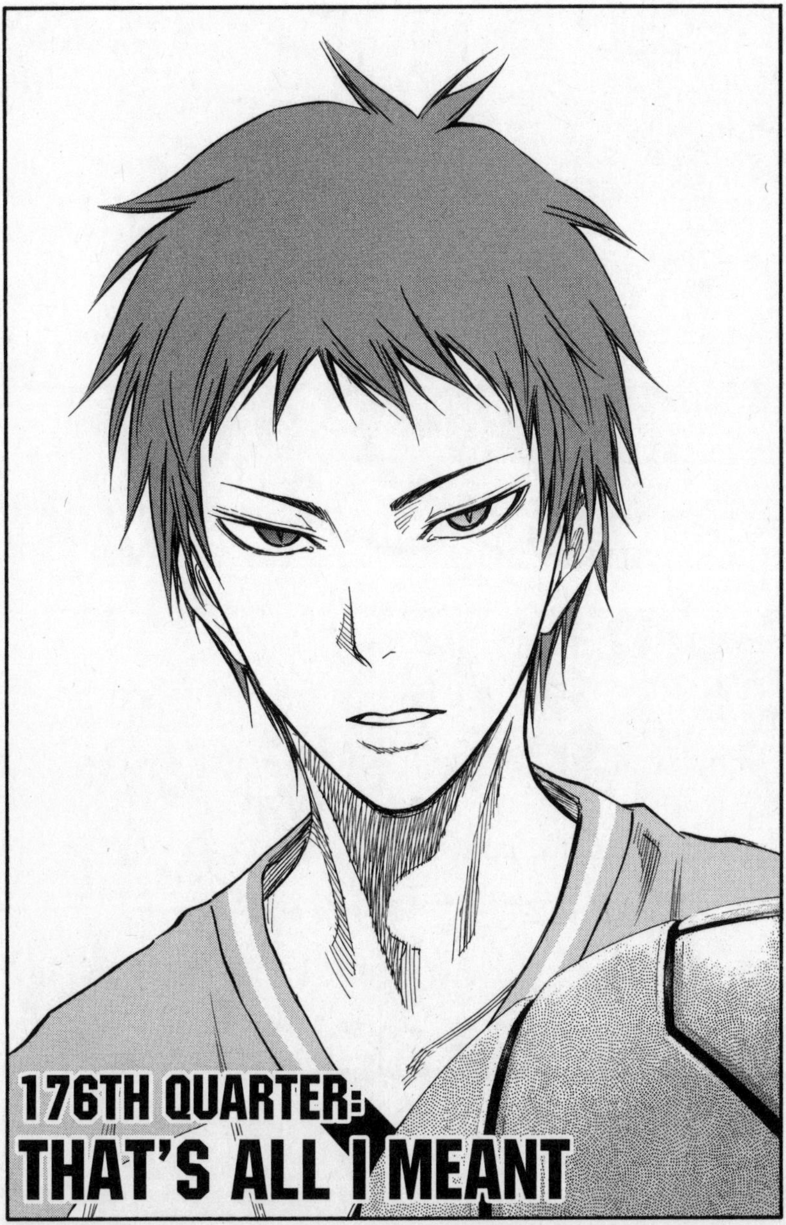
176TH QUARTER:
THAT'S ALL I MEANT

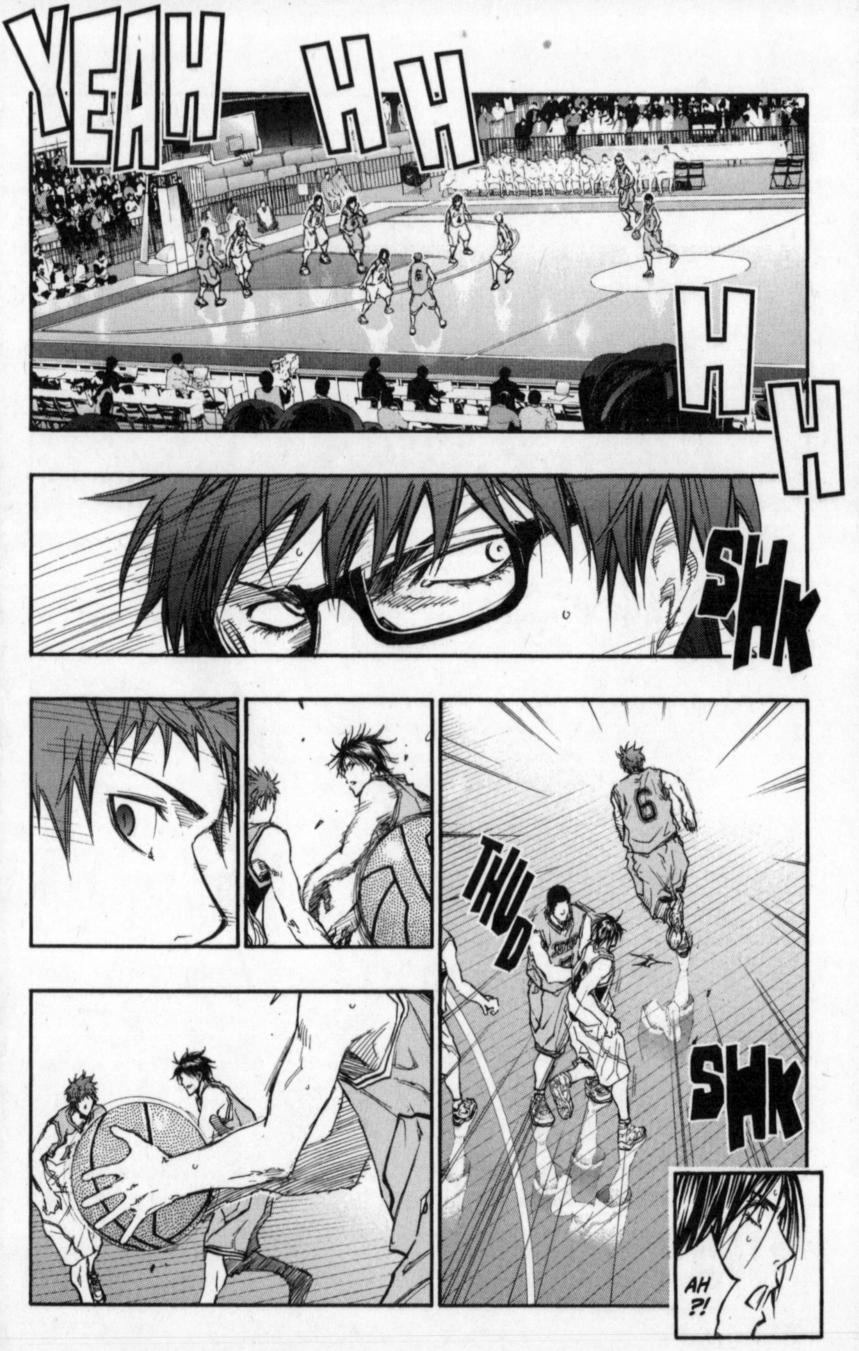
YEAHHHHHH
SHK
THUD
SHK
AH ?!

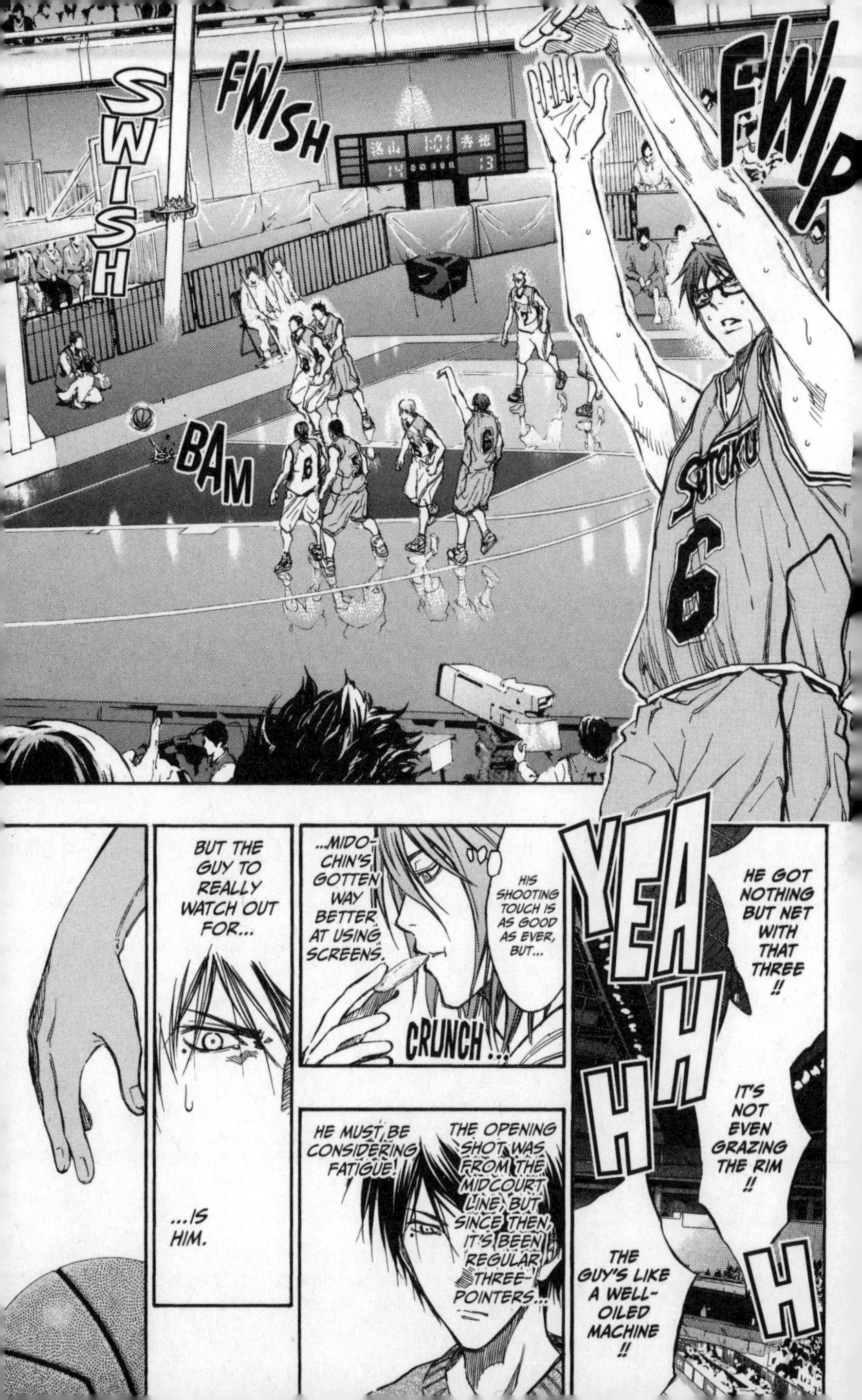
FWIP
FWISH
SWISH
BAM
YEAHHHH
HE GOT NOTHING BUT NET WITH THAT THREE!!
IT'S NOT EVEN GRAZING THE RIM!!
THE GUY'S LIKE A WELL-OILED MACHINE!!
HIS SHOOTING TOUCH IS AS GOOD AS EVER, BUT...
...MIDO-CHIN'S GOTTEN WAY BETTER AT USING SCREENS.
CRUNCH...
THE OPENING SHOT WAS FROM THE MIDCOURT LINE, BUT SINCE THEN, IT'S BEEN REGULAR THREE-POINTERS...
HE MUST BE CONSIDERING FATIGUE!
BUT THE GUY TO REALLY WATCH OUT FOR...
...IS HIM.

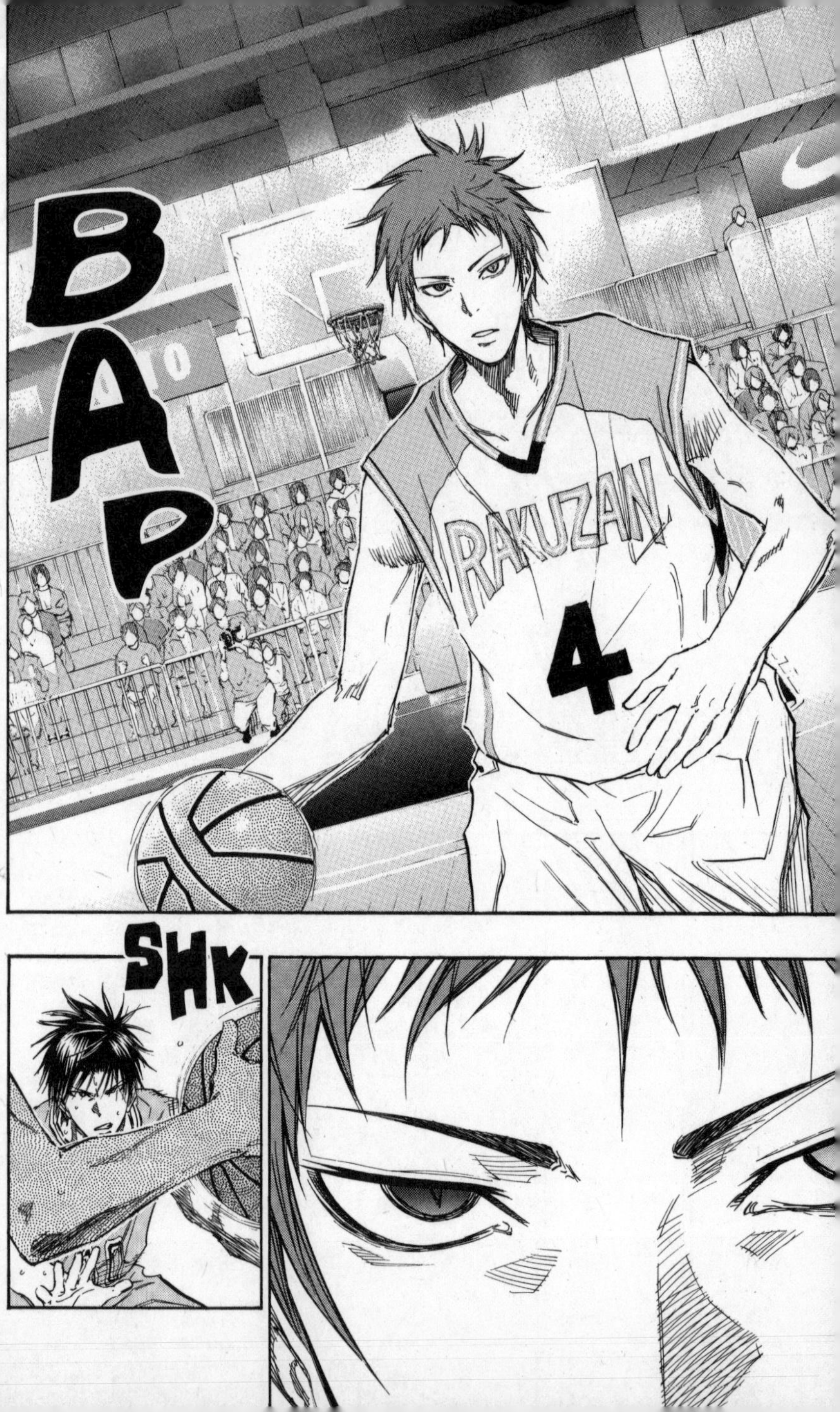
BAP
RAKUZAN
4
SHK

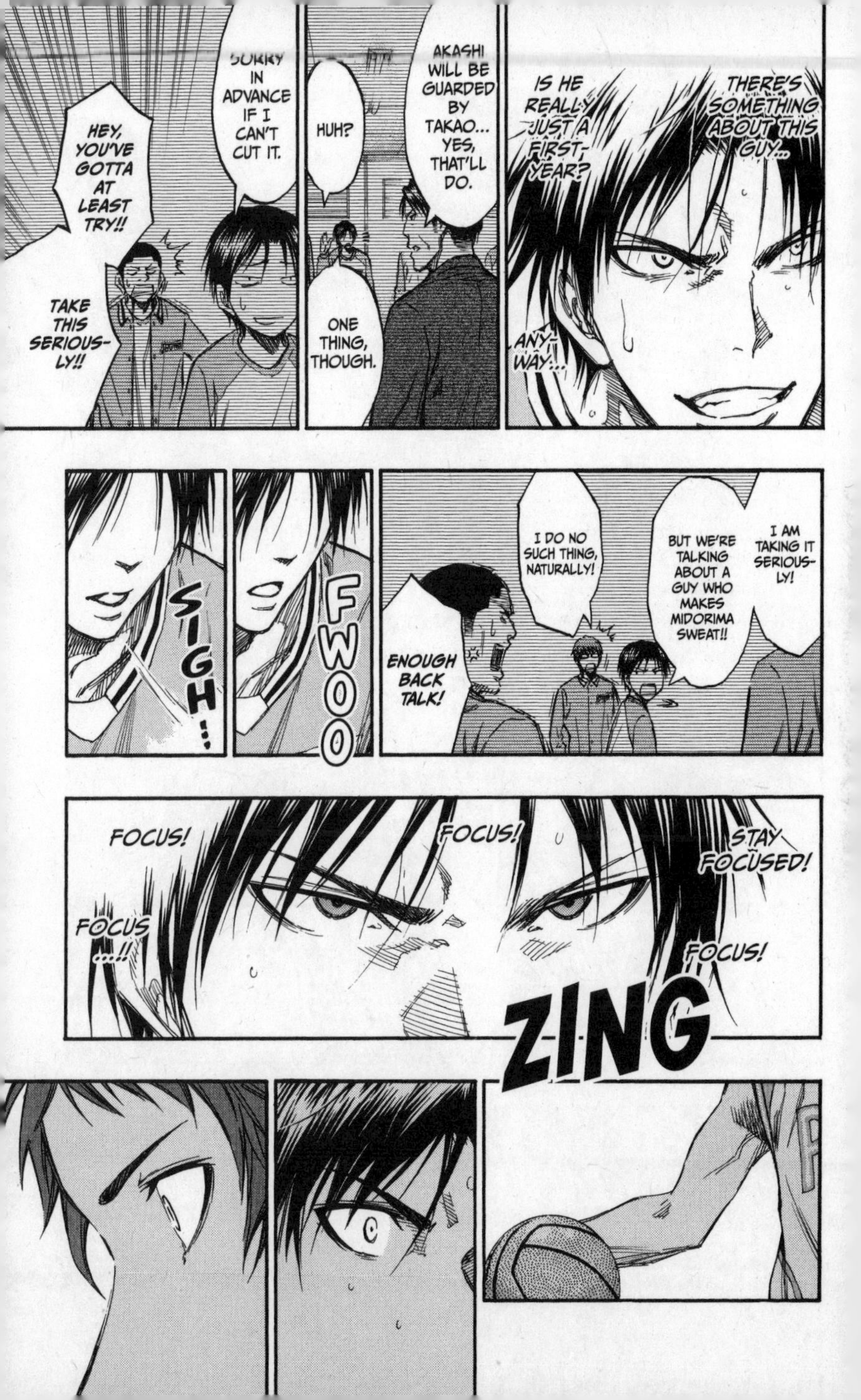
THERE'S SOMETHING ABOUT THIS GUY...
IS HE REALLY JUST A FIRST-YEAR?
ANYWAY...
AKASHI WILL BE GUARDED BY TAKAO... YES, THAT'LL DO.
HUH?
ONE THING, THOUGH.
SORRY IN ADVANCE IF I CAN'T CUT IT.
HEY, YOU'VE GOTTA AT LEAST TRY!!
TAKE THIS SERIOUSLY!!
I AM TAKING IT SERIOUSLY!
BUT WE'RE TALKING ABOUT A GUY WHO MAKES MIDORIMA SWEAT!!
I DO NO SUCH THING, NATURALLY!
ENOUGH BACK TALK!
FWOO
SIGH...
STAY FOCUSED!
FOCUS!
FOCUS!
FOCUS...!!
FOCUS!
ZING

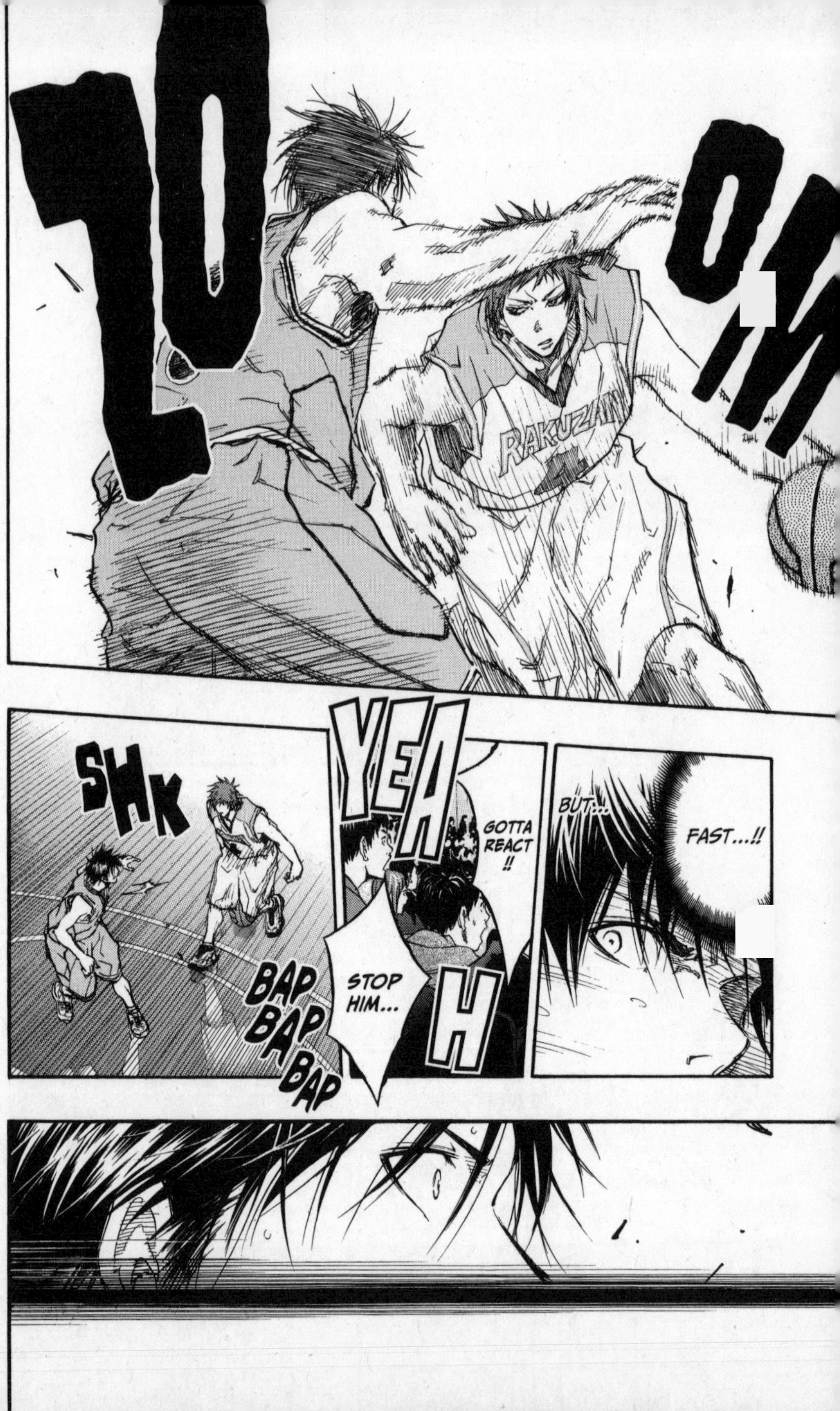
ZOOM
BUT...
FAST...!!
YEAH
GOTTA REACT !!
STOP HIM...
SHK
BAP BAP BA BAP

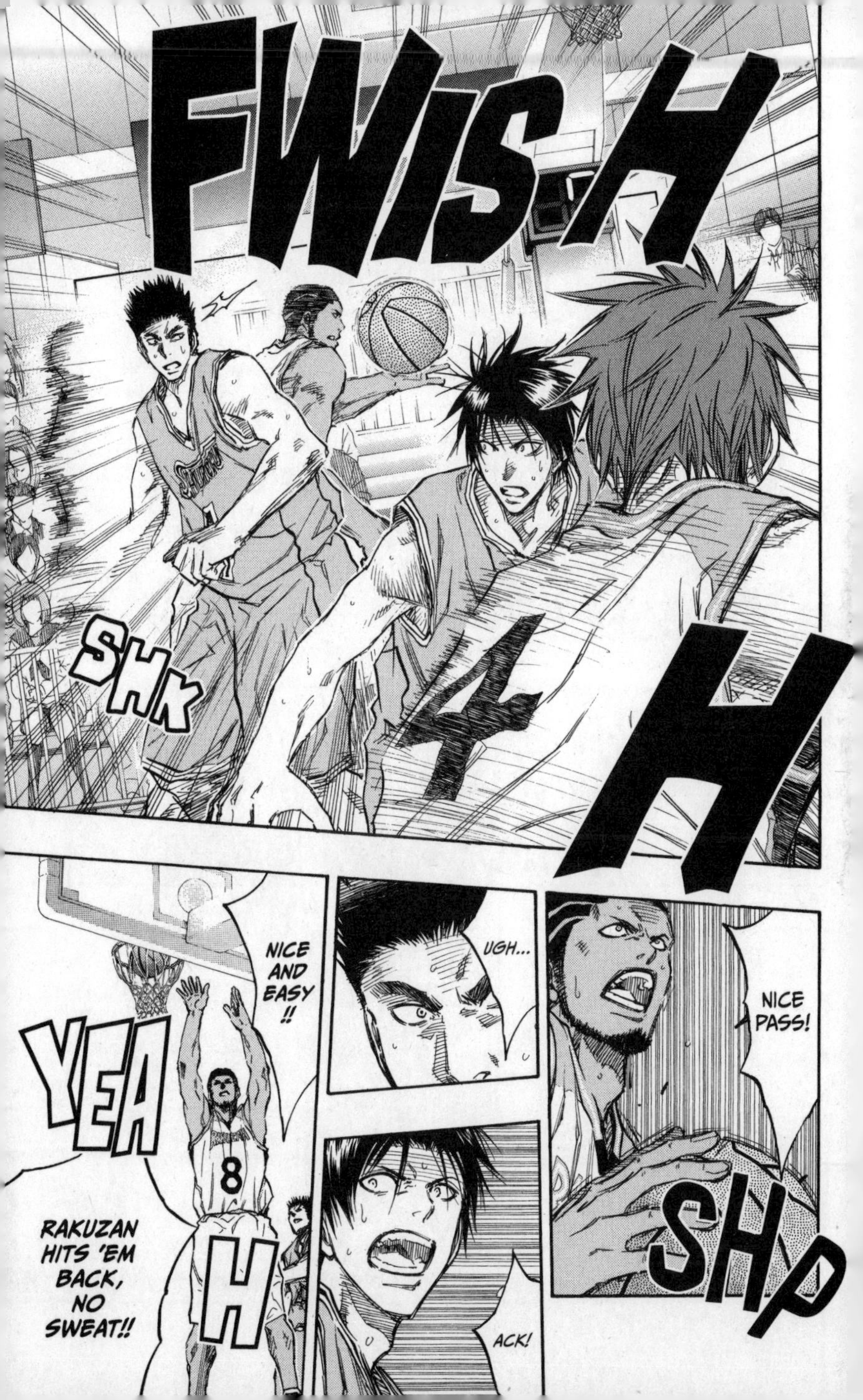
FWISH
SHK
H
NICE PASS!
SHP
UGH...
ACK!
NICE AND EASY!!
YEAH
RAKUZAN HITS 'EM BACK, NO SWEAT!!

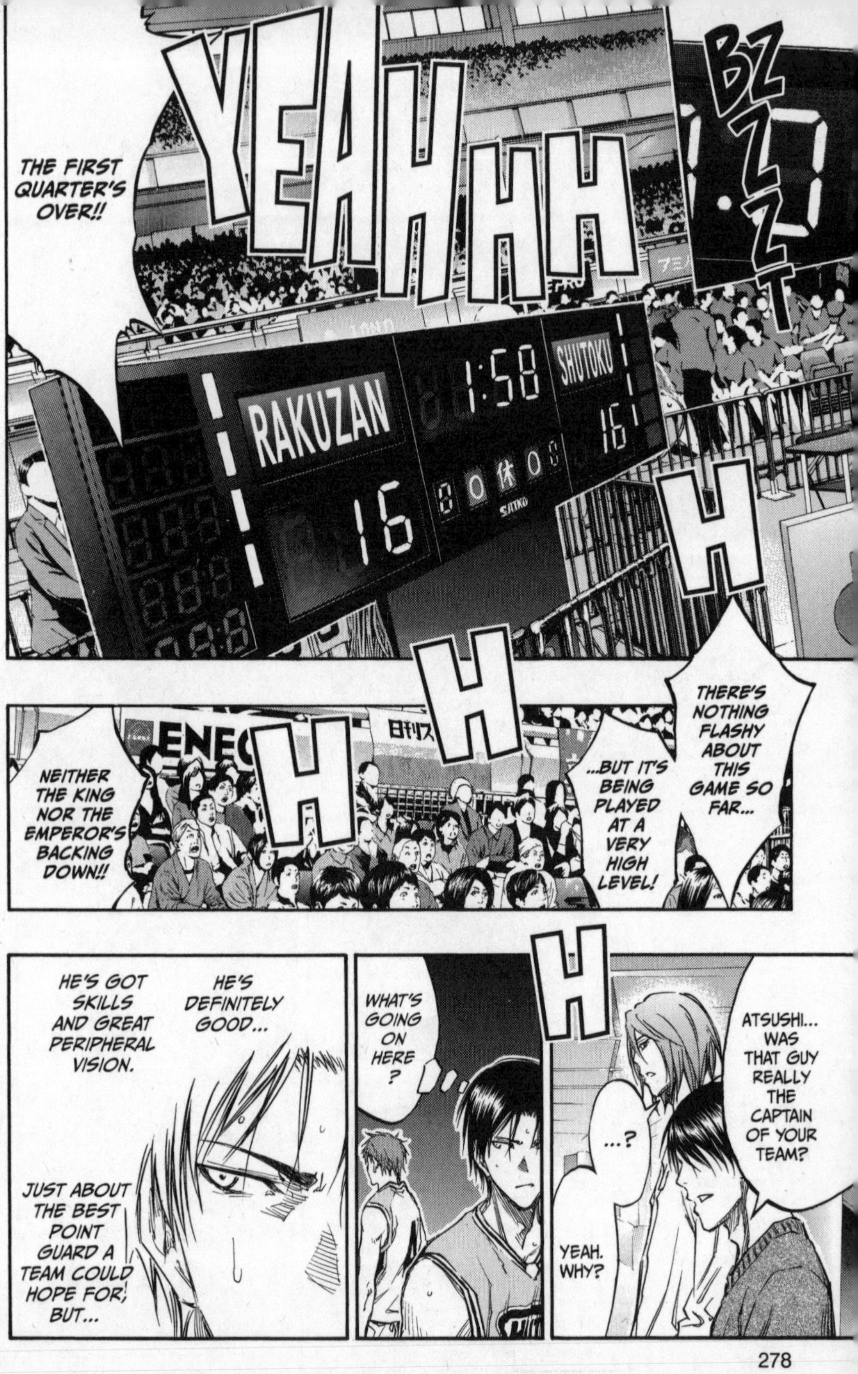
BZZZZT
YEAHHHH
SHUTOKU
1:58
16
RAKUZAN
16
THE FIRST QUARTER'S OVER!!
H
H
H
THERE'S NOTHING FLASHY ABOUT THIS GAME SO FAR...
...BUT IT'S BEING PLAYED AT A VERY HIGH LEVEL!
NEITHER THE KING NOR THE EMPEROR'S BACKING DOWN!!
H
ATSUSHI... WAS THAT GUY REALLY THE CAPTAIN OF YOUR TEAM?
...?
YEAH. WHY?
WHAT'S GOING ON HERE?
HE'S DEFINITELY GOOD...
HE'S GOT SKILLS AND GREAT PERIPHERAL VISION.
JUST ABOUT THE BEST POINT GUARD A TEAM COULD HOPE FOR, BUT...

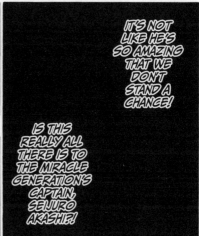

IT'S NOT LIKE HE'S SO AMAZING THAT WE DON'T STAND A CHANCE!

IS THIS REALLY ALL THERE IS TO THE MIRACLE GENERATION'S CAPTAIN, SEIJURO AKASHI?!

THIS IS GOING WELL.

Rakuzan High Coach
EIJI SHIROGANE

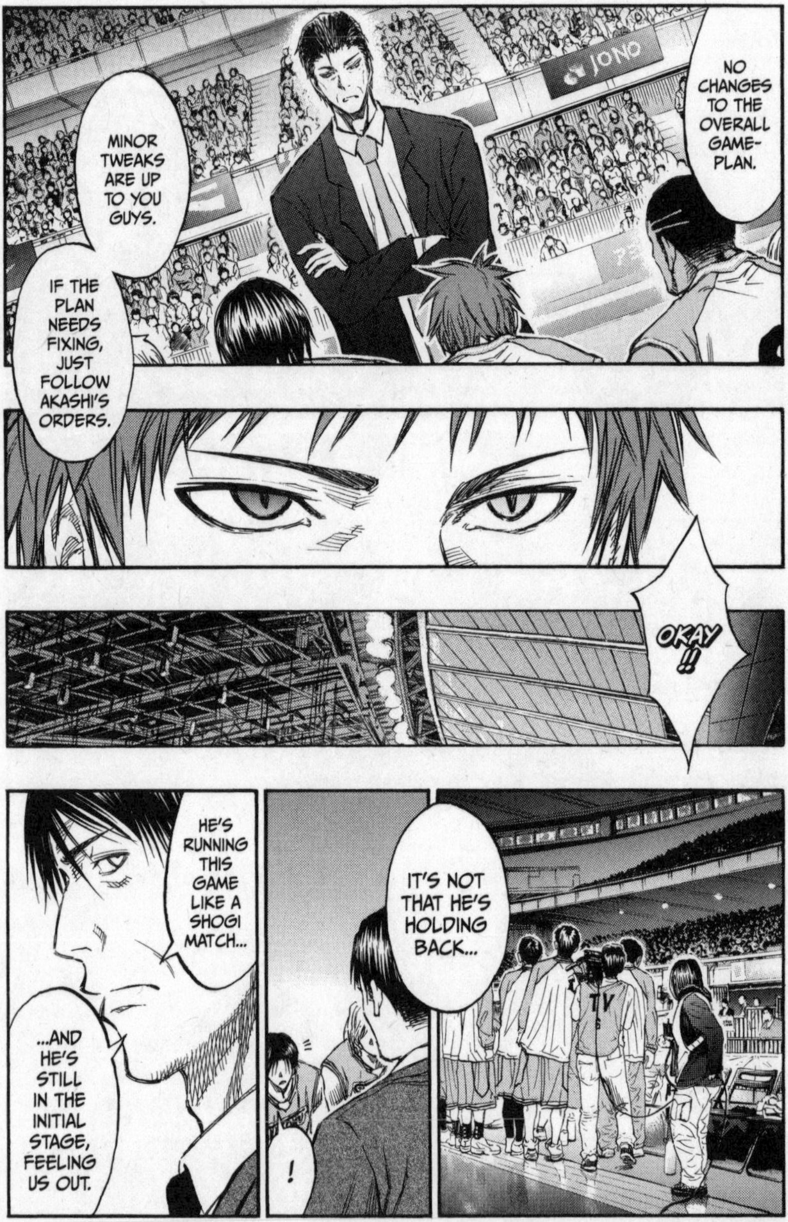
NO CHANGES TO THE OVERALL GAME-PLAN.
MINOR TWEAKS ARE UP TO YOU GUYS.
IF THE PLAN NEEDS FIXING, JUST FOLLOW AKASHI'S ORDERS.
OKAY!!
IT'S NOT THAT HE'S HOLDING BACK...
!
HE'S RUNNING THIS GAME LIKE A SHOGI MATCH...
...AND HE'S STILL IN THE INITIAL STAGE, FEELING US OUT.

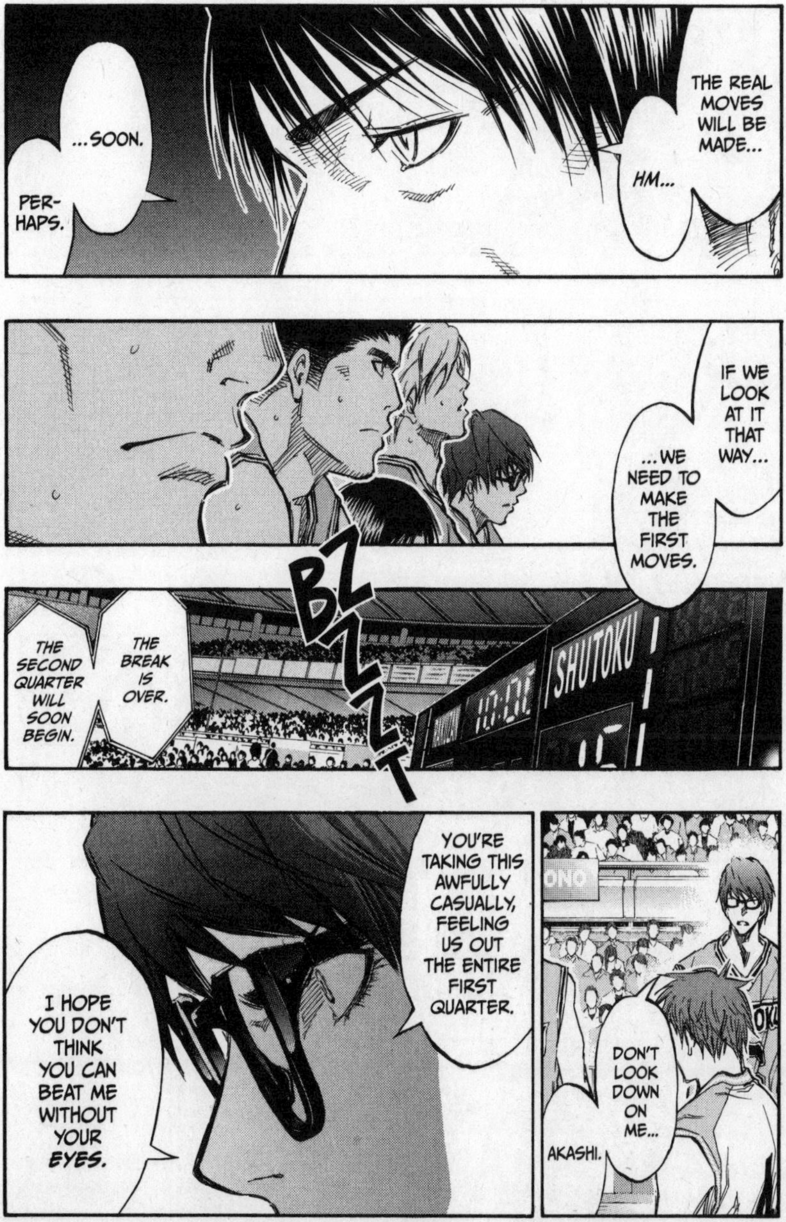
THE REAL MOVES WILL BE MADE...
...SOON.
HM...
PER-HAPS.
IF WE LOOK AT IT THAT WAY...
...WE NEED TO MAKE THE FIRST MOVES.
BZZZZT
SHUTOKU
THE BREAK IS OVER.
THE SECOND QUARTER WILL SOON BEGIN.
DON'T LOOK DOWN ON ME...
AKASHI.
YOU'RE TAKING THIS AWFULLY CASUALLY, FEELING US OUT THE ENTIRE FIRST QUARTER.
I HOPE YOU DON'T THINK YOU CAN BEAT ME WITHOUT YOUR *EYES*.

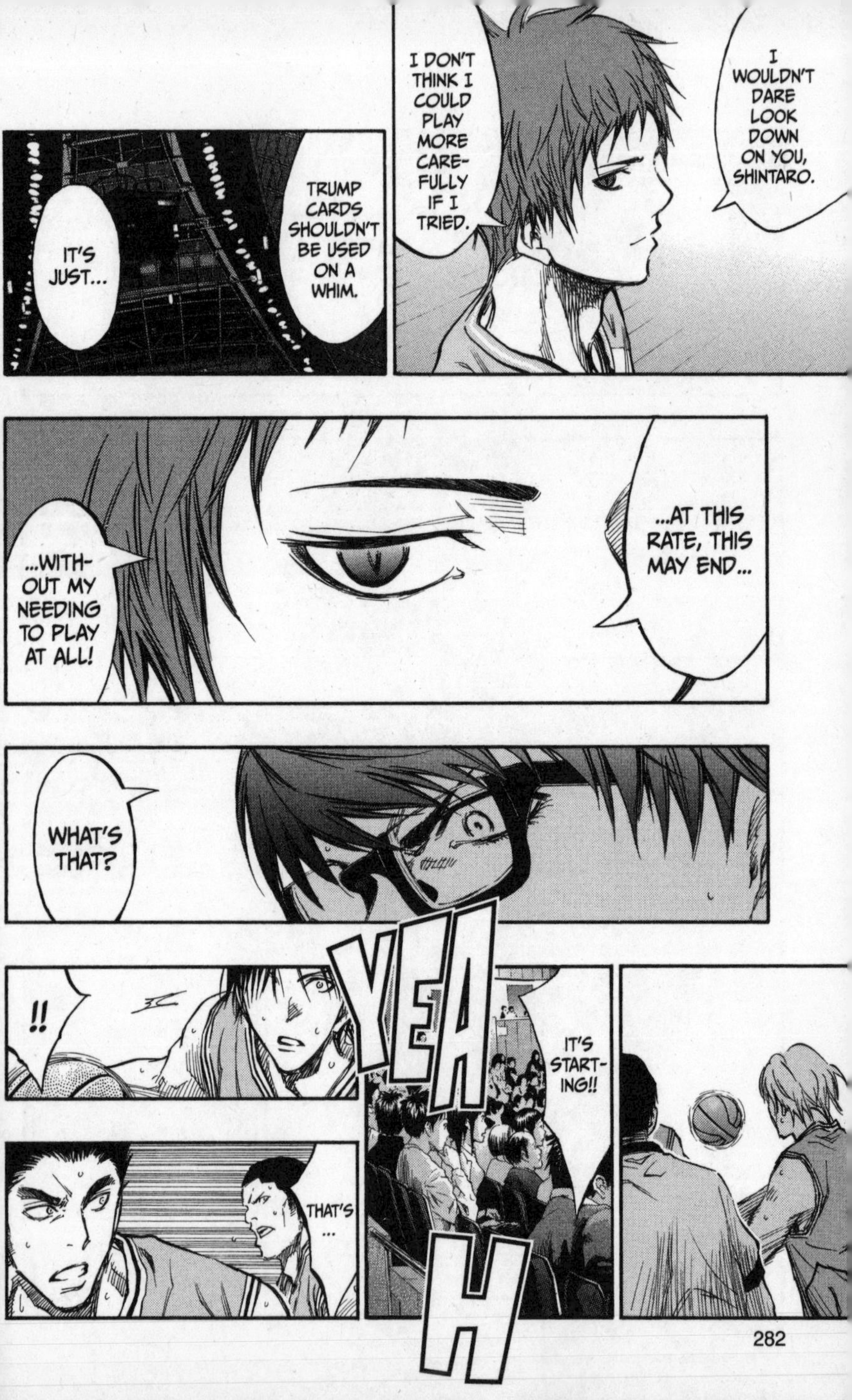
I WOULDN'T DARE LOOK DOWN ON YOU, SHINTARO.
I DON'T THINK I COULD PLAY MORE CARE-FULLY IF I TRIED.
TRUMP CARDS SHOULDN'T BE USED ON A WHIM.
IT'S JUST...
...AT THIS RATE, THIS MAY END...
...WITH-OUT MY NEEDING TO PLAY AT ALL!
WHAT'S THAT?
IT'S START-ING!!
YEAH
!!
THAT'S ...

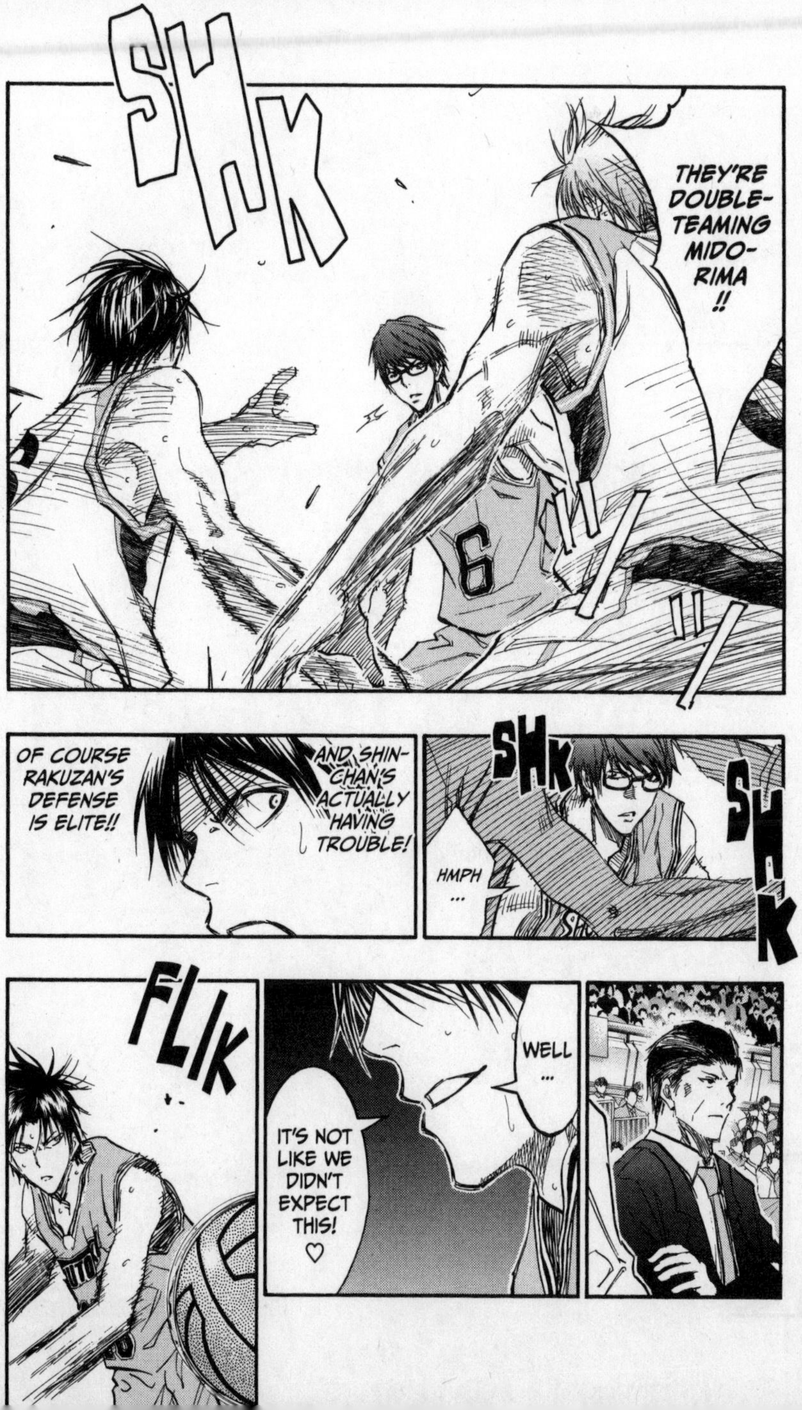
SHK
THEY'RE DOUBLE-TEAMING MIDORIMA!!
SHK
SHK
HMPH...
AND SHIN-CHAN'S ACTUALLY HAVING TROUBLE!
OF COURSE RAKUZAN'S DEFENSE IS ELITE!!
WELL...
IT'S NOT LIKE WE DIDN'T EXPECT THIS! ♡
FLIK

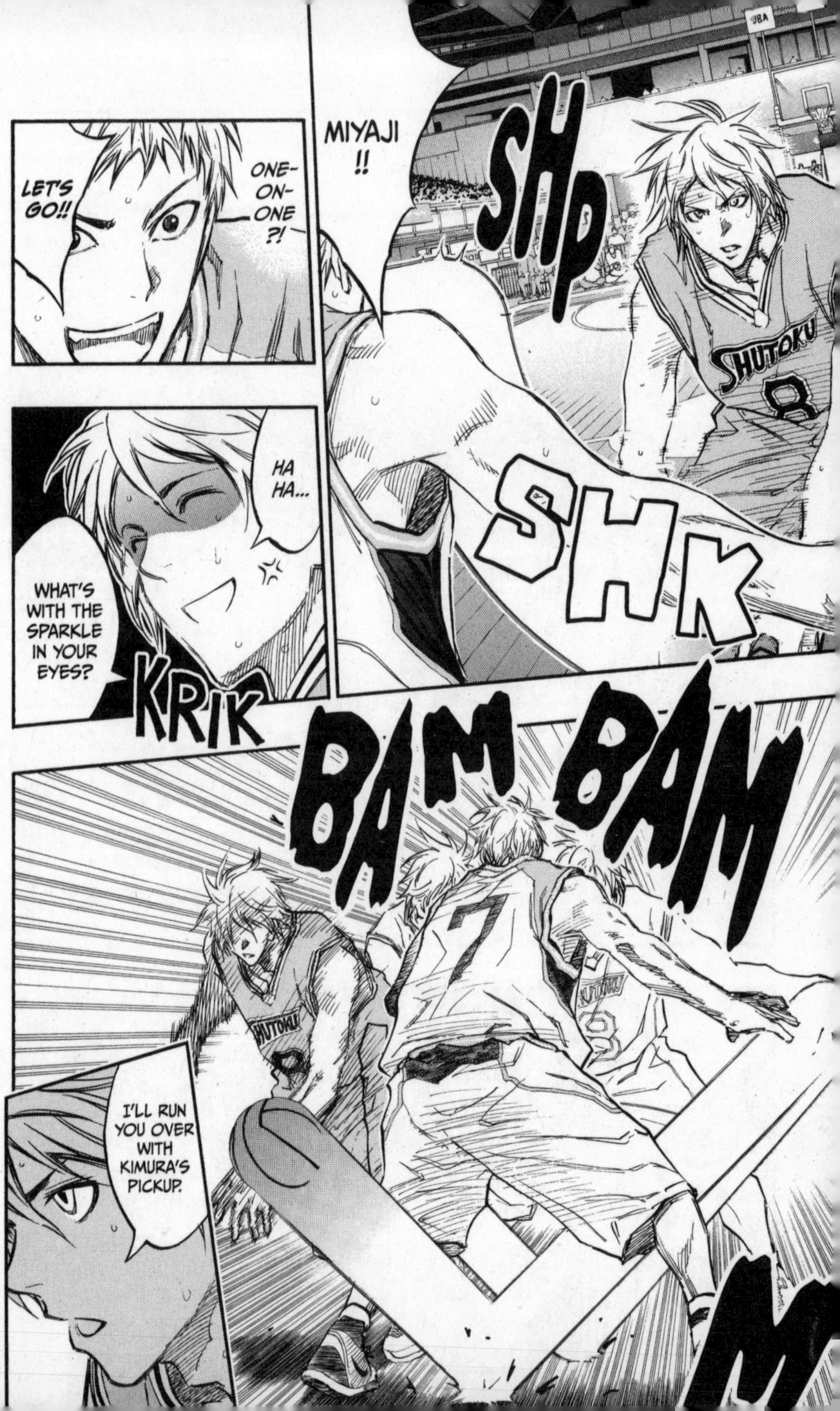
SHP
MIYAJI !!
ONE-ON-ONE ?!
SHK
LET'S GO!!
HA HA...
WHAT'S WITH THE SPARKLE IN YOUR EYES?
KRIK
BAM BAM
I'LL RUN YOU OVER WITH KIMURA'S PICKUP.

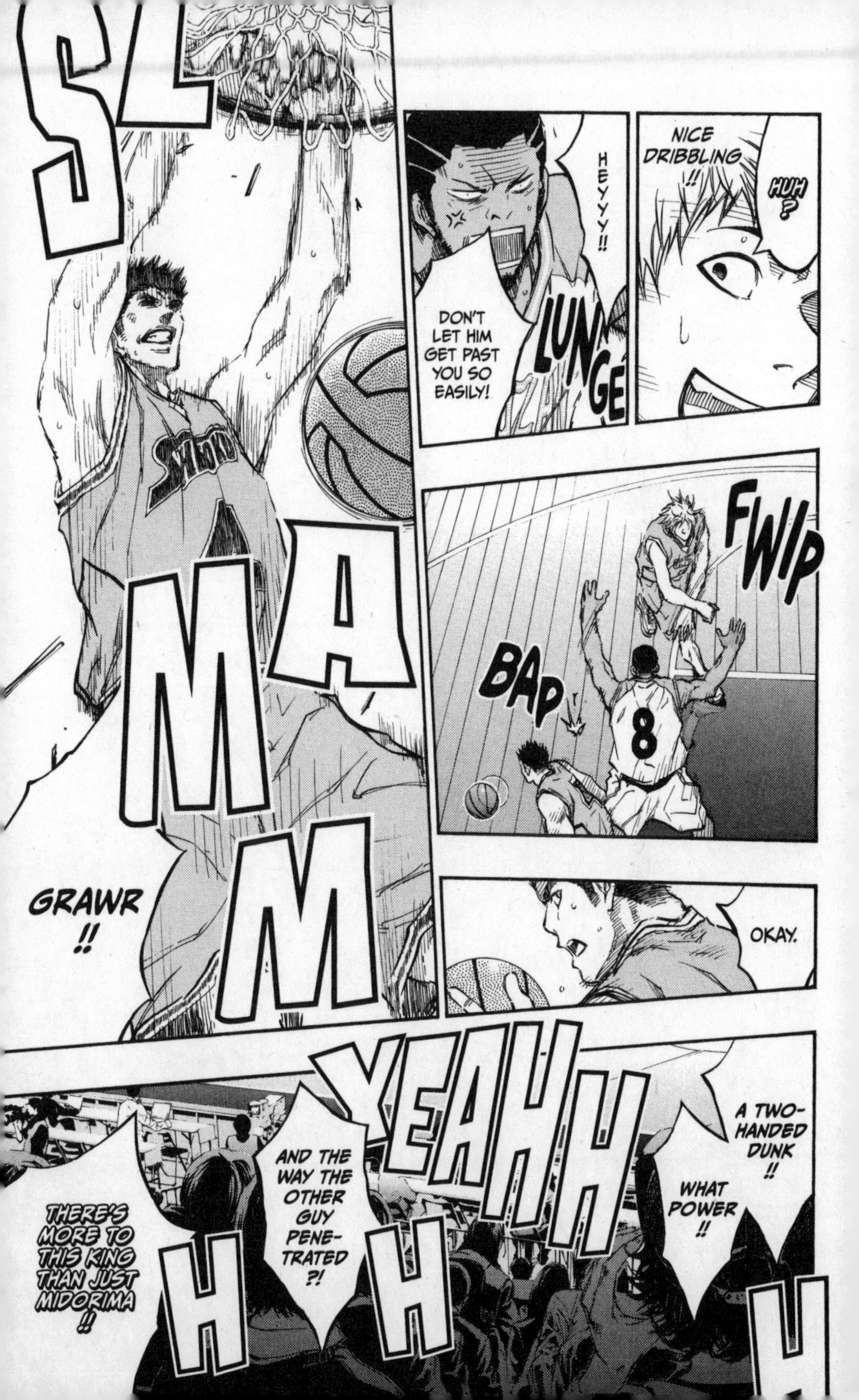
NICE DRIBBLING!!
HUH?
HEYYY!!
DON'T LET HIM GET PAST YOU SO EASILY!
LUNGE
FWIP
BAD
OKAY.
SLAMM
GRAWR!!
A TWO-HANDED DUNK!!
WHAT POWER!!
YEAHHHHH
AND THE WAY THE OTHER GUY PENE-TRATED?!
THERE'S MORE TO THIS KING THAN JUST MIDORIMA!!

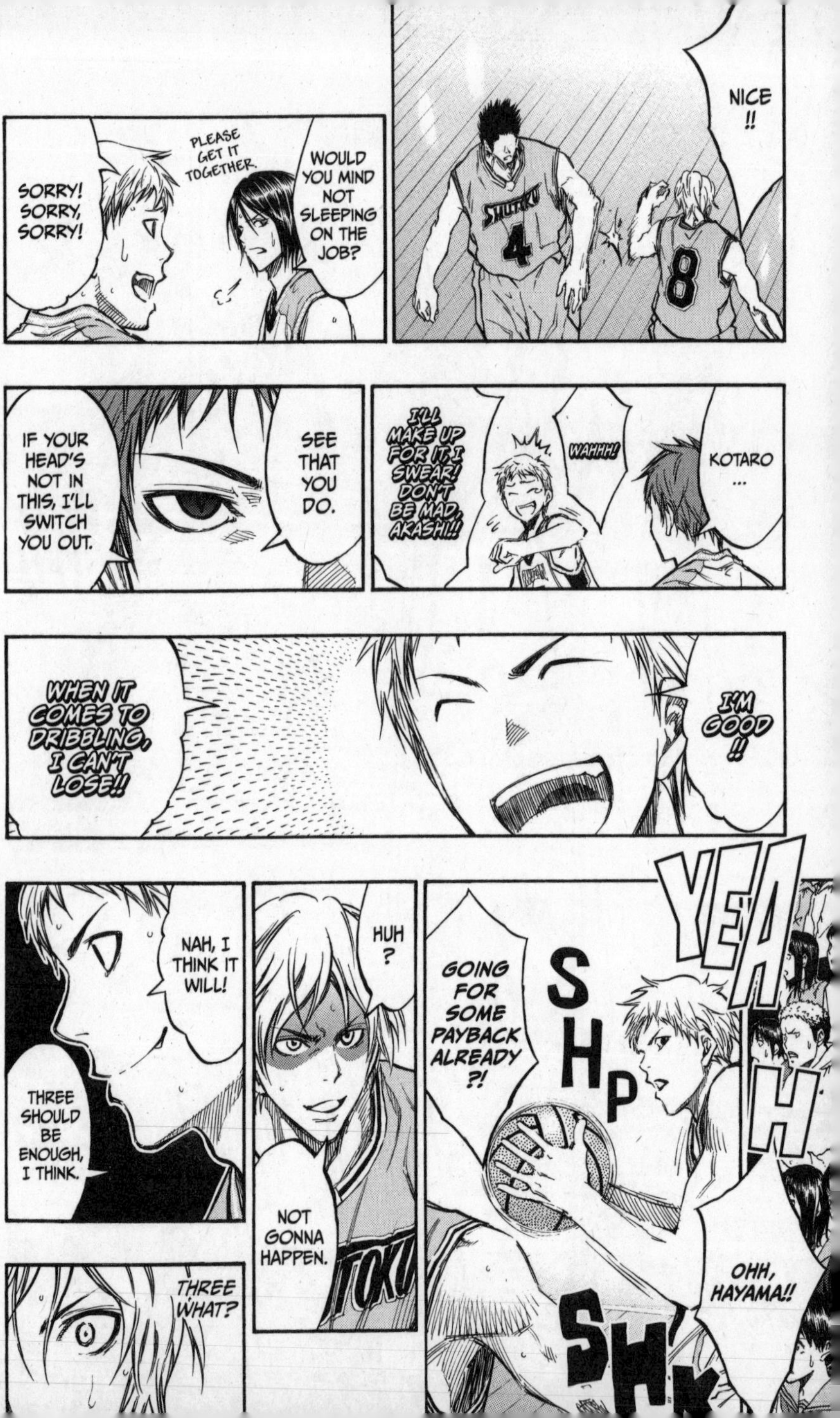
NICE !!
WOULD YOU MIND NOT SLEEPING ON THE JOB?
PLEASE GET IT TOGETHER.
SORRY! SORRY, SORRY!
KOTARO ...
WAHHH!
I'LL MAKE UP FOR IT, I SWEAR! DON'T BE MAD, AKASHI!!
SEE THAT YOU DO.
IF YOUR HEAD'S NOT IN THIS, I'LL SWITCH YOU OUT.
I'M GOOD !!
WHEN IT COMES TO DRIBBLING, I CAN'T LOSE!!
YEAH
GOING FOR SOME PAYBACK ALREADY ?!
SHP
OHH, HAYAMA!!
SHK
HUH ?
NOT GONNA HAPPEN.
NAH, I THINK IT WILL!
THREE SHOULD BE ENOUGH, I THINK.
THREE WHAT?

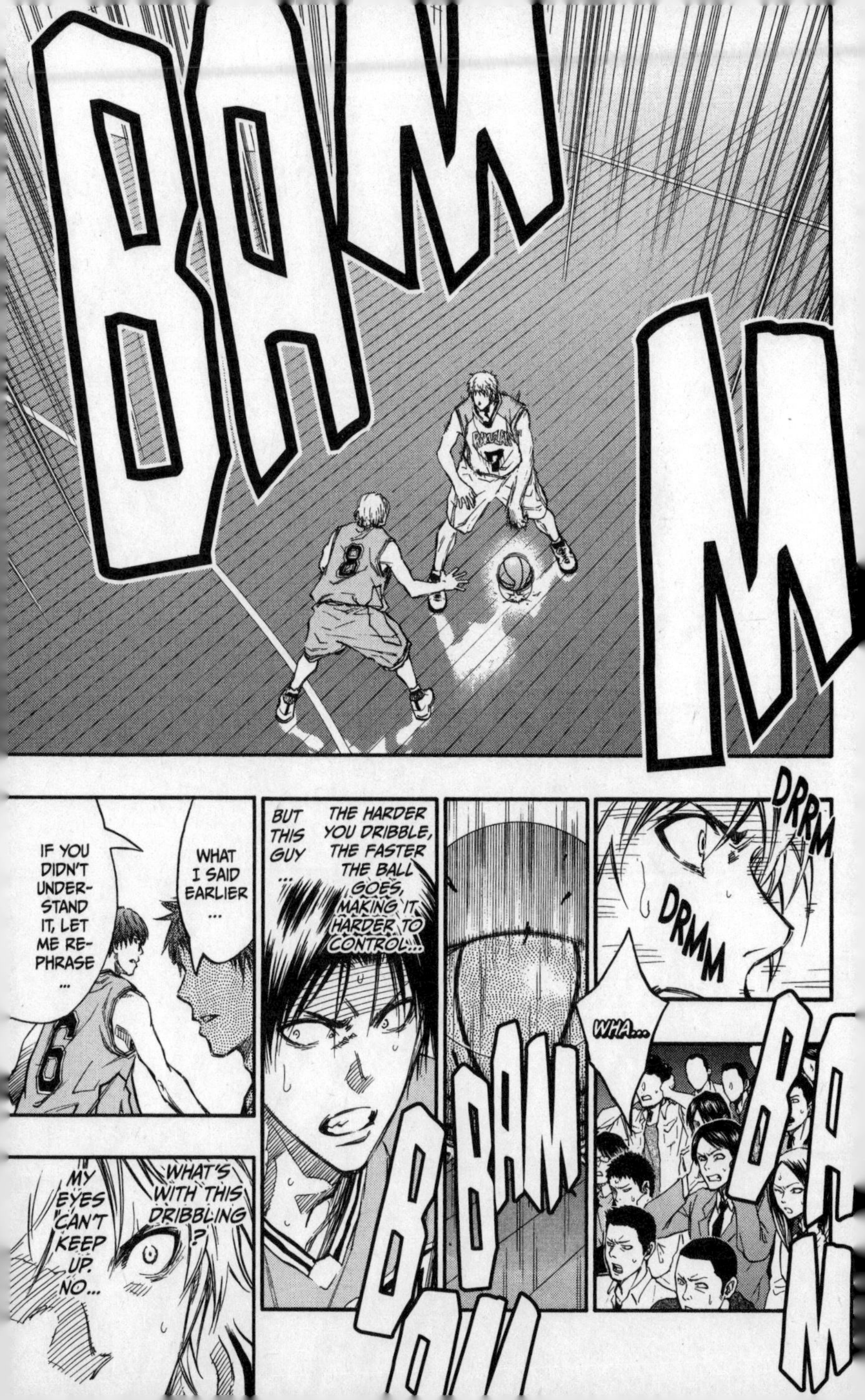
BAMM
DRRM
DRMM
WHA...
BAM
BAM
BAM
THE HARDER YOU DRIBBLE, THE FASTER THE BALL GOES, MAKING IT HARDER TO CONTROL...
BUT THIS GUY...
WHAT I SAID EARLIER...
IF YOU DIDN'T UNDER-STAND IT, LET ME RE-PHRASE...
WHAT'S WITH THIS DRIBBLING?
MY EYES CAN'T KEEP UP. NO...

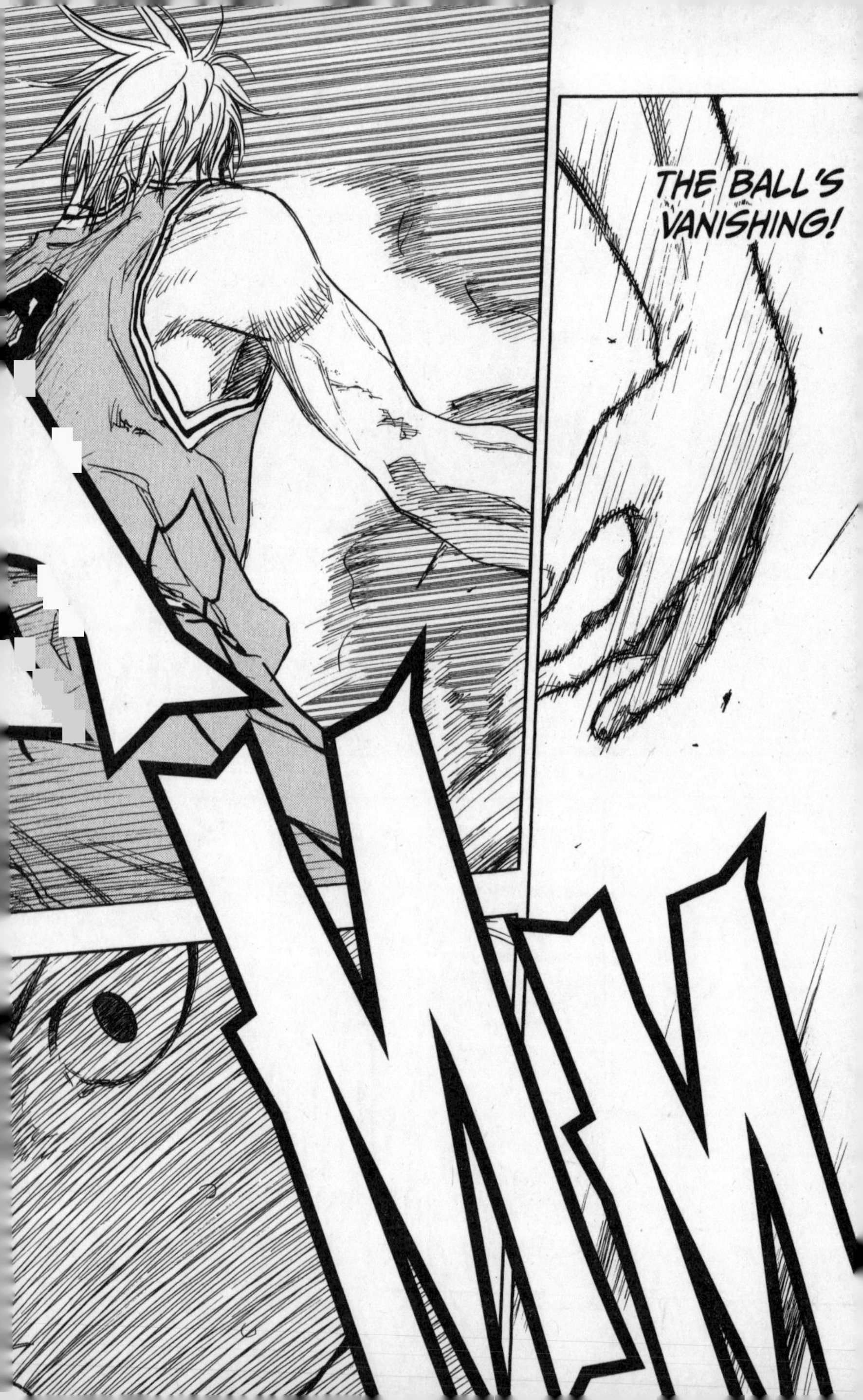
THE BALL'S VANISHING!

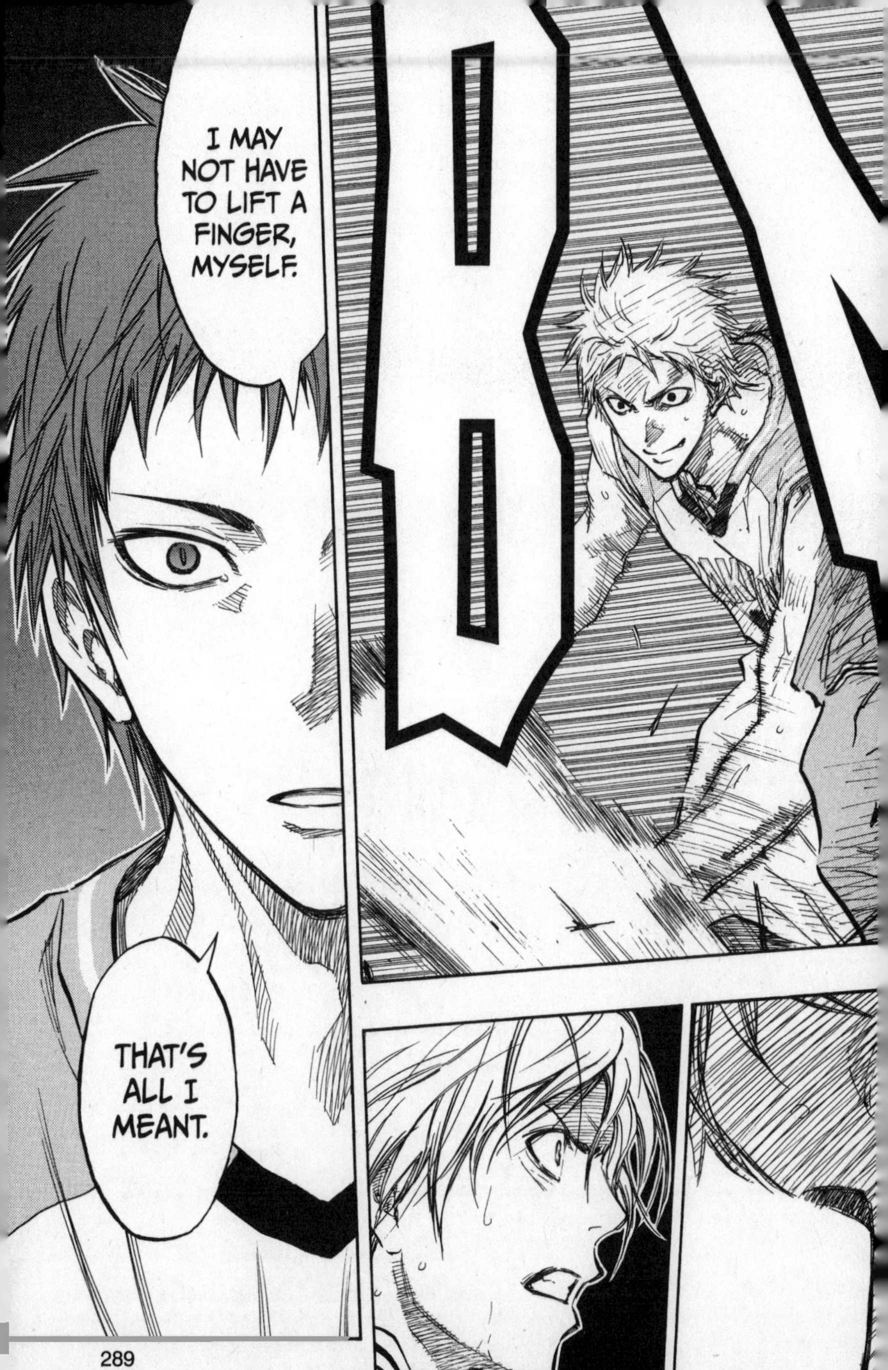
I MAY NOT HAVE TO LIFT A FINGER, MYSELF.
THAT'S ALL I MEANT.

KUROKO'S BASKETBALL BLOOPERS

TAKE 10

HIS SHOOTING IS AS GOOD AS EVER, BUT...
...MIDO-CHIN'S GOTTEN WAY BETTER AT USING SCREENS.
YUM YUM STICKS
POTATOTARD
MOUNTAIN OF FINISHED SNACKS
HE ALWAYS SNACKS ENDLESSLY LIKE THIS, BUT...
...CAN HE REALLY KEEP IT UP UNTIL THE GAME ENDS ?!
CRUNCH
CRUNCH
MUNCH
MUNCH
MIGHT NOT HAVE ENOUGH.

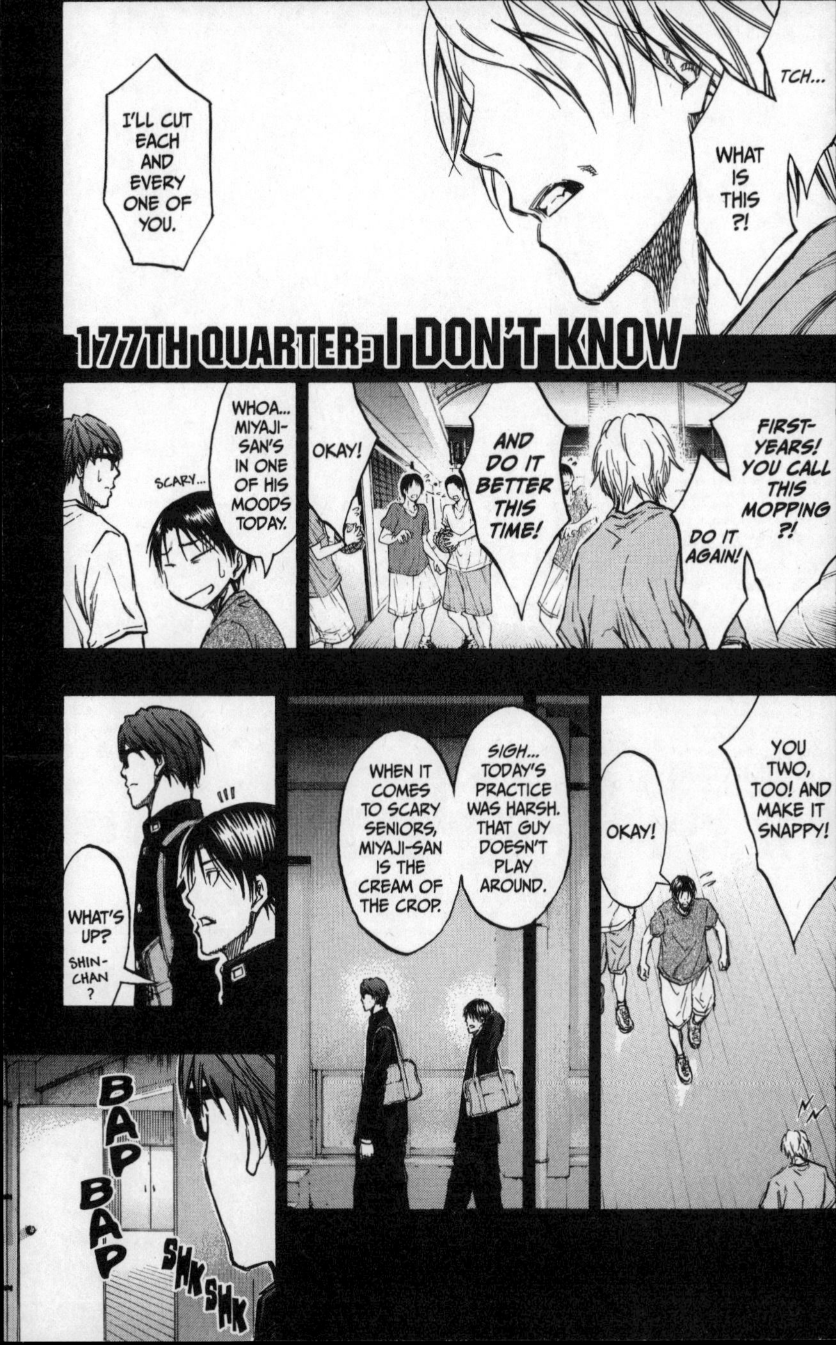
TCH...
WHAT IS THIS?!
I'LL CUT EACH AND EVERY ONE OF YOU.
177TH QUARTER: I DON'T KNOW
FIRST-YEARS! YOU CALL THIS MOPPING?!
DO IT AGAIN!
AND DO IT BETTER THIS TIME!
OKAY!
WHOA... MIYAJI-SAN'S IN ONE OF HIS MOODS TODAY.
SCARY...
YOU TWO, TOO! AND MAKE IT SNAPPY!
OKAY!
SIGH... TODAY'S PRACTICE WAS HARSH. THAT GUY DOESN'T PLAY AROUND.
WHEN IT COMES TO SCARY SENIORS, MIYAJI-SAN IS THE CREAM OF THE CROP.
WHAT'S UP? SHIN-CHAN?
BAP BAP BAP BAP
SHK SHK

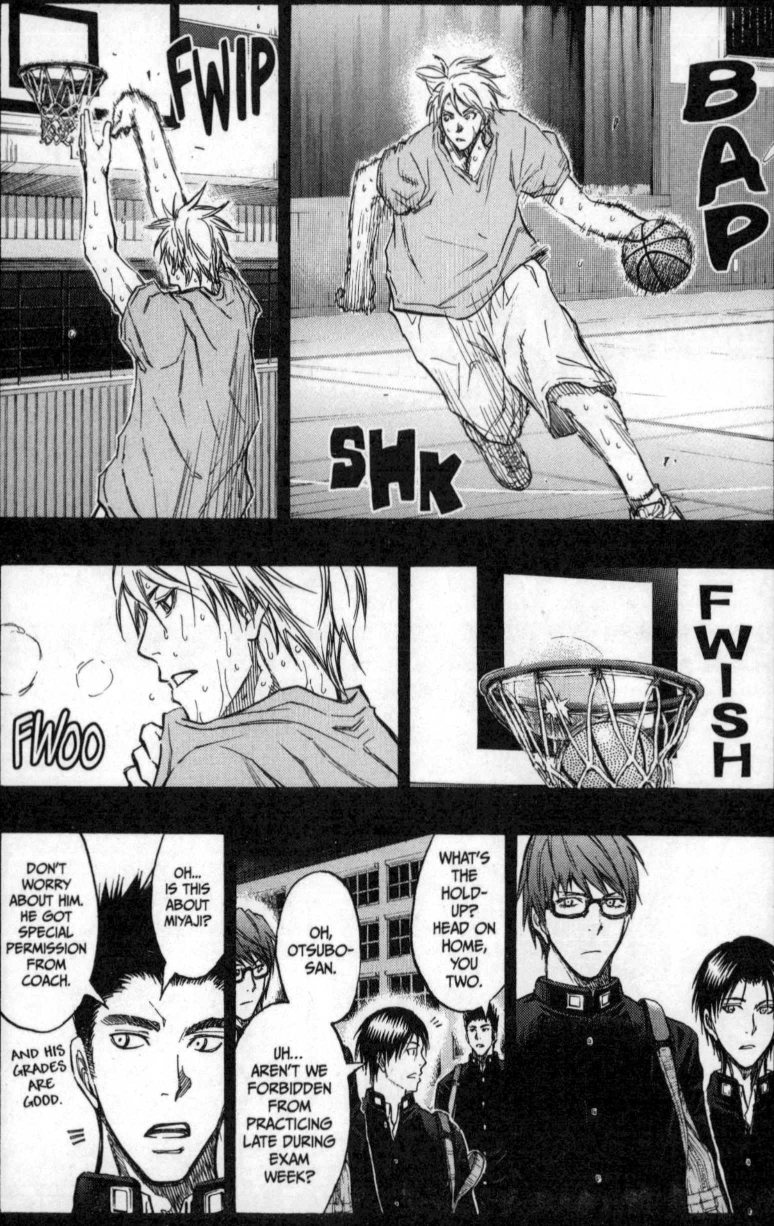
BAP
SHK
FWIP
FWISH
FWOO
WHAT'S THE HOLD-UP? HEAD ON HOME, YOU TWO.
OH, OTSUBO-SAN.
UH... AREN'T WE FORBIDDEN FROM PRACTICING LATE DURING EXAM WEEK?
OH... IS THIS ABOUT MIYAJI?
DON'T WORRY ABOUT HIM. HE GOT SPECIAL PERMISSION FROM COACH.
AND HIS GRADES ARE GOOD.

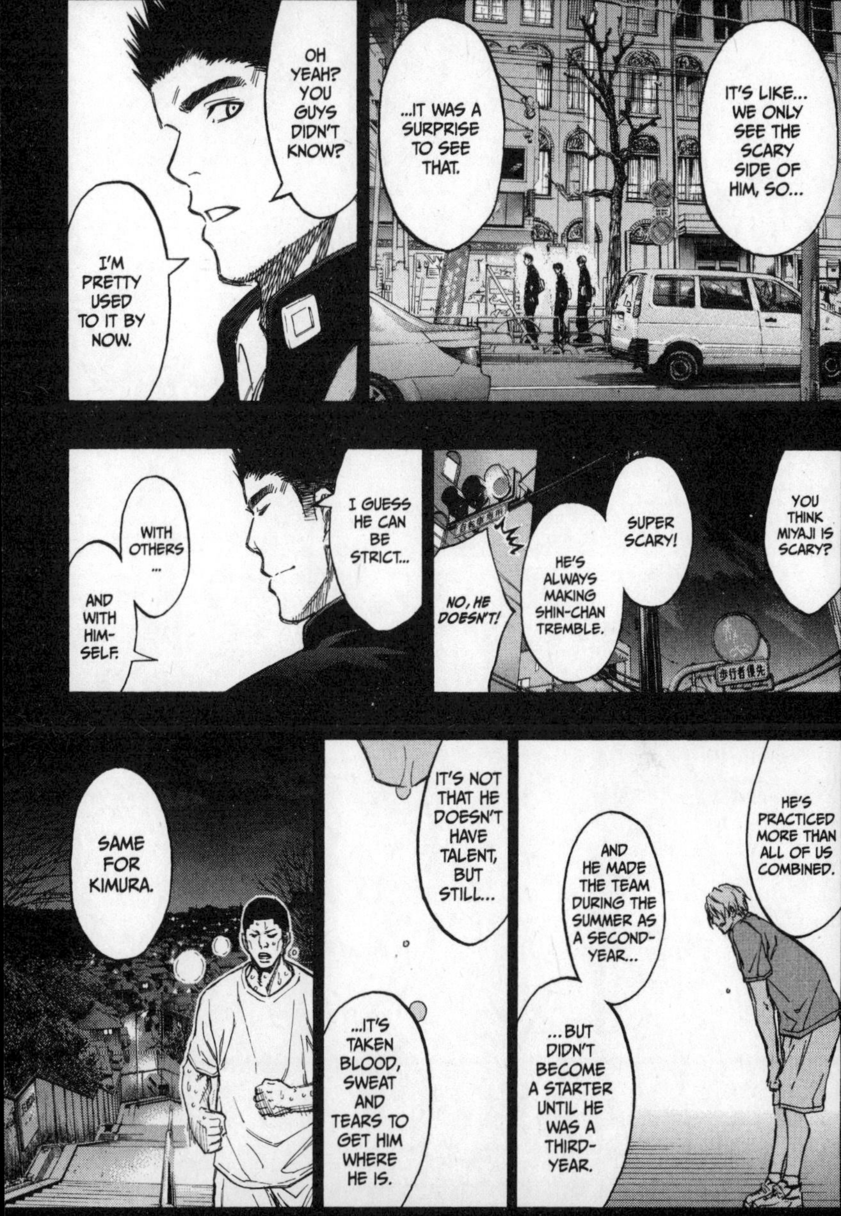
IT'S LIKE... WE ONLY SEE THE SCARY SIDE OF HIM, SO...
...IT WAS A SURPRISE TO SEE THAT.
OH YEAH? YOU GUYS DIDN'T KNOW?
I'M PRETTY USED TO IT BY NOW.
YOU THINK MIYAJI IS SCARY?
SUPER SCARY!
HE'S ALWAYS MAKING SHIN-CHAN TREMBLE.
NO, HE DOESN'T!
歩行者優先
I GUESS HE CAN BE STRICT...
WITH OTHERS...
AND WITH HIM-SELF.
HE'S PRACTICED MORE THAN ALL OF US COMBINED.
AND HE MADE THE TEAM DURING THE SUMMER AS A SECOND-YEAR...
...BUT DIDN'T BECOME A STARTER UNTIL HE WAS A THIRD-YEAR.
IT'S NOT THAT HE DOESN'T HAVE TALENT, BUT STILL...
...IT'S TAKEN BLOOD, SWEAT AND TEARS TO GET HIM WHERE HE IS.
SAME FOR KIMURA.

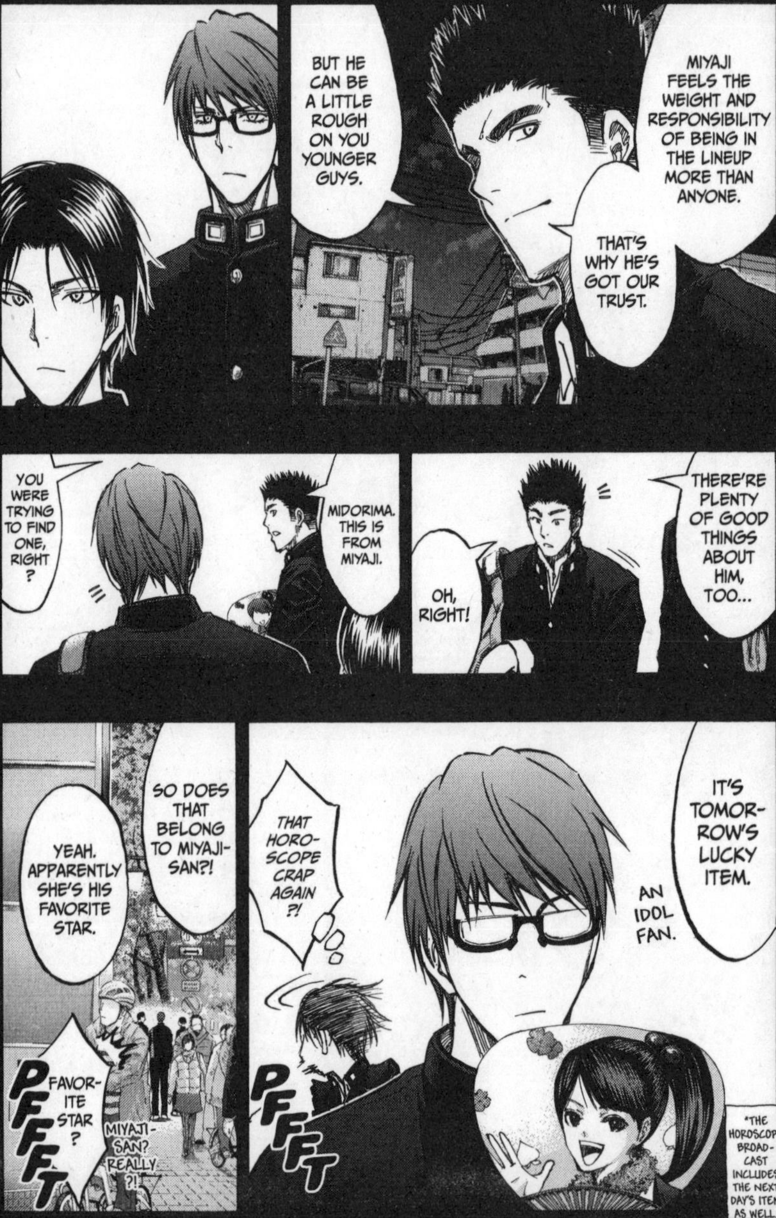
MIYAJI FEELS THE WEIGHT AND RESPONSIBILITY OF BEING IN THE LINEUP MORE THAN ANYONE.
THAT'S WHY HE'S GOT OUR TRUST.
BUT HE CAN BE A LITTLE ROUGH ON YOU YOUNGER GUYS.
THERE'RE PLENTY OF GOOD THINGS ABOUT HIM, TOO...
OH, RIGHT!
MIDORIMA. THIS IS FROM MIYAJI.
YOU WERE TRYING TO FIND ONE, RIGHT?
IT'S TOMORROW'S LUCKY ITEM.
AN IDOL FAN.
THAT HOROSCOPE CRAP AGAIN?!
PFFFT
*THE HOROSCOP BROAD-CAST INCLUDES THE NEXT DAY'S ITEM AS WELL.
SO DOES THAT BELONG TO MIYAJI-SAN?!
YEAH. APPARENTLY SHE'S HIS FAVORITE STAR.
FAVORITE STAR?
MIYAJI-SAN? REALLY?!
PFFFT

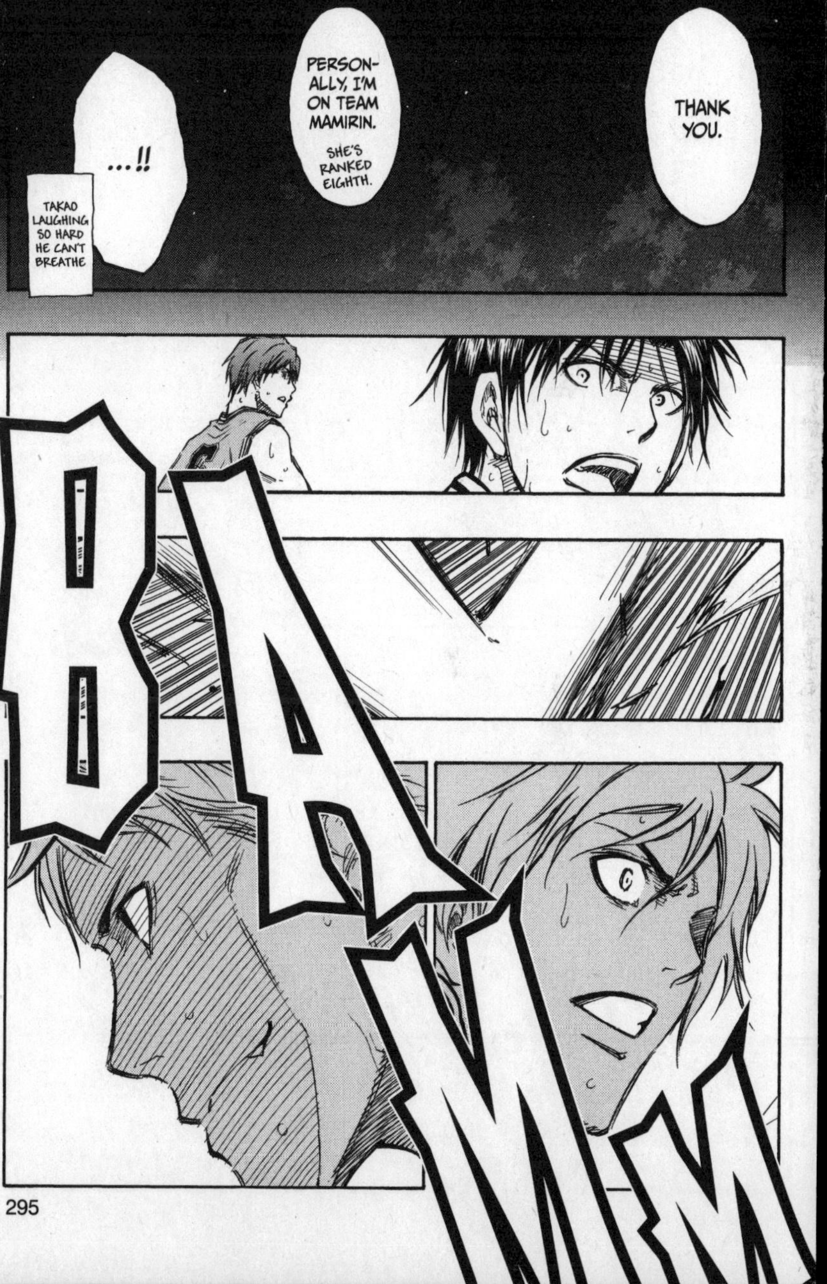
THANK YOU.
PERSON-ALLY, I'M ON TEAM MAMIRIN.
SHE'S RANKED EIGHTH.
...!!
TAKAO LAUGHING SO HARD HE CAN'T BREATHE
BAMM

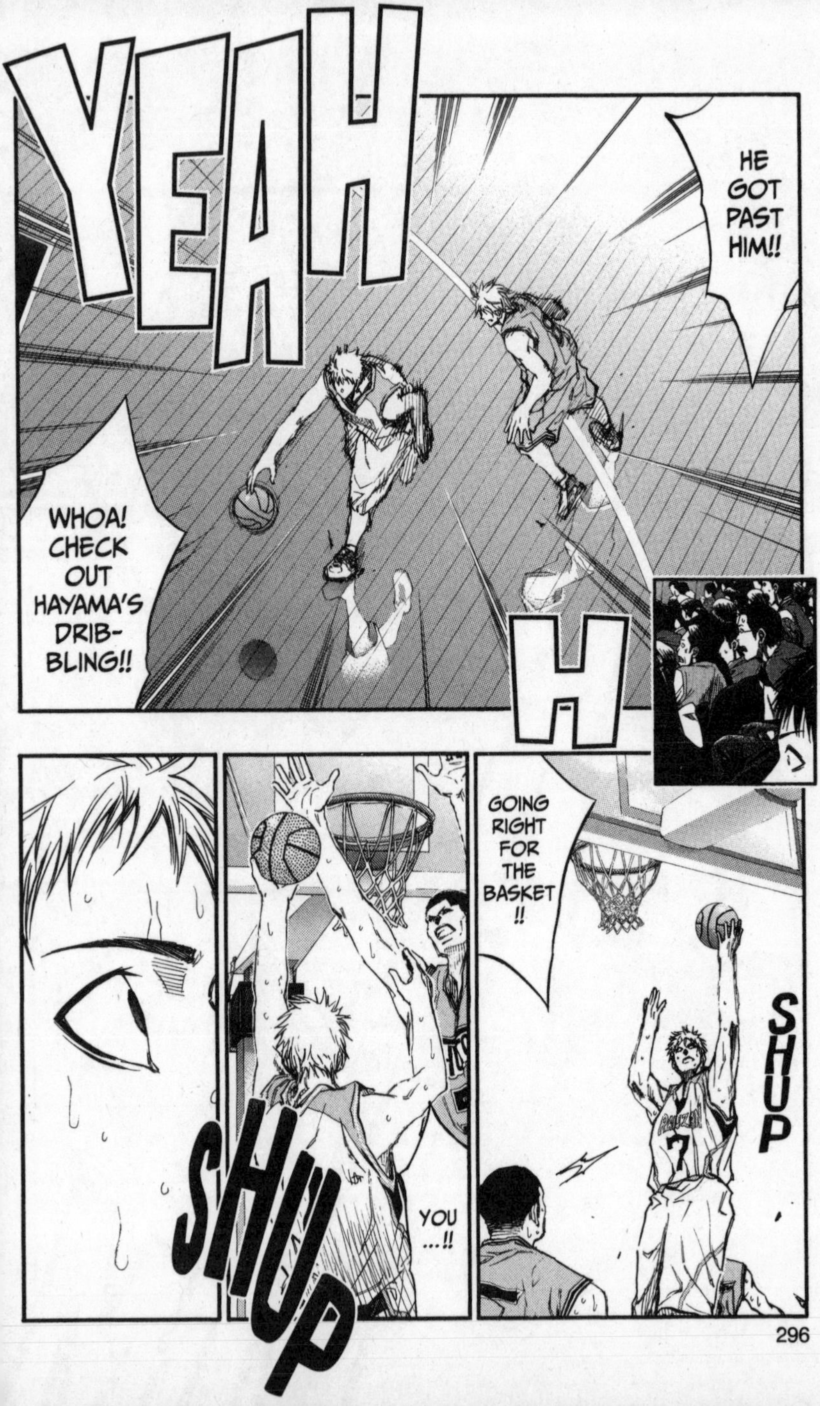
HE GOT PAST HIM!!
YEAH
WHOA! CHECK OUT HAYAMA'S DRIB-BLING!!
H
GOING RIGHT FOR THE BASKET!!
SHUP
YOU ...!!
SHUP

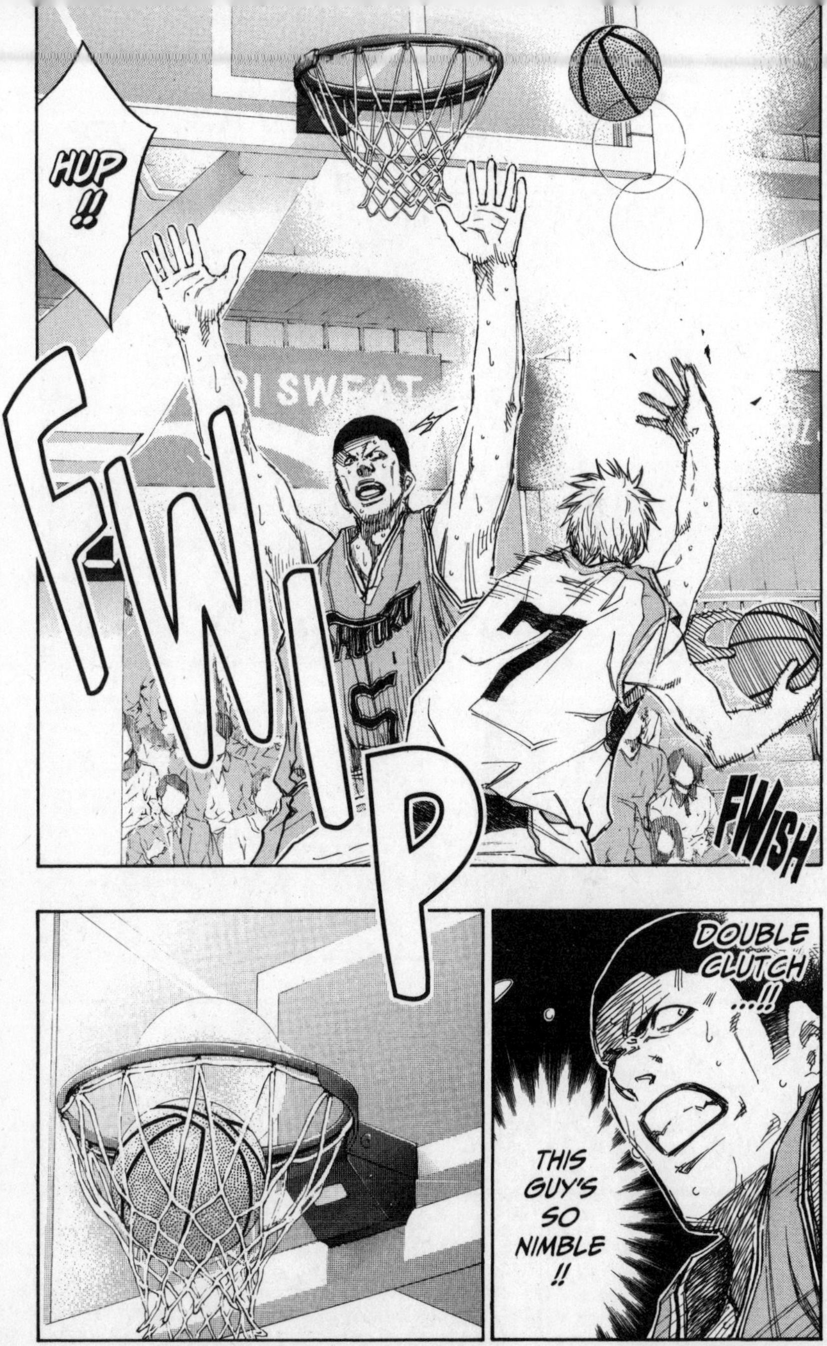
HUP!!
FWIP
FWISH
DOUBLE CLUTCH...!!
THIS GUY'S SO NIMBLE!!

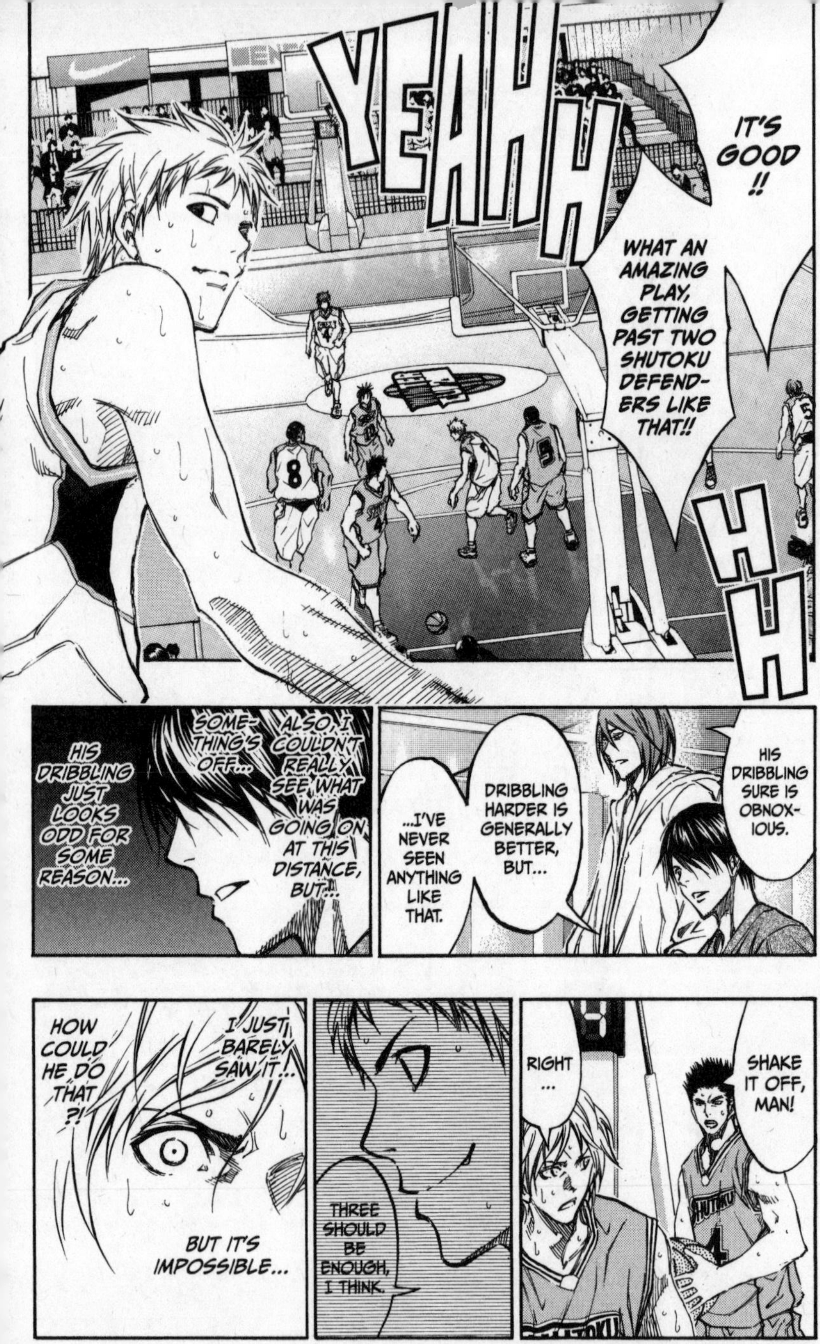
IT'S GOOD!!
WHAT AN AMAZING PLAY, GETTING PAST TWO SHUTOKU DEFENDERS LIKE THAT!!
YEAHHHHH
HIS DRIBBLING SURE IS OBNOXIOUS.
DRIBBLING HARDER IS GENERALLY BETTER, BUT...
...I'VE NEVER SEEN ANYTHING LIKE THAT.
ALSO, I COULDN'T REALLY SEE WHAT WAS GOING ON AT THIS DISTANCE, BUT...
SOMETHING'S OFF...
HIS DRIBBLING JUST LOOKS ODD FOR SOME REASON...
SHAKE IT OFF, MAN!
RIGHT...
THREE SHOULD BE ENOUGH, I THINK.
I JUST BARELY SAW IT...
HOW COULD HE DO THAT?!
BUT IT'S IMPOSSIBLE...

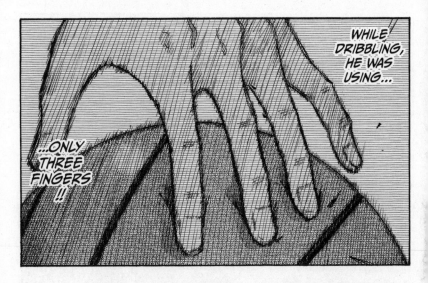

WHILE DRIBBLING, HE WAS USING...

...ONLY THREE FINGERS !!

THE SECRET BEHIND HIS STRONG DRIBBLING MUST BE...

...HOW HE FOCUSES ALL THE POWER IN HIS BODY INTO HIS FINGER-TIPS...

SO IF HE'S USING ONLY THREE...

...DOES THAT MEAN...

...HIS DRIBBLING CAN STILL BE TAKEN UP A COUPLE NOTCHES?!

HOW ?!

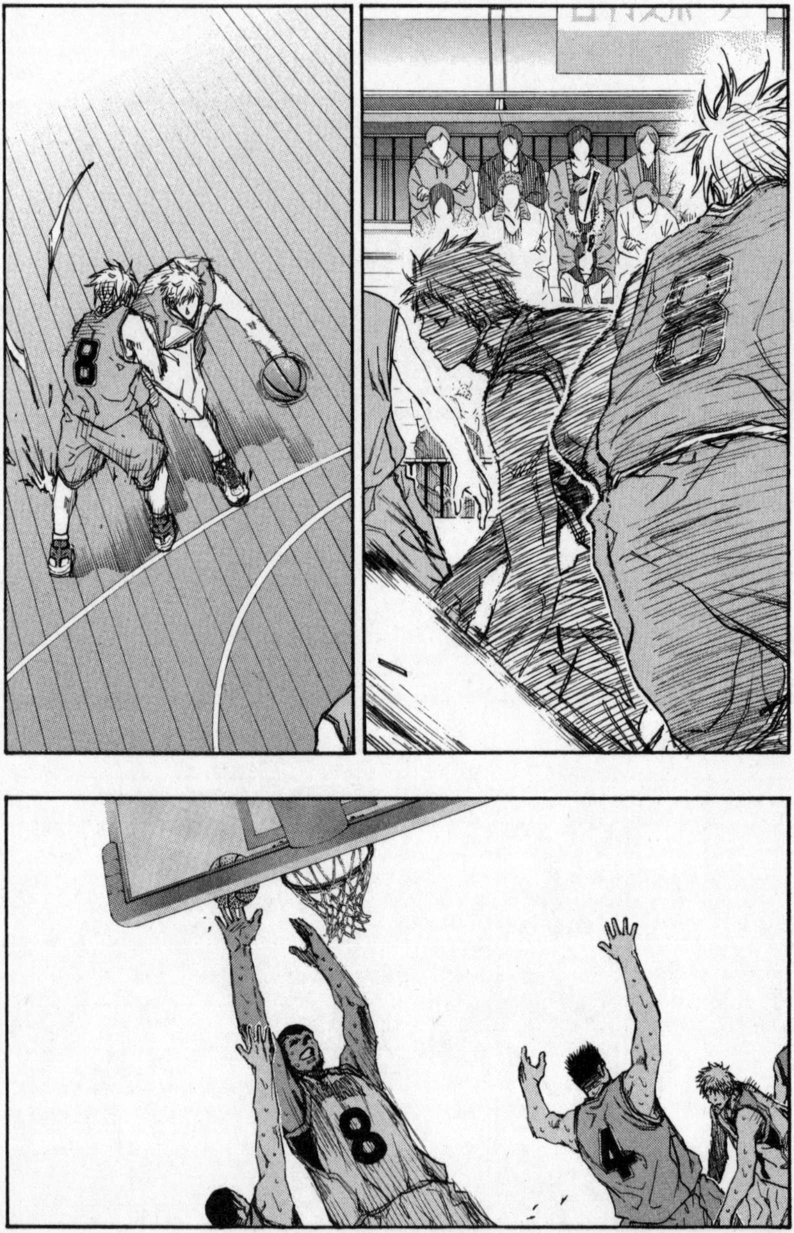

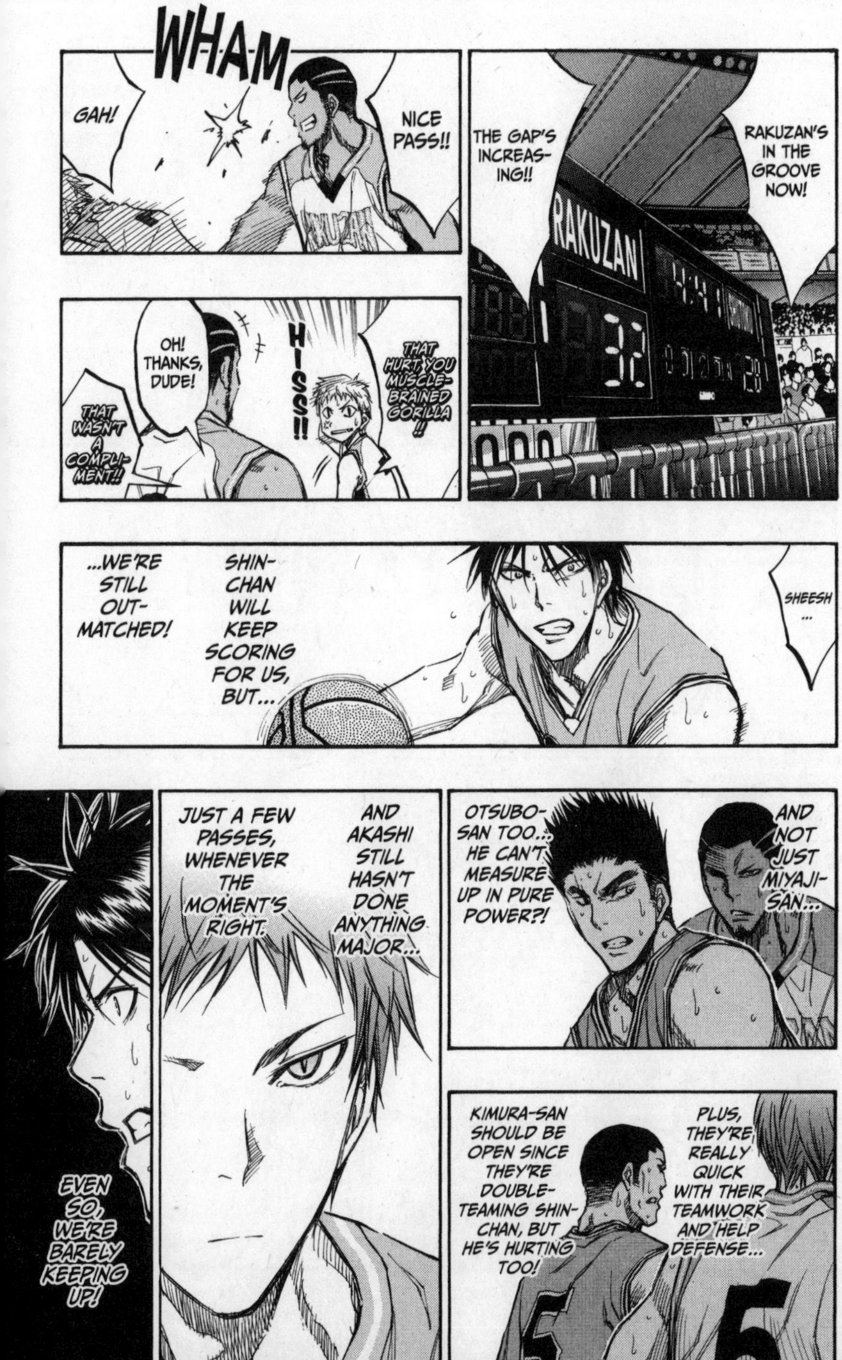
RAKUZAN'S IN THE GROOVE NOW!
THE GAP'S INCREAS-ING!!
RAKUZAN
WHAM
NICE PASS!!
GAH!
THAT HURT, YOU MUSCLE-BRAINED GORILLA!!
HISS!!
OH! THANKS, DUDE!
THAT WASN'T A COMPLI-MENT!!
SHEESH...
SHIN-CHAN WILL KEEP SCORING FOR US, BUT...
...WE'RE STILL OUT-MATCHED!
AND NOT JUST MIYAJI-SAN...
OTSUBO-SAN TOO... HE CAN'T MEASURE UP IN PURE POWER?!
PLUS, THEY'RE REALLY QUICK WITH THEIR TEAMWORK AND HELP DEFENSE...
KIMURA-SAN SHOULD BE OPEN SINCE THEY'RE DOUBLE-TEAMING SHIN-CHAN, BUT HE'S HURTING TOO!
AND AKASHI STILL HASN'T DONE ANYTHING MAJOR...
JUST A FEW PASSES, WHENEVER THE MOMENT'S RIGHT.
EVEN SO, WE'RE BARELY KEEPING UP!

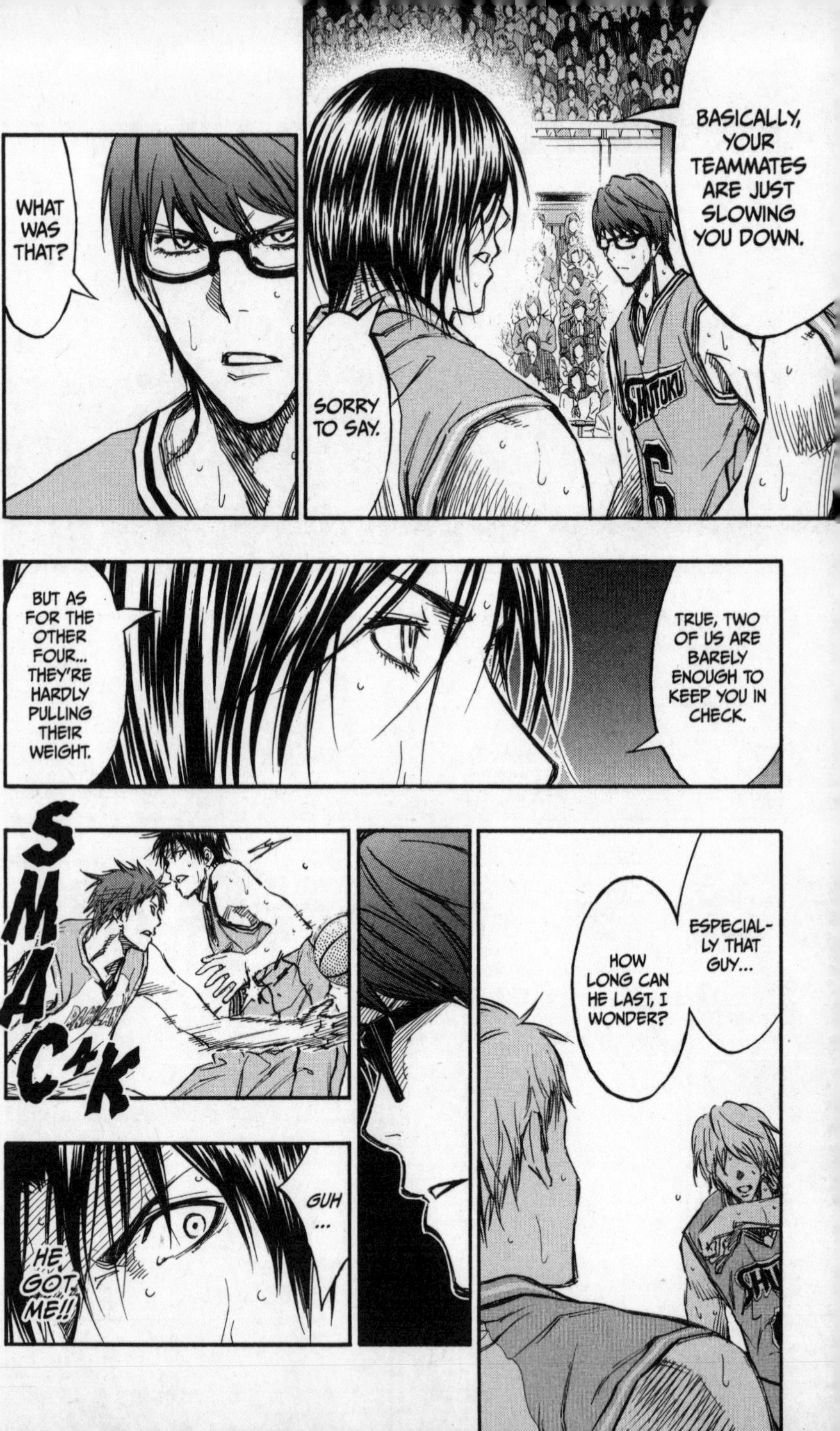
BASICALLY, YOUR TEAMMATES ARE JUST SLOWING YOU DOWN.
SORRY TO SAY.
WHAT WAS THAT?
TRUE, TWO OF US ARE BARELY ENOUGH TO KEEP YOU IN CHECK.
BUT AS FOR THE OTHER FOUR... THEY'RE HARDLY PULLING THEIR WEIGHT.
ESPECIAL-LY THAT GUY...
HOW LONG CAN HE LAST, I WONDER?
SMACK
GUH ...
HE GOT ME!!

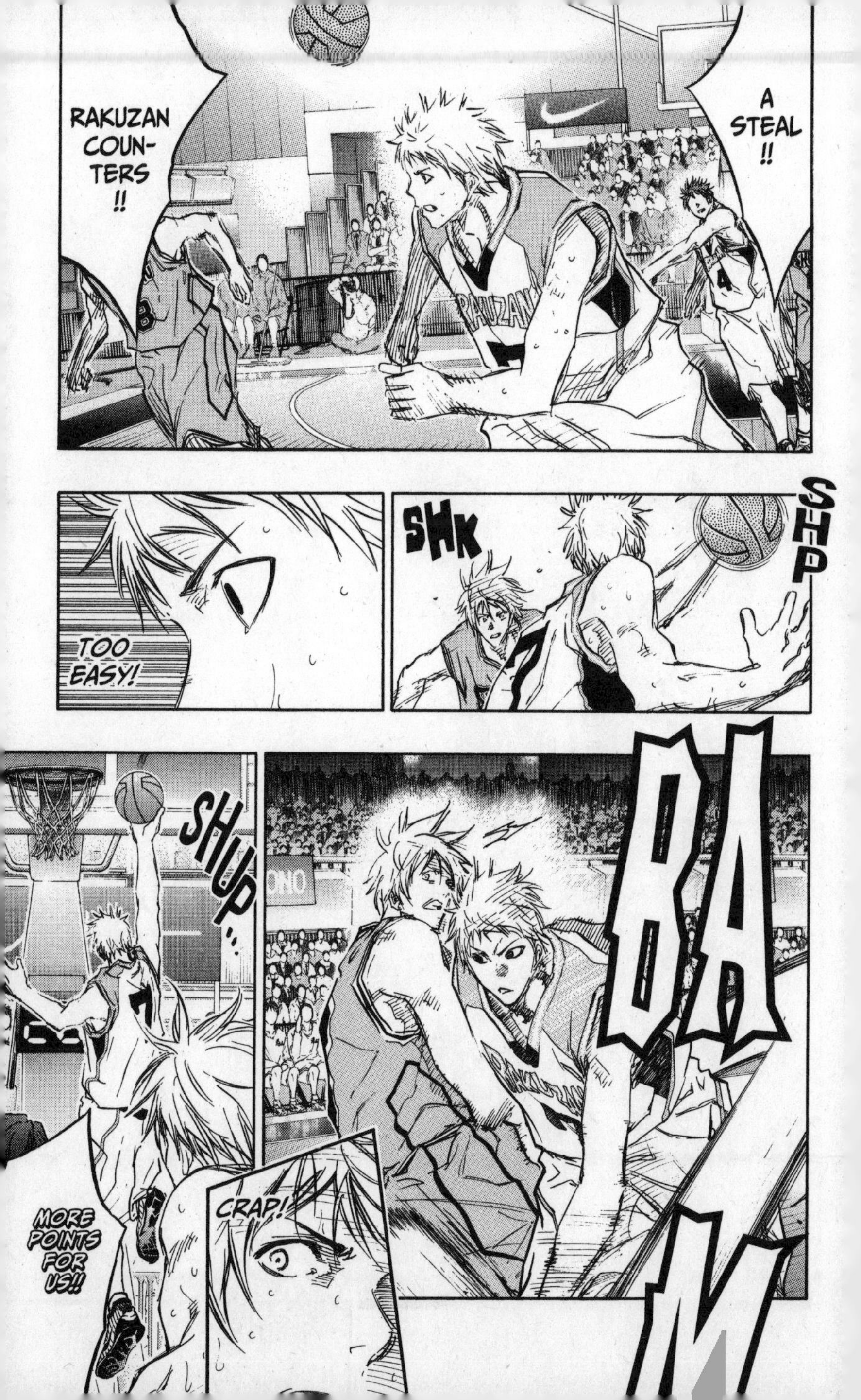
A STEAL!!
RAKUZAN COUNTERS!!
SHP
SHK
TOO EASY!
BAM
CRAP!
SHUP...
MORE POINTS FOR US!!

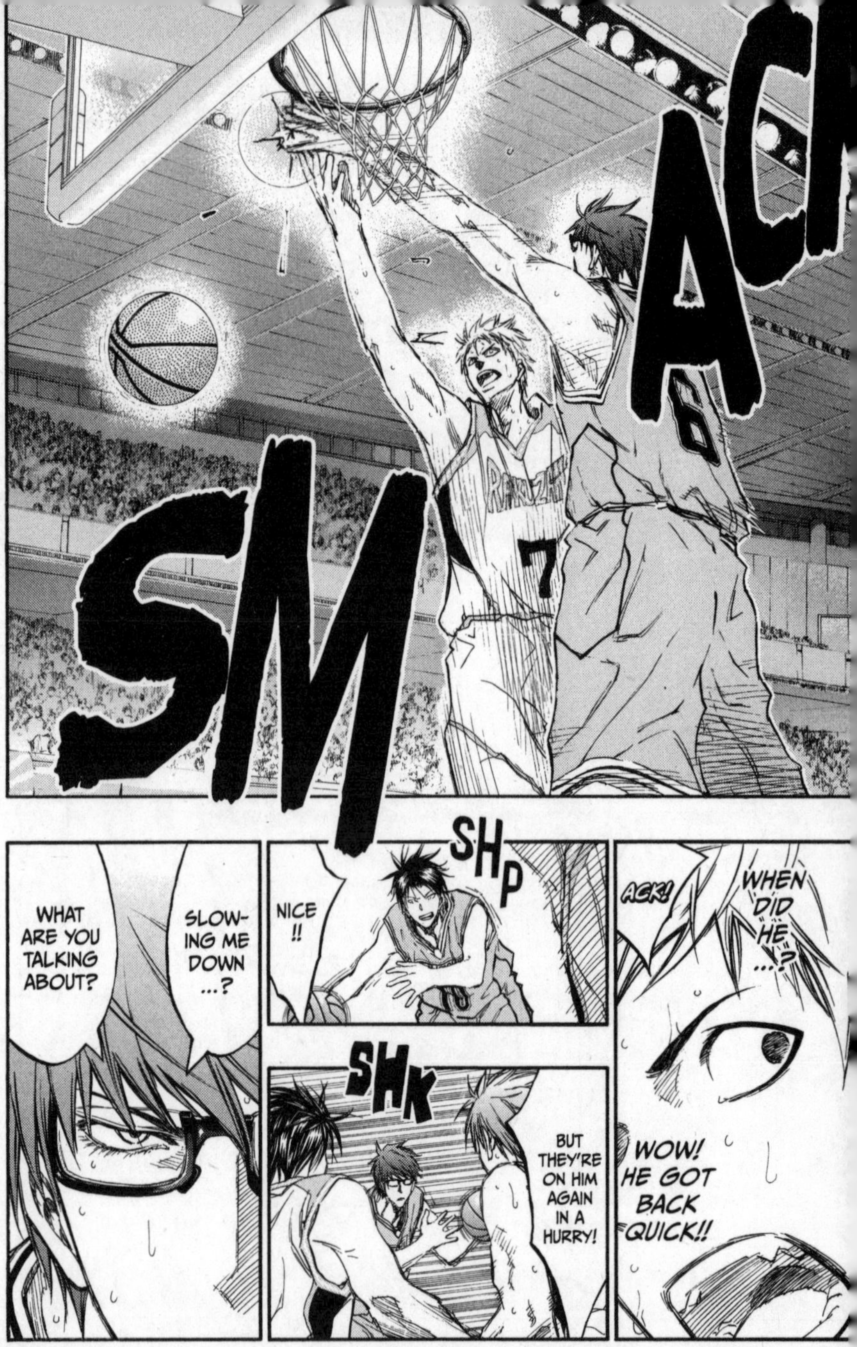
SMAC
WHEN DID HE ...?
ACK!
WOW! HE GOT BACK QUICK!!
SHP
NICE!!
SHK
BUT THEY'RE ON HIM AGAIN IN A HURRY!
SLOWING ME DOWN ...?
WHAT ARE YOU TALKING ABOUT?

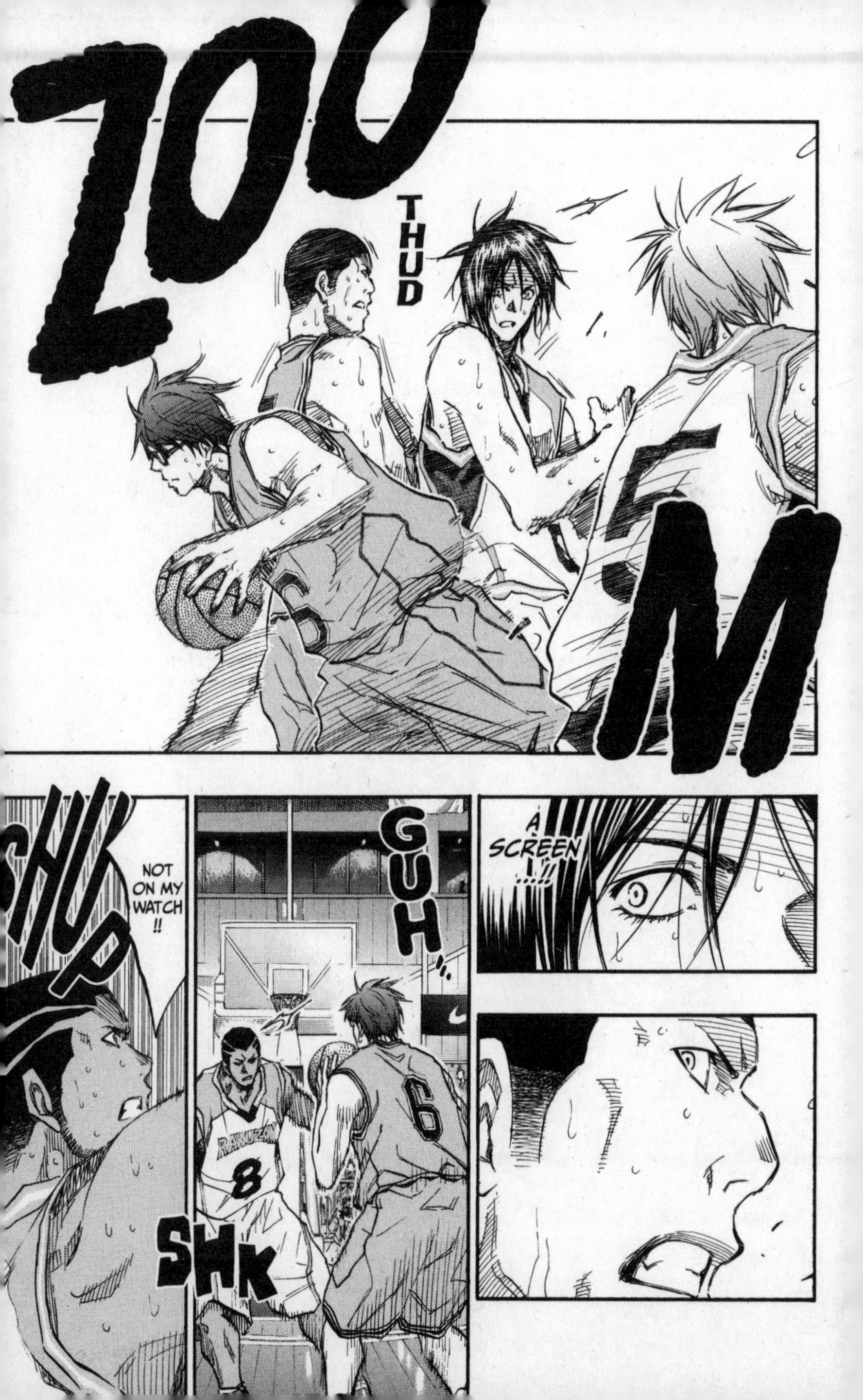
ZOOM
THUD
A SCREEN ...!!
GUH..
SHK
SHUP
NOT ON MY WATCH !!

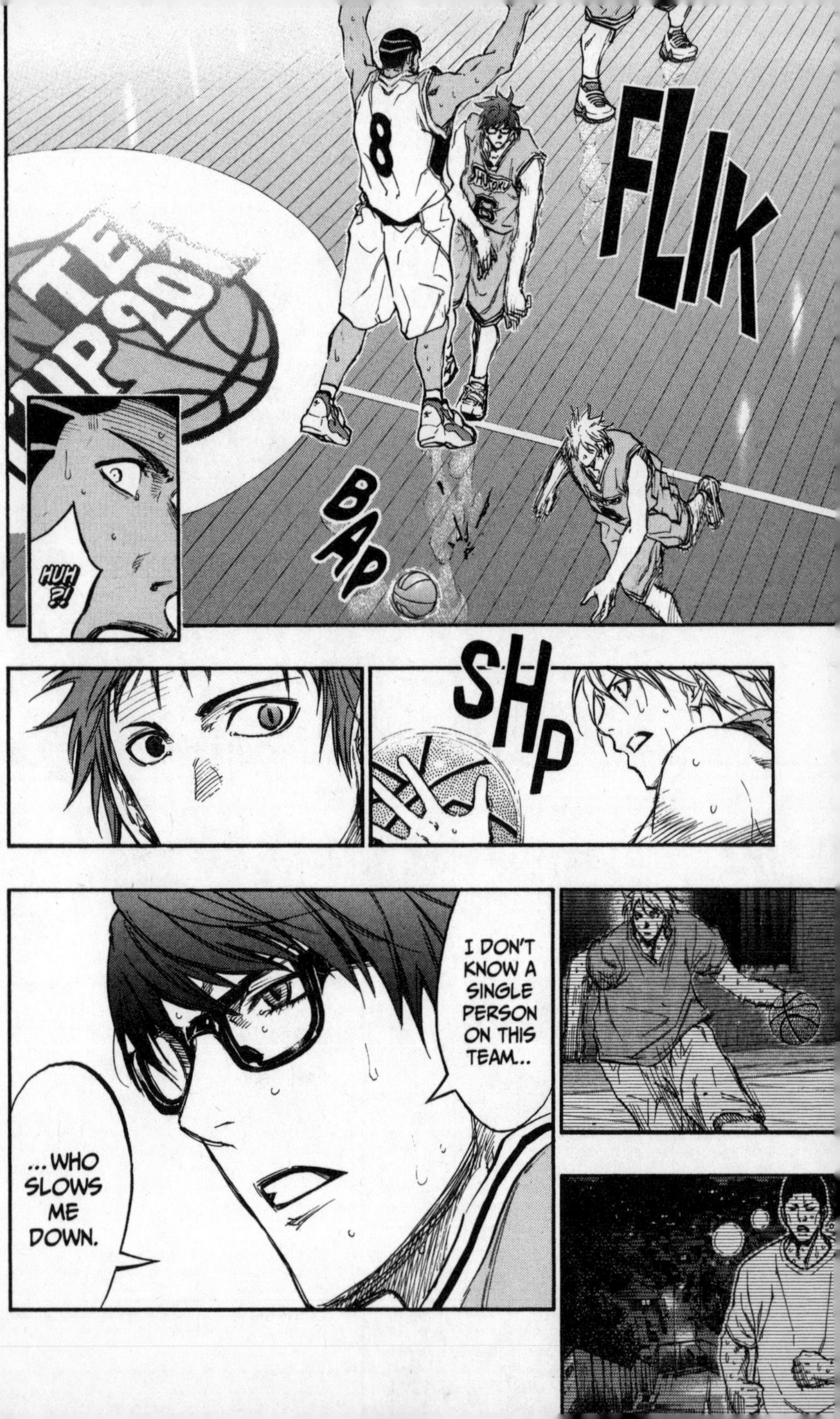
FLIK
BAP
HUH ?!
SHP
I DON'T KNOW A SINGLE PERSON ON THIS TEAM...
...WHO SLOWS ME DOWN.

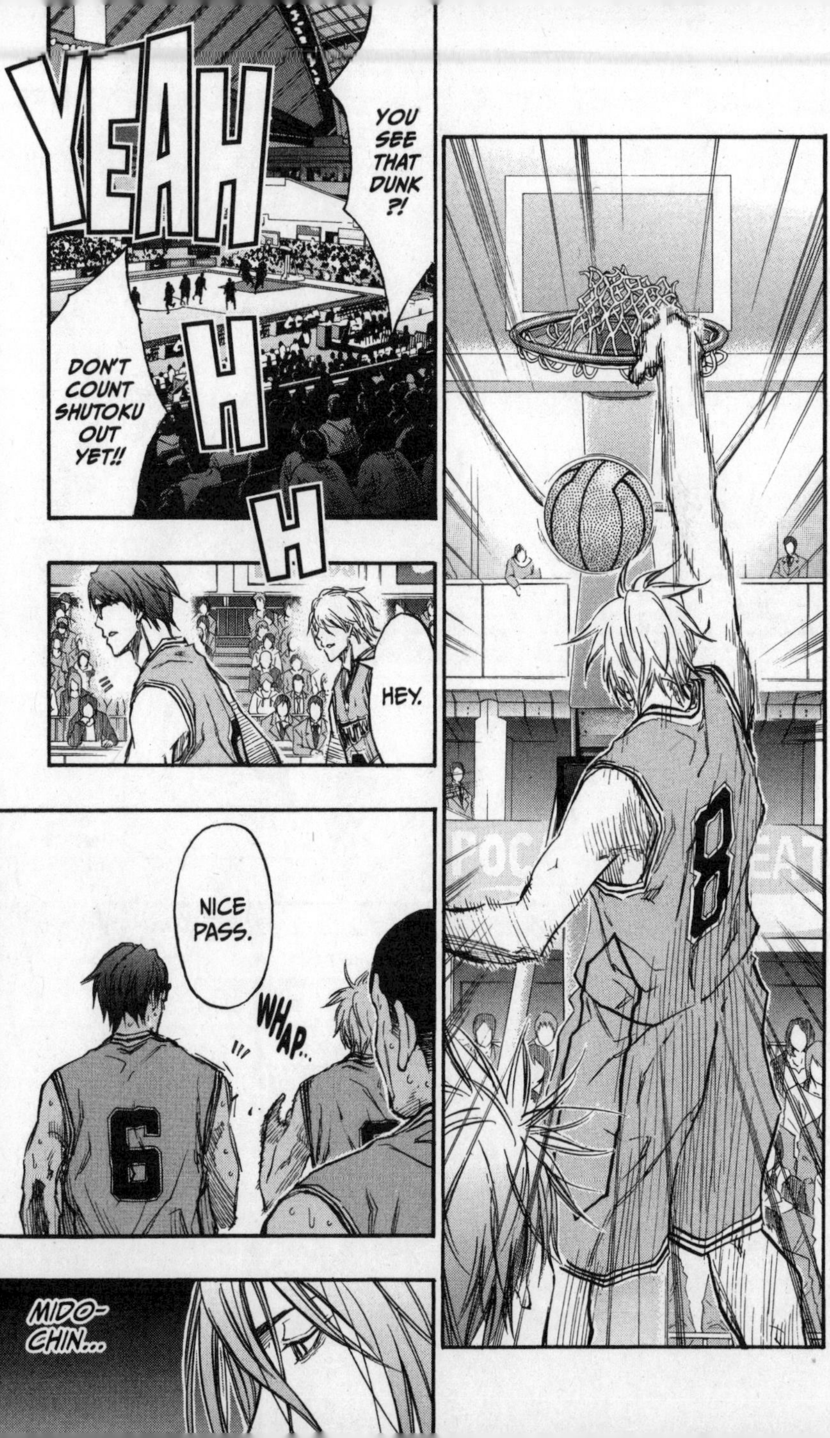
YOU SEE THAT DUNK?!
YEAHHH
DON'T COUNT SHUTOKU OUT YET!!
HEY.
NICE PASS.
WHAP...
MIDO-CHIN...

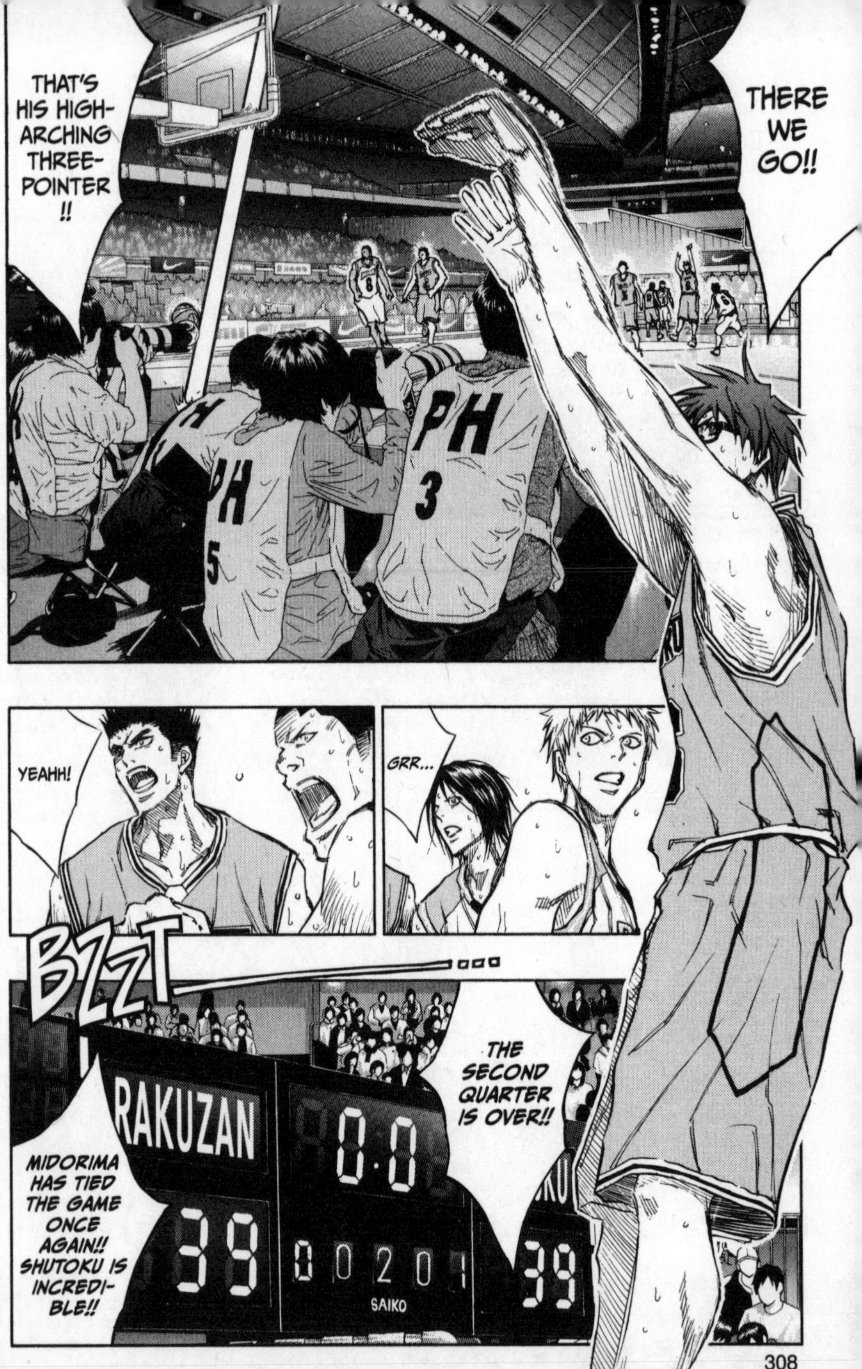
THERE WE GO!!
THAT'S HIS HIGH-ARCHING THREE-POINTER!!
GRR...
YEAHH!
BZZT
THE SECOND QUARTER IS OVER!!
MIDORIMA HAS TIED THE GAME ONCE AGAIN!! SHUTOKU IS INCREDIBLE!!
RAKUZAN
39
39
SAIKO

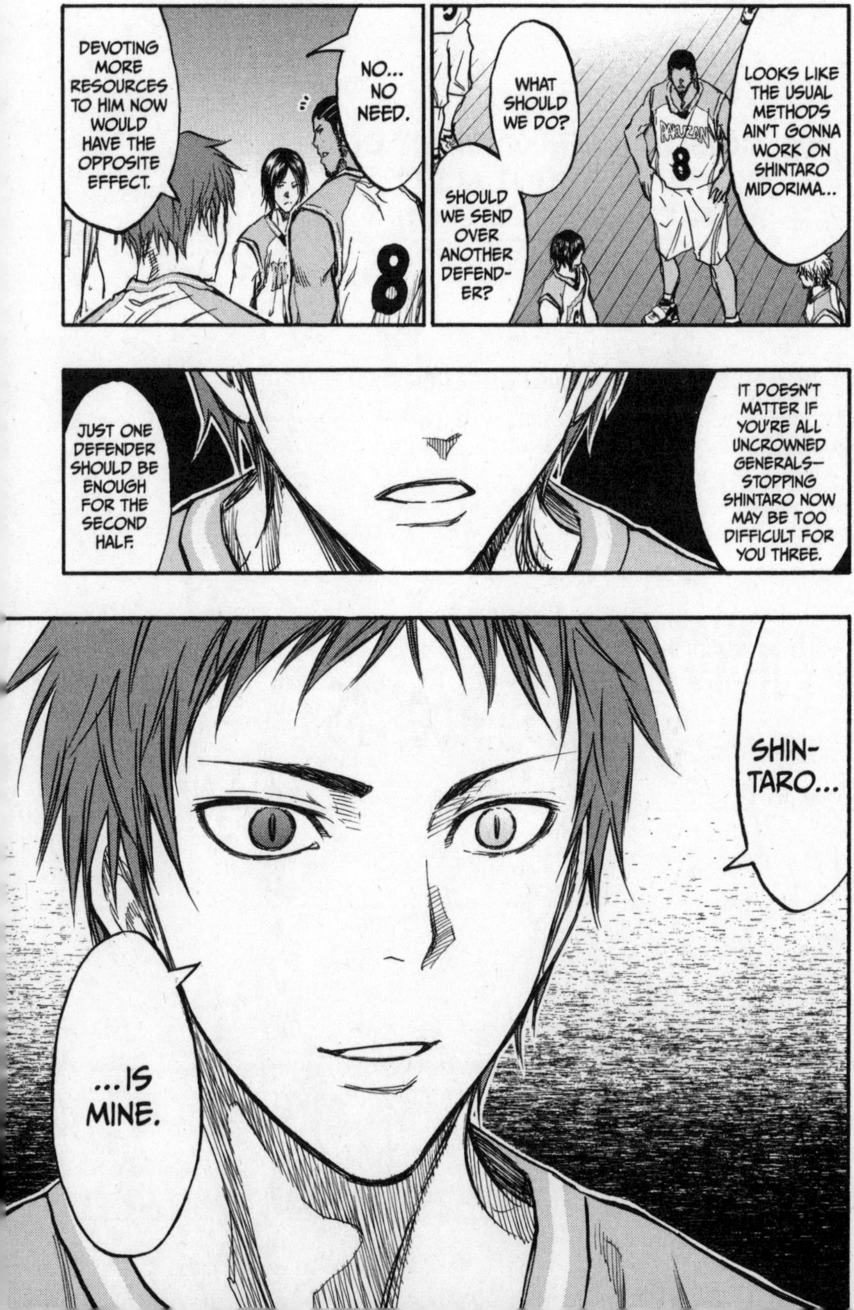
LOOKS LIKE THE USUAL METHODS AIN'T GONNA WORK ON SHINTARO MIDORIMA...
WHAT SHOULD WE DO?
SHOULD WE SEND OVER ANOTHER DEFENDER?
RAKUZAN
NO... NO NEED.
DEVOTING MORE RESOURCES TO HIM NOW WOULD HAVE THE OPPOSITE EFFECT.
IT DOESN'T MATTER IF YOU'RE ALL UNCROWNED GENERALS—STOPPING SHINTARO NOW MAY BE TOO DIFFICULT FOR YOU THREE.
JUST ONE DEFENDER SHOULD BE ENOUGH FOR THE SECOND HALF.
SHIN-TARO...
...IS MINE.

KUROKO'S BASKETBALL Q&A W/ HALFWAY-DECENT ANSWERS

Q. MOMOI AND RIKO CAN'T COOK, BUT WHAT ABOUT ALEX?
(FLOWER ARRANGER from YAMAGATA PREFECTURE)

A. HER SPECIALTY IS BARBECUE.

KUROKO'S BASKETBALL BLOOPERS
TAKE 7

AN IDOL FAN.
IT'S TOMORROW'S LUCKY ITEM.
IDOL ?!
THAT GUY'S AN IDOL ?!

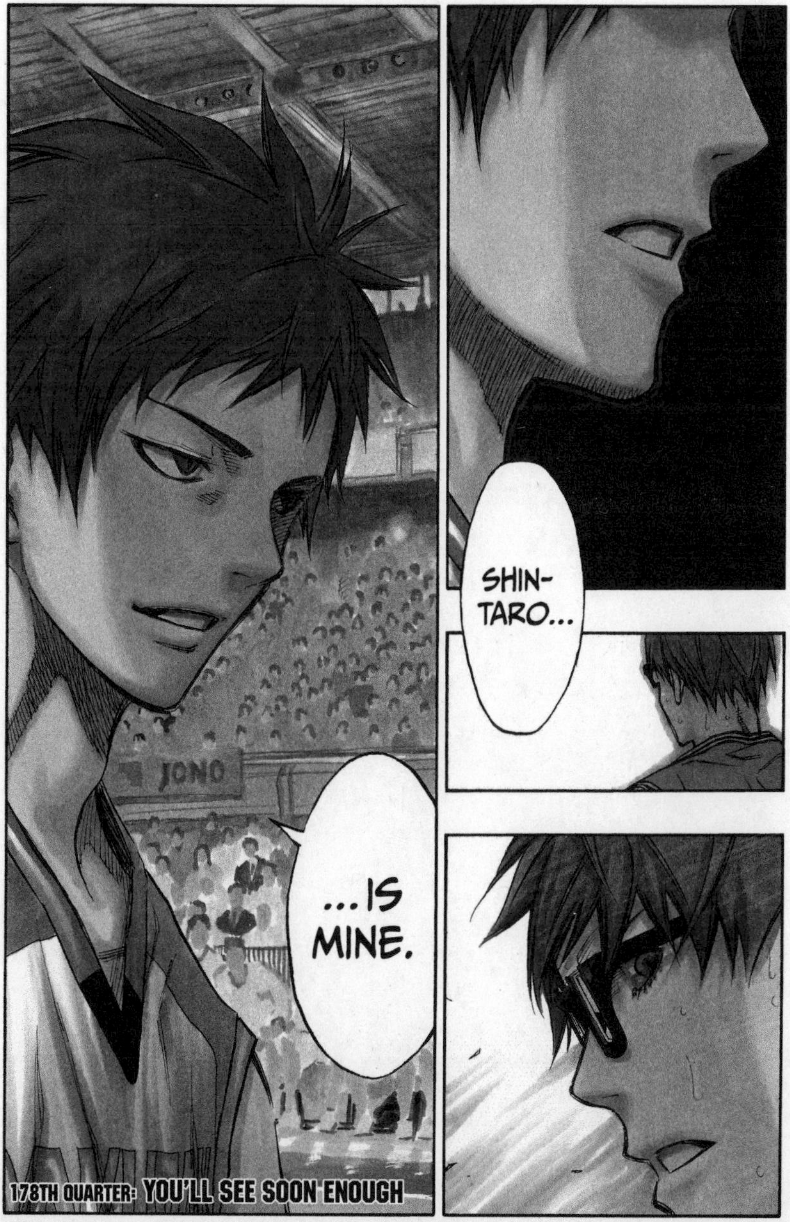
SHIN-TARO...
...IS MINE.
178TH QUARTER: YOU'LL SEE SOON ENOUGH

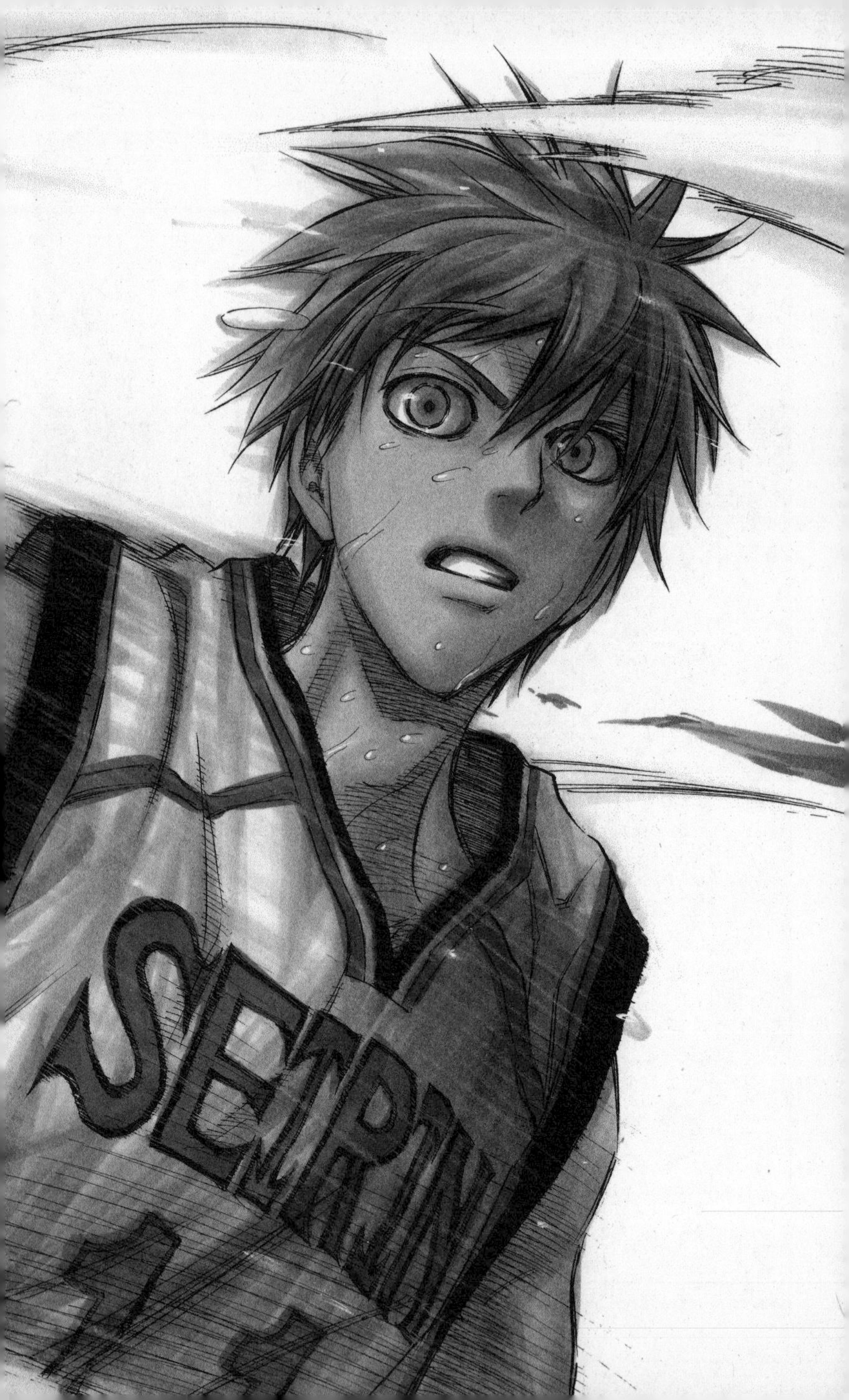
SEIRIN

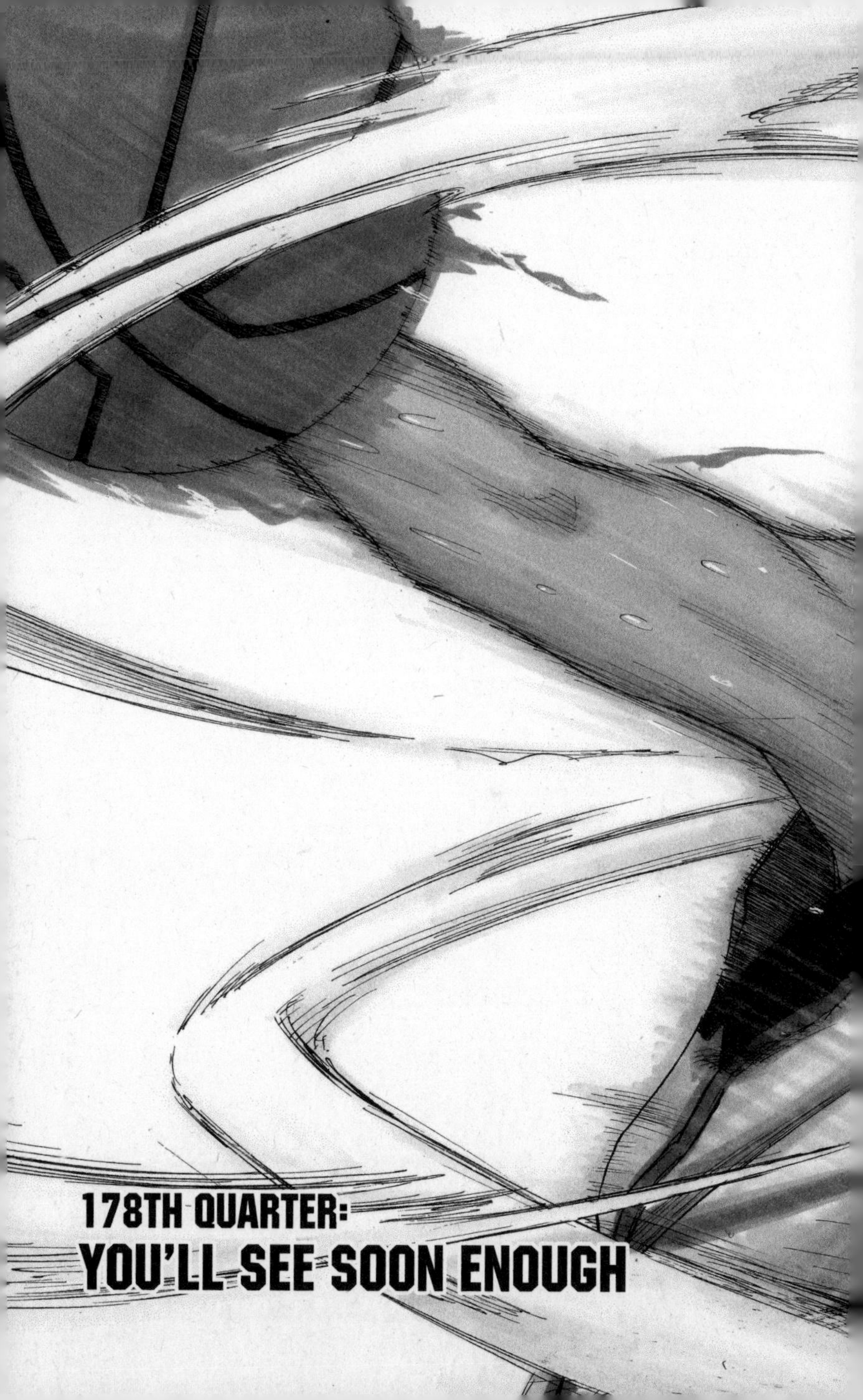
178TH QUARTER:
YOU'LL SEE SOON ENOUGH

Kuroko's
BASKETBALL

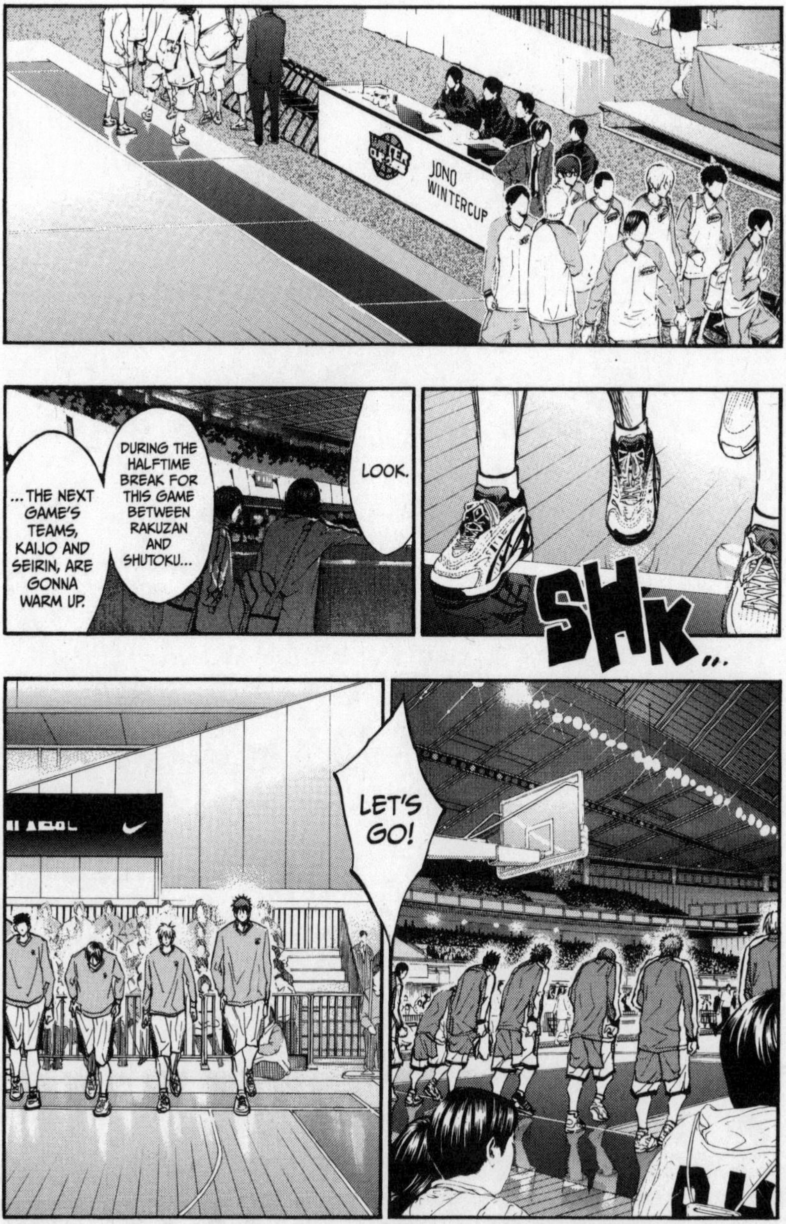
JONO WINTERCUP
SHK...
LOOK.
DURING THE HALFTIME BREAK FOR THIS GAME BETWEEN RAKUZAN AND SHUTOKU...
...THE NEXT GAME'S TEAMS, KAIJO AND SEIRIN, ARE GONNA WARM UP.
LET'S GO!

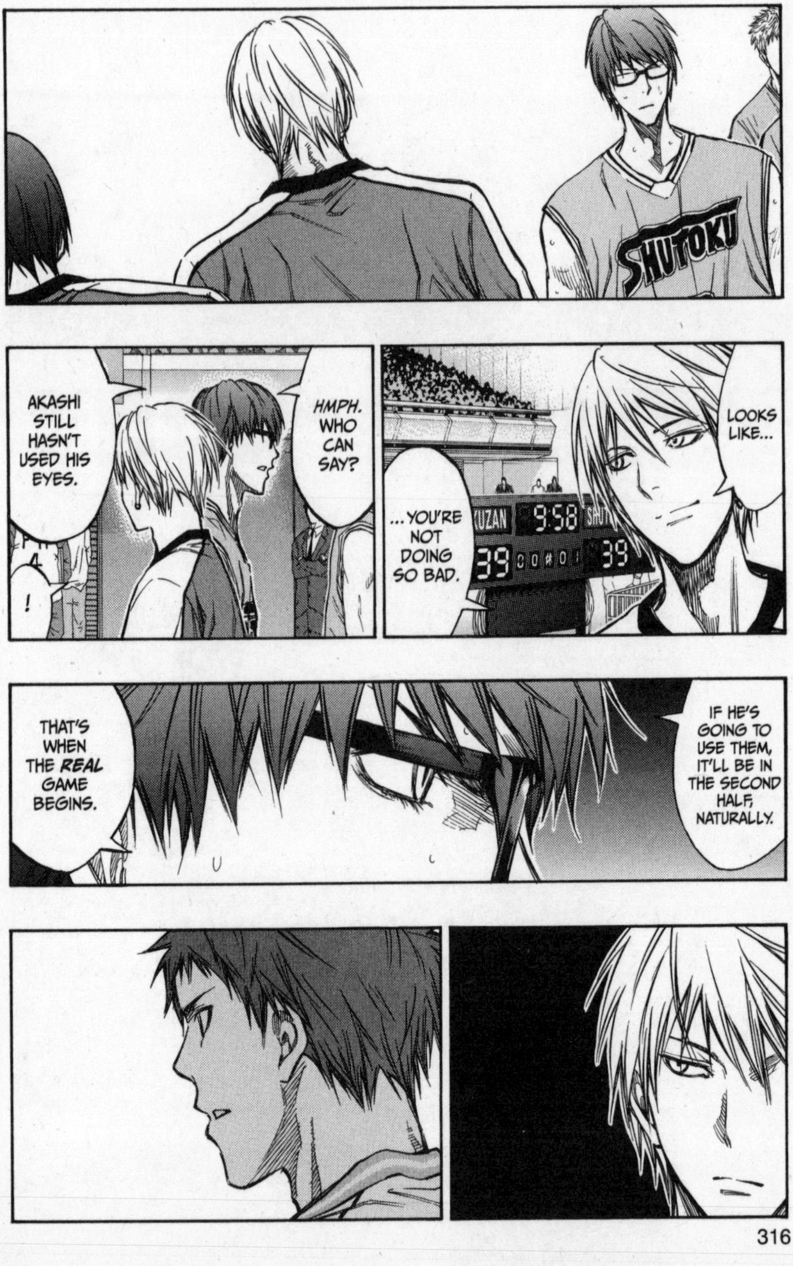
LOOKS LIKE...
...YOU'RE NOT DOING SO BAD.
HMPH. WHO CAN SAY?
AKASHI STILL HASN'T USED HIS EYES.
!
IF HE'S GOING TO USE THEM, IT'LL BE IN THE SECOND HALF, NATURALLY.
THAT'S WHEN THE *REAL* GAME BEGINS.

HEY... I HAVEN'T SEEN YOU SINCE THE OPENING CERE-MONY...
TETSU-YA.
YOU'RE RIGHT...
AKASHI-KUN.
SO THIS IS RAKUZAN AND SEIJURO AKASHI...
THEY'RE CERTAINLY SOME-THING ELSE...

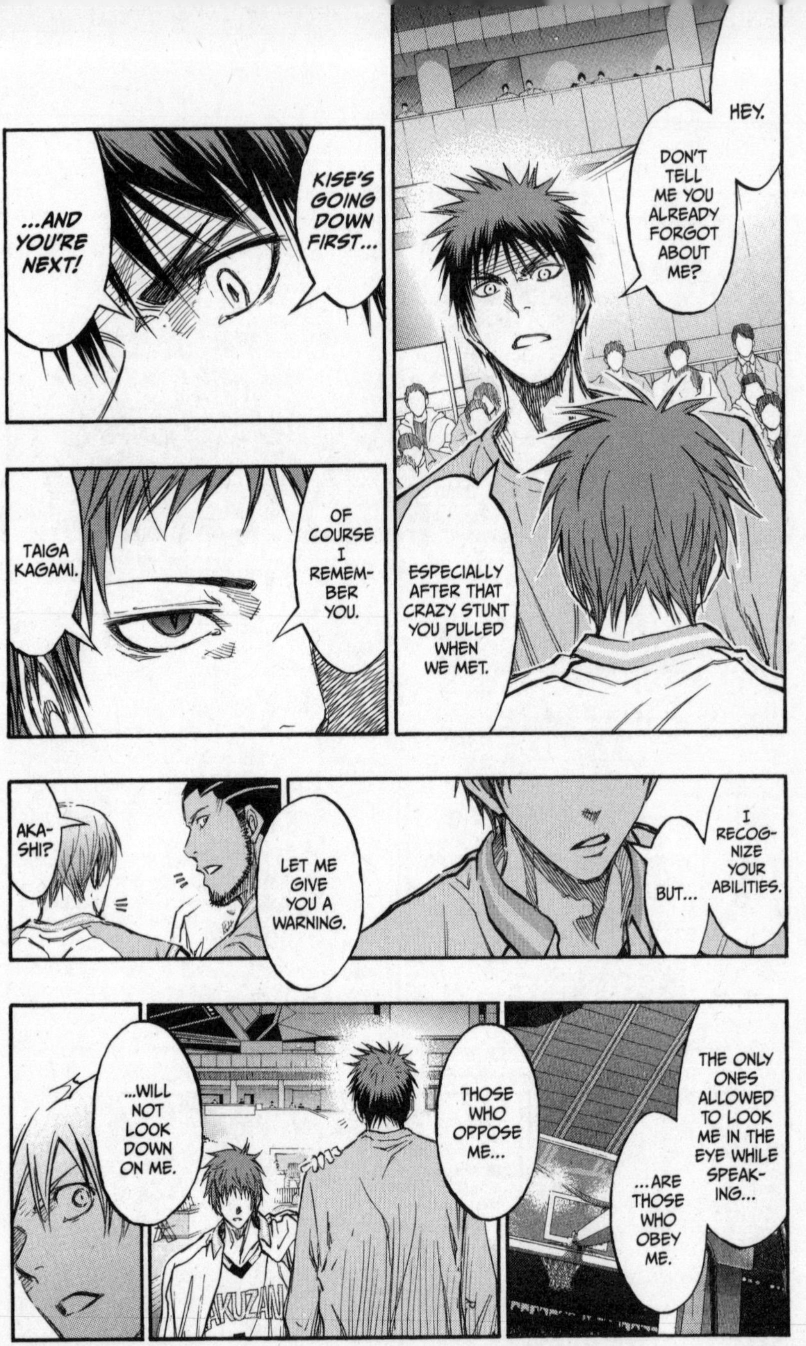
HEY.
DON'T TELL ME YOU ALREADY FORGOT ABOUT ME?
ESPECIALLY AFTER THAT CRAZY STUNT YOU PULLED WHEN WE MET.
KISE'S GOING DOWN FIRST...
...AND YOU'RE NEXT!
OF COURSE I REMEMBER YOU.
TAIGA KAGAMI.
I RECOGNIZE YOUR ABILITIES.
BUT...
LET ME GIVE YOU A WARNING.
AKASHI?
THE ONLY ONES ALLOWED TO LOOK ME IN THE EYE WHILE SPEAKING...
...ARE THOSE WHO OBEY ME.
THOSE WHO OPPOSE ME...
...WILL NOT LOOK DOWN ON ME.
RAKUZAN

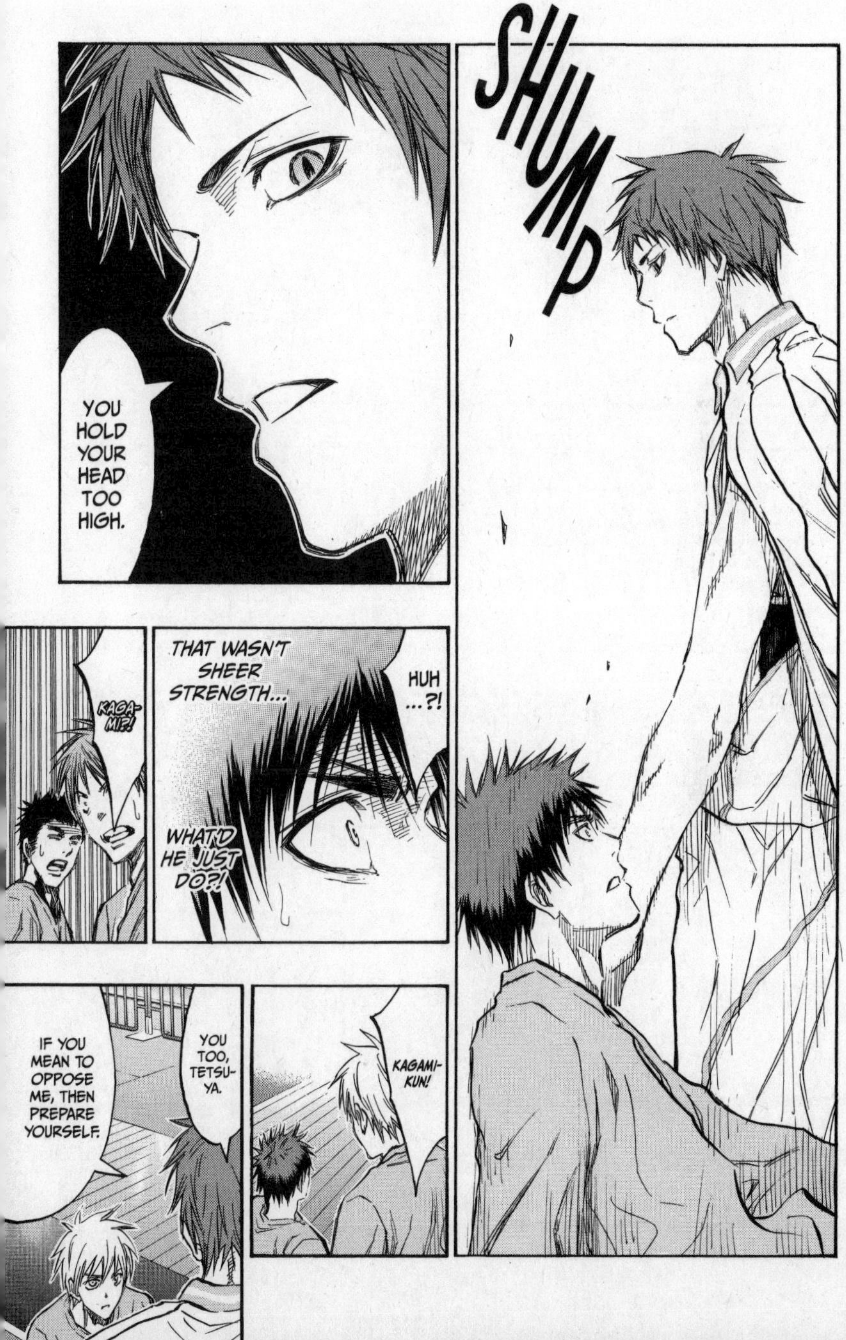
SHUMP
YOU HOLD YOUR HEAD TOO HIGH.
HUH ...?!
THAT WASN'T SHEER STRENGTH...
WHAT'D HE JUST DO?!
KAGA-MI?!
KAGAMI-KUN!
YOU TOO, TETSU-YA.
IF YOU MEAN TO OPPOSE ME, THEN PREPARE YOURSELF.

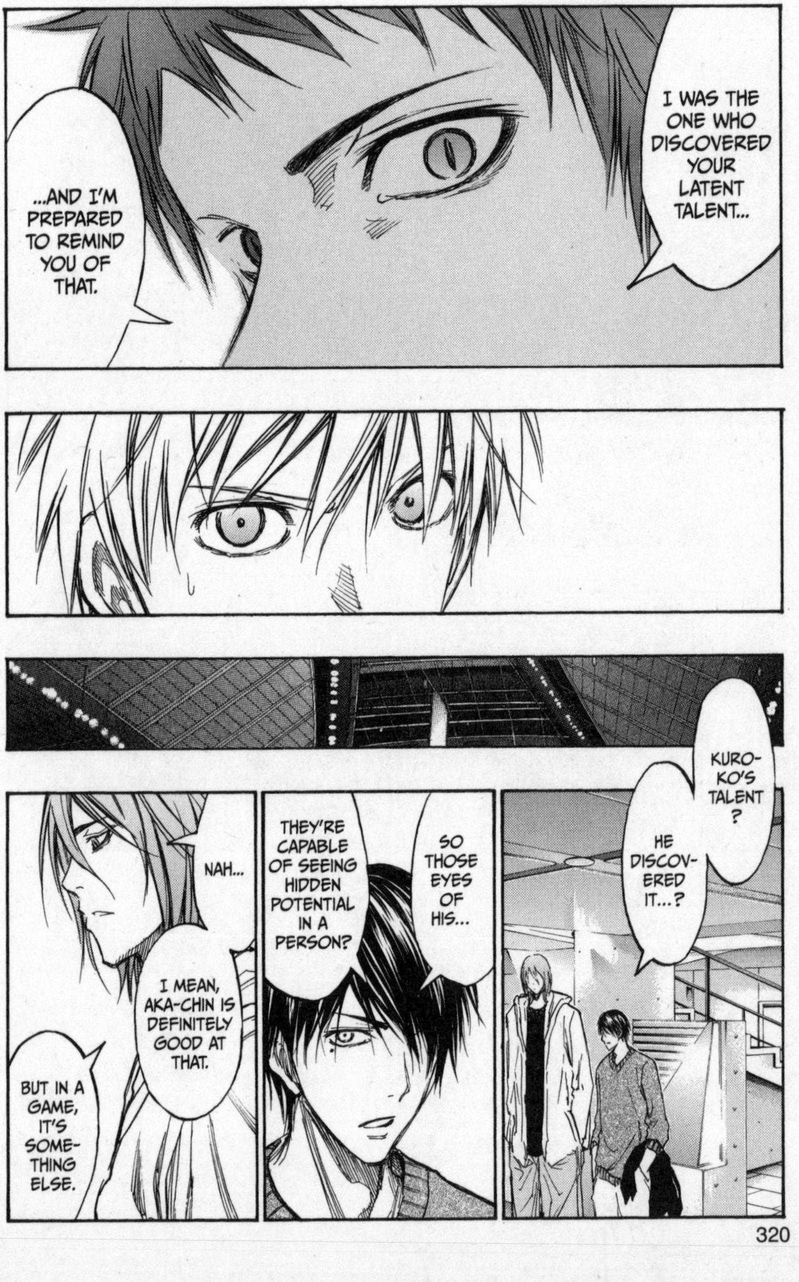
I WAS THE ONE WHO DISCOVERED YOUR LATENT TALENT...
...AND I'M PREPARED TO REMIND YOU OF THAT.
KURO-KO'S TALENT?
HE DISCOV-ERED IT...?
SO THOSE EYES OF HIS...
THEY'RE CAPABLE OF SEEING HIDDEN POTENTIAL IN A PERSON?
NAH...
I MEAN, AKA-CHIN IS DEFINITELY GOOD AT THAT.
BUT IN A GAME, IT'S SOME-THING ELSE.

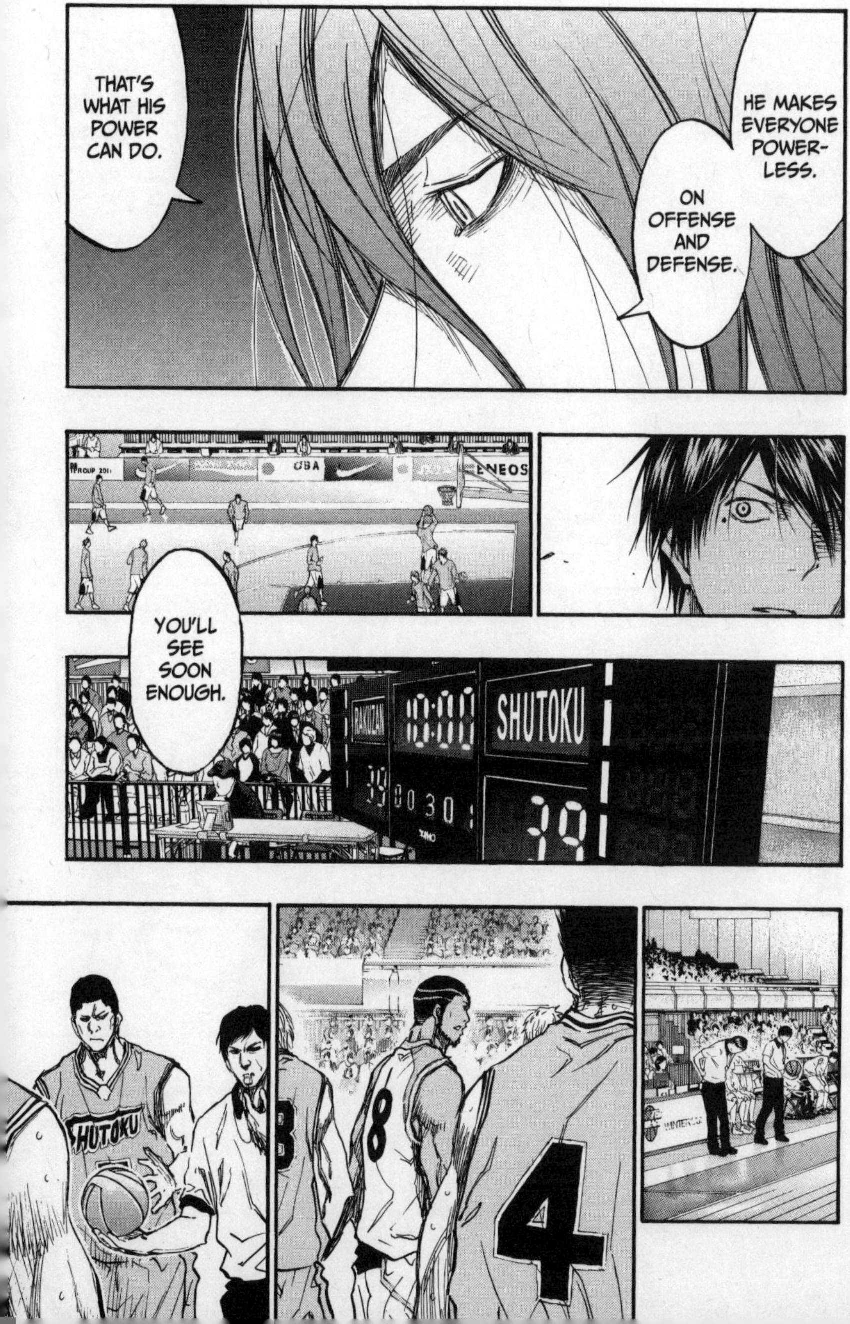
HE MAKES EVERYONE POWER-LESS.
ON OFFENSE AND DEFENSE.
THAT'S WHAT HIS POWER CAN DO.
ENEOS
YOU'LL SEE SOON ENOUGH.
SHUTOKU
SHUTOKU

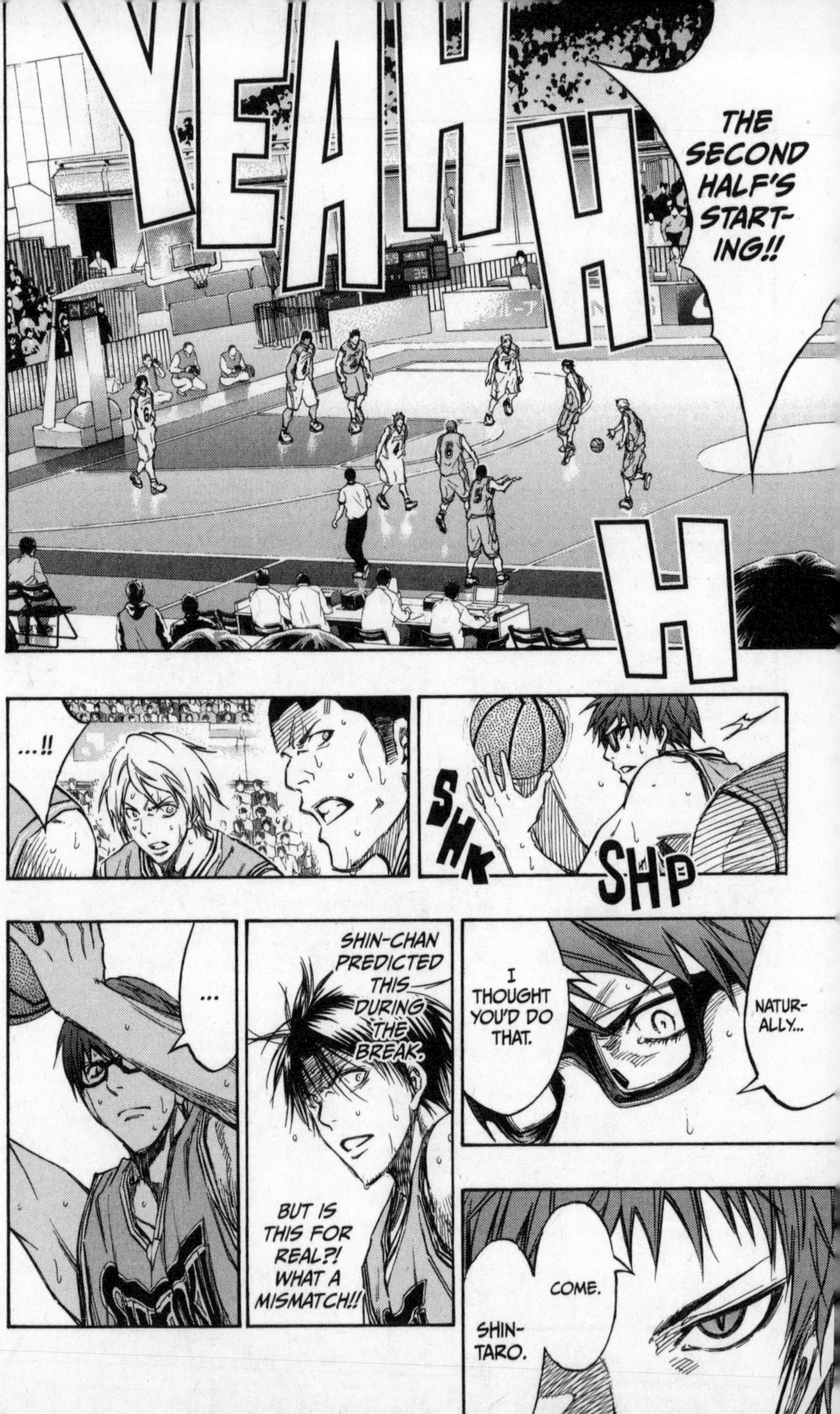
THE SECOND HALF'S STARTING!!
YEAHHHH
SHK
SHP
...!!
NATURALLY...
I THOUGHT YOU'D DO THAT.
COME.
SHINTARO.
SHIN-CHAN PREDICTED THIS DURING THE BREAK.
BUT IS THIS FOR REAL?! WHAT A MISMATCH!!
...

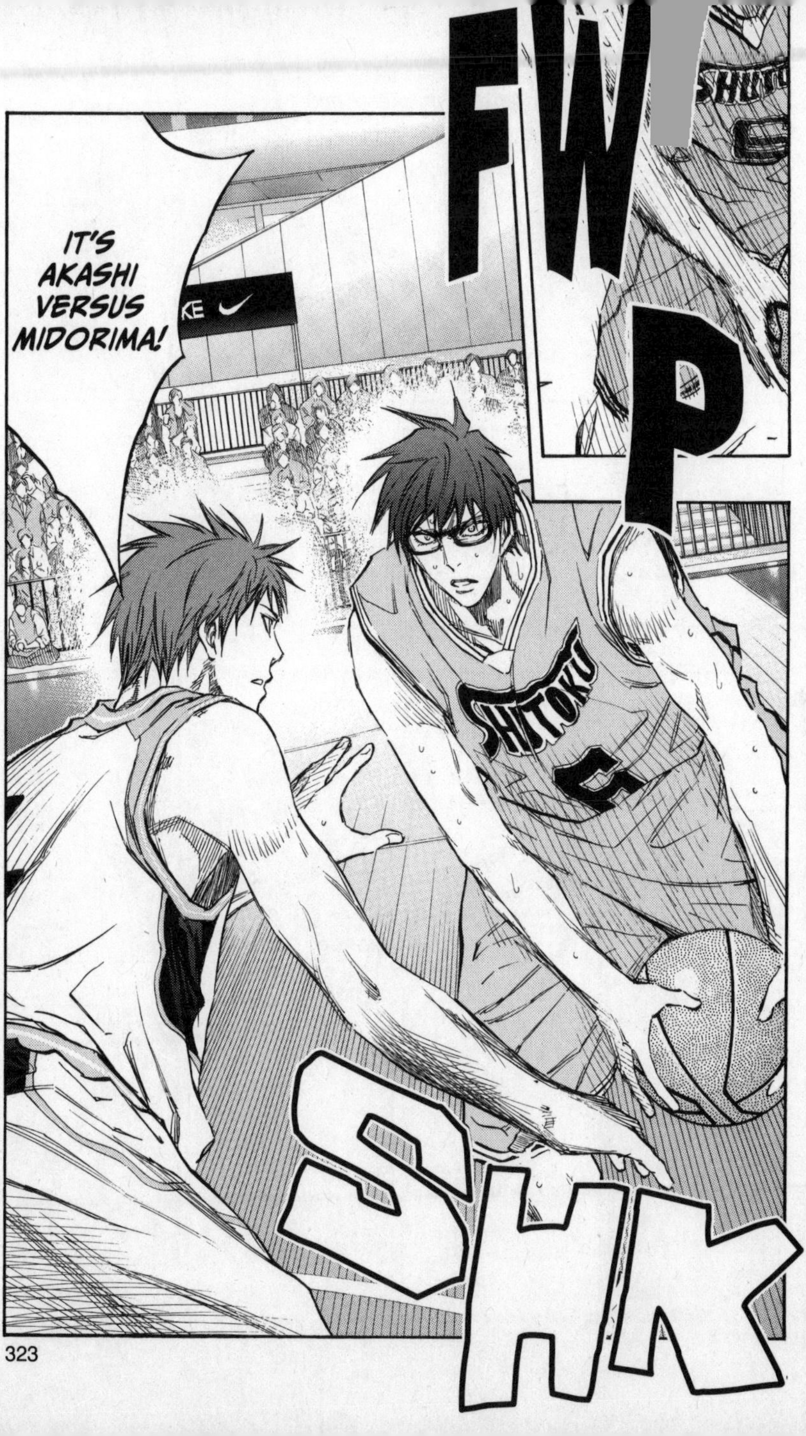
FWP
IT'S AKASHI VERSUS MIDORIMA!
SHUTOKU
SHK

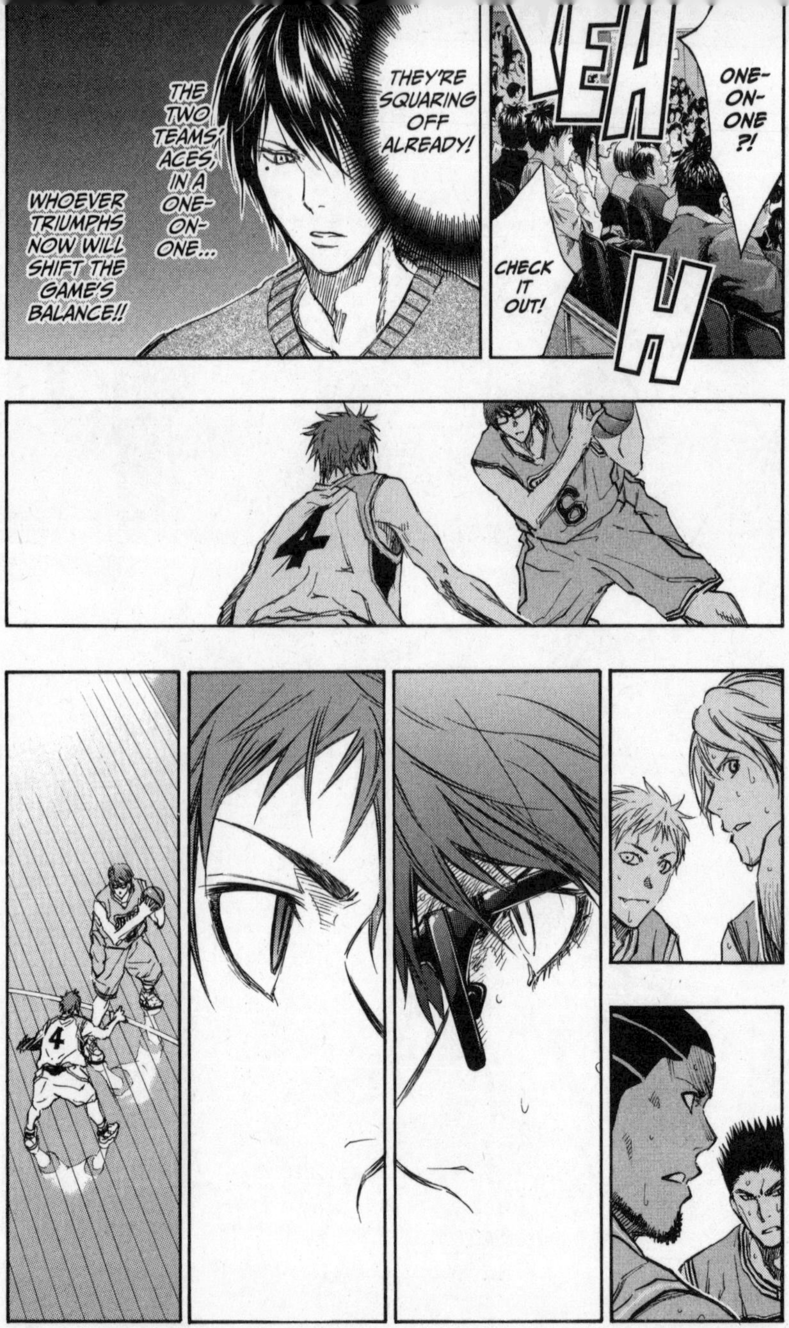
ONE-ON-ONE?!
YEAH
CHECK IT OUT!
THEY'RE SQUARING OFF ALREADY!
THE TWO TEAMS' ACES, IN A ONE-ON-ONE...
WHOEVER TRIUMPHS NOW WILL SHIFT THE GAME'S BALANCE!!

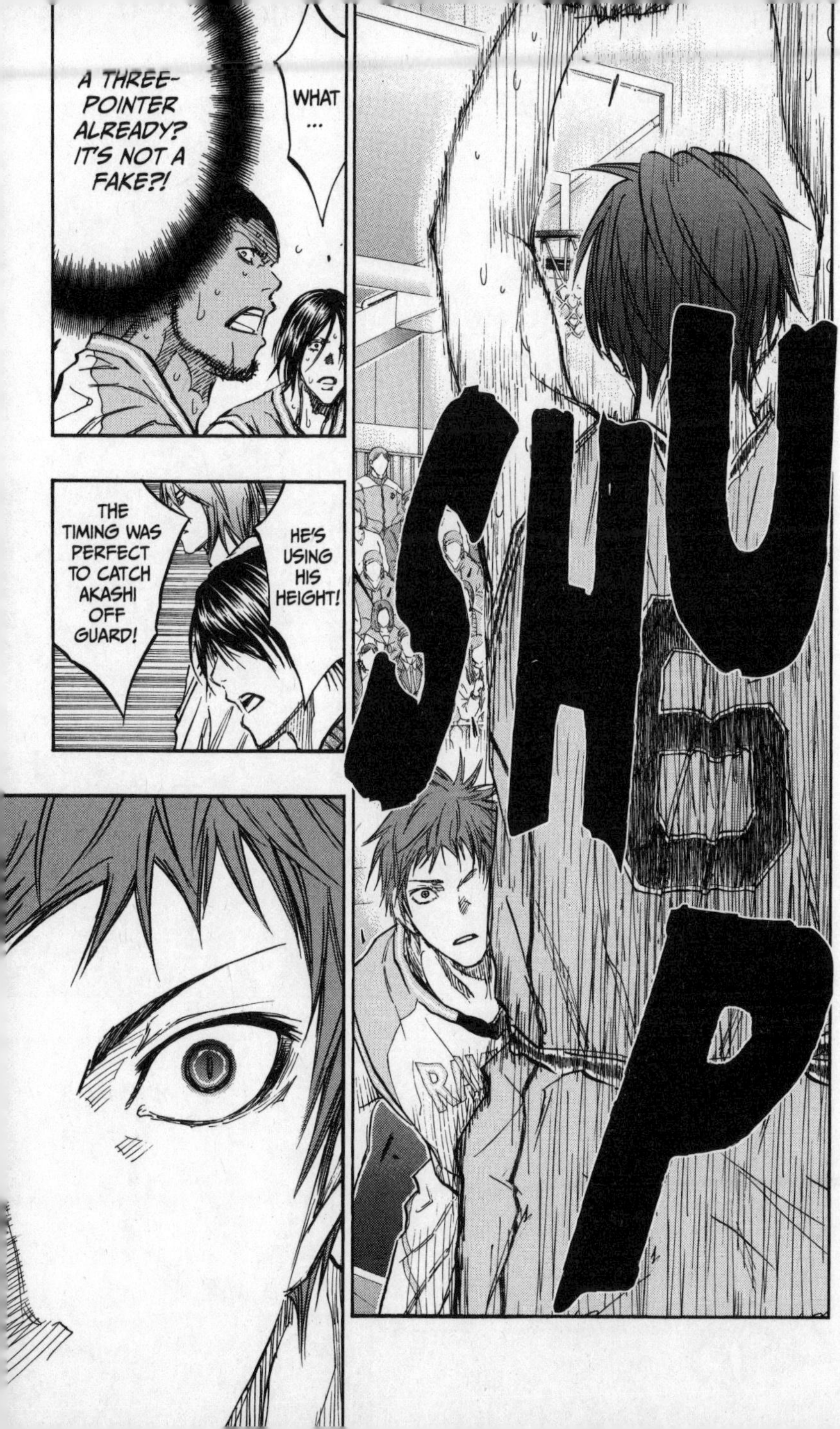
SHUP
WHAT ...
A THREE-POINTER ALREADY? IT'S NOT A FAKE?!
HE'S USING HIS HEIGHT!
THE TIMING WAS PERFECT TO CATCH AKASHI OFF GUARD!

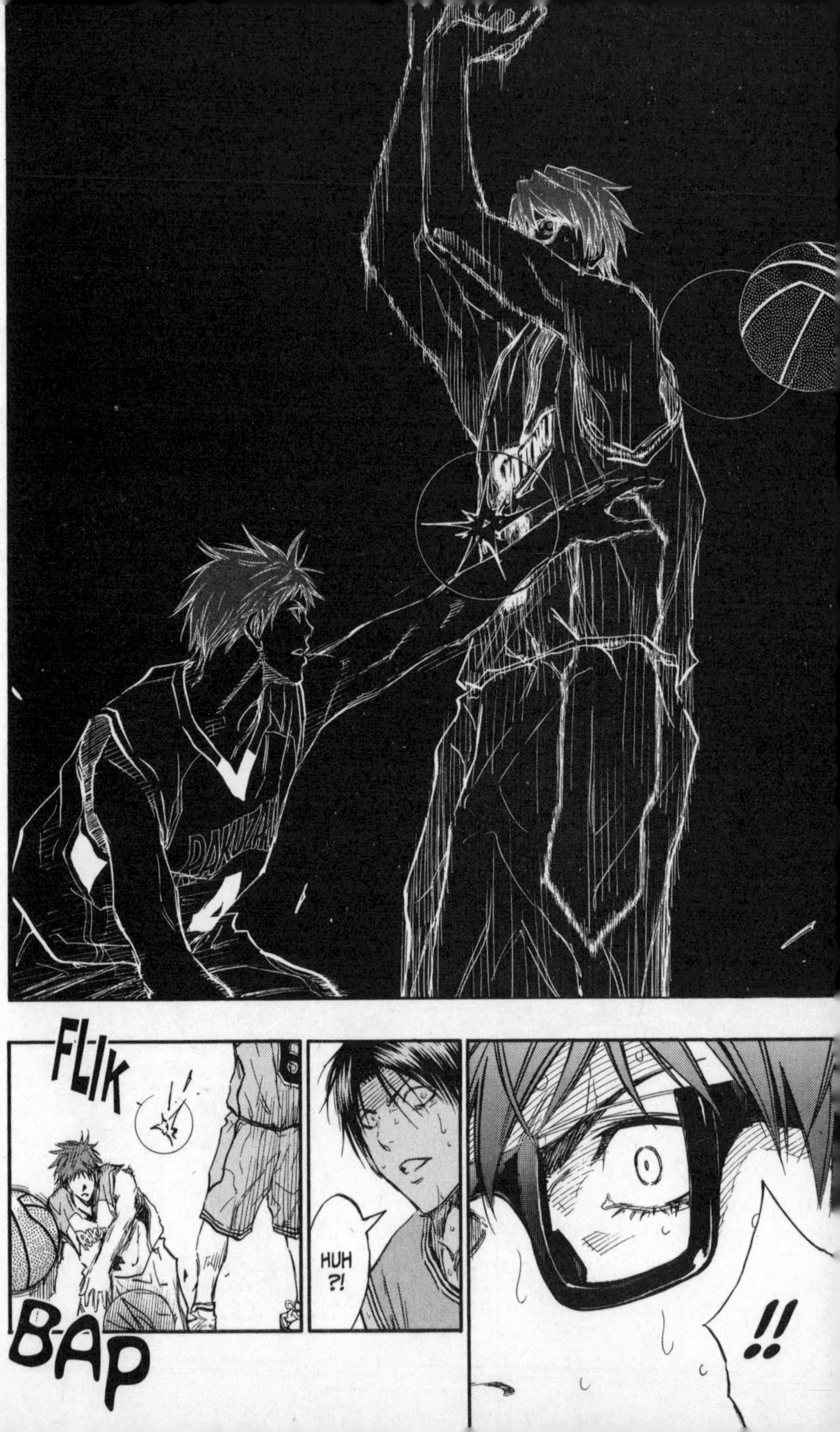
!!
HUH ?!
FLIK
BAP

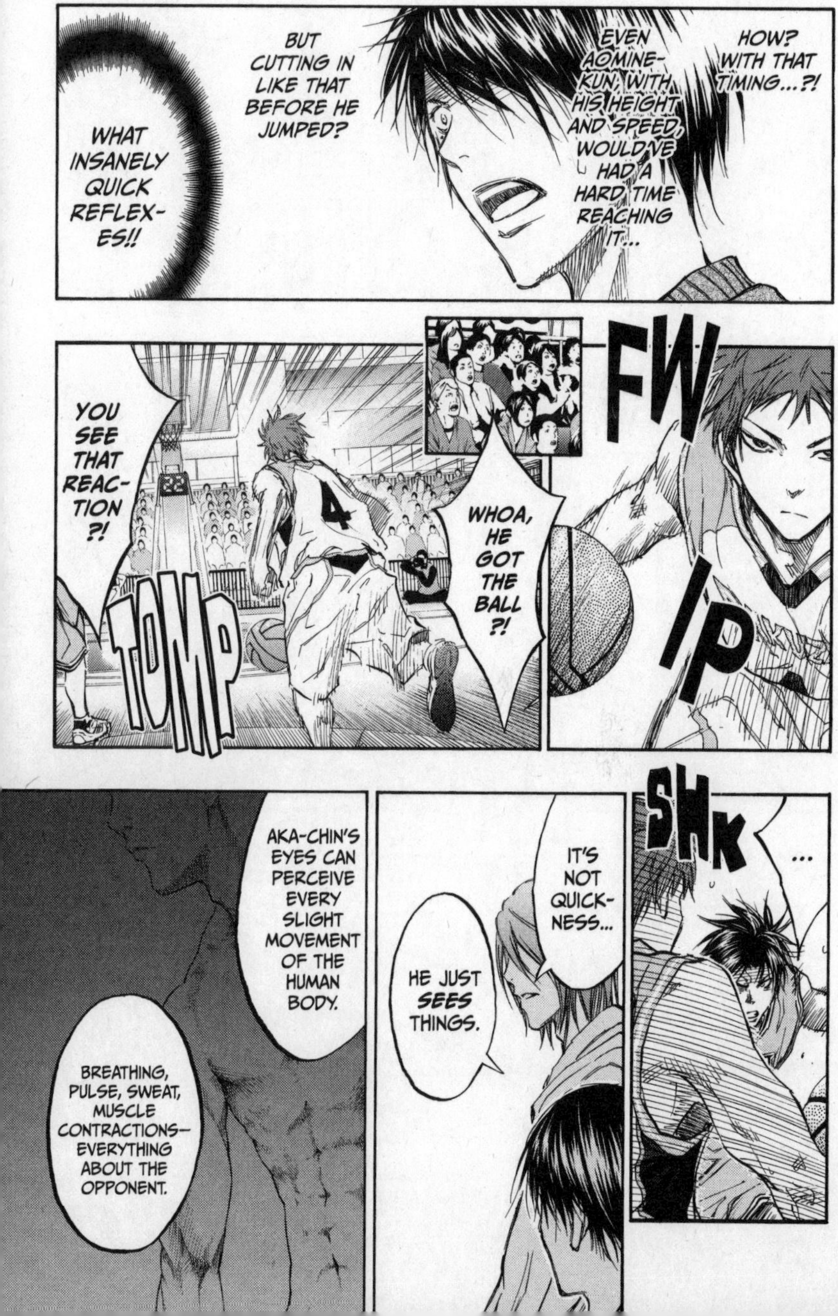
HOW? WITH THAT TIMING...?!
EVEN AOMINE-KUN, WITH HIS HEIGHT AND SPEED, WOULD'VE HAD A HARD TIME REACHING IT...
BUT CUTTING IN LIKE THAT BEFORE HE JUMPED?
WHAT INSANELY QUICK REFLEXES!!
FWIP
WHOA, HE GOT THE BALL?!
YOU SEE THAT REACTION?!
TOMP
SHK
...
IT'S NOT QUICKNESS...
HE JUST SEES THINGS.
AKA-CHIN'S EYES CAN PERCEIVE EVERY SLIGHT MOVEMENT OF THE HUMAN BODY.
BREATHING, PULSE, SWEAT, MUSCLE CONTRACTIONS— EVERYTHING ABOUT THE OPPONENT.

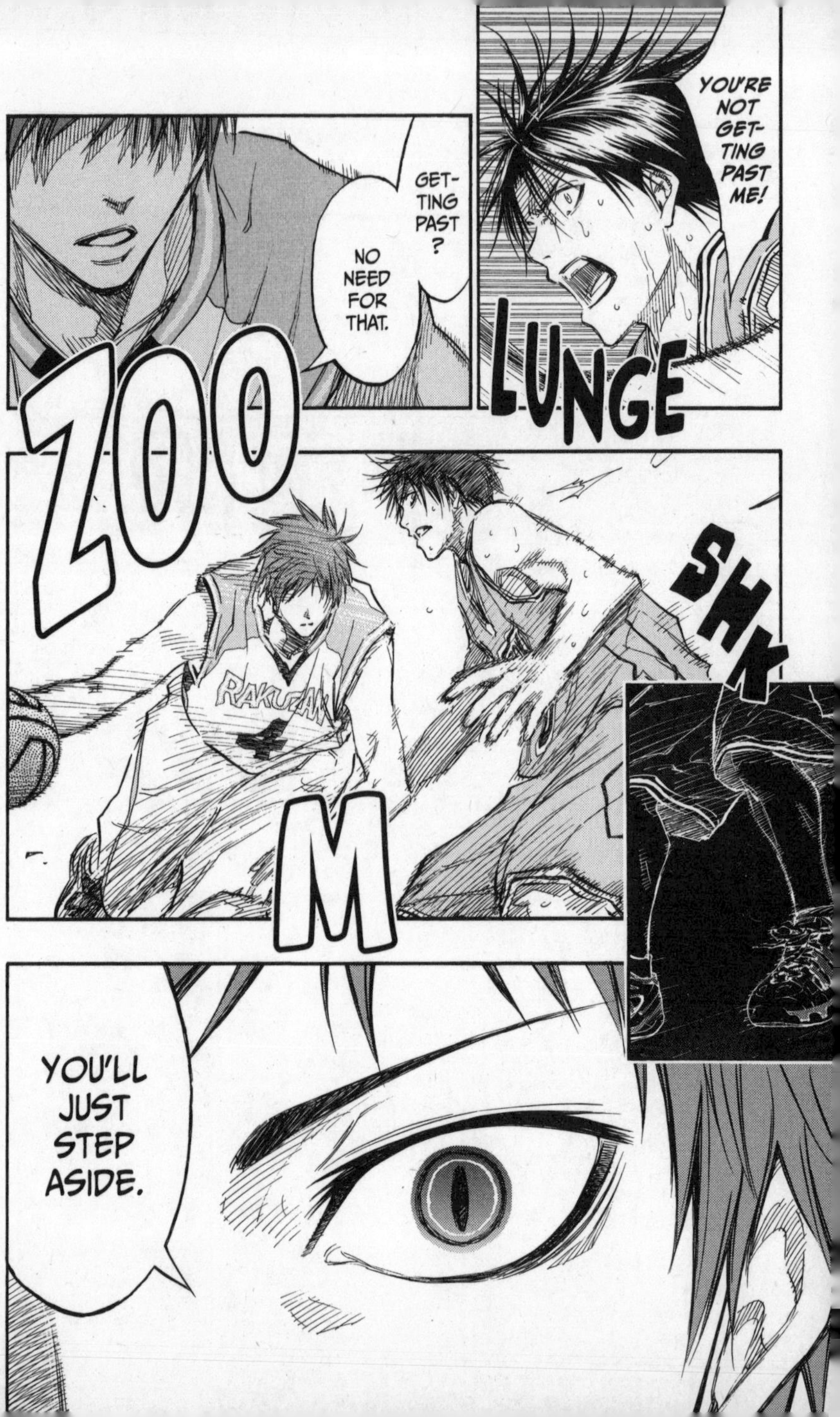
YOU'RE NOT GET-TING PAST ME!
LUNGE
GET-TING PAST?
NO NEED FOR THAT.
ZOOM
SHK
YOU'LL JUST STEP ASIDE.

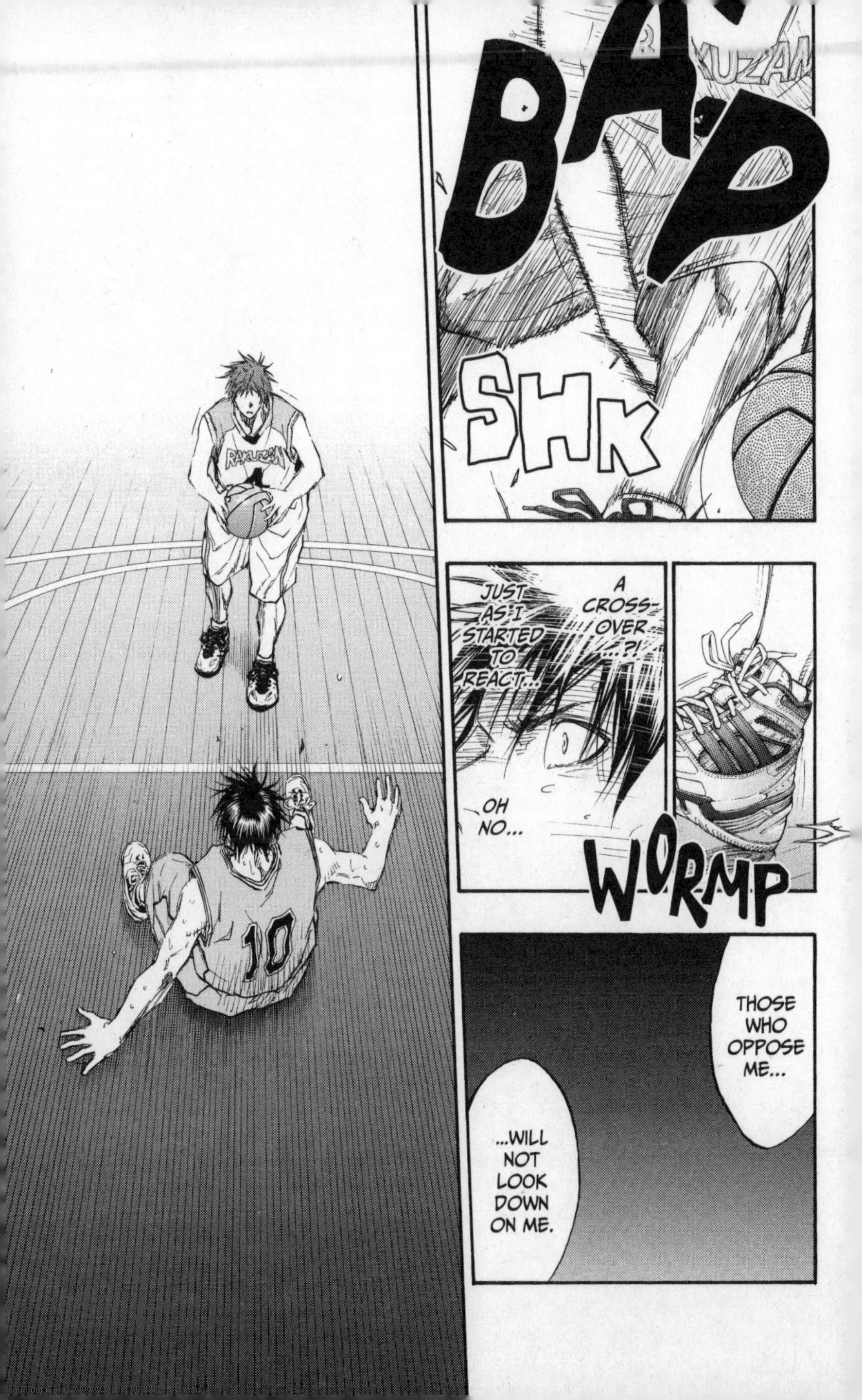
SHK
WORMP
A CROSS-OVER...?!
JUST AS I STARTED TO REACT...
OH NO...
THOSE WHO OPPOSE ME...
...WILL NOT LOOK DOWN ON ME.

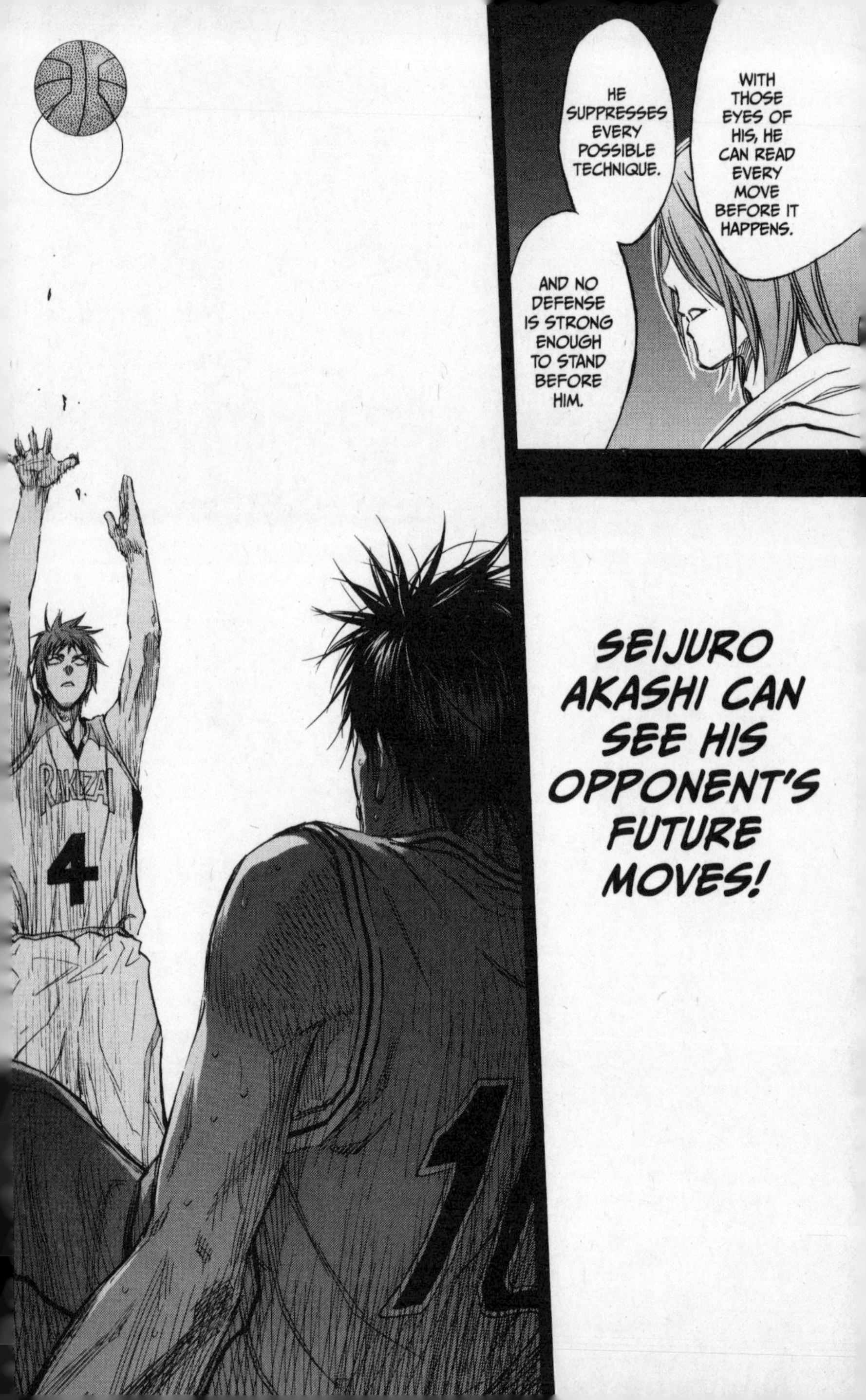
WITH THOSE EYES OF HIS, HE CAN READ EVERY MOVE BEFORE IT HAPPENS.
HE SUPPRESSES EVERY POSSIBLE TECHNIQUE.
AND NO DEFENSE IS STRONG ENOUGH TO STAND BEFORE HIM.
SEIJURO AKASHI CAN SEE HIS OPPONENT'S FUTURE MOVES!
RAKUZAN
4

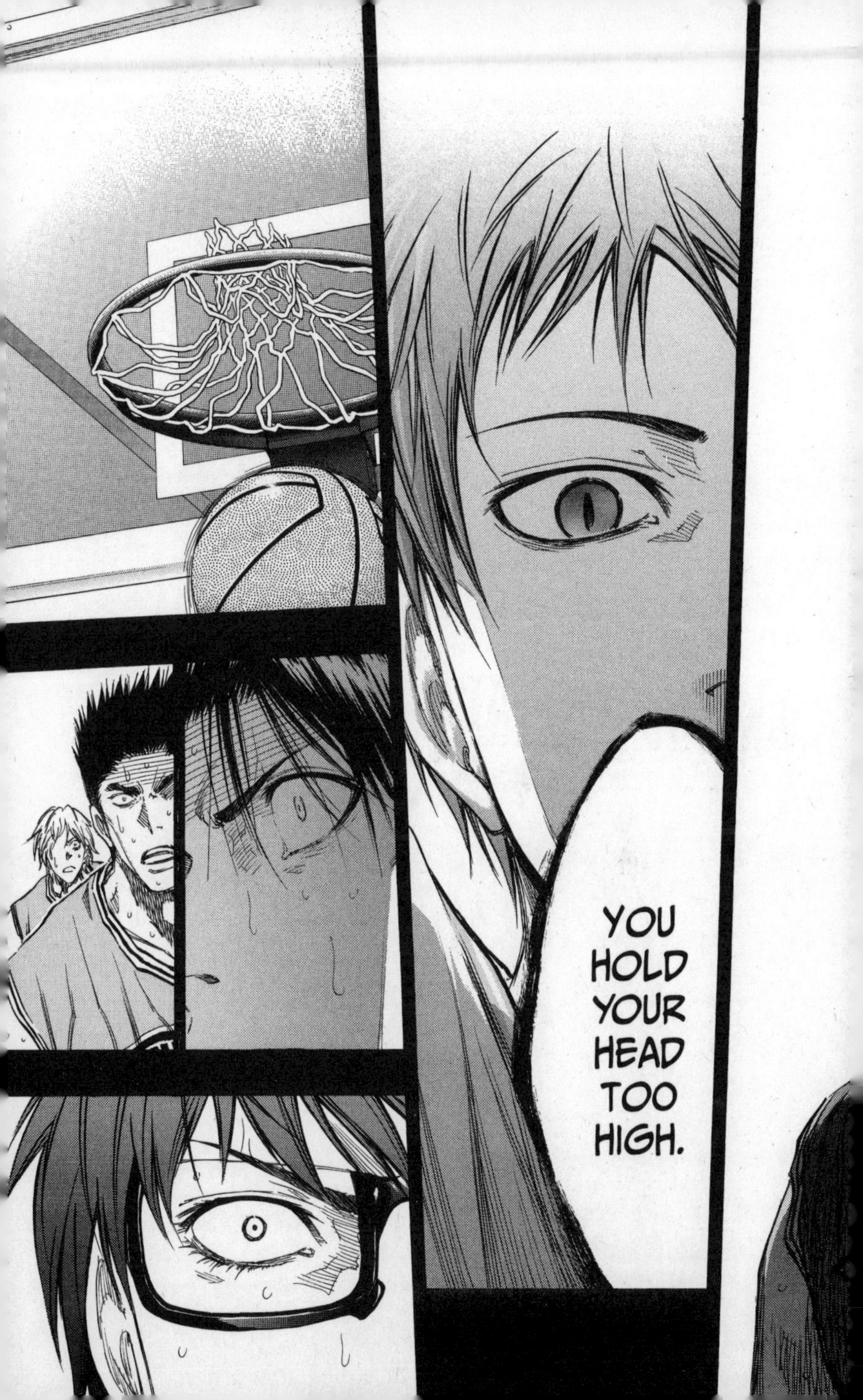
YOU HOLD YOUR HEAD TOO HIGH.

KUROKO'S BASKETBALL BLOOPERS

TAKE 2

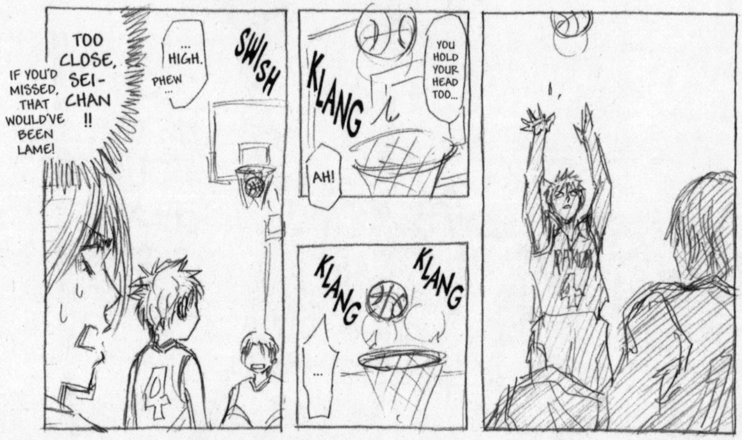
YOU HOLD YOUR HEAD TOO...
KLANG
AH!
KLANG
KLANG
...
SWISH
... HIGH.
PHEW ...
TOO CLOSE, SEI-CHAN !!
IF YOU'D MISSED, THAT WOULD'VE BEEN LAME!

179TH QUARTER: HAVEN'T GIVEN UP

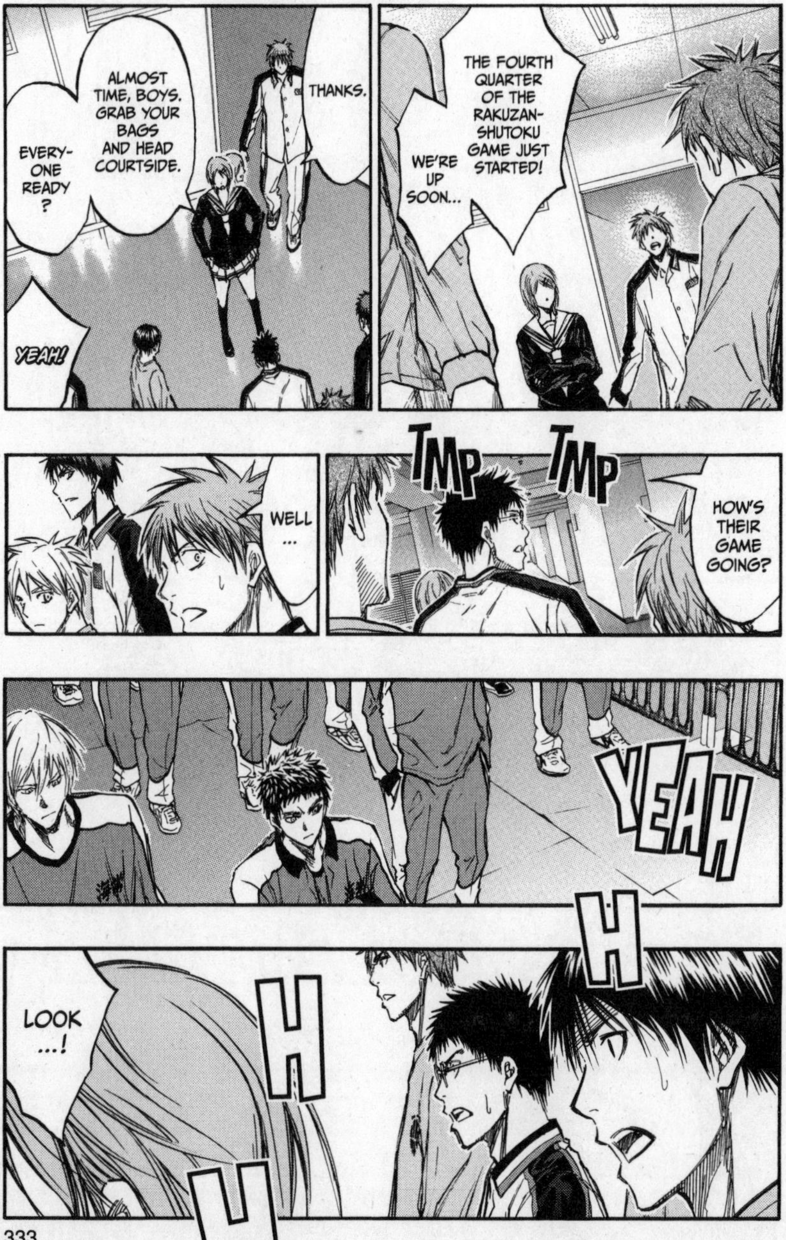

THE FOURTH QUARTER OF THE RAKUZAN-SHUTOKU GAME JUST STARTED!
WE'RE UP SOON...
THANKS.
ALMOST TIME, BOYS. GRAB YOUR BAGS AND HEAD COURTSIDE.
EVERY-ONE READY?
YEAH!
TMP
TMP
HOW'S THEIR GAME GOING?
WELL ...
YEAH
H
H
H
LOOK ...!

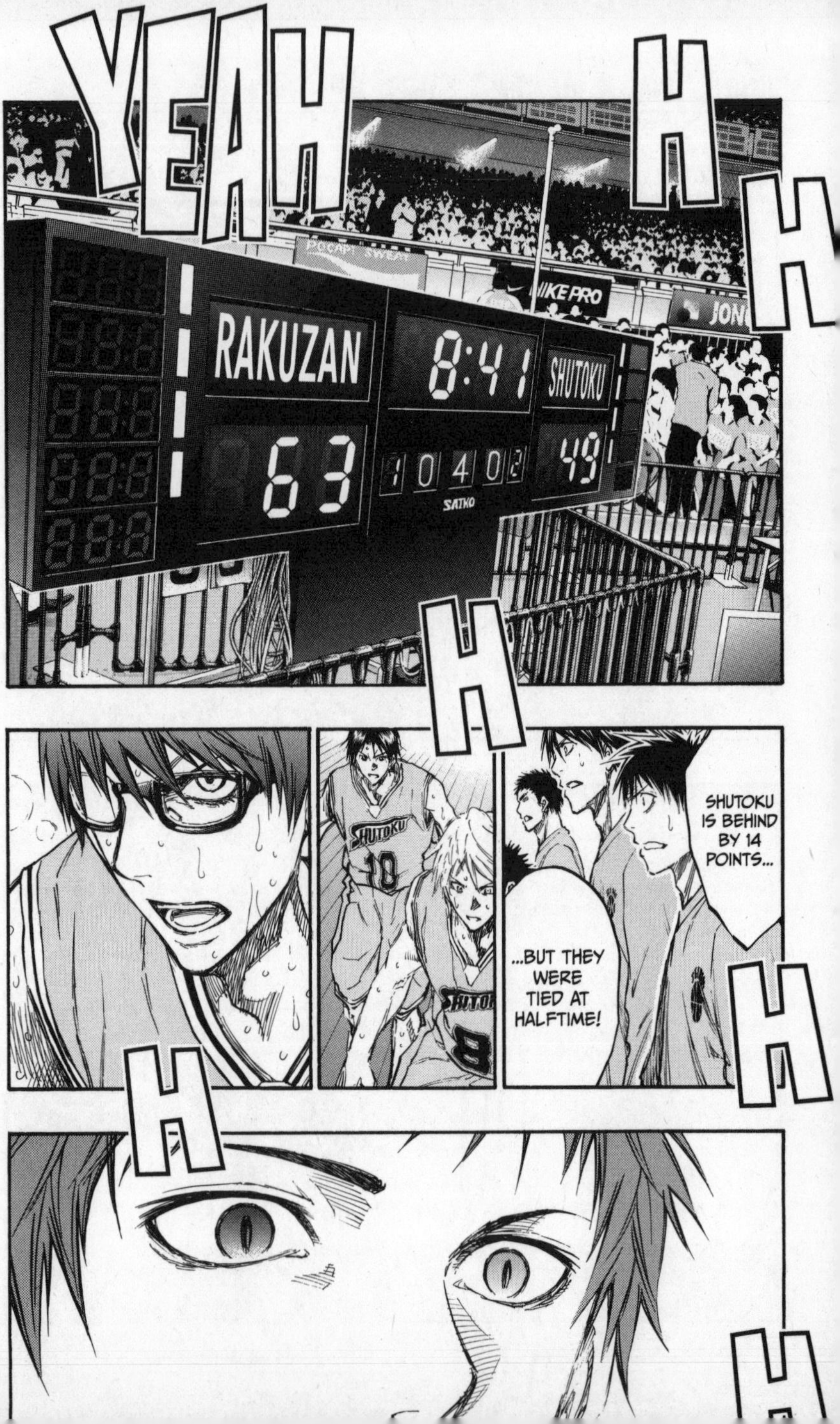
YEAH
HHHH
RAKUZAN
8:41
SHUTOKU
63
49
NIKE PRO
SHUTOKU IS BEHIND BY 14 POINTS...
...BUT THEY WERE TIED AT HALFTIME!
HHHH

179TH QUARTER: HAVEN'T GIVEN UP

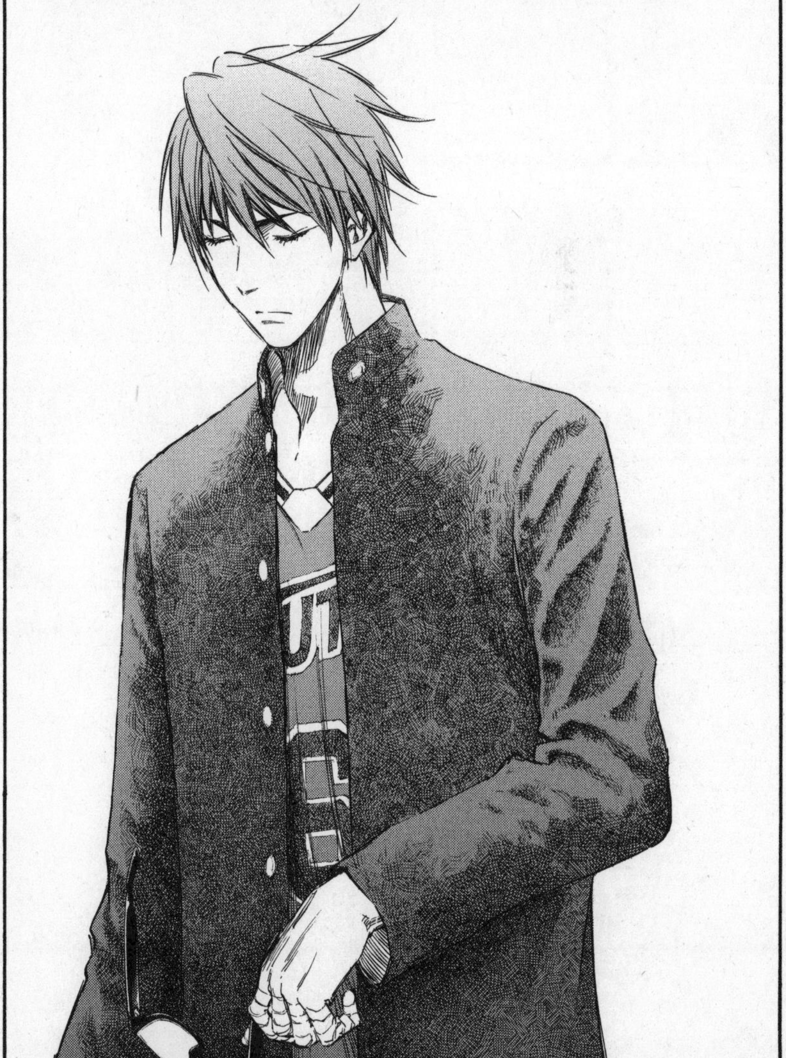

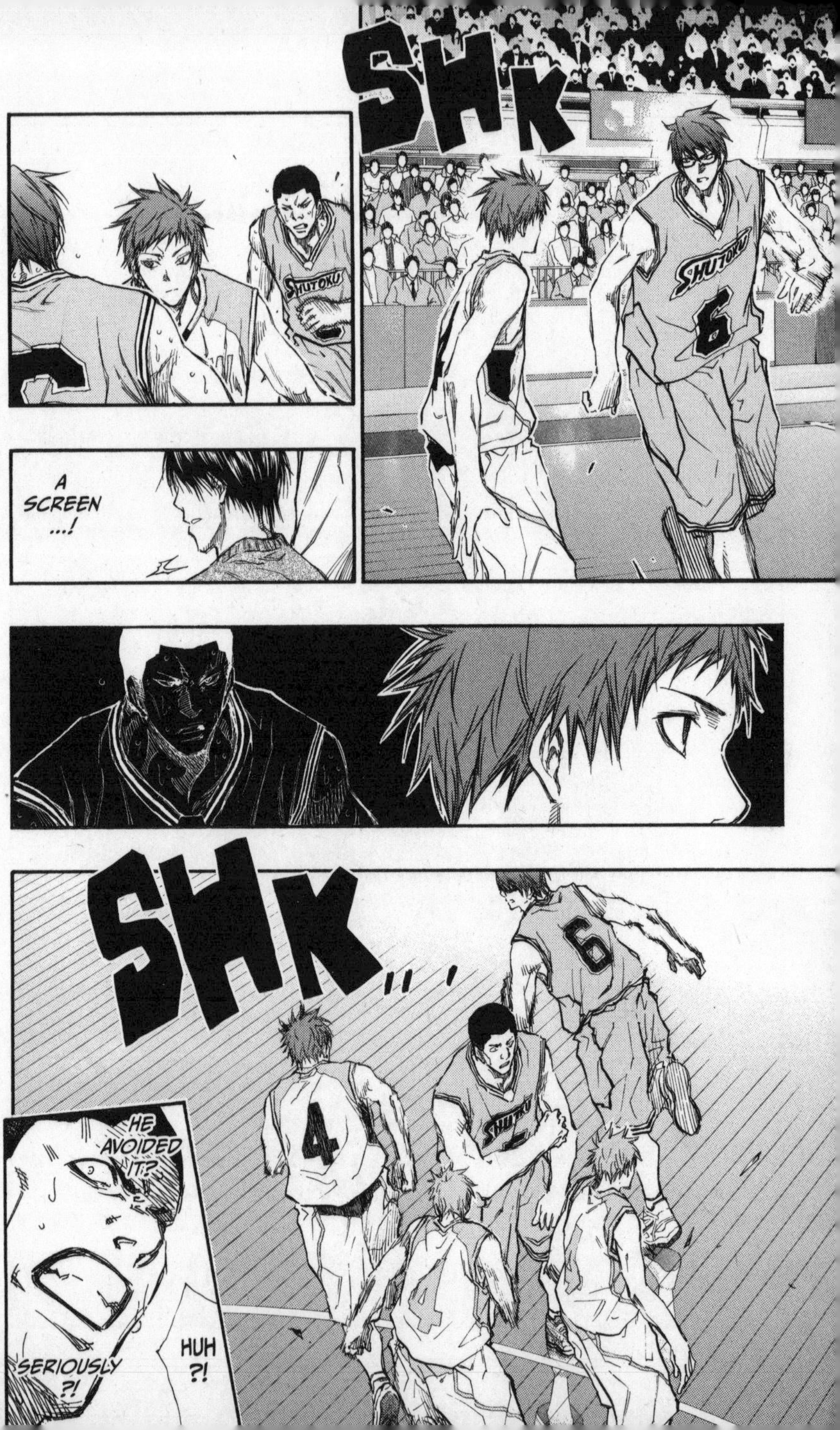
SHK
A SCREEN ...!
SHK...
HE AVOIDED IT?
HUH ?!
SERIOUSLY ?!

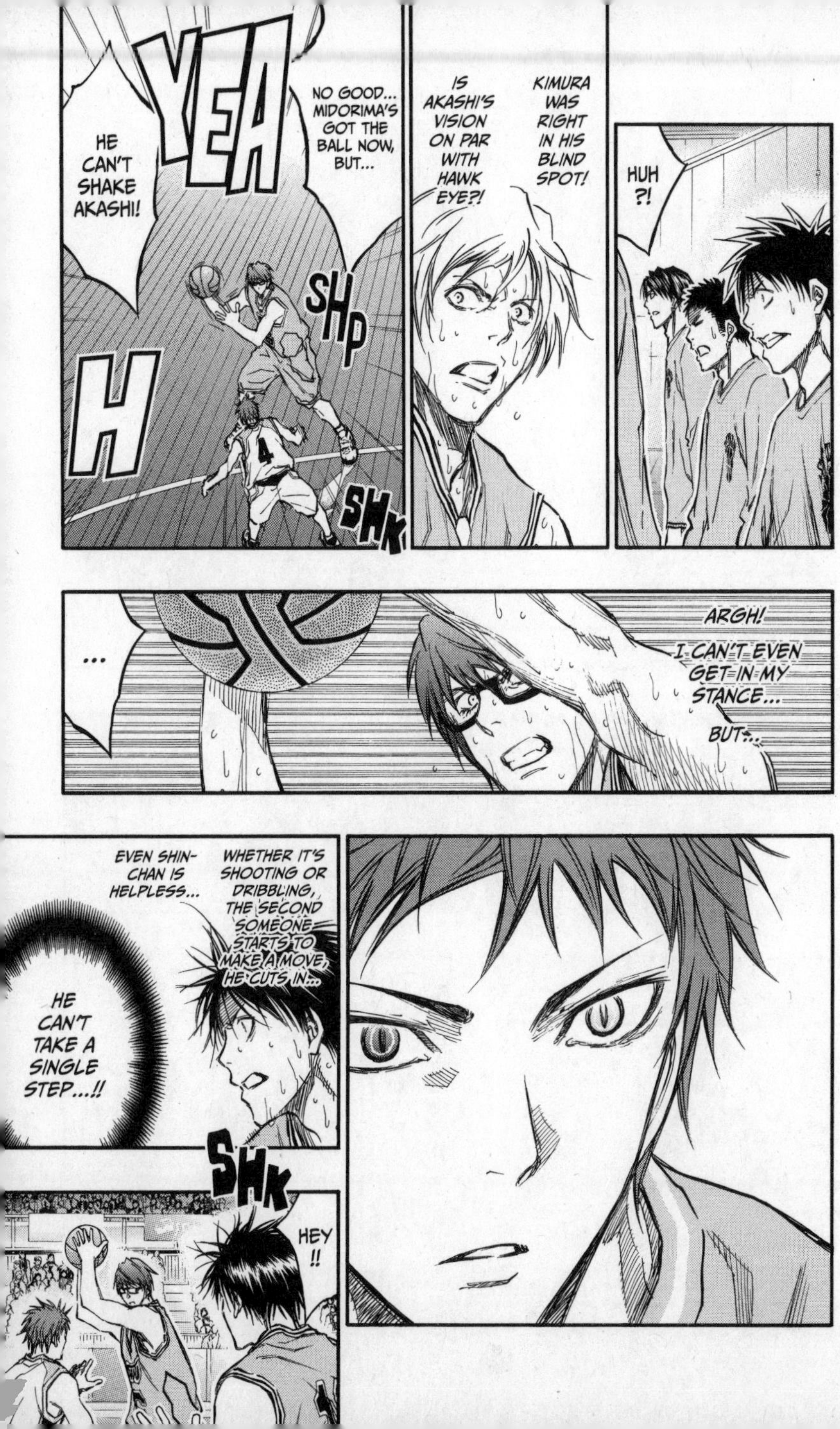
HUH ?!
KIMURA WAS RIGHT IN HIS BLIND SPOT!
IS AKASHI'S VISION ON PAR WITH HAWK EYE?!
NO GOOD... MIDORIMA'S GOT THE BALL NOW, BUT...
YEA
HE CAN'T SHAKE AKASHI!
SHP
H
SHK
ARGH!
I CAN'T EVEN GET IN MY STANCE...
BUT...
...
WHETHER IT'S SHOOTING OR DRIBBLING, THE SECOND SOMEONE STARTS TO MAKE A MOVE, HE CUTS IN...
EVEN SHIN-CHAN IS HELPLESS...
HE CAN'T TAKE A SINGLE STEP...!!
SHK
HEY !!

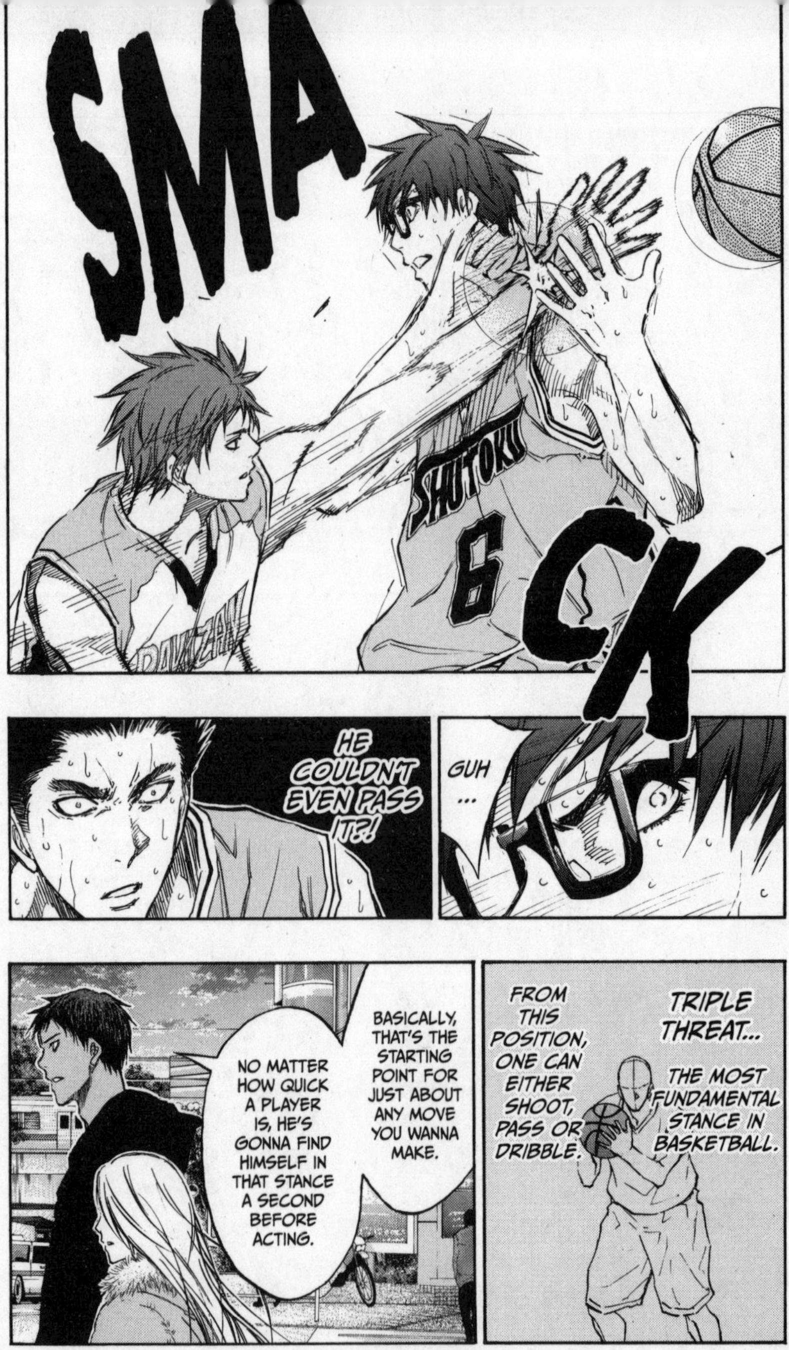
SMA
CK
GUH ...
HE COULDN'T EVEN PASS IT?!
TRIPLE THREAT...
THE MOST FUNDAMENTAL STANCE IN BASKETBALL.
FROM THIS POSITION, ONE CAN EITHER SHOOT, PASS OR DRIBBLE.
BASICALLY, THAT'S THE STARTING POINT FOR JUST ABOUT ANY MOVE YOU WANNA MAKE.
NO MATTER HOW QUICK A PLAYER IS, HE'S GONNA FIND HIMSELF IN THAT STANCE A SECOND BEFORE ACTING.

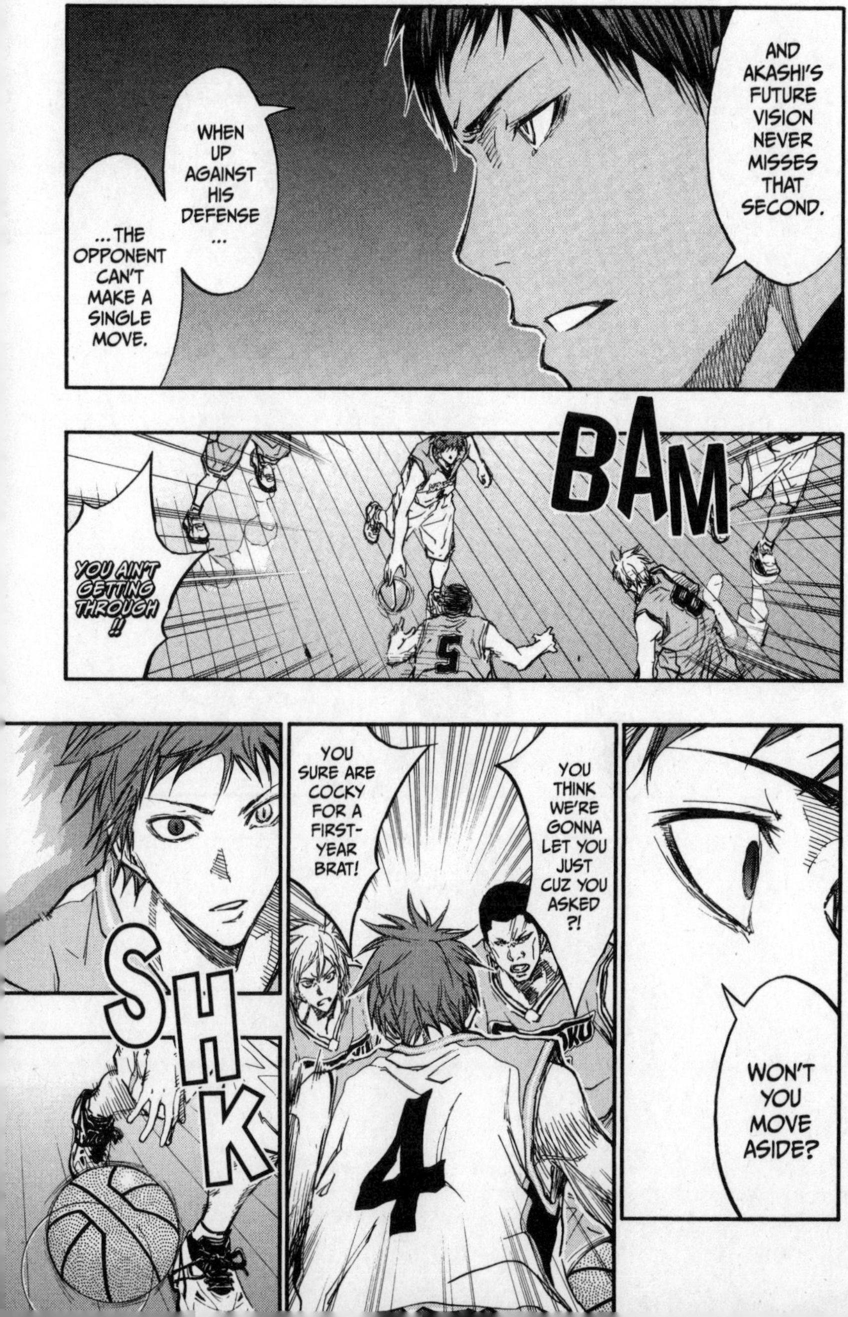
AND AKASHI'S FUTURE VISION NEVER MISSES THAT SECOND.
WHEN UP AGAINST HIS DEFENSE ...
...THE OPPONENT CAN'T MAKE A SINGLE MOVE.
BAM
YOU AIN'T GETTING THROUGH !!
WON'T YOU MOVE ASIDE?
YOU THINK WE'RE GONNA LET YOU JUST CUZ YOU ASKED ?!
YOU SURE ARE COCKY FOR A FIRST-YEAR BRAT!
SHK

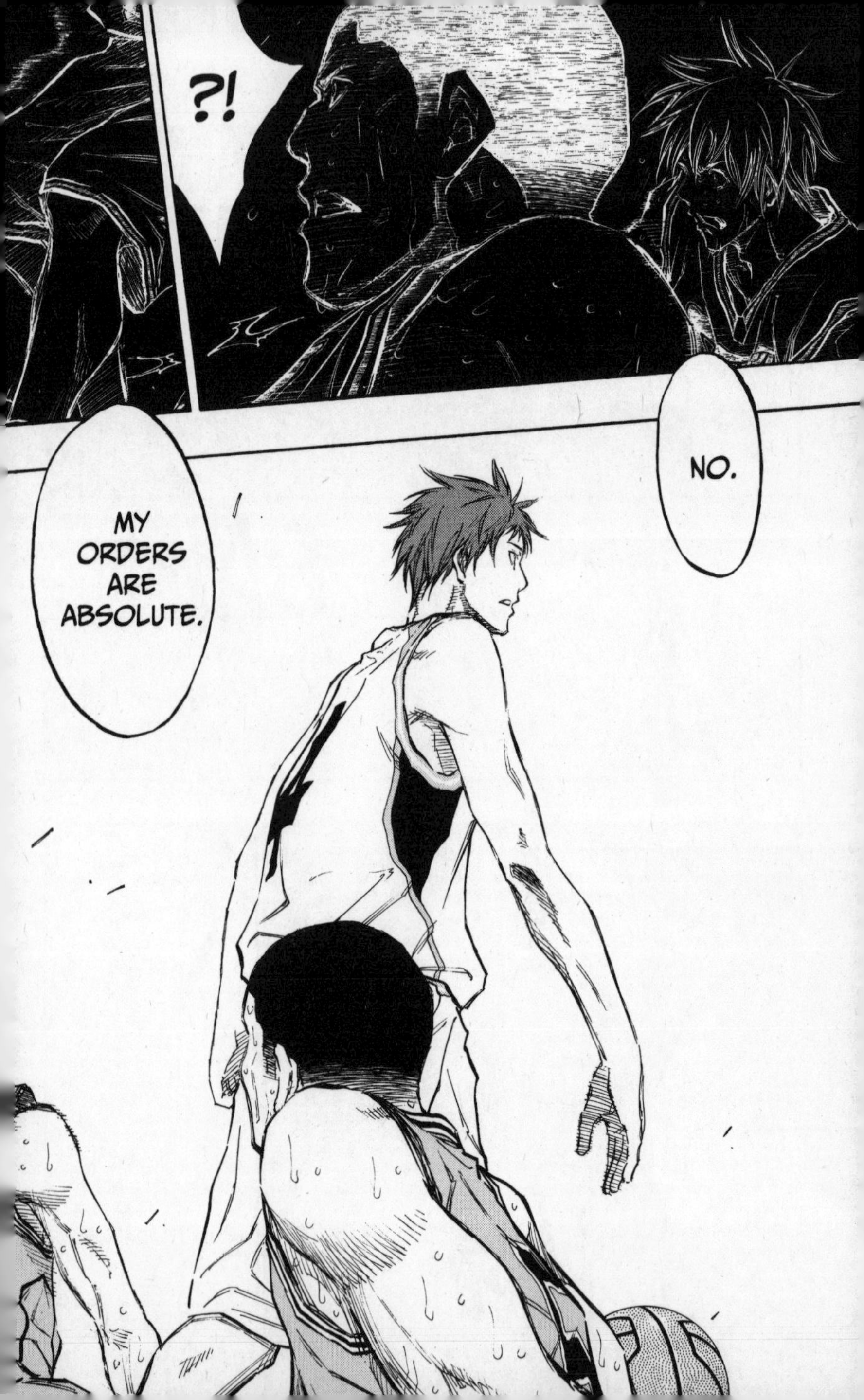
?!
NO.
MY ORDERS ARE ABSOLUTE.

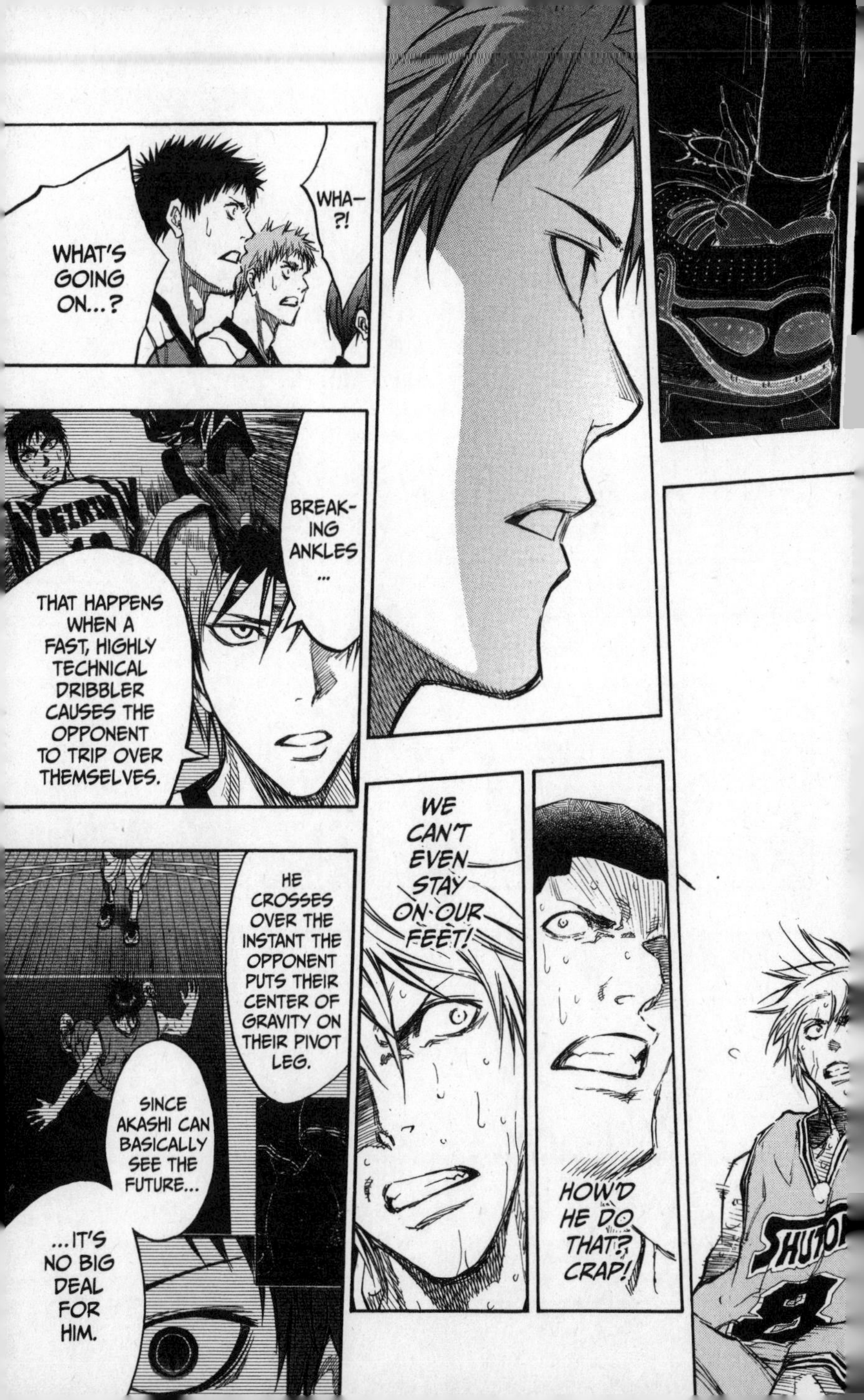
WHA- ?!
WHAT'S GOING ON...?
BREAKING ANKLES...
THAT HAPPENS WHEN A FAST, HIGHLY TECHNICAL DRIBBLER CAUSES THE OPPONENT TO TRIP OVER THEMSELVES.
HOW'D HE DO THAT?! CRAP!
WE CAN'T EVEN STAY ON OUR FEET!
HE CROSSES OVER THE INSTANT THE OPPONENT PUTS THEIR CENTER OF GRAVITY ON THEIR PIVOT LEG.
SINCE AKASHI CAN BASICALLY SEE THE FUTURE...
...IT'S NO BIG DEAL FOR HIM.

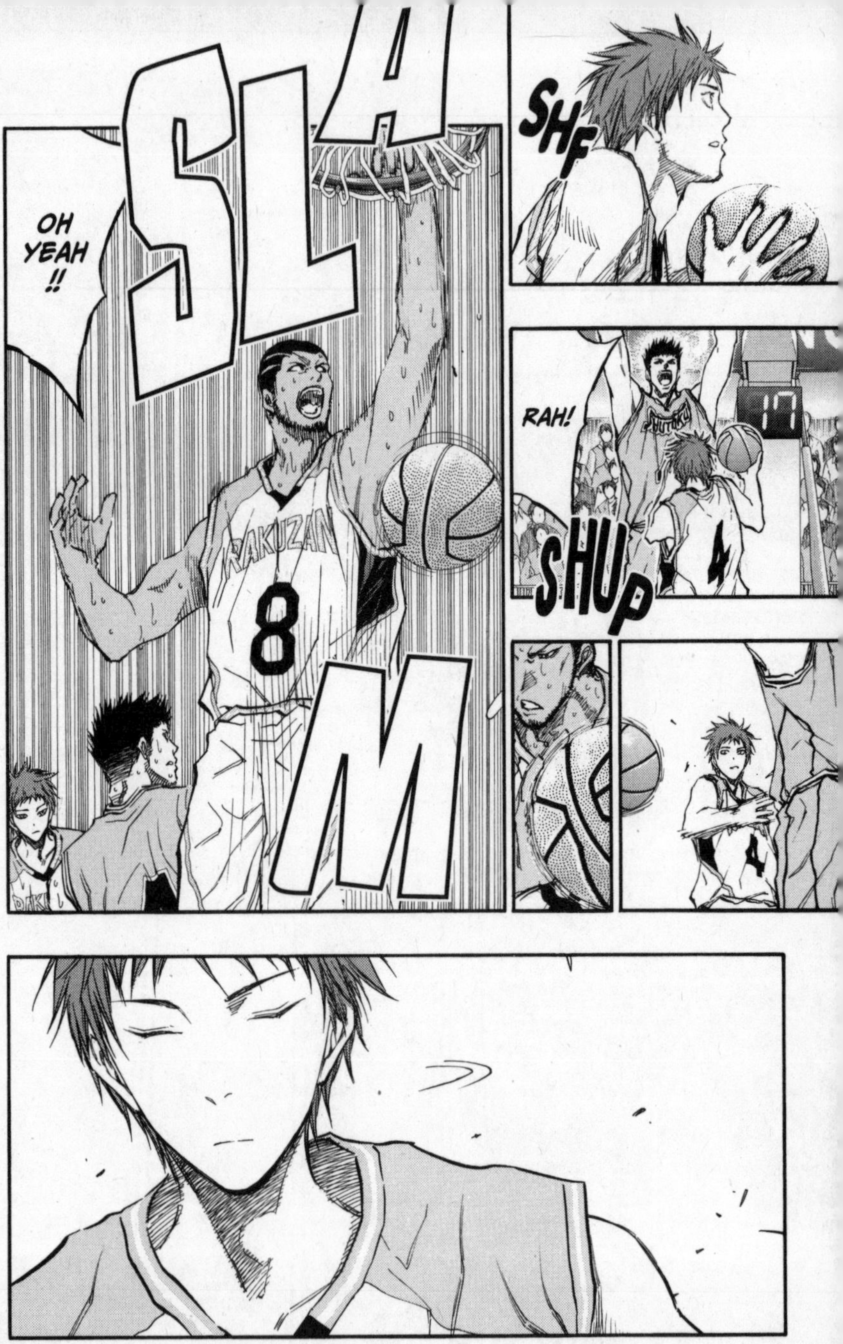
SHF
RAH!
SHUP
SLAM
OH YEAH!!

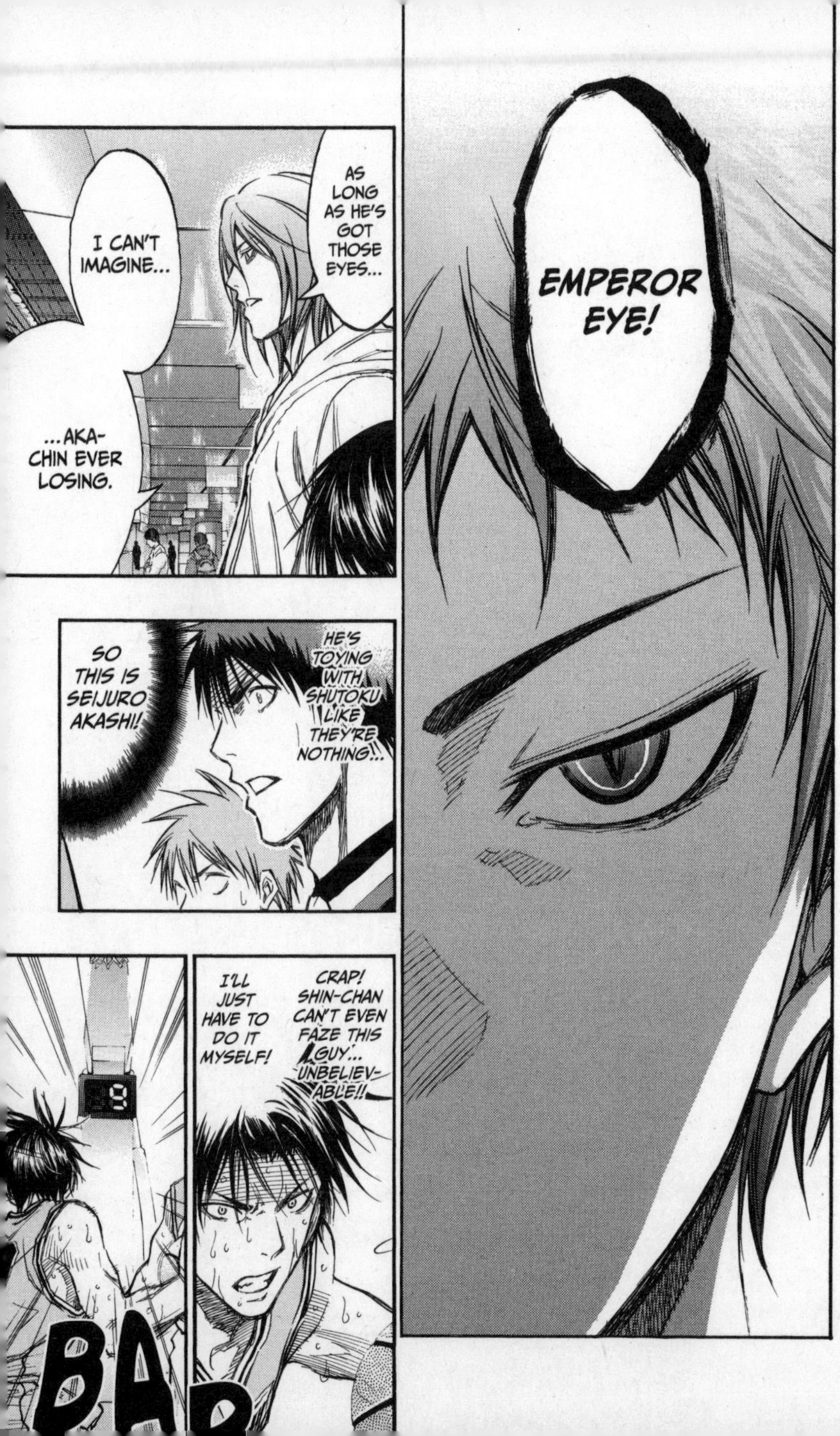
EMPEROR EYE!
AS LONG AS HE'S GOT THOSE EYES...
I CAN'T IMAGINE...
...AKA-CHIN EVER LOSING.
HE'S TOYING WITH SHUTOKU LIKE THEY'RE NOTHING!!...
SO THIS IS SEIJURO AKASHI!
CRAP! SHIN-CHAN CAN'T EVEN FAZE THIS GUY... UNBELIEV-ABLE!!
I'LL JUST HAVE TO DO IT MYSELF!
BA

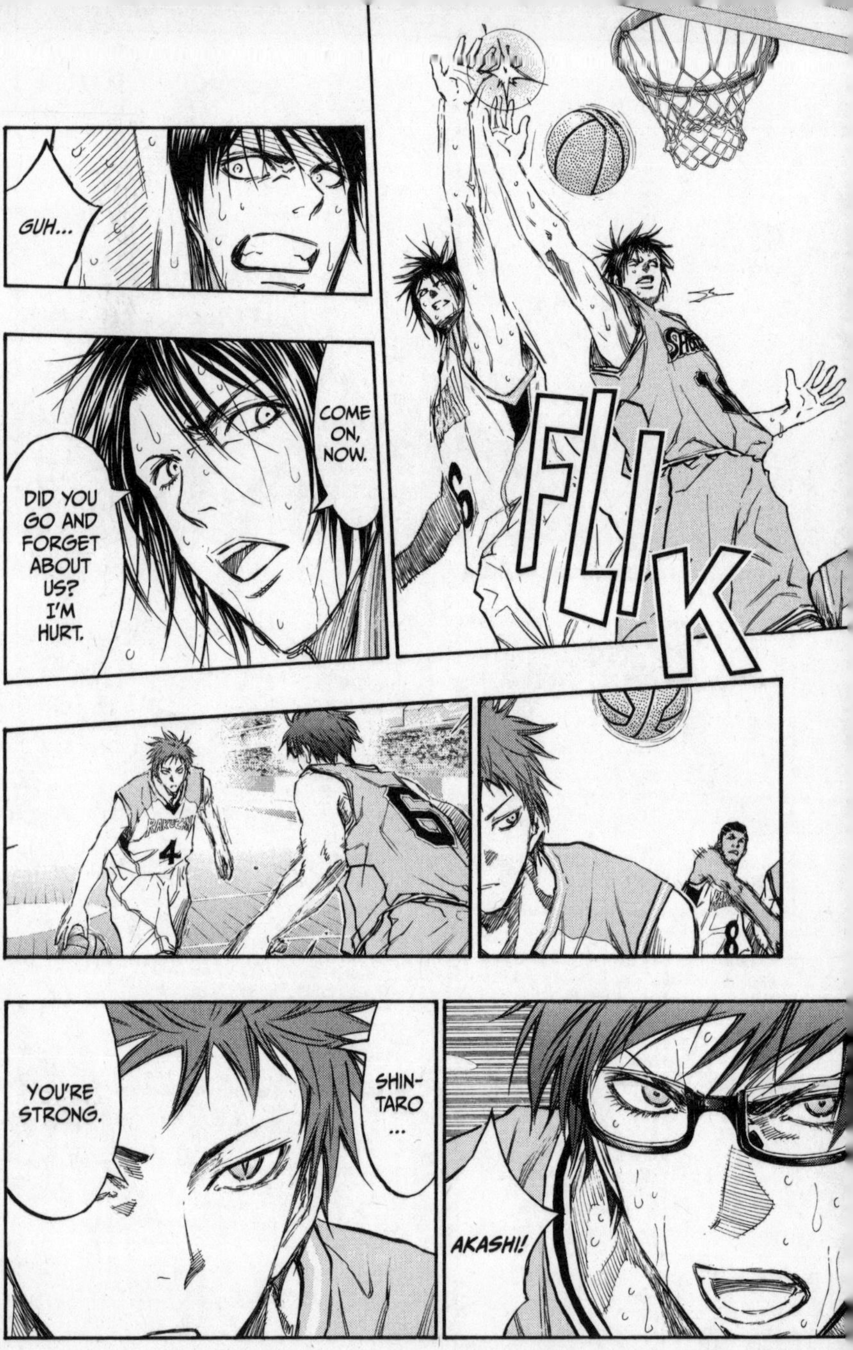
FLIK
GUH...
COME ON, NOW.
DID YOU GO AND FORGET ABOUT US? I'M HURT.
AKASHI!
SHIN-TARO ...
YOU'RE STRONG.

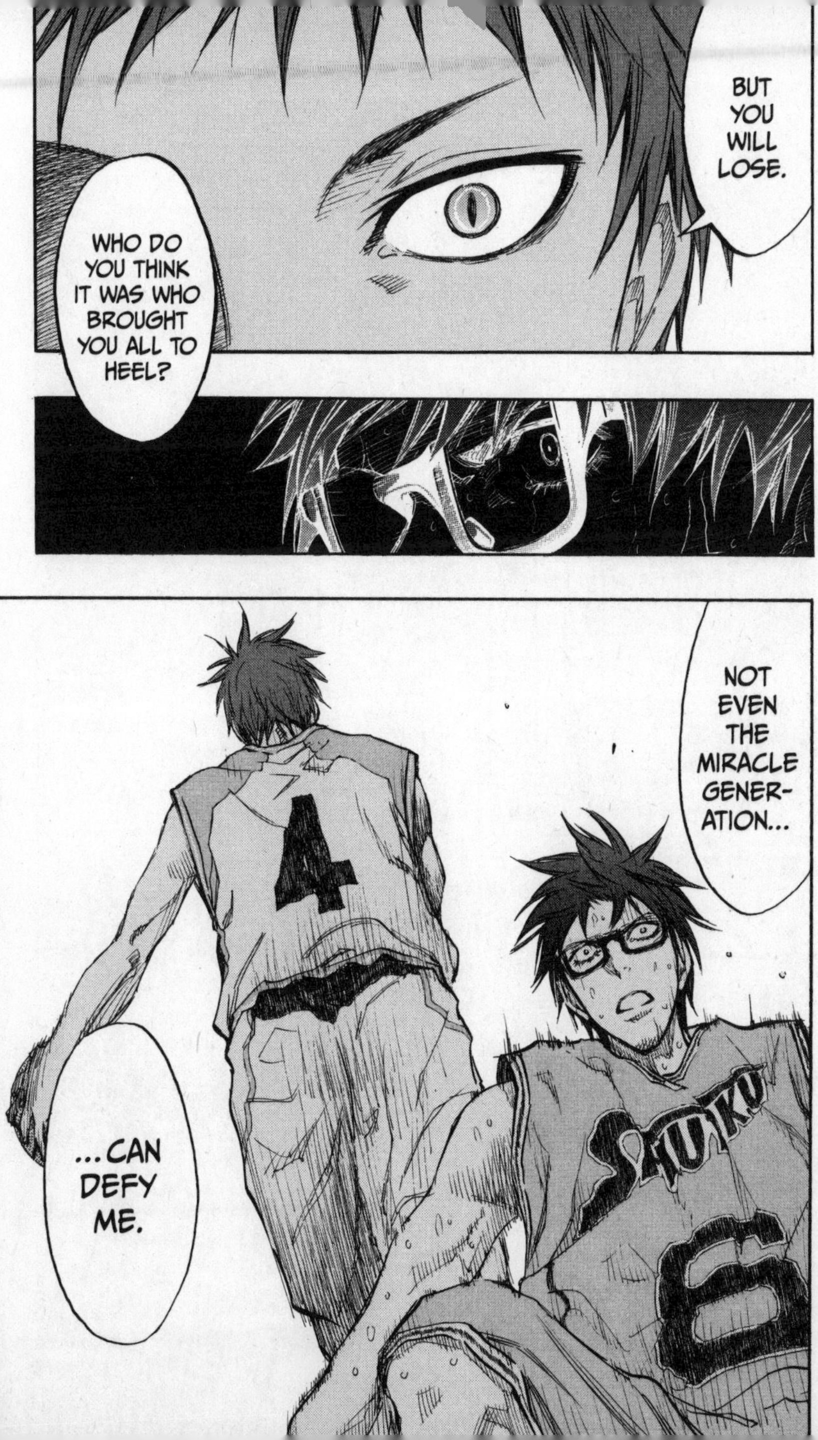
BUT YOU WILL LOSE.
WHO DO YOU THINK IT WAS WHO BROUGHT YOU ALL TO HEEL?
NOT EVEN THE MIRACLE GENER-ATION...
...CAN DEFY ME.

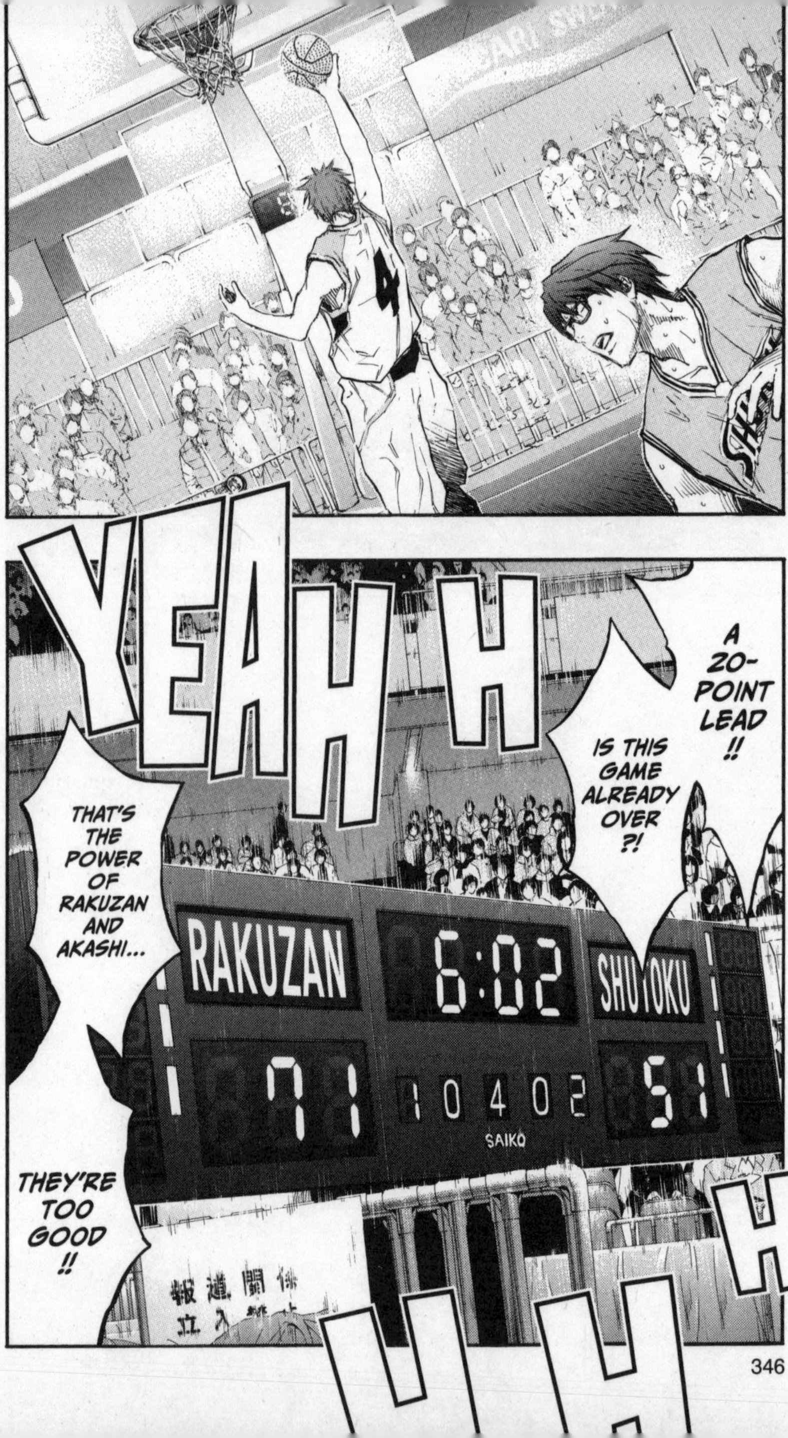
YEAHH
A 20-POINT LEAD!!
IS THIS GAME ALREADY OVER?!
THAT'S THE POWER OF RAKUZAN AND AKASHI...
RAKUZAN
6:02
SHUTOKU
71
10402
51
SAIKO
THEY'RE TOO GOOD!!
HHHH

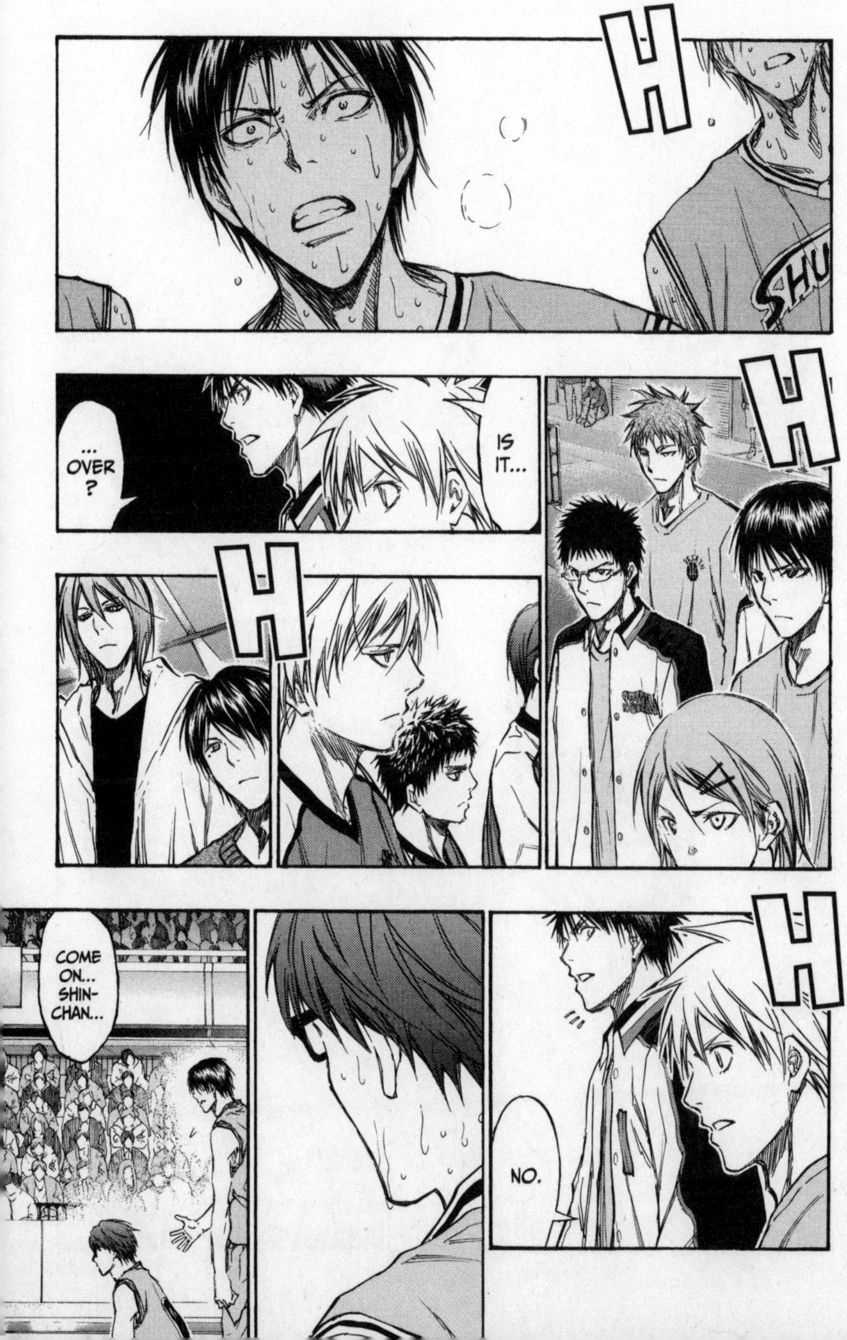
H
H
IS IT...
...OVER?
H
H
NO.
COME ON... SHIN-CHAN...

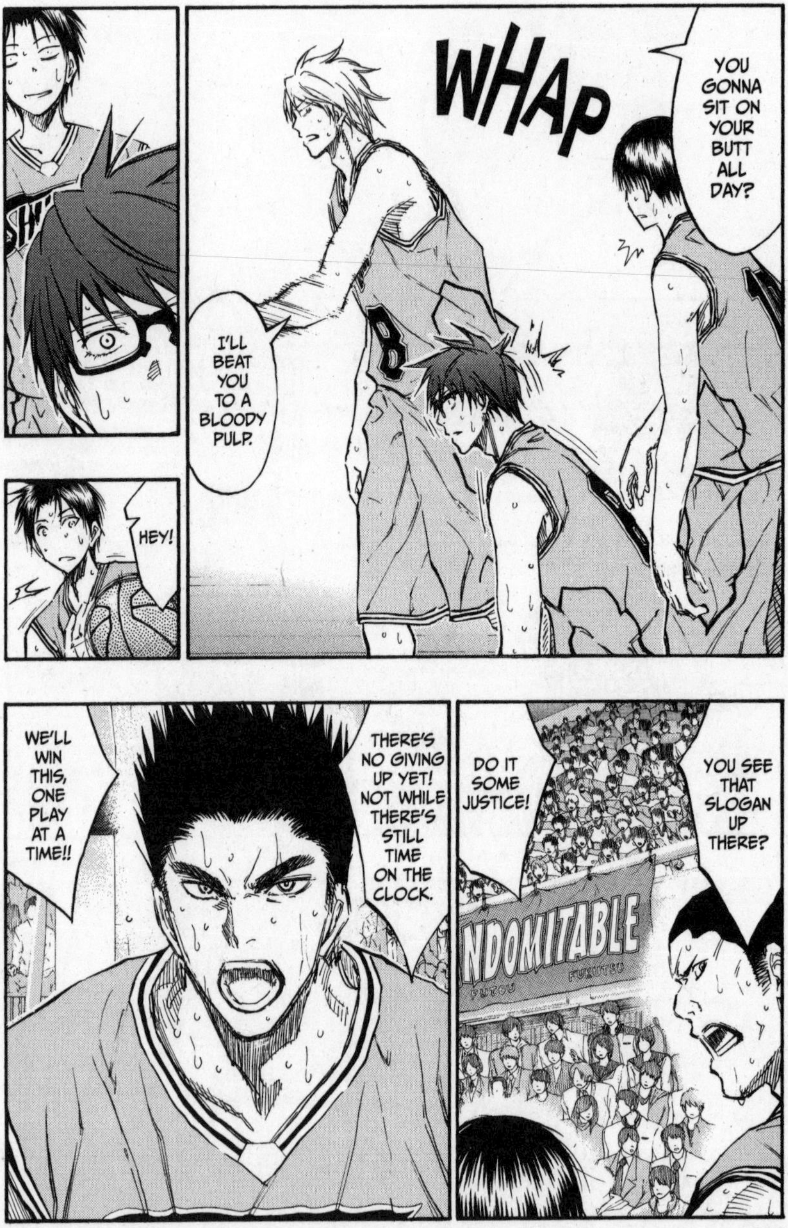
YOU GONNA SIT ON YOUR BUTT ALL DAY?
WHAP
I'LL BEAT YOU TO A BLOODY PULP.
HEY!
YOU SEE THAT SLOGAN UP THERE?
DO IT SOME JUSTICE!
NDOMITABLE
FUKUTSU
THERE'S NO GIVING UP YET! NOT WHILE THERE'S STILL TIME ON THE CLOCK.
WE'LL WIN THIS, ONE PLAY AT A TIME!!

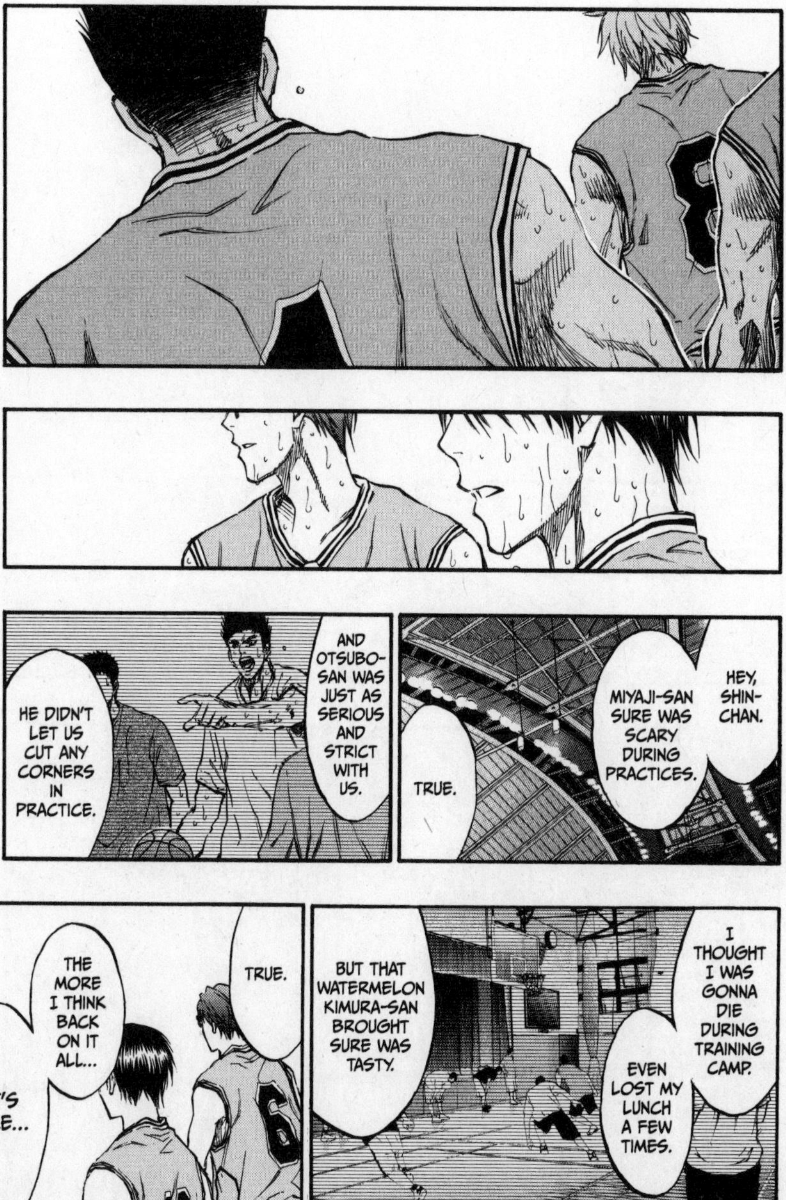
HEY, SHIN-CHAN.
MIYAJI-SAN SURE WAS SCARY DURING PRACTICES.
TRUE.
AND OTSUBO-SAN WAS JUST AS SERIOUS AND STRICT WITH US.
HE DIDN'T LET US CUT ANY CORNERS IN PRACTICE.
I THOUGHT I WAS GONNA DIE DURING TRAINING CAMP.
EVEN LOST MY LUNCH A FEW TIMES.
BUT THAT WATERMELON KIMURA-SAN BROUGHT SURE WAS TASTY.
TRUE.
THE MORE I THINK BACK ON IT ALL...
IT'S LIKE...

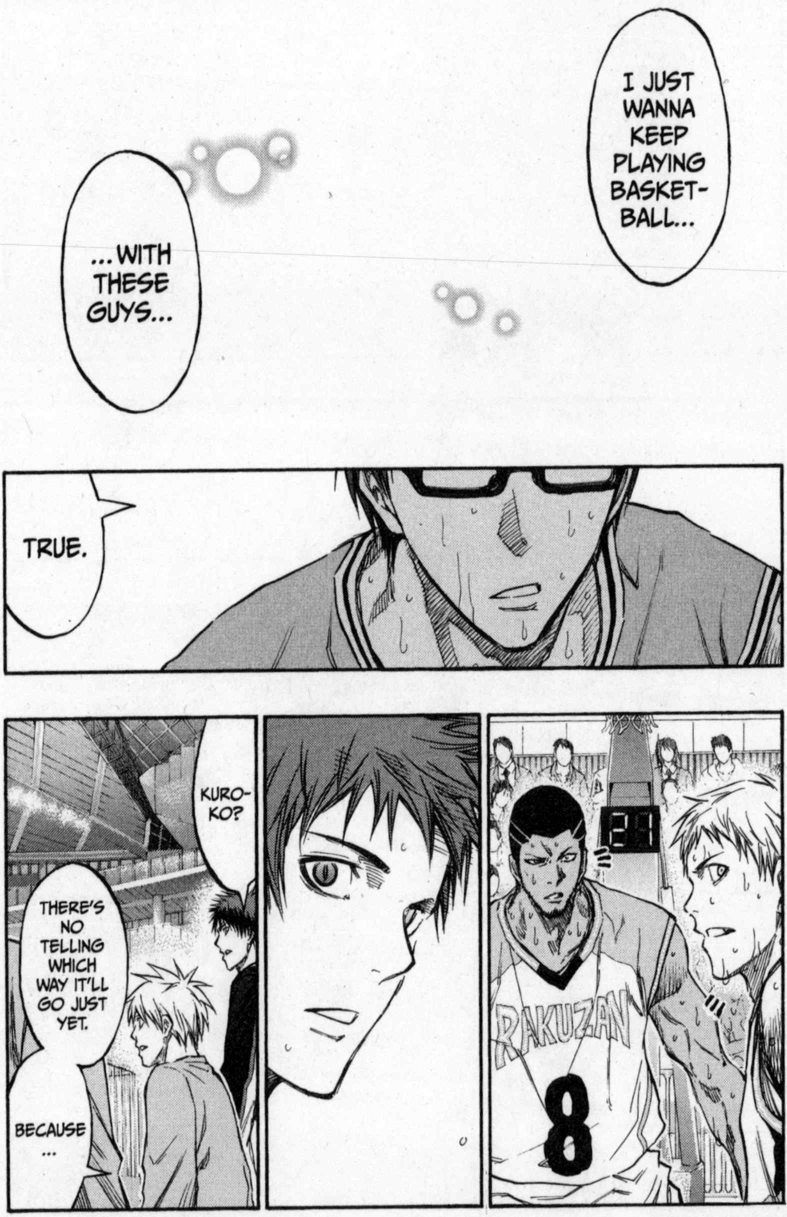
I JUST WANNA KEEP PLAYING BASKET-BALL...
...WITH THESE GUYS...
TRUE.
KURO-KO?
THERE'S NO TELLING WHICH WAY IT'LL GO JUST YET.
BECAUSE...
RAKUZAN
8

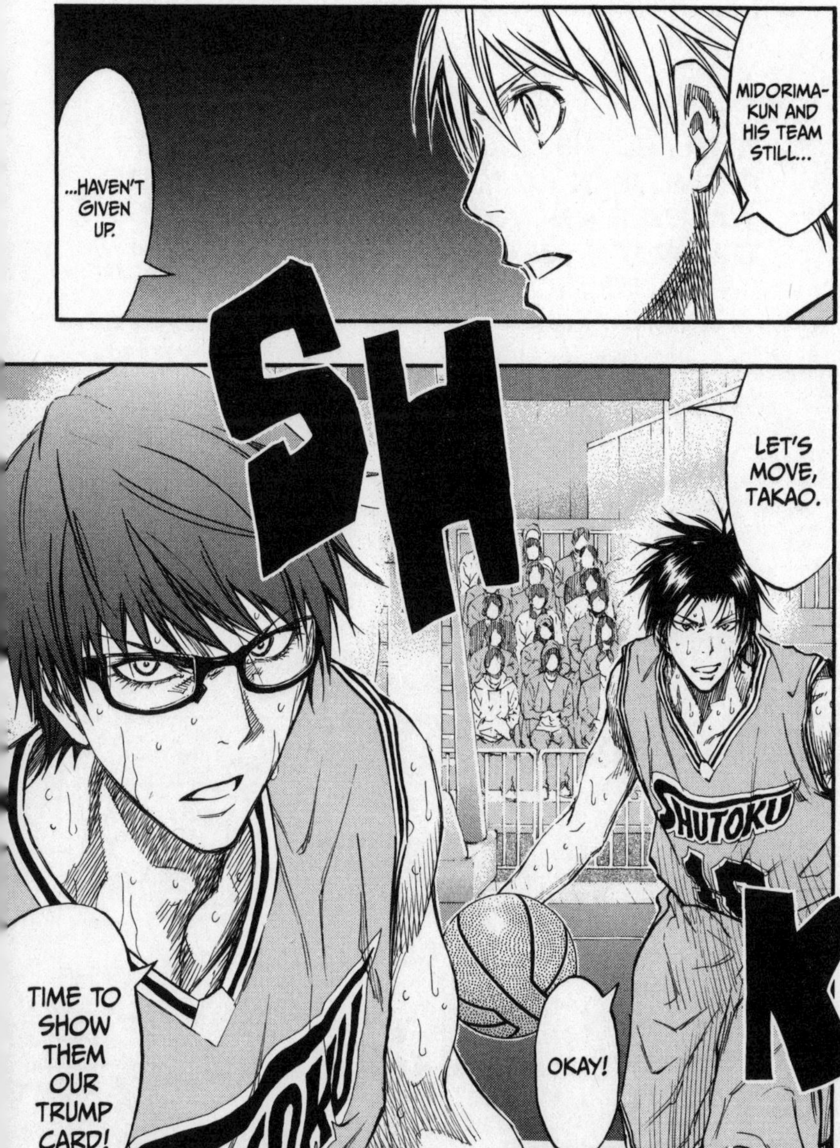
MIDORIMA-KUN AND HIS TEAM STILL...
...HAVEN'T GIVEN UP.
LET'S MOVE, TAKAO.
SHK
OKAY!
TIME TO SHOW THEM OUR TRUMP CARD!

KUROKO'S BASKETBALL Q&A (W/ HALFWAY-DECENT ANSWERS)

Q. WITH ALL THE TEAMS AND PLAYERS THAT SHOW UP IN *KUROKO'S BASKETBALL*, DO YOU EVER ASK YOURSELF, "WAIT, WHAT'S THIS GUY'S JERSEY NUMBER AGAIN?"
(AYACHI from TOKYO)

A. ALL THE TIME.

KUROKO'S BASKETBALL BLOOPERS (TAKE 2)

YOU SEE THAT SLOGAN UP THERE?
FAIL...
I'M SORRY, BUT I CAN'T.
DO IT SOME JUSTICE...
OH ...
DROOP...

180TH QUARTER: KINDA LIKE YOU TWO

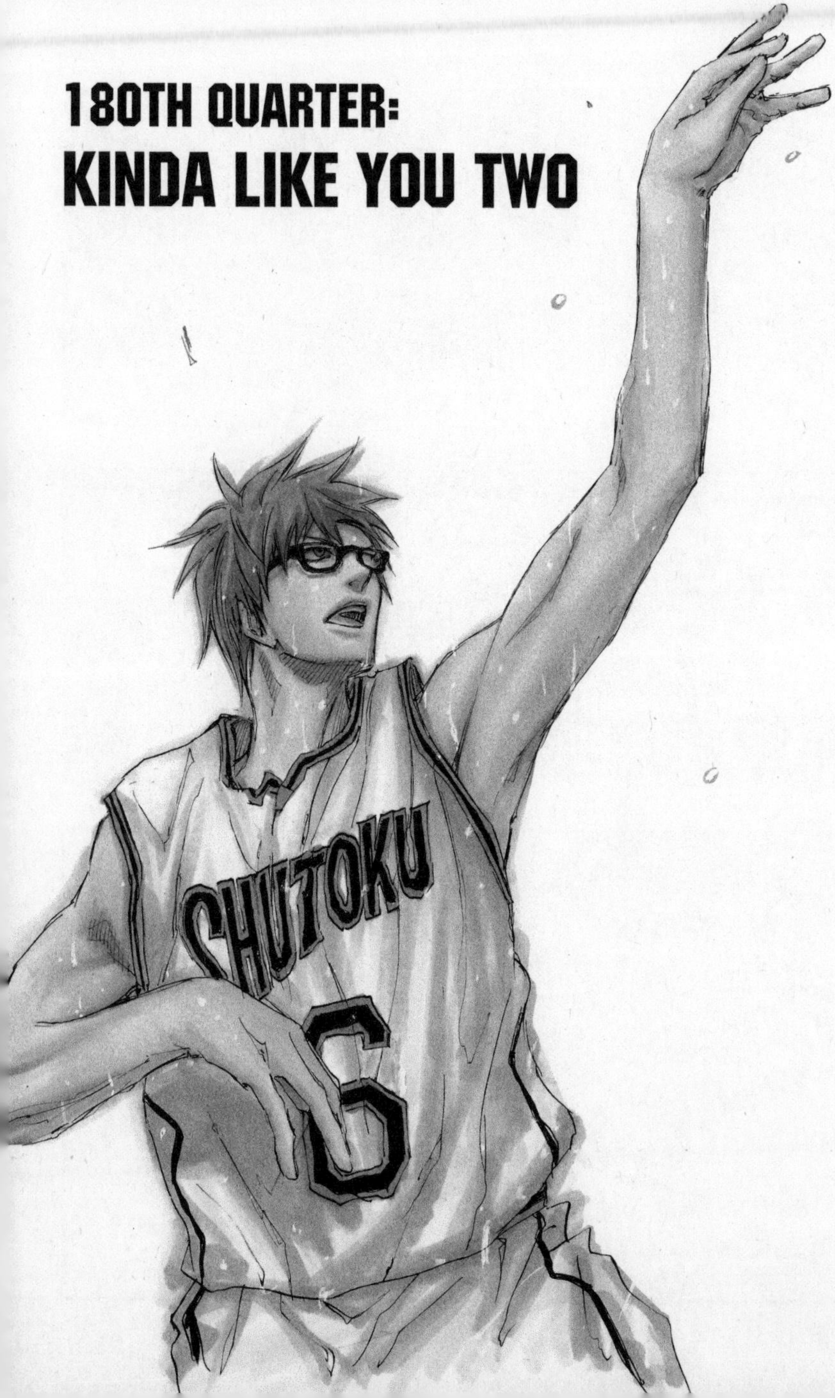
SHUTOKU
6

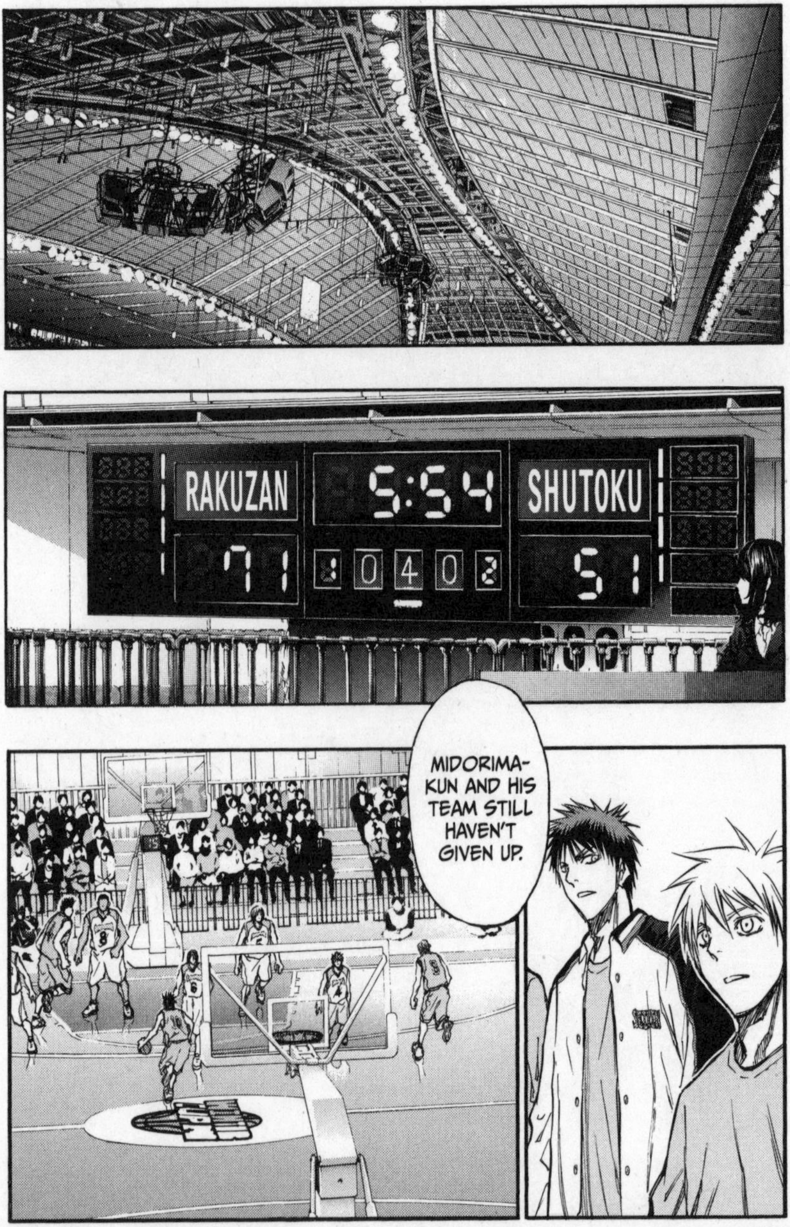
RAKUZAN
5:54
SHUTOKU
71
51
MIDORIMA-KUN AND HIS TEAM STILL HAVEN'T GIVEN UP.

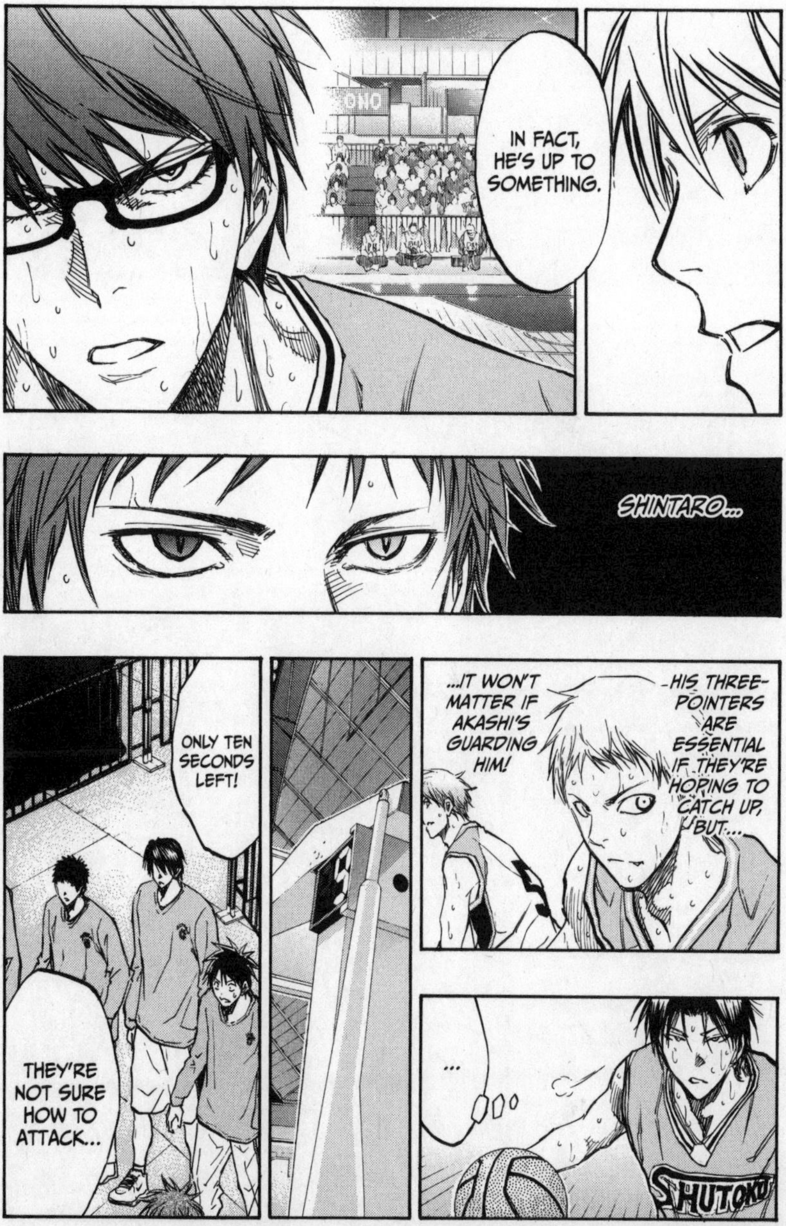
IN FACT, HE'S UP TO SOMETHING.
SHINTARO...
-HIS THREE-POINTERS ARE ESSENTIAL IF THEY'RE HOPING TO CATCH UP, BUT...
...IT WON'T MATTER IF AKASHI'S GUARDING HIM!
...
ONLY TEN SECONDS LEFT!
THEY'RE NOT SURE HOW TO ATTACK...

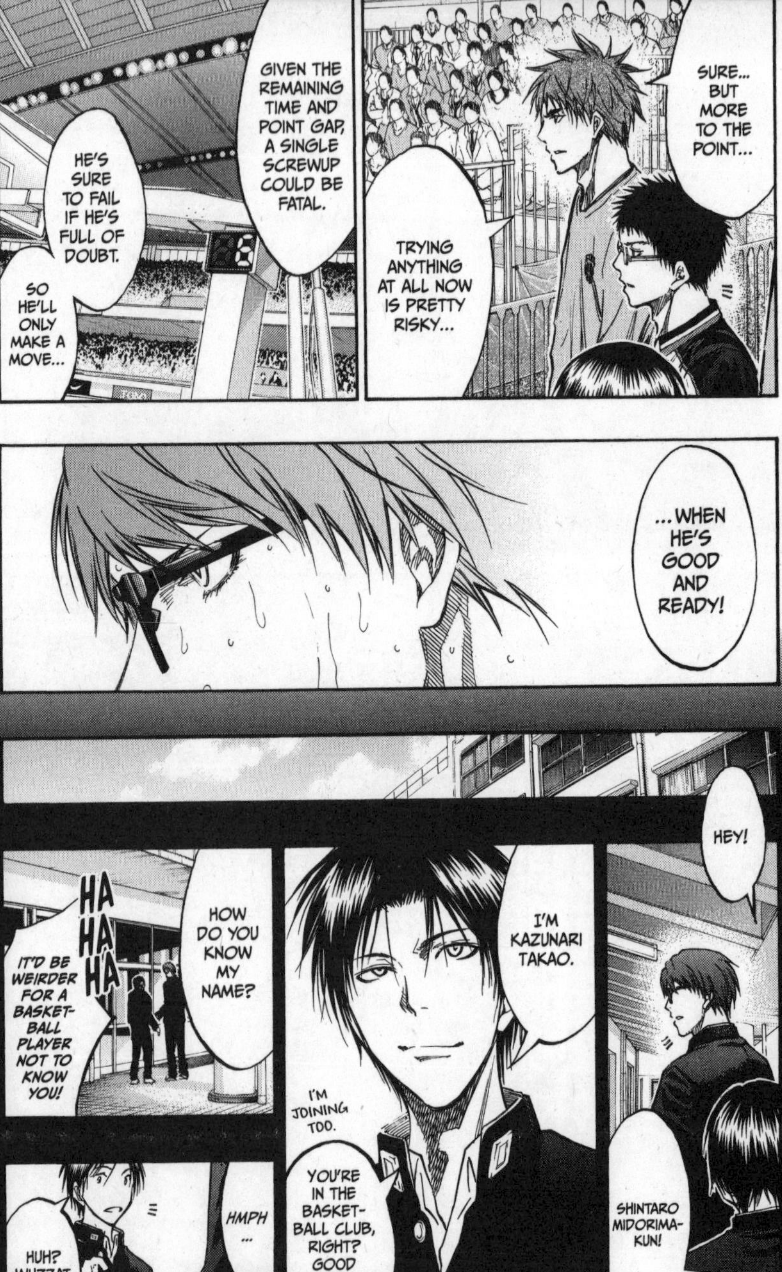
SURE... BUT MORE TO THE POINT...
TRYING ANYTHING AT ALL NOW IS PRETTY RISKY...
GIVEN THE REMAINING TIME AND POINT GAP, A SINGLE SCREWUP COULD BE FATAL.
HE'S SURE TO FAIL IF HE'S FULL OF DOUBT.
SO HE'LL ONLY MAKE A MOVE...
...WHEN HE'S GOOD AND READY!
HEY!
SHINTARO MIDORIMA-KUN!
HOW DO YOU KNOW MY NAME?
HAHAHA
IT'D BE WEIRDER FOR A BASKETBALL PLAYER NOT TO KNOW YOU!
I'M KAZUNARI TAKAO.
I'M JOINING TOO.
YOU'RE IN THE BASKETBALL CLUB, RIGHT? GOOD TO BE WORKING WITH YA!
HMPH...
HUH? WUZZAT?

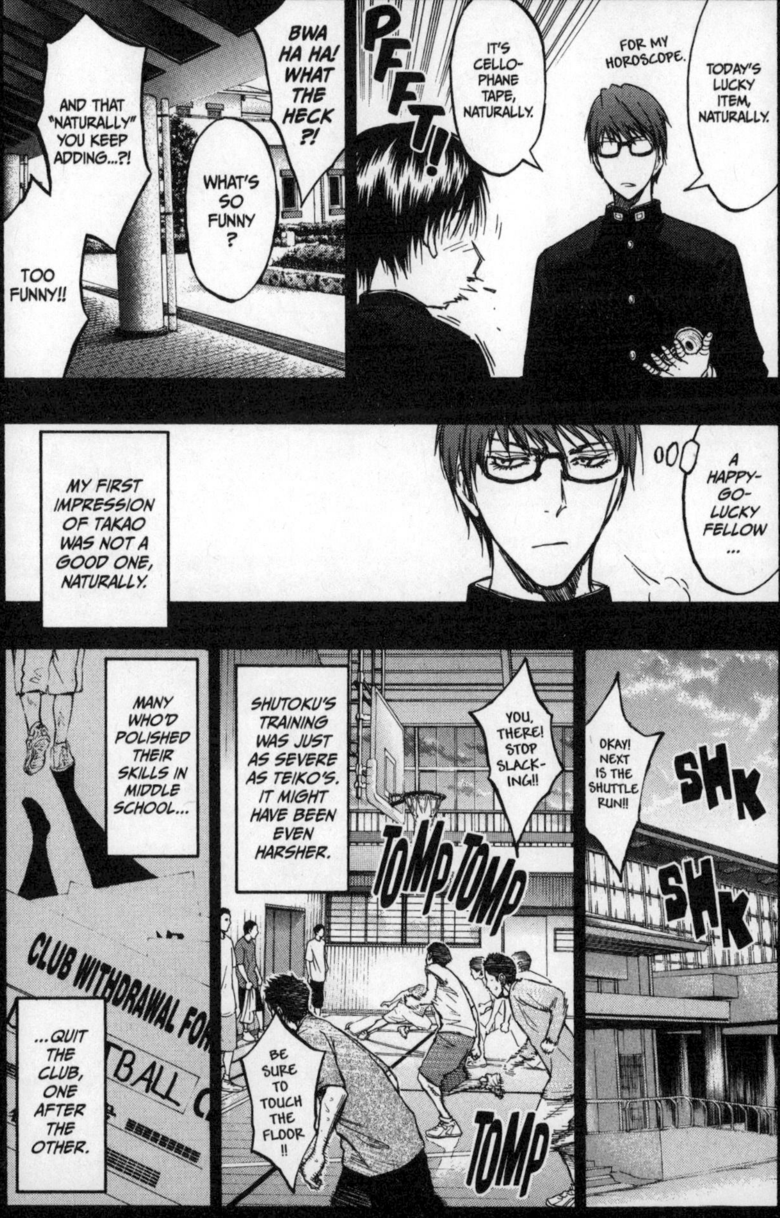
TODAY'S LUCKY ITEM, NATURALLY.
FOR MY HOROSCOPE.
IT'S CELLOPHANE TAPE, NATURALLY.
PFFT!!
BWA HA HA! WHAT THE HECK?!
WHAT'S SO FUNNY?
AND THAT "NATURALLY" YOU KEEP ADDING...?!
TOO FUNNY!!
A HAPPY-GO-LUCKY FELLOW...
MY FIRST IMPRESSION OF TAKAO WAS NOT A GOOD ONE, NATURALLY.
SHK
SHK
OKAY! NEXT IS THE SHUTTLE RUN!!
YOU, THERE! STOP SLACKING!!
SHUTOKU'S TRAINING WAS JUST AS SEVERE AS TEIKO'S. IT MIGHT HAVE BEEN EVEN HARSHER.
TOMP TOMP
BE SURE TO TOUCH THE FLOOR!!
TOMP
MANY WHO'D POLISHED THEIR SKILLS IN MIDDLE SCHOOL...
CLUB WITHDRAWAL
...QUIT THE CLUB, ONE AFTER THE OTHER.

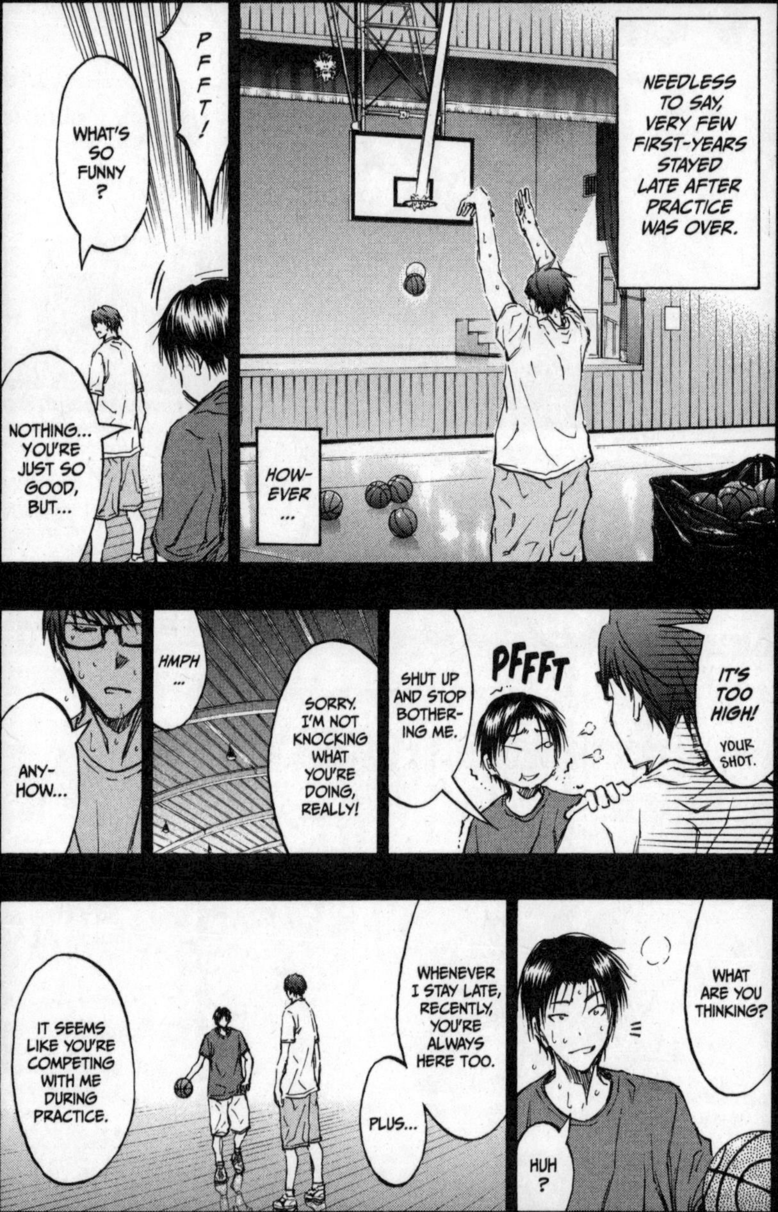
NEEDLESS TO SAY, VERY FEW FIRST-YEARS STAYED LATE AFTER PRACTICE WAS OVER.
HOW-EVER...
PFFFT!
WHAT'S SO FUNNY?
NOTHING... YOU'RE JUST SO GOOD, BUT...
IT'S TOO HIGH!
YOUR SHOT.
PFFFT
SHUT UP AND STOP BOTHER-ING ME.
SORRY. I'M NOT KNOCKING WHAT YOU'RE DOING, REALLY!
HMPH...
ANY-HOW...
WHAT ARE YOU THINKING?
HUH?
WHENEVER I STAY LATE, RECENTLY, YOU'RE ALWAYS HERE TOO.
PLUS...
IT SEEMS LIKE YOU'RE COMPETING WITH ME DURING PRACTICE.

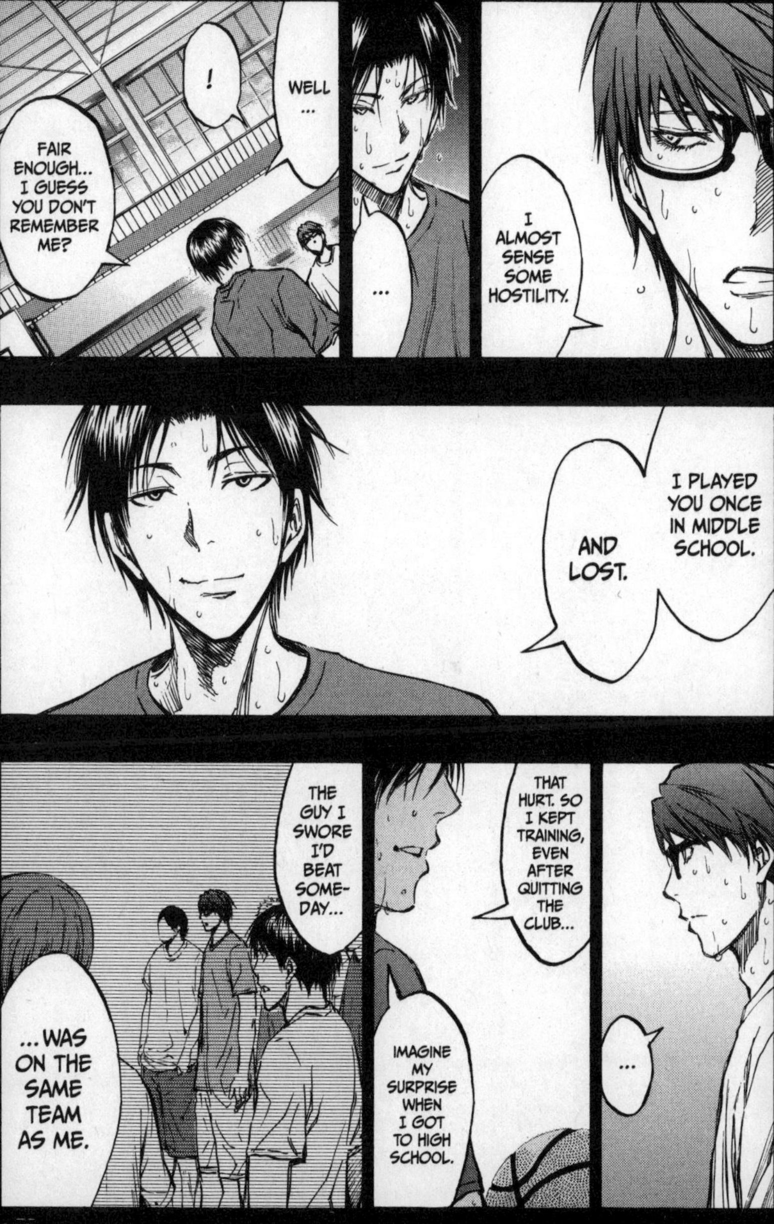
I ALMOST SENSE SOME HOSTILITY.
...
WELL ...
!
FAIR ENOUGH... I GUESS YOU DON'T REMEMBER ME?
I PLAYED YOU ONCE IN MIDDLE SCHOOL.
AND LOST.
...
THAT HURT. SO I KEPT TRAINING, EVEN AFTER QUITTING THE CLUB...
IMAGINE MY SURPRISE WHEN I GOT TO HIGH SCHOOL.
THE GUY I SWORE I'D BEAT SOME-DAY...
...WAS ON THE SAME TEAM AS ME.

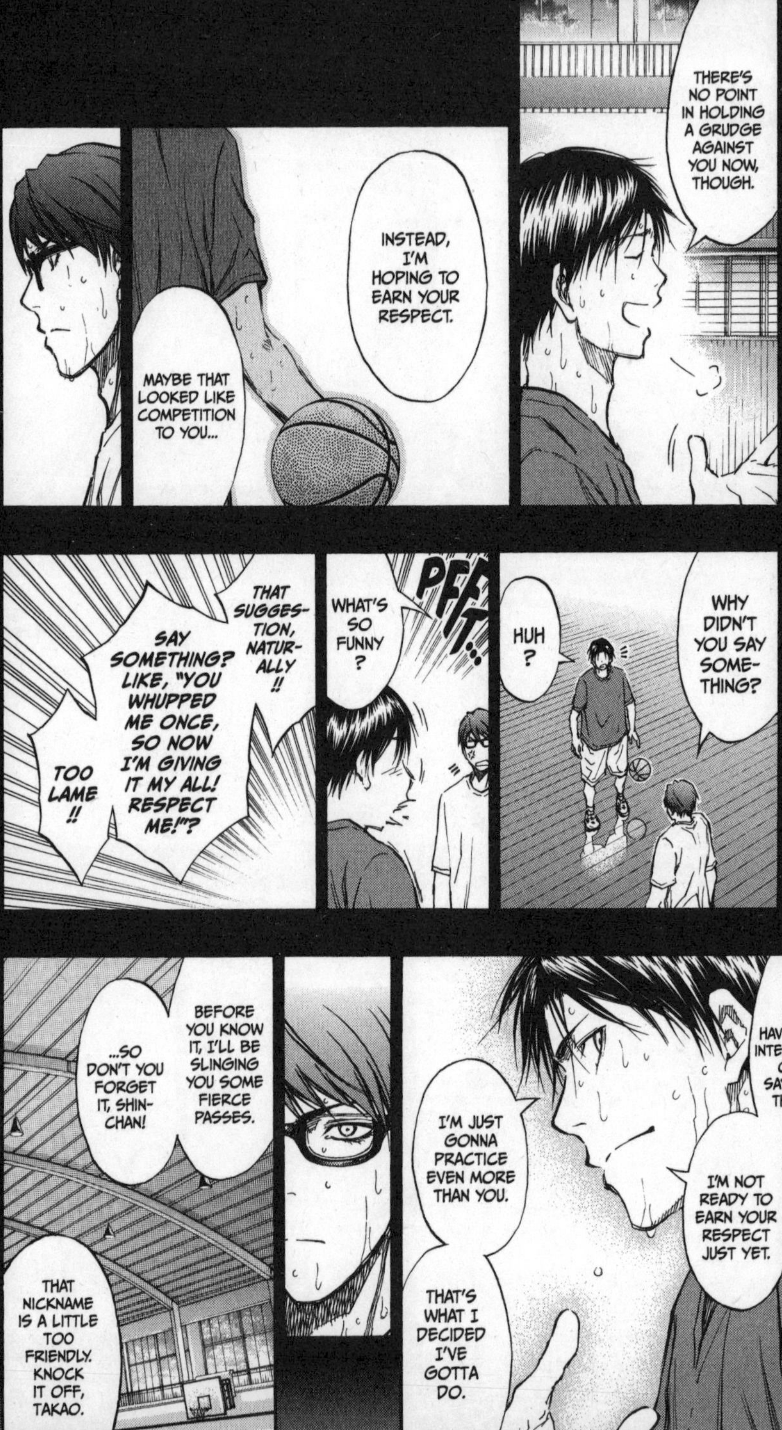
THERE'S NO POINT IN HOLDING A GRUDGE AGAINST YOU NOW, THOUGH.
INSTEAD, I'M HOPING TO EARN YOUR RESPECT.
MAYBE THAT LOOKED LIKE COMPETITION TO YOU...
WHY DIDN'T YOU SAY SOME-THING?
HUH ?
PFFT!!
WHAT'S SO FUNNY ?
THAT SUGGES-TION, NATUR-ALLY !!
SAY SOMETHING? LIKE, "YOU WHUPPED ME ONCE, SO NOW I'M GIVING IT MY ALL! RESPECT ME!"?
TOO LAME !!
I HAVE NO INTENTION OF SAYING THAT.
I'M NOT READY TO EARN YOUR RESPECT JUST YET.
I'M JUST GONNA PRACTICE EVEN MORE THAN YOU.
THAT'S WHAT I DECIDED I'VE GOTTA DO.
BEFORE YOU KNOW IT, I'LL BE SLINGING YOU SOME FIERCE PASSES.
...SO DON'T YOU FORGET IT, SHIN-CHAN!
THAT NICKNAME IS A LITTLE TOO FRIENDLY. KNOCK IT OFF, TAKAO.

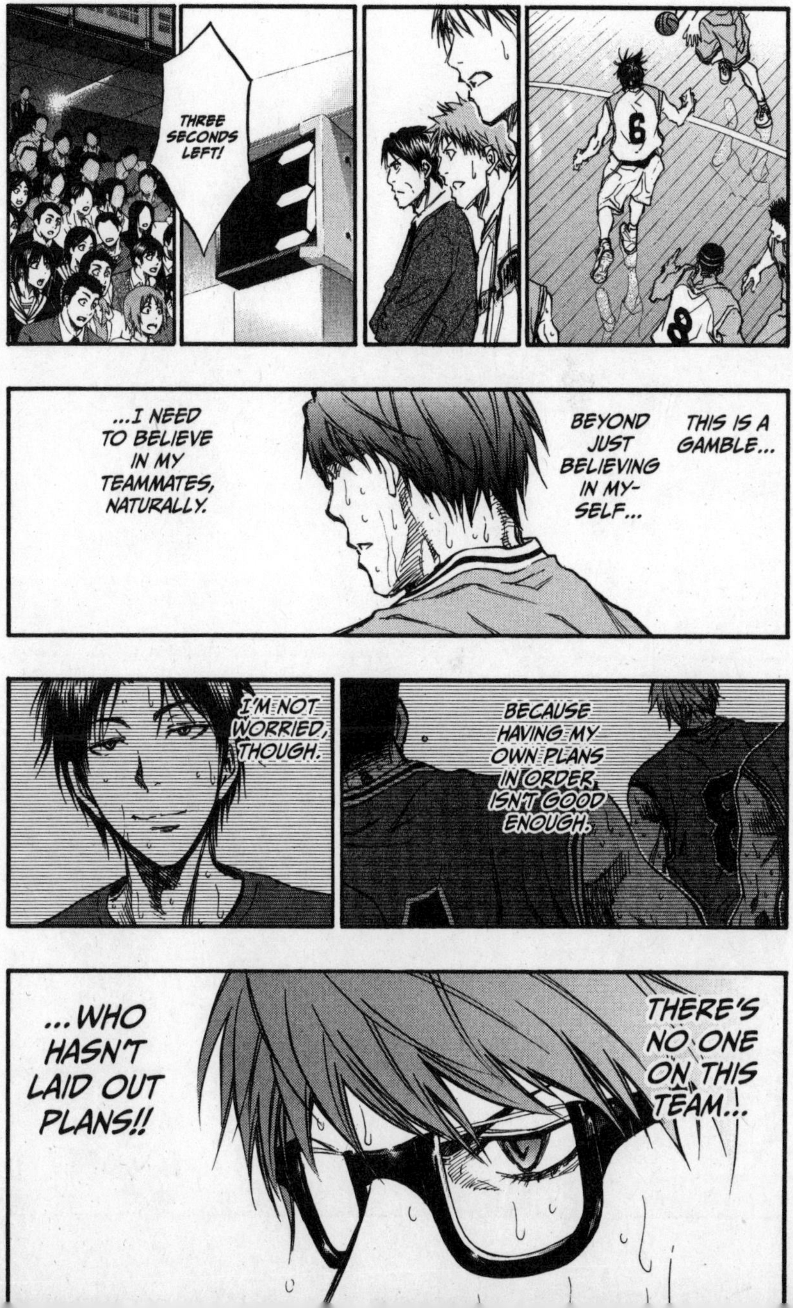
THREE SECONDS LEFT!
THIS IS A GAMBLE...
BEYOND JUST BELIEVING IN MY-SELF...
...I NEED TO BELIEVE IN MY TEAMMATES, NATURALLY.
BECAUSE HAVING MY OWN PLANS IN ORDER ISN'T GOOD ENOUGH.
I'M NOT WORRIED, THOUGH.
THERE'S NO ONE ON THIS TEAM...
...WHO HASN'T LAID OUT PLANS!!

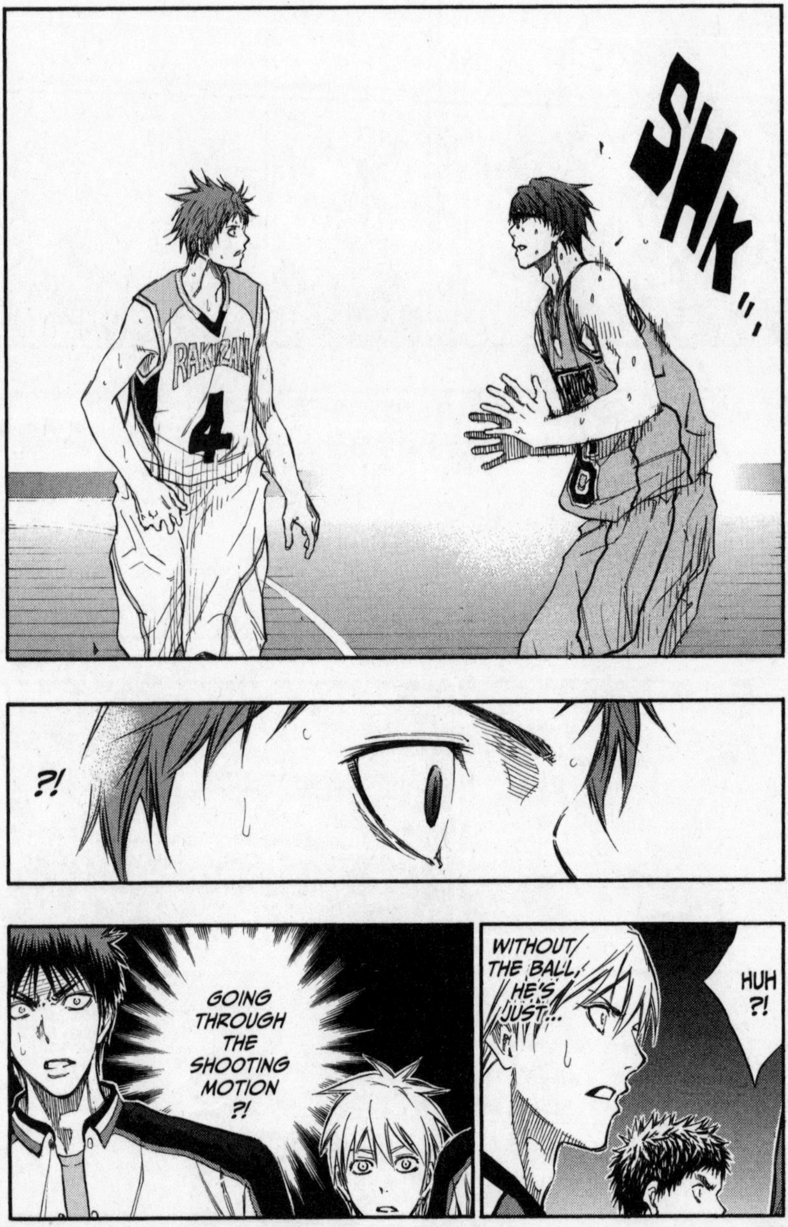
SHK...
?!
HUH ?!
WITHOUT THE BALL, HE'S JUST...
GOING THROUGH THE SHOOTING MOTION ?!

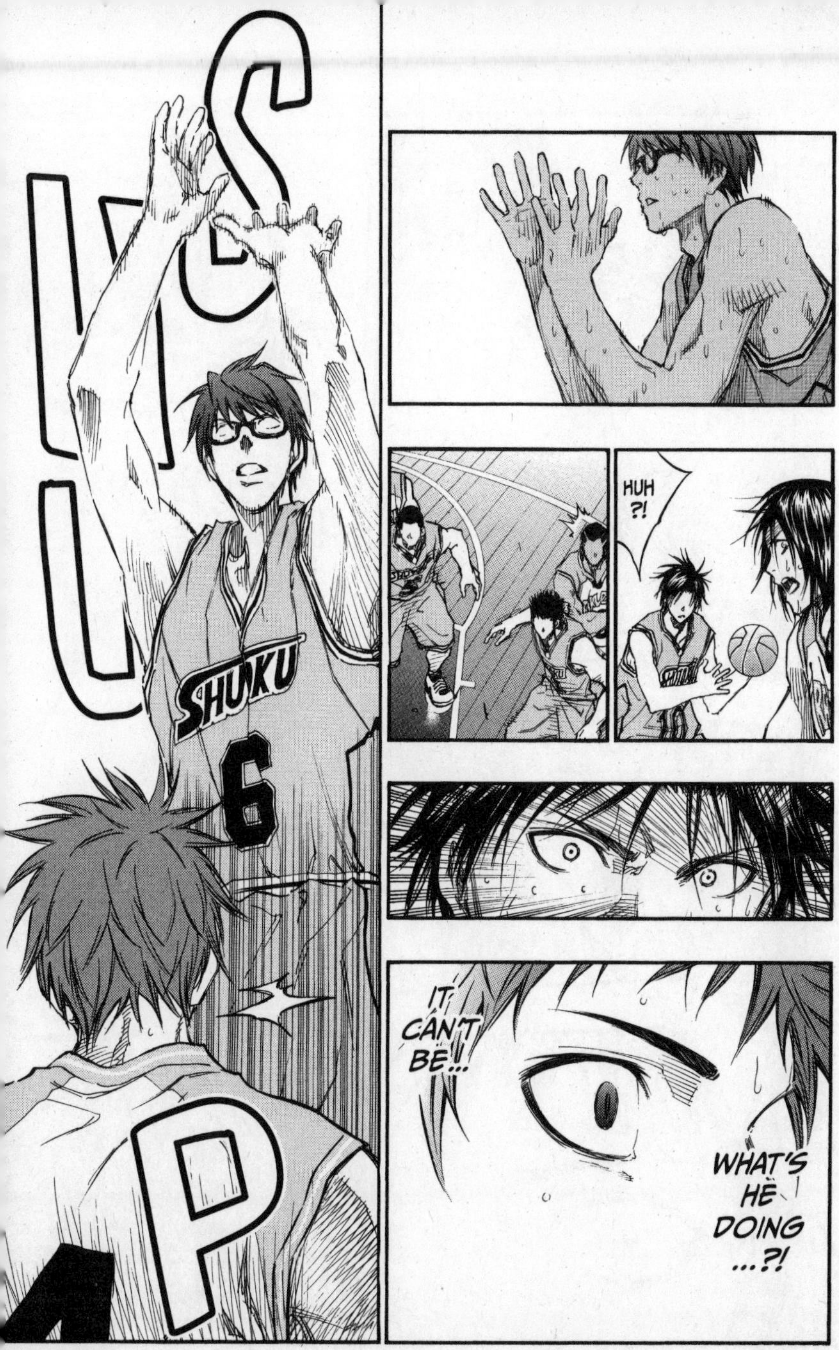
HUH ?!
IT CAN'T BE...
WHAT'S HE DOING ...?!
SHUP
SHUKU
6

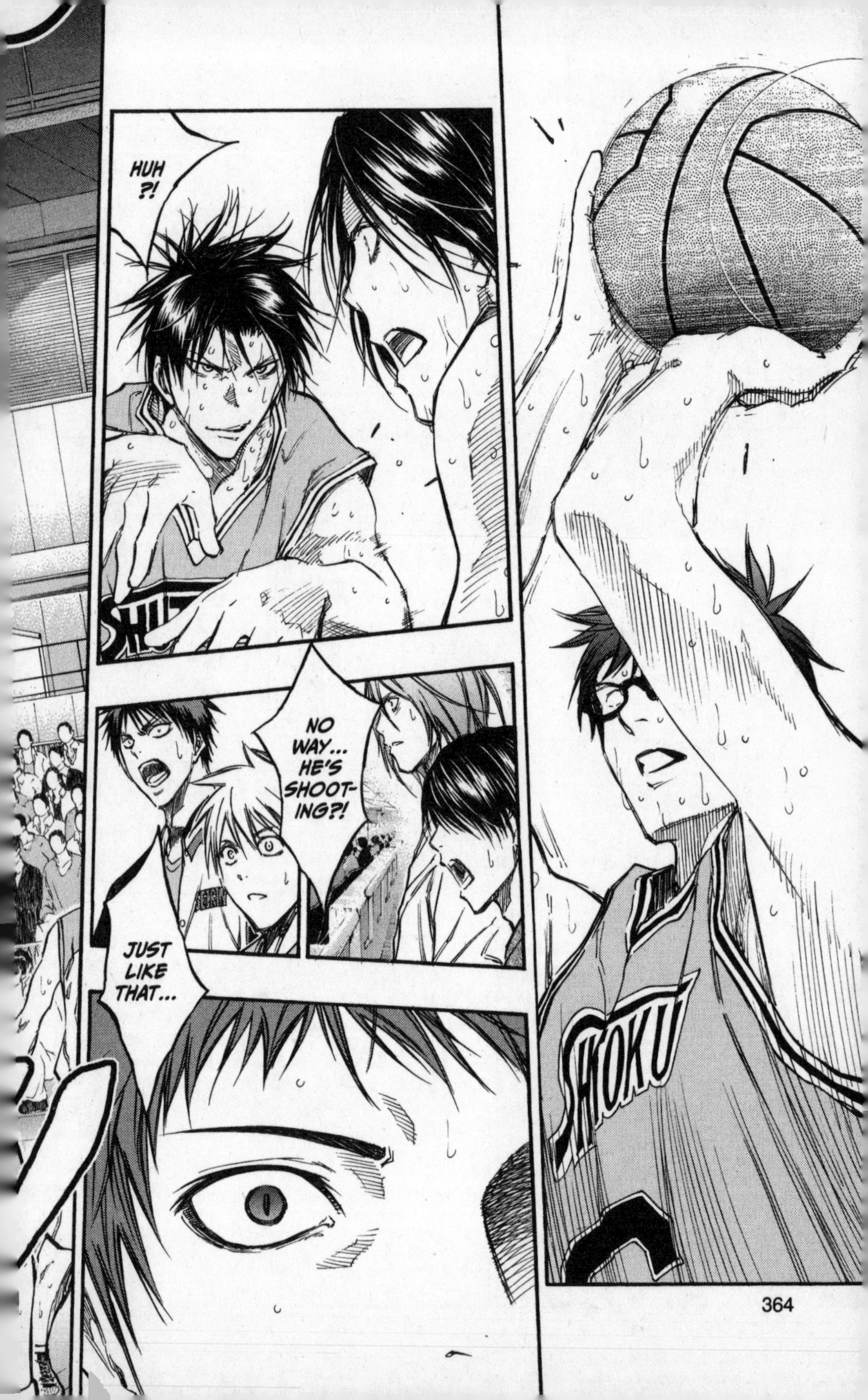
HUH ?!
NO WAY... HE'S SHOOT-ING?!
JUST LIKE THAT...

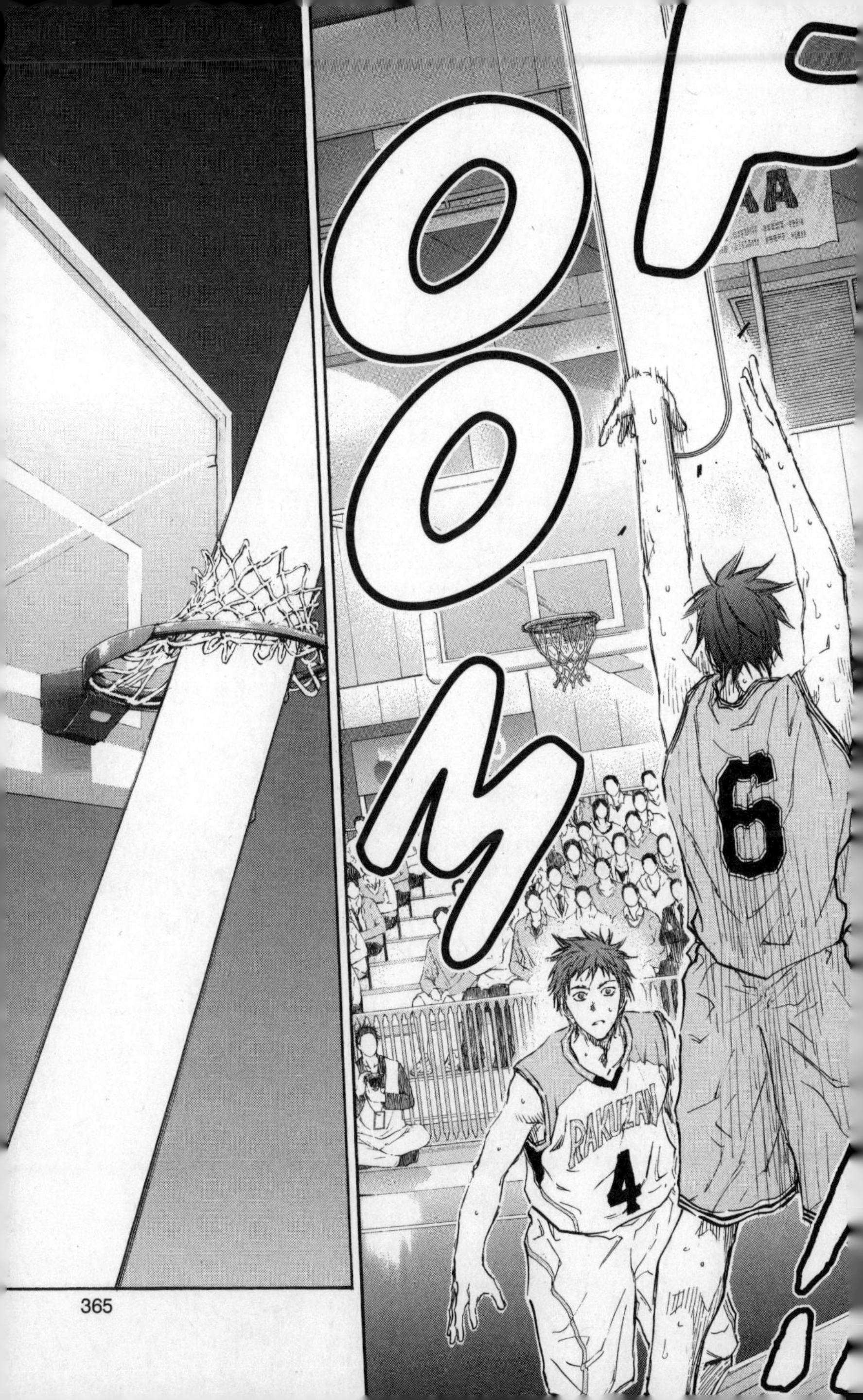

WOOOM
RAKUZAN
4
6

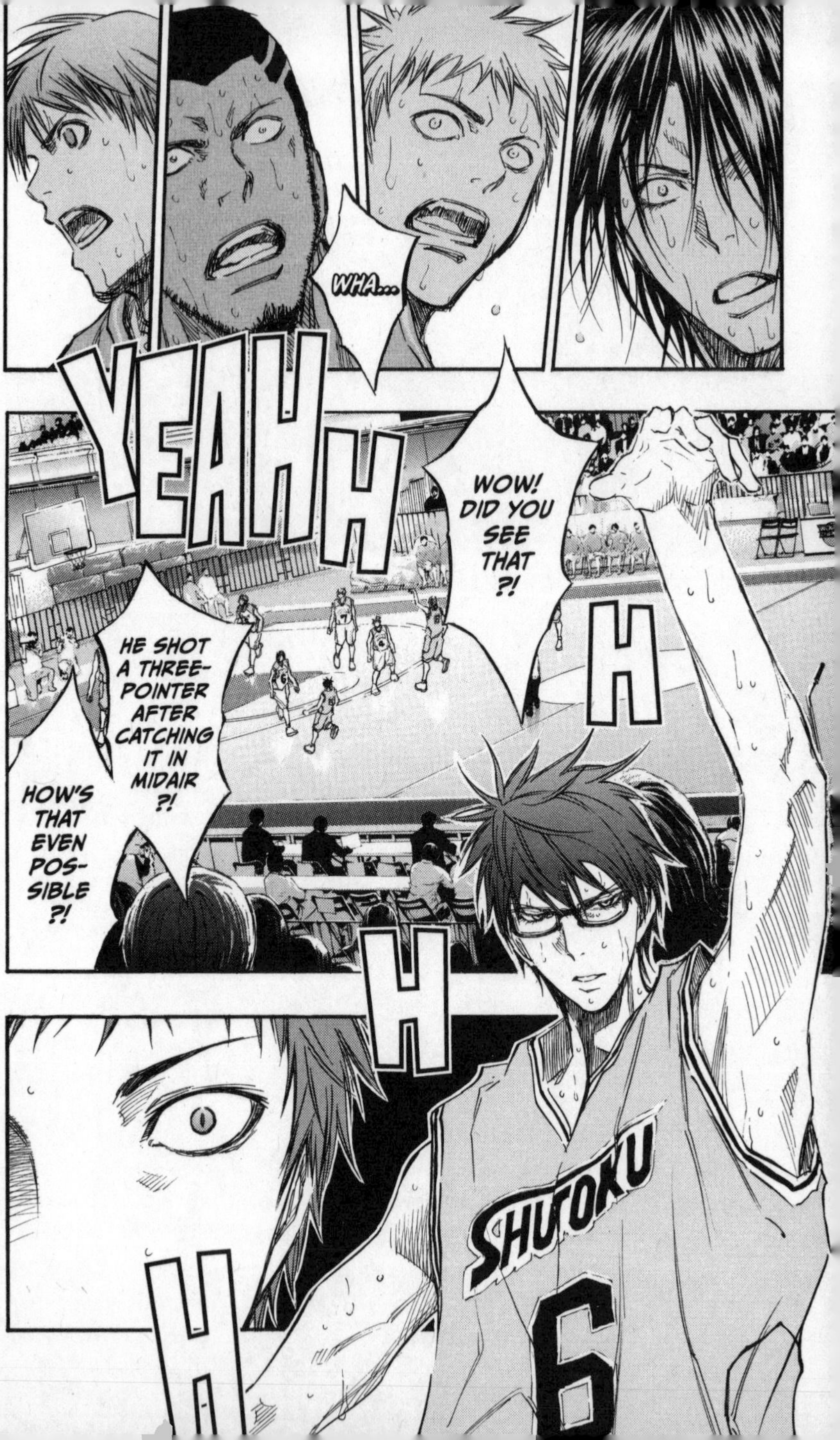
WHA...
YEAHH
H
H
H
WOW! DID YOU SEE THAT?!
HE SHOT A THREE-POINTER AFTER CATCHING IT IN MIDAIR?!
HOW'S THAT EVEN POSSIBLE?!
SHUTOKU
6

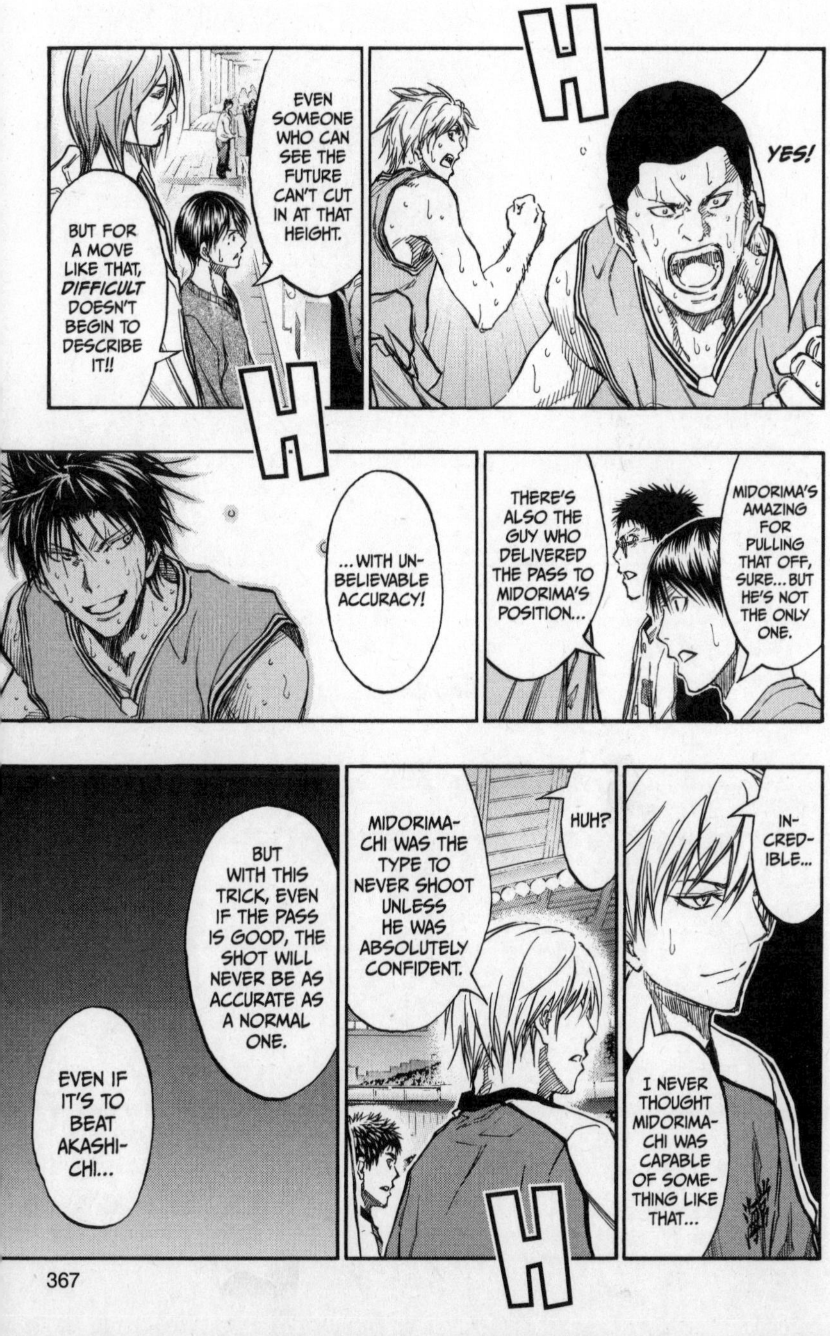
H
YES!
EVEN SOMEONE WHO CAN SEE THE FUTURE CAN'T CUT IN AT THAT HEIGHT.
BUT FOR A MOVE LIKE THAT, *DIFFICULT* DOESN'T BEGIN TO DESCRIBE IT!!
H
MIDORIMA'S AMAZING FOR PULLING THAT OFF, SURE... BUT HE'S NOT THE ONLY ONE.
THERE'S ALSO THE GUY WHO DELIVERED THE PASS TO MIDORIMA'S POSITION...
...WITH UNBELIEVABLE ACCURACY!
INCREDIBLE...
I NEVER THOUGHT MIDORIMACHI WAS CAPABLE OF SOMETHING LIKE THAT...
HUH?
MIDORIMACHI WAS THE TYPE TO NEVER SHOOT UNLESS HE WAS ABSOLUTELY CONFIDENT.
H
BUT WITH THIS TRICK, EVEN IF THE PASS IS GOOD, THE SHOT WILL NEVER BE AS ACCURATE AS A NORMAL ONE.
EVEN IF IT'S TO BEAT AKASHICHI...

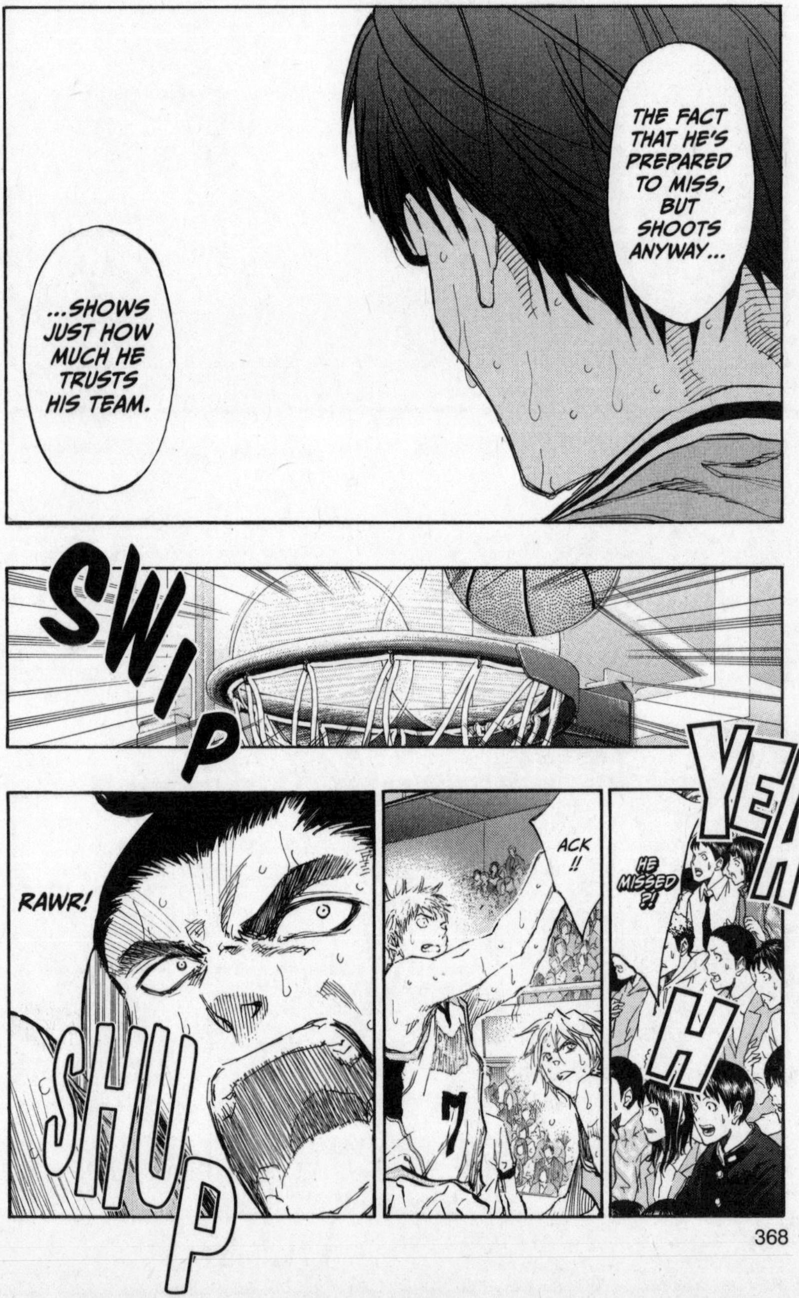
THE FACT THAT HE'S PREPARED TO MISS, BUT SHOOTS ANYWAY...
...SHOWS JUST HOW MUCH HE TRUSTS HIS TEAM.
SWIP
YEAH
HE MISSED?!
ACK!!
RAWR!
SHUP

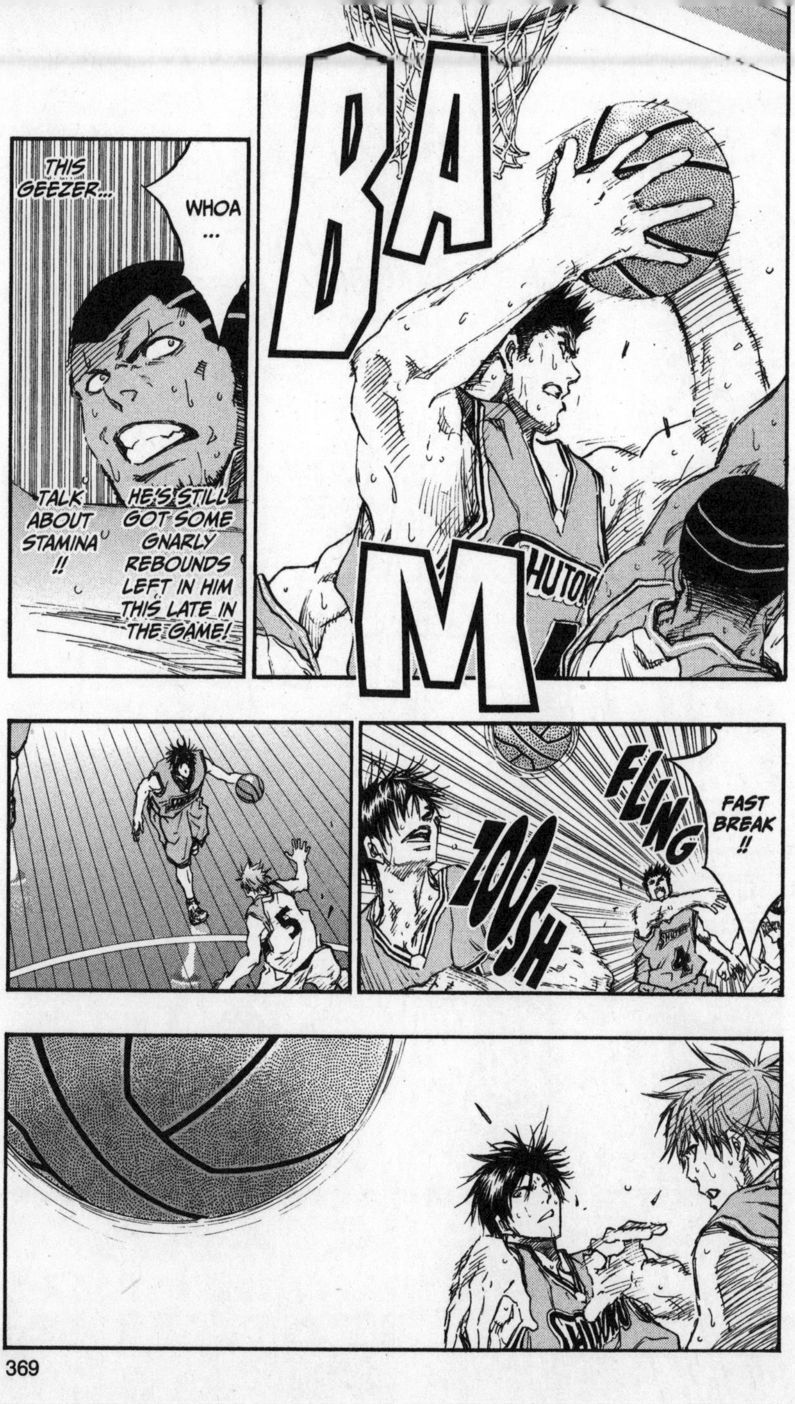
BAM
WHOA ...
THIS GEEZER...
HE'S STILL GOT SOME GNARLY REBOUNDS LEFT IN HIM THIS LATE IN THE GAME!
TALK ABOUT STAMINA!!
FAST BREAK!!
FLING
ZOOSH

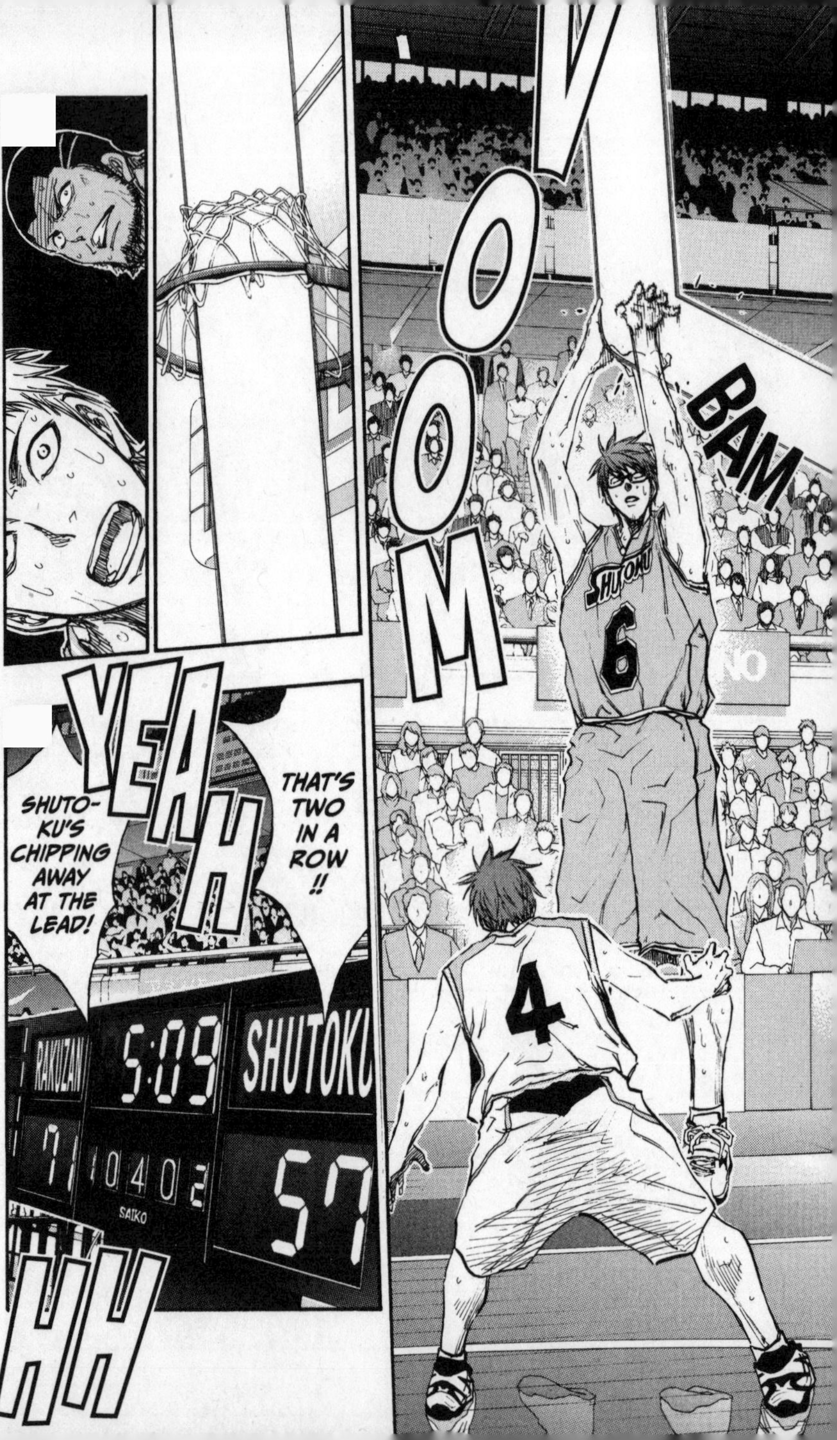
VOOOM
BAM
SHUTOKU
6
NO
4
YEAH
THAT'S TWO IN A ROW !!
SHUTOKU'S CHIPPING AWAY AT THE LEAD!
RAKUZAN
5:09
SHUTOKU
0402
57
SAIKO
HH

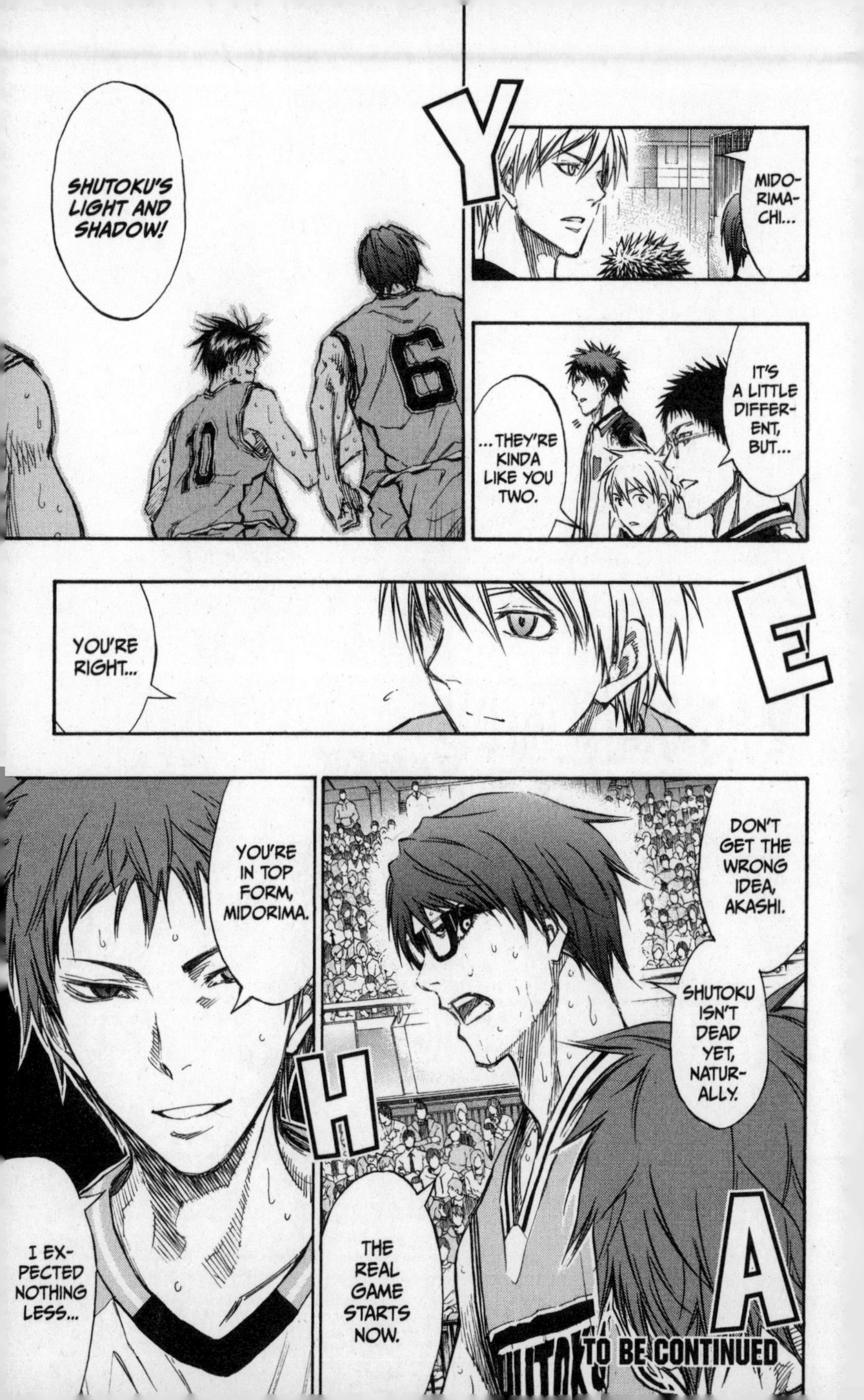
Y
MIDO-RIMA-CHI...
IT'S A LITTLE DIFFER-ENT, BUT...
...THEY'RE KINDA LIKE YOU TWO.
SHUTOKU'S LIGHT AND SHADOW!
E
YOU'RE RIGHT...
DON'T GET THE WRONG IDEA, AKASHI.
SHUTOKU ISN'T DEAD YET, NATURALLY.
THE REAL GAME STARTS NOW.
A
H
YOU'RE IN TOP FORM, MIDORIMA.
I EX-PECTED NOTHING LESS...
TO BE CONTINUED

KUROKO'S BASKETBALL BLOOPERS

TAKE 3

KAME-
HAMEHA
...?!

IT'S
NOT
THAT
!!

MIDO-
RIMA

INCRED-
IBLE,
SHINTARO
...

T
E
N
S
E
...

Coming Next Volume

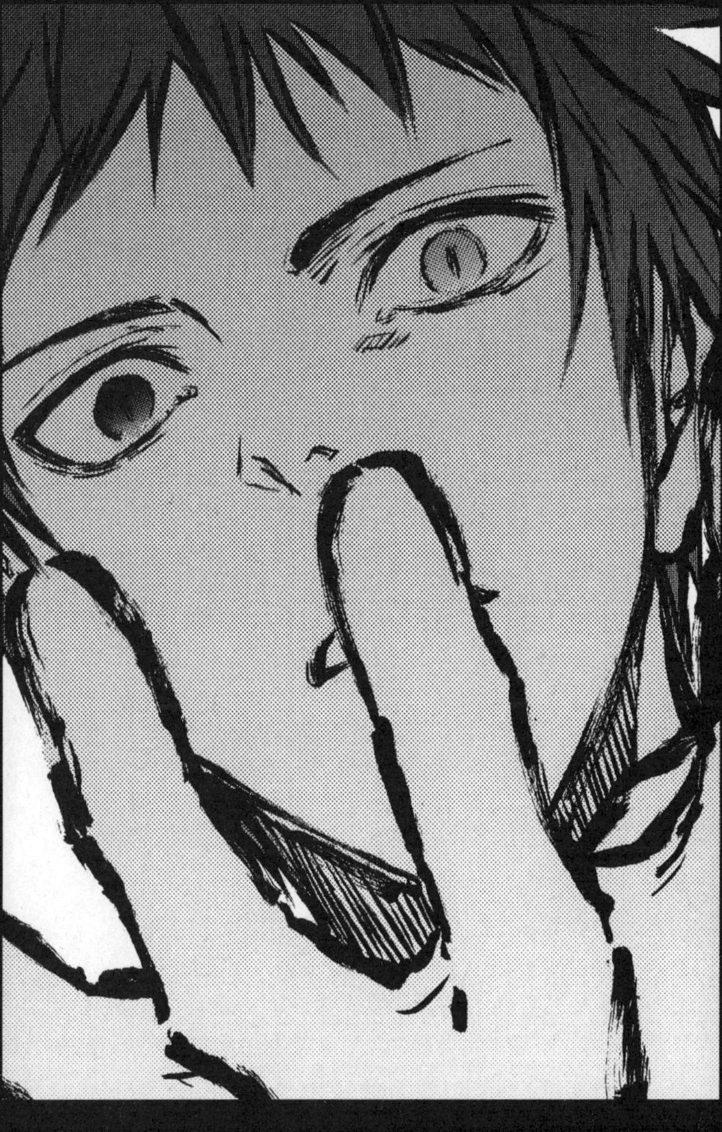

Midorima's taking on Akashi in a Miracle Generation showdown! Who will carry his team to victory?!

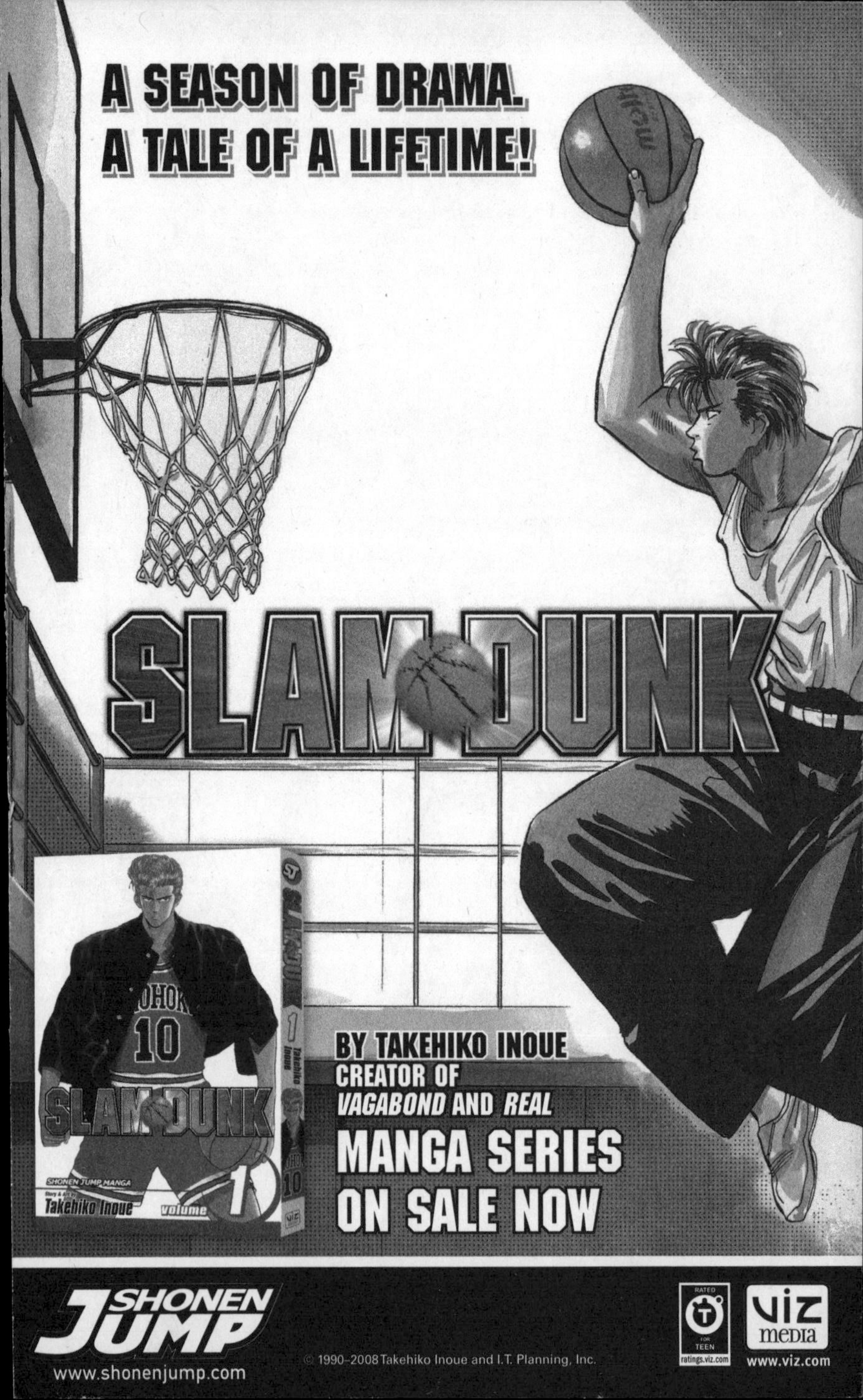
A SEASON OF DRAMA.
A TALE OF A LIFETIME!
SLAM DUNK
SLAM DUNK
SHONEN JUMP MANGA
Story & Art by
Takehiko Inoue
volume 1
SLAM DUNK 1 Takehiko Inoue
BY TAKEHIKO INOUE
CREATOR OF
VAGABOND AND REAL
MANGA SERIES
ON SALE NOW
SHONEN JUMP
www.shonenjump.com
© 1990–2008 Takehiko Inoue and I.T. Planning, Inc.
RATED T FOR TEEN
ratings.viz.com
VIZ media
www.viz.com